Pearson New International Edition

Evaluating Practice: Guidelines
for the Accountable Professional
Martin Bloom Joel Fischer John G. Orme
Sixth Edition

PEARSON®

Pearson Education Limited
Edinburgh Gate
Harlow
Essex CM20 2JE
England and Associated Companies throughout the world

Visit us on the World Wide Web at: www.pearsoned.co.uk

© Pearson Education Limited 2014

All rights reserved. No part of this publication may be reproduced, stored in a retrieval system, or transmitted in any form or by any means, electronic, mechanical, photocopying, recording or otherwise, without either the prior written permission of the publisher or a licence permitting restricted copying in the United Kingdom issued by the Copyright Licensing Agency Ltd, Saffron House, 6–10 Kirby Street, London EC1N 8TS.

All trademarks used herein are the property of their respective owners. The use of any trademark in this text does not vest in the author or publisher any trademark ownership rights in such trademarks, nor does the use of such trademarks imply any affiliation with or endorsement of this book by such owners.

ISBN 10: 1-292-04195-1
ISBN 13: 978-1-292-04195-7

British Library Cataloguing-in-Publication Data
A catalogue record for this book is available from the British Library

Printed in the United States of America

Table of Contents

1. Integrating Evaluation and Practice
Martin Bloom/Joel Fischer/John G. Orme — **1**

2. Basic Principles of Conceptualization and Measurement
Martin Bloom/Joel Fischer/John G. Orme — **27**

3. Specifying Problems and Goals
Martin Bloom/Joel Fischer/John G. Orme — **53**

4. Developing a Measurement and Recording Plan
Martin Bloom/Joel Fischer/John G. Orme — **81**

5. Behavioral Observation
Martin Bloom/Joel Fischer/John G. Orme — **125**

6. Standardized Scales
Martin Bloom/Joel Fischer/John G. Orme — **155**

7. Logs
Martin Bloom/Joel Fischer/John G. Orme — **201**

8. Reactivity and Nonreactive Measures
Martin Bloom/Joel Fischer/John G. Orme — **221**

9. Selecting a Measure
Martin Bloom/Joel Fischer/John G. Orme — **233**

10. Basic Principles of Single-System Designs
Martin Bloom/Joel Fischer/John G. Orme — **243**

11. Baselining
Martin Bloom/Joel Fischer/John G. Orme — **275**

12. From the Case Study to the Basic Single-System Design: A-B
Martin Bloom/Joel Fischer/John G. Orme — **289**

13. The Experimental Single-System Designs: A-B-A, A-B-A-B, B-A-B
Martin Bloom/Joel Fischer/John G. Orme — **305**

14. Multiple Designs for Single Systems
Martin Bloom/Joel Fischer/John G. Orme — **329**

15. Changing Intensity Designs and Successive Intervention Designs
Martin Bloom/Joel Fischer/John G. Orme — **353**

16. Designs for Comparing Interventions
Martin Bloom/Joel Fischer/John G. Orme — **371**

17. Selecting a Design
Martin Bloom/Joel Fischer/John G. Orme — **387**

18. Basic Principles of Analysis
Martin Bloom/Joel Fischer/John G. Orme — **405**

19. Visual Analysis of Single-System Design Data
Martin Bloom/Joel Fischer/John G. Orme — **429**

20. Not for Practitioners Alone
Martin Bloom/Joel Fischer/John G. Orme — **445**

21. References
Martin Bloom/Joel Fischer/John G. Orme — **473**

Index — **491**

INTEGRATING EVALUATION AND PRACTICE

PURPOSE: This chapter presents an introduction to evaluation-informed practice through use of single-system designs (SSDs), a method used by helping professionals to evaluate practice. In this chapter we present the basic characteristics of single-system designs, compare this evaluation method with the classical research methods, and summarize the entire evaluation process and this book with a flowchart showing which chapters will discuss which portions of the whole process. We also present an introduction to evidence-based practice, and describe the ways in which evidence-based practice and evaluation-informed practice can be integrated. Our main purpose in this chapter is to encourage you to recognize the feasibility and the desirability of evaluating your own professional services—in whatever community setting you may work and using whatever theory guides your practice. This is a goal that we will identify as scientific practice, the combination of a sensitive and caring practitioner with the logical and empirical strengths of the applied social scientist.

Introduction to Single-System Designs
    A Primer on Single-System Designs
        Specifying the Target (Problem or Objective/Goal)
        Measuring the Target by Forming Its Operational Definition
        Baseline and Intervention Phases
        Repeated Measures
        Practice Designs
        Evaluation Designs
        Analysis of the Data
        Decision Making on the Basis of Findings
Single-System Designs and Classical Research: The Knowledge-Building Context

Evidence-Based Practice
    Steps in Evidence-Based Practice
Integrating Evaluation-Informed Practice and Evidence-Based Practice: The PRAISES Model
Single-System Evaluation, Qualitative Research, and Quantitative Research
Advantages of Using Single-System Designs in Practice
A Walk through the Evaluation Process
Summary

From Chapter 1 of *Evaluating Practice: Guidelines for the Accountable Professional*, Sixth Edition. Martin Bloom, Joel Fischer, John G. Orme. Copyright © 2009 by Pearson Education, Inc. All rights reserved.

INTRODUCTION TO SINGLE-SYSTEM DESIGNS

The title of this book, *Evaluating Practice,* says it all: Everything we present in this text is intended to facilitate your use of evaluation methods in your practice, that is, the systematic, ongoing, and more or less objective determination of whether we are obtaining the objectives and goals of practice that we set with our clients. This is a critical function of practice, especially as it is going to be conducted in this age of managed care that demands tangible evidence of effectiveness (Vandiver & Corcoran, 2007; Bolen & Hall, 2007). Virtually all the helping professions require their practitioners to evaluate their practice and their students to learn how to evaluate (Fisher, 2004; NASW, 1996; O'Donohue & Ferguson, 2003). For example, the accrediting body of schools of social work requires that all students be taught how to evaluate their own practices (Council on Social Work Education, 2003), and the Codes of Ethics of social work, clinical psychology, and counseling require evaluation of all intervention programs and services (O'Donohue & Ferguson, 2003; NASW, 1996).

We call this emphasis on evaluation in practice *evaluation-informed practice*, because it refers to the use of formal and systematic evaluation methods to help you assess, monitor, and evaluate your cases and inform you and the client about decisions that can be made to improve your results. Although there are many ways we as practitioners receive information about what happens with our clients, it is the primary thesis of this book that *evaluation-informed practice,* because of its systematic and logical approach, comprises a major increment over other methods in helping us achieve effective practice. In fact, there is an emerging, methodologically strong body of evidence which shows that such routine monitoring and receipt of feedback as in evaluation-informed practice can reduce deterioration, improve overall outcome, and lead to fewer intervention sessions with no worsening of outcome for clients making progress (i.e., increased cost-effectiveness) (e.g., Faul, McMurty, & Hudson, 2001; Lambert, 2007; Lambert et al., 2002, 2003; Harmon et al., 2007).

The primary method of evaluation that is the backbone of evaluation-informed practice is *single-system designs*, the topic of this book. Single-system designs essentially involve continuing observation of one client/system before, during, and after some intervention. By *client/system* we mean one or more persons or groups being assisted by a helping professional to accomplish some goal. These goals may involve preventive, protective, promotive (the three aspects of primary prevention), interventive, or rehabilitative practices. And these practices may be delivered by social workers; psychologists; people in nursing, medicine, or the allied health fields; or professionals in education or other helping professions. For simplicity of discussion, we will use the term *client* to refer to individuals, groups, or other collectives, as the context will make clear. And we will use the term *practitioner* to refer to any helping professional. The term *treatment*, although widely used, is problematic because it is a medically oriented word that assumes a medical model of disease causation that may not be suitable to the full range of social and psychological concerns. So, we will mainly use the term *intervention* for discussions of practice that may include medical treatment, social services, psychotherapy, community change efforts, educational methods, and the like. The context of our discussion will determine what practice term we use.

We suggest that you start this book by reading the case example of graduate students learning to use single-system designs that we have included on the CD-ROM that comes with this book. We consider that case as the Prologue to the book. Insert your CD, click on "Student Manual," "PDF File" and "Prologue from Evaluating Practice (5th ed.)." Double click on this file to open it. As we illustrated in the case presented in the Prologue, using single-system evaluation, you can learn what the client's problems and potentials are before the intervention. You can identify the client's objectives and goals. From this understanding of problems and goals, you can specify a target or targets for intervention. We use the word *target* to refer to clients' concerns, problems, or objectives that have been clearly specified as the focus of our interventive efforts. Combining this knowledge of the client's situation both with our theories of human behavior and behavior change and with the relevant research base, you can construct and implement a workable intervention plan.

Then we *monitor* the interventive process; that is, we check progress against the client's objectives in order to know whether to change our intervention: Should we do more than, the same as, or less than we are doing, or should we do something completely different? This is the heart of the evaluation process, making use of the rapid feedback of information for present and future helping.

Finally, we can determine whether the overall outcome was successful in terms of the client's objectives and goals in the social context. We will use the term *evaluation* to refer to this special analysis of outcomes, in contrast to *monitoring* the process of intervention.

There are a number of simple conventions for graphing the flow of events with regard to a particular client problem. We often obtain a reference point (or more likely, a pattern of points), called a *baseline*, of a given problem before any intervention occurs. We then can compare changes in the target against the baseline during and after intervention. We repeat these same measures on a regular basis, using a *chart* to examine client change. Using certain conventions described in this book, we can determine for the ongoing intervention whether there is significant change occurring—in either the desired or undesired directions—in order to make suitable adaptations in the intervention. We also can have an empirical and rational basis for termination: when statistical significance is aligned with clinically or socially meaningful changes in the client's situation, as predicted by one's practice theory. This process is the essence of scientific practice—the use of science, scientific methods, and findings from scientific research—that we hope will result in a relatively objective guide to sensitive practice changes and outcomes. This is not a lock-step approach to practice and evaluation, but one that does require considerable thought and flexibility.

And that's it! The basic principles of single-system designs actually are few and simple. The principles can be combined in numerous ways to fit the needs of a given case or situation. The information obtained can be reasonably objective, and the sense of knowing how matters are proceeding is positively exhilarating. That's the fun part, assuming that the case is going well. If it isn't, then you need to know about this as soon as possible, so you can change intervention techniques or directions.

Now, let us turn to a discussion of specifics that we just summarized in the preceding paragraphs.

A Primer on Single-System Designs

For many years helping professionals dreamed about integrating theory, research, and practice in the belief that the more clearly their theories could be stated and tested in the real world, the better their practice would be. Unfortunately, it has been difficult to create this integration, primarily because the technologies needed were not available. The global concepts used in some theories were difficult to define in concrete terms. In classical, experimental/control group research designs, immediate feedback was almost impossible to achieve. Thus, when reasonably objective but relatively easy methods of evaluation, such as single-system designs, were developed, the helping professions had the tools for which they had long hoped.

The phrase *single-system designs* refers to a set of logical and empirical procedures used to observe changes in an identified target (a specified problem or objective of the client) that is measured repeatedly over time. This relatively new evaluation technology has been described using a number of terms, all of which are about equivalent for our purposes. These terms include intensive or idiographic research, single N or $N = 1$ research, single-subject research or single-subject design, single case-study design, time-series research, single-organism research, single-case experimental design, and the term we will use in this book, single-system designs. We use this term because it emphasizes the person-in-the-environment as a useful perspective for scientific practice. A given system—one person alone, but often one or more persons and/or groups interacting in ordinary life situations—is the object of evaluation and intervention. Changes are sought in either the person or persons involved, and/or the relevant social or physical environments. Thus, single-*system* designs refer to evaluating practice with the relevant parts of a whole system, which could range from an individual to a family to a group to a community to any size system.

Explicit interventions typically are guided by a practice theory or by specific principles of practice; consequently, using single-system designs, we can learn what intervention techniques work well under what conditions. However, there are no particular intervention models (like behavior therapy) that alone are suited for single-system designs. Single-system designs are not attached to any particular theory of intervention. The single-system design model is "theory independent" in this sense; that is, the design can be used with just about any intervention theory or approach. Single-system designs have been used by, among others, psychoanalytically-oriented practitioners (Dean & Reinherz, 1986); practitioners working with groups (Johnson, Beckerman, & Auerbach, 2001) and families (Bentley, 1990); practitioners using systemic, problem-solving approaches (Hall, 2006); cognitive-behavioral practitioners (Humphrey & Brooks, 2006); practitioners conducting parent-child interaction therapy; practitioners using narrative/music therapy (Strickland, 2006); practitioners using task-centered and motivational interviewing (Fassler, 2007); practitioners using paradoxical intention (Kolko & Milan, 1983); and so on. In fact, we will use examples from a variety of theoretical orientations throughout this book to illustrate the adaptability and flexibility of single-system designs.

Usually, but not always, single-system designs employ a before/during and/or a before/during/after approach to compare the patterns of two or more states of one client/system. The before-intervention state (baseline) is used as a frame of reference for changes occurring in the during-intervention and/or after-intervention state. Because the same client/system is involved throughout the service period, the practitioner looks for differences in that system's target events and, with a powerful enough evaluation design, tries to determine whether his or her efforts produced these differences.

Now, let's examine the basic characteristics of all single-system designs.

Specifying the Target (Problem or Objective/Goal). A fundamental rule of any professional practice requires that you identify the problem: What are we going to try to change? In practice, this often involves client and practitioner interactions that define the problems and objectives in the given situation, as well as the strengths and resources with which they have to work.

Something important goes on when clients and practitioners discuss the presenting problems and objectives and goals (what we hope to accomplish). The clients express their concerns, and practitioners simultaneously conceptualize and empathize. Practitioners conceptualize when they abstract and generalize the patterns of client behaviors (thoughts, feelings, and actions), which are given some label (a concept) representing that class of experiences. For example, the practitioner sees a client's head slumped to the chest and the teary eyes, and hears the client talk of not sleeping well and losing interest in food and sex. The practitioner forms an initial hunch that the client may be depressed, which directs the practitioner to look for and test additional factors known to be associated with depression. Thus, concepts act as the building blocks of theory, or at least of some general principles, which in turn serve as guides to practice. It is essential to be clear about how you conceptualize because the class labels you identify lead you to bodies of information that in turn guide your practice. A fuzzy concept can lead you in unfruitful directions. Accurate conceptualizing represents the practitioner's first contribution to the helping process.

Simultaneously with conceptualizing, practitioners also empathize; they actively listen to clients, cognitively and emotionally attempting to understand the meanings of these problems and objectives, and then reflect this understanding to the clients with warmth and genuineness. These are the core skills for any helping practice (Fischer, 1978; Norcross, 2002; Norcross & Hill, 2004). Scientific practice includes sensitive, empathic awareness of client problems and strengths, which constitute the practitioner's second contribution to the helping process. Both conceptualization and empathy help the practitioner to specify what is happening in the client situation.

It is important to note that no finite list of problems or objectives will ever be a comprehensive picture of the whole person or group involved. Instead, a few specified targets are chosen and represent indicators of the whole, as a compromise between feasibility and comprehensiveness. Schön (1983) describes presenting problems as "indeterminate messes"—complex, changing, fluid experiences that constitute the human condition. While case situations are often messy in this way, the practitioner tries to create some order with them to make the problems amenable to change. In effect, the practitioner is a problem constructor, assembling and recombining elements of the "mess" with the client until both share a common perception of the problem and how to solve it. As this process of problem construction continues, the mess may become more manageable. The client and practitioner may see progress—in part because they have agreed on ways of talking about or identifying problems and strengths in the client's situation. This is a critical step in problem solving.

Measuring the Target by Forming Its Operational Definition. By means of the problem construction process we just described, the broad problem and/or objective can be changed into a specific target that the practitioner will seek to influence when it is restated as an operational definition. By specifying what operations or measurement procedures we will use to define the target—how often it occurs, in what intensity, and so on—both client and practitioner can be clear about what they are dealing with. These actual procedures of measurement are called the *operational definition*. Changes in this target will provide feedback to the practitioner and client regarding progress toward problem resolution.

But, we want to emphasize that the measurement procedures used in single-system designs are generally quite simple, and they are used only to the extent that they can help the practitioner make decisions about changes in the client's situation. Moreover, there are formal scales and do-it-yourself procedures available to measure just about every possible target, no matter what the practitioner's theoretical orientation. We present many case examples illustrating the range of measures throughout this book.

Baseline and Intervention Phases. A phase is a time period during which a particular activity occurs. In general, there are two types of phases, baseline phases and intervention phases. The targets are measured in both phases, but during a baseline phase, no target-focused intervention is implemented, whereas during an intervention phase, one or more target-focused helping practices are introduced.

The baseline phase involves the planned, systematic collection of information regarding the target, typically before a given intervention is begun. Usually, you collect such information at the very beginning of the case as you are trying to understand the nature and extent of the problems and strengths in the client's situation prior to intervening. You also may return to baseline conditions during the course of service, such as when one intervention appears not to be working well and the practitioner needs a fresh perspective in identifying changes in the client's situation. These baseline or nonintervention phases constitute the core of single-system evaluation; changes in the pattern of data between baseline and intervention phases provide the key evaluation information.

Students and practitioners frequently ask whether any baseline situation can ever be free of some intervention. The answer requires that the distinction be made clearly between the relationship-building interactions that are not precisely structured in a way to bring about specific changes and the interventions that are intended to change specific aspects of the client situation. Practitioners rightly believe that they are providing a useful service while they are building a trusting relationship with the client. But this trust or rapport generally is a means to an end, which is problem resolution; rapport is not necessarily an end in itself. This vital relationship often provides the basis for implementing an intervention and for helping the client to make changes in his or her life; it may also provide sensitive information whereby the environment may be changed to benefit the client (see Bohart & Greenberg, 1997).

Formal interventions, on the other hand, are *planned* changes in which practitioners perform certain actions with regard to their clients, to other people, or to situations, in order to achieve specified objectives. Thus, we expect changes that occur as a result of these formal interventions to be far greater than those that would occur in the baseline phase, precisely because these planned interventions are *added* to the rapport-building and relationship-building activities in the baseline. Of course, the practitioner maintains these trusting relationships during the intervention.

Repeated Measures. The heart of single-system evaluation is the collection of repeated information on the target problems or objectives. This is what is meant by a time-series design. Either the practitioner, the clients, or relevant others observe the same target problem over regular time intervals such as every day or every week—whatever is appropriate to the given problem—to see whether any changes are taking place between the "before phase" (the baseline phase), and the "during phase" (the intervention phase), and/or in the "after phase" (the follow-up phase) of the intervention. This is the basis of monitoring progress to determine whether changes are needed in the intervention program, a process that is critical to guiding practice and making sound practice decisions.

Practice Designs. Whatever practice methods and theories are used, they should be clearly described. Thus, if the overall results are positive, you would know what exact services were delivered and under what conditions those results were produced. In this way, you would be able to build a repertoire of effective methods, as well as communicate clearly with others who might wish to use these same methods. Equally important, it is useful to know what does *not* work with a given kind of client in a given situation, so that we won't repeat our less effective methods.

There should also be clear conceptual linkages between the identified targets and the specific interventions chosen to affect them. For example, if one were dealing with depression—a cognitive, physiological, and affective state with certain typical associated behaviors, often correlated with various kinds of environmental factors—then one's intervention approach would need to take account of these cognitive, physiological, affective, behavioral, and environmental factors. A given intervention approach need not directly act on all of these factors, but it should have a rationale for what it does direct the practitioner to act on, and how it presumes those factors on which there is no planned action would be influenced.

A *practice design* is the sum of systematic and planned interventions chosen to deal with a particular set of targets to achieve identified objectives and goals. Such a design may be a translation of an existing theory or set of principles of behavior change adapted to the context of a given client, or it may be newly constructed by the practitioner (see, e.g., Thyer, 2001).

Evaluation Designs. In general, research designs are arrangements for making or structuring observations about a situation in order to identify lawful relationships (e.g., that a certain variable seems to vary consistently with another variable). *Evaluation* designs are special types of research designs that are applied to the evaluation of practice outcomes. Single-system designs, as one type of evaluation design, involve arrangements in which repeated observations before, during, and/or after intervention are compared to monitor the progress and assess the outcome of that service. All single-system designs permit an analysis of patterns of change in client problems; some of the more complex designs also allow you to infer whether the practitioner's efforts may be causally responsible for the identified changes.

Analysis of the Data. Unlike other forms of evaluation, single-system designs rely on several unique types of analysis. First, a simple visual analysis of changes in the data on the chart on which all data are recorded (i.e., from baseline through intervention periods) may indicate improvement, deterioration, or even no change, providing feedback as to whether the intervention should be maintained or revised; this is the *monitoring* function of single-system designs.

Also, a visual analysis of the data that reveals marked positive differences between baseline and intervention is sometimes used as the basis for overall accountability in the case; this is the *evaluation* function of single-system designs. Statistical analyses also may be used for more precise statements of outcome, and in most cases, computers can facilitate statistical analyses.

Decision Making on the Basis of Findings. The ultimate purpose of doing single-system evaluations is to be able to make more effective and humane decisions about resolving problems or promoting desired objectives. That means that we will consider the visual and the statistical analyses of the intervention, along with an analysis of the social or clinical import of these events in order to guide our practice decisions. A judgment about human activities involves more than the "facts" of the matter; it involves the values that are activated by these events. Single-system analyses offer ways to test hypotheses about portions of the client situation in order to receive rapid feedback. We assume as an axiom of practice that the better the information you have about the case, the more likely you are to make better service decisions.

And there you have it. These basic points are simple, but there are plenty of variations and complications, as you will read in the rest of this book. Single-system designs are approximate methods to determine whether certain practice objectives have been achieved. In exchange for the relative simplicity of methods and the rapidity of feedback, we give up some of the power that can be attained in classical research designs. However, by use of more powerful single-system designs, it is possible to do some sophisticated and rigorous evaluation. We are advocating that everyone learn to use the basic designs, even with their limitations. We also hope to motivate some to use more sophisticated designs because of their power, and because sometimes we need to know whether we caused changes in the target to occur, information that the more sophisticated designs can provide.

Evaluation is simply that part of good practice that informs the practitioner about how well the intervention is proceeding relative to the original objectives. But evaluation also encourages the practitioner to be clear about the targets of intervention, as well as about the helping activities themselves. Evaluation-informed practice using single-system designs means that our evaluation efforts help guide practice decisions in a dynamic fashion.

Because evaluation seems to imply research, statistics, mathematics, and computer science technology, it does raise ghosts that are fearful to some practitioners and students. But this misses the point, because it is the *logic* of clear thinking and acting that is essential to evaluation, not a bunch of difficult and esoteric technologies. Good practitioners carefully observe and subjectively evaluate their own practice. This may be why they are good practitioners—they benefit from this precise observation and accurate feedback as they monitor the progress of their clients. The single-system methodology adds to these subjective evaluations by providing everyone with a common language and more or less objective procedures for doing what good practitioners have long done.

Good practice is holistic practice. It involves a systematic framework for conducting the actual steps of intervention; consideration of the role of theory and ethics; and a way to measure, monitor, evaluate, and guide what we do in practice. We have tried to be as honest and as accurate as possible an account of how new students may proceed (and sometimes stumble) through that process. There are, indeed, complex issues that must be worked out with each and every case. That is one of the great challenges of evaluation-informed practice.

But we want to assure you, based on our own practice and the practice of our students and colleagues, that with experience comes greater expertise, and with greater expertise comes enhanced competence in wending your way through some of the obstacles to humane and effective scientific practice.

SINGLE-SYSTEM DESIGNS AND CLASSICAL RESEARCH: THE KNOWLEDGE-BUILDING CONTEXT

The focus of this book is almost exclusively on single-system designs. Many readers have probably had some exposure to research methods, but this exposure is more likely to have involved what is called "classical" methods, in which experimental groups are compared with control groups in laboratories or field settings, or where large-scale surveys are conducted. Typically, these methods depend on the aggregation of data from groups of people; for example, one would find the mean of the group rather than look at any one person's scores. Then comparisons are made between different groups of persons; for example, the average score of one group that received an intervention is compared with the average score of another group that did not. These methods frequently use a variety of statistical procedures and computer software to process the large amounts of data collected from the participants in the research.

Such classical methods are extremely powerful and useful, particularly in generalizing research results to similar populations, one of the vital functions of science. The classical group designs are also effective in ruling out alternative explanations of results (e.g., Shadish, Cook, & Campbell, 2002). In fact, most program evaluations are conducted using classical research methods, providing absolutely critical information to practitioners about the effectiveness of different intervention programs (see Royse, Thyer, Padgett, & Logan, 2006; Unrau, Gabor, & Grinnell, 2007; Cone, 2001, for excellent overviews of the methods and issues in evaluating practice outcomes). So, classical research and evaluation methods are at the heart of evidence-based practice decisions, as we will see in the next section.

However, these classical designs are not useful for many of the situations with which most practitioners are *immediately* concerned. While controlled, experimental, and quasi-experimental designs evaluate the differences between groups from pretest to posttest, a time period that can range from weeks to months, single-system designs provide immediate information on virtually a daily basis so that you can monitor changes (and lack of changes) in the client's problem situation and guide your practice accordingly. This is the crucial information a practitioner uses to make decisions about whether to maintain or change his or her intervention. And *that* is at the core of evaluation-informed practice.

We have summarized the similarities and differences between these models of research and evaluation—the classical experimental/control group design on the one hand, and the single-system design on the other—in Table 1. We also have drawn the classical and the single-system designs in Figure 1, comparing their basic ingredients. By following the research and the evaluation processes from left to right, and then from the top to the bottom of Figure 1, you can see the parallels and the differences that are also described in a different form in Table 1.

In general, then, there are different roles for each of these approaches: Single-system designs are best used to monitor, guide, and evaluate practice in field situations, whereas the results of experimental/control

Table 1 Comparison of single-system designs and experimental/control group designs

Characteristic	Single-System Designs	Experimental/Control Group Designs
1. Number of clients involved	One individual, group, or collectivity.	At least two groups are involved. Ideally, these groups are randomly selected from a common population and randomly assigned to groups to control between-group variability.
2. Number of attributes measured	Limited to a number feasibly collected by the client, practitioner, or others. Usually a large number of issues are assessed before selecting the specific targets, few in number.	Variable, depending on the purpose of the study. Usually a medium to large number of items is asked of a large number of persons by research interviewers or others.
3. Number of measures used for each attribute	Variable. Ideally, multiple measures of the same attribute would be used (cf. Shadish, Cook, & Campbell, 2002).	Variable. Ideally, multiple measures of the same attribute would be used (cf. Campbell & Fiske, 1959).
4. Number of times measures are repeated	Data are collected frequently in regular intervals before, during, and sometimes after (follow-ups) the intervention. Assumes variability in behavior across time (cf. Chassan, 1979).	Data are collected only a few times, usually once before and once after intervention, and one follow-up. Assumes relatively static state of human behavior, which may be representatively sampled in research.
5. Duration of research	Variable, depending on whether time-limited services are provided wherein the duration is fixed, or whether an open-ended service is given; depends on needs of client.	Fixed time periods are usually used.
6. Choice of goals of research	Goals are usually chosen by the client and agreed to and made operationally clear by the practitioner.	Goals are often chosen by the researcher, occasionally in consultation with the funding agency, practitioner, or community representatives.
7. Choice of research design and its review by others for ethical suitability	The practitioner usually selects the particular design and has no professional review except by the practice supervisor, if that.	The researcher chooses the design, but usually has to submit the design and instrumentation to peer review (e.g., Human Subjects Review Committee).
8. Feedback	Feedback is a vital ingredient of single-system designs; it is immediately forthcoming as progress is monitored, and the service program may be modified accordingly. This permits the study of process as well as outcome. Systematic recording opportunities are present.	There is almost no feedback in the group design until the entire project is completed, lest such information influence events under study. Little information is given about process in studies of outcome.
9. Changes in research design	Changes are permitted. Any set of interventions can be described as a "design," but some designs are logically stronger than others. Flexibility of design is a major characteristic of single-system designs.	Changes in research design are not permitted. Fixed methods are used as exactly as possible across subjects. Standardized instruments and trained interviewers are often employed.
10. Use of theory as guide to practice	Variable. In ideal form, some clear conceptual rationale is used to give meaning to the set of operational procedures.	Variable. In ideal form, some clear hypotheses are derived from a theory that gives direction to the entire project.
11. Use of comparison groups in arriving at the evaluation	The relatively stable baseline period would have continued, it is assumed, had not the intervention been made. Therefore, the single-system design uses its "own control" by comparing outcomes from the intervention period with the preintervention baseline.	Ideally, a control or contrast group is randomly selected from a common population and randomly assigned on the assumption that it will represent what likely would have occurred to the experimental group had the intervention not been made.
12. Reliability	Usually achieved through having a second observer make ratings where possible. Internal consistency used with standardized measures, along with conventional methods of measuring reliability where necessary.	All the basic methods of measuring reliability can be used: reliability of tests (test-retest, alternative forms, split-half) and interobserver agreement.

Table 1 (continued)

Characteristic	Single-System Designs	Experimental/Control Group Designs
13. Validity	The closeness of the measures, especially direct measures, to the ultimate outcome criteria increases the opportunity for validity, while various pressures toward distortion in reporting decrease that opportunity.	All basic methods of measuring validity can be used: face validity, content validity, criterion-related validity, and construct validity.
14. Utility of findings for intervention	Direct and immediate. May include involvement of client as well as practitioner in collecting and interpreting data and modifying intervention.	Indirect. Probably will not affect clients of the present project, but may be useful for the class of subjects (or problems) involved.
15. Targets of intervention and measurement	Ideally, should be important life events, but single-system designs are susceptible to trivialization in choice of targets. Emphasis is on knowledge-for-immediate-use, but some efforts concern knowledge-building issues.	Variable, depending on the purpose of the study. Can include important life events or targets of theoretical interest (and low immediate-practice utility). Emphasis is more likely to be on knowledge for knowledge-building, but with some efforts on knowledge-for-use.
16. Kinds of data obtained	a. Descriptive data on the system in question, providing norms for that system. b. Change for that individual system. c. If the design permits, inferences of causal or functional relationships between independent and dependent variables, but susceptible to many alternative explanations for given outcomes.	a. Descriptive data, providing normative information. b. Scores, grouped or averaged, thus masking individual patterns of change (Chassan, 1979). c. Experimental designs provide strong logical bases for inference of causality and generalizability (Shadish, Cook & Campbell, 2002).
17. Costs	Relatively low. A small amount of time and energy must be expended in designing the evaluation and carrying it out, but this may be routinized as part of the empirically guided practice itself. Essentially a do-it-yourself operation.	Relatively high. Most group designs require research specialists separate from the practitioners involved, as well as expenses for data collection, analysis, and report writing. Computers typically are used.
18. Role of values in the research	Clients' values are incorporated in the choice of targets and goal-setting procedures. Practitioners remain "agents of society" in accepting or modifying these goals and in helping client/systems to attain them.	Researchers or funders generally control the values expressed in the research—the goals, instruments, designs, and interpretations.
19. Limitations	Statistical and logical considerations and limitations (such as generalizability of results) are not yet well-explicated; indeed, there are many differences of opinion among specialists in the field. There is an increasingly large body of exemplars that can be modeled available to practitioners from all theoretical orientations. Ethical issues abound (e.g., use of baselines vs. immediate practice).	Problems remain concerning practitioners reading, understanding, and using scientific information stemming from group designs. Ethical issues (e.g., withholding treatment from controls) are still not resolved among practitioners. Resistance to large-scale research by minorities is increasing.
20. Prospects	Optimistic. The literature on single-system designs is expanding rapidly. Freedom from major funding needs and the relative simplicity of the task—and the teaching of the task—may stimulate more practice research and evaluation with single-system designs. It is now potentially possible for every practitioner to evaluate every case on every occasion. *All of this is the heart of evaluation-informed practice.*	Optimistic. Greater care in selecting populations and problems seems likely. Funding of large-scale research suffers in times of economic scarcity. New research journals should stimulate communication of current research. *All of this is the heart of evidence-based practice.*

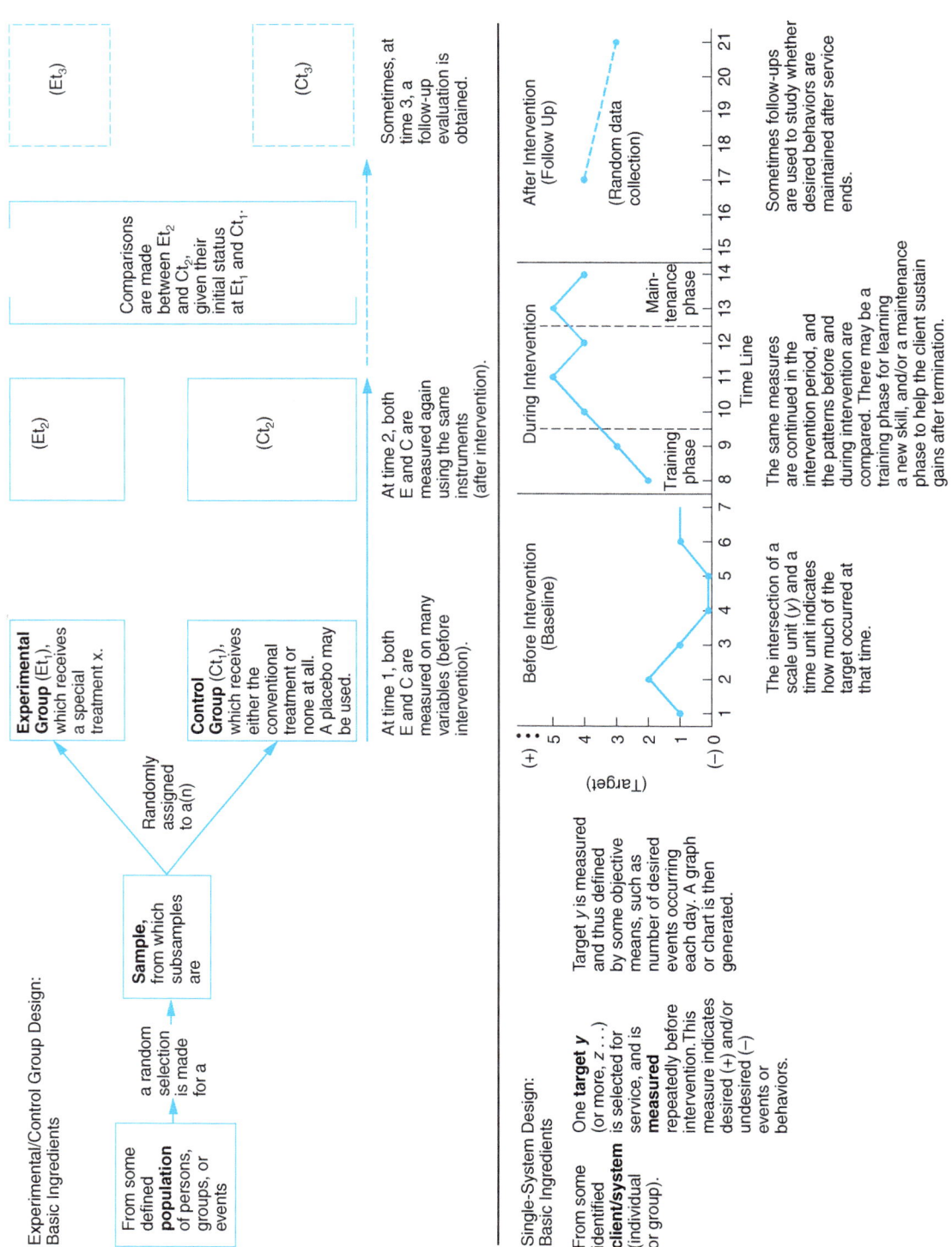

FIGURE 1 Schematic diagrams comparing the basic ingredients of experimental/control group designs and single-system designs.

group research are best used as the basis for selecting interventions based on demonstrated evidence of the effectiveness of the program or technique studied. From a different perspective, single-system designs are more useful for formative program evaluation (research focused on evaluating and improving a specific program) whereas classical research is more useful in summative evaluation (research focused on knowledge that can be generalized to apply to decision making in other programs or situations) (Royse et al., 2006; Unrau, Gabor, & Grinnell, 2007). Single-system designs can even be used to suggest hypotheses to be tested in classical research. At any rate, the strengths of the *differences* between each approach — single-system designs and classical research—are precisely why it is important to understand the major contributions of both perspectives for effective, evaluation-informed, and evidence-based practice.

Because the remainder of this book describes single-system designs, let's try to do a brief summary here of the classical methods. The classical methods, and particularly, the group, experimental, and quasi-experimental control group designs, aggregate data to produce descriptions about group characteristics—what the average person in a group is like. Aggregate methods provide little or no information about single clients or specific groups of clients, which often is of greatest interest to the practitioner. In fact, variability of effects in group studies (e.g., some clients doing better while other clients are doing worse) is often hidden in average scores. Changes in specific people are rarely presented, and so it seems that for many practitioners, the individual client or treatment group gets lost in the shuffle.

Classical studies usually involve measures at the beginning and end of long time periods, with little or no information about changes in the interim. Typically, many variables are measured at the same time, although not necessarily the ones that fit any particular client. The eventual outcomes may come too late to affect the participants in the study, although the knowledge so derived may help others in the future.

It is precisely because classical methods and single-system design methods contribute different kinds of information that it is of critical importance to practice what some authors suggest as *combining* both methods in the same study to benefit from each type of strength (Benbenishty, 1988, 1989; Jayaratne, 1977; Nugent, 1987, 1988, 1991b).

We know of few practitioners who do not claim to be effective at least some of the time. What they may be seeking is a method to demonstrate their claims for effectiveness and sensitivity. We believe that the single-system design approach may be one answer to their search because these relatively easy methods are so directly and immediately useful to practice, and yet provide a relatively objective basis for measuring the effectiveness of their interventions and for making corrections in practice to improve their effectiveness.

EVIDENCE-BASED PRACTICE

Evidence-based practice (EBP) is one of the most important developments in the helping professions—including medicine, nursing, social work, psychology, public health, counseling, and all the other health and human service professions—for many decades (Briggs & Rzepnicki, 2004; Brownson et al., 2002; Dawes et al., 1999; Dobson & Craig, 1998; Gilgun, 2005; Roberts & Yeager, 2004; Sackett et al., 2002). That is because evidence-based practice holds out the hope for practitioners that we can be at least as successful in helping our clients as the current available information on helping allows us to be. Both the importance and the multidisciplinary nature of EBP can be seen in the Roberts and Yeager (2004) compendium, *Evidence-Based Practice Manual*, a collection of chapters describing the meaning, methods, and examples of EBP.

Evidence-based practice represents both an ideology and a method. The *ideology* springs from the ethical principle that clients deserve to be provided with the most effective interventions possible. The *method* of EBP is the way we go about finding and then implementing those interventions (see, e.g., manuals on EBP methods by Gibbs, 2003; Cournoyer, 2003; and Rubin, 2008; see also www.evidence.brookscole.com/index.html). *Evidence-based practice represents the practitioner's commitment to use all means possible to locate the best (most effective) evidence for any given problem at all points of planning and contacts with clients.* This pursuit of the best knowledge includes extensive computer searches, as described below (Gibbs & Gambrill, 2002).

Evidence-based practice is an enormous challenge to practitioners because the methods of locating the most effective interventions go beyond, or are more rigorous than, even those of *empirically based practice*. Thus, for example, where a practitioner using empirically based practice might be satisfied with locating two or three controlled studies as evidence of effectiveness (Chambless et al., 1996, 1998), practitioners using EBP will do whatever it takes to locate *all* studies of effectiveness on a particular problem, typically using *reviews* of research on intervention effectiveness, and then critically assessing the studies in those reviews for evidence of validity and utility for practice. The emphasis in EBP is on the comprehensiveness of the search and critical evaluation of the results, all in as close collaboration with clients as possible, including sensitivity to socially and culturally relevant approaches to intervention (Ancis, 2003; Mio & Iwamasa, 2003; Sue & Sue, 2004).

The EBP model has spawned a huge amount of literature, including methods of education and critical thinking for this rigorous form of practice (Crisp, 2004; Gambrill, 2005; Gira et al., 2004; Howard et al., 2003); EBP skill-training manuals (Rubin, 2008; Bisman & Hardcastle, 1999; Cournoyer, 2003; Gibbs, 2003; Weisz & Hawley, 1998); issues and challenges regarding EBP (Norcross et al., 2005; Gibbs & Gambrill, 2002); *principles* of change that work (Castonguay & Beutler, 2006); manuals presenting procedural guidelines for applying intervention techniques (LeCroy, 2008; Van Hasselt & Hersen, 1996); evidence-based assessment (Hunsley & Mash, 2008); evidence for an empirical foundation for the most effective relationship factors (Norcross, 2002; Norcross & Hill, 2004); evidence-based internships (Thomlison & Corcoran, 2008); evidence-based practice in groups (Macgowan, 2008); and methods for intervention planning and assessment (Beutler & Groth-Marnat, 2003; Beutler & Mailik, 2002; Haynes & O'Brien, 2000; Hersen, 2004; Hunsley & Mash, 2008; Lopez & Snyder, 2003; Mash & Terdal, 1997; Seligman, 2004; Vance & Pumariega, 2001; Woody et al., 2004).

Most importantly, the EBP movement has produced an outpouring of literature on the most effective procedures for prevention and intervention (Abramovitz, 2006; Antony et al., 2005; Antony & Barlow, 2001; Barlow, 2001a, b; Barrett & Ollendick, 2004; Bellack, 2006; Bloomquist & Schnell, 2002; Carr, 2000; Corcoran, 2003, 2004; Cormier, Nurius, & Osborn, 2009; Dobson & Craig, 1998; Dugus & Robichaud, 2006; Dulmus & Rapp-Paglicci, 2005; D'Zurilla & Nezu, 2006; Fisher & O'Donohue, 2006; Fisher, Kelley, & Lomas, 2003; Fonagy et al., 2003; Freeman & Power, 2006; Gambrill, 2006; Gullotta & Blau, 2007; Gullotta & Bloom, 2003; Hersen & Bellack, 1999; Hoffman & Otto, 2007; Hoffman & Tompson, 2002; Kazantzis & L'Abate, 2006; Kazdin, 2005; Kazdin & Weisz, 2003; Kendall, 2005; Lambert, 2004; Liddle et al., 2002; Levkoff, 2006; Lyddon & Jones, 2001; MacDonald, 2001; Marlatt & Gorman, 2005; Mash & Barkley, 2006; Nathan & Gorman, 2007; O'Donohue et al., 2003; O'Hare, 2005; Reiser & Thompson, 2005; Roberts & Yeager, 2006; Roberts & Yeager, 2004; Rosqvist, 2005; Roth & Fonagy, 2004; Rygh & Sanderson, 2004; Silverstein et al., 2006; Stout & Hayes, 2004; Thyer & Wodarski, 2007; Wedding et al., 2005).

Our view of evidence-based practice is that it depends on the successful integration of the two primary types of research we discussed and compared in the previous section: single-system designs as the heart of evaluation-informed practice and experimental and quasi-experimental controlled group designs that form the basis for practitioners' decisions about what procedures are the most effective for a particular case. Indeed, the importance of systematic evaluation with each and every case, once you have selected the best available program, can be seen in one compelling fact: The evidence is clear that even interventions selected on the basis of several randomized, controlled studies cannot be assumed to be effective with each and every client. The research clearly shows that both characteristics of clients (Clarkin & Levy, 2004) and characteristics of practitioners (Beutler et al., 2004) can have profound effects on outcomes. Cultural, socioeconomic, ethnic, and a host of other demographic and interpersonal variables can keep what seems like the perfect intervention from doing what one might expect given the reported results in the literature.

We believe the *evidence-based* practice model and the *evaluation-informed* practice approach, in a sense, "complete" each other. One uses a systematic and comprehensive search of the empirical literature to find what works best; the other provides methods for ongoing monitoring, guiding, and evaluating client progress. People and their situations are complex. So many things can go wrong during an intervention, even given the best of relationships, that the evidence-based practitioner always monitors and evaluates progress with every case and situation so as to be able to tell how well the intervention is—or is not—progressing. Thus, to be a well-rounded evidence-based practitioner, we strongly recommend the use of single-system designs to allow you, the practitioner, to receive regular feedback on how well your clients are doing and to make changes accordingly. This is particularly so given the recent evidence that we mentioned earlier in this chapter that routine monitoring and receipt of feedback that is characteristic of evaluation-informed practice can reduce deterioration and improve overall outcome (Faul, McMurty, &

Hudson, 2001; Lambert, 2007; Lambert et al., 2002, 2003). In other words, the evidence seems to support the idea that evaluation-informed practice fits the bill as an integral partner of evidence-based practice.

The essence of successful practice is to help resolve client problems and to attain client objectives, without creating problems for others or new problems for the client. Probably the most clear and socially accountable way of determining whether our practice is successful is through systematized, relatively objective, evaluation methods that can be replicated (repeated) by others. This is part of the science of practice; professional action that is informed by the best available information, guided by techniques of demonstrated effectiveness, and combined with objective evaluation components, all within the context of professional values.

Yet, this focus on the science of evidence-based and evaluation-informed practice is not intended to rule out other crucial aspects of practice. The art and creativity of practice, and the values and philosophy undergirding practice that make it humane and caring, we believe can be combined with the empirical/scientific orientation to produce what we call the *scientific practitioner*. Here, then, is our definition of the scientific practitioner. Such a practitioner combines the following elements in his or her practice:

1. Using the results of research and evaluation to the extent possible to select intervention techniques and other procedures that have evidence of effectiveness, and use of techniques without such evidence, only with caution; this is the heart of evidence-based practice;

2. Systematic monitoring and evaluation of his or her practice with each and every case, particularly through use of single-system designs; this is the heart of evaluation-informed practice;

3. Having the skills and attitudes—the commitment—to keep learning, to keep searching for new and more effective ways to serve consumers;

4. Conducting practice as a problem-solving experiment, a project in which little or nothing is assumed as known or given, with the core task of the practitioner being investigation and discovery; and, above all,

5. Maintaining a commitment in words and deeds to the ethics and values of the helping professions, a sensitivity, care, and concern for the well-being, rights, and dignity of clients and consumers.

In other words, the scientific practitioner is a person who is strongly concerned with humane helping that is provided in the most effective manner possible. Each element—the scientific, the ethical, and the practice—clarifies and reinforces each other. None can be minimized in favor of the other without detriment to the whole.

Now, obviously, scientific practice featuring evidence-based and evaluation-informed practice involves a complicated and broad set of commitments, including precise information retrieval, evaluation, use of effective interventions, and ethics and values. While we have argued the importance of integrating all of these components. If one is to engage in evidence-based practice, or any practice for that matter, it is probably obvious that one must evaluate that practice to provide a foundation for any claims to effectiveness.

As you can probably guess, we believe that thinking about evaluation during the course of practice will help to sharpen the thinking of practitioners and offer insights that cannot easily be attained in other ways. However, we want to emphasize that if ever occasions arise when the procedures of evaluation interfere with some specific intervention practice, our ethics tell us there is no choice but to put those intervention concerns first. We should do nothing (in the name of research or evaluation) that harms clients or their chances for successful service. Because the primary goal of evaluation is to improve practice, we do not believe in sacrificing the meaning and relevance of practice on the altar of scientific rigor. We believe, however, that occasions involving serious conflicts between practice and evaluation are rare. As we will try to show, in the great majority of situations, evaluation will help us to think clearly and act effectively and humanely on behalf of our clients.

Use of this form, or the more extensive planning format in Woody et al. (2004), will help ensure a well-rounded, sensitive approach to being the best possible practitioner.

STEPS IN EVIDENCE-BASED PRACTICE

The importance of evidence-based practice suggests to us that we should present a brief overview of the actual procedures involved in conducting evidence-based practice. Therefore, we will summarize in this section some of the far more detailed information on conducting evidence-based practice that you can find in skill-training manuals (e.g., Rubin, 2008; Gibbs, 2003; Cournoyer, 2003). We present these procedures as a series of steps.

Before we present these steps, however, we want to recognize with you the enormous challenge to most practitioners presented by this approach, and the large amount of time and stress that can be involved in applying these steps in a conscientious fashion. We hope you will remember, then, the following two possibilities that may help mitigate some of that pressure in applying evidence-based practice. First, one possibility is that you begin your pursuit of EBP gradually. You might want to start, sort of in an exploratory way, with just one case to try using evidence-based practice. Assess for yourself the time and effort that applying these evidence-based practice steps takes in that case. This way, you can properly gauge the costs and benefits of EBP. (Of course, we hope you will reap a huge amount of benefits in applying evidence-based practice with that first case in that you will see demonstrable, positive changes for your client.) Then, you can gauge just what resources you will need to apply EBP with subsequent cases. We are certain that each application will become easier as you gain experience, as with any new approach, including using single-system designs.

The second possibility to keep in mind actually depends on the kinds of services you provide in your organization. In many organizations, the caseloads include similar problems, admittedly with variations among individual clients. This may mean that one review of the literature to ascertain what may be useful for evidence-based practice may be generalizable to many of your cases. That is a huge savings in your time and energy in conducting these steps. In fact, as you will see, there inevitably will be client problems and situations where the literature is only minimally helpful, and in which inspiration for the best approach will come from your own experiences and those of your colleagues.

So, keeping those possibilities in mind, following are the steps involved in evidence-based practice.

Step 1. Develop a Question. This isn't as easy as it first may appear. The question may be as complicated as: What are the key factors affecting homelessness? or as focused as: What intervention works best with a given problem? For example, we may be working with clients with overwhelming anxiety. We would want to ask questions such as: What are the best methods for assessing anxiety, and What interventions work best with what different types of anxiety? We also want to be aware in seeking answers to our practice questions that characteristics of the client, practitioner, setting, and other environmental variables play an important part in getting the clearest and best answers to our questions. An intervention that cannot be adjusted to account for cultural differences among clients may not be the best answer to your question.

Step 2. Find the Evidence. The heart of evidence-based practice is in the search process, trying to find the best answers to the questions we ask. The largest part of the manuals available on EBP is devoted to this search process. Here, we can only provide a brief summary of search procedures.

There are three ways of finding evidence, all of them connected to the way we use the literature. Further, all of them also are connected to our use of the Internet, one of the trademarks of the evidence-based practitioner. The first two methods consist of finding published reviews of the research literature, while the third method involves do-it-yourself reviews.

The first method of finding the evidence is to find a meta-analytic review. *Meta-analyses* are quantitative reviews of the literature. A meta-analysis seeks to find all published (and sometimes unpublished) studies on a topic and synthesizes the results by finding a common metric to report the results of all the studies. That common metric is called an effect size, symbolized by a single statistic, most typically, d. The higher the effect size, the greater is assumed to be the impact of the intervention. Because of the importance of the decision for our clients about what is and what is not evidence-based, we recommend that practitioners be especially cautious in making that decision by using larger and less common effect sizes to try to ensure that such a decision is well-grounded in the evidence. To that end, we recommend that an effect size of .80 be the minimum one that practitioners use as a guideline for deciding what is evidence-based and what may not be. An effect size of .80 is regarded by many as large (Cohen, 1988), and also is relatively uncommon in the meta-analytic literature (Lipsey & Wilson, 1993). For meta-analyses with effect sizes lower than .80, we recommend that you use extra diligence and caution in applying the results. (For an excellent introduction to both meta-analyses and systematic reviews, described below, see Littel, Corcoran, & Pillai, 2008).

The second method of finding evidence is to find a published traditional or narrative review of the literature. In their more rigorous forms, these are called *systematic reviews*. These reviews also attempt to collect all available studies, but rather than conducting a quantitative analysis, either simply present the results of several studies or add to that by analyzing the methodologies of those studies. Then, a conclusion about effectiveness is drawn by logical (rather than quantitative) means. This is sometimes called the "box-score" method because the reviewer often just adds up the total of positive studies and negative studies and presents a conclusion.

For these reviews, too, we recommend a great deal of caution in accepting a conclusion about what is evidence-based. We recommend that unless 80% or more of the published studies are positive, extreme caution be used in making a conclusion that a procedure is evidence-based. (80% is the same percentage we use for accepting a measure as reliable, that is, consistent. The same principle applies here.) For reviews with a lower percentage of positive studies, once again we advise due caution in applying the results.

Here are a couple of hints about using the results of these traditional reviews. First, if the reviewer does not *analyze* the studies but only *describes* the results presented by the original authors of the studies, your confidence in accepting the conclusions should be decreased because there would be no way of knowing from the review whether the methods of the studies affected the results.

Second, if the reviewer only presents the results of the studies with positive outcomes, this may mean he or she has not done a comprehensive search. Thus, your confidence in the conclusions of that review should be greatly decreased. (Presentation of only positive results is actually a very common practice in book chapters on the effectiveness of different intervention techniques.) Obviously, an incomplete search can be a sign that the reviewer was selectively looking only for results that corroborate the reviewer's opinions.

The third method is to conduct a review of all the available evidence yourself. This method clearly is the most time-consuming and difficult of the three methods. But you will find, unfortunately, that many of the questions you pose in your search for the evidence simply have not been reviewed by others or that the reviews are out-of-date. (We define out-of-date reviews as those roughly three or more years old, an admittedly stringent criterion.) Therefore, you will have to do additional work yourself, either by supplementing older reviews or by finding all of the evidence yourself. (From our own experience in attempting to find evidence-based interventions, we know exactly how frustrating that can be.) The key challenge in conducting your own review is to try to ensure the review is comprehensive enough to incorporate all the literature. To that end, you may have to use different data bases and multiple search terms to ensure that all possible search options were pursued. To help in this type of search and the searches for published reviews, we present in Table 2 a number of the prime Internet sources for conducting such searches.

Step 3. Analyze the Evidence As if it is not enough to *find* the evidence, now you have to *analyze* it. For analysis of individual studies, this means having more than just a passing understanding of research design and methodology, as well as the commitment to putting in the time to apply your understanding to the analysis of studies. This means knowing about, let's say, the difference between experimental and quasi-experimental designs (hint: it's random assignment); understanding that there is a hierarchy of evidence from which one might make inferences about effectiveness, ranging from experimental designs to uncontrolled case studies; understanding whether the statistics used in a study are appropriate or inappropriate; and so on (see Rubin, 2008, for an extensive description of this hierarchy and what can be gleaned from each "level" of evidence). This is called research consumerism, and it is one of the reasons all education programs in the helping professions place so much emphasis on research methods classes.

Table 2 Internet sites for evidence-based practice searches

1. We recommend that two of the first sites you visit are the Campbell Collaboration at www.campbellcollaboration.org [go to C2 and scroll down for reviews] for reviews of the effects of social and behavioral interventions and the Cochrane Collaboration at www.cochrane.org for systematic reviews of the effects of health care interventions, including many reviews of psychosocial interventions
2. If you still have connections with your university, such as maintaining your university email address, you may still be able to use their data bases at no charge. If that is so, we highly recommend that you locate the data base called **EBSCOHost.** This data base contains over 20 databases, including *Academic Search Primer* that has full text (complete for downloading) articles from over 4,500 journals. For example, one of the data bases in EBSCOHost is *Psychology and Behavioral Sciences Collection* which alone has 575 full text journals available; this data base is particularly useful for members of the helping professions (your library may have a different version called *PsycINFO*).
3. Most readers probably are aware of Google for everyday searches. Google has a specialized feature called **Google Scholar** that is free and can be used to find research and other publications on many of the topics of interest for evidence-based practice. You can enter just one or two words as your search term (e.g., "meta-analysis and depression") or you may even enter an entire question to ensure broader coverage (e.g., "What are the most effective interventions for depression?").

How can one be a good consumer of research and hence evidence-based if one cannot properly analyze the studies that will guide decisions?

We understand that in the hard reality of everyday work in an organization, we simply are not going to be able to find rigorous empirical research to provide the evidence for all of our questions. Therefore, we recognize that some "evidence" may be considered weak by some standards. Thus, when we discuss evidence, we simply mean the *best* evidence that is available, starting with rigorous empirical research, of course, but including other sources when such research is not available. The decision to apply the available evidence is made with the understanding that the decision is the best one that could be made under the circumstances, and that careful evaluation of each case will reveal the wisdom of that choice. (We highly recommend the new book by Rubin, 2008, as an excellent introduction to analyzing research for evidence-based practice.)

Step 4. Combine the Evidence with Your Understanding of the Client and Situation. Although the process of arriving at an evidence-based practice decision is complex, it becomes even more interesting when we consider how to adapt it to the current client/problem/situation configuration. If all the evidence that is accumulated is based on a population that is different from the client with whom you are working, then you will have to find the best way to adapt what you found in the literature to the context in which you are working. The number of such contextual variables that could affect your decision are numerous, including ethnic and cultural differences, income level and income security, housing and family situation, and so on. We suggest that you take each piece of the evidence from your information search and ask: How specifically will this fit with my client? What can I do to make it more suitable to my client? (Clarkin & Levy, 2004, and Beutler et al., 2004, go into detail about making suitable adaptations from a research literature to your own specific case, especially with regard to the effects of different client and practitioner characteristics.) For example, using interventions originally used with preschoolers may be modified to assume more cognitive sophistication in elementary school students; dealing with views of unmarried mothers as suitable caretakers of their children may differ by ethnicity; different cultures may permit more or less child tending by older siblings. Your conceptual mapping of the situation will have to take into consideration these kinds of perspectives.

Step 5. Application to Practice. In a sense, this might be the easiest part of evidence-based practice. Once the decision is made to implement the material you have identified as evidence-based, all that's left to do is to implement that material. Of course, a practitioner might find that he or she does not have sufficient knowledge to immediately implement the techniques identified as evidence-based; therefore, a period of familiarization will be necessary. This can be greatly eased by maintaining in one's possession some of the books described earlier that present the intervention techniques that have been found to be effective in proceduralized manuals; that is identifying the specific steps involved in implementing an intervention technique (e.g., LeCroy, 2008).

Step 6. Monitor and Evaluate Results. Even with interventions that have the soundest base of evidence, evaluation of the application in practice is necessary. Perfect results are never guaranteed, and that is how and why evaluation-informed practice is so crucial to evidence-based practice. We, as practitioners, must always be accountable for our efforts. And the primary way we demonstrate that accountability, once an evidence-based decision is implemented, is through our systematic and careful monitoring and evaluation of that application. Of course, evaluation-informed practice and single-system designs are the focus of the rest of this book, so we hope that you will be highly skilled in the application of these evaluation procedures.

INTEGRATING EVALUATION-INFORMED AND EVIDENCE-BASED PRACTICE: THE PRAISES MODEL

Although we have argued that it is critically important to integrate evaluation and practice, it still remains for us to provide examples of precisely how that integration might occur. We have described evidence-based practice as using the best evidence at *all* points of planning and contact with the clients. And it is exactly these points that have to be operationalized clearly in order for you to understand not only how evaluation-informed and evidence-based practice can be integrated, but identifying every point in the overall intervention process—from first contact to follow-up—where they *can* and *should* be integrated.

To that end, we present in Figure 2, the PRAISES Model, a framework for integrating evaluation-informed and evidence-based practice (Fischer, 1986). We understand that at first glance, this framework can be somewhat intimidating, as it may look more like a General Motors wiring diagram than a flowchart for use by helping professionals. But we want to assure you, on the basis of well over two decades of teaching using the PRAISES Model, that this framework is very useful and quite adaptable. Here's why: A careful look at the flowchart will show that the flowchart actually is a compilation of virtually all the steps many practitioners go through any way, but in this case, systematized in a flowchart that is intended to add a more structured nature to those steps.

Indeed, to that end, the PRAISES Model is an attempt to integrate, structure, and systematize the process of evidence-based practice, while highlighting the interrelationships among interventive practices and evaluation in the overall process. Let's just briefly describe some of the characteristics of this framework and the ways in which they illustrate and enhance evidence-based practice.

1. *Empirically based.* To the extent possible, this framework attempts to enhance development of the empirical base for evidence-based practice. As we have pointed out, the empirical base of evidence-based practice has two meanings. The first is the use of the results of research to guide selection of interventions that have demonstrated effectiveness. The second meaning is in the careful and systematic evaluation of the effects of our interventions. This framework highlights the points of planning and contact with the clients where evaluation-informed and evidence-based decisions need to be made. In other words, every time the practitioner plans to see the client, he or she should have a handle on what the empirical evidence says about that contact (e.g., the very first interview; the very last interview; or the follow-up contact).

2. *Integrative.* The PRAISES Model flowchart integrates essentially all practice and evaluation activities. This is the basis for our earlier assertions that good practice incorporates good evaluation. There are no distinctions made between evaluation and practice in the flowchart. Only the different activities required at each step are described. In fact, you will be able to see in the PRAISES Model flowchart all the evaluation steps that are described in this book and summarized at the end of this chapter.

3. *Eclectic.* This framework is based on the assumption that the knowledge base of practice in the helping professions is both pluralistic and eclectic. It is pluralistic in the sense that knowledge is derived from many sources. It is eclectic in that only the best available knowledge is derived from those sources. Eclecticism refers to the use of clear, precise, systematic criteria to select knowledge. In particular, this relates to the empirical base of evidence-based practice in that, whenever possible, evidence-based practice is comprised of a variety of procedures and techniques selected largely on the basis of evidence of effectiveness and applied with people and situations where the evidence indicates that such application has a good chance of producing a successful outcome.

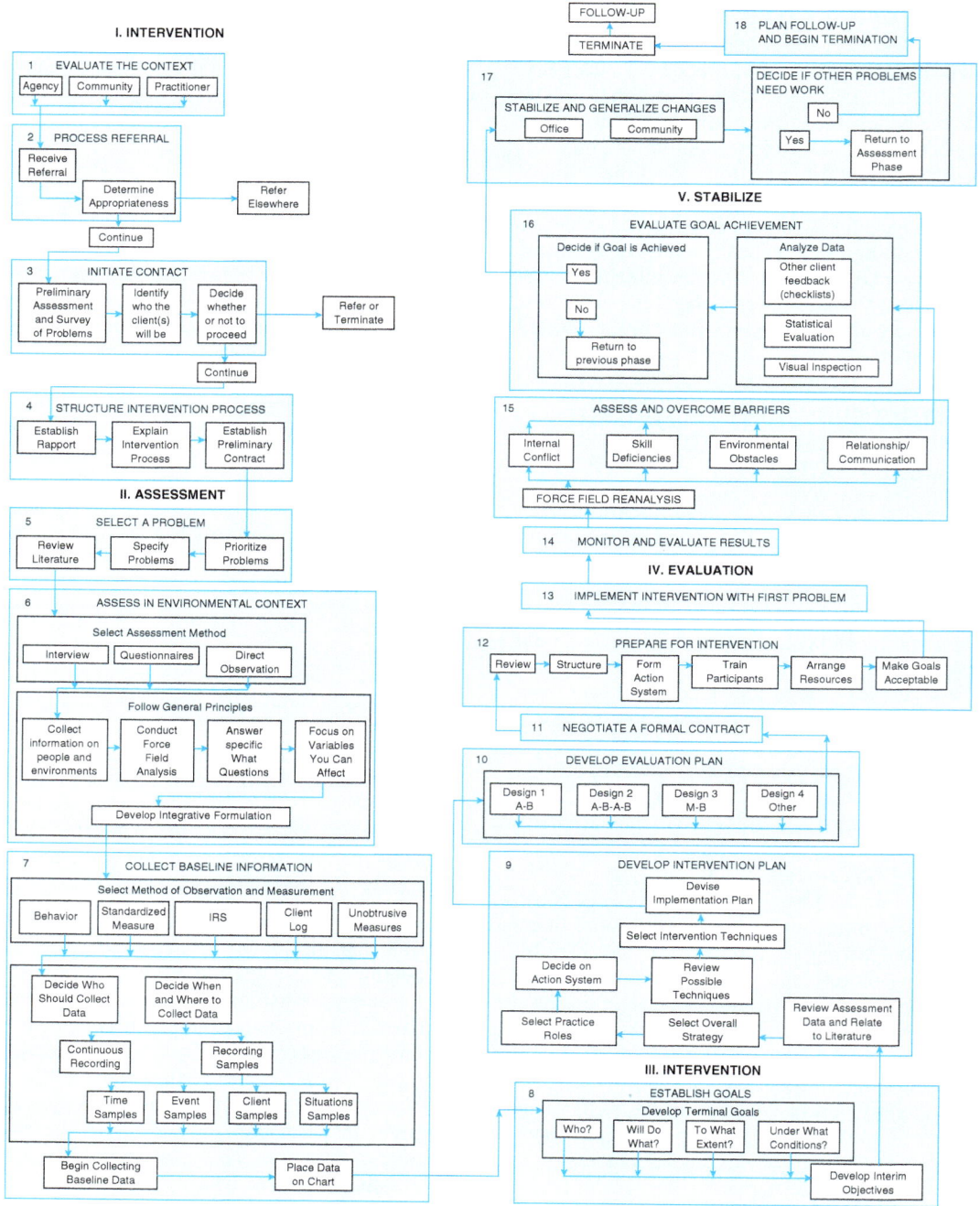

FIGURE 2 The PRAISES Model: A framework for integrating evidence-based and evaluation-informed practice.

Of course, it is not always possible to achieve this ideal with each and every problem/situation. But as an organizing principle of evidence-based practice, it seems like a worthwhile goal to shoot for. More concretely, this framework is intended to apply whatever the theoretical orientation, methods, or approach of the user.

4. *Systematic.* This framework is an attempt to systematize practice. This means clearly identifying the various phases of practice and organizing them in a step-by-step sequence. In fact, one of the most important characteristics of practice is being systematic: in how goals are defined, in how intervention techniques are selected, in how outcome is monitored, and so on. It also appears to make sense to try to organize the diverse activities of practice into a logical sequence that runs from initial contact to termination and follow-up.

Although we describe the process of practice in the flowchart as a sequence of steps within phases, we do not intend to prescribe a rigid, lock-step approach to practice. For example, depending on the problem or situation, the length of time for any step could vary considerably, the steps could overlap, or a particular step might not even occur at all. Indeed, despite the fact that a number of steps are described, the essence of professional practice using this framework must be flexibility: selecting what is done on the basis of a specific client/problem/situation configuration. This attempt to organize that process is intended to bring some order and structure into the subtleties and contradictions of real-life practice. Importantly, this framework has been found to be a very useful device for newer practitioners, providing them with an anchor as they learn how to engage in evidence-based practice.

5. *Accountable.* This framework is an attempt to add to our professional accountability as practitioners. It brings the entire process of practice out into the open for scrutiny by others. It points out and builds into practice the necessity for carefully evaluating results with every case, and this is the very *heart* of accountability.

6. *Way of thinking.* The PRAISES Model is intended, perhaps more than anything else, to illustrate and enhance a way of thinking about practice: systematic, data-based, outcome-oriented, structured, flexible depending on the needs of the client, evidence-based, informed by ongoing evaluation, and up-to-date with the relevant literature. All of this is grounded in the ethics and values, the scientific humanism, that underlie the philosophy and practices of the helping professions.

The PRAISES Model is comprised of five major phases and 18 steps, each of which is divided into component parts. The term "PRAISES" is an acronym for the five phases. The entire flowchart of the PRAISES Model is presented in Figure 2. Following is a summary of the phases and the 18 steps.

PHASE I. PRe-Intervention

1. Evaluate the context
2. Process the referral
3. Initiate contact
4. Structure

PHASE II. Assessment

5. Select problem
6. Conduct assessment
7. Collect baseline information
8. Establish goals

PHASE III. Intervention

9. Develop intervention plan
10. Develop evaluation plan
11. Negotiate contract
12. Prepare for intervention
13. Implement intervention

PHASE IV. Systematic Evaluation

14. Monitor and evaluate results
15. Assess and overcome barriers
16. Evaluate goal achievement

PHASES V. Stabilize

17. Stabilize and generalize changes
18. Plan and implement termination and follow-up

SINGLE-SYSTEM EVALUATION, QUALITATIVE RESEARCH, AND QUANTITATIVE RESEARCH

With the recent renewed interest in qualitative research, as contrasted with the traditional quantitative research, the questions arise: How does single-system evaluation fit? Is it more like qualitative or quantitative research, or is it different from both of them (but for different reasons)? Our answer: Yes, to all of the above. To explain this paradoxical response, let us first define terms.

Unfortunately, it is not easy to define "qualitative research." An anthology by Sherman and Reid (1994), containing over 40 discussions or examples of qualitative research, reveals enormous differences of opinion even among respected qualitative researchers. The following working definition, therefore, is a sympathetic interpretation of the discussions in Sherman and Reid's anthology: *Qualitative research,* at its core, is a set of philosophical ideas and empirical methods for identifying and describing some human experience, based on spoken or written words, and/or observable behaviors *alone,* that is, without forcing a preconceived theoretical position or set of values onto the experience. Instead, the observer tries to be as sensitive as possible to the client's experience—in spite of the cultural and psychosocial differences that may stand between them—and to report this experience as fully as possible so that others who haven't had the same experience may understand. This means that units of analysis—what one pays attention to—will differ according to the observer; there are few traditional "laws of research" operating, unless it is to understand the situation as fully as possible as it is lived by the persons involved.

From this naturalistic experience of the person-in-situation, qualitative researchers develop subjective themes, categories, classifications, and topologies that verbalize their understanding, a rich and "thick description" (cf. Laird, 1994, pp. 175–189) of the many layers and textures of the experience. This holistic description can then be used to contribute to a kind of empirical understanding of a more nearly realistic human experience. This qualitative knowledge, or heuristic approach (Tyson, 1994, pp. 89–112), then can be used by applied social scientists for a more nearly valid description of human concerns, and eventually as a guide to evaluating in realistic terms, the outcomes of interventions. Qualitative research is too new to have cumulated a large body of qualitative outcome studies, but the Sherman and Reid anthology, among others, begins to identify such studies.

Some researchers in the qualitative community sharply criticize certain aspects of quantitative research: For example, its assumption that the methods of the natural sciences are superior to all others and should be used in the social sciences; its putting research values above treatment values, which could harm the helping process due to its inevitable intrusiveness; its attempt to separate all values and biases from the human enterprise of research and to assume we can have independent, objective knowledge of any human situation; and its erroneous seeking of universal truths, while disregarding as pesky annoyances the contexts of human actions (Tyson, 1994; Heineman-Pieper, 1994). Single-system designs are designated as a kind of quantitative research, according to these critics, and thus are heir to all of these criticisms.

In contrast, there are more than enough definitions of quantitative research. We offer our own equally sympathetic interpretation: *Quantitative research,* at its core, is a set of philosophical ideas and empirical methods for identifying and describing some human experience, based on spoken or written words, and/or observable behaviors, by using the cumulative understanding and common language of prior researchers. By adhering as closely as possible to shared procedures—such as defining terms in operational definitions, using clearly defined hypotheses to test implications of existing theory, and presenting results in standardized numeric and statistical terms—the results of investigation will be open to common understanding (by suitably trained persons) and replication. From this standardized experience of some specific portion of the person-in-situation, quantitative researchers develop more or less objective pieces of information that can be combined to create larger networks of understanding, codified in revised theories and new hypotheses for further testing. Thus, there emerges a knowledge base that can be used by applied social scientists for solving human problems and concerns. There are a large number of quantitative studies which have been used by helping professionals for many years as the basis for selecting a guiding practice theory and a substantiated method of practice.

Quantitative researchers have responded to the barbs of qualitative critics more than they have offered full-blown critical analyses of this heuristic approach. However, quantitative researchers do ask critical questions such as these: If qualitative research is so good, show us the results in tangible effects that have helped clients; if you can't clearly (i.e., operationally) define the nature of a problem, it may not exist for any practical purpose of trying to resolve that problem (Hudson, 1982); if qualitative research relies so heavily on individualizing people and situations, how does it avoid biases and how can results be corroborated, cumulated, and/or generalized?

As you can see, the vital differences between the definitions of qualitative and quantitative research lie in what the researcher brings to the experience, and what the researcher takes from the experience. The quantitative researcher brings cumulated shared understandings and standardized procedures, and takes away numerical and statistical information that is interpreted in terms of abstract theories and value assumptions. The qualitative researcher brings as few preconceptions as possible, and takes away a richer, more subjective interpretation of what the human experience is all about, some of which may be summarized in numerical and statistical forms. What they both share is the *research* component, a knowledge-building perspective using certain kinds of ideas and methods. Neither approach *requires* that the obtained knowledge be used in human affairs.

We now can ask the question: What is single-system evaluation, with reference to making connections to either qualitative or quantitative research . . . or both . . . or neither? We proposed earlier that single-system evaluation may be all of the above. Now, we can explain. First, we emphasize that evaluation is very different from research, even though it shares some of the same methods and ideas. The differences make all the difference. Evaluation largely is obtaining information for use by practitioners to modify their practices so as to more nearly move in the direction of enhancing client goal attainment. Building knowledge is not its primary goal; however, the results of evaluation studies may help to build practice knowledge, and may contribute to forming research hypotheses that require testing using research methods. So, let us give a sympathetic definition, parallel to the issues discussed previously.

Evaluation—and particularly *single-system evaluation*—is a set of philosophical ideas and empirical methods for working with clients in identifying and describing some human experience—a problem or concern that is important (valuable) to the client—based on direct observations in client–practitioner interactions, and/or spoken or written words, using both the practitioner's own human experience and past training in the language and methodology of practice.

These "descriptions" then form the basis for evaluating the success of interventions applied to the client's experiences. By being a sensitive human being and a trained observer—these seem to be quintessential for the qualitative researcher—the practitioner can enter a situation and form a trusting relationship with a client. With the client, the practitioner can then identify and prioritize problems and concerns (i.e., the preferences or values of the client), and can begin to formulate professional ways to address them (based on past experiences and training). As part of good practice, the practitioner will engage the client to participate in as many aspects of the helping process as possible, including the monitoring of targeted concerns, so as to have corrective feedback on developments. This monitoring will involve operational procedures and numbers—important for the quantitative researcher. From this interchange over time, the client and practitioner hope to move toward problem resolution, along with training of the client for self-maintenance and empowerment after the direct intervention period has ended. The practitioner also may reflect on the intervention process for what other information it suggests, with the possibility of building an efficacious repertoire of practices for use with other clients.

Thus, single-system evaluation partakes of both qualitative and quantitative methods, and yet it is different in important ways from both of them. Perhaps the most useful way to characterize these similarities and differences is by reference to Lang's (1994, pp. 265–278) insightful analysis on ways of distinguishing qualitative research and practice. Briefly, Lang distinguishes an action, or *knowledge-using* approach, from a pure-science, or *knowledge-building,* approach. The data processing cycle for *knowledge-using* involves abstracting and then generalizing from the concrete data of practice, so as to match the given case to some existing practice theory. Then the practitioner uses the logical predictions from the theory as strategies for guidance back in the concrete world. The *knowledge-building* cycle is longer; it incorporates the abstracting and generalizing steps, but then goes on to categorize and eventually conceptualize—which is the building of new theory, the goal for the *knowledge-building* approach. It does not necessarily cycle back, especially immediately, to the real world to influence the events from which it began.

Although we accept this general model distinguishing knowledge building from practice, we submit that single-system evaluation applies to both. Yes, the action, or *knowledge-using* cycle does operate, but it doesn't merely stop back at the concrete world. It may, under some structured conditions, provide a broader perspective on what has been attained in terms of categorizing and eventually conceptualizing these events into a revised practice theory that can be cycled back for use with new clients. Single-system evaluation procedures comprise one such set of structured conditions that encourages practitioners to build efficacious repertoires of practice and the practice theory ideas needed to apply them. However, all practitioners are not obliged to build new practice theory; it is simply an option if they wish to contribute to the knowledge development of the helping professions. Therefore, *we hold that single-system designs are partly qualitative and partly quantitative enterprises, but more importantly, they are knowledge-using enterprises on behalf of our clients.*

ADVANTAGES OF USING SINGLE-SYSTEM DESIGNS IN PRACTICE

Many characteristics of single-system designs will assist you to practice more effectively and humanely. Here, we summarize some of these points, noting also that these characteristics address—and we think overcome—many of the problems practitioners see regarding practice applications of traditional, classical, practice research.

1. Single-system designs can be built into almost every practice situation, usually without disrupting the intervention, because these designs emphasize good practice characteristics, such as clear identification of the presenting problems.

2. Single-system designs provide reasonably objective and systematic information for monitoring changes in client conditions over time so that you, the practitioner, can adapt appropriately and in a timely fashion. Important targets and special factors (placed on charts) don't get lost in the shuffle because they are all there on the charts. This continuous record differs considerably from traditional pretest and posttest group designs.

3. Single-system designs focus on the individual client or system, mirroring the unique changes in the practice situation, rather than reflecting *average* scores as with group research designs. This is truly client-focused evaluation, permitting both relative objectivity in data gathering and close involvement with the unique case.

4. Single-system designs are practitioner-oriented in the here-and-now situation. They provide vital feedback on what the practitioner needs to know to move the case in desired directions. They are flexible designs, capable of changing as new events occur in the client's circumstances, including allowing new targets. Traditional group designs cannot be changed once the study has begun.

5. Single-system designs can be used to assess the case or situation by clarifying what seem to be the relevant factors in the problem, such as the frequency and intensity of a problem and where and when the problem occurs. This, in turn, will lead to the selection of more appropriate interventions.

6. Some single-system designs can be used to test hypotheses or ideas regarding the relationship between specific intervention procedures and client changes, ruling out some alternative explanations and allowing an inference regarding causality: Was your intervention program responsible for the change in the target problem?

7. Single-system designs are essentially theory independent—or, more accurately, theory neutral—in the sense that they are usable by practitioners adhering to just about any practice theory. They can be applied to the practice of any practitioner who can be reasonably clear about what targets and what interventions are being used, and who is willing to obtain ongoing measures on these targets.

8. Single-system designs are relatively easy to use and to understand. They can be applied within the same time frame that you are currently using in seeing clients. (Often, you can share your charts with clients as motivators of continuing progress or clarification of the nature of the problems.) Once you understand the basics, there is relatively little time spent on the mechanics of single-system designs. (Students have reported a threshold effect; it takes some initial effort to learn about single-system designs and to implement them at first, but once you cross that threshold, it is much easier thereafter.)

9. The use of single-system evaluations in entire agencies largely can avoid the imposition of outside researchers coming to evaluate your work. Because clients and others are intrinsically involved

in constructing and implementing single-system designs, there is a high level of intellectual and professional honesty in their use. The closeness of the measures to the client's problems produces a type of validity that cannot be matched in group designs.

10. Single-system designs provide a model for demonstrating our accountability to ourselves, our clients and consumers, our funding sources, and our communities. Use of these evaluation methods with numbers of clients can lead to new practice hypotheses that can further the knowledge base of the profession.

11. Finally, a recent meta-analysis (a quantitative review of research), involving large-scale experimental research (e.g., Lambert, 2007) has shown that formally monitoring client progress and providing feedback to the practitioner, as in single-system designs, not only can reduce deterioration but also can have a positive effect on overall outcome. Now *that* is an enormous boost to the importance of evaluation-informed practice using single-system designs.

A WALK THROUGH THE EVALUATION PROCESS

Our ultimate goal is to convince you of the value of single-system designs in furthering your practice, for yourself, your clients, and society. We hope to show you how to integrate the steps of this evaluation process into your practice so that it is an automatic reaction to think clearly about the presenting problem, to ascertain more or less objectively the extent of that problem, to consider possible causal/maintaining factors, and to plan specific interventions that have some chance of making the changes the client desires. All of this is part of both good practice and good evaluation. Just as you are learning or have learned how to practice well, so we hope you will learn how to evaluate well in connection with whatever type of practice you are using.

Thinking about and working with this problem-solving process will become second nature after you study this material in the classroom or in the field. Likewise, evaluation will become second nature—and closely identified with your practice steps—once *this* material is carefully studied.

The problem-solving process will never fit exactly in all your cases, but it will be a point of departure in thinking systematically about the situation. Evaluation also will help you to think clearly and systematically because it raises the very questions that make for clear thinking: Specifically, what are the scope and nature of the presenting problem? What exact interventions should be tried with it? What concomitant changes are occurring when the intervention is present or absent? Are the problems changing with use of the intervention, or do more intense or different interventions need to be considered? Has the problem been resolved effectively and humanely? These are questions at the heart of evaluation-informed practice, but they are also vital questions that practitioners ask about practice in general. Indeed, good practice inevitably includes good evaluation.

One way to visualize this sequence of practice and evaluation is through the flowchart, a graphic presentation of the actions, decisions, and exchanges of information in a given process. You already have seen how we used a flowchart to illustrate the PRAISES Model. Now, we want to use another flowchart to provide a specific guide to the topics and chapters in this book.

As with the PRAISES Model, use of this flowchart is not intended to present a rigid sequence of events. There will be occasions when we go back to an earlier step to consider new problems or new ways of measuring problems or change the order of some of the steps, but the general flow will help to provide a sense of direction and purpose amid all the ebbs and flows of the client's life.

Figure 3 is a flowchart of the evaluation process as contained in this book. Each of the main components of the evaluation process—conceptualization and measurement, design, and analysis and decision making—plus an introduction (evaluation context) and a conclusion (challenges) is a major block in the flowchart. Each block represents one of the parts, and most of the subunits, as noted, reflect either a complete chapter or a section of a chapter. Note that there are some commonalities across the three major evaluation blocks: Each part is introduced by a "basic principles" chapter. Then other chapters follow and provide specific applications of these basic principles. Each part is concluded by a chapter on how to select from among the alternative applications.

Integrating Evaluation and Practice

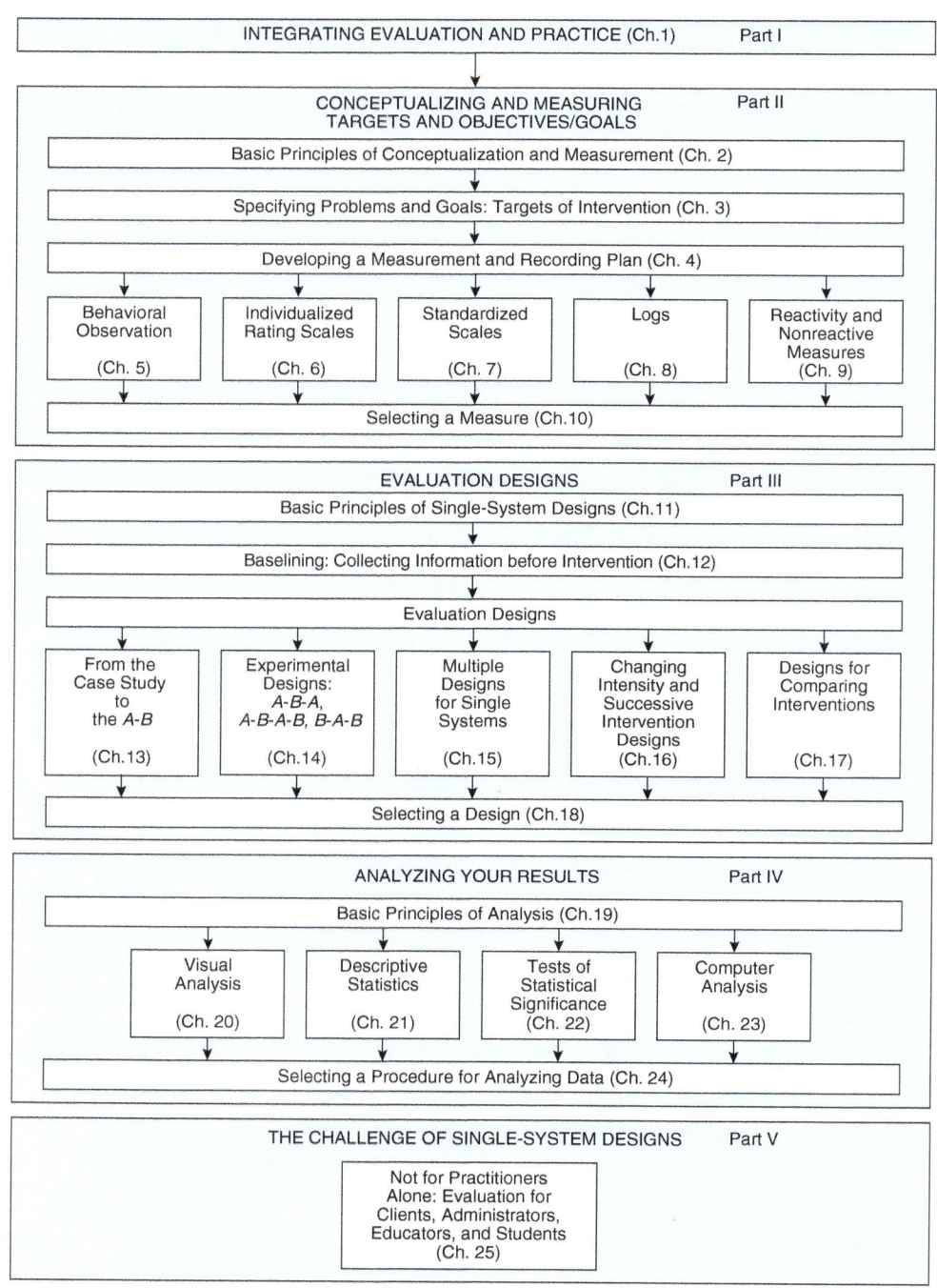

FIGURE 3 Flowchart showing the organization of this book.

The first major component of the evaluation process involves conceptualization and measurement. Before you can begin to measure a problem, you need some understanding of the basic principles of measurement. One of the major bridges connecting evaluation and practice—specification of problems and goals. In this chapter we describe how to move from the often vague and nebulous problems with which we are initially faced in practice to clearer, more precise statements regarding both the nature of the problem and the goals we are aiming for with each client-system.

We discuss the preliminary steps you should take in developing a recording plan, including who should do the recording, when and where the recording should take place, and deciding how many problems to record. We also present an introduction to recording and to managing cases with computers, using the computer program called CASS that is included with this book.

Summary

This chapter provided an overview of and introduction to the topic of—integrating evaluation and practice through the use of single-system designs—what we call evaluation-informed practice. The chapter began with a brief overview of basic characteristics of single-system evaluation methods. This was followed by a comparison of single-system evaluation methods with the methods of classical research. This was followed by an introduction to evidence-based practice and the PRAISES Model for integrating evaluation-informed and evidence-based practice. We then examined the issue of qualitative and quantitative methods in single-system designs. We then summarized the many advantages for practice of single-system designs. The chapter concluded with a flowchart of the entire evaluation process, as presented in this book, to be used as an introduction to and overview of the rest of the chapters.

BASIC PRINCIPLES OF CONCEPTUALIZATION AND MEASUREMENT

PURPOSE The purpose of this chapter is to introduce you to the key characteristics of measurement tools and to help you evaluate them for use in your own practice. We discuss the use and importance of conceptualization in practice, as well as key measurement characteristics such as reliability, validity, utility, directness, and administration of measures. The basic point of this chapter is this: Without good measurement, you cannot do good evaluation or good practice.

Introduction
What Is Conceptualization?
What Is Measurement?
   Levels of Measurement
      Nominal Level
      Ordinal Level
      Interval Level
      Ratio level
   Advantages of Measurement
Definition as a First Step in Measurement
   Conceptual Definitions
   Operational Definitions
Can Everything Be Measured?
Key Characteristics of All Measures
   Measurement Error
      Random Measurement Error
      Systematic Measurement Error
      Importance of Measurement Error
   Reliability
      Test–Retest Reliability
      Alternate-Forms Reliability
      Internal-Consistency Reliability
      Interobserver Reliability
      Standard Error of Measurement (SEM)
      What Is "High" Reliability?
      Which Type of Reliability Should You Use?
   Validity
      Face Validity
      Content Validity
      Criterion Validity
      Construct Validity
      Which Type of Validity Should You Use?
   The Relationship between Reliability and Validity
   Factors Influencing Reliability and Validity
      Administration Procedures
      Populations
   Utility
      Relevance to Intervention Planning
      Ease of Use
      Accessibility
   Direct and Indirect Measures
Summary

From Chapter 2 of *Evaluating Practice: Guidelines for the Accountable Professional*, Sixth Edition. Martin Bloom, Joel Fischer, John G. Orme. Copyright © 2009 by Pearson Education, Inc. All rights reserved.

INTRODUCTION

Because the purpose is to illustrate the usefulness of evaluation in practice, we want to avoid a lot of traditional research jargon. Most research books seem to be written with the belief that the potential readers are primarily other researchers instead of people whose callings may be oriented toward other pursuits, such as the helping practices.

However, there are a number of principles that are important for you to understand in order to use evaluation methods effectively in practice. Many of these principles have to do with the measurement processes. The repeated measurement of the client concerns that are the targets of our interventions is at the heart of single-system evaluation, and, therefore, it is important to know how to select the most accurate and practical measures from the measurement tools we'll be presenting. This is important because, the better the information, the more likely it is that the service will be effective and humane.

This chapter presents a review of the key considerations that should underlie your selection and use of every measurement procedure. First, we define measurement. Next we discuss the importance of identifying what we intend to measure. We then tackle the rather thorny question: Can everything be measured? Finally, we move to a review of the basic characteristics of measurement tools; that is, guidelines for selecting measures and interpreting the results of those measures.

Many of the principles of single-system evaluation that we describe in this chapter are the same for more traditional research methods as well. We will, however, try to point out where the applications are different.

In all, we hope to provide you with enough information in this chapter to (a) understand our use of these terms in subsequent chapters, and (b) encourage you to employ these principles in selecting and using the measurement tools we present. As you make decisions regarding what measures to use in practice, we hope you will evaluate these measures according to the guidelines we present in this chapter.

The helping professions run on energy supplied by theories and research and are guided by professional training and ethics, as expressed in one's personal style and experiences. In order to translate abstract theory and empirical research into terms usable by the helping professional, we need to introduce this on measurement with a brief discussion of concepts—the stuff that makes up theories and evaluation methodology.

WHAT IS CONCEPTUALIZATION?

Conceptualization is the process of finding general behavior patterns among the bits and pieces of specific situations in everyday life. We see a person's bowed head, a sad expression on his face, a physical compression of his whole body; we hear about his not eating well, taking no enjoyment in ordinary life events, feeling unhappy, having no sense of a personal future. But we *conceptualize* this set of events with the abstract term *depression* in order to connect all of our experiences into one linguistic basket as well as to connect, by means of this concept and going through appropriate information retrieval systems, with the writings of experts in this mental health area who can help us understand what is going on (theories and research on normal human development and psychopathology) and provide some suggestions about ways of dealing with it in our client (evidence-based practices).

This linguistic basket is constructed by a process of *abstraction*—identifying some portion of the observed event that appears to be significant for the future concept, and *generalizing* that portion into a new entity, the concept. For example, a man with a bowed head is not engaging in typical adult behavior, so we can infer that something must be going on in his life that makes him "weighted down" physically. The same is true of the physical compression of his body (bent over, arms crossed in front). The sad expression on his face suggests that whatever is going on in his life is not pleasant to him, and so on, with each observation.

The resulting concept may have no specific connection with any of the pieces of life events that went into its construction, but there is something (abstract and general) that links it with each of these separate client attributes or events. For example, the concept *depression* has been studied widely (because it is one of the most common experiences in mental illness), so that there are many descriptions of it. While there may be other concepts that fit some or most of the experiences we observed, the concept of depression seems to be a first good educated guess—literally, a guess—which itself requires further testing. From research, we know that many common adult behaviors, such as sexual desire and performance, are reduced for a person who is depressed. We could explore this kind of empirical information with the client, and, if confirmed, then it would add one more piece of evidence that this concept does in fact cover all of the known facts related to the client in this situation.

A *concept* may be defined as an abstract idea about some portion of the universe, which is neither true nor false, but only useful to someone to some degree. Concepts pull together separate pieces of our stream of experiences, thereby imposing some degree of order in an unruly universe. However, keep in mind that all concepts are arbitrary constructions, not underlying truths of nature.

When two or more concepts are joined together with logical modifiers (such as *and, not*, etc.), we get *propositions*, which may be of several types. *Hypotheses* are propositions that make predictions and are used to guide evaluation-informed practice and research activities. Typically, these hypotheses are derived from some body of theory. One type of proposition asserts some *causal linkage* (e.g., "A causes B"). This type of proposition may be tested for truth or falsity, which can be helpful to the practitioner in field settings. Related to this causal statement is the *correlational proposition* that two items are related, but not necessarily in a causal way. Another type of proposition is the *assumption*, a proposition that is a given, or taken for granted, in a particular study. Assumptions are not tested; they are used to get our logical machinery going. Without assumptions, we would have to test every proposition before using it in a logical network. Finally, another type of proposition is the *value statement*, which is simply an expression of preference and cannot be proven to be true or false.

Theory is composed of systems of concepts and propositions that describe some portion of the universe succinctly, explain how things work within that portion, and predict the likely trajectory of events concerning that part of the world. So, for example, Bandura's widely used social/cognitive theory (Bandura, 1986) suggests that behavior will likely occur when people know about some situation (knowledge), know how to act in that situation (skill), want to see certain changes in the status quo (motivation provided by anticipated future desired change), and most important, believe that they have self-efficacy, which is the belief that they can do the specific task. When these four conceptual elements are in place, then we are likely to observe the behavioral change, according to the theory. However, merely having this abstract road map is not enough for helping professionals. This system of concepts and propositions is a logical model needing translation into specific professional action.

This translation of social cognitive theory to practice involves providing knowledge about the specific issue, giving the skill training needed to make the behavior changes, acquainting the individual with future states to which he or she can aspire, and most important, enhancing the individual's sense of self-efficacy. Based on Bandura's (1986) research, there are four ways to enhance self-efficacy, in order of effectiveness: (1) provide mastery experiences of some relevant portion of that task; (2) provide vicarious learning relevant to that task from the actions of others; (3) offer verbal lessons or lectures; and (4) help the individual experience physiological feedback (such as relaxing when anxious, since being relaxed is antagonistic to the feelings of being tense with anxiety). Therefore, a *translation of theory/research into practice strategy* involves taking the concept and identifying specific actions that would constitute an instance of that abstract concept. For example, teaching assertiveness to a shy person constitutes giving that person needed skills relevant to his or her life concerns.

Thus, a theory is a kind of road map to some area of human experience that may be useful to get predictable and testable ideas on how to move through that territory. A theory may be a more or less reliable guide, and some eclectic thinkers prefer to assemble evidence-based practice knowledge on a topic, rather than rely on abstract ideas as such. But even eclectic thinking requires that we understand the conceptual nature of the task at hand, for making connections with bodies of empirical studies. For others, conceptualizing some piece of experience (like the client's problem) permits the practitioner to connect with bodies of theory and research that may shed some light on the problem and offer suggestions for ways to address it.

From our professional education, we also learn a bit of humility, that there are many definitions of most concepts, such as depression, each composed of patterns that emphasize more of one set of events rather than some other set of events that have attracted the attention of other theorists. Theories are neither true nor false; they may provide fruitful predictions that can be tested for their correctness. A major purpose of single-system designs, the topic of this text, is to test the correctness of practice hypotheses derived from theories, research, or practice wisdom, but to do this in the context of helping our clients.

So, conceptualization is the way we name patterns or regularities among events we observe in client situations. The names (concepts) and the ways in which these names are combined (in propositions, such as hypotheses, value statements, and assumptions) often influence how we think about the client situation and perhaps connect these ideas with those others discussed in the theoretical or empirical literature, which may provide guidance for practice. Concepts may lead us to discover an empirical literature with useful techniques of intervention that are quite independent of theory (Fischer, 1993). So, in either case, it is important to think about what we are observing in the client situation and to identify patterns or regularities whose "names" may lead us to other people's approaches to dealing with these target events.

Some theories, like the psychoanalytic approach, apply complex concepts to subtle human behaviors as they lead to complex strategies of intervention. Other theories, like the behavioral approaches, apply relatively simple, more observable concepts to observable human behaviors, as a lead to specific intervention strategies. There are, of course, many kinds of theories in between. In all cases, the practitioner looks for regularities in the problem behaviors the client and situation present. These patterns are named with knowledge of similarly patterned names in the literature, so that the practitioner can connect with this other literature on similar patterns and suggested interventions based on their evaluated experiences.

How should we conceptualize? Ask yourself these kinds of questions with regard to the regularities or patterns you are noticing: (1) Do you notice that the same kinds of verbs are being used in describing several situations, for example, verbs about violence, shyness, or fear, regardless of the situation? (2) Look at the nouns that are linked with these verbs—who or what is involved with the verbs? Are they common across several situations? You may have to use synonyms to find patterns, but beware that you may also have two or more patterns. (3) Now look at the kinds of sentences (propositions) that you use as you connect nouns and verbs regarding two or more situations. If these propositions are similar, then use the common verbs or nouns as your key terms to enter a search for information on your computer, either on theories using these terms as a central part of their system or on empirical studies addressing these terms.

WHAT IS MEASUREMENT?

Once we conceptualize, we try to translate our concepts into measures. Measurement is generally thought of as the process of assigning labels to certain characteristics of things according to a set of rules. The "things" may be people (especially their thoughts, feelings, or actions), objects, or events. The most common type of label is numbers. In some circumstances, such as with young children or developmentally disabled persons, suitable innovations are used—such as pictures of faces to indicate how one is feeling—and these choices of faces would then be translated into numbers for analysis.

The measurement "rules" refer to steps for assigning labels in an explicit and consistent manner. For example, you can make a rule to count every occurrence of a certain behavior in a given time period, or to ask a client to indicate how often a target occurs by selecting one of the following categories:

1 = Rarely or never
2 = Some or a little of the time
3 = Occasionally or a moderate amount of the time
4 = Most or all of the time

Levels of Measurement

There are four different levels of measurement and each provides a different type of information. You need to understand the information conveyed by each level in order to interpret your own and other people's measurements correctly and analyze the results of single-system designs (e.g., some statistics are designed to be used only with certain levels of measurement). These levels of measurement are termed nominal, ordinal, interval, and ratio.

Nominal Level. Nominal-level measures provide information about whether one observation is qualitatively different from another or a person is in one category or another, for example, male or female. These categories, by definition, are mutually exclusive. For example, a person might be married at one time and single at another time, and different numbers could be assigned to the person depending on his or her current marital status (e.g., 0 = single, 1 = married). Diagnostic systems (e.g., American Psychiatric Association, 2000; Kirk, 2005) that assign individuals to diagnostic categories provide another example of nominal-level measurement. In any case, if a person has different values at different times for a nominal-level variable, it indicates a change (e.g., a different marital or diagnostic status), but not that the person has more or less of some characteristic (e.g., a value of 1 would not indicate a greater marital status than a value of 0).

Ordinal Level. Ordinal-level measures provide the same information as nominal-level measures, *plus* information about the relative amount of one observation compared with another. Basically, the categories are rank-ordered on a scale from less to more for some target. For example, each week the number of marital arguments for a couple might be classified into one of the following categories:

1 = Rarely or never
2 = Some or a little of the time
3 = Occasionally or a moderate amount of the time
4 = Most or all of the time

If the frequency of arguments was assigned a 4 one week, and a 3 the next, this would indicate that the frequency was different from one week to the next, and that the frequency was less during the second week. However, the change from 4 to 3 would not necessarily be the same as a change from 3 to 2 or from 2 to 1, because for ordinal-level measures the adjacent intervals are not necessarily equal.

Interval Level. Interval-level measures provide the same information as ordinal-level measures, *plus* the adjacent intervals are equal, so it's possible to determine *how much* more of some characteristic is possessed by a person. The Fahrenheit scale for measuring temperature is an example of an interval measure because the difference between 0 and 1 degree is the same as the difference between 50 and 51 degrees. Examples of true interval measures are difficult to find in social work and the social sciences, although often it's reasonable to use standardized scales and other measures with the assumption that they are interval-level measures. Among other things, this allows more sophisticated data analyses, including many of the most commonly used statistical procedures.

Ratio Level. Ratio-level measures provide the same information as interval-level measures, *plus* they have a defined zero point that has some intrinsic meaning. In contrast to ratio measures, a score of zero on a standardized scale that one assumes provides an *interval-level* measurement usually does not indicate the complete absence of some characteristic such as depression, problem-solving ability, or marital satisfaction. Examples of ratio measures include the amount of time spent caring for an elderly parent or the amount of time spent with a child or spouse.

Advantages of Measurement

In a way, measurement is just a more formalized way of clarifying the observations that you make every day in practice, no matter what level of measurement is used. After all, before beginning an intervention program you need to decide whether a problem exists. You want to know when it is appropriate to modify an intervention during the course of providing the service. And before terminating an intervention program you need to decide whether the problem is resolved to an acceptable degree. When you make these decisions you are measuring whether a problem is present or absent, and (in a rough way) perhaps the severity of the problem. Practitioners who make qualitative judgments about clients are in fact using a type of measurement (nominal level). What we are suggesting is that practitioners use the most accurate and informative, yet practical, measurement strategies available.

Measurement has several advantages, but these all stem from the fact that it requires you to develop explicit criteria or *rules* for determining the status of a target (e.g., its existence, intensity, frequency). Some of the advantages are: (a) The criteria provide clear guidelines for helping you evaluate where you are going with your intervention programs and to monitor changes to provide feedback on success or even failure. Indeed, using measurement will reduce the chances that you will fool yourself into thinking that things are going better than they really are, which can happen because of the often observed human tendency to avoid signs of failure. (b) You will need to talk with your clients about their targets and goals in detail in order to develop criteria for assessing change. This exchange can increase the chances of a successful intervention because it can lead to active client involvement and agreement on targets and goals over time. (c) Having criteria for determining the status of a target will put you in a better position to get consultation from your colleagues because it will be easier to give them accurate information about client targets.

The value of measurement is that it allows you to be more precise and systematic in evaluating what you are doing. (This assumes that before you decide how you will measure a problem, you are specific in defining it.) Measurement allows you to classify events, observing them to know when, how often, how intense or how long, or even whether they are occurring. Measurement aids you in being clear in describing and communicating to others what you are doing. Measurement, in other words, to the extent that it makes your practice more objective, and to the extent that it does indeed increase the precision of what you do, is a key to enhancing the effectiveness and efficiency of your practice efforts (Faul, McMurty, & Hudson, 2001).

As we've only hinted about, a number of considerations enter into the measurement process. We will discuss many of these in relation to the specific measurement procedures. At this point, however, it's important to note that depending on how you deal with some of these considerations, you can actually enhance the measurement process by providing more accurate measures, or distort the process by providing biased measures. Your job as a scientific practitioner is to conceptualize problems clearly, select "good" measurement methods (accurate, sensitive to such factors as the client's gender and ethnic background), and then use the measures in ways that will provide the most useful evaluation. The bulk of this chapter is devoted to taking a look at guidelines that you can use to evaluate measures for your practice, and the following chapter will be devoted to the process of specifying targets and goals.

DEFINITION AS A FIRST STEP IN MEASUREMENT

Conceptual Definitions

To measure something we first need to define what it is we're trying to measure. Two types of definitions are important: conceptual and operational definitions. A *conceptual definition* (sometimes called a nominal definition) is found in a dictionary, defining a concept by using one set of words—like synonyms—to define another word or set of words. For example, you might conceptually define "child neglect" (following Polansky, Chalmers, Buttenweisser, & Williams, 1981, p. 15) in this way:

Child neglect may be defined as a condition in which a caretaker responsible for the child either deliberately or by extraordinary inattentiveness permits the child to experience avoidable present suffering and/or fails to provide one or more of the ingredients generally deemed essential for developing a person's physical, intellectual, and emotional capacities.

Operational Definitions

However, how do you know whether child neglect occurred and, if it occurred, to what extent? For this you need an *operational definition*. An operational definition is one that assigns meaning to a concept (e.g., child neglect) in terms of *the activities or operations necessary to measure it*. Operational definitions are the "working definitions" of what you are trying to measure. Some concepts are easy to measure, such as the number of times a child cries, whereas other concepts are difficult to measure and may make use of *indicators* of an abstract concept, for example, a standardized scale may be used to measure depression. In either case, we attach numbers to the most meaningful set of activities that describe the client's situation. An operational definition of child neglect might involve asking a client or someone familiar with the client the following questions, assigning a value of 0 to each "no" response and a value of 1 to each "yes" response, and then summing the response values across questions (Combs-Orme & Orme, 1986) to provide an overall measure—the operational definition—of child neglect, as in the following example:

1. Have you sometimes left young children under 6 years old home alone while you were out shopping or doing anything else?

2. Have there been times when a neighbor fed a child (of yours/you were caring for) because you didn't get around to shopping for food or cooking, or kept your child overnight because no one was taking care of him/her at home?

3. Has a nurse or social worker or teacher ever said that any child (of yours/you were caring for) wasn't being given enough to eat or wasn't being kept clean enough or wasn't getting medical care when it was needed?

The fit between our conceptual and operational definitions usually won't be perfect. For example, you can probably think of additional questions that should be asked to measure child neglect. You can probably also think of reasons why answers to the three questions shown might be inaccurate. No matter how you operationalize and measure child neglect, or anything else for that matter, your operationalization will never be a complete and perfect representation of your conceptual definition—it will always contain some error. It's important to understand the different types of measurement errors that can occur so that you can avoid them or reduce them whenever possible, or minimize these errors when you select measures and when you interpret the results of your measures. Before we discuss measurement error, though, let's think about an even more fundamental question: Can everything be measured?

CAN EVERYTHING BE MEASURED?

Many years ago, the psychologist Robert Thorndike said that if something exists, it exists in some quantity; if it exists in some quantity, then it can be measured. Based on these ideas, Hudson (1978) proposed what he calls the "first axioms of treatment." These are: (a) If you cannot measure the client's problem, it does not exist; and (b) if a problem doesn't exist, that is, if you cannot measure the client's problem, you cannot treat it. Hudson stated these as universal propositions, then challenged readers to refute them by citing only one concrete exception.

We are not going to address here a number of philosophical implications of these arguments, such as how indirect an indicator of a problem can we accept as measuring the real problem. But, the practice implications of Hudson's axioms are directly relevant. We view these arguments as appropriate challenges to professional practice, especially with regard to the need to clarify and specify (operationalize) the targets of our interventions.

However, the argument might run, isn't it possible that many of the problems with which we deal in practice are just too subtle or too complex and changeable to measure? We challenge you on this one. Try this exercise. List as many problems as you can that you think you can't measure. Go over that list and see how many of those "unmeasurable" problems are in fact measurable with one of the procedures we describe. We think you'll be happily surprised.

Our point of view on this is that if a problem is too subtle or complex to measure, it just may be too subtle or complex to work with in practice. If a problem is meaningful to the client, then you have to have some means of grasping what it is the client is facing and for what he or she needs help. Otherwise, there will be no way of knowing how well you're doing with your intervention program or the extent to which you have reached your client's goals.

However, if you're saying that it's *difficult* to measure many of the problems with which you're working, that's something else. Certainly, many problems are rather complex or even vague to begin with, but if a problem exists it can be measured. That is the crux of the situation. Part of your job as practitioner is to identify the measurable components of a problem. This is part and parcel of practice no matter what your theoretical orientation. Although we present detailed guidelines on how to go about doing this, let's take a closer look at this issue right now.

Because many clients present their concerns in rather vague and amorphous terms, your job is to help clients clarify and specify their concerns. One way of doing this is to identify those parts of the problem that can serve as measurable *indicators* of the problem, so that you can measure them to gather feedback on the success of your interventions. These "measurable indicators" should be real parts of the problem, personally, interpersonally, organizationally, or socially significant and not selected only because they're measurable. Thus, the key step in the process of measuring anything that exists is finding indicators of the problem that are typical or representative of the problem and accessible to measurement.

Part of the discomfort with the assertion "anything that exists can be measured" is the concern among some practitioners about what the term *measurable* means. *Measurable* doesn't refer just to observing overt behaviors. There are a number of measurement tools available to measure the whole gamut of problems you may be faced with in practice—everything from feelings to thoughts to behaviors to community activities and archival records of past actions. Once you see the range, potential, and flexibility of these procedures, we think you'll agree that all of the problems that you're likely to face in your practice are, indeed, measurable.

So we would argue that if a problem exists, the problem, or reasonably close indicators of it, can be measured. However, we recognize that some problems are difficult to measure. The important question for the practitioner is how to measure them in the best possible way.

KEY CHARACTERISTICS OF ALL MEASURES

When a practitioner makes a judgment about the problems of a client, how does the practitioner know he or she is "reading" the problem consistently from one time to the next, or is reading the problem accurately, or the extent to which he or she is talking about the problem that truly is troubling the client? Most of us develop a number of devices to double-check by looking for external, independent confirmation to assure consistency. The point is that there are direct analogies between what you do in practice to ascertain that you are being accurate and consistent, and what you do in evaluation, particularly with single-system designs. This is to say, once again, that what makes for good practice also makes for good evaluation.

In the remainder of this chapter, we discuss a number of the key characteristics that you would want to address in selecting, using, or developing a measurement procedure. As we noted previously, it is probably impossible to cover every characteristic of measurement devices in just this chapter. So, we've attempted to select those which should be most helpful for you, and which you can actually use. The characteristics that we discuss are reliability, validity, utility, and directness; these characteristics are actually strategies, or ways of telling just how good a measure is at measuring the target or concept. Thus, if you can meet these criteria to a high degree, you can be confident that you are providing measurement that is as free from distortions and error as possible.

Measurement Error

A client's score on a measure can result from different things. It might result just from the real or true amount of whatever it is you are trying to measure (e.g., the amount of child neglect, the amount of marital satisfaction). This is what you would like, and it's easy to assume that this is the whole story. Unfortunately, there are other plausible explanations for why a client might get a particular score. It's useful to think about two categories of alternative explanations.

Random Measurement Error. Most measures have an element of random error. Random, in this sense, means haphazard or by chance. Unfortunately, this is a little different from the use of the term *random* that you probably are familiar with, such as in random selection and random assignment, where *random* refers to a systematic and scientifically based process. Let's take an example. Suppose that you're using a standardized scale to measure the magnitude of a client's depression on a weekly basis. The client's mood might get better or worse from week-to-week due to any number of haphazard factors (careless errors in reading, interpreting, and answering questions on the scale from week-to-week; changes from week-to-week in the time of day the measure was completed). So, to some extent the measured level of depression might fluctuate randomly from week-to-week, but the average level of depression over time wouldn't be influenced because random errors cancel each other out over time. However, depression scores would be more variable over time than they would be if there was no random error and this makes it more difficult to detect intervention effects.

Systematic Measurement Error. Systematic error is a tendency to err in a particular way, and so sometimes it's referred to as *bias*. For example, suppose again that you're using a standardized scale to measure the magnitude of a client's depression on a weekly basis. Let's say that the client completes the measure in the evening, the time of day the client is most depressed. The average level of depression over time would be systematically higher than if more representative times were selected.

Importance of Measurement Error. Why should we care about the extent to which a measure has random or systematic measurement error? The answer is that we would like to know how much measured or observed change in a client's problem is due to actual change in the problem. To the extent that change or a lack of change is due to extraneous factors such as measurement error, the results of your measures are difficult to interpret and to use in monitoring and evaluating your interventions, and hence in helping your clients. *The basic issue is that measurement error can lead to erroneous practice decisions and less effective practice.* Random measurement error can cause us to miss intervention effects entirely, beneficial or detrimental. Systematic measurement error can cause us to miss intervention effects, and it also can cause us to underestimate or overestimate intervention effects. Can you see how much this could distort or misdirect your practice?

So, how do you know the extent to which a measure has random and systematic measurement error?

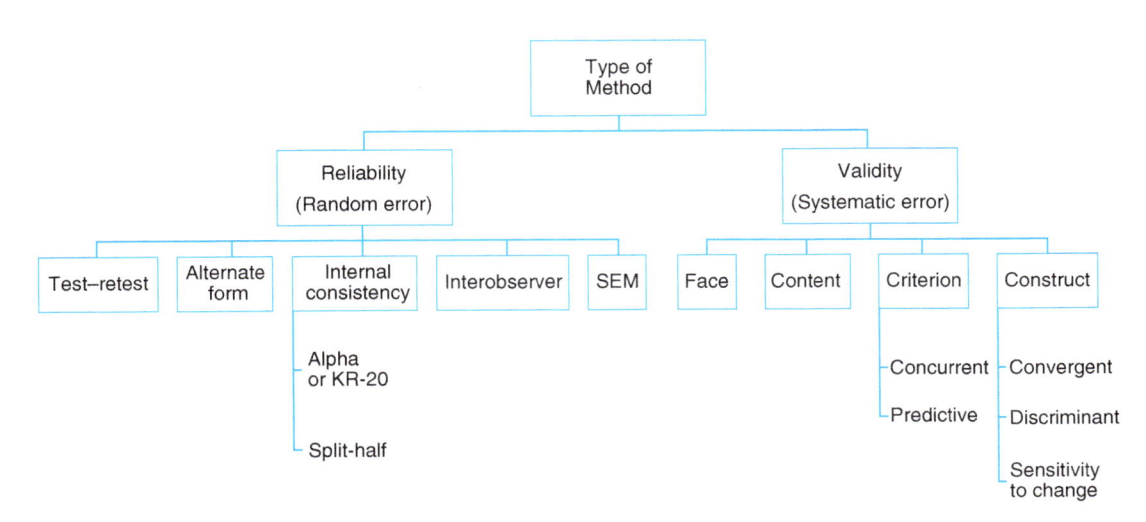

FIGURE 1 Methods to determine measurement error.

The *reliability* of a measure indicates the extent to which a measure contains random measurement error, and the *validity* of a measure indicates the extent to which a measure contains systematic measurement error. Reliability and validity are two of the most important criteria by which the adequacy of measures are judged. To understand how to select and use measures you need to understand these concepts, and you need to know how reliability and validity are determined and interpreted. Figure 1 shows the different methods used to determine reliability and validity, and we'll now turn to these different methods.

Reliability

Random measurement error will lead to inconsistencies in measuring things. For example, two people observing the same event might report that different things occurred. The same question asked of the same person on two different occasions might elicit two different answers. Phrasing two questions about the same thing in slightly different ways might result in different responses from the same person.

The word *reliability* is a general term for the *consistency* of measurements, and unreliability basically means inconsistency due to random measurement errors (American Educational Research Association et al., 1999; Anastasi & Urbina, 1997; Nunnally & Bernstein, 1994). In general, we find out if a measurement is consistent by repeatedly and independently measuring the same people (or sometimes things) under the same circumstances. To determine the consistency of measurements the same event might be observed by two observers, the same question might be asked of the same person on two different occasions, or the same question might be asked in two slightly different ways.

A test of reliability requires first that observations be independent and second that they be made under the same circumstances, so it's necessary to have some understanding of these two requirements. *Independence* means that one measurement doesn't influence another measurement. For example, if two observers talked about what they observed before they decided what to record, the measurements wouldn't be independent. If people remembered their answer to a question asked at one time, and this first answer influenced their answer to the same question at a second time, the measurements wouldn't be independent. The phrase *under the same circumstances* means that the measurement is made under the same conditions. For example, if we had a client complete a depression scale in a crowded, noisy, waiting room and then in a quiet, private, comfortable office, the circumstances clearly wouldn't be the same. Therefore, there are degrees of "independence" and "sameness" of circumstances, and those examining reliability should seek to attain the highest levels of each, as circumstances permit.

Different types of measurement inconsistencies exist (e.g., between observers, between times, between questions), and, therefore, different types of reliability have been distinguished. In addition, a measurement strategy might be consistent (i.e., reliable) in one way but not in another. Therefore, it's actually best to think of the reliabili*ties* of a measure. For example, two observers might not agree about the frequency of a child's prosocial behavior observed in a videotape, but each observer might be consistent over time in the frequency of prosocial behavior recorded. The different types of reliability that we'll discuss include test–retest reliability, alternate-forms reliability, internal-consistency reliability, interobserver reliability, and the standard error of measurement (SEM). However, before discussing these types of reliability and validity, we must discuss the correlation coefficient, the statistic usually used to quantify and report the reliability and validity of measures.

A *correlation* tells us whether and how two variables are related. For example, if parents' knowledge of child development increases with the number of children they have, then child development knowledge and number of children are said to be positively correlated. A positive correlation means that people with high values on one variable (e.g., number of children) tend to have high values on another variable (e.g., scores on a measure of child development knowledge). Two variables also can be negatively (or inversely) correlated. For example, if parent–child conflicts decrease as parents' knowledge increases, then parent–child conflicts and child development knowledge are correlated negatively. A negative correlation means that people with low values on one variable tend to have high values on another variable. Finally, two variables might be uncorrelated. If two variables are uncorrelated, values on one variable are not related to values on another variable. For example, if parents with few children are just as knowledgeable about child development as parents with many children, then the number of children tells us nothing about how knowledgeable parents will be about child development.

A correlation can range from –1.0 (negative correlation) to +1.0 (positive correlation). The sign of a correlation indicates whether the variables are correlated positively or negatively, and a correlation of 0 means there's no linear relationship at all between two variables. The absolute value of a correlation (i.e., the actual number, ignoring the plus or minus sign) indicates the strength of the relationship—the larger the absolute value, the stronger the relationship. Therefore, a correlation of –.80 indicates a stronger relationship than a correlation of +.50 because the sign of the correlation is ignored when determining the strength of the relationship. The following web site provides a useful and fun interactive exercise that illustrates different aspects of the correlation coefficient: **www.stat.uiuc.edu/courses/stat100/java/ GCApplet/GCAppletFrame.html**.

Test–Retest Reliability. Test–retest reliability is determined by independently measuring the same group of people (or things) with the same measure on two different occasions under the same circumstances. The correlation between the first and second administration of the measure indicates the test–retest reliability or the *stability* of a measure.

What does an estimate of test–retest reliability indicate? A high value tells us that the measure provides consistent results over a certain time period; for example, those who have high scores the first time are likely to have high scores the second time. Another way of thinking about high test–retest reliability is that it indicates that the measure is not very susceptible to random changes in individuals from one time to the other (e.g., changes due to fatigue, emotional strain, worry, illness, recent pleasant or unpleasant experiences), or to the measurement environment (e.g., changes due to who is present in the environment, or to noise, room temperature, or other distractions).

Test–retest reliability is particularly important for single-system evaluation because you will be administering your measures or making your observations repeatedly before and during intervention. If your measurement or observation tool is not stable, changes that come about may be a result of changes in the measurement tool itself. With a stable measure you can be more confident that you are recording real changes in the behavior, feelings, attitudes, and so forth that are being measured.

There are some things that can make the test–retest reliability of a measure appear higher or lower than it really is, and you need to remember these things when interpreting the test–retest reliability of a measure. First, reliability is determined from *independent* repeated observations of the same subjects under the same circumstances. Sometimes the process of retesting violates the requirement of independence, that is, that the second measurement not be affected by the first. Individuals may be less interested, motivated, or anxious during the second measurement because they're already familiar with the measurement procedure. If the time interval between test and retest is fairly short, people might remember their initial responses and simply repeat many of the same responses they gave the first time. Finally, the initial measurement may change the response. For example, a questionnaire assessing marital satisfaction may raise questions people never thought about before, which might heighten their interest in certain issues and stimulate the development of definite opinions; consequently, a "Don't Know" response on the first questionnaire may be replaced by a "Definitely Agree" response on the second.

A second possible problem with test–retest reliability has to do with the requirement that the measurements are made under the same circumstances. One important way that circumstances can change is for genuine change to occur in whatever is being measured (i.e., change due to influences unrelated to the measurement). For example, administration of a depression inventory on two occasions separated by a 1-year interval may result in low test–retest reliability because the depression, in fact, lessened.

The test–retest reliability of any measurement strategy could be determined using many different time intervals between test and retest. Most often you will want to be assured that the measure is reliable over the time interval in which you are interested for your particular case. In general, though, the shorter the test–retest interval, the more likely it is that the first measurement will have an effect on the second one; the longer the interval, the more likely it is that real change will have occurred. Unfortunately, it's often difficult to know whether two measurements are independent. In general, the time interval should be long enough for the effects of the first measurement to wear off, but not long enough for a significant amount of real change to occur. For example, it's reasonable to expect marital satisfaction, depression, self-esteem, and other similar concepts to remain stable over relatively short periods of time (e.g., 1 or 2 weeks), but not long periods of time (e.g., 1 or 2 years). In contrast, it's reasonable to expect different types of aptitudes (e.g., general intelligence, artistic ability) and other similar constructs to remain stable over relatively longer periods of time. Therefore, overall, there's no one time interval that is best, because some things change faster than others, and some things are forgotten more easily than others.

Your own evaluation of an individual client also can provide some evidence of the test–retest reliability or stability of a measure as used with your particular client. This just involves visually examining the pattern of results over time for a given client. If a relatively "flat" pattern of observations is obtained during a phase (e.g., baseline), this would provide some evidence for the test–retest reliability or stability of the measure, if it's reasonable to assume that the observations are independent. However, if a "flat" pattern is not found, don't automatically fault the measure, because it might be that real change occurred in the target, or the circumstances changed under which the measurements were made. But a fluctuating baseline at least should make you stop and think about the reliability of your measure.

Alternate-Forms Reliability. Alternate-forms reliability, and internal-consistency reliability, which will be discussed next, are primarily concerned with the consistency with which we measure concepts. Concepts are abstract and generalized terms about classes of events and many client problems are reframed as concepts (e.g., child neglect, depression, problem-solving ability, marital satisfaction, antisocial behavior). For example, consider the following selected items designed to measure the concept of marital satisfaction (Hudson, 1997):

1. I feel that my partner is affectionate enough.
2. I feel that my partner and I get along very well together.
3. I feel that my partner is a comfort to me.

Each item is taken to be an indicator of the concept of marital satisfaction, and we hypothesize that someone who answers affirmatively to one will probably answer affirmatively to the others. However, no single item would be sufficient to measure the concept, just as no single person will represent a group of people, because marital satisfaction is a complex and multidimensional phenomenon. So, to measure concepts we need to find a sufficient number of indicators that are typical or representative of the array of events described by the concept.

Alternate-forms reliability involves the administration of two forms of a measure that are constructed according to the same specifications (e.g., they have the same number of items; items expressed in a similar form; items of equal difficulty; and comparable instructions, format, illustrative examples, and time limits), but the actual content of the items is different.

The reason for doing this is to see whether the two sets of items designed to measure the same concept actually do measure the same concept. A high correlation between alternate forms tells us that people respond consistently to the different forms of the measure (i.e., different sets of indicators), suggesting that the different forms of the measure do measure the same concept. Thus, the measure is said to be consistent (reliable) because both forms agree regarding measurement of the concept.

Internal-Consistency Reliability. It is also possible to examine the extent to which the same results would be obtained with different samples of items without having to devise and administer two versions of a measure. Methods for doing this involve the administration of a single set of items to a group of people, and an examination of the extent to which people respond consistently to the different items contained in the measure. This type of reliability is called internal-consistency reliability, and it basically refers to the extent to which parts of a measure (items or even entire halves of the measure) are homogeneous or measure the same thing. There are two types of internal-consistency reliability that you're likely to see reported—split-half reliability and coefficient alpha.

Split-half reliability is determined by dividing the items in a measure into two groups containing an equal number of items (most often the even-numbered items are used for one half and the odd-numbered items for the other half, so this is sometimes called "odd–even reliability"), computing a score for each person on each half of the measure, and determining the correlation between scores on the two halves of the measure. The correlation between the two halves only indicates the reliability of one-half of the measure, and so a correction formula is applied to this correlation to provide the reliability of the whole measure, and this corrected correlation is the split-half reliability of the measure. A high split-half value indicates that people respond consistently to both halves of the measure (hence the term "internal-consistency"), indicating that the different halves of the instrument measure the same concept.

Coefficient alpha is a statistic used to quantify internal-consistency reliability and it is by far the statistic most often used and reported for quantifying internal consistency reliability. Like split-half reliability, higher values indicate greater internal consistency reliability. Essentially, alpha is just the average intercorrelation among a set of items, weighted by the number of items (coefficient alpha is sometimes called Cronbach's alpha after its developer, or KR-20, which is a specialized version of coefficient alpha). Coefficient alpha provides more information about internal consistency than split-half reliability, so in general it is the more useful of the two. Like split-half reliability, a high value of coefficient alpha suggests that the results obtained with a measure don't depend on the particular items used. A high value of coefficient alpha also indicates that a person responds fairly consistently to all of the items in a measure (i.e., those who have high scores on one item are likely to have high scores on other items), and this in turn suggests that the items all measure the same concept; that is, they're homogeneous. The *homogeneity* of a set of items is important because most measures are designed to measure a single concept (e.g., family cohesion, depression), and coefficient alpha provides one indication of the extent to which this is accomplished.

Interobserver Reliability. The different types of reliability discussed so far are important to understand in order to select measures that already are available, to understand and avoid different types of measurement error (e.g., inconsistency over time due to changes in the measurement conditions), and to properly interpret results from the measures that you do use. Interobserver reliability (or, as it's sometimes called, interrater reliability) refers to the extent to which two or more observers are consistent with each other when they independently observe or judge the same thing. The consistency with which two or more people observe or make judgments about a client's behavior is actually something you might test yourself when you use single-system designs, so it's important to understand in some detail.

Interobserver reliability has been used most extensively to determine the extent to which two observers agree in their observations about whether, how often, or how long overt behaviors occur. For example, two observers (say, husband and wife) might record the amount of time their child spent doing homework, the number of parent–child arguments, or the amount of time the family spends together. The degree of agreement between the husband and wife could then be determined as one method of assessing the adequacy of the information collected.

In general, interobserver reliability is quantified using either a correlation coefficient, which we discussed earlier, or some measure of agreement, such

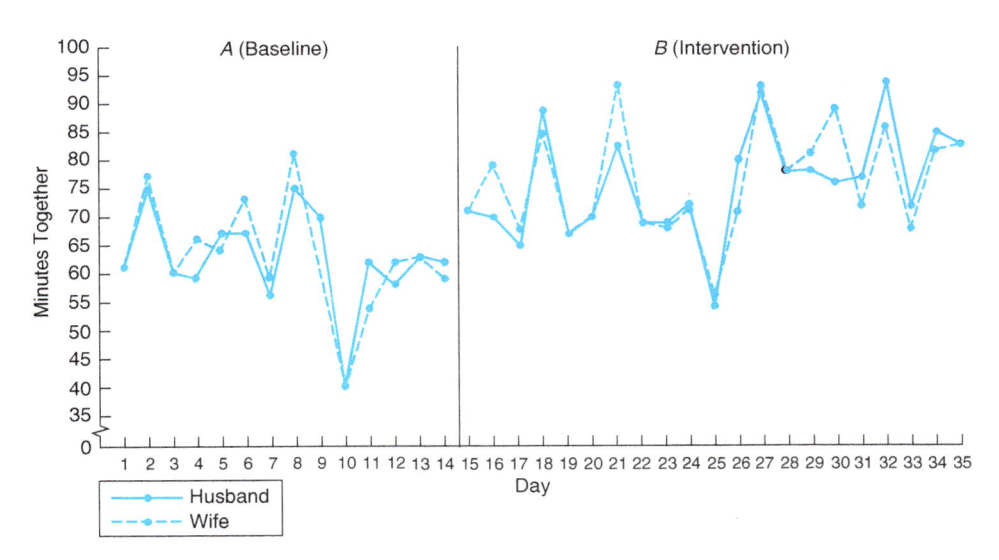

FIGURE 2 Interobserver reliability in measuring satisfying time together.

as percentage of agreement or kappa. *Percentage of agreement* refers to the percentage of times both observers agree with each other in their observations, for example, that a given behavior occurred five times in an hour. (*Kappa* and other such measures of agreement are statistics that correct for agreement that would be expected just by chance; Fleiss, Levin, & Paik, 2003.) In any case, a high value of interobserver reliability indicates a high degree of consistency between observers. We provide instructions on how to compute interobserver reliability, and how to enhance interobserver reliability by carefully giving clear instructions and training to observers.

Correlations or different indexes of agreement provide precise estimates of interobserver reliability. A less precise, but still useful way to examine the extent to which two or more observers provide comparable information over time, is to graph the information from the different observers on the same chart, and visually determine whether the information is comparable. For example, suppose that a husband and wife seek help because they are dissatisfied with their marriage, and one of their major complaints is that they don't spend enough time in mutually satisfying activities. You ask them to independently record the amount of time spent in mutually satisfying activities each day. Two weeks of baseline information is collected, and then an intervention designed to increase the amount of mutually satisfying time spent together is implemented. The day-to-day pattern of results shown in Figure 2 shows a high degree of correspondence in husband–wife reports of the amount of time spent in mutually satisfying activities, indicating that this information is reported reliably by each member of this couple.

We recognize that it's not always realistic for you to find two observers in order to do this reliability check. If the client and a relevant other are both available and willing to record (the secondary recorder only in certain situations), that would be great. But in other circumstances, no one else might be available. Then, the second recorder might be you. You might make home visits, once in the baseline period and once in the intervention, and do some recording yourself. Then your recording could form the basis for the reliability check. Or, you could set up a situation in the office in which you and the client role-play and record.

Standard Error of Measurement (SEM). The SEM usually should not be used to compare the adequacy of different measures. This is because the SEM is in part determined by the scale range of the measure, and therefore you can't directly compare the SEM from different measures unless they have the same range of scores, or unless you convert scores into a percentage (by dividing the SEM by the score range and multiplying by 100). But, in general, if you want to compare the reliability of different measures, use other reliability coefficients.

The SEM is useful for interpreting changes in scale scores over time for individual clients. That is, the SEM lets you address the question of whether change in a scale score from one time to another is more than you would expect just based on measurement error alone (i.e., reliable change) (e.g., Bauer, Lambert, & Nielsen, 2004).

What Is "High" Reliability? Reliability figures are generally presented either as correlations or as percentage of agreements (with the exception of the SEM). In either case a 0 indicates a totally unreliable measure, and a 1 indicates a perfectly reliable measure. Reliability estimates based on correlations can fall in the range from −1.00 to +1.0, but it is very unusual for a zero to happen, and when it does it simply indicates that the measure is unreliable.

Hunsley and Mash (2008) provide useful recent guidelines for judging reliability, and you should make these judgments based on the preponderance of the available evidence. For test–retest reliability (i.e., correlations):

Adequate = .70 over a period of several days to several weeks
Good = .70 over a period of several months
Excellent = .70 over a period of a year or longer

For internal consistency reliability (i.e., coefficient alpha):

Adequate = .70 to .79
Good = .80 to .89
Excellent = .90 or greater

For interobserver reliability (i.e., kappa) (see Fleiss et al., 2003, for somewhat less stringent criteria):

Adequate = .60 to .74
Good = .75 to .84
Excellent = .85 or greater

What Type of Reliability Should You Use? Given these several types of reliability, how do you know which one to use to evaluate a measure? Sometimes you will be able to examine the interobserver reliability of the measures you use, but typically you won't be in a position to examine other types of reliability. Therefore, when you select existing measures for use with your clients you should determine whether evidence exists in the literature for the reliability of the measures. It's important to look for existing evidence of short-term test–retest reliability (stability) for most types of measures, especially for use with single-system designs, and interobserver reliability for measures based on direct observations. You should look for estimates of internal-consistency reliability for standardized scales, and especially for estimates of coefficient alpha (or KR-20), although estimates of split-half reliability also can be useful. Finally, if you intend to use two or more forms of a measure (and this is rare in the conduct of single-system designs), you should look for evidence of alternate-forms reliability.

Validity

The reliability of a measure indicates only whether something is being measured consistently, but that "something" may or may not be the variable we're trying to measure. Validity is the degree to which evidence and theory support the proposed interpretation of scores derived from measures. The process of validation involves accumulating evidence to provide a sound scientific basis for proposed score interpretation (AERA et al., 1999).

Validity is perhaps the most important measurement consideration of all because validity involves knowing whether a measurement procedure actually does what it's supposed to. Does it measure what it's supposed to measure? Does it predict what it's supposed to predict? Does a measure really accomplish its aims? These are the key questions one would ask in evaluating a measure for possible use. While both reliability and validity are important, without being sure that a measure indicates what we want it to indicate, it's almost irrelevant whether the measure is consistent. That is, validity is a crucial guideline that you will want to look for when choosing an instrument. So, we believe it's important to review some of the ways you might assess the validity of a measure.

It's probably obvious that different measures have different purposes. Because this is so, it also seems logical to assume that the purpose of the measure would determine the type of method needed for establishing its validity. For some measures, it's relatively easy to establish validity. For example, asking a client his age to the nearest birthday generally produces an answer that seems apparently valid, at least on the face of it. But presenting a client with a scale to measure depression or family conflict may be a different matter altogether.

Face Validity. The first method of determining validity, face validity, refers to the opinion by the developer of a measure, by some expert, or by you, that an instrument measures what it intends to measure. For example, take a look back at the three questions designed to measure marital satisfaction: I feel that my partner is affectionate enough, . . . get along very well, . . . is a comfort to me. . . . In your judgment, do they look like they measure marital satisfaction? If so, you would say the measure has face validity.

There's no standard method for determining face validity, no way to quantify it, and no standard against which to determine how much of it we should have. For these reasons, face validity is sometimes called "faith" validity because it requires us to place considerable faith in the person who decides whether a measure has validity.

In some cases you might not even want to use a measure that has only face validity (e.g., a set of subtle questions measuring alcohol and drug use might be labeled a Health Practices Questionnaire; Sisco & Pearson, 1994). The argument here is that if clients or perhaps even observers know what is being measured, they can distort their responses more easily. On the other hand, face validity cannot be dismissed entirely because it implies that, on the "face" of it, you or someone else has made a judgment that some instrument appears to be measuring what it purports to. After all, if you ask clients to complete a questionnaire or record certain behaviors or events in their lives, and if these requests don't seem to the clients to be related to the problem for which they're seeking help, the clients might be reluctant to cooperate.

Content Validity. Content validity refers to the extent to which the questions or behaviors selected for measurement are representative or are a biased or limited sample of what you intend to measure. Content validity assumes that a good description of the content domain exists. For example, look back at the three child-neglect questions such as, "Have you left young children under 6 years old home alone while you went shopping?" etc., and suppose that you used these questions to measure child maltreatment in general (i.e., neglect and abuse). These questions represent too limited a sample of questions concerning child maltreatment because they don't include questions concerning important aspects of child maltreatment. For example, questions about physical and sexual abuse aren't included, and this exclusion would introduce a systematic source of error (i.e., invalidity) into the measurement of child maltreatment. However, although these questions might not be valid for measuring child maltreatment, they might be valid for other purposes; that is, measuring child neglect.

Content validity refers to how adequately content is sampled, but so do alternate-forms and internal-consistency reliability. What is the difference? Reliability refers to the extent to which measurement is due to *random* error (i.e., inconsistency), and validity refers to the extent to which measurement is due to *systematic* error. Unreliability due to content sampling refers to random errors in the selection of the questions asked or the behaviors observed. Invalidity due to content sampling refers to systematic errors in obtaining information about the concept in question, as opposed to some other concept. For example, the three questions on child neglect mentioned previously very well might consistently measure something (e.g., child neglect), but not what is intended (i.e., child maltreatment). People might respond consistently (i.e., reliably) to the three questions (e.g., those who answer yes to one question might answer yes to the other two questions, and therefore coefficient alpha would be high), and they might respond consistently over time. What is being measured consistently, though, is not child maltreatment but perhaps just child neglect, because of a systematic error (i.e., a biased sample resulting from the exclusion of questions concerning physical and sexual abuse).

Issues of content validity arise in the construction and selection of a measure supposedly addressing a concept you have in mind (like "child abuse"). So, content validity is an important consideration for you to apply with many of the measures we'll be presenting. If you observe a type of behavior (e.g., the frequency with which a family can successfully resolve family problems), you would want to make sure that you're adequately sampling the range of family problems, locations, or situations in which problems occur, or times during which the problems may be occurring, in other words, that the sample of events is representative of the range of possible events. In evaluating a standardized scale, you would want to evaluate whether the items on the scale appear representative of all the content that could reasonably be included. Similarly, in using individualized rating scales and logs you want to be sure that the scales or logs you construct with your client are really tapping the range of problems, locations, and times during which the problem might occur.

When selecting or developing a measure, first establish the definition and essential features of the concept to determine the content validity of a measure (e.g., a measure of parenting knowledge might include subsets of questions concerning child health and safety, discipline, and child development which you have defined as essential for your purposes with a given client). You won't know whether the measurement operations include the essential features of a concept and exclude irrelevant features if you don't have a definition against which to judge the measurement operations.

Content validity also is determined in other ways. Frequently, experts in the particular area are asked to provide feedback on the content validity of a measure during its development (e.g., a measure of knowledge of normative child development may be sent to developmental psychologists). This approach is often useful, but remember that experts are fallible and don't always provide perfect advice.

Content validation involves a more systematic approach to the conceptual and operational definition of a concept than does face validity, but still there are no standard procedures for determining content validity or quantifying it, and no standard against which to determine how much of it you should have. Ultimately, the validity of a measure must be empirically tested and demonstrated. Now, we turn to this issue.

Criterion Validity. The criterion validity of a measure refers to its ability to predict an individual's performance or status on certain outcomes (AERA et al., 1999; Anastasi & Urbina, 1997). The performance or outcome that a measure is designed to predict is called a "criterion," and the validity of the criterion must already be established because it is the standard against which the measure is validated. In short, criterion validity involves a testable public prediction.

Criterion validity usually is determined by collecting scores on the measure being validated and on the criterion, and determining the correlation between the measure and the criterion. The higher the correlation between the measure and the criterion, the better the criterion validity. There are two types of criterion validity, concurrent and predictive.

Concurrent validity refers to the ability of a measure to predict an individual's *current* performance or status. Concurrent validity can be determined in several different ways depending on the purpose of the measure being validated. One way is to examine the correlation between an existing validated measure (i.e., the criterion) and another measure of the same concept that was developed as a simpler, quicker, or less expensive substitute for the available measure. For example, suppose that a self-report measure of the recency, quantity, and frequency of marijuana, cocaine, and opiate use is developed. Results of a urine toxicology analysis for drug of abuse might be used as the criterion against which this self-report measure is compared. Both measures would be administered at about the same time to the same group of people, and the correlation between the two measures would be determined. A high correlation between the two measures would provide evidence of the concurrent validity of the new self-report measure.

Another way concurrent validity is determined is by examining the extent to which a measure predicts current performance in a criterion situation. This is important if the measure is intended as a substitute for direct measurement of the actual criterion situation. For example, suppose that a questionnaire measure of child behavior problems was developed not as a simpler, quicker, or less expensive substitute for an available questionnaire measure, but rather to predict existing observable behavior problems in a classroom situation. The questionnaire might be completed by the children's teachers, and classroom observers might observe the behavior problems. A high correlation between the questionnaire and observational measures would provide evidence of the concurrent validity of the questionnaire measure.

A final way concurrent validity is determined is to examine whether a measure distinguishes between groups known to have different amounts of whatever is supposedly measured. This type of concurrent validity is sometimes called *known-groups* validity. (It's also sometimes called *discriminant validity*, but we use this term in a different way in the following section.) For example, our behavior problem questionnaire could be used with children in special classes for those with behavior problems and with children in regular classrooms. If the results indicated that the average behavior problem score for students in special classes was significantly higher than the average score for children in regular classrooms, the concurrent validity of the questionnaire would be supported.

One particular reason known-groups validity is important is because a measure that is sensitive to a known-groups contrast also should be sensitive to intervention effects comparable to the difference between the groups (Lipsey, 1990).

Sometimes we can examine the concurrent validity of a measure with individual client systems. Suppose that a mother and father seek help because their son is doing poorly in school. One major problem seems to be that he doesn't complete his homework, and this becomes a target of intervention. Each school day he has a homework assignment in each of six subjects, and you ask him to record the number of completed homework assignments each day. You're concerned about the accuracy of his self-reports, so you check with the boy's teachers on randomly selected days (because it would be too difficult for everyone concerned to do this every day), and the teacher reports are used as the criterion against which the accuracy of the self-reports is judged. Three weeks of baseline information is collected, and then an intervention is implemented that is designed to increase the number of completed homework assignments. As shown in Figure 3, there was perfect agreement between self-reports and teacher reports for 10 of the 13 checks (10/13 × 100 = 77% agreement), and this provides support for the concurrent validity of the self-reports.

Predictive validity refers to the ability of a measure to predict or forecast some future criterion, for example, performance on another measure, prognostic reaction to an intervention program, performance in some task of daily living, grades in school, suicide attempts, and so on. The key here is to determine how useful your measure will be in predicting some future characteristic or behavior of an individual. Such predictive knowledge might allow you to identify those at high risk for certain problems, and you might then work to prevent the problems (e.g., a child's risk of entry into foster care, a child's risk of being physically abused, an adolescent's risk of discontinuing contraception). The simplest way to determine predictive validity would be to correlate results on a measure at one time with the criterion information collected at a later time.

As an example of predictive validity, suppose that your questionnaire measure of child behavior problems was developed to predict the development of future child behavior problems. The questionnaire might be administered at the beginning of the school year, and the number of behavioral problems might be determined at the end of the school year by examining various school records (e.g., number of suspensions, calls to parents). A high correlation between the measure and the criterion would provide evidence of the predictive validity of the measure.

Construct Validity. Construct validity is the approximate truth of the conclusion that your operationalization accurately reflects its construct (Shadish, Cook, & Campbell, 2002). Construct validity is the overarching type of validity, and other types of validity can be subsumed under it. Just because the name given to a measure suggests that it measures a particular

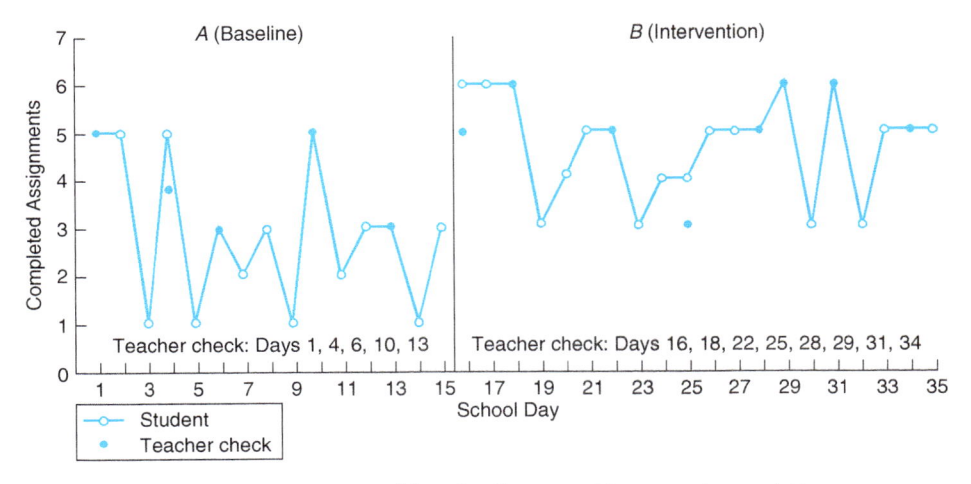

FIGURE 3 Concurrent validity of self-reported homework completion.

concept (e.g., "marital satisfaction," "child maltreatment," etc.) doesn't necessarily mean that it does. Remember that a particular measure is an operational definition of a concept, and the operations (questions, observations, etc.) might not fully or accurately represent the construct. In general, there are two ways in which this can happen: Either the measure doesn't measure all that it's supposed to measure (e.g., a measure of child maltreatment that fails to measure sexual abuse), or it measures something that it's not supposed to measure (e.g., a questionnaire measure of marital satisfaction whose scores depend in part upon how well the respondent can read, and therefore, in part measures the ability to read).

In developing or testing a measure, a researcher uses the theory underlying the concept being measured to set up hypotheses regarding the behavior of persons with high or low scores on the measure (Anastasi & Urbina, 1997). The hypotheses are then tested to see whether the validity of the measure is supported. An examination of the construct validity of a measure assumes that there are well-developed theories or hypotheses about the relationships of the concept being measured to other concepts.

Three different types of construct validity hypotheses are usually tested, and these correspond to three different types of construct validity. These include an examination of whether a measure (a) correlates in a predicted manner (i.e., either positively or negatively) with variables that theoretically it should correlate with (*convergent validity*), (b) does *not* correlate significantly with variables that theoretically it should not correlate with (*discriminant validity*), or (c) changes in a predicted manner (i.e., increases or decreases) in response to an experimental intervention (*sensitivity to change*) (Anastasi & Urbina, 1997).

If a measure is highly correlated with another measure of the same concept, it is said to have *convergent validity* (Anastasi & Urbina, 1997; Campbell & Fiske, 1959). For example, a new self-report measure of household safety precautions for children (e.g., the installation of smoke alarms and locks on medicine cabinets) should be positively correlated with existing measures of household safety precautions. Convergent validity evidence based on correlations between measures using different measurement methods (e.g., self-reports and independent observations) is especially important. For example, a correlation between a new self-report measure of parental safety precautions and an independent observer's observation of these precautions would provide stronger evidence of convergent validity than a correlation with an existing self-report measure. The reason for this is that measures using the same method might be correlated because they measure related concepts, *or* because they use the same method. For example, two different self-report measures might be correlated because they both measure a parent's ability or willingness to report the implementation of safety precautions, not because they both measure the actual implementation of safety precautions.

Convergent validity is demonstrated not just by correlations between different measures of the same concept; more generally, it's demonstrated if a measure is correlated in a predicted manner with variables with which it theoretically should correlate. For example, a parental self-report measure of household safety precautions for children should be correlated negatively with the number of child injuries that have occurred in the home, and positively with parental knowledge of accident risks and prevention strategies (Fickling, 1993).

Evidence concerning whether a measure is correlated with related variables, or changes in response to an intervention, is not sufficient to demonstrate the construct validity of a measure. It's also necessary to have evidence that a measure is not correlated significantly with variables with which it theoretically should not be correlated, and this type of evidence provides support for what is known as the *discriminant validity* (sometimes called divergent validity) of a measure (Anastasi & Urbina, 1997; Campbell & Fiske, 1959). For example, if a self-report measure of safety precautions is highly correlated with a measure of self-esteem, responses might depend partially on a person's self-esteem instead of just on safety precautions. That is, self-esteem and safety precautions theoretically should not be correlated.

Discriminant validity is not just demonstrated by the absence of a correlation between a measure and other variables, though, but is also demonstrated if the magnitude of the correlation suggests that the measure is measuring a distinct concept. For example, a measure of self-esteem and a measure of depression might be correlated positively (higher depression is often associated with lower self-esteem), but if the measure of depression is as highly correlated with a measure of self-esteem as it is with other measures of depression, it would suggest a problem with the measure of depression.

When you select or design a measure for your practice, be especially skeptical in thinking about its discriminant validity. You should consider the extent to which the scores on a measure are determined by the amount of the intended concept (e.g., the actual safety precautions implemented) or by other extraneous variables (e.g., reading ability, a desire to present oneself in a socially desirable light). These extraneous variables present threats to the discriminant validity of a measure, and measures that are sensitive to the influence of extraneous variables are undesirable because they don't just measure what is intended. It would be safe to say that all measures are influenced by extraneous variables (i.e., variables other than the one supposedly measured) to some extent. The issue is the extent to which this occurs, and the effect this has.

There are a variety of extraneous variables that present possible threats to the construct validity of measures, and an understanding of these will help you make better decisions in the selection and use of measurement strategies. For example, some types of self-reports are biased by the desire to present oneself in a socially desirable manner. Some types of observations are biased by observers' expectations about what is observed (e.g., expectations based on client characteristics such as race, age, gender, social status). To some extent these possible threats are specific to particular methods of measurement (e.g., self-reports, observation), and in our discussion of particular measurement methods we'll highlight these possible threats.

Reactivity is an example of one such possible threat. Reactive measures are those about which the client is aware and to which the client "reacts." Reactivity means changes that come about in the client or in the problem due to the act of measurement itself—the client "reacts" (Fritsche & Linneweber, 2006; Webb et al., 1981). To the extent that reactivity occurs, the observation or monitoring process leads to change in the target even if an intervention doesn't occur or doesn't have any effect. Conversely, in the absence of reactivity the measurement itself does not bring about change in what you are measuring. If a target changes simply because it's measured, you obviously would have a difficult time separating the effects of an intervention from the measurement of the target.

There are a number of types of reactivity, as well as ways of overcoming or diminishing reactivity. Because this is a very important topic, we've devoted ways of minimizing reactivity and to the range of measures that minimize or eliminate reactivity. For now, in selecting a measure, when everything else is equal (which, of course, it rarely is), try to use the least reactive measure possible. That is, try to use nonreactive measures when you can, or if you're using more than one measure, try to include at least one nonreactive measure.

Construct validity also is demonstrated if a measure changes in a predicted manner in response to an intervention (Anastasi & Urbina, 1997; Lipsey, 1990). Such changes provide evidence that a measure is *sensitive to change*, and in the selection of a measure to evaluate client change this is especially important. The point here is that if changes really do occur in a target, you want to be sure that your measure will be able to pick them up. An insensitive measure, by definition, is one that won't indicate change even though actual changes have come about. Of what value is a measure that will not be responsive (sensitive) to changes that occur?

It's not always possible to know in advance whether a measure will be sensitive to change, although with standardized scales, such information sometimes is available from studies that have used the measure to evaluate interventions similar to the one you plan to evaluate (e.g., Hunsley & Mash, 2008). Measures that have shown change in previous research and evaluations in a sense have proved themselves sensitive to some change, but you should do what you can to try to obtain a sensitive measure. For example, if you have a choice between counting behaviors that occur often and those that occur rarely, all other matters being equal, use the one that occurs more often. It will be more sensitive to changes, and hence, a more accurate representation of what is occurring. This is because a high-frequency behavior is likely to be more responsive to small changes and can both increase or decrease, while a low-frequency behavior largely can only increase and may be responsive only to major changes. Or, a standardized scale that asks for ratings of emotions or behaviors over the course of the past 6 months might not be sensitive to ongoing changes brought about by an intervention. Finally, measures of some constructs can be more or less sensitive depending on who provides the information; for example, youth self-report measures of depression are more sensitive than the parent versions (Dougherty, Klein, Olino, & Laptook, 2008). In some ways, determining the sensitivity of a measure could be reflected in the absence of any changes in the measure during baseline, even though the client reports major events occurring in his or her life. Then, it might be a matter of finding another measure during the baseline period that will more accurately represent what is taking place.

Sometimes we can examine the construct validity of a measure with individual client systems. As an example, suppose that a client seeks help because he is depressed and he is dissatisfied with his marriage. You decide to measure depression using the Beck Depression Inventory (Beck, Steer, & Brown, 1996), which is a self-report depression scale, and the Hamilton Rating Scale for Depression (Hamilton, 1980; Rush, First, & Blacker, 2008), which is a practitioner-completed depression scale. For both depression measures, higher scores indicate greater depression. You measure marital satisfaction using the Index of Marital Satisfaction (IMS) (Hudson, 1997), a self-report measure for which higher scores indicate greater *dis*satisfaction. Each measure is completed weekly. After a 3-week baseline, a 7-week intervention designed to ameliorate depression is implemented, and this is followed by a 7-week intervention designed to ameliorate marital distress. Results are shown in Figure 4, and the following patterns provide evidence of construct validity (an open circle represents IMS scores, a square represents BDI scores, and a solid circle represents HRS-D scores):

1. The week-to-week pattern of change in depression is similar for the BDI and the HRS-D; when BDI scores go up, HRS-D scores also go up; and when BDI scores go down, HRS-D scores also go down. Therefore, the BDI and the HRS-D appear correlated over time, suggesting that they measure the same thing and providing support for the convergent validity of the two measures. This evaluation doesn't provide evidence of the convergent validity of the IMS because only one measure of marital satisfaction was used, but it would be possible to obtain such evidence if another method of measuring marital satisfaction was included (e.g., practitioner judgment of the client's marital satisfaction).

2. The week-to-week pattern of change in IMS scores doesn't follow exactly the same pattern as BDI and HRS-D scores, but IMS scores do appear somewhat related, as would be expected. The fact that the IMS pattern is somewhat different suggests that it measures something different from either the BDI or the HRS-D, and this provides support for the discriminant validity of the BDI, HRS-D, and IMS. That is, if the week-to-week pattern of change was the same for each measure, this would suggest that they all measure the same problem (e.g., perhaps just generalized distress), instead of distinct problems.

3. The BDI, HRS-D, and IMS scores decrease when the intervention designed to ameliorate depression is implemented (i.e., the *B* phase), but the decrease in BDI and HRS-D scores is larger than the decrease in IMS scores. When the intervention designed to ameliorate marital distress is

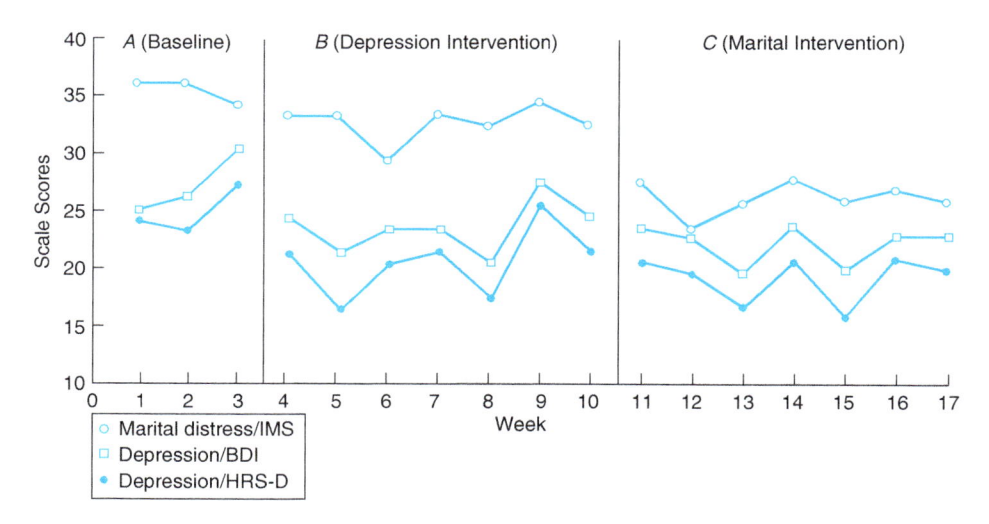

FIGURE 4 Construct validity of the BDI, HRS-D, and IMS.

implemented (i.e., the *C* phase), BDI, HRS-D, and IMS scores decrease further, but the largest decrease occurs for the IMS scores. This pattern of change between phases suggests that the BDI, HRS-D, and IMS change in a theoretically predicted manner in response to an intervention, which in turn suggests that they're sensitive to "real" change in the problems they attempt to measure.

Which Type of Validity Should You Use? Given these several types of validity, how do you know which one to use to evaluate an instrument? In the first place, we've presented them in a rough order of increasing importance. Thus, if a measure has high predictive validity, that would be much more important to know than whether a measure has face validity. Evidence concerning construct validity may make a measure even more useful because it will be related to a specific theoretical framework.

Perhaps a more basic guideline is this: In evaluating the validity of a measure for possible selection, one can probably place most confidence in the measure that has information about all the forms of validity. The measure obviously will be most useful if one is certain it has high face and content validity and that it can be safely used to make accurate predictions about the performance of an individual at the present time or in the future. In addition, consider the quality and quantity of the evidence available concerning the validity of a measure, especially when the evidence has been replicated by independent investigators; the quality and quantity of evidence available for different measures varies considerably. Finally, remember that a measure usually is not completely valid or invalid in general, but rather more or less valid for a particular purpose (e.g., a self-report depression scale may provide a valid measure of depression for adults but not children). So, the purpose of the measure should be considered in deciding what type of validity is relevant and the extent to which that validity pertains.

The Relationship between Reliability and Validity

First, you need to decide whether something is being measured consistently before you try to discover what it is that is being measured. If something isn't being measured consistently, it doesn't really make any sense to try to discover what that something is. So, if a measure isn't reliable, don't spend your time deciding whether it's valid. An unreliable measure will have little or no validity. If the scores on a measure are due just to chance events (i.e., random measurement error—unreliability) that are unrelated to what you're trying to measure, the measure cannot be correlated with anything, cannot show change in response to an intervention, and so cannot be a valid measure of anything. For example, if you flipped a coin to "measure" whether a client had a problem or you rolled a die to "measure" the degree of the problem on a 6-point scale, you wouldn't expect these "measures" to be correlated with anything, and you wouldn't expect them to be sensitive to any changes brought about by an intervention.

On the other hand, there is a continuum of reliability; most measures are not absolutely reliable or absolutely unreliable. Some measures have low or moderate reliability. As a general rule, though, any lack of reliability in a measure tends to lessen its validity.

Even if a measure is reliable, it may or may not be valid. Don't make the mistake of thinking that because a measure is reliable it will be valid. Think back to the example of the use of the neglect questions to measure child maltreatment. Reliability is necessary but not sufficient for validity.

Figures 5 and 6 illustrate reliability and validity. In Figure 5, the target is hit pretty consistently in the same spot, but not in the correct spot, the center (i.e., reliable but not valid). In Figure 6, the target is hit reliably and in the correct spot (i.e., reliable and valid).

If the criterion and construct validity of a measure are demonstrated, you can assume that it is to some

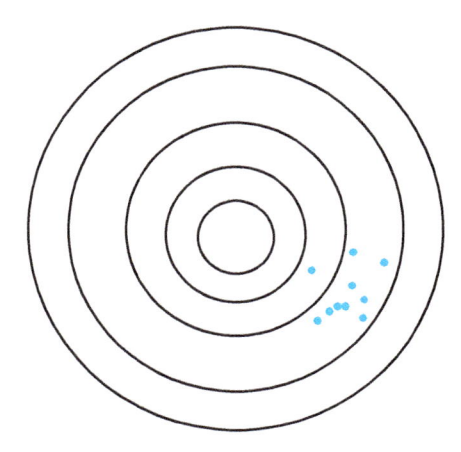

FIGURE 5 Reliable but not valid.

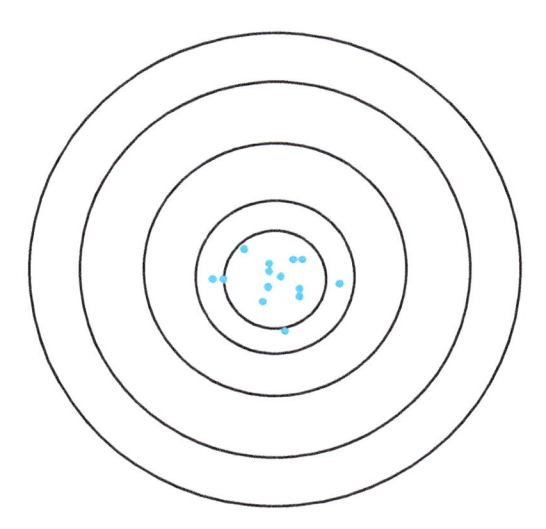

FIGURE 6 Reliable and valid.

extent reliable; if it contained too much random measurement error, it probably would not show such consistent relationships (Anastasi & Urbina, 1997). Therefore, if one can demonstrate that a measure has good validity, its reliability can be assumed and becomes a secondary issue. So, why are researchers concerned with reliability? The reliability of a measure is relatively easier to determine than its validity, and if you find that a measure has very low reliability there's no need to examine its validity: An unreliable measure cannot be valid. Conversely, if a measure has very poor validity, it is irrelevant that it may have high reliability.

Factors Influencing Reliability and Validity

We've mentioned a variety of factors that influence the reliability and validity of measures (e.g., the adequacy with which behaviors or questionnaire items are sampled, consistency in the domain from which behaviors or questionnaire items are sampled, reactivity), and we discuss other factors specific to particular measurement methods. However, there are two additional factors that can influence the reliability and validity of most measures: the procedures for administering a measure and the population for which estimates of reliability and validity are obtained.

Administration Procedures. Any condition that's irrelevant to the purpose of a measure can potentially introduce random or systematic measurement error. Therefore, to the extent possible, try to structure measurement conditions that reduce measurement error, and try to maintain uniform measurement conditions over time.

Various types of ambiguities and distractions can produce random measurement error and reduce the reliability of a measure. For example, asking clients or observers to report information under uncomfortable, chaotic, noisy, distracting conditions can reduce reliability. Ambiguity in the instructions provided to clients or observers also can reduce reliability. Therefore, give clients or observers careful and well-planned instructions for the use of measures, and make the conditions under which measurements are obtained as conducive to accurate measurement as possible.

The conditions of measurement also can decrease validity. For example, a questionnaire designed to elicit information about alcohol consumption, or some other highly sensitive type of information, might be valid when administered under certain conditions (e.g., individually, with guarantees of confidentiality), but it might not be valid when administered under other conditions (e.g., in the presence of a family member). Under the first condition the questionnaire might be a valid measure of alcohol consumption, but under the latter condition the questionnaire might just measure the degree to which someone is willing to disclose sensitive information in the presence of family members.

Systematic changes in measurement conditions also can introduce systematic measurement error and reduce the validity of a measure. For example, suppose that during baseline a client rated her depression each evening, but after the beginning of intervention the client rated her depression each morning. Suppose further that the client was more depressed in the evening than in the morning. This would make it look like the intervention had a positive effect even if it didn't. Therefore, in order to make valid comparisons across repeated measurements, the measures ideally should be obtained under similar conditions (e.g., in terms of time, place, instructions, assessor). In particular, avoid change in the conditions of measurement that coincide with the introduction of an intervention, because it will be difficult to tell whether the change in the measurement conditions or the introduction of the intervention caused any observed change.

Populations. The validity with which a target is measured can differ depending on numerous characteristics of clients, including racial and ethnic identity, national origin, cultural background, language preference, gender, age, sexual orientation, disability status, religion, extent of spirituality, and socioeconomic status (e.g., Dana, 2005; Davis & Proctor, 1995; Gilbert, 2003; Paniagua, 2005; Rubio-Stipec, Canino, Hicks, & Tsuang, 2008; Suzuki & Ponterotto, 2008). A reasonable question to ask when evaluating a measure, "is whether performance differs as a function of any of these demographic factors" (Malgady & Colon-Malgady, 2008, p. 41) (e.g., see Baden & Wong, 2008, for a good discussion of these issues with the elderly and Fontes & O'Neill-Arana, 2008, for a good discussion of these issues in the context of assessing child maltreatment). This has been referred to variously as "multicultural assessment validity" (Ridley et al., 2008), "validity generalization" (Hunsley & Mash, 2008), and as an issue of "fairness in testing and test use," that is, an ethical issue (AERA et al., 1999; Ridley et al., 2008).

Multicultural assessment validity can be enhanced or compromised in a number of ways. For example, the content or language of the items on a scale may give unfair advantage to one group over another, for example, items developed and written in English and then translated inappropriately into another language (Padilla & Borsato, 2008) or, more generally, measures developed within one cultural context and administered to individuals who are not acculturated to that context (Okawa, 2008; Rivera, 2008). The format of standardized scales (e.g., rating scales, true-false, multiple-choice) may be unfamiliar or offensive to individuals from some cultures (Okawa, 2008). The method used to administer a measure may disadvantage one group compared to another; for example, computer-based assessment may be problematic for those with insufficient access to, experience with, and confidence in using computers (Ahluwalia, 2008). The construct measured may have different meanings for different groups; for example, quality of life, parenting practices, marital discord, depression, and other constructs can mean something quite different in different cultures (Utsey & Bolden, 2008; Okawa, 2008). Normative scores (e.g., clinical cutting scores) developed on majority group populations may not be appropriate for individuals who differ from this population (Malgady & Colon-Malgady, 2008; Okawa, 2008). So, in evaluating, selecting, using, and interpreting results of a measure keep these issues in mind.

The facts are that many standardized measures are initially developed using white college students; white, middle-class individuals; or other unique populations that may not be representative of the normative population of interest (e.g., measures of couple distress developed and tested with white, middle-class married couples might or might not be useful for measuring couple distress in couples from different ethnic or socio-economic groups, or for gay and lesbian couples; see Snyder, Heyman, & Haynes, 2008). Thus, because the validity of a measurement procedure can vary depending on a variety of client characteristics, practitioner knowledge about and sensitivity to client diversity in a whole range of areas is critically important. These areas include, for example, client values and preferences in child-rearing practices, care of the elderly, religious beliefs, sexual orientation, willingness to disclose intimate information to and receive help from professionals, and, of course, ethnic and cultural differences. It also argues for the importance of using multiple measurement methods and multiple sources of information to measure a client's targets, and for the importance of verifying the validity of the measurement strategies used with a particular client whenever this is possible and practical.

These issues also require the ultimate in what might be called *population/person sensitivity* from the practitioner (see Pack-Brown & Williams, 2003, for their discussion of critical decision making in multicultural settings). First, you have to be careful to find measures that are specific to the client's concerns or that have been used with people from the client's group. In this way, you can use the measures with confidence in this application, knowing they're valid and appropriate. Second, if this is not possible, you have to try to find, or construct, measures that are appropriate for the client. (We provide some guidelines in subsequent chapters for doing just that.) Finally, if the first two suggestions are impossible to implement, in this particular application you may have to go ahead and use one or more measures about which you don't have total confidence, interpreting them with sensitivity and due caution regarding their possibly inappropriate interpretation.

Utility

Reliability and validity are important criteria by which to judge the accuracy of a measurement strategy. However, these are not the only criteria that are important, especially when selecting and using measurement tools for single-system evaluation. It's also important to consider evidence concerning how measures might be used to improve the decisions you make about your clients, the outcomes experienced by your clients, and the extent to which the measures are efficient, cost-effective, and acceptable to clients. These issues have to do with the *utility* of a measure (Hunsley & Mash, 2008). Unfortunately, as Hunsley and Mash note, little research exists concerning these issues and, typically, a determination of the utility of measures must be made on the basis of how likely a measure is to improve outcomes experienced by clients. For an exception, see the work of Lambert and his colleagues, which shows that routine monitoring and receipt of feedback to therapists based on clients' completion of the Outcome Questionnaire (www.oqmeasures.com) can reduce deterioration, improve overall outcome, and lead to fewer treatment sessions with no worsening of outcome for clients making progress (i.e., increased cost-effectiveness) (Lambert, 2007; Lambert et al., 2002, 2003; Harmon et al., 2007).

Relevance to Intervention Planning. The most basic reason for measuring client targets is to improve client outcomes. Accurate measurement is not an end in and of itself. The ultimate consideration in selecting a measure is how useful it will be to the success of the intervention. Therefore, the extent to which a measure increases the chances that a client problem will be resolved should be considered an important criterion for the selection and use of a measure. Thus, the measure you select should, as accurately as possible, closely reflect the problem, and it also should be reasonable to expect that the measure clearly will reflect change resulting from the intervention.

In the selection of a measure you might ask yourself the following questions to determine how a measure facilitates intervention decisions:

1. Does the measure help in deciding whether a client has a particular problem or the extent to which the problem exists?
2. Does the measure help in deciding what may be affecting or maintaining the problem?
3. Does the measure help in selecting the most effective intervention strategy?
4. Does the measure help in deciding whether a target is improving or deteriorating, so that any necessary modifications in the intervention plan can be undertaken?

In most cases a single measure won't meet all of these criteria, but a measure should meet one of these criteria to a high degree and one other to at least a moderate degree.

Ease of Use. Single-system designs require the repeated measurement of client targets over time. Therefore, the ease with which a measure is used becomes an important consideration. The question here is whether the client, practitioner, relevant other, or independent evaluator will be able and willing to use a given measure and, more specifically, use it within the context of single-system evaluation (e.g., Applegate, 1992; Campbell, 1988, 1990; Faul, McMurty, & Hudson, 2001).

There are several considerations in deciding the ease with which a measure can be used. These include the time it takes to administer, score, and interpret the measure, and characteristics of the client. For example, clients might be irritated, overwhelmed, or bored with the repeated completion of standardized scales, or they may be unable to read or understand the questionnaire. Practitioners or other observers might get worn out or bored with making certain types of observations, or a standardized scale might be time-consuming for a practitioner to score and interpret.

There has been an increasing recognition of the importance of the ease with which measures can be used in practice. This recognition has led to the development and dissemination of an amazing number of measures that can be used relatively easily on a repeated basis.

Accessibility. The accessibility of a measure is also an important criterion. Some measures are difficult to obtain; for example, they might be expensive. They might not be available for use by some professionals (e.g., some measures are only available to psychologists with appropriate training). It might be difficult and time consuming to locate and obtain copies of the measures.

Again, fortunately, there are an increasing number of source books that describe a wide variety of different types of measures and, in some cases, even provide copies of the measures.

Direct and Indirect Measures

Reliability, validity, and utility are important criteria by which to evaluate a measurement strategy, but one final consideration involves the extent to which your measure is a direct measure of the client's target. When the target that is measured is the same as the target of interest, the measure is "direct." When the target that is measured is in some way different from the target of interest, the measure is "indirect," and less valid because it is necessary to make inferences about the target of interest (Cooper, Heron, & Heward, 2007). For example, if you are interested in measuring the negative consequences of drinking, don't use measures of the quantity, frequency, and patterns of alcohol consumed; the same amount of alcohol consumed by different people can have different negative consequences (Green, Worden, Menges, & McCrady, 2008). (Of course, this is the same reason you would not use a measure of the negative consequences of drinking as a way to measure the quantity, frequency, and patterns of alcohol consumed.) Or, if you are interested in the subjective evaluation of marital dissatisfaction, don't use behavioral measures of relationship dysfunction; the same behaviors are evaluated differently by different people and across different cultures (Snyder, Heyman, & Haynes, 2008).

It's important to note that we're not trying to rule out the use of indirect measures. Indeed, many individualized rating scales, standardized scales, and unobtrusive measures are indirect measures. We are suggesting, though, that there may be priorities in selecting measures, and that for the reasons described previously, direct measures deserve a higher priority than indirect measures. But indirect measures may be the measures of choice (a) when direct measures are not available, (b) when the client is unable or unwilling to use them and no one else is available for direct observation, or (c) when other reasons prevent the use of direct measures.

Summary

This chapter began by introducing you to the general notion of conceptualization and measurement. We argued that although all practitioners might not rely on measurement in a formal sense, all practitioners do engage in a wide variety of measurement-like activities. The question isn't whether you will rely on measurement in your practice, but whether you will rely on the best possible measurement strategies. Therefore, the bulk of this chapter focused on key characteristics of measures—principles that you can use as guidelines to select the best possible measures and use them in a way that is appropriate for your own practice. The following criteria were discussed: reliability, validity, utility, and directness.

If you select an existing measure to evaluate your client you should critically examine the evidence of the reliability and validity of the measure. Figure 1 provides you with an overview of the possible information that you should look for to judge the adequacy of the measure, although given your purpose in using a measure it might not be necessary to have information on each of these different types of reliability and validity (e.g., alternate-forms reliability isn't necessary unless alternate forms are required; predictive validity isn't necessary unless you plan to use the measure to make predictions). In addition to considering the reliability and validity of the measure, you should consider whether the measure was tested with people who are similar to your client, and whether the measure is feasible for your use.

Using an existing measure with established reliability and validity can provide considerable confidence that a target is measured reliably and validly. However, even if you decide to use an existing measure with established reliability and validity, it's useful to examine how reliable and valid it is with your particular client. The reason this is useful is that the circumstances under which the reliability and validity of measures are typically determined are different in important ways from the way a measure is used in practice.

SPECIFYING PROBLEMS AND GOALS

Targets of Intervention

PURPOSE This chapter presents guidelines on how to develop clear and specific targets of intervention. This process usually involves moving from a client's concerns, which often are described vaguely although deeply felt, to operationally defining problems, then objectives and goals. We use the term *target* to refer to these specifically defined objects of preventive or interventive services. We also discuss setting goals in groups, the use of statistics to set goals, and Goal Attainment scaling as a method of establishing goals.

Introduction: From General Problems to Specific Targets of Intervention
Specifying Client Concerns: Identifying and Clarifying Problems and Potentials
    Preliminary Steps in Identifying Targets
        Survey Client Concerns: Starting Where the Client Is
        Select a Target
        Prioritize Targets
    Guidelines for Going from the Vague to the Specific: Operational Definition of the Target of Intervention
        Clarity
        Countability
        Verifying Sources
        Dereify
        Increasing and Decreasing
        Measurability
    Case Illustrations of Operationalized Targets
Specifying Goals and Objectives
    Definition of Terms: Goals and Objectives
    Components of Specific Goal Statements
        Who?
        Will Do What?
        To What Extent?
        Under What Conditions?
    Using Statistics to Set Goals
Using Goal Attainment Scaling (GAS) to Establish Goals
    Basic Guidelines for Using GAS
        Collecting Information
        Designation of Problem Areas
        Predictions for Each Problem Area
        Follow-Up "Interview"
Setting Goals in Groups
Problems and Issues in Setting Goals
    Anticipate Negative Outcomes
    Who Sets the Goals?
    Anticipate Impediments
    Case Illustrations of Goals in the Context of Problems and Interventions
Summary

From Chapter 3 of *Evaluating Practice: Guidelines for the Accountable Professional*, Sixth Edition. Martin Bloom, Joel Fischer, John G. Orme. Copyright © 2009 by Pearson Education, Inc. All rights reserved.

INTRODUCTION: FROM GENERAL PROBLEMS TO SPECIFIC TARGETS OF INTERVENTION

There is a profound truth in the saying that "well defined is half solved" in that if we can clearly identify what our problem is, we have taken a major step toward its solution. This saying strongly applies to practice and the evaluation of practice because all forms of professional service begin with the questions: *What client problems or issues need to be resolved and what goals need to be achieved?*

We don't mean to imply that specifying the problem is necessarily the most important aspect of practice, only that it is the essential beginning step. Obviously, if a practitioner did not have effective intervention skills, specifying problems from now until doomsday would be useless. But experience with many groups of students and practitioners informs us that the identification and clarification of client problems and goals are difficult because of the many ways one might try to get hold of these complex human events. Our purpose in this chapter is to help you identify specific targets of intervention from the sometimes confusing mass of client concerns. This specification will not only help practice, it will also facilitate the use of the evaluation methods we describe in this book.

We use the term *target* to refer to the specific object of preventive or interventive services that is relevant in a given situation. We have chosen this neutral term because there are several ways to think about what aspects of the client's life situation we want to influence. We will distinguish among client problems, goals, objectives, and targets. We also will continue to discuss the process of operationalization. When you state problems or goals in specific, measurable terms, you are operationalizing a target of intervention. Operationalizing (or constructing an operational definition) means that you clearly specify the actions you would go through in order to observe or measure the client's problem.

Let's begin with an example. A client tells the practitioner that she "feels depressed all the time." She recognizes that some events in her life are going to be difficult and resistive to change, but she would prefer not to be depressed so much of the time. Note that you can begin to identify a problem (the depressed feelings), and following from this, you can also tentatively identify a goal (her preference not to be so depressed, or expressed in the positive, to be happier than she currently is much of the time). Her problematic experience does not demonstrate the intensity of these feelings or under what circumstances they occur. Indeed, while the client keenly feels her depression, she is somewhat vague about its nature as well as what goals she would like to attain. The practitioner needs more specific information on which to formulate a target of intervention.

So, you might operationalize this target of intervention by asking the client to complete a standardized scale that measures the extent and intensity of depression. Or, you might unobtrusively record the number of times the client cries during the interview hour, where crying is seen as an indicator of the intensity of her depression. Or, you might ask her to record in a log not only the times she feels depressed during the coming week, but also what events occurred before, during, and after the times she felt depressed. The point here is that there are many ways to specify measurable operations that indicate the nature and extent of the target, in this case, depression. Which ones you select depend on the nature of the case, but they become the operational meanings of the term *depression* throughout the period of service.

It is difficult to deal with global problems, and practitioners may feel overwhelmed or frustrated in the attempt. Being clear and specific about the problems and goals lends itself to selection of both specific intervention procedures and specific measures related to these identified problems and goals. By repeating such measures, you can know explicitly what changes are occurring in the target and adopt suitable responses. This chapter discusses how you can get to a reasonable, sensitive, and accurate specification of the problems on which you might be working in a particular case.

In suggesting that practitioners should be specific, we are not suggesting that you ignore complex problems or goals. Rather, we urge you to be as clear and precise as possible in specifying what those problems and goals are and in finding ways that they can be measured or observed. This may mean breaking down a complex problem into component parts, if possible. As each component is changed, the entire complex of problems becomes modified.

Likewise, by encouraging the specification of problems, we do not suggest that meaning be sacrificed for rigor, for example, by setting up irrelevant or trivial goals merely because they are easy to measure. *A goal that is irrelevant or trivial to the client's situation is equally unimportant to evaluate.* Indeed, we believe that specifying problems and goals can be very relevant to practitioners and clients because it leads to more precise selection of intervention methods and related procedures, clearer evaluation of results, and more effective services (e.g., Faul, McMurty, & Hudson, 2001).

SPECIFYING CLIENT CONCERNS: IDENTIFYING AND CLARIFYING PROBLEMS AND POTENTIALS

In this section, we focus on client's problems and potentials that will ultimately be the target of our intervention. Our task will be to move from an area of concern felt by the client as problematic to a target on which client and practitioner can agree to work. This target may involve interventive action to decrease a given set of events, to build on strengths, or both. There is no one right way to do this; rather, keep your eye on the approach that we are proposing. It will serve you in a wide variety of contexts.

We again want to emphasize that when we discuss problems or issues, we mean concerns in the life of the client or client-system that can be turned into targets for intervention. That includes identifying strengths and potentials that can be built upon. In fact, we hope you will do everything possible to focus on the strengths of the client or system you are trying to help (Lopez & Snyder, 2003). This means several things: (1) accentuating the positive when selecting targets (e.g., focusing on regular school attendance rather than truancy, so as not to emphasize or reinforce dysfunctional behavior); (2) looking at measuring strengths to be increased by your interventions rather than problems to be decreased; and (3) overall, it means identifying specific strengths in a person or situation as a focus for your measurement, intervention, and evaluation efforts. Thus, a high measurement priority is to look for the strengths in people in difficult situations and attempt to build on them rather than focusing on a person's weaknesses and limitations.

Preliminary Steps in Identifying Targets

There are several steps you might take in the process of specifying a problem. We will review these here, with the understanding that we are obviously not attempting to deal with the entire assessment phase of practice or even with all of the implications of early contacts with clients (Groth-Marnat, 2003; Haynes & Heiby, 2003). We are only carving out a chunk of the process—identifying and specifying problems.

Survey Client Concerns: Starting Where the Client Is.
The first step on the path toward specifying problems begins when you attempt to review all the matters of concern to the client, referring agency, and/or relevant others. This is not the assessment proper; rather, it is a preliminary survey of problems and a discussion with those concerned, involved, or affected about how they perceive these problems. We suggest making a written list of all the concerns, perhaps adding any that you yourself might observe.

It might be useful at this initial stage to use a checklist to help the client identify problems. The checklist is simply a preset list of problems that a client can check off if he or she has a concern about one or more of them. You or your agency may want to develop your own checklist for conducting a preliminary survey of client problems. There are several ways to do this. First, you could simply list many of the problems commonly seen in your agency and ask the client to check off whether he or she wants help with them (see Figures 1, 2, and 3 for abbreviated examples of such a form for clinical, consultative, and community work).

Another type of checklist—actually, one that could be combined with the checklists shown—simply lists relevant others and asks the client to check those with whom he or she may have special concerns, as in the abbreviated example in Figure 4.

Name		Date
Yes	No	Do you want help with:
___	___	Managing your money?
___	___	Being less anxious?
___	___	Having more friends?
___	___	Feeling better about yourself?
___	___	Controlling your anger?

FIGURE 1 Example of a problem checklist for clinical practice.

Name		Date
Yes	No	Do you want help with:
___	___	Understanding family dynamics?
___	___	Specifying the problems?
___	___	Developing an intervention plan?
___	___	Overcoming client resistance?

FIGURE 2 Example of a problem checklist for use in consultation.

```
_____   _____
Name                      Date

  Yes        No         Does your organization need
                        help with:
_____   _____         Increasing participation?
_____   _____         Getting new members?
_____   _____         Running meetings?
_____   _____         Securing funds?
```

FIGURE 3 Example of a problem checklist for community work.

```
_____   _____
Name                      Date
```

Put a check in front of any of the relationships that seem to bother you. Circle the checks for those which bother you the most.

_____ Mother   _____ Child   _____ Friend
                                                (same sex)
_____ Father   _____ Employer   _____ Friend
                                                (opposite sex)
_____ Spouse   _____ Co-worker   _____ Neighbor

FIGURE 4 Example of a checklist for problem relationships.

Finally, your initial problem survey form could simply consist of open spaces in which you ask the client to list the problems or people with whom they are having the most difficulty, as in Figure 5.

Remember, you are still doing a preliminary survey of problems, so at this point it is not necessary to go into too much detail about each concern. At the end of this part of the session go over the list with the client to ensure that it is complete.

Select a Target. Unless you are lucky enough to be meeting with an individual or group that has presented only one problem for you to work on, it is likely that you will have to make some initial selections from among several concerns presented earlier by the client. The importance of this cannot be overstated. It has been our observation that one of the greatest roadblocks to effective practice is the failure of some practitioners to partialize problems, that is, to focus on one problem and attempt to be as specific as possible in defining it. Often problems are stated vaguely or globally, leaving the practitioner and client with a feeling of tremendous frustration as

```
_____   _____
Name                      Date
```

Please list below the problems or people that most concern you. Try to give one or two specific examples of the problem for each.

Problem 1: _____
           _____

  Example: _____
           _____

Problem 2: _____
           _____

  Example: _____
           _____

FIGURE 5 Example of an open problem list.

they attempt to manage a problem that, as the client defines it, is essentially unmanageable.

Although selecting a problem generally comes rather early in the overall assessment process, it is important to note that this is not the only place in the process where problem selection may go. This may be largely a matter of your personal preference, theoretical orientation, or approach to practice. Some practitioners prefer to select a problem after a more comprehensive assessment has been conducted on the grounds that only after the assessment has been completed can they make an intelligent judgment as to priorities. Other practitioners prefer to select a problem prior to the formal assessment process on the grounds that this problem selection then provides clear and specific guides regarding what to assess. Either way, some selection and priority-determining process must be conducted. It's up to you to decide at what point you will engage in this activity.

Essentially, problem selection involves two steps: (a) determining the priorities within the problem/situation (which we consider to be a preliminary step), and (b) specifying the problem per se, or moving from the vague to the specific, which will take up a large section of this chapter.

As we mentioned earlier, we view targets simply as areas about which the client is concerned. Thus, the "problem" may be something the client wants to decrease (e.g., an undesired behavior or lack of cooperation of community agencies) or an asset or strength that the client wants to build on or increase (e.g., a desired behavior or the number of community members participating in meetings). In some instances you may have the option of defining a concern from either viewpoint—a problem involving decreasing support for an activity is also one involving increasing support. As a general strategy, we recommend focusing on strengths or assets when possible and attempting to increase or build on these strengths or assets, rather than trying to decrease deficits. There are three basic reasons for this: (a) it is generally easier (and more effective) to build on strengths and increase behaviors than it is to decrease negative or undesired behaviors; (b) by focusing on increasing positive behaviors, you will be more likely to marshal support from the client and others, since trying to decrease negative behaviors often produces concomitant negative emotional reactions; and (c) philosophically, for the helping professions, it is more compatible with our values to take a strengths or positive perspective than a problem or negative perspective.

Prioritize Targets. The first step in selecting a problem or area of concern on which to work is to review the written list of concerns that you developed earlier with the client. The task then becomes one of negotiating with the concerned parties regarding what concern(s) to work on. The point here is not to select one concern only for the sake of selection, but to select one concern because this is the best way to marshal resources. If you and the client have the time, energy, and resources, more than one problem may be attacked at the same time. Whether in a clinical, organizational, or community context, we suggest that you attempt to negotiate to work first with the problem that meets as many of the following criteria as possible (Brager & Specht, 1973; Sundel & Sundel, 1975): (a) It is one that clients prefer to start with or about which they are most concerned; (b) it has the greatest likelihood of being changed; (c) it is relatively concrete and specific; (d) it can be readily worked with, given your resources; (e) it has the greatest chance of producing the most negative consequences if not handled; (f) it has to be handled before other problems can be tackled; and (g) changes in the problem will result in tangible, observable changes for those involved, thereby perhaps increasing the participants' motivation to work on other problems.

Once the problem (or problems) is selected, the next step is to define the problem as specifically as possible in terms that make it measurable and clearly susceptible to change. This topic is discussed in detail in the following section.

Guidelines for Going from the Vague to the Specific: Operational Definition of the Target of Intervention

In initial contacts with clients, practitioners often hear problems such as, "My son is immature"; "I don't know what to do with my life"; "My husband and I don't communicate"; "Something's wrong but I'm not sure what"; "I'm pretty shy." Very few clients spell out their specific problems precisely in clear, observable terms. Instead, most often people apply labels to themselves or others, talk about general characteristics, or simply use vague, hard-to-decipher terms.

The task of the practitioner in situations such as these is to help the client operationalize problems, that is, redefine them in more precise, measurable (observable) terms. This will aid in assessing the problem to see what factors may be affecting it. It will also help the client and practitioner have a clearer understanding of and agreement about the nature and occurrence of the problem so that they can take action on it and so that they will agree on what is to be changed. Furthermore, stating the problem in observable terms means the client and practitioner will be able to evaluate their progress. Thus, the problem becomes operationalized as the *target* of intervention.

Obviously, all problems can't be succinctly specified, as though they occurred in a few minutes' time with a discrete beginning and end. Even so, use of this model will at least help you identify those situations, and also help clarify some of the conditions that may be affecting particular occurrences of the problem; for example, what antecedents may elicit it, what consequences may follow it.

There are a number of guidelines to use in stating problems more specifically and precisely in order to convert them into targets. We suggest you consider each of these as a way of thinking about how to add more precision to your definition of problems.

Clarity. Most clients have a great deal of difficulty being clear about describing the problem or about describing where, when, or how often it occurs. The job of the practitioner in these cases is to help translate vague or even inaccurate descriptions into specific and accurate ones.

Think of how often you've heard the terms *hostile, suspicious, immature, anxious, aggressive*. What do you do with those terms?

First, ask the client to give concrete examples of the occurrence of the problem. For example, if a teacher describes Jane as being immature, he or she may mean one or more of several things: she talks too much, she talks out of turn, she doesn't talk enough, she gets out of her seat without permission, she doesn't get out of her seat when asked to, she fights with other children, she doesn't fight back when attacked. Asking the client for concrete examples (e.g., "What does Jane do when she is acting immature?"), thereby operationalizing the problem, will give both the practitioner and the client a clearer idea of what the problem actually is.

Second, the practitioner can ask the client to try to identify when and where the problem occurs, perhaps to actually observe and record its occurrence. This can be done through a combination of simply trying to recall its occurrence, or better yet (because of its greater objectivity), through recording the problem using any of the measures described in subsequent chapters, or by asking the client to keep a log.

Third, you might consider doing a functional analysis of the relationship between the problem and personal, interpersonal, or environmental events that could be affecting (or controlling) the occurrence of the problem (e.g., Cooper, Heron, & Heward, 2007). Think of this as the *A-B-C* model. *A* refers to antecedents of the problem. Ask the client what happened just before the occurrence of the problem, who was there, and what he or she said and did. These antecedents could include the client's thoughts about the occurrence of some event; these thoughts might lead the client to perceive the event as positive or negative and could lead to the next step in the functional analysis.

B refers to the behavior or the actual occurrence of the problem. What actually happened? What did the client or others do or say that led to the definition of *B* as a problem? You and the client might even roleplay the situation so that you would have a clearer picture of the problem.

C refers to consequences. Here you ask the client to identify what happened as a result of the occurrence of *B*. What did the client and others do or say? Were there environmental factors that could have reinforced the client for the occurrence of the problem so that its occurrence would actually be strengthened?

Not only will an *A-B-C* analysis help you clarify the problem, it may give you some preliminary ideas about intervention. For example, if certain circumstances (*A*) consistently elicit the problem (*B*), or consistently reinforce it (*C*), you will have some ideas that could direct you to make changes in those antecedents or consequences.

Countability. Gottman and Leiblum (1974, p. 53) state, "Anything that occurs, occurs with some frequency and can therefore be *counted*." If you think of counting simply as checking over or keeping track of each occurrence of some problem, you'll see how this can be helpful in specifying problems. When you think in terms of counting, you will begin to start thinking in terms of how often does the problem occur, and for how long does it occur. Answers to questions such as these will provide specific referents for the problem, turning vague, global statements into specifics and helping you pinpoint the problem. The focus in counting is on what the client (or person or organization with which the client is concerned) actually does. The focus is on "how long," "how often," "what," and "when" issues rather than only on "why" issues, which are generally interpretive, subjective, and/or difficult to answer.

This process helps to focus on specific occurrences rather than on generalizations or motives. The husband who complains that his wife doesn't care about what goes on around the house may really mean, "She doesn't help with the dishes after dinner." The parent concerned that the child is not living up to his or her potential may really mean, "He doesn't accurately complete all his math homework."

Verifying Sources. One way of thinking about specification is to try to establish a *verifying source*—a way of knowing, when possible, that the problem does in fact exist, and a way for documenting when, where, and how often it occurs. This could mean asking the spouse to observe the client's behavior, using agency records to verify impressions with regard to service load, or using school records to document a child's attendance or grades. If there are no specific verifying sources available, think of the use of this guideline in this way: If there *were* people available who could act as verifying sources, would they be able to document the existence and occurrence of the problem? In other words, think of the problem in terms of the possibility of two or more people being able to agree on its occurrence. Although this is not possible for all problems (e.g., private thoughts), when it is possible and when agreement between client and practitioner is reached, you should have a more precise idea of the nature of the problem. If not, the problem may be too vaguely defined.

Dereify. One major impediment to defining problems in specific terms and with real-world referents is called *reification*, which refers to the treating of abstractions or constructs as though they were real things.

Any number of concepts that we commonly use to explain problems are examples of reification and often keep us from both specifying the problem and taking action on it. Consider the following examples (Hudson, 1976):

"Mrs. Johnson's problems arise from a deficient ego."

"Ethel hallucinates because she is psychotic."

"Julie became pregnant because she is promiscuous."

"John rocks back and forth because he is autistic."

"Bill abandoned his family because he is an inadequate father."

"Sam hit her because he is hostile."

"Marie socked her brother because she is aggressive."

In all of these examples problems were described and explained by labels (constructs) that actually did not have real-world referents. This suggests circular reasoning: Ethel hallucinates because she is psychotic and she is psychotic because she hallucinates. In none of these examples could you actually intervene with the presumed explanation. On the other hand, you could intervene if you were to focus on the specific problem or behavior contained or implied in the statements.

There is a simple way to do this. If you are having difficulty specifying problems, check whether you are reifying them. See if you really are simply treating an abstraction as though it were an actual thing. If you are, then you really cannot take action on it. (How does one intervene with an abstraction?) And if you are, try this: Simply convert the abstraction into an adjective. Instead of saying, "Marie is aggressive," try something like, "Marie demonstrates aggressive *behaviors*." Instead of saying, "Billy is immature," say, "Billy demonstrates immature *behaviors*." The next step is to identify what those behaviors are and then to describe the situation in which the behavior occurs. Then you will be on your way.

Increasing and Decreasing. One way of helping you specify problems is to think of them in terms of concerns to be increased or decreased. This is related to the idea that you would want to decrease undesired situations, while you would want to increase desired ones (i.e., build on strengths). Thinking of what needs to be increased and decreased almost automatically helps you pinpoint and specify problems. Such an orientation can help guide you toward being specific, because it requires answers to the questions: "What specific strength should we increase?" and "What specific problem should we decrease?" The more global or vague the problem definition, the more difficult it is to answer those questions. Defining problems in terms of increasing or decreasing them—for example, decreasing the number of aggressive behaviors that Marie performs—is also valuable as a guide to selection of intervention techniques, since a number of techniques have been developed and described in terms of their focus on increasing or decreasing behaviors, thoughts, or feelings. For example, how should we go about decreasing the number of aggressive behaviors that Marie has been performing?

Measurability. Our final suggestion involves simply taking a perspective on how to think about problems. That is, begin to consider different ways a given problem can be, or has been, measured. When we discuss defining problems in observable or measurable terms, we are not only speaking about overt behaviors. Many problems are simply not overt behaviors. But there has to be some way to keep track of the occurrence of the problem. Thus, one of the key guidelines to think about when helping clients define their problems is how these might be sensitively, but more or less objectively, measured, including how other practitioners have measured them sensitively in the past. We emphasize that we want measures that are sensitive to the reality of the client's problems; never sacrifice meaning for the sake of measurement. Measured targets should be personally, interpersonally, organizationally, or socially significant, not just measurable. But try to be as objective as possible under the circumstances. And we suggest you think of measurability in terms of the measurement ideas.

For example, if Ben's problem is that he is feeling depressed because he and hundreds of his teaching colleagues were dismissed because state funds for education were reduced, then the measurement of those feelings of depression will be limited to what the client observes and reports. Yet, there are a number of ways that the problem can be measured. The client could count negative (depressive) thoughts or more positively, he could count the nondepressed intervals between negative thoughts. (The interventive emphasis here then might be on expanding such nondepressed intervals, a positive-oriented target, as well as increasing reality-oriented efforts at reemployment.) Or, the practitioner might devise an individualized rating scale with the client to keep track of activities he likes to do, with the goal of increasing these activities in place of spending time on depressive thoughts. Or, there are standardized measures to help Ben and his practitioner keep an accurate track of the extent and nature of Ben's depressed feelings. Or, a client log could be kept to indicate where the nondepressed (and the depressed) behaviors occur; when they occur most frequently (or least frequently); how often they occur on a given day; who is present when they occur; and what happens just before, during, and after the nondepressed (and the depressed) intervals occur. This set of questions represents the kinds of issues that measurability seeks to identify.

These guidelines parallel the issues Paul and Elder (2004) call "universal intellectual standards of critical thinking." These are standards that are applied to thinking "whenever one is interested in checking the quality of reasoning about a problem, issue, or situation" (Paul & Elder, 2004, p. 7). The standards are comprised of questions one asks to ensure that the standards, and, hence, critical thinking, are applied to every problem/situation. The questions include those that may be asked of clients and relevant others by practitioners and those that would be considered by practitioners themselves in considering whether they have done an adequate job in understanding a problem or situation. These standards, and the associated questions, can be applied not only in specifying problems, but also in conducting thoughtful, analytic assessments.

The standards and questions, from Paul and Elder (2004), are as follows:

Clarity: Could you elaborate further? Could you give me an example? Could you illustrate what you mean?

Accuracy: How could we check on that? How could we find out if that is true? How could we verify or test that?

Precision: Could you be more specific? Could you give me more details? Could you be more exact?

Relevance: How does that relate to the problem? How does that bear on the question? How does that help us with the issue?

Depth: What factors make this a difficult problem? What are some of the complexities of this issue? What are some of the difficulties we need to deal with?

Breadth: Do we need to look at this from another perspective? Do we need to consider another point of view? Do we need to look at this in other ways?

Logic: Does all this make sense together? Does your first paragraph fit in with your last? Does what you say follow from the evidence?

Significance: Is this the most important problem to consider? Is this the central idea to focus on? Which of these facts are most important?

Fairness: Do I have any vested interest in this issue? Am I sympathetically representing the viewpoints of others?

Case Illustrations of Operationalized Targets

In this section, we present some operational definitions of problems that some students and practitioners have selected for their cases. Along the way, we suggest some variations in how these targets might have been operationalized for different kinds of contexts. The point of this section is to present some real examples of targets—operationalized problems on which client and practitioner could work.

Angelica (a second-year graduate social work student) had a practicum at a senior citizen center, where a problem emerged regarding serving the noon meal. Volunteers were only too happy to get trays of food for older persons who came in for lunch, but the agency staff thought this fostered an unhealthy dependence, as most of these diners could get the trays themselves. Also, the seniors complained of long waits in line. Therefore, the intervention involved calling a table at a time to come through the lunch line. (Volunteers helped those who truly couldn't manage for themselves.) The first operationalized target constituted the number of elderly persons who went through the lines themselves on a given day, compared to the number of able elderly persons. Two weeks before intervention, the nutritionist for the agency counted the number of elderly persons who carried their own trays. She continued to do this during the intervention period. The second target was the satisfaction level of the participants in the luncheon program. This was measured once a week by a short survey of the elderly as they were leaving the dining area: (a) How was the food today? ("very good," "good," "adequate," "not so good," "poor"); (b) Was waiting in line for food a problem today? (ranging from "yes, very much," through three steps to "no, not at all"); and (c) Did you enjoy being with your friends today during lunch? ("yes, very much," through three steps to "no, not at all"). The proportion of satisfied customers (the average of "satisfied" responses on the three questions for each individual summed over all lunch eaters) was noted on the charts before and during the intervention period.

Barbara (an undergraduate social work student) was working with the parents of a severely developmentally disabled child who were frustrated at his inability to get dressed and ready for school on time. The problem of dressing correctly was operationalized to mean putting on in the correct order all of the clothes the parents had laid out the night before in a line on the bedroom floor. The parents were simply to observe their child and note the number of clothes not put on or put on in the wrong order, and record this on a chart each day. The second problem, the parents' frustration, was operationalized by the number of times either of them yelled at their son in the morning regarding his being on time for the school bus. This, too, was recorded by both parents independently (to determine interrater reliability); the data were brought in to the practitioner once a week when they met to discuss the problems. (The parents could also have kept a diary of their feelings of frustration, but this may have required more cooperation than the parents were thought to be willing to give.)

Francis was a counselor at an alcoholic recovery center run by the city. A young man was referred to this center for his alcohol abuse problems that were combined with his abusive behavior toward his girlfriend. When he was sober, he was not abusive toward her, but sometimes, when he had too much to drink, she reported that he exhibited behaviors that she found very unpleasant to the point where she tried to break up with him. At that time, although sober, he was very upset and became abusive. She called the police and events escalated to the point where he was placed under court order to stay away from her, and to go through the alcohol control program at this center on a daily basis for 6 weeks.

The counselor saw need for several measures (operational definitions). First, on his drinking, she obtained his self-report. This was not considered to be a completely satisfactory indicator of his true behavior, so he was required to take a breathalyzer test each time he came to the session. Note that these two measures of alcohol use serve several functions; the breathalyzer is taken as the most nearly objective measure of alcohol in his blood, while the self-report is taken partly at least as an indicator of validity in reporting his own behavior. Eventually, the daily breathalyzer test will be stopped, while the self-reports will be continued; there will be random breathalyzer tests to ascertain his continued valid reporting. This is also an example of how the criterion validity of self-reported alcohol use could be examined.

The counselor also was concerned about the abusive behavior, but since the client was ordered to stay away from his former girlfriend, the counselor decided to measure the client's thoughts about abusing her. The measure was a list of questions that the client answered before the session at the alcohol center. It asked whether he had thought about his girlfriend in the time since the last session and, if so, whether he thought about being abusive toward her. (This report was confirmed indirectly by analysis of the content of the therapeutic session in which the client's feelings were discussed in several different ways. The therapeutic discussion was seen as the best available indicator of the validity of the client's self-reports.)

George was a graduate student in a research class and kept records on himself as a client. He admitted being very anxious about being in a research class, so much so that he thought it interfered with his doing his schoolwork effectively. He decided to operationalize anxiety by a self-anchored scale that ran from "bouncing butterflies in stomach, very uncomfortable feelings about self as adequate student in research class," to "fluttering butterflies in stomach, somewhat uncomfortable about self as adequate student in research class," to "no butterflies in stomach, feeling reasonably comfortable with self as adequate research student." He also turned in weekly homework, and recorded his grades as a measure of his actual competence at a given research assignment. (This student did very well in class, partly, he noted, because he was watching not only his level of anxiety, but also his grades at corresponding times. He learned that his anxiety was generally in excess of his actual quality of work in class.)

Irene was a practitioner in a rural mental health agency. Her task was to document that the special bus service for the elderly was working adequately to maintain the service. What "adequate" meant became something of a political football because the county administrators who made this decision were never able to give her an exact figure of the minimum needed to continue the service. Irene reviewed the bus censuses for the past few years and estimated that at least 40 customers a week would be necessary because, when fewer took the special buses, there were complaints from the administrators. Thus, 40 customers a week became the operational definition of "adequate." Then it was a simple matter to try some interventions, such as information campaigns, to get at least that minimum number. She was able to increase ridership, and apparently 40 was about the right number, since the county administrators voted to sustain the bus service another year.

Jack is a social work student who interned at a hospital for the mentally ill. Within a few days of his arrival, several residents at the hospital died, and there was a pervasive sadness in the facility. Jack wondered how this chance event affected the other residents, so he developed a small evaluation project, which he cleared with the appropriate staff. He did some checking into the literature and found a standardized scale designed to measure a respondent's anxiety about death (Lonetto & Templer, 1983, as cited in Fischer & Corcoran, 2007b, p. 827). He found that this scale had norms for psychiatric patients as well as "normal" adults, so he could compare his results against those of known groups. He also noted that the reliability of this instrument was good (a 3-week test–retest correlation of .83), and that validity was fair (correlating .74 with the Fear of Death Scale, another well-studied instrument). He compared a sample of older residents with a group of patients who were admitted after the rash of deaths, and found marked differences—the older residents were more anxious than the newly admitted residents. This led the hospital staff to intensify discussions of death with older residents rather than ignoring the unpleasant subject.

These examples can be multiplied in great numbers, but they all share some basic characteristics in how they operationalized the problem: First, whatever measures were used had to reflect a commonsense view on the nature of that problem. That is, all of these measures were indicators of the problem, and to be successful, they had to be as close as possible to the problem without being burdensome for anyone to use.

Second, the measures involved thoughts, feelings, and actions of individuals, as well as collective actions of groups or clusters of people. When there was any reasonable doubt, the practitioner attempted to verify both the validity of the measure and its reliability or consistency. It would make no sense to measure something if what was measured and how it was measured were in doubt.

Third, these practitioners had to be careful about whom they asked to collect the data. Sometimes they did it themselves, but more often they involved the clients or others in the situation. Some data had to be collected by the client, as no other person could accurately report about feeling states, for example. But other times, there were options on who could do the measuring, and the choice was made on the basis of available resources and the willingness of participants.

Fourth, no miracles were performed in selecting these measures, and most were reasonable, homemade varieties. Of course, already available standardized measures will sometimes fit the measurement needs of a case, as we illustrated. But the point of this section is to emphasize that every practitioner can come up with some reasonable and innovative measures customized to the situation at hand. It does take thought, but this is the same type of thinking that goes into the overall assessment of case problems and goals.

SPECIFYING GOALS AND OBJECTIVES

Goals usually emerge from discussions about client problems, but it is important to keep these two ideas distinct. Problems involve what currently hurts or disturbs the client; goals are preferences about the future. Goals indicate what the client would prefer to happen, to do, or to be, when the intervention is completed.

Goals specify what kinds of changes are desired and, thus, in what direction the intervention should move. Perhaps, most importantly, goals provide the standard or frame of reference for evaluating whether the client is moving, and whether the destination is met. Thus, goals provide the opportunity for ongoing feedback during the process of intervention, as well as the reference point for deciding whether the end has been attained.

Unfortunately, goals are frequently stated in abstract or vague terms, what Mager (1972) calls *fuzzies*. They may point in the direction of the desired outcomes, but they don't tell us "how to know one when you see one." Here are some familiar fuzzies: "to communicate clearly within the family," "to develop an awareness of oneself," "to feel a sense of accomplishment in one's activities," and so on. These are all perhaps desirable characteristics, but we really can't tell when they have been accomplished. Thus, we need to clarify how goals can be used in evaluating practice.

Definition of Terms: Goals and Objectives

Previously, we briefly defined *goals* as statements about what the client and relevant others (family, peers, friends, the practitioner) would like to happen, or to do, or to be when the intervention is completed. This definition of goals is taken in the sense of an ultimate end of action, against which the results of the intervention are to be compared. Thus, we could view these as *ultimate goals*, or goals related to ultimate *outcomes* for the *client* (Rosen, 1993).

Most of the time, though, it is not possible to go directly from a problem to the ultimate goal. Rather, it is necessary to move first through a sequence of manageable steps or subgoals. Rather than moving from *A* to *Z*, we move from *A* to *B* to *C* and so on. We use the terms *intermediate goals*, *objectives*, or *outcome objectives*, to refer to these subgoals or intermediate goals. Outcome objectives simply are limited or intermediate versions of the ultimate goal and are defined in exactly the same terms as goals. For example, a goal might be to increase the initiation of communication by 50% over a period of 10 weeks, as measured by an increase in the number of times a client initiates a comment to a family member at the dinner table, while the objective might be to increase the initiation of communication by 10% the first two weeks, an additional 10% the next two weeks, and 10% more for each week until the 50% goal is met. Also, it should be clear that goals and objectives are relative terms. What may be an objective for one client may be a goal for another.

In accord with the vast bulk of literature, when we use the terms *objectives* or *goals*, we are referring to outcomes for the *client* rather than interventive activities or tasks in which you as practitioner will be engaged. That is, all goal and objective statements refer to client or client/system attainments. The practitioner's activities, tasks performed, or steps taken can be specified in a separate statement that may be useful in agency accounting purposes, but is not included as a client goal or objective as such.

An important guideline in goal selection is that you should have some logical reason to expect that the intervention will have an effect on the selected targets. For example, if knowledge of child injury risk is selected as a target for a child welfare client, there should be some reason to believe that your intervention will increase this knowledge. It is not very efficient to measure something that isn't really the focus of, or is unlikely to change due to, your intervention efforts. More important though, targets that aren't the focus of an intervention will not be valid indicators of the effectiveness of that intervention, and so they can give a misleading impression of the effectiveness of the intervention. In particular, a target that isn't the focus of an intervention is unlikely to improve in response to that intervention, and this can give the misleading impression that the intervention is ineffective.

The remainder of this chapter focuses on how to establish specific client objectives and goals. We first describe the components of specific goal statements and then briefly discuss how to use statistics and other procedures such as Goal Attainment Scaling to establish goals. The chapter concludes with a review of some of the problems and issues involved in goal setting.

We should point out here that, as with selection of problems, there may be a number of different points in the assessment/intervention process at which you would logically establish goals. Some practitioners do this early in their contacts with the client, especially when the goals are reasonably clear, and then keep their assessment focused on the specific area of the goal statement. Other practitioners prefer to wait until after the assessment and baselining periods are completed in order to have more precise information about the factors affecting the problem (and, hence, the goal).

By placing "goals" in the same chapter as "problems," we do not mean that selecting goals is necessarily the next step in the process. What we are suggesting, though, is that goals are directly related to the problem and should reflect that relationship.

We also recognize that setting goals can be a more complicated process than what we describe here. There can be numerous pressures and points of view intruding on the goal-setting process, such as the client's, the practitioner's, the agency's, and, in some cases, such as mandated service, the community's. We will discuss this later in this chapter in the section on "Problems and Issues in Setting Goals." For now, we would mainly like to emphasize the idea that it is part of the role of the practitioner to balance these different pressures in a way that makes the most sense in any given situation and in a way that will enhance services and outcomes for the client.

Components of Specific Goal Statements

With many clients you probably will be able to arrive at some general or global goal statement relatively easily. For example, the program administrator may want to make his agency more effective, the woman may want her husband to be more sexually responsive, and the father may want his son to be less obnoxious. The first step with general statements such as these is to specify just what the problem is. Once that is accomplished, the practitioner's task is to develop some clear and specific outcome objectives and goals that can serve to guide the rest of the intervention process.

Such goals and objectives should have at least four components (Gottman & Leiblum, 1974; Brown & Brown, 1977). They should specify *who, will do what, to what extent*, and *under what conditions*. Try to develop specific outcome goals for each problem encountered. Thus, you may need multiple goals for one general problem area. For example, school problems could lead to specific goals in relation to studying, attendance, peers, or relationships with teachers. Each would contain all four of the following components.

Who? Objectives and goals should be stated in terms of intermediate and ultimate outcomes for the *client*. One problem we sometimes run into is goals stated in terms of what the *practitioner* will do. These are not appropriate as outcome goals. However, the practitioner's procedural steps may be appropriate intervention methods, that is, what the practitioner hopes to do or establish in order to facilitate achieving objectives. At the least, the practitioner should be able to distinguish between procedural interventive steps and outcome goals and be aware that outcome goals should be stated in terms of what the client will do or be like when intervention is completed. That is, it would not be an appropriate goal statement to say, "I will provide supportive therapy to decrease the client's depression." Decreasing the depression might be an excellent goal, but providing therapy designed to decrease a component of the depression is part of the intervention plan, not the goal for the client.

Will Do What? A most important part of establishing goals is to attempt to state them in performance terms. In other words, attempt to state what clients actually will be *doing* to show that they have achieved the goal.

The key point here is that this performance should be stated in measurable terms. If the goal cannot be observed in some way—whether by counting the actual behaviors involved or by use of a scale or other instrument—then it will be impossible to evaluate the success of the intervention, that is, whether the goal was achieved.

Again, when we talk about "measurable performance," we are not saying all performances must be overt behaviors. Some "performances" are overt and some are covert (e.g., cognitive activities, such as remembering the names of acquaintances at the senior citizen center).

It may be best to think in terms of *indicators* when trying to decide whether a goal involves a performance or an abstraction. An indicator refers to the idea that you have some *direct way* that will indicate the presence of the alleged performance. This direct way then becomes the key measurement indicator and could involve actual observation of an overt behavior, a score on a standardized test, or a self-report on an individualized rating scale.

It might be helpful once again to think in terms of increasing or decreasing the targeted problem. This might give you a handle on stating the goal in terms of what the client will be doing (or thinking or feeling), linking interventions with this goal, and suggesting ways of measuring outcome. For example, a client believes that she is a poor socializer and has not been able to meet eligible men. Her goal is to become a reasonable socializer to increase the possibility of finding an appropriate mate. The phrase *reasonable socializer* is her own term, so the practitioner requested that she provide some indicators of when she would feel she is a reasonable socializer. She worked out with the practitioner several indicators: when she would be able to initiate a conversation with a stranger, sustain it for at least 10 minutes, and then terminate it with the possibility of continuing at some later time. These specifications of the phrase *reasonable socializer* helped the practitioner formulate some interventions directed at initiating, sustaining, and terminating conversations. The measurement of these indicators included the client's self-report of social activities at parties, whether she initiated conversations with strangers, how long they lasted, and whether she defined these relationships as ones in which she could reinitiate conversations later. The set of these three actions formed an operational definition of "reasonable socializer." Even though these indicators are very subjective, they are clearly reportable, if the client is willing and able to provide the information.

Try to state your goals in positive rather than negative terms. This gives the client a positive mind-set, identifying a goal in terms of something attainable so that each step forward is itself reinforcing the client's constructive efforts. This point is especially important for clients with problems that are socially disapproved, such as child abuse, alcohol abuse, drug abuse, and so on. Instead of asking how many times the parent hit the child, or how many drinks a person had that day, you might ask, "How many minutes did you and your child spend together having fun today?" or, "How many times did you call an AA buddy when you felt the urge to take a drink?" Measured objectives such as these clearly reinforce some possible interventive plans, while at the same time obtain useful information measuring process and outcome.

To What Extent? The purpose here is to attempt to establish how well and how often the target event occurs. In other words, you will want to establish a level of performance that will be acceptable. Without this you may never know whether the goal was achieved to anyone's satisfaction. For example, the goal might be to lose 30 pounds, to answer 80% of the questions successfully, or to maintain a conversation with your spouse for 15 minutes.

This is one place where taking a baseline is particularly important. The baseline establishes the level of occurrence of the target event prior to intervention and is used for comparison with changes in the target during the intervention program. The goal or desired level of performance can be set in comparison with the baseline level. Or, it can be set in terms of some other standard, for example, weight within a "normal" range, a passing test score, and so on.

It is here, too, that the notion of outcome objectives (subgoals or intermediate outcomes) is probably most important. The key question regarding criterion level is: Can the client achieve the goal (do the activity, perform the behavior, and so forth)? In evaluating this it is important to set interim objectives that the client will be able to achieve. Make sure the first objective is realistically achievable. If you err, err on the side of setting the first objectives too low rather than too high. Achievement of these objectives will then serve as additional reinforcement or motivation for continuing on to the next step. Indeed, under most circumstances, the objective will be defined as exactly the same as the goal, but in smaller quantities.

For example, if the ultimate goal is the one in the prior example involving a young woman's social skills and her engaging in conversation with a man, the first objective might be to say hello to a man in passing, the next to ask a man for directions, and so on for progressively increasing periods of time. Or, if the ultimate goal is to score 30 on a depression scale, where higher scores mean more depression, the objective for the second week might be to score 75 (reduced from 90 at baseline), and the objective for the fourth week might be to score 50.

These objectives or intermediate outcomes should be set in ways that are as close to achieving the goal as possible, but that are comfortable and realistic for the client. Furthermore, all of the objectives do not have to be set in advance at the same time, since success or failure in achieving one objective can provide information on what the next objective should be.

Under What Conditions? The fourth component of goal setting is to specify the conditions and situations under which the desired behavior or activities will occur. You may find that the desired behavior will occur (or should occur) only in specific situations (e.g., at school, but not at home). You should try to set up as clearly as possible under what occasions it *should* occur. If it does not occur in all the desired situations, then you can make its occurrence in other situations intermediate objectives to the final goal of occurrence in all relevant situations. Thus, an ultimate goal (outcome) might be for arguing to be eliminated under all circumstances, and the intermediate objectives might be for arguing to be decreased or eliminated in a sequential way in each setting in which it occurred.

When you are thinking about conditions for the behavior to occur, consider at least the following three: where would it occur, when should it occur, and with whom? This specificity will greatly aid in developing clear and achievable goals.

Using Statistics to Set Goals

One of the frustrating choices for a practitioner intent on being specific in setting goals is deciding where to set the criterion for success. It's generally a good idea, when possible, to be precise in identifying what you are shooting for in terms of an actual target. Sometimes this is easy. For example, in a weight-loss program, you can pretty much aim at losing a specific number of pounds. In other situations, you might know exactly what you're after (having 20% of the community attend each meeting, no wetting of the bed at night, ability to maintain an erection for at least 5 minutes during intercourse, etc.). If you are using standardized measures, some actually have a cutoff or "cutting point," so that when the score gets to that point, in comparison with other people who have taken the test (norms), you have some degree of assurance that the problem has diminished. In all of the previous situations it would be possible to select a specific goal with a specific criterion level (lose 15 pounds, 0 wet nights, score of 30 or less on a questionnaire).

But sometimes this isn't so easy. In many situations it's very difficult to go beyond saying, "I want to increase participation" or "I want to decrease her depression" or "I want to see that they 'communicate more.'" What recourse do you have for being more specific under these circumstances?

In these situations we recommend the use of statistics. Now, don't panic. We don't mean anything horrendous or complicated. Our point in this chapter is simply to inform you about this possibility, and to explain what it means with regard to goals.

When we say that these statistical procedures can help you set goals, we mean something quite specific. Goal setting is usually done in the context of client and societal values or physical realities. For example, you may not be allowed to keep your child if you exceed some social standards for permissible disciplinary actions, and you won't be allowed to become a pilot if your vision isn't good enough.

However, sometimes there are no natural markers, and social values are not clear; for example, how many arguments between spouses are "too many?" What intensity of feeling between two intimates constitutes "love?" What level of morale must exist for the agency to have a "good working environment?" The practitioner has to make decisions based on the events in the situation even when social values are not clear.

Statistics provide one way of making decisions. In effect, we connect a statistical difference (such as change in the intervention period of some amount from that in the baseline period) with a practical or social difference, that the (desired) change could not have happened by chance alone and therefore we should pay attention to changes of this magnitude.

We are not saying that the amount of difference between baseline and intervention that is in the desired direction is the value we wish to achieve per se, only that this clearly definable change is in the right direction and, let us assume, could not have happened by chance alone. Whether it is a meaningful change in the everyday world when no other norms or rules are available is another question, calling for feedback from participants. For example, if the spouses mentioned previously argue only half as much as they used to before intervention, is this meaningful? So, statistics provide only a partial handle to hold when other methods come up short.

With some statistics you can compute just from the baseline data how much change would have to take place in order for the change to be statistically significant. With these procedures, you use the baseline information to set a level for the intervention phase at which the change will be statistically significant. Then, when you get data from the intervention phase of your program, you just plot it on your chart and see whether it is significant. (There are simple procedures for doing this, some not much more complicated than drawing a line.) If the data do reach significance, you can conclude that your goal has been met. Thus, you would set a goal at the baseline of achieving a statistically significant change in the target, from the baseline to the end of the intervention phase.

We realize that there is more to life than statistical significance, and that the practical significance of the change can be much more important. But, as a shorthand guide, you might want to use statistics to establish goals. Examples of such goals might be a statistically significant increase in participation or a statistically significant decrease in depression score. This would minimize the problem of having to use some arbitrary goal-setting procedure.

USING GOAL ATTAINMENT SCALING (GAS) TO ESTABLISH GOALS

One widely used method for establishing and tracking goals is called Goal Attainment Scaling. Goal Attainment Scaling (GAS) is a system devised by Kiresuk and Sherman (1968) to assist in goal definition and goal measurement. GAS was originally developed as an assessment approach for individual clients. Since its inception, however, it has been applied to goal-setting activities not only for individuals, but for organizations as well, in a broad range of human service agencies (Beidel, 1988; Kagle & Kopels, 2008; Kiresuk & Garwick, 1979; Kiresuk, Smith, & Cardillo, 1993; Neuman, 2002; Wade & Neuman, 2007). The approach has been used by members of many of the helping professions, including psychologists, social workers, counselors, veterinarians, psychiatrists, and nurses, and across virtually all fields of interpersonal helping (Fisher & Hardie, 2002; Malec, 1999; McLaren & Rodger, 2003; Mitchell & Cusick, 1998; Newton, 2002; Persons & Fresco, 2008; Shefler, Canetti, & Wiseman, 2001; Snyder, Heyman, & Haynes, 2008; Sladeczek et al., 2001).

The basic GAS procedures involve identifying client problems, assigning individualized weights to those problems, estimating the client's expected outcome (the "goals") for each problem area, obtaining follow-up scores on actual outcomes for each problem area, and averaging outcomes across all problems for each client or all clients within a given program.

The following sections attempt only to highlight the basic procedural guides for using GAS to supplement the previous material and as a way of helping you specify goals. More detailed information addressing issues and problems for each of the steps is available in the references, and Hurn, Kneebone, and Cropley (2006) provide a recent review of GAS.

Basic Guidelines for Using GAS

Four basic steps for GAS have been described by Kiresuk and Garwick (1979): (a) collection of information about the person or organization for which goals will be scaled, (b) designation of the major areas where changes would be feasible and helpful, (c) development of specific predictions for a series of outcome levels for each major area, and (d) scoring of outcomes at follow-up.

Collecting Information. This step of the process varies by practitioner, setting, and type of problem with which you may be working. Standard sources of assessment information are used (GAS does not prescribe any specific methodologies), including interviews, direct observation, questionnaires, reports from those in the environment, and/or any methods of data collection prescribed by a particular agency.

Designation of Problem Areas. Once assessment data are collected, the GAS format suggests you break these down into a series of "problem areas." Using the methods for specifying problems described in this chapter, you would identify those positive areas or strengths that should be increased and those undesired areas that should be decreased. All of the problems are listed and priorities set along the lines described earlier.

Your agency may wish to specify in advance a list of problem areas. For example, Benedict (1978) lists some 21 problem areas appropriate for a family service agency. Some of these are interpersonal conflicts, reactive emotional distress, problem solving, problems of role transition, human sexuality, child rearing/child care, and so on. Each of these is described and then examples are provided of possible specific program goals. For example, for reactive emotional distress, a specific measure might be number of days per week client reports having no thoughts fearing end of marriage; for problem solving, percentage of mutually agreed-upon decisions that client takes some actions on; for problems in role transition, number of times that mother does not "hassle" daughter for spending time with friends on weekend.

For each problem area, a continuum or scale of behaviors is developed. This scale is placed on a form called the Goal Attainment Follow-Up Guide in which each vertical scale represents a scale of outcomes related to a problem area for a client (Kiresuk & Garwick, 1979). Figure 6 presents a blank Goal Attainment Follow-Up Guide. Room also could be left at the bottom of the page for comments on verifying sources (who would verify reports of success), time limits, presenting problems, and intervention plans.

Any number of scales or problems can be used. Each problem area is given a title, which may be relatively general (e.g., "employment"). The problem can then be described in more specific but brief terms under the title at the top of each scale. However, the remainder of the information on each scale should be as specific and objective as possible.

Because the client's problems have been prioritized, it is possible also to weight each one in the

Specifying Problems and Goals: Targets of Intervention

Goal Attainment Follow-Up Guide

Levels of Predicted Attainments	Scale Headings and Scale Weights				
	Scale 1: _____ (weight$_1$ = ____)	Scale 2: _____ (weight$_2$ = ____)	Scale 3: _____ (weight$_3$ = ____)	Scale 4: _____ (weight$_4$ = ____)	Scale 5: _____ (weight$_5$ = ____)
Most unfavorable outcome thought likely					
Less than expected success					
Expected level of success					
More than expected success					
Most favorable outcome thought likely					

FIGURE 6 Basic Goal Attainment Follow-Up Guide.

space next to the title (weight$_1$ = ___). Any one- or two-digit number can be used here, with a higher number indicating a more significant problem. It is sometimes helpful to imagine a scale of 1 to 20, with 20 being the most significant. Without the weights, each scale or problem is seen as equally relevant.

Predictions for Each Problem Area. The GAS framework is intended to operate within a time limit. Thus, a specific follow-up point (which can be determined for each case and in accord with agency standards) should be set for each scale or problem area. Then, a series of predictions is made for each scale. These predictions actually are the goals for the client. For each scale, it is likely that a number of variables are applicable as indicators of change. The purpose here is to select the one that is most desirable to be used as a measure—it is most directly representative of the problem, easy to measure, and its measurements can be reliable. Any of the measures described in this book can be selected for this variable, for example, a specific behavior or scores on a scale.

As should be clear, for each one of these variables, a range of outcomes is possible—from very negative to very positive. The goal here is to try to make predictions about this variable in line with the statements along the left edge of the Follow-Up Guide. Thus, each variable, or goal, is described according to "the most favorable outcome likely," "more than expected level of outcome," "expected level of outcome," "less than expected level of outcome," to "the most unfavorable outcome thought likely." Figure 7 presents a completely filled-in Goal Attainment Follow-Up Guide with weights on a scale from 1 to 20.

The most important point on the scale is the midpoint or "expected level." This is intended to be the most realistic prediction of outcome based on the expected date at which that goal can be reached. This is the part of the scale that is developed first, since it is the "most likely" outcome. The other outcome levels are developed after the expected level.

This part of the process—ranging from operationalizing the problem to making predictions—is really the trickiest part of using GAS, although with experience at doing this for each case or situation, most practitioners can become rather adept. Kiresuk and Garwick (1979) suggest that with practice, the guide can be constructed in 15 to 30 minutes.

The operationalized variables that make up each of the scales have potential for use in single-system evaluation (Yarbrough & Thompson, 2002). That is, because each of the problem areas is supposed to be operationalized according to specific, observable measures, one or more of these can be used to collect

Goal Attainment Follow-Up Guide

Levels of Predicted Attainments	Scale 1: School Attendance (weight$_1$ = 20)	Scale 2: Anxiety; Scores on S-A Scale (weight$_2$ = 12)	Scale 3: Self-Esteem Scores on Scale (weight$_3$ = 10)	Scale 4: Family Agreements (weight$_4$ = 15)	Scale 5: Suicide (weight$_5$ = 20)
Most unfavorable outcome thought likely	0%	Daily average rating of 9 on 9-point scale	Weekly score of 80–100 on 100-point scale	0 agreements	Client commits suicide
Less than expected success	25%	Average rating of 7 or 8	Score of 70–79	1 agreement	Client acts on at least 1 suicidal impulse
Expected level of success	50%	Average rating of 5 or 6	Score of 51–69	2–3 agreements	Client has suicidal ideas 3 or more times per day
More than expected success	75%	Average rating of 3 or 4	Score of 31–50	4 agreements	Client has suicidal ideas 1 or 2 times per day
Most favorable outcome thought likely	100%	Average rating of 1 or 2	Weekly score of 30 or below (clinical cutting point)	5 or more family agreements	Client has no suicidal ideation

FIGURE 7 Basic Goal Attainment Follow-Up Guide as illustrated by an adolescent client at a family service agency.

data for a baseline, placed on a chart, and used for regular feedback to help guide your intervention. Thus, GAS can be used as a context to help establish goal statements, and the results of the repeated collections of data on the target problem can be used for regular monitoring, between the point when the guide is constructed and the follow-up actually conducted.

Follow-Up "Interview." The last part of the process is the evaluation of outcome. This can be done by the practitioner with the client, by other agency staff members, or by others in the environment. Because the expected length of intervention is preset, this part of the process should come as no surprise to anyone involved. However, since this evaluation may involve an interview by someone unfamiliar with the case or by someone very involved with the case, care should be taken to train the interviewer to do whatever is possible to avoid overly subjective or biased evaluations.

To record the level of success achieved, a check or an asterisk can be inserted in the appropriate box of the Follow-Up Guide. For example, if the "expected level of success" is achieved on a self-esteem scale, a check mark can be placed in that square on the scale.

It is here that the use of single-system designs and other procedures can have important cross-validating purposes. That is, you will have a built-in check on the results obtained on your Goal Attainment Follow-Up Guide. In fact, if the problem areas are broken down into more or less objective, or highly specific, variables, outcome will be relatively easy to determine and distortion kept to a minimum.

One of the problems with GAS is it contains no built-in systems for organizing or standardizing regular feedback, a serious potential problem if GAS is to be used with single-system designs (see Mackay & Sommerville, 1996, for critique). Thus, although few practitioners would wait until the "follow-up interview" to secure feedback, GAS does not present an organized framework for collecting such data. Thus, the use of repeated measures on at least one of the target problems, in a single-system design fashion, will provide ongoing feedback as to whether the problem is indeed changing. On the other hand, a recent review of the research on GAS found strong evidence for its reliability, validity, and sensitivity (Hurn, Kneebone, & Cropley, 2006). Therefore, it is clear that there is firm evidence for recommending the use of GAS as an adjunct to the use of single-system designs.

SETTING GOALS IN GROUPS

Throughout, we allude to the fact that many practitioners use single-system designs with groups; indeed, we try to illustrate these designs with individuals, groups, families, neighborhoods, work organizations, and even larger communities. The underlying principles are the same for any client system, but experience has taught us that we must provide some additional observations on using these evaluation designs with groups for both conceptual and procedural reasons.

It is difficult to identify and operationalize goals for any client, but when group goals are at stake, it seems to be even more difficult (see Paritzky & Magoon, 1982, for a review of the use of GAS with groups). This may be because fewer practitioners have been trained to think about groups as groups, or about the problems or objectives of groups, whether formally or informally organized. Even when some group-level objective can be conceived of, there may be additional problems in operationalizing it because the actions of several people are involved all at once.

These are real difficulties, but they are manageable to some degree. The following discussion pulls together some of the thinking and research from the literature on establishing goals and objectives with groups.

First, we should distinguish true group problems and objectives from the individual problems and objectives of people who may be seen in groups. A true group problem might include a divorcing family when the legal action of divorce will affect each member of the group as roles are changed within that family. It would also affect each person's feelings, thoughts, and actions. But as a family group, there would be targets reflecting the set of interrelationships of "the family," in addition to targets reflecting the feelings of the husband and the wife, as well as of any children. "Staying married" would be one such collective target; "number of arguments between spouses," "amount of free time spent in satisfying family activities," "proportion of assigned chores completed by each member of the household" could be others. There is nothing mysterious about these group (or family) factors; they are natural to the family in the sense that they are part of ordinary family life and functioning. Some set of such factors would constitute "family life," and their breakdown might indicate the nature and extent of problems that had to be dealt with in considering divorce counseling.

Other types of groups, such as family life education groups, disseminate information and render skills training. Each participant in a family life education meeting might have his or her own objectives, and the distance they progress might also be measured. As a group, it would be possible to take the average score from some standardized scale administered to all the participants. These are somewhat arbitrary choices the practitioner makes, seeking always to reflect as fully and faithfully as possible the nature of the group being evaluated.

Multiple indicators of success in residential youth care and treatment have been described by Whittaker, Overstreet, Grasso, Tripodi, and Boylan (1988). Their proposals are interesting for several reasons: (a) They view success as occurring at different stages of the service cycle, from intake to post-discharge placement, and (b) they propose a variety of perspectives on residential services. Table 1 is adapted from their paper. While individuals are necessarily involved, the use of rates or percentages indicates a collective phenomenon to which individual behaviors contribute, but which reflect how the entire group is reacting to the entire service experience. These indicators are simply the sum of individual scores.

Other indicators can be truly reflective of the group and are probably greater than the sum of individual scores. For example, group morale can be viewed as some multiple score based on the interactions of members with one another, not just the sum of each member's liking to be in the group. It might also be useful to keep track of communication patterns, who talks to whom and how much, as these patterns may also shift as the group begins to form its own structure.

Still another example of a group goal would be when a recreational group is formed to include one or two predelinquent youths who will be exposed to positive peer norms. The general behavior patterns in the group reflect the dominant norms, and comparisons might be made as to how closely individuals identify with those norms over time, with the goal being higher group scores (closer identification) on the measure of those norms.

In general, we are proposing that, where possible, the group objectives and goals be identified and operationalized. In addition, it may be very useful to collect individual scores on related topics so that the relative status of each individual may be compared with the group as a whole (cf. Benbenishty, 1989). If group norms are related to individual behavior in enjoyable ways, but without putting an individual in se-

Table 1 Indicators of success in residential services

Stage	Criterion of Success	Operational Indicators
Intake	Placement in a less restricted environment	Percent of clients diverted from more restricted settings (e.g., jail)
Treatment	Decrease in violent acting out Acquisition of prosocial skills	Rate of assaults in the facility (Average) life skills progress from baseline to highest level attained by each individual
Discharge	Planned discharge occurred	Percent of clients who have completed the program without premature termination
Postplacement	No recidivism	Percent of clients who remain in less restrictive environment in community Percent of clients adjudicated

rious conflict with the group, then an individual's score that shows a discrepancy with the norm may suggest the need for extra counseling or enhanced group efforts to help this particular individual.

An interesting example from a student case involved the establishment of a senior citizen support group at a new high-rise building where no one felt "at home." A measure of the cohesion of the group was the number in attendance at any given weekly meeting. Individual measures of discontent with the housing situation were obtained from standardized questions asked of the residents in weekly interviews with the student. Thus, two different phenomena were observed—cohesion and discontent—but positive changes in the former were observed to precede positive changes in the latter, as the student hypothesized.

PROBLEMS AND ISSUES IN SETTING GOALS

There are several problems and issues in establishing objectives and goals that could impede progress. You should be prepared to deal with these in negotiating goals with your client.

Anticipate Negative Outcomes

You will want to help the client anticipate the impact of achieving his or her goals. You and the client will have to evaluate the effects that changes in the client are likely to have on others in his or her environment. Have others actually received some form of reinforcement or gratification from the client's undesired behavior? Is it possible that the changes in the client will lead to some negative occurrence for the client (e.g., will being more assertive lead to being fired)? Say an agency director wants to increase the number of minority clients in his or her agency's caseload. Is the staff trained and prepared to deal with a changing caseload? The point of all this is to attempt to anticipate results and to examine them with clients or others in their environment. In this way, either negative impacts may be minimized, or at least clients will be prepared to deal with them.

Who Sets the Goals?

Because goal setting is largely a value judgment—a statement of what is desired—whenever possible the client should have the major, if not the sole, say in setting goals. This is not to say the practitioner does not have an important role in setting the goals, for example, in helping the client be more specific about just what he or she wants. Furthermore, this influence is likely to be greatly increased when the client is confused, unsure, incapable of speaking for himself or herself (e.g., an infant), or simply unable to decide. Indeed, the client may even have a specific goal in mind at initial contact, but the practitioner's expertise in collecting assessment information may broaden the client's perspective and even lead to a negotiated revision in goals. In addition, agencies or even communities may have their priorities, and these priorities may be evident in the goal-setting process.

Perhaps the key principle here is that *whenever possible* the client should have the predominant say in establishing goals. When this is not completely possible, it is the practitioner's responsibility to be sensitive to the client's interests and desires and to balance them against other pressures. At the least the practitioner can try to see that those interests are kept uppermost in any decision about goals. This is particularly true when there is pressure being put on the client or practitioner by outside sources (e.g., from relevant others or referring sources) to develop goals that conform to their needs or wishes.

A related issue has to do with being sure the goals are acceptable to both client and practitioner and perhaps the agency (Brown & Brown, 1977). Self-defeating, destructive, or illegal behaviors may all be put on the table for discussion and negotiation. This can occur not only when the practitioner is dealing with a client who may have been referred from another source or who is a mandated client (e.g., in a prison, school, or hospital), but also in a situation in which the client simply appears to be making poor choices. At the least it is the practitioner's responsibility to provide as accurate and as honest information as possible in evaluating how workable the goal is.

Anticipate Impediments

Because a number of issues can arise during the goal-setting process, it's always a good idea to try to anticipate problems. In reviewing this section, a number of questions, in part modified from Gambrill (1977, p. 175), could be useful as a checklist to see whether the major conditions of establishing specific goals have been set:

1. Have specific behaviors, thoughts, feelings, or activities been identified?
2. Have initial intermediate objectives been set?
3. Are objectives and goals attainable?
4. Is it clear who will be changing?
5. Could two or more people agree on whether a task has been accomplished?
6. Is it clear under what conditions the desired activities will be performed?
7. Are the goals stated in positive terms and not in terms of what the client won't be doing?
8. Are performance criteria identified? (Will it be clear when a goal or objective has been accomplished?)
9. Is there any way the goal or objective could be satisfied in an unsatisfactory way (e.g., completing homework by copying someone else's)?
10. Are there any possible negative consequences to achieving the goal?
11. Are the goals and objectives stated as client outcomes rather than in terms of what you (the practitioner) will do?
12. Is the goal acceptable to you, the client, relevant others?

Case Illustrations of Goals in the Context of Problems and Interventions

It would be impossible to list all of the possible problems and goals clients present. Instead, we have presented a framework for specifying problems and goals as a means of understanding where the client is and of seeking to help the client resolve problems and thereby attain the desired goals.

In addition, it may be instructive to consider the following sketches of cases, summarized in Table 2. We have combined many of the elements of scientific practice, a translation of the client's concerns into a more or less objectively definable problem (target) with its verifying source, and the goals or objectives we seek to attain in the resolution of that problem. Interventions are suggested that are clearly connected with the targeted problem. (These examples are taken from student cases and simplified for exposition.)

Note that in some of these examples there is a one-to-one listing of concern/problem/goal. In others, there may be several goals or objectives for one problem, or there may be several problems for one general concern. The point is to capture the meaning of the situation so that the set of problems represents a fair and full sense of the client. We can never measure everything about the client's problems or goals, but we can hope to *sample* these so that our intervention deals with *representative* indicators of the client's problems and hopes. If desired outcomes occur under

Table 2 Case illustrations of client concerns, operationalized problems, goals, and interventions

Client Concerns	The Problem/Goals Operationally Defined	Verifying Source	The Goal of the Intervention	Intervention Methods as Linked to Problem
1a. Joe's parents are concerned that he is skipping school. The truancy officer has issued a formal warning to Joe and his family.	1a. The number of days per week that Joe does not attend school when he should be present.	1a. School records.	1a. Joe to attend school 5 full days a week as appropriate.	1a. Arrange that Joe walk to school with three friends, eat lunch with them, and walk home together (peer support).
1b. Joe has been getting failing grades in his major subjects.	1b. The number of F-grades Joe gets in English, math, history, and science.	1b. Teacher's grade book.	1b. Joe to get passing grades in every major subject (D or better).	1b. Arrange for Joe to study with his friends. Parents permit Joe extra late hours on weekend for each passing grade.
1c. Joe is unhappy because he can't get any girls from school to go out with him.	1c. The number of dates Joe has with girls in his class per month.	1c. Client's report.	1c. Joe would like to have at least two dates a month.	1c. Joe enters interpersonal skills training group related to social skills.
2a. A family agency has gradually had a reduction in number of clients, which threatens the continuation of the agency.	2a. The number of active cases per month, as compared with the previous 5 years' client census.	2a. Agency statistics.	2a(1). Increase the number of referrals from other agencies by 50% per month.	2a(1). Send brochures of agency programs to practitioners in likely referring agencies.
			2a(2). Increase agency visibility through a community health fair.	2a(2). Publicize and run a health fair at local high schools.
			2a(3). Initiate new program where there is an identified need for which staff has qualifications.	2a(3). Do needs survey in the community and design a helping project according to results.
2b. Agency staff morale has been poor.	2b(1). The number of practitioners leaving the agency per month.	2b(1). Agency records.	2b. Reduce practitioner turnover by 50%.	2b. Involve practitioners in agency policy and program making.
	2b(2). The practitioners completed a self-report (anonymous) measure of morale once a month.	2b(2). Agency records.		

3a. Mary feels depressed.	3a. Mary's score on a standardized depression test.	3a. The practitioner scores the test.	3a. Mary's scores should decrease to below the clinical cutoff.	3a. and 3b. Family therapy session dealing with mother–daughter relationship and how to problem solve so as to keep disagreements under control. (Mother also takes course on Parent Effectiveness Training.)
3b. Mary and her mother get into a lot of arguments about her rights and responsibilities.	3b. The number of times Mary and her mother argue each week.	3b. They bring in a score sheet to the weekly appointment.	3b. Mary and her mother will try to reduce the number of arguments per week by half, to the point of no arguments.	
4a. Drugs are becoming a major problem in the neighborhood, as connected with several break-ins (to steal money for drugs).	4a. Number of drug-related thefts in the neighborhood.	4a. Police records.	4a. Reduce theft to zero.	4a. Neighborhood patrols (groups of citizens walking the neighborhood by shifts day and night, reporting suspicious events to police).
4b. The elderly residents express fears of leaving their homes at night.	4b. Attendance at regular neighborhood (evening) functions.	4b. Minutes of the neighborhood council.	4b. Increase involvement of neighbors in weekly activities.	4b. Each resident to bring one plan to encourage neighbors to attend social functions. Others to patrol the streets protecting homes.
5a. Miss E (age 90) has stopped coming down for (obligatory) meals at Senior House. She appears to be incoherent at times. Staff and friends are concerned.	5a. Number of meals taken at dining hall per week indicating measure of nutritional health.	5a. Census taken by director of Senior House each night, at dinner.	5a. Miss E to eat a balanced diet.	5a(1). Appear at Miss E's door with small gifts and short conversations in order to build rapport and gain her trust.
5b. Number of times she is overheard by staff to be speaking incoherently.	5b. Report by director while chatting with residents at dinnertime.	5b. Miss E to be as coherent as she is capable of being.	5a(2). Then invite her to tea and have conversations about diet, etc. Try to reinterest Miss E in eating with a new set of friends.
			5b(1). Try to make sure Miss E has balanced diet. If incoherence continues, arrange for medical contact.

(continued)

74

Table 2 (continued)

Client Concerns	The Problem/Goals Operationally Defined	Verifying Source	The Goal of the Intervention	Intervention Methods as Linked to Problem
				5b(2). Physician to examine Miss E to ascertain extent of physiological/medical problems and to provide treatment.
6a. Bill and Elaine are going to a family life education program to learn effective parenting skills for when their baby gets older.	6a. Number of times they use rational explanations as appropriate responses to family stimulus situations, rather than ordering responses.	6a. Each spouse keeps score on self and other spouse, and records results.	6a. Bill and Elaine want to make rational responding a natural part of their child-rearing patterns—at least 80% of the time.	6a. Each spouse will positively reinforce the other for correct response, and merely indicate (without censure) incorrect responses.
6b. Elaine also wants to learn some stress management skills, as her law position demands long hours and heavy duties.	6b. Number of times Elaine completes the appropriate number of muscle-relaxing and deep breathing exercises at her office per day.	6b. Self-report.	6b. Elaine wants to be able to relieve work-related stress any time it occurs at the office or home, even though the work-load itself probably won't be lightened for some time.	6b. Every time Elaine feels strain in her neck or back she will do relaxation exercises.
7a. P.S. 99 wants to create a drug-free school environment for the junior and senior high students.	7a. Number of students observed smoking cigarettes on campus.	7a. Faculty or maintenance personnel observation.	7a. Increase the number of students who selected allowable alternative highs to feel great in socially acceptable ways.	7a. Sponsor group activities in which allowable alternative highs are encouraged, which are antagonistic to and inhibitory of the antisocial highs.
	7b. Number of students observed to be high on drugs (dazed look, slurred speech, etc.).	7b. Faculty or nursing staff observation.	7b. Increase knowledge of problems associated with substance abuse.	7b. Conduct small group seminars and activities related to substance abuse education.
	7c. Number of students observed to be drunk while at school.	7c. Faculty or nursing staff observation.		
	7d. Number of students affirming that they have not used drugs in the past week.	7d. Self-report.		
	7e. Number of students affirming that they have had an allowable alternative high—from sports, art, religion, etc.—in the past week.	7e. Self-report.		

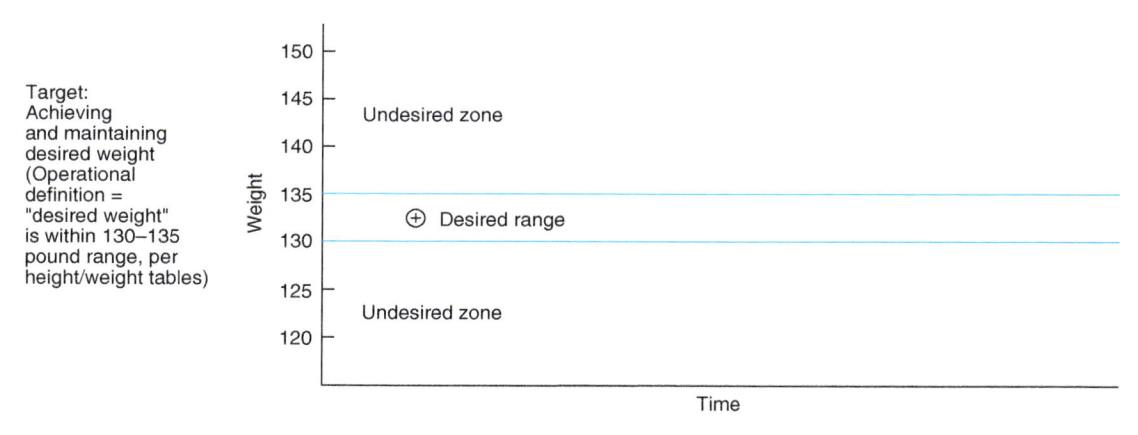

FIGURE 8 Goals of service indicated by reference to preestablished norms. Weights above or below the desired range are considered undesirable.

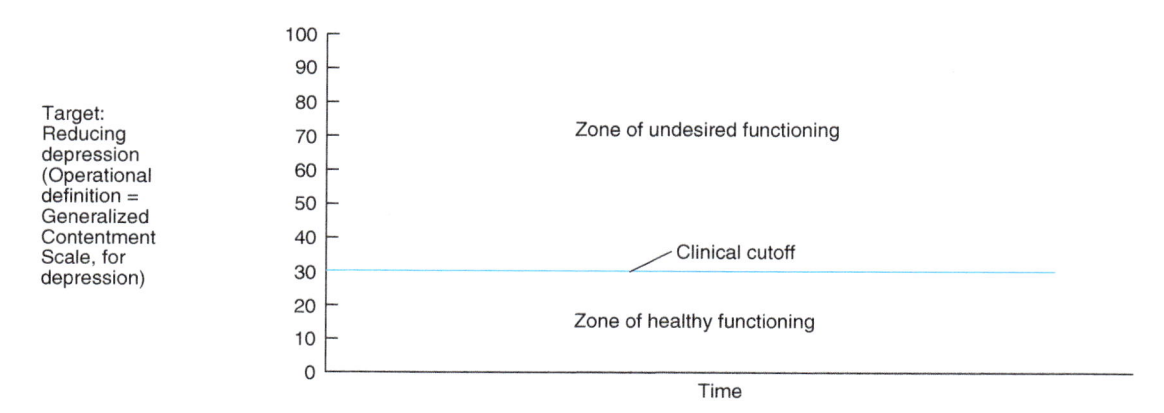

Target: Achieving and maintaining desired weight (Operational definition = "desired weight" is within 130–135 pound range, per height/weight tables)

FIGURE 9 Goals of service indicated by reference to measures on standardized test or scale. In this case, the clinical cutoff is an empirically derived line indicating the separation of problematic and nonproblematic functioning.

Target: Reducing depression (Operational definition = Generalized Contentment Scale, for depression)

these conditions, then there should be some socially significant changes occurring to the client and/or the situation—even though not everything may be resolved.

Another way to represent goals and objectives specifically is illustrated in Figures 8 through 11. Four targeted problems are represented on these charts. The valued objectives or client preferences are reflected in the way the chart is constructed. Figure 8 presents the objective of maintaining a certain range of weight; the lines indicating the upper and lower limits of this range represent the values of the client. Figure 9 uses a clinical cutoff, a line separating persons whose scores are like those with known problematic conditions from persons who do not show these problems. This approach applies norms developed on large numbers of persons to setting goals in the given case.

Figure 10 indicates one of many statistical approaches to establishing preferred behaviors with the goal of getting as many observations below the dotted line as possible. The point is that we make a rough estimate from what we know about the client's current behavior to what patterns of change must occur to exhibit improvements over the problematic behavior. This is a statistical way

Specifying Problems and Goals: Targets of Intervention

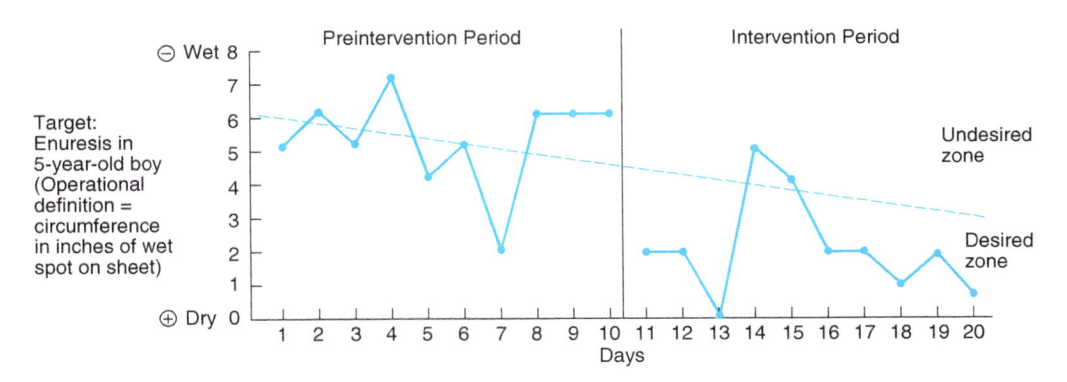

FIGURE 10 Goals of service established by a statistical procedure (described in Chapter 21) by which the preintervention data are compared with the intervention data.

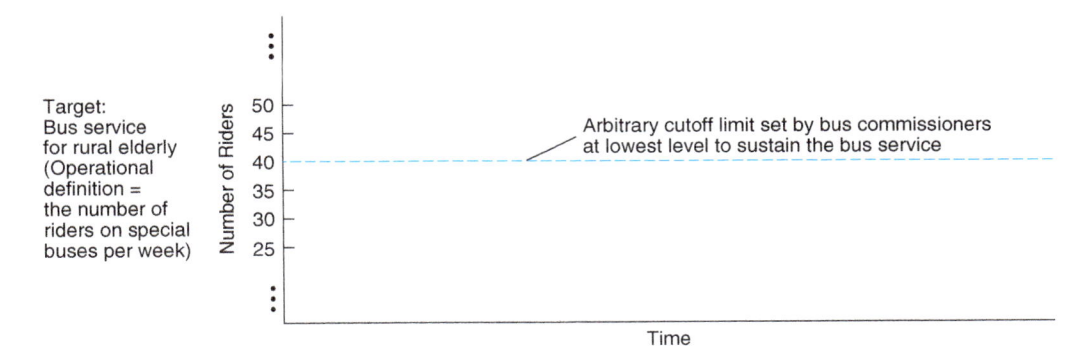

FIGURE 11 Goals of service established by arbitrary rules. The number of riders set as a cutoff has nothing to do with cost recovery: The bus operation is heavily subsidized. Rather, this decision seems to have been political. Nonetheless, it is a real limit in terms of practical decisions.

to construct preferences, that is, improvements over the current problematic situation.

Figure 11 represents the weakest approach to indicating preferences, objectives we aim for in order to claim some improvement over the preintervention situation. In effect, we make a good guess of what we should aim to achieve as a goal in a given situation. We might rationalize this choice in various ways, but because we don't have any objective basis for the choice, it is simply a plausible but arbitrary objective. This is better than nothing because it gives us something to aim at, but it would be preferable to have a sounder basis for selecting our objectives and goals.

The final illustrations of cases combine client concerns, operationally defined problems as targets of intervention, the verifying sources of these targets, goals and objectives, and the interventions used. It is important to note that one can get to specific targets of intervention or prevention from either problems or goals. Table 3 summarizes these two ways in which targets may be specified.

The third question in Table 3 brings the two paths of inquiry together and moves the discussion to an evaluative frame of reference, for which single-system designs become an appropriate tool for answering the question. The single-system design includes both a conceptual statement (the naming of the target variable) and an empirical component (the operational definition of that target). Either path, or both together, can help you identify some specific target and its operational definition.

Table 3 The specification of targets of intervention from an analysis of client problems and/or goals and objectives

Professional Service Begins with the Question, How Can We Help the Client? The Answer Involves Exploring Two Paths Regarding Client Concerns:

PROBLEMS as One Origin Point in Constructing Targets of Intervention

1a. What are the client's general areas of concern for which professional services were sought (survey the problem area)? "What are the difficulties you (the client) are experiencing?"

1b. Select one general concern and describe all of the topics within it, or representative types of problems within that domain.

1c. Take one illustrative problem—the highest priority problem—and indicate:
 - Who? (what client or relevant other)
 - Does what? (more or less of some specific activity)
 - To what extent? (specify how much more or less of the problem behaviors are involved)
 - Under what conditions? (Where? In what settings?)

3. How will you know whether the target (either a specified problem or a specified objective/goal) changes in the desired direction?

GOALS as Another Origin Point in Constructing Targets of Intervention

2a. What are the client's general and long-range goals (relative to the issues that brought the client and the practitioner together)? What would the client like to change? "What would you (the client) be doing, thinking, or feeling differently at that time?"

2b. What are the short-term intervening steps or objectives that may lead to the goal? What has to get done first? Then what second? Third? And so on.

2c. In order to achieve a given goal or objective, indicate:
 - Who? (what client or relevant other)
 - Does what? (more or less of some specific activity)
 - To what extent? (specify what criterion levels are to be used)
 - Under what conditions? (Where? In what settings?)

Summary

Being specific in identifying problems and goals is a crucial link among assessment, intervention, and evaluation activities. In this chapter, we started with client concerns—both those that are undesired and should be decreased and those that are desired and should be increased. Then we reviewed the rationale for being more precise and specific about defining problems and, later, establishing goals and objectives. We stated our belief that unless you can measure a problem, you cannot objectively evaluate how well you are resolving it. Focusing first on being specific in defining problems, we suggested several guidelines for using more precise problem definitions. Included in these were clarity, use of verifying sources, counting, dereification, focus on increasing and decreasing problems, and measurability. We also presented some examples of specific problems drawn from actual cases.

In the section on developing objectives and goals, we distinguished between problems ("what is") and goals ("what we prefer"). We also discussed the differences between goals (as ultimate outcomes) and objectives (intermediate outcomes). We clarified that outcome objectives are the actual stepping stones to the ultimate goals. We then discussed the key components of goal statements as including who, will do what, to what extent, under what conditions. We described how to use statistics to define goals and how to set goals in groups, and we presented a brief review of Goal Attainment Scaling (GAS), a widely used method of establishing goals. We then concluded the chapter by describing some problems in goal setting, with a checklist to anticipate those problems.

The Intervention Plan is a form you can use to practice implementing what you are learning. You can use the form with a real or imaginary client, on your computer in Microsoft Word, or printed out as a paper form.

DEVELOPING A MEASUREMENT AND RECORDING PLAN

PURPOSE This chapter provides guidelines for developing a plan to measure client problems after the targets have been selected using the guidelines provided in Chapter 3. A measurement plan involves deciding who, where, when, and how to measure targets, and a good plan makes it more likely that all of the measurement bases are covered. This chapter also provides guidelines for developing a plan to record the information generated by the measurement plan, including introduction to use of a personal computer program called Computer Assisted Social Services (CASS) to help you in recording and managing your caseload. The recording plan also involves graphing the information you collect on an ongoing basis in order to document, communicate, and monitor client progress so that you can make any needed changes in your intervention in a timely fashion.

Introduction
    Advantages of a Systematic Recording Plan
Steps in Developing a Recording Plan
    Select a Method of Measurement
    Decide Who Should Collect Data
        Client
        Practitioner
        Independent Evaluators
        Relevant Others
        Enhancing Cooperation in Recording
    Decide When and Where to Collect Data
    Decide How Often Data Should Be Collected
    Decide How Many Targets to Record
    Standardize Recording Procedures
    Begin Collecting Baseline Information
Charting: Putting Your Information on Graphs
    Presenting Data on the Chart
    Phases
Problem-Oriented Records (POR)
    Basic Guidelines for Using the POR
        Data Base
        Complete Problem List
        Initial Plans
        Monitoring Progress
Use of Computers in Evaluation and Practice
    Some Advantages and Disadvantages of Using Computers
Summary
Computer Assisted Social Services (CASS): A User's Guide
Appendix: Installing Cass

From Chapter 4 of *Evaluating Practice: Guidelines for the Accountable Professional*, Sixth Edition. Martin Bloom, Joel Fischer, John G. Orme. Copyright © 2009 by Pearson Education, Inc. All rights reserved.

INTRODUCTION

After targets have been selected, it's necessary to develop a plan for their measurement. A measurement plan involves deciding *who* (e.g., the practitioner or the client), *where* (e.g., the agency or in the client's natural environment), *when* (e.g., once a day or once a week), and *how* (e.g., a standardized questionnaire or the observation of behavior) to measure targets. These decisions are important because they influence the adequacy with which targets are measured. Some people are in a better position than others to provide information about some targets (e.g., a teacher might be in a better position than a practitioner to provide information about the way a child interacts with his or her peers). Some times and places provide a more representative picture of a target than others (e.g., the observation of a child's interaction with her peers at school might provide a more representative picture of her social skills than role playing in the practitioner's office). Some methods provide a better picture of a target than others (e.g., a client's rating of his self-esteem might provide a better picture of his self-esteem than an observation of his overt behavior).

Even if a good measurement plan is carried out, to make the best use of the information, it must be recorded in a way that allows it to be used to document (e.g., to funding sources), communicate (e.g., to supervisors and consultants), and monitor client progress in a way that will let you make needed and timely changes in your intervention. Usually this just involves charting the information on a graph, as we've illustrated in earlier chapters, and as we discuss in more detail in this chapter. However, there are also exciting developments using personal computers not only to graph the results of single-system designs, but also to easily store, retrieve, and manipulate recorded information in ways that are useful to practitioners and administrators. We'll discuss some of these developments.

As you probably know from your own practice, it's possible to successfully help someone without developing a plan for measuring and recording his or her concerns. If that's true, then why go through all the bother of setting up such a plan? Isn't the measurement and recording process an unnecessary intrusion into the practitioner and client relationship? Aren't records just a form of mechanical busywork?

We believe that setting up systematic recording plans is a useful and accurate way of establishing the effectiveness and efficiency of interventions. We recognize that the ethics of professional practice require accountability. You therefore must document the success of your interventions and even provide evidence about possible negative results that arise after your interventions. Data obtained from recordings serve this need for documentation.

To be sure, there are alternatives to systematic record keeping. Mainly, these involve less-structured impressions of the practitioner and the client that changes did (or did not) come about. Indeed, in some situations these impressions may be the only data available. But they also have their limitations. First, they tend to be imprecise; they may fail to measure a slow but steady change. Second, they are often inaccurate; there are too many possible distortions of the information when vague, subjective impressions are relied upon as the sole source of outcome information.

Advantages of a Systematic Recording Plan

It's advantageous to use a systematic recording plan for several reasons:

1. It enhances assessment and intervention planning, particularly by providing a focus on specific targets and goals.
2. It allows the practitioner to determine client progress and to record plateaus or regression.
3. It can alert the practitioner to the need for changes in the intervention program.
4. It can motivate the client and practitioner as they see the results of their work.
5. It can keep track of small but steady changes that might be overlooked.
6. It can provide data that can be analyzed to determine the range of effective interventions for different clients.
7. It can provide evidence about the effectiveness of your practice.
8. It allows you to demonstrate your accountability.

The remainder of this chapter focuses on the steps you would take in setting up a recording plan, shows you how to chart the data from your recording plan, and includes a brief discussion of recording using a method called the Problem-Oriented Record (POR). The chapter concludes with an overview of computerized recording followed by instructions on how to use the CASS computer program included with this book.

STEPS IN DEVELOPING A RECORDING PLAN

The whole process of recording should be built into the procedural guidelines that you ordinarily use as you collect and assess various sources of information about the client and target, starting prior to intervention. In other words, we suggest that the recording methods we describe should be as much an integral part of your preintervention activities as any of the activities that you typically engage in before your intervention plan is formulated. Thus, recording is an integral part of practice.

The recording plan grows out of your initial assessment of a client's targets, your hunches and the client's wishes about what needs to be done, and your preliminary review of the situation.

Select a Method of Measurement

Once the target or situation is specified adequately, the next step is to decide how it is to be observed and to select a method of measuring it. As we have suggested, it's best to try to use at least two different methods to measure a target whenever possible. For example, you might want to observe target behaviors and have the client evaluate the more subjective nature of the targets using an individualized rating scale. Of course, selecting a method of measurement is also based on who is available to record. Thus, these two steps—selecting a method and deciding who will use it—actually occur at roughly the same point in the process.

Decide Who Should Collect Data

An important consideration in setting up a baseline and recording plan is deciding just who should collect data. This can be the client, the practitioner, an independent professional (such as a colleague or a trained observer), someone else in the client's environment, or some combination of these (e.g., the practitioner using unobtrusive measures of changes in the client's target while the client collects his or her own self-report data). A key question you should always ask yourself in making this decision is whether the person can and will provide accurate information.

Client. There are a number of advantages to having clients report about their own situation, and we present information on such measures in the following chapters. Clients, whether they're individuals or members of groups or families, obviously are present when the problem is occurring, so they are in a uniquely favorable position to observe their own behavior. In fact, in some instances only the client can record target information (e.g., his or her own thoughts or feelings, or private behaviors that occur when a client is alone). Also, the client may be highly motivated to change the target and therefore may be willing to do the necessary recording. In addition, self-reports are often convenient and relatively easy to obtain, and you can get a wealth of information from self-reports. Finally, with the exception of behaviors that are illegal and consequently defined as problems independently of the client, the client defines whether a problem exists, and so the client's perspective is especially important.

Client reports also have some potential limitations and disadvantages. First, the client, perhaps out of a long-term habit, may not be aware of the occurrence of the target, and even your best efforts to help the client become aware (perhaps through role playing of the target to increase awareness) may not succeed. Second, clients may not be able to provide the needed information because they are too disabled or too young. Third, the client simply may not want to provide information, or may wittingly or unwittingly provide inaccurate information; clients might tell you what they think you want to hear, especially in situations in which you are in a position to give or withhold valued social sanctions and the client's reports might influence your decisions (e.g., a parent may not admit abusing a child to a child protective services worker, knowing that the worker is legally mandated to report this information). You may do your best to motivate the client (see the final section of this chapter), but that also may fail.

Finally, clients' recording of their own target may have a reactive effect so that the target might change during the baseline simply due to the effects of recording. Although one way to handle this is to extend the period of time over which baseline data are collected, this may not always be possible.

In some cases the client may be the only source of information about a target (e.g., if the target is a cognition or private event), but the client may not want to systematically collect baseline information on the target. For example, the client may be under stress and might be impatient to initiate intervention and go about the business of addressing his or her concerns (this impatience is often shared by the practitioner). Yet, interventions that are plunged into without adequate preparation may be doomed to failure. Thus, as part of that preparation, recording in general, and baseline recording in particular, provides some of the foundation for enhancing your potential for more effective intervention.

Even though we all might agree on this principle, we still might have difficulty in persuading the client. It's our belief, however, that recording is important enough in most instances to be viewed as a prerequisite of intervention. This means that the practitioner should strive to involve the client or relevant others in collecting data.

The success or failure of recording may very well depend on the way the practitioner presents it to the client. First, the practitioner should not throw the baselining and recording tasks at the client (or whomever is to collect the data) before some rapport has developed in the relationship and the client and practitioner begin to develop mutual trust. This is true whether the "client" is an individual, a small group, or a large agency. Too many projects have failed because the practitioner forced recording tasks on the client prematurely.

Second, recording should be explained as integral to intervention; that is, it should be clear to the client that effective assessment and intervention rely heavily on the collection of data.

Third, the procedure should be explained as clearly and precisely as possible. Of utmost importance is the amount of certainty and confidence the practitioner expresses in regard to baselining and recording in general. It would be hard for any of us to accept the task of recording (or any other task for that matter) from someone who appears uncertain about its usefulness.

Fourth, the practitioner can motivate the client to participate in any number of ways, including providing encouragement and support for the client's participation, conveying warmth and appreciation for efforts at cooperation, displaying empathy for the realistic constraints and concerns that the client expresses about recording, and by doing whatever is possible to remove any obstacles so as to facilitate recording (see Fischer & Gochros, 1975, Chapter 9, for a number of other suggestions).

Finally, if the target that is selected for recording is particularly annoying to the client, he or she may be more motivated to change it. It's important to be as certain as possible that the target is also amenable to change (so that the client won't get discouraged), and that above all, the method of recording is not aversive and perhaps is even enjoyable.

There are two other options a practitioner has if the client won't cooperate and collect information. The first is to go ahead and begin intervention anyway. This assumes, at a minimum, that assessment information collected from other sources is adequate to select the appropriate intervention and that an alternative method of evaluating success is also available.

The second option, when all else has been tried to include the client in the program, including exploration with the client of possible barriers to recording, is to terminate the relationship and possibly refer the client elsewhere. Although this option is not widely used in the helping professions and is not a popular choice, it nevertheless must be considered by the practitioner who is interested in effective and efficient use of time. This might be the option selected when not obtaining information will so obviously interfere with the assessment and intervention program that even normally effective results could not be expected. Under these conditions, when it would not be possible to expect that the client can be helped, it seems unreasonable and unfair to both client and practitioner to continue the relationship. For example, parents whose child has severe behavior problems may be unwilling to record their interactions with the child, making it impossible to assess the reasons for the child's problems, and therefore making it impossible to develop an adequate intervention.

Practitioner. Practitioners also can collect and record useful information about clients. In a way practitioners are in a unique position to observe and understand clients because of their professional training and experience, familiarity with the client, and the ease of recording unobtrusively. Therefore, we present information on data collection methods for practitioners in the following chapters.

There are potential problems and limitations of practitioners' reports. The validity of the data may vary with how the practitioner perceives the information will be used (e.g., for evaluating progress for accountability purposes). The data may be biased because of the practitioner's desire to succeed (e.g., the bias might be a function of how much time and effort were expended with a given client). In addition, the practitioner might not always be present when the problem occurs, since most problems obviously don't occur only or mainly during office or home visits.

Independent Evaluators. Other professionals, such as your colleagues, supervisor, or outside consultants, can sometimes provide valuable assessments of your clients. For example, you might have a colleague review a random sample of audiotapes or videotapes of your sessions with a client, or even interview your client. Independent evaluators have the advantage that they are less personally invested in a client and so they might be able to provide a more accurate, less biased assessment. Some evaluators may even receive special training in recording procedures. However, the fact that independent evaluators are less involved with a client also can be a disadvantage because they are less familiar with the client. Also, in busy agencies it simply might not be possible to have your colleagues provide independent assessments of your clients except on a limited basis.

Relevant Others. There are numerous people in a client's environment who interact with the client on a day-to-day basis and who might be able to provide valuable information about a client: *in homes*—parents, spouse, children, siblings, or other members of an extended family such as grandparents; *in the schools*—teachers, aides, parents, volunteers, classmates, recreation workers, cafeteria workers, school counselors, or social workers; *in institutions and hospitals*—house parents, psychiatrists or other physicians, psychologists, nurses, aides, secretaries, occupational and other specialty therapists, volunteers, social workers, other residents of the institution, or other nonprofessional staff such as cafeteria workers.

There are a number of advantages to having relevant others provide information about a client. First, the ultimate goal of your intervention efforts is to improve the way clients function in their day-to-day environment, and relevant others are often in a unique position to provide information about clients' real-world functioning. Second, some interventions are interpersonally based (e.g., in treatment of couples and families), and so the perspective of other involved parties is especially pertinent in judging the success of an intervention. Third, it may be possible for others to observe the target as it "naturally" occurs, unobtrusively, without producing a reactive effect. Finally, someone in the environment may be extremely motivated to collect data because the target is especially distressing to him or her. (See Fischer & Gochros, 1975 for guidelines for helping select, motivate, and train someone from the client's environment to do the recording.)

Information from relevant others can be valuable, but there are some potential problems and limitations with using relevant others to record. First, some clients simply don't have relevant others, or they may not want you to collect information from relevant others. Second, relevant others may be unwilling to cooperate, or they may "fudge" their recording depending on how they see its use. Third, the reason that makes relevant others so useful a data source—their day-to-day relationship with the client—also might bias their responses. Fourth, relevant others simply might not know enough about a particular client's target to provide adequate information (e.g., a relevant other might know that a client who abuses alcohol still drinks, but not how much). Fifth, sometimes it can be time-consuming and otherwise expensive to collect information from relevant others. Finally, if the client has access to information provided by relevant others it can prove embarrassing and even harmful to the client's relationship with relevant others (e.g., asking a person to collect information about the extent to which a neighbor abused his or her children).

In all, then, you sometimes have to weigh the pros and cons of all the factors, use whoever is available and willing to record, and try to minimize the negatives and maximize the positives as previously described. Also, typically, no individual is a perfect source of information, so it's best to collect information from various sources. If the bulk of the information from different sources is consistent, you can have greater confidence in the information; if the bulk of the information isn't consistent, at least you'll know that you have to proceed with some caution in making decisions from your information.

Enhancing Cooperation in Recording. There are several additional criteria you might use in deciding who should do the recording:

1. Be certain the recorder understands the value and purpose of recording.

2. Be certain the recorder accepts the value and purpose of recording.

3. Be certain the recorder will be present when the target occurs.

4. Be certain the recorder clearly understands just *what* is to be recorded. (If not, this means the practitioner must train the recorder in observing the target.)

5. Be certain the recorder knows how to record. (This, again, always necessitates training.)

6. Be certain the recorder has the necessary equipment available.

7. Be certain the recorder is motivated and/or willing to record. (If not, the practitioner's task is to develop a situation in which the necessary motivation can be produced, whether this is through support and encouragement by the practitioner or others, or through the development of a mini-intervention program to see that the recorder is reinforced for his or her efforts.)

We cannot overemphasize how important it is to adequately prepare the person who will be doing the recording, no matter which of the methods you select. We strongly recommend that you work to establish rapport and trust with that person. Don't ram the recording task down his or her throat. Once rapport is established, present the task clearly and confidently as an integral part of the overall program. The more uncomfortable you appear with the recording assignments, the more likely it is that someone else will be reluctant to take the responsibility for recording.

Explain the relevance of the information you're requesting. You might want to say that you need a baseline to evaluate what you do, just as a physician needs blood pressure, heart rate, and other readings before starting a treatment program. If the information you're asking for doesn't seem relevant, it might be difficult to convince recorders that the client will be better off if they provide accurate reports. Don't ask for information that isn't relevant, but make sure its relevance is understood by the person being asked for information.

Explain the importance of recording confidently, matter-of-factly, and as clearly and precisely as possible. Don't make it seem like a heavy burden, and be sure it isn't. Be certain that the recorder understands that the success or failure of the intervention may depend on collecting baseline information and information after intervention has begun. The confidence with which you request information may influence the accuracy of the information. Sometimes practitioners who aren't experienced in the use of measures in practice request this information in an uncertain, embarrassed, and apologetic fashion. This might suggest to the recorder that the task really isn't all that important or that it's indeed unreasonable to ask for the information; the recorder might act accordingly and provide less than complete or accurate information. If you believe that the information you're requesting is important, convey this to the recorder; if you don't believe it's important, don't ask for it.

A client, relevant other, or even an independent evaluator might want to provide complete and accurate information but might be reluctant to do so because he or she doesn't know who will have access to the potentially embarrassing information that was requested. Therefore, it's important to provide assurances that the information will be kept confidential to the limit of the law. However, don't inadvertently deceive the person by implying that such information is completely confidential (e.g., the client might have access to information provided by a relevant other). Numerous exceptions exist to the privilege of confidentiality and you need to be careful to not promise a greater degree of confidentiality than you can guarantee (Bloom & Orme, 1993; Kagle & Kopels, 2008).

Even if someone is willing and motivated to provide requested information, he or she might not have the necessary information. For example, under the right circumstances a client seeking help with alcoholism might be willing to tell you how much alcohol he consumed on most days in the previous month, but it's quite likely also that he might not be able to remember. A mother being investigated for child neglect might be willing to tell you when her child achieved certain developmental milestones, but often a parent doesn't remember this information. Therefore, the accuracy of information depends upon whether the recorder has what you need. You should ask yourself, and the recorder, whether he or she is able to provide the needed information. After all, if you ask a person for information that he or she doesn't have, you might get an answer, but it might be an inaccurate guess.

Try to emphasize how important it is that the recording doesn't interfere with the "natural occurrence" of the target (the reactive effect). Be certain that the recorder attempts to be as unobtrusive as possible; give suggestions about how to do that. Emphasize the importance of the recorder being honest

Recorder's Name
_____

Practitioner's Name   Date _____
_____

Client's Name
_____

	Yes	No
1. Is the target problem clearly defined?	____	____
2. Has the recorder practiced observing the problem?	____	____
3. Is the recorder accurate in his or her observations?	____	____
4. Is all data collection equipment available?	____	____
5. Are the sheets for collecting data properly dated and labeled?	____	____
6. Does the recorder know where to collect data?	____	____
7. Does the recorder know when to collect data?	____	____
8. Does the recorder have any unanswered questions or problems about collecting data?	____	____
9. Does the recorder know how and where to contact the practitioner if problems arise?	____	____

FIGURE 1 Data collection checklist.

and accurate. Be certain that the recorder—whether the client or someone else—doesn't think that he or she can "help" the program by being a trifle "overgenerous" with how he or she views the target.

Your reaction to the information provided by a client is another factor that can influence the accuracy of the information. For example, you might subtly show surprise or disapproval in response to a client's report, and consequently the client might subsequently provide less accurate information. You also want to avoid subtly but inadvertently encouraging a client to report improvement even when it doesn't occur. You should be careful not to suggest possible replies, although you should reinforce the recorder for his or her thoroughness and effort.

Finally, make sure the recorder is adequately prepared to collect data. Take the time to explain the task, and be sure that the recorder understands the instructions. When appropriate, you might ask the recorder to restate the instructions as a means of gauging understanding. In any case, encourage the recorder to ask questions whenever something isn't clear, and be sure not to give the recorder the impression that you're hurrying, because this might discourage him or her from asking much-needed questions. Also, you need to be sure that you're knowledgeable about the measurement task and prepared for any question the recorder could ask you. You might even want to develop a list to go over with the recorder before he or she begins. This list could include all the items that should be checked before recording begins (Gelfand & Hartmann, 1975). An example of such a checklist is provided in Figure 1, but you can make changes or add items to suit the needs of your own situation. If "no" is checked for any item, you would then go back and see that the item is accomplished.

Decide When and Where to Collect Data

In the best of all possible practice worlds, practitioners would be able to have information on all their clients' targets all of the time. In some instances (e.g., total institutions) this may indeed be possible; in many other instances this is highly unlikely. Often it's either impractical or simply impossible to collect information about the occurrence of a target every time it occurs. But a decision about this issue should be made *before* the actual recording begins.

The first guideline with regard to when to record is to try to record when and where the action occurs. If you're recording actual behaviors, this is perhaps obvious. With other forms of measurement you can work to see that whatever the recording device or instrument used, the measures are recorded as close to the actual occurrence of the problem as possible. That is, try to avoid a long delay between the occurrence of a problem and its recording (e.g., don't ask a parent to record child misbehaviors at the end of the day). The goal here is to try to minimize possible distortions of memory.

Deciding when to record depends mainly on the nature of the target and the measure you're using; therefore, in each of the chapters dealing with the different measurement procedures we describe specific information about how to decide when to use that particular measure. However, as a preliminary guideline, try to get as clear and representative a picture of the target problem as possible.

The key is the term *representative*. You don't want to collect information on a problem that would misrepresent how often or how intensely it occurs. For example, when recording behaviors, you would want to make sure that you understand the full range of occurrences of the problem, and that you're not underestimating it because you have decided to collect information only in one location or at one time. Similarly, if you're asking the client to note feelings of loneliness, you have to decide whether the client should record several times a day or only once a day, say, in the evening. This could give a distorted view of his or her feelings if that particular time of day has been identified as a particularly lonely time.

Decide How Often Data Should Be Collected

As a general guideline, data should be collected as often as possible without becoming tiresome, boring, aversive, or overwhelming to whoever is collecting the data. Care should be taken to see that you're not putting too much of a burden on the record keeper, that the repeated collection of information is not producing a reactive effect on the target, and that the recorder isn't changing the way he or she records or views the target halfway into the project.

Repeated measures, as we said earlier, are part of the essence of what single-system designs are all about, because you can establish and track *over time* the range and level of occurrence of a target. This gives you the clearest and best picture of what is happening to that target. These repeated measures should be collected prior to and during intervention and, we hope, at some follow-up period selected by you and the client.

Repeated measurement during baseline, intervention, and follow-up may not be possible all of the time, although we believe that it's possible most of the time. There are times when complications arise that affect your ability to measure a target repeatedly during baseline, intervention, or follow-up (e.g., a life-threatening situation arises during baseline, such as the physical abuse of a child, that requires immediate intervention and therefore precludes the prospective measurement of the target during baseline). Under such conditions we suggest that you do whatever you can to get as much of an accurate picture of the client's problems as possible. You should try to at least measure the target once prior to intervention so you have a rough preintervention estimate of the target, once at or near the end of intervention so you have a rough estimate of whether the criterion for termination is met, and once at follow-up so you have a rough estimate of whether change was maintained. At best, such *single-point measures* provide suggestive information, but we definitely do not recommend them as the methods of choice, because they don't provide sufficient information to evaluate an intervention or to assess or monitor targets in order to make needed and timely changes in an intervention.

While you should try to do the best you can with the resources available, we believe the tremendous utility of repeated measures makes them the key priority for single-system evaluations. As we said before, repeated measures will give you the clearest picture of what is happening to the client problem(s).

No matter how often data are collected, you should select regular predesignated times or conditions for the data to be recorded, and you should make it clear to the person who is to record the data just exactly when and under what conditions data are to be recorded. For example, you should make it clear whether a client should rate anxiety at regular intervals (e.g., each day), at preselected times (e.g., before going to sleep in the evening), or when faced with selected critical incidents (e.g., prior to having a job interview).

Decide How Many Targets to Record

The basic guideline for all recording is to try to keep the whole procedure simple. You don't want to overburden the recorder (your client, you, a relevant other) with the task. This is particularly true when it is the recorder's first attempt at recording. You don't want to create confusion or frustration by making the process too complicated.

A rule for selecting the number of targets to be recorded is: When in doubt, do less. It would be unreasonable to ask anyone to record more than two or three separate targets at most, unless perhaps there are existing records (e.g., in a school) that would make such recording manageable. In most situations it is probably best to focus on one problem area at a time. This also allows the practitioner to develop a thorough intervention plan focused on one area at a time.

Of course, one problem area (say, marital discord) may encompass several specific targets (e.g., communication, sex, finances). Thus, it may be possible to record more than one aspect of the same problem. For example, you might ask the client to record both the number of positive thoughts he or she has about himself or herself and the number of negative thoughts. Or you might ask the client to record the number of angry feelings and to evaluate the intensity of the anger on a separate scale. Similarly, if the target involves a configuration of factors dealing with interpersonal skills and anxiety, you might ask the client to record the number of contacts he or she has with someone of the opposite sex, to rate the intensity of the anxiety he or she experienced, and to evaluate the negative or positive thoughts he or she experienced with each contact. Such recording, all focused on one problem, would still provide information on several targets: overt behaviors, feelings, and thoughts.

Another example of collecting data on several aspects of one problem is not only to record the occurrence of some problem, but also to note when it occurred and under what circumstances in order to assess controlling conditions.

If there's still some doubt as to what target to focus on for recording, try to pick one that may be representative of the others. That is, if the target you select seems to give a clear picture of the entire configuration, or at least typifies it, you probably made a good choice. If you do decide to record only one target, select one that: (a) has the most practical advantages, (b) is relatively amenable to the recording process, (c) is clear and readily identifiable, and (d) is most direct and objective.

Focusing on recording only one target shouldn't limit you. You might want to select several measures of that target; for example, behavioral observation, an individualized rating scale, and a standardized questionnaire to get a clear picture of the target.

We know that the realities of practice are such that in most cases you're confronted with a host of targets. Indeed, you are probably usually working with several targets at the same time. It may be possible to record information for each of those, perhaps using a different person to collect data on each. On the other hand, the best you can do may be to work with several targets, but only record one of them. If this is the case, then we suggest you use some of the previously stated guidelines in selecting which one to record (e.g., representativeness, availability of resources for recording). Thus, in some situations the main criteria regarding how many targets to record may involve practicality: willingness and availability of people to record; time and energy of the recorders; complexity of the target (e.g., ability to clearly identify a recording method); and the time and energy you have to devote to the task of setting up recording methods.

Standardize Recording Procedures

The time (e.g., morning or evening), place (e.g., client's home or the practitioner's office), and method (e.g., self-administered or practitioner-administered questionnaire) you use to measure a client's targets can influence your results. Therefore, if the time, place, or method used changes over time, it becomes difficult to disentangle these changes from real changes in the problem. Therefore, ideally, you should use the same time, place, and method to measure a particular client's targets over time.

It's especially important that you avoid changes in the time, place, or method of measurement that coincide with a change in treatment conditions (e.g., change from baseline to intervention). When measurement procedures change at the same time that treatment conditions change, it's difficult to determine the effect of the change in treatment conditions. For example, during baseline a client might rate his or her depression in the late afternoon, a time when he or she feels especially upset. If for some reason when the intervention is implemented he or she begins to rate depression in the morning, a time when he or she feels much better, any improvement observed in the problem after the intervention begins might be due either to the intervention, or to the change in the time of rating.

Sometimes it isn't possible to use the same time, place, and method of measurement over time for a client. Clients, relevant others, and sometimes even busy practitioners, forget to complete self-administered questionnaires at appointed times, or they complete them in different settings. Computers sometimes don't work, requiring the substitution of the tried-and-true paper-and-pencil method of data collection. When such changes occur, you should note the differences and try to take them into account when interpreting results. You'll just have to make a judgment concerning the extent to which a pattern of results over time was due to real changes or to changes in the time, place, or method of measurement.

Begin Collecting Baseline Information

Once you have completed the preceding steps, you're ready to begin collecting baseline information. Many of the decisions and issues that we have described may seem overwhelming at first and may indeed prove to be overwhelming the first one or two times you try collecting data. However, we're confident that with experience both the decisions and the actual act of recording information will grow to be less complicated and more rewarding.

We hope you are already convinced of the advantages of recording during the baseline and intervention periods. Once you try recording with a client and continue to use it with subsequent clients, we hope you not only will become convinced of the ultimate practicality of recording, but will also build it into your practice with every client. Hence, the last steps are to start baselining, continue to record once your intervention program begins, and start to enjoy the fruits of your labor—more precise assessments, clearer evaluations, and the potential for enhancing your effectiveness.

CHARTING: PUTTING YOUR INFORMATION ON GRAPHS

The information that you collect for the baseline and subsequent intervention periods, as we mentioned earlier, could be collected and tabulated in any number of ways, ranging from records of agency intakes, to a client's scores on a questionnaire, to a family's count of communications. Yet, in this more or less raw form (e.g., just a bunch of scores or tallies on a 3" × 5" card), these data may not be helpful because they may be too complicated or jumbled. Furthermore, it seems desirable to have a standardized system for recording and checking changes for a variety of quite different forms of information.

Charting is probably the most convenient and desirable way to make the data you collect both useful and standardized. Now, if you're not one for statistics or mathematics, and the notion of charting conjures up all sorts of fears, don't stop reading. Charting—or graphing as it's sometimes called—is a convenient, simple, helpful way for you and your client to make some sense out of the data you collect.

The most important guideline for recording is to make sure the data will be *used*. Charting is perhaps the best method to help you attain that goal, since charting involves a pictorial representation of changes in the target from the onset of baselining to the termination of intervention. But charting also helps the assessment process, as changes in the data reveal patterns in factors that may affect the target.

Charting has another value. It can serve as feedback to the client and to the practitioner. This feedback can help motivate, support, and reinforce efforts to change, maintain willingness to participate in the program, and generally encourage the involvement of those concerned. The chart also can be a constant reminder of the goals and objectives of intervention.

Charting generally involves transferring the data you collect onto a piece of paper (preferably lined graph paper because it makes the charting process easier and more precise) and then displaying the chart in a prominent place (perhaps chosen by the client) so that it can be seen often. If your client is collecting data and placing this information on a chart at home, the chart might be placed on a refrigerator or some other area that people walk by frequently. If the data are for an organization, you can put the chart on the main bulletin board. Don't skimp on the space you use on the piece of charting paper. Spread the chart out along the width of the entire paper. (Remember to use these same guidelines if you're teaching your client how to record and chart.)

Graphs of client targets are easy to draw by hand, but a variety of easy-to-use personal computer programs also are available that will generate and easily update high-quality single-system design-type graphs even faster than you can draw them by hand. SINGWIN is an excellent example of such a program, and in Part IV we describe how it can be used in more detail. SINGWIN will compute virtually all of the statistics described in this book, and will do so with far more speed and accuracy than any of the hand calculations will allow. You will find, we hope, that SINGWIN is very user friendly, even for novices, and will make graphing and analyzing single-system design data not so much a challenge as a delight. SINGWIN is increasingly recognized (Beaulaurier, 2005; Davis, 2007) and used across disciplines for teaching and to analyze the results of single-system data (e.g., Barrett & Wolfer, 2001; Bradshaw, 2003; Bradshaw & Roseborough, 2004; Johnson, Beckerman, & Auerbach, 2001; Jindani & Newman, 2006; Mauszycki & Wambaugh, 2008; Miller, Combs, Fish, Bense, Owens, & Burch, 2008; Rock & Cooper, 2000; Wambaugh & Ferguson, 2007). We think that you, like others, will find that it is easy to use and helpful in evaluating your practice and understanding practice evaluation (Conboy et al., 2000).

The Computer Assisted Social Services (CASS) system (Nugent, Sieppert, & Hudson, 2001; Nurius & Hudson, 1993), which is described in this book, is another good example of a computer program that graphs single-system data, and we discuss it in more detail later in this chapter. Among other things, CASS administers standardized scales to clients, scores these scales, and graphs the results in a single-system design format.

As another example, many agencies now have spreadsheet programs such as Excel. Excel can be used easily to graph the results of single-system designs (Carr & Burkholder, 1998; Grehan & Moran, 2005; Hillman & Miller, 2004; Lo & Konrad, 2007; Moran & Hirschbine, 2002; Patterson & Basham, 2006). (Grehan & Moran [2005], Hillman & Miller [2004], and Moran & Hirschbine [2002] can be downloaded for free from "The Behavior Analyst Today" web site located at www.behavior-analyst-online.org/newBAT/index.html2). Once there, click on "Index," search for the correct volume and issue, and scroll to the particular article. Excel also can be used to compute many of the statistics used in the analysis of single-system data.

Presenting Data on the Chart

There are standardized methods for use of charts, so all charts can be interpreted roughly in the same terms (e.g., Cooper, Heron, & Heward, 2007; Kennedy, 2005; Thyer & Myers, 2007). Also, as noted previously, Excel can be used easily to graph the results of single-system designs and articles describing how to do this also describe how to construct single-system design charts.

First, draw two straight lines at right angles, one horizontal and one vertical, joined at the lower left corner. There are some conventions as to what these lines represent, and we suggest following these conventions. The horizontal line or axis (sometimes called the abscissa) always refers to time elements. The time elements always begin on the left and move to the right. The period of time you use depends on how often you collect data. The most typical time unit is days. But if you collect a great deal of information (e.g., about organizations), you might want to average the data over some period of time, say, a week. Similarly, if the target doesn't occur frequently, you might want to count all the occurrences of the target that week and use the week as the basic unit for your horizontal axis. Each unit on the timeline is considered a "point"; thus, a baseline of 15 days has 15 points. Several charts illustrating different time elements are displayed in Figure 2.

If you do decide to average or group data, you must be aware that you may be hiding factors that can help your assessment. It's much more difficult to investigate factors that are related to daily changes in a behavior when you average or group the data over a week. On the other hand, if the baseline data are extremely variable, grouping the data can produce a more stable baseline, making the data more amenable to analysis. Furthermore, if you group data, you will probably need to extend the baseline so that you can achieve more than the minimal number of data points.

Figure 2 illustrates two charts (2a & e) using days as the time unit. (The days can be numbered or the actual dates can be placed on the chart.) Note that each time unit is denoted by a hatch mark on the horizontal axis, and the marks are equidistant. The time unit you select should be written under the line.

The vertical axis (sometimes called the ordinate) represents the target. The hatch marks on this axis also should be equidistant. The label you use for the target should be entered to the left of the axis. If you're dealing with large numbers, your increments on the vertical axis should vary accordingly (see Figure 2). Ordinarily the "0" (indicating no occurrences of the

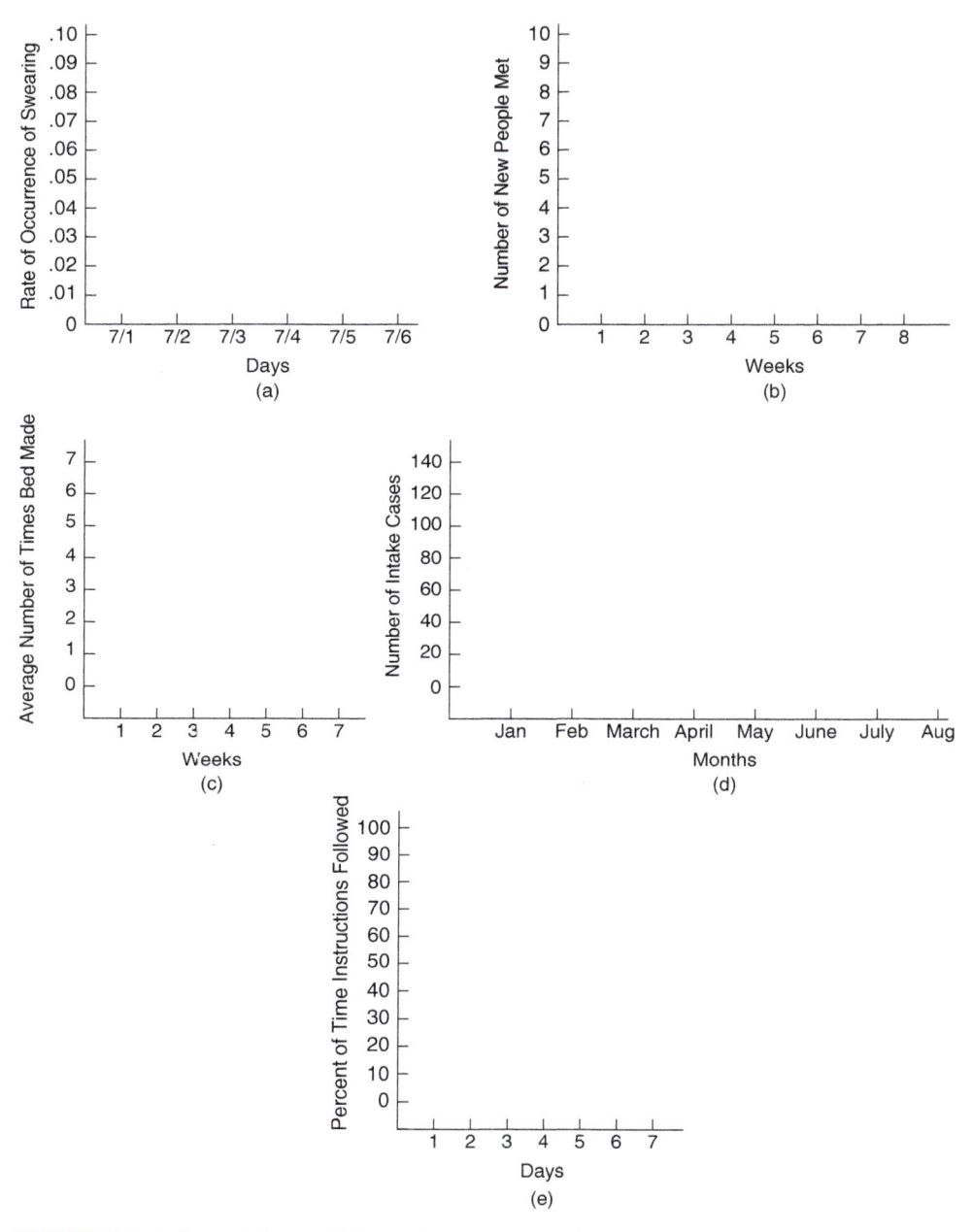

FIGURE 2 Variations of data and time units as presented on charts.

target) is placed on the vertical axis, where it intersects the horizontal axis, as in Figure 2a and b. However, it's also possible to place the 0 above the horizontal axis using the first hatch mark on the vertical axis, as in Figure 2c–e; it sometimes presents a clearer picture, since the data then don't run into the horizontal axis.

The key question at this point is what form of data to use. You have several choices: absolute numbers (e.g., number of days of school attended, number of practitioner-client contacts); percentages (e.g., percentage of time an entire family spends together); rates (when the time periods for collection of data vary or scores (e.g., scores on a problem-solving questionnaire from 0 to 100). The method of plotting information on the chart represents the way you define the target and how you actually collect the data. Several variations of data and time units are presented in Figure 2.

The last step in using the chart is to plot the data. Over each number on the horizontal axis (time), put a dot next to the appropriate number on the vertical axis (target). You will be placing the dot alongside the value (e.g., the number of times the target occurred, the scale score for that time period, etc.) for the target recorded during that time period. This continues until there's a dot for all time periods. The dots are then connected by a line so that the patterns can be more readily seen. This is depicted in Figure 3.

What if the client is sometimes not able to record (or even forgets)? These data should still be plotted on the chart, and they're represented either by omitting the lines between the time periods before and after data *were* recorded or by connecting the dots with a dotted rather than solid line. Of course, with days missing, you should use a little more caution in interpreting any patterns on the chart, since it would be difficult to know whether those days would have continued the pattern. This process is depicted in Figure 4 with Days 3 and 6 missing.

If the target could not possibly have occurred at all (e.g., disruptive behavior in the schools could not

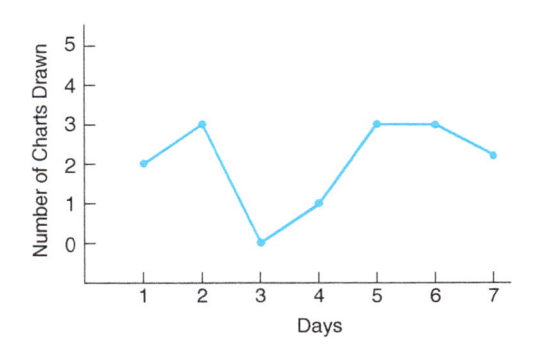

FIGURE 3 Chart illustrating the complete labeling and plotting process.

occur on weekends), those days are not entered on the chart (see Figure 5).

In some situations, though, you might want more than one chart to depict different parts of the same target. For example, if the goal of the program is to increase a client's number of positive self-references and to decrease the number of negative self-references, you might want to depict each of these on separate charts.

Under some circumstances you might want to depict two or sometimes three different measures on the same chart. This is useful to determine whether the different measures "vary together" over time. As a hypothetical example, suppose that a Task-Centered approach (Fortune, 1985; Reid, 1978) is used with a client who

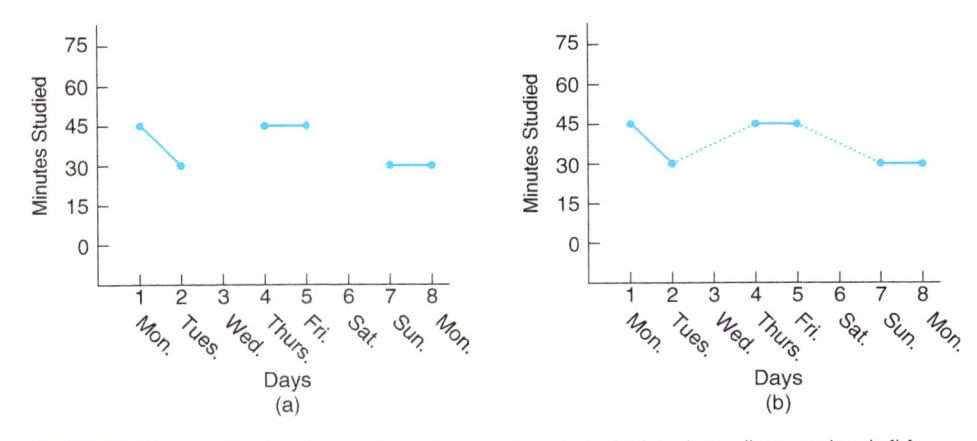

FIGURE 4 Two methods of recording missing data: (a) missing data—lines omitted; (b) missing data—dotted line.

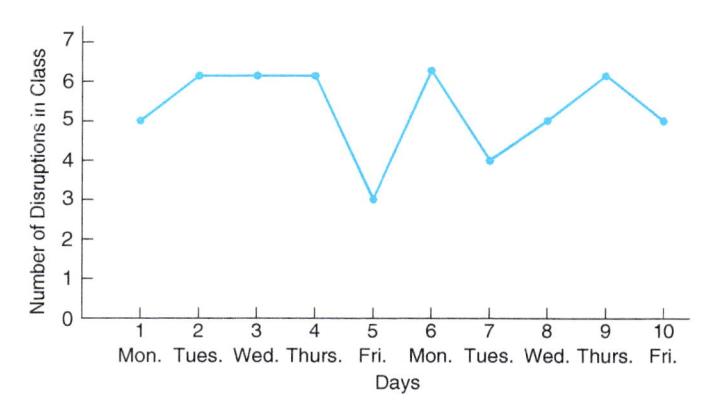

FIGURE 5 Chart illustrating number of disruptions in class with weekends omitted.

is dissatisfied with his or her job, but whose goal is to keep the job and increase job satisfaction. Each week the client and practitioner jointly select a task for the client to undertake at work to improve job satisfaction (e.g., discussing job assignments with the supervisor), and the client is asked to rate the success in carrying out the week's task on the following Task Achievement Scale (Reid, 1977, p. 289; Reid & Hanrahan, 1988): (1) not achieved or minimally achieved; (2) partially achieved; (3) substantially achieved; (4) completely achieved. Also, each week the client is asked to rate job satisfaction on the following 5-point scale: (1) not at all satisfied; (2) somewhat satisfied; (3) moderately satisfied; (4) very satisfied; (5) extremely satisfied. The objective was to at least "substantially" achieve the tasks (i.e., a rating of 3 or greater), and the ultimate goal was to have a job satisfaction rating of at least 4.

Results of this example are shown in Figure 6, and they show that as task achievement increases during the intervention phase job satisfaction also increases. They also show that for Weeks 7 and 8 both the objective and ultimate goals were achieved.

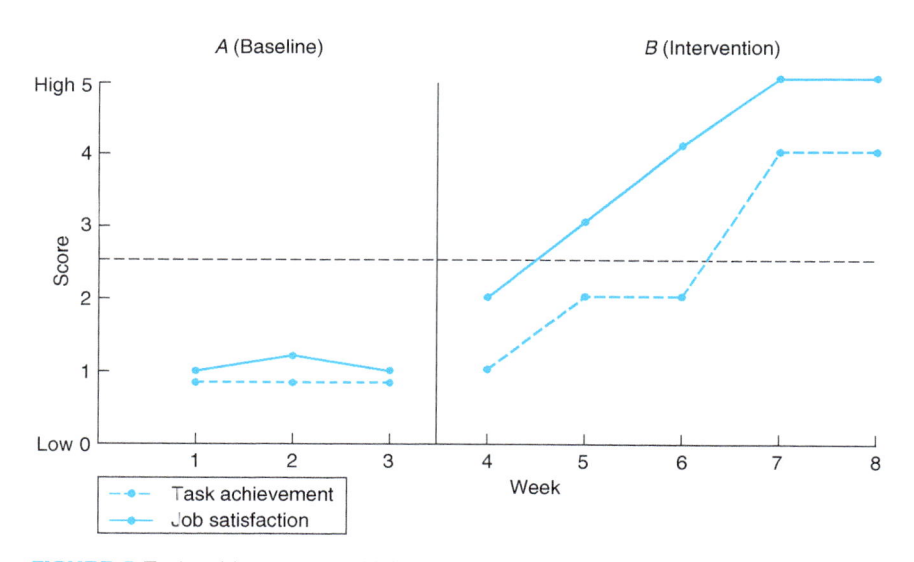

FIGURE 6 Task achievement and job satisfaction.

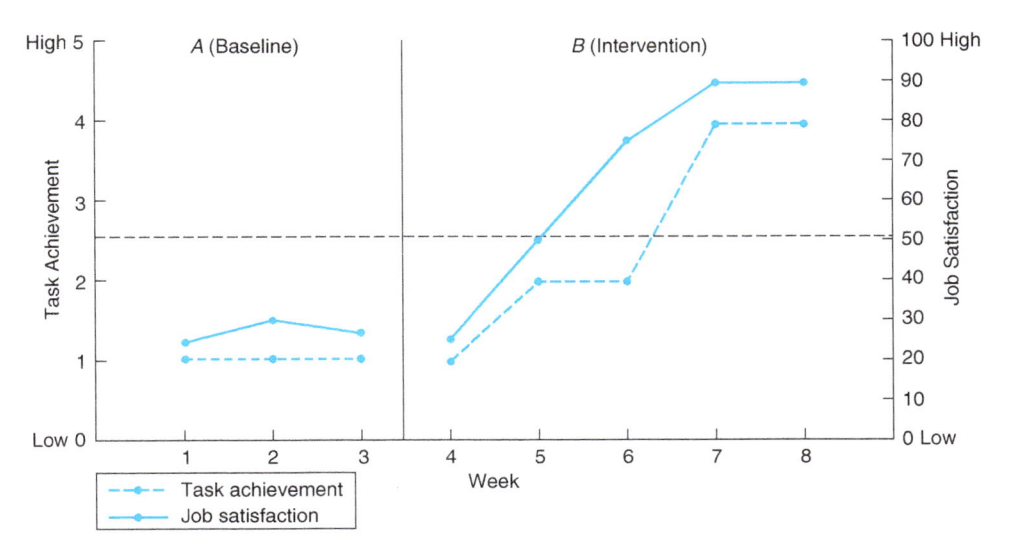

FIGURE 7 Task achievement and job satisfaction.

The results shown in Figure 6 also illustrate what is called *concomitant variation*. Concomitant variation exists if two or more events change together: if they consistently increase or decrease at the same time (i.e., they're positively correlated), or one consistently increases while the other decreases (i.e., they're negatively correlated). Concomitant variation is important because it can suggest causal connections between events. For example, the results shown in Figure 6 suggest that task achievement increases job satisfaction. However, *it's risky to assume that one event causes another just because the events are correlated*. It might be, for example, that the more satisfied the client is with his or her job, the more likely he or she is to complete tasks, or it might be that some other factor is causing task achievement and job satisfaction to change (e.g., increased marital satisfaction).

If two or more measures are depicted on the same chart, and the scales for the two measures are about the same (e.g., a 4-point scale for one measure and a 5-point scale for the other measure), it's reasonable to use just one vertical axis to represent the scale, as illustrated in Figure 6. If the scales for the different measures are very different, it's useful to use separate vertical axes to represent the different measures. To read these more complicated graphs, try looking for one line of data at a time to get a sense of its flow before comparing it with another line of data. Suppose that in the example just discussed job satisfaction was measured using a standardized questionnaire with a range of values from 0 to 100. In this situation it would be best to use two vertical axes to depict the different measures. An example of how this could be done is shown in Figure 7. First examine each line (task achievement and job satisfaction) separately; then you can compare them to each other.

Although most charts you will use and see in the literature present the data as they occur in each time period—say, giving the number of times a target occurs each day or how long it occurs—another possibility for charting is to use *cumulative charting*. Cumulative charting involves adding each time period's recorded data to the data of the periods before it. This is a good method to use when you wish to emphasize progress, because the trend of the data is always upward (you're adding each time period's total to the total of the time periods before it). In this case you can evaluate change by looking at the slope of the line; the steeper the slope, the higher the occurrence of whatever you've targeted for change. Figure 8, adapted from Fischer and Gochros (1975), illustrates a cumulative chart of cleanup activities. The first week involved 10 hours of cleanup activities. The second week involved 7 hours of cleanup activities, and this number was added to the first week's activities. The third week's cleanup activities involved some 5 hours, and this number was added to the first 2 weeks' sum for a total of 22 hours of cleanup activities during the first 3 weeks. This total is the baseline. As the figure shows, there was a dramatic change in the slope of the line once intervention started.

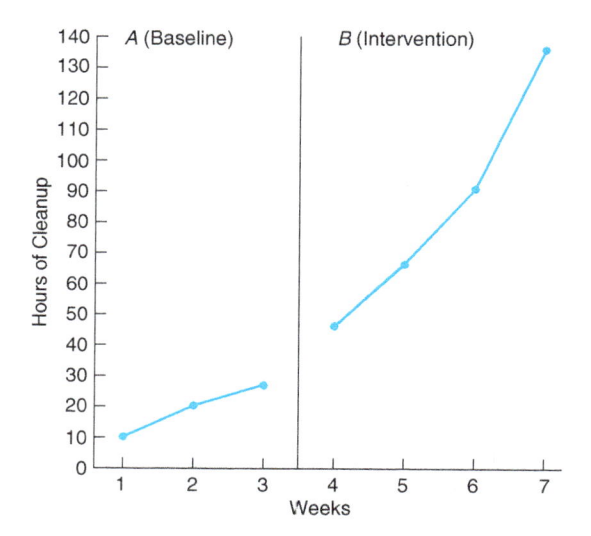

FIGURE 8 Cumulative hours of cleanup activities by Blue Cottage during the cleanup campaign.

Another way of displaying data on the charts is the bar graph. This is most typically used in group situations; for example, where group averages or aggregate data are reported. Figure 9 illustrates a bar graph concerned with a class's weekly average score on a test for the first 5 weeks of the semester.

Phases

One advantage of charts is that they can help you clearly identify the different aspects of your total intervention program virtually from your first involvement with the client. The chart necessitates that you distinguish among various phases of your contact with the client. A *phase* refers to any relatively distinct part of the client's overall program from first to last contact. The most commonly used distinction between phases is between baseline and intervention. However, phases also can refer to the onset and termination of different types of interventions with the same client.

Phases are usually separated on the chart by a vertical line. They also should be labeled in the appropriate section of the chart. It's customary to use a letter to designate different phases of intervention. Conventional notation for designating phases is that A always stands for baseline, and subsequent letters of the alphabet (B, C, and so on) each stand for different but specific interventions. Combining two earlier interventions simply calls for using both of the earlier letters. These could consist of separate intervention techniques or several techniques integrated into a package.

Let's say you conduct a baseline (A) and then begin your intervention (B). Feedback from your chart indicates that it's not working. You switch to a new intervention (C). Then you decide to combine the two interventions in an attempt to enhance overall effects (BC). This process is charted in Figure 10.

In some articles in the literature, you will see subscripts used along with letters (e.g., $A_1 - B_1 - A_2 - B_2$). These subscripts only refer to the first or second (and so on) implementation of exactly the same phase. Thus, A_1 is the first baseline and A_2 is the second, while B_1 is implementation of the intervention the first time and B_2 is implementation of exactly the same intervention the second time.

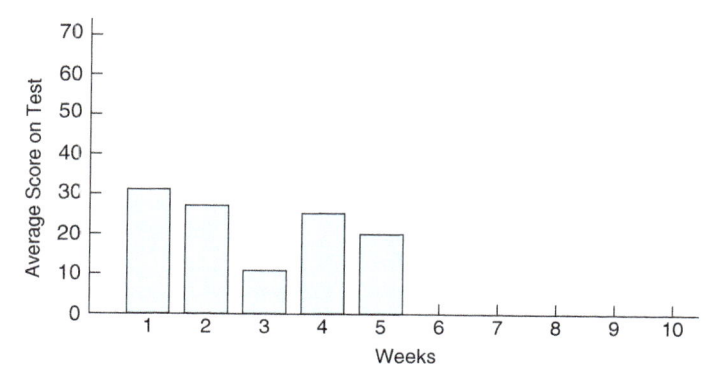

FIGURE 9 Bar graph of class weekly average score on a test.

Developing a Measurement and Recording Plan

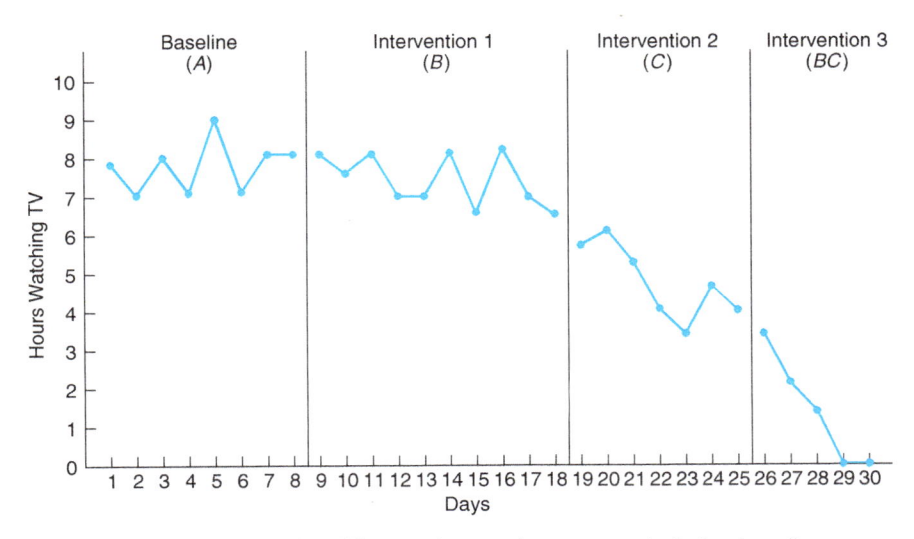

FIGURE 10 Chart illustrating different phases of a program including baseline (A), intervention 1 (B), intervention 2 (C), and a combination of interventions 1 and 2 (BC).

Another variation in notation is the use of *superscripts* (e.g., $A - B^1 - B^2$). Superscripts refer to changes in the *intensity* of either the intervention or the goals.

Although we use the letter *A* to denote baseline and subsequent letters of the alphabet to indicate interventions, there's another system of labeling that we'll briefly describe in case you come across it in the literature. This is the system used by Shadish, Cook, and Campbell (2002) in which they label repeated observations or measurements *O* and interventions *X*. Thus, a design incorporating baseline and intervention periods (*A–B*) might be labeled $OOO\ X\ OOO$ or $O_1 O_2 O_3 O_4\ X\ O_5 O_6 O_7 O_8$. Similarly, an $A - B - A - B$ design (baseline-intervention-baseline-intervention) might be labeled $OOO\ X_1\ OOO\ X_2$ or simply $O\ X_1\ O\ X_2$.

These are the basics of the notation system.

PROBLEM-ORIENTED RECORDS (POR)

One of the great values of recording for single-system designs is precisely that these records can be used with just about any type of agency recording format. In fact, we believe use of the recording methods we describe here will actually make your other recording jobs easier. This is because you will have clearly specified targets and goals and regularly collected information on changes in targets throughout your contact with the client, both during your assessment (during which the baseline occurs) and intervention.

For example, one recording format that is commonly used in many organizations is the Problem-Oriented Record (POR); it sometimes is called the Problem-Oriented Log or POL (Burrill, 1976; Grant & Maletzky, 1972; Kane, 1974; Martens & Holmstrup, 1974; Ryback, 1974; Sheafor, Horejsi, & Horejsi, 1991; Weed, 1968). Originally developed in an attempt to systematize and reform medical records (Bhopal, 1981; Margolis et al., 1984; Savage, 2001), the POR has been widely adopted in a number of human service organizations. Hence, we provide a description of the POR and the way it can be used to supplement single-system designs.

The basic purpose of the POR is to provide, in a standardized format, information that is directly related to the problem being dealt with by the practitioner. It's therefore thought to be helpful in the attempt to document and evaluate services. The POR basically requires that (a) client problems be specified clearly, (b) an intervention plan be specified, and (c) progress be monitored and recorded at regular intervals.

Basic Guidelines for Using the POR

The POR is composed of four major parts: (a) data base, (b) complete problem list, (c) initial plans, and (d) monitoring progress.

Data Base. The data base essentially is the information that you collect as part of the assessment. This, of course, is standard operating procedure for all professions. The POR, however, focuses on an important requirement in the development of a data base: The types of data to be collected must be clearly defined in advance, based on the typical range of problems and needs and requirements of your agency or practice setting. This is an attempt to ensure that the data base meets uniform minimum standards of the quality and quantity of information needed in order to produce a sound assessment. This can then lead to a sound decision regarding intervention plans (Martens & Holmstrup, 1974).

The data base, because it's defined in advance, necessitates systematic collection of information. However, each agency or organization has to decide what kind of data base would be most productive to further its aims and to enhance its selection of interventive methods. Obviously, an agency specializing in foster care arrangements would need a data base different from the kind used by an agency specializing in cases of sexual abuse.

Similarly, the theoretical orientation of the practitioner might dictate collection of a different set of data to constitute the data base. Thus, the data base could include everything from practitioner observations to reports of individuals in the client's environment to checklists and inventories.

The data base can and should be added to as the evaluation proceeds. Care must be taken to ensure that it is clearly defined, not overinterpreted (i.e., that impressions don't stray too far from observations), complete, representative of actual problem occurrences, and representative of observations of all members of the professional team (if a team is involved), and that plans are specified to continue to collect data if the data base is incomplete.

Because the data base is developed prior to intervention, it can be used to provide suggestions for selecting one or more of the problems for more intensive and repeated observations, and for charting on a graph for evaluation using single-system designs.

Complete Problem List. The next step in use of the POR is to develop a complete problem list. This problem list is based on the information obtained from the data base. Each problem should be numbered and that number can be used to refer to the problem throughout the rest of the record. The numbered problem list becomes the first page and table of contents of the record. Highlighting the problem list in this way keeps problems from being overlooked as intervention proceeds.

The problem list is constructed on the basis of what you and the client have agreed should be focused on; the items are recorded in order of priority. The problem list should include all problems that the practitioner and client can identify. No problems should be eliminated or dropped by erasure; instead, a line can be drawn through the original problem with an arrow followed by the modified problem or the term *dropped* or *resolved*. It is probably best not to note problems in terms of diagnosis, since this may lead to confusion, labeling, or different perceptions by different practitioners. Instead, the problem should be defined as precisely and specifically as possible, using guidelines.

The problem list can be constructed in different ways depending on the needs and priorities of the given agency. It is probably best, though, to include, at a minimum, a problem number, the name of the active problem, the date it was defined (when the practitioner found out about it), the inactive status (resolved or improved), and the date the problem was resolved.

Initial Plans. Once problems are listed, all subsequent notes should refer to a specific, numbered problem. You should also record the basis for all subsequent information and for all decisions.

There are three basic components to the plans. The first is further assessment. In this part of the record, new or additional information (and its source) that bears on the specific problem under consideration is listed. This could include elaboration of the conditions causing or maintaining the problem. It might even include an example of the problem, when and where it occurred, who was present, and so on.

The second component is a clear statement of the goal, plus a statement of the system you will use to monitor progress. Remember, simply stating the problem (lack of sleep) may not have anything to do with the goal (e.g., to diminish a client's anxiety over a job interview so that he or she will be able to sleep). Actually, almost any of the material in this book—ranging from goal selection to measurement to design options—can be used to monitor progress.

The third component involves establishing an intervention plan. For each problem, a specific plan is developed. The intervention plan should include who will intervene, for how long, what intervention techniques will be used, what role the practitioner will be functioning in, and what tasks the client must undertake. The notes may even indicate the basis for the selection of those particular intervention techniques (e.g., reference to articles in the literature demonstrating effective use of those techniques with the particular problem under concern).

The initial plans also may include other categories, such as anticipated time limits, resources, potential barriers to effective intervention and plans for overcoming those barriers, and so on.

Monitoring Progress. The final component of POR is the notes that one takes as progress is monitored. As with other parts of the POR system, these notes should be dated, numbered, and titled.

A suggested POR format for these progress notes is known by the acronym *SOAP*.

The first component is **S**ubjective data. These are statements of the problem from the point of view of the client, practitioner, and others, including thoughts, feelings, and concerns. These data are subjective in that they're difficult or impossible to verify.

The second component is **O**bjective data. These are all important objective data related to a particular problem. These objective data could include observations (what was observed, not interpretations of the observations), test results, attendance reports, demographic data related to the problem, medications taken, and so on.

The third component of the progress notes is **A**ssessment. This is the synthesis and analysis of the subjective and objective data as related to a particular problem. The assessment is also intended to identify and evaluate new obstacles or resources as they may affect intervention. The assessment obviously is ongoing and is intended to provide information to bolster, or, if need be, change the intervention plan.

The fourth component of the notes is progress with the intervention **P**lan. Here, continued use or changes in the intervention procedures are identified as the case proceeds, and specific dates and plans to review progress are identified. If there are no changes in the overall plan, the practitioner would note this. This section, however, also would include short-range plans; for example, what is to be done in the next week.

An example (from Kane, 1974, p. 416) of a progress note for a child (John) whose problem has been identified as "uncontrollable at home," would be:

Subjective: Mrs. X states that she feels more relaxed about John, and John reports less quarreling at home. He claims he doesn't feel as "uptight."

Objective: Mrs. X has been attending a parents' group at the Q Agency since May 1. Her attendance has been perfect, and the group leader reports that she has been actively involved. The worker has observed her using the new ideas she has learned in discussing a problem with John.

Assessment: The problem seems much diminished.

Plan: (1) No further direct intervention after the group ends in 2 weeks, (2) review in 1 month to determine if the summer vacation brings new stress, (3) evaluate at that time for removal to inactive list.

An additional component of the progress notes would be the termination summary. This would follow the same format shown above, but would also include the final evaluation of the extent to which the goal was achieved, the reason for termination, and follow-up and maintenance plans.

While there are few data on the reliability of the POR, it appears to be a good example of the attempt to systematize recording beyond the methods used in many organizations. Single-system designs can be used in complementary ways with the POR, especially with regard to providing a system for monitoring progress to provide the basis for the more or less objective data needed in order to evaluate change with the POR (i.e., the O in the SOAP) model.

POR is used in many agencies in an integrated fashion with other procedures. One of the best examples of this is the Lutheran Social Services of Wisconsin and Upper Michigan (W. Benedict, personal communication, 1986). This agency uses a program called "Evalutreat," which actually integrates the POR and Goal Attainment Scaling (GAS) and other evaluation techniques. Evalutreat combines an agency's case recording and program evaluation functions into a unified process in a way that can satisfy most case recording requirements.

USE OF COMPUTERS IN EVALUATION AND PRACTICE

As the prices of personal computers continue to drop, and programs for their use become more accessible and easy to use, it is inevitable that practitioners in the human services will come to rely on personal computers to help manage and enhance their practice (Schoech, 2008). Computers increasingly are becoming a crucial part of evaluation and practice. In fact, one might argue that recent advances in computer technology have revolutionized the way practitioners engage in practice and evaluation. This development has been hastened by three major phenomena: (1) the increasing sophistication of users of computers—computers are available at home and at work, and more and more people are becoming familiar with their use; (2) the incredible drop in prices of personal computers, making them more accessible to people than ever before; and (3) recognition by practitioners of the value of computers for evaluation and practice. Indeed, some practitioners feel completely hampered in their practice and evaluation activities if they are denied access to their computers for even a short time. (You can include the authors in this latter group.)

Recent reviews of computer technology tools and applications illustrate the wide range of activities for which computers currently are used in practice (Berger, 2006; Butcher, Perry, & Hahn, 2004; Finn, 2008; Jindani & Newman, 2006; McNutt, 2008; Patterson, 2008; Richard & Gloster, 2006; Schoech, 2008). These activities include single-system evaluation, of course; computer-assisted assessment; online support; e-therapy; virtual reality assessment and treatment programs; decision support systems; marketing and fundraising; community organizing/development; political advocacy; web-based surveys and data collection; and risk assessment. And, of course, we would add that computers are at the heart of finding and analyzing information for evidence-based practice.

Most prominently, we also included two complete computer programs, **Computer Assisted Social Services (CASS),** which we will discuss later in this chapter, and **SINGWIN,** a program to help you store, retrieve, organize, communicate, disseminate, graph, and analyze single-system design data.

We also want to encourage you to explore the Internet and to take advantage of the vast resources available there. To begin, open the Internet browser program on your computer, such as Mozilla Firefox or Microsoft Internet Explorer, and type in the following address in the top window: www.pearsonhighered.com/bloom and then hit "Enter." This will bring you to the web site for this book. It will provide you with an overview of the book, allow you to connect directly with sites devoted to CASS and CAAP, provide you with links to other interesting sites, and, if you click on "Technical Support," will provide you with technical information about SINGWIN and give you an email address where you can get technical support for this program.

Personal computer programs are available not only to graph the results of single-system designs, but also to easily store, retrieve, organize, communicate, disseminate, and analyze recorded information for practitioners, supervisors, and administrators (e.g., Patterson, 2008; Patterson & Basham, 2006; Richard & Gloster, 2006; Schoech, 2008). However, because there are so many, it's impossible to describe all the different computer programs for the management of client data. This is a rapidly growing area, so you should look for current developments in journals such as *Journal of Technology in Human Services, Social Science Computer Review, Behavior and Information Technology*, and *Computers in Psychiatry/Psychology*; on the Internet in such places as CUSSnet (www.uta.edu/cussn/cussn.html), and Human Service Information Technology Applications (HUSITA) (www.husita.org); and in software and book review sections of professional journals.

Another tremendous resource on the Internet is called *Information for Practice* developed by Gary Holden. An archive that is updated monthly, this site contains information pertinent to all human service professionals on topics including government, measurement, social work, psychology, social science, and many more. All you have to do is type the following address into your browser and hit "Enter" and you'll be there: www.nyu.edu/socialwork/ip. You can subscribe to this free, Internet-based information service for human service professionals by sending a blank email message to *join-information-for-practice@forums.nyu.edu*.

Finally, there are several books that are excellent resources for finding sites on the Internet that can be helpful to professionals: *Research Navigator Guide: The Helping Professions* (Kjosness, Barr, & Rettman, 2004), *Information Technology for Social Work* (Schiller, 2005), and *The Insider's Guide to*

Mental Health Resources Online (Grohol, 2004). For online updates to the Grohol book, visit the site **www.insidemh.com**.

Because CASS is focused on helping you manage case records, this chapter features the CASS program, and there is an extensive CASS User's Guide at the end of this chapter.

Some Advantages and Disadvantages of Using Computers

There are some concerns raised by the use of personal computers to manage client data (e.g., Ahluwalia, 2008; Butcher, Perry, & Hahn, 2004; Schoech, 2008). Computers require start-up time in learning the operation of the computer and the particular software program. They also require a financial investment in the computer equipment and software. In addition, eliciting information via computer may seem intimidating and impersonal to some clients. Also, eliciting information via computer may disadvantage clients with visual, hearing, or motor difficulties; clients with insufficient access to and experience with computers; and clients with literacy or language barriers. However, it is increasingly possible to adapt the presentation of materials to those with special needs (e.g., through computer synthesized speech and voice recognition). Extra care needs to be taken to ensure that clients understand the task at hand and are able to respond appropriately.

The personal computer management of client data does have some important benefits, as suggested by the following description of CASS and other related personal computer software (see also Berger, 2006; Butcher, Perry, & Hahn, 2004; Nurius & Hudson, 1993; Patterson & Basham, 2006; Schoech, 2008). Computers can increase the speed and efficiency with which information is managed and feedback is available, and this can free up time to deliver services. They also can increase the standardization and accuracy with which measures are administered and scored. Even the most conscientious practitioner can make mistakes in scoring measures, and these mistakes can lead to incorrect practice and evaluation decisions. Computers can and have been used to identify clients who are "off track" for a positive outcome and to improve positive outcomes and reduce negative outcomes for such clients (e.g., Lambert, 2007). Finally, computers can be used to aggregate and analyze data (e.g., across clients within an agency).

Summary

This chapter presented the basic principles involved in developing a measurement and recording plan. We first discussed how to decide who, where, when, and how to measure targets. Then we discussed guidelines for developing a plan to record the information generated by the measurement plan. The recording plan involves charting the information you collect on an ongoing basis in order to document, communicate, and monitor client progress to permit any needed changes in your intervention in a timely fashion. Also, we discussed the use of the Problem-Oriented Record (POR), a commonly used recording device that can be used along with single-system designs. Finally, we briefly described computerized recording in general, and one of the programs that is included with this book, CASS, in particular. The CASS User's Guide begins on the following page.

CASS

COMPUTER ASSISTED SOCIAL SERVICES (CASS)

A User's Guide

CASS was developed for human service practitioners, and it provides a good example of a comprehensive, easy-to-use, personal computer program that simplifies and enhances the recording, storage, retrieval, and organization of client data. CASS is the general name of this program, but there is another program included with CASS named CAAP (Computer Assisted Assessment Package). It's important to distinguish between CASS and CAAP and their different functions at the outset.

CAAP is used by *clients* to:

- Complete scales
- View scale scores
- View graphed scale scores

CASS is used by *practitioners* to:

- Manage client files (e.g., create, edit, and read files)
- Manage scales completed by clients using CAAP (e.g., view and graph scale scores)
- Manage scales completed by clients by hand (e.g., input and score scale data)
- Manage service tasks for individual clients and overall for an agency or group of practitioners who use CASS (e.g., define and redefine tasks, monitor task completion)
- Manage client casenotes (e.g., create, edit, and read casenotes)
- Manage how information is presented to clients using CAAP (e.g., edit menus of scales presented, add new scales)

CAAP administers almost any type of standardized scale or test to your clients, and it automatically scores it, charts the results in a single-system design format, updates the information for a client each time a measure is completed so you can monitor client progress over time using CASS, and stores the information in the computer. An especially notable feature is that, although CAAP comes with ready-to-use scales, you can add an almost unlimited number of additional scales, including ones constructed by you or your agency. Therefore, it's possible to use CASS to construct a tailor-made package of computer-administered instruments for use in your practice.

Essentially, CASS automatically retrieves, organizes, and saves client-completed scale data from CAAP, and it lets you view and manipulate (e.g., graph) this information. Furthermore, CASS lets you enter and otherwise manage other client information, such as service tasks and casenotes.

A notable feature of CASS and CAAP is that information is stored so that only you or someone you designate can access the program and client information. Clients and practitioners are assigned unique passwords that must be used to enter the system, and scale scores and other information are encrypted so that only you or someone you designate will have access to the information.

CASS is designed to be used by practitioners with minimal knowledge of personal computers, and CAAP is designed to be used by clients with minimal knowledge of personal computers and with minimal instruction from you. To this end CASS and CAAP are Windows-based systems with on-screen menus that walk you and your clients through the program. (A computer menu is just a set of choices from which users select what they want to do.) Also, CASS and CAAP have extensive online, context-sensitive help that can be read on-screen or printed.

Here we would like to introduce you to CASS and its numerous features. **However, before you can work through the exercises here you need to install CASS and CAAP. The installation procedure is described in the Appendix at the end of this User's Guide**.

We assume that you know very little about computers, and we apologize in advance if this isn't the case. There are a few things that you need to know at the outset, but if you've used Windows before you probably already know these.

Before starting, first be sure to familiarize yourself with the basic operations of your computer (e.g., location of your A drive, "Enter" key, "Ctrl" key, and ← ↑ → ↓ keys). In particular, find out what version of Windows your computer uses (e.g., 95, 98, 2000, ME, XP); CASS probably installs best on computers running Windows 95 and 98.

Also, you'll need to know the following terms to install and use this software:

- "Click" means use your mouse to move the arrow you see on your screen to a certain word or place on the screen, and then click the *left* mouse button once.
- "Right-click" means use your mouse to move the arrow you see on your screen to a certain word or place on the screen, and then click the *right* mouse button once.
- "Double-click" means use your mouse to move the arrow you see on your screen to a certain word or place on the screen, and then click the *left* mouse button *twice quickly*.

WARNING: If CASS does not run according to the following instructions, as a last resort you might have to reinstall the program, as shown in the Appendix at the end of this User's Guide.

STARTING CASS

▶ Double-click the CASSWIN icon (the city scene) on your desktop.

▶ When the following window appears, enter *walmyr* for the User ID, press the Tab key, and enter *scales* for the password. (When you type scales it will appear as ******.) Note that the User ID and password must be entered using all lowercase letters.

▶ After you've entered the User ID and password, click "OK" and the "Password Entry" window will disappear. We'll refer to the resulting screen (not shown) as the start screen.

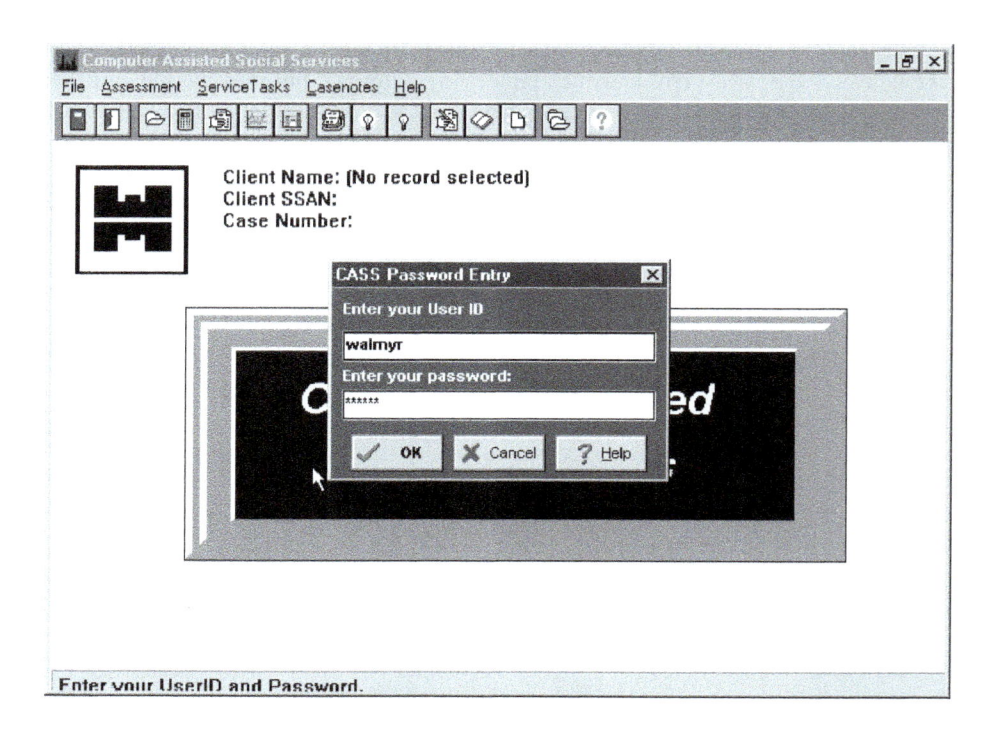

Notice the menu bar items at the top of the screen shown (i.e., "File," "Assessment," "Service Tasks," "Casenotes," and "Help"). You can click any of these items and menus will be displayed. We'll discuss these menu bar items and menus below. Also, note the buttons below the menu bar. These give you another way of doing the same things you can do with the menus. When you move the arrow to one of these buttons, after a short pause a note appears describing its purpose.

CREATING A NEW CLIENT RECORD

▸ Click "File" and "Create New Client Record."

The "Add a New Client Record" window will appear, but the boxes will be empty. In our example, we entered the information in the boxes; here are the conventions used to enter this information (if you click "Help" on the following window you'll also get essentially this same information):

- **Case Number.** *The case number you assign to a new client record must be unique.* If you enter a case number that already exists you will obtain a "Key Violation" message. *Note:* If you ever get a "Key Violation" message, click on the "OK" button to remove the

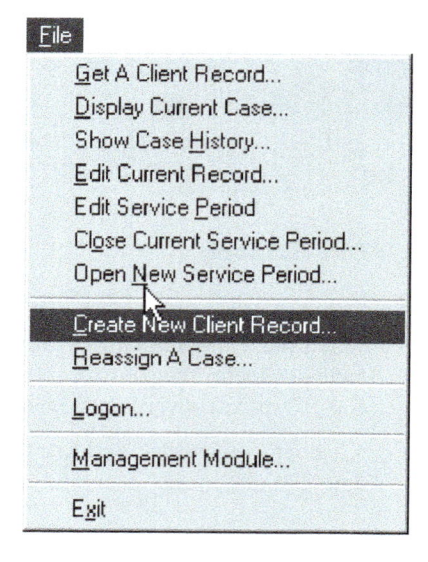

key violation message and then click on the "Cancel" button. Once you have entered the case number, press the Tab key to move to the next field.
Note: The client's case number must begin with a number or a letter, it cannot exceed 15 characters in length, and no other symbols are allowed. You also must plan your case numbering system with great care. Once you enter a new case number into the data base, it is difficult to change.

- **Honorific.** Type into this field the honorific title you wish to use for the client. The most frequently used honorific titles are Mr., Ms., Mrs., and Dr., but you may enter any other honorific title.
- **Client's Name.** Enter the client's first, middle, and last name in the designated data entry fields.
- **SSAN.** The client's Social Security Account Number, or SSAN, is a critically important identifier and it must be entered using the dash separator. Please always use the form, 000-00-0000 (e.g., 123-45-6789).
- **Birth Date.** Always enter the client's date of birth as Mo/Da/Year (e.g., 04/25/1944). Always use *four-digit years* with CASS.
- **Gender.** Always use the gender codes of *Male* or *Female*. You can click the down arrow in the drop-down combo box for gender and then click on the correct choice. That will ensure correct spelling and coding.
- **Ethnicity.** When entering the client's Ethnicity always enter *White, Black, Hispanic, Asian, Native American,* or *Other*. You can click the down arrow in the drop-down combo box for Ethnicity and then click on the correct choice. That will ensure correct spelling and coding.
- **Education.** Enter the number of years of school that were completed by the client. For example, a client who completed high school and four years of college would typically have completed a total of 16 years of schooling. In that case you would enter the number 16.
- **Income.** The income field should always contain the *total annual gross family income in thousands* of dollars. For example, a family with a total annual gross income of $47,834.00 would be entered as 47,834. Do not enter the dollar sign. (Entering the income in thousands means moving the decimal point three places to the left.)
- **Marital Status.** When entering the client's marital status, always enter *Never married, Married, Divorced, Separated, Widowed,* or *Other*. You can click the down arrow in the drop-down combo box for marital status and then click on the correct choice. That will ensure correct spelling and coding.
- **Number of Times Married.** Enter the number of times the client has married. Enter 0 if the client has never married.
- **Years with Spouse or Partner.** Enter the number of years the client has resided with a current spouse or partner. Enter the number 0 if the client is not currently residing with a spouse or partner.
- **Children in the Home.** Enter the number of children who are residing in the client's home.
- **Household Size.** Enter the total number of persons residing in the client's home or apartment, including the client.
- **Worker EN.** Enter the employee number of the practitioner to whom this case will be assigned. For our purposes here you can make up any number you like.
- **Supervisor EN.** Enter the employee number of the supervisor to whom this case will be assigned. For our purposes here you can make up any number you like.
- **Client Password.** Enter the password that you will give to the client for use with the Computer Assisted Assessment Package (CAAP) program. Don't forget this password.

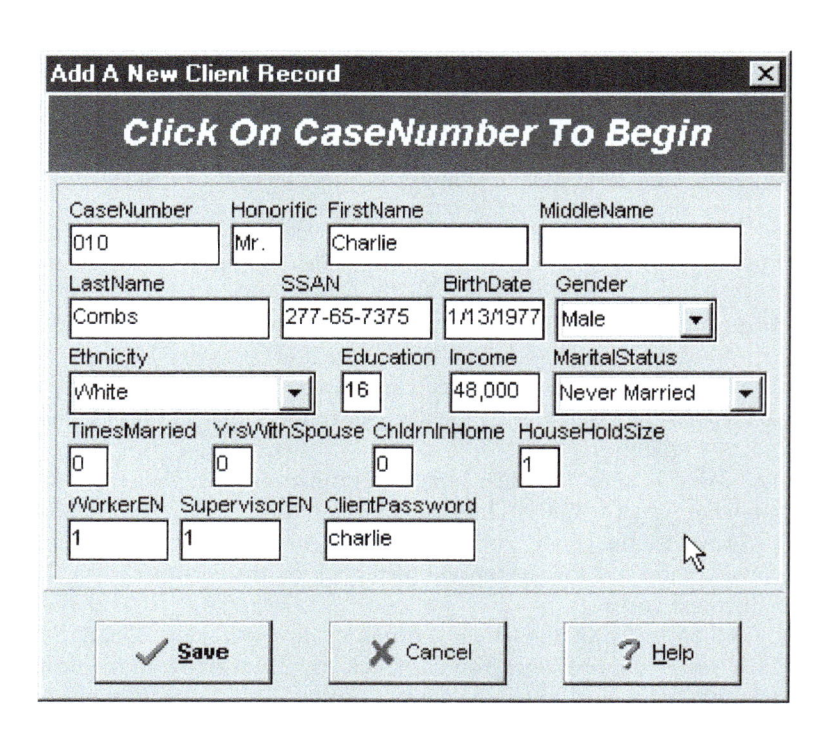

▸ Click "Save" when you're finished entering the client's information and the following window appears.

▸ Click "OK" and the "Service Code" window will appear with the client's name and case number, but "Primary," "Secondary," and "Tertiary" service will be blank.

Be sure that the first time you create a new client record you click "Help" on the window below and carefully read the instructions for selecting a service code. After doing this, enter a service code or codes. We clicked "Depression" and then "Problems at Work."

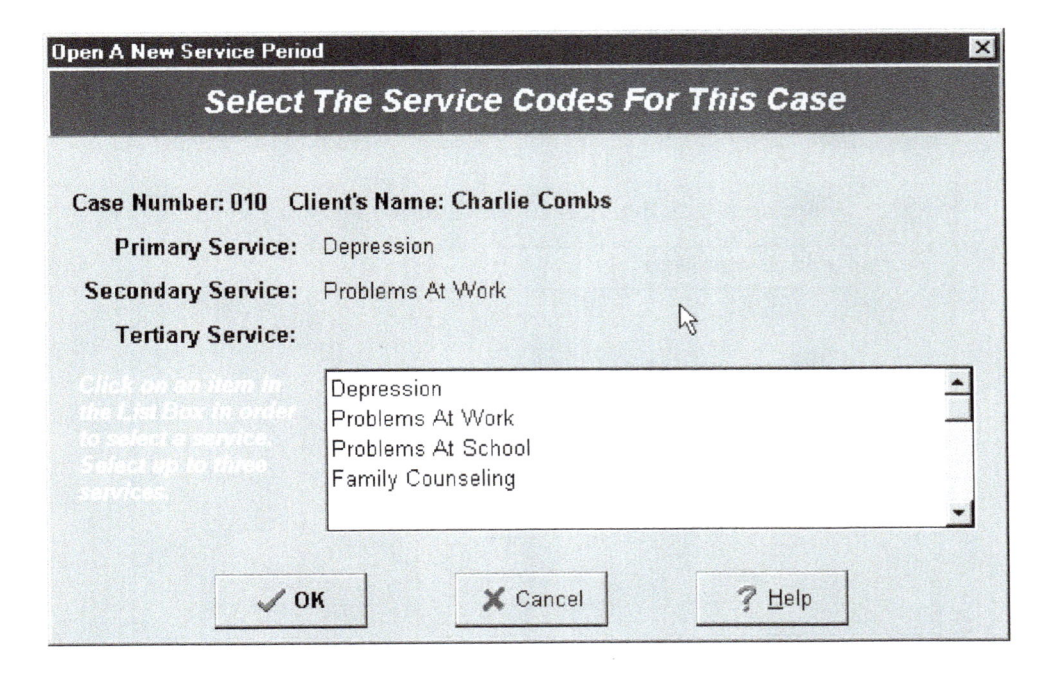

▶ Click "OK" and a verifying window will appear.

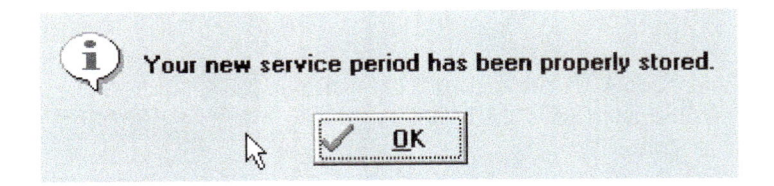

▶ Click "OK" and the "Service Task" window will again appear, except now "Enter Task Here" and "Date Due" will be entered in the boxes.

Be sure that the first time you create a new client record you click "Help" on the window shown here and carefully read the instructions for entering a service task. After doing this, enter a service task and date. We entered "Reduce workload," moved the arrow to "Date Due," and entered 1/31/2003 for the date. (Be sure you use the full year for the date, i.e., "2003" rather than "03.")

Add Service Tasks For This Case

Describe a task that must be completed for this case.

Reduce workload

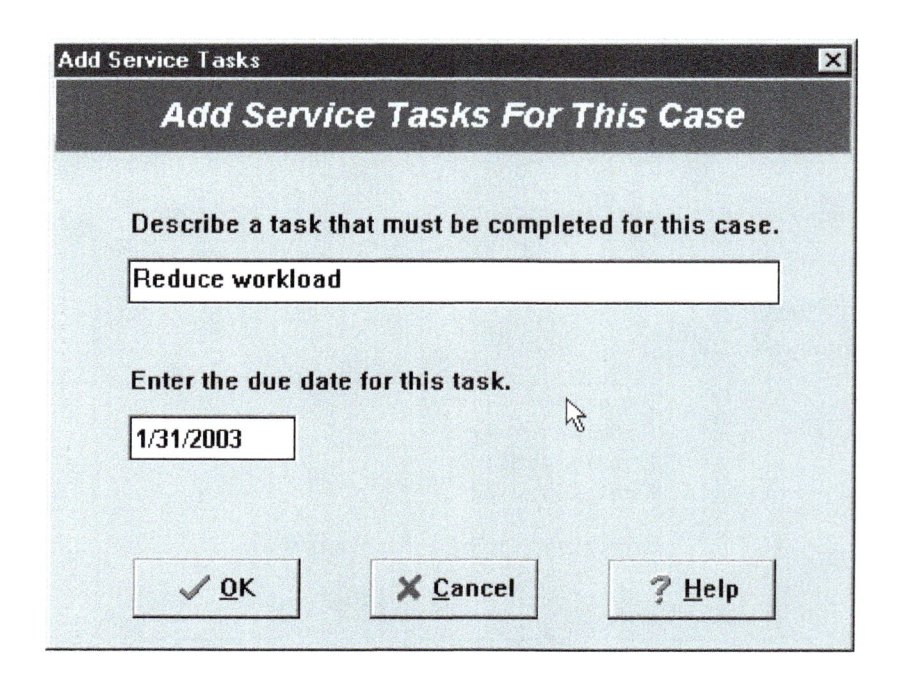

Enter the due date for this task.

1/31/2003

[OK] [Cancel] [Help]

▶ Click "OK" and you'll be returned to the start screen.

GETTING A CLIENT RECORD

One of the first things you'll need to do when you use CASS is to get a client record. Here's how you do this.

▶ Click "File" and "Get A Client Record." The list of client records will appear (SAMPLE1 and SAMPLE2 come with the program).

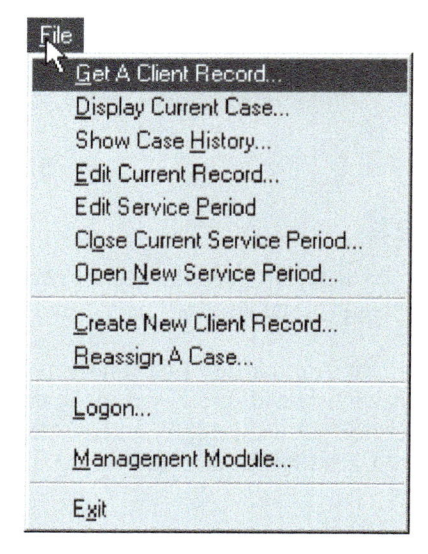

File menu:
- Get A Client Record...
- Display Current Case...
- Show Case History...
- Edit Current Record...
- Edit Service Period
- Close Current Service Period...
- Open New Service Period...
- Create New Client Record...
- Reassign A Case...
- Logon...
- Management Module...
- Exit

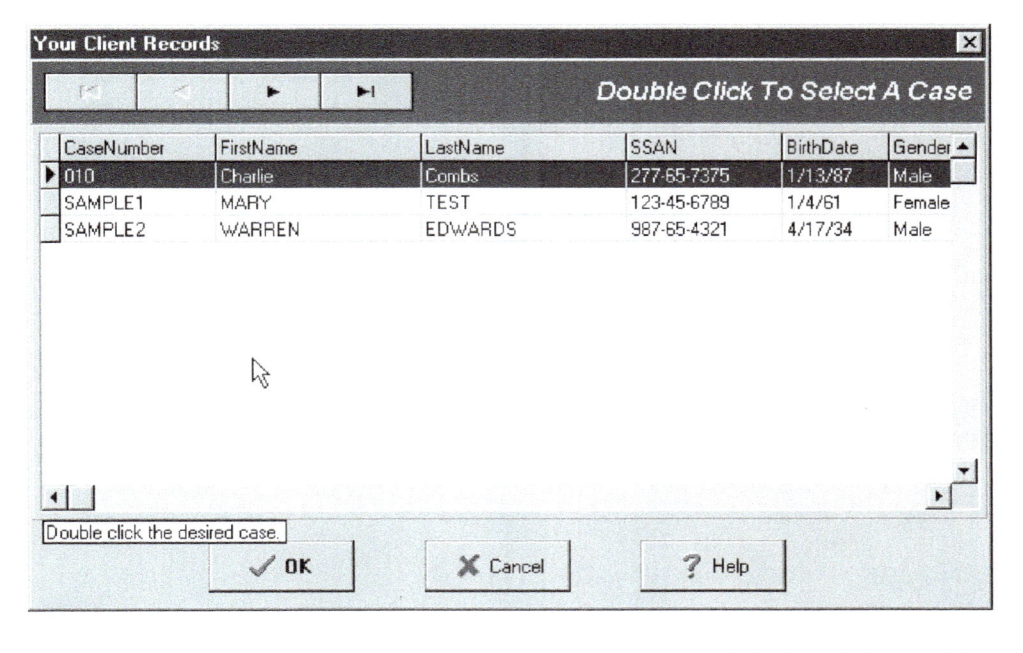

▸ Move the arrow to the row with listing Case Number "010" and double-click, or click once and then click "OK."

The service period list will appear. (You also can click "Help" on the window anytime you see a "Help" button on a window. This provides help with the task at hand. (One exception to this rule is in the "Select A Service Period" window.) If you try to return to the service period and receive a message that it is currently in use, try the steps on page 114 (If Locked Out). Also see page 118; you can click on "Utilities" and "Unlock A Client Record" for help.

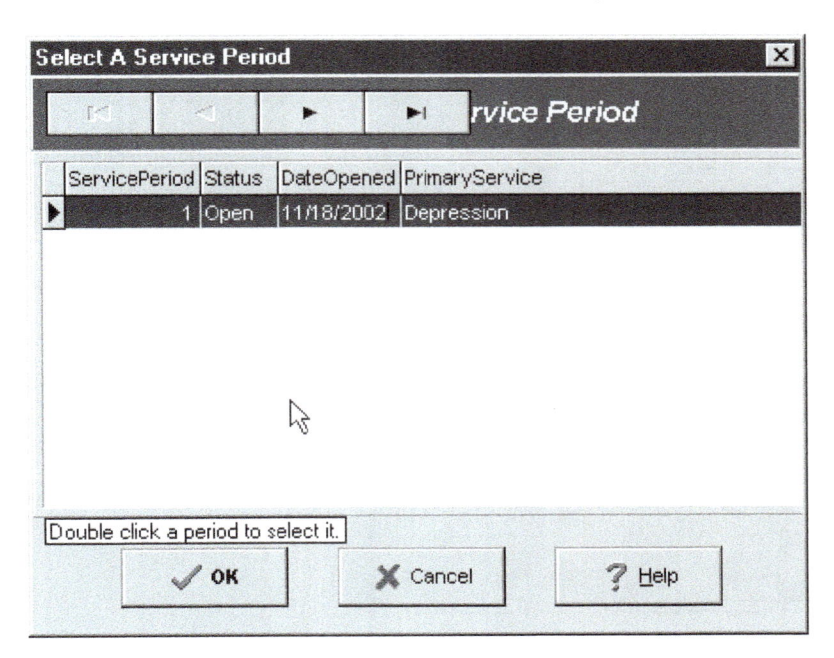

109

▶ Double-click the line with the service period information, or click once and then click "OK."

This service period will be selected and you'll be returned to the start screen. Basic client information now is listed on this screen.

Client Name: Mr. Charlie Combs
Client SSAN: 277-65-7375
Case Number: 010 Service Period: 11/18/2002

WARNING: When creating client records or opening service periods, be sure that all dates are past dates, that is, prior to the date you actually enter this information on the computer.

GETTING CLIENT CASE INFORMATION

After you get a client record, but before you use it, we think it best to check to make sure that you're using the correct record. Here's how you do this.

▶ Click "File" and "Display Current Case."

The table of case information will appear. Click "Close" to return to the start screen.

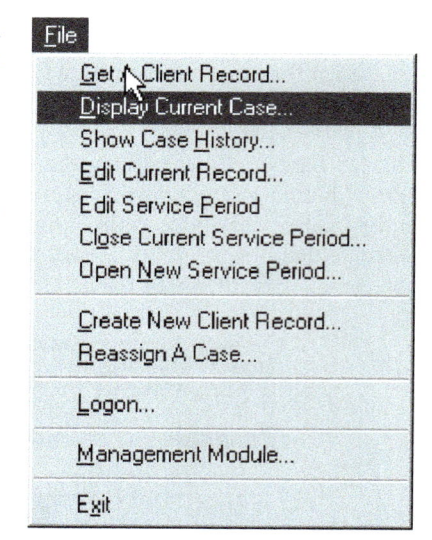

CASENOTES

Often you'll need to write, edit, and print casenotes for clients. It's possible to do this with CASS using the "Casenotes" menu.

▶ Click "Casenotes" and "Create New Casenote." (We assume that you have opened the record for Charlie.)

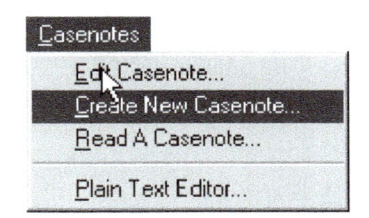

You can start typing your casenotes in the window that appears.

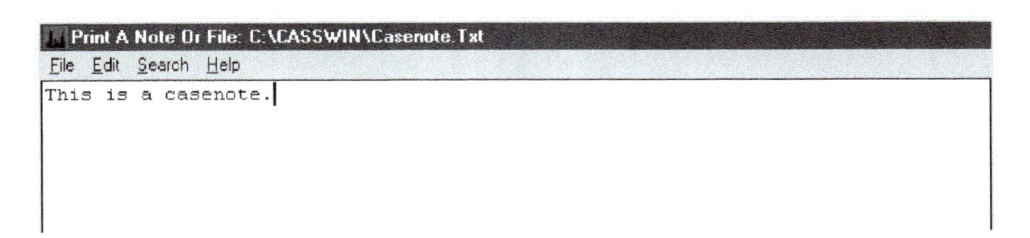

▶ Click "Edit" to do various editing tasks.

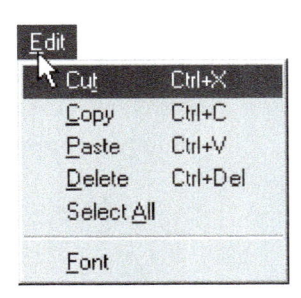

▶ Click "Search" to find or replace information in this casenote.

▶ Finally, when you're finished, click "File" to save, exit, or print your casenotes.

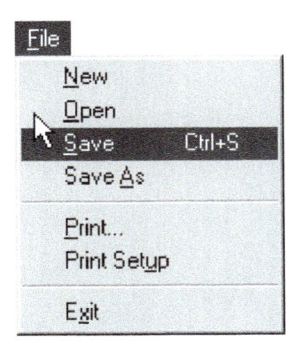

▶ After you have created and saved a casenote for a client you can then click "Casenotes" and edit or read that casenote, or edit it using any word processor.

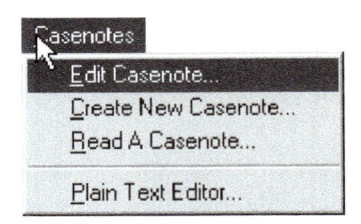

If you have any trouble printing a window in CASS (or any other program), use the following "Print Screen" procedure.

1. Hit the "Print Screen" key on your computer keyboard (usually the upper right row of keys).
2. Click "OK" if a message pops up telling you that you're copying the page.
3. Exit CASS (or CAAP).
4. Open your word processing program (e.g., MS Word).

5. Hit "Edit" then "Paste."
6. Hit "File" then "Print."

Returning to Casenotes

Saving Casenotes
1. Click "File."
2. Click "Save As."
3. In the "Save As" window, enter the file name for the casenote (e.g., "MaryTest" for SAMPLE1).
4. Click "OK."

WARNING: You can only write one casenote per case per day because the notes are tracked by date.

Retrieving and Editing Casenotes
1. Open the client record.
2. Click "Casenotes" (at top).
3. Click "Edit Casenote."
4. The next window is "Select a Service Period." Click on service period, then click "OK." The casenote you click on will appear.
5. Make your corrections, then click "File" and "Save."
6. Click "File," then "Exit."
7. "Store a Finished Casenote" window will appear.
8. Enter the title of your casenote (e.g., MaryTest), then click "OK."
9. Click "Store It."

If Locked Out (e.g., "Case Record in Use" message)
1. Click "File."
2. Click "Management Module."
3. Click "Utilities."
4. Click option to "Unlock A Client Record."
5. Click "Unlock" on "Unlock A Client Record" window.

TASK MANAGEMENT

Practitioners often ask clients to do "homework." CASS lets you specify and track these service tasks. This is a very important feature of CASS because it adds to every practitioner's accountability.

▶ Click "Service Tasks" and "Task Completion Review."

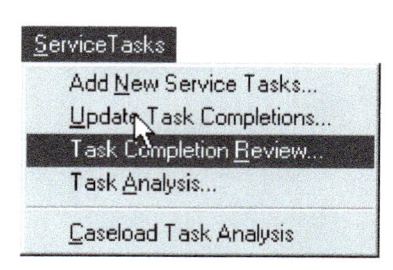

The "All Tasks For This Case" list appears.

▶ Click "Close" to return to the start screen.

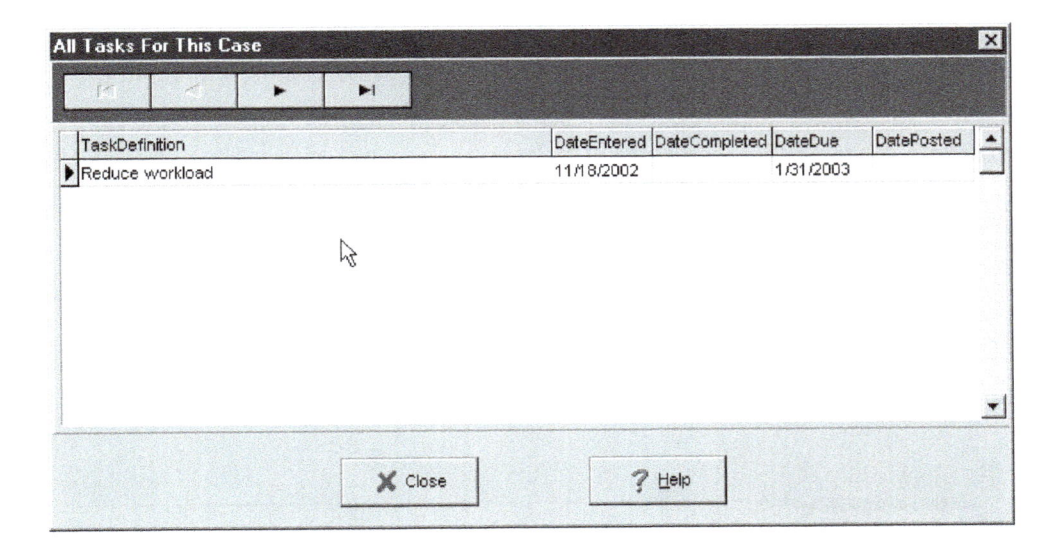

▶ Click "Service Tasks" and "Task Analysis."

The "Task Analysis For This Case" information appears. We encourage you to try all aspects of this task management function of CASS. It will add to your pleasure of discovery and accomplishment, while giving you additional tools to help you become an accountable professional.

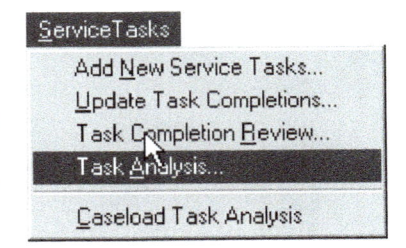

▶ Click "Close" to return to the start screen.

Note: If you click on "Add New Service Tasks" when you want to add a new activity, be sure to use the full year when CASS requires the date (e.g., "2003," not "03.")

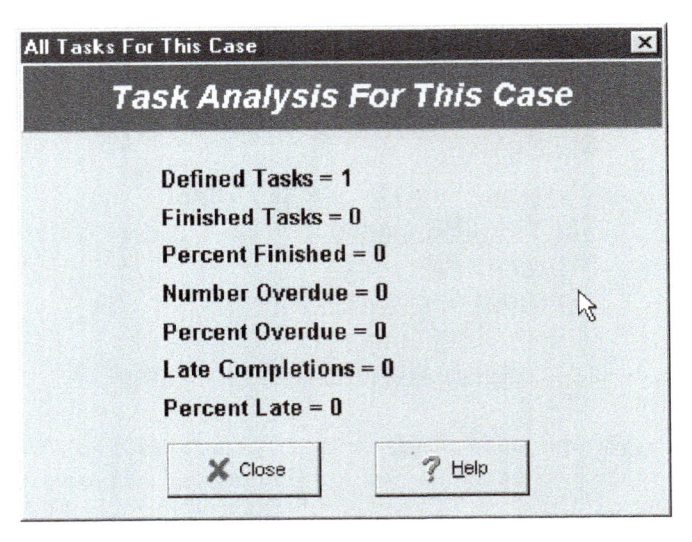

WARNING Once an open service period is closed, you cannot change any of the information in it. You can review the information, but you cannot change it. Be sure to check all information in an open service period for correctness and accuracy before closing it.

ONLINE HELP

Online, context-sensitive help is available at many places in CASS, as you've already seen. Also, it's possible to get help with a wide range of topics and to print this information.

▸ Click "Help" and "CASS Help."

The table of contents appears.

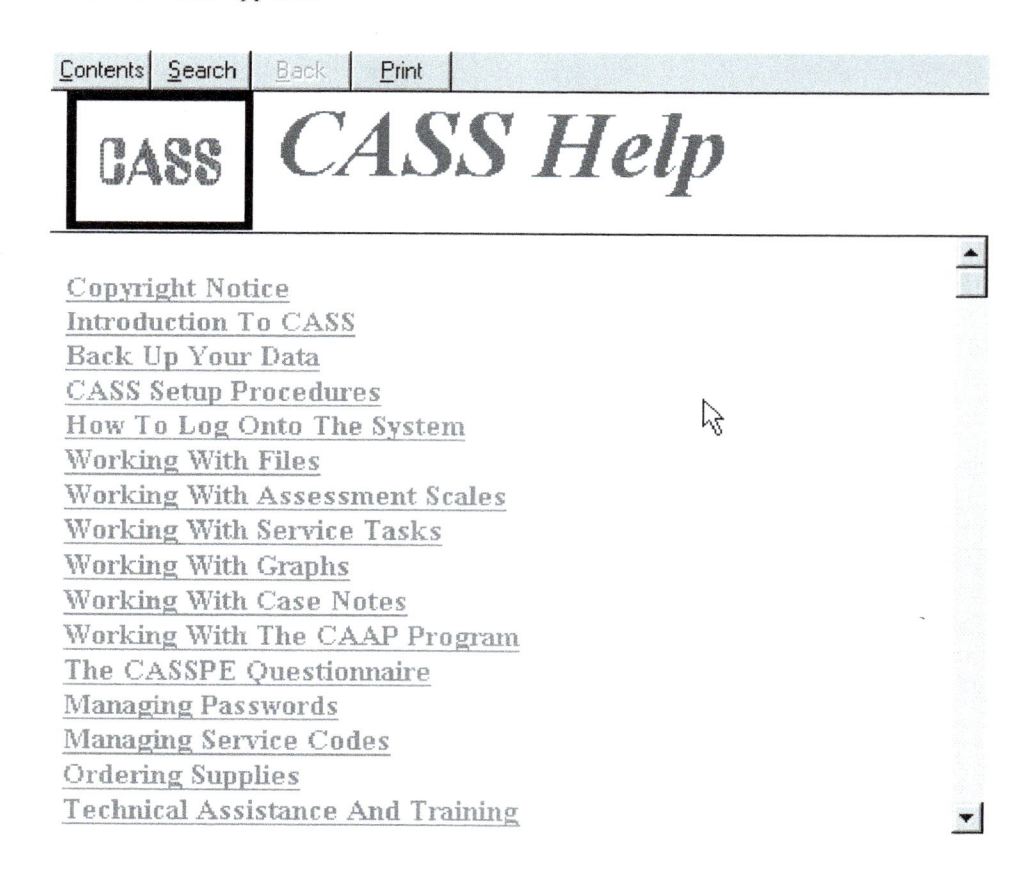

We urge you to open these help files and read at least the first six topics before attempting to use the CASS program. You will find most of the procedures explained and your questions answered in advance. This will greatly facilitate your use of CASS.

When you locate a "Help" topic, move the arrow to it, click, and more detailed information about that topic appears. For example, click "Back Up Your Data" and the following window appears. You can explore how to back up your data by clicking on "Contents."

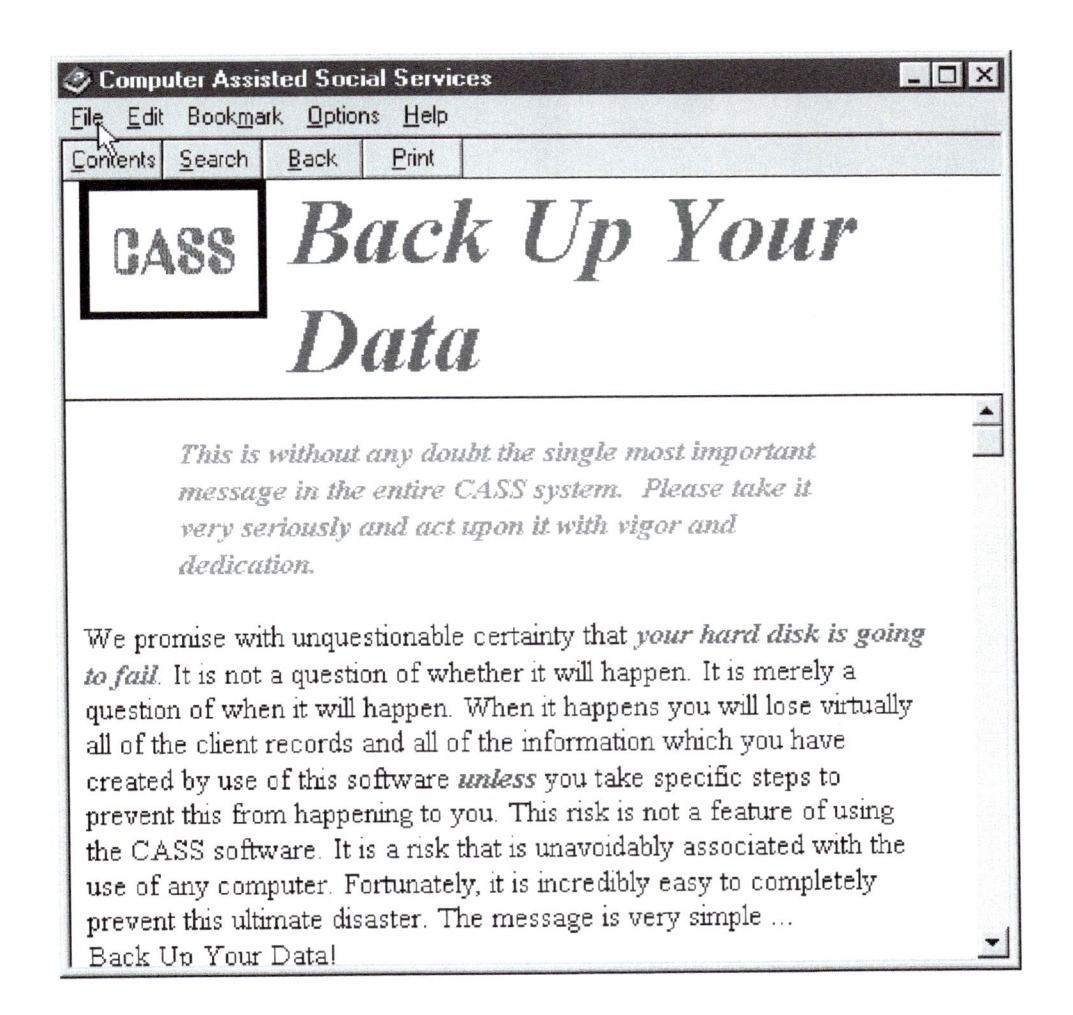

▸ Click "Print" if you want to print this information. Click "Contents" if you want to return to the table of contents. Click "Search" if you want to search for a particular topic. Click the "X" in the upper right-hand corner when you're ready to return to the start screen.

USING THE MANAGEMENT MODULE

CASS lets you change the appearance of scale menus, add new scales, and prepare different types of order forms and correspondence to the publisher. The "Management Module" is used for these tasks. (Please note that some aspects of the "Management Module" were not functioning at the time of publication.)

▶ Click "File" and "Management Module."

The "Manager's Module" screen (not shown) appears.

▶ Click "Scales" and a menu appears.

This menu is used to edit scale menus and to add new scales.

▶ Click "Utilities" and another menu appears.

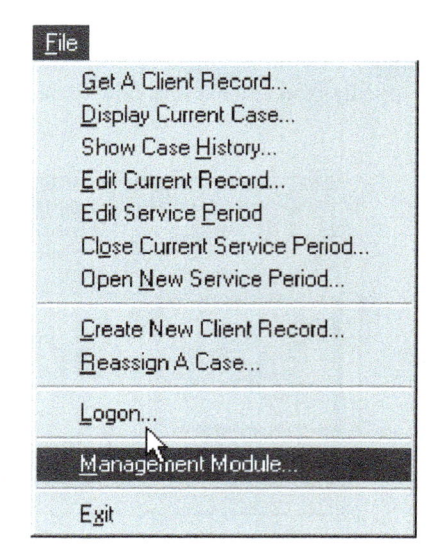

This menu is used to write a letter to the publisher, show a list of people in your agency permitted to use this software, define and keep track of the types and frequency of services provided to clients, define and manage the service tasks used (e.g., homework assignments), and unlock closed client records.

▶ Click "Supplies" and a menu appears.

To use CAAP to administer a scale to a client, and to use CASS to score this scale, you must purchase a "scoring credit" from the publisher. However, the program comes with some scoring credits for a selected number of scales. When you order additional scoring credits, use CASS to prepare the order form. Then mail or fax that order form to the publisher, WALMYR (the address is in the Appendix to this guide). They will then send you an unlocking code. This menu is used to determine the number of available credits, to order credits, to get a list of available scales and their costs, to install the credits, and to keep track of all of this. (*Note:* At the time of publication of this edition, these credits were not available. Hopefully, they will be available in the future.)

▶ Click "Supplies" and "Display Scale Scoring Credits" to get a list of the available scales and the number of existing scoring credits for each scale.

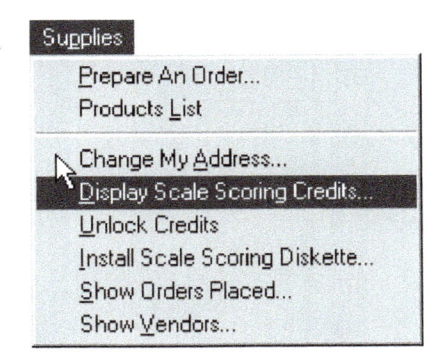

Supplies
- Prepare An Order...
- Products List
- Change My Address...
- Display Scale Scoring Credits...
- Unlock Credits
- Install Scale Scoring Diskette...
- Show Orders Placed...
- Show Vendors...

▶ Click the down (▼) and up (▲) arrows on the window to scroll through this list.

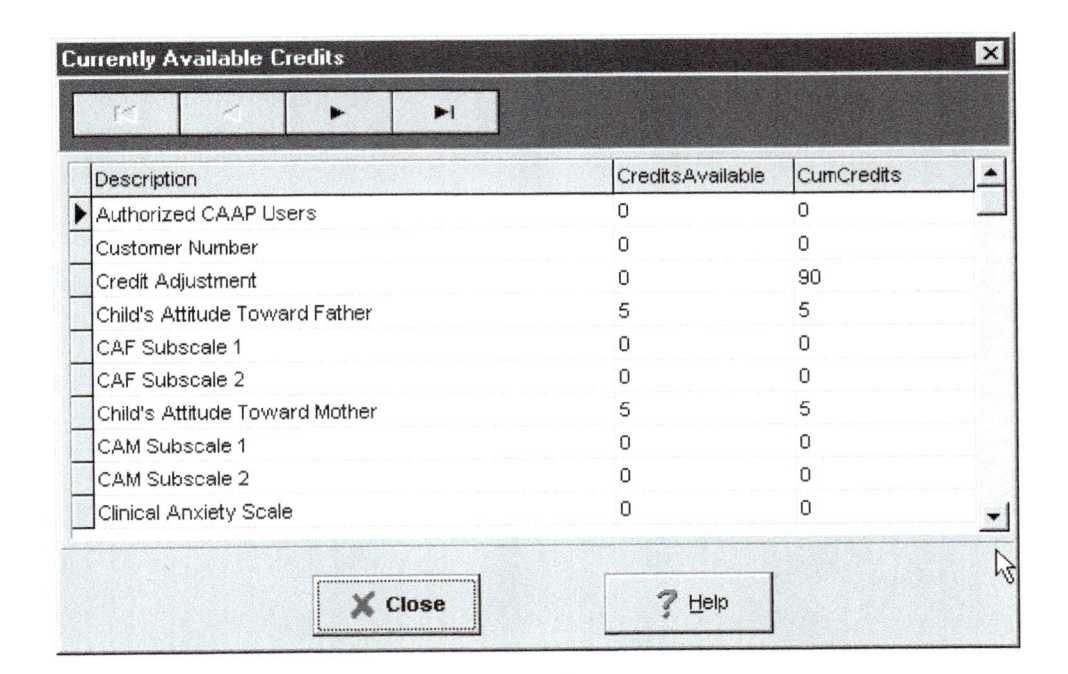

Currently Available Credits

Description	CreditsAvailable	CumCredits
Authorized CAAP Users	0	0
Customer Number	0	0
Credit Adjustment	0	90
Child's Attitude Toward Father	5	5
CAF Subscale 1	0	0
CAF Subscale 2	0	0
Child's Attitude Toward Mother	5	5
CAM Subscale 1	0	0
CAM Subscale 2	0	0
Clinical Anxiety Scale	0	0

[Close] [Help]

▶ Click "Close" to close this window and return to the "Manager's Module" window (not shown).
▶ Click "Exit" to return to the start screen.

EXITING CASS

▶ Click "File" and "Exit" to exit the program.

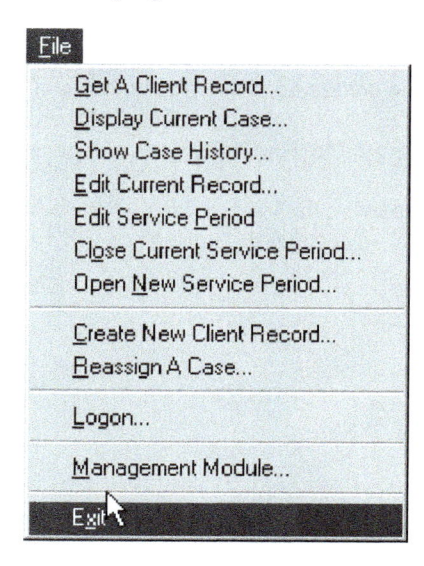

APPENDIX: INSTALLING CASS

DOWNLOADING CASS/CAAP FROM THE INTERNET

CASS and CAAP also can be downloaded from the Internet at the site for this book. Follow these steps:

1. Go to www.pearsonhighered.com/bloom.
2. Click on "CASS."
3. In the first window, click on the "New Folder" icon on the tool bar.
4. Click on "Open" in the next window.
5. Follow the instructions for downloading.
6. Repeat for CAAP.
7. Install both programs. Follow the installation instructions on the computer.

WARNING: Once you have installed the CASS software and it is working properly, you should never reinstall it. To do so will wipe out all of your client data because a full reinstall will replace all of your data tables with the ones supplied by the software.

▶   Insert the CD that came with the book. Wait until the following window appears, then click "Install CASS."

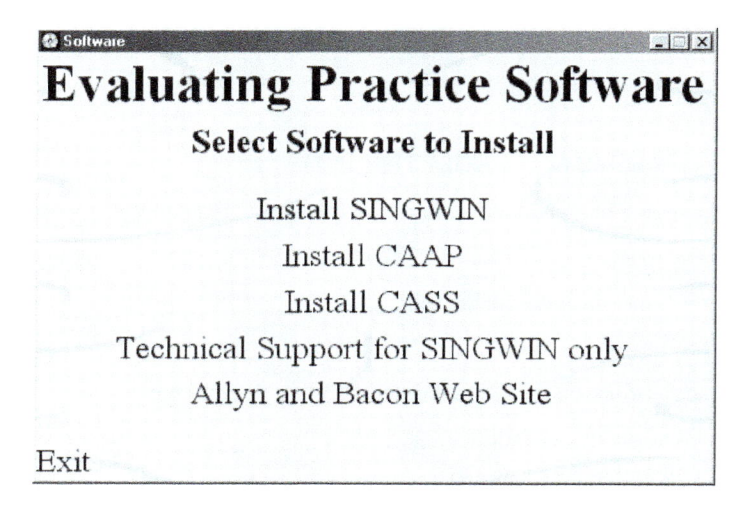

Evaluating Practice Software
Select Software to Install

Install SINGWIN
Install CAAP
Install CASS
Technical Support for SINGWIN only
Allyn and Bacon Web Site

Exit

▶   Click "Yes" in response to the confirmation question.

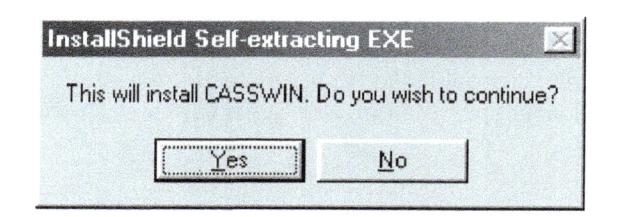

InstallShield Self-extracting EXE
This will install CASSWIN. Do you wish to continue?
Yes   No

▶   Click "Next" at each of the subsequent windows until you reach the "User Information" window. Enter your name and company (or school or agency) in the appropriate boxes and then click "Next."

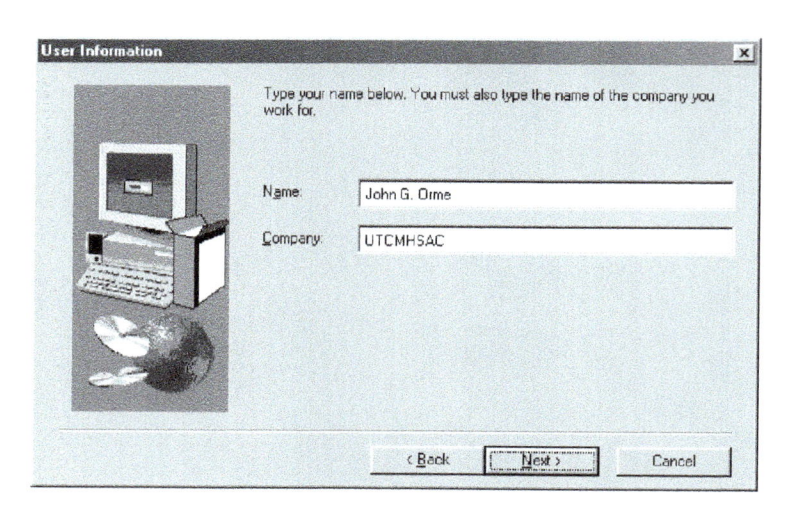

User Information
Type your name below. You must also type the name of the company you work for.

Name: John G. Orme
Company: UTCMHSAC

▸ Click "Next" at each subsequent window until you reach the "Setup Complete" window. Click "Finish" on this window.

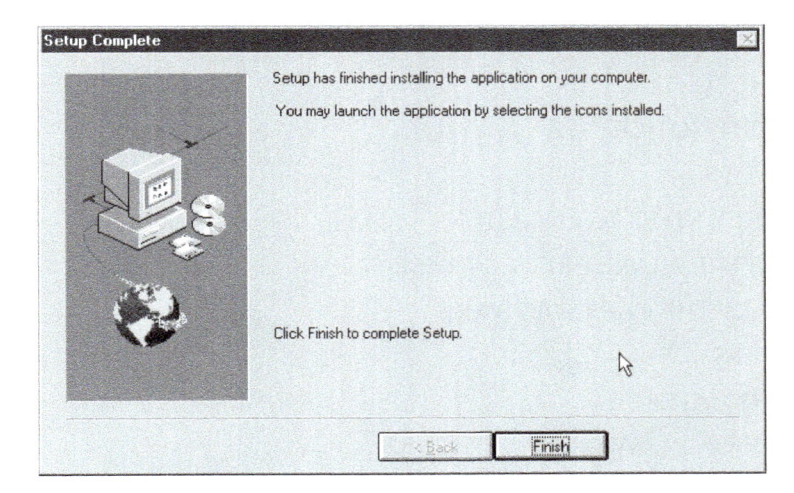

▸ Move the cursor to "CASSWIN." Hold down the left mouse button and drag the icon (the night scene) to your desktop. This will create a shortcut on your desktop for easy access to CASS. Then click the "X" in the top right corner of the screen.

▸ To install CAAP, repeat the prior steps, but click "Install CAAP" in place of "Install CASS." You also can drag the CAAP icon (the clasped hands) to your desktop.

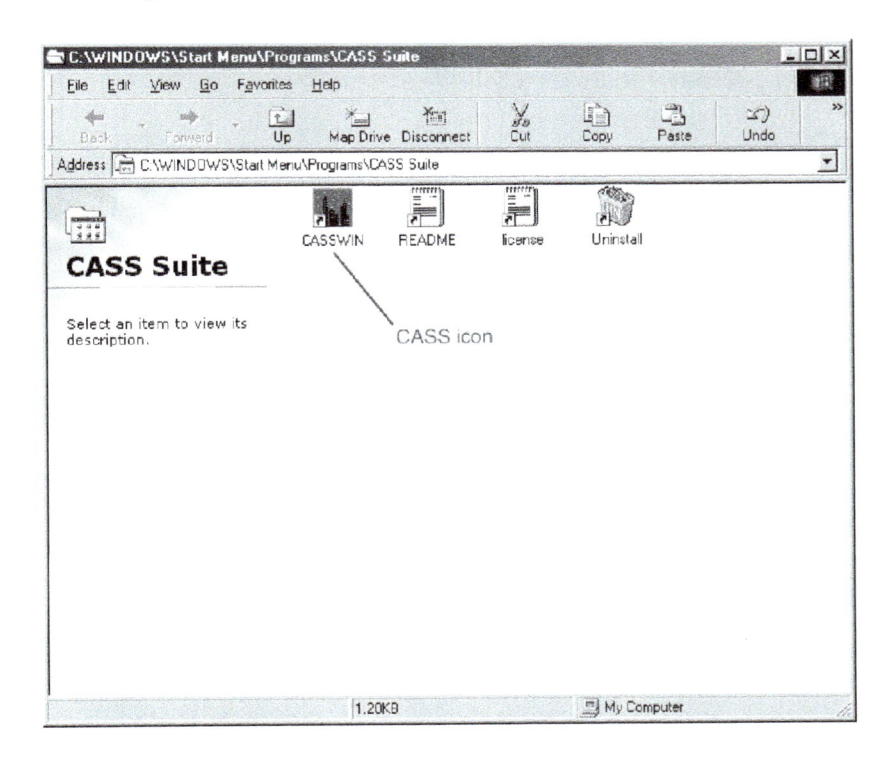

INTRODUCTION TO USING CASS (REPRINTED FROM CASS)

Urgent! Read This Entire File Before Using CASS

1. WELCOME TO CASS
2. COPYRIGHT NOTICE
3. LEGAL NOTICE
4. SOFTWARE AND FILES LOCATIONS
5. LOADING THE SHARE.EXE PROGRAM
6. SETTING UP THE CASS SOFTWARE
7. NEXT STEPS
8. TRAINING MATERIALS
9. YOUR LOGON PASSWORD
10. NETWORK INSTALLATION

1. WELCOME TO CASS

When you install and begin using the Computer Assisted Social Services or CASS software, we believe you will then have the world's premier computer-based case management, quality assurance, and applied measurement package at your fingertips.

This version of the CASS software is provided to you without fee in order to help you get the most out of the client assessment scales that you purchase from our company.

You can order assessment scales at the following address:
WALMYR Publishing Co.
P.O. Box 12217
Tallahassee, FL 32317-2217
Voice: (850) 383-0045
Fax: (850) 383-0970
Email: Walmyr@Walmyr.com
Internet: www.walmyr.com

Scoring Assessment Scales

The CASS software will enable you to score WALMYR's commercial assessment scales and store the results in your client records. A number of these scales are included in the program for several trial uses. However, in order to continue to use these features of the system, you must purchase additional commercial assessment scales that you wish to use with your clients. It is illegal to copy or reproduce copyrighted commercial assessment scales.

2. COPYRIGHT NOTICE

The Computer Assisted Social Services (also known as the CASS software) is copyrighted, produced, and distributed by the WALMYR Publishing Company. You may copy and distribute this version of the software provided you make exact copies of the original distribution diskettes, you do not sell the software, you do not charge any fees for its use, and you do not make any changes of any kind to the software or its documentation. You may not copy or distribute any upgrade diskettes that are later sent to you by the publisher.

The Computer Assisted Social Services (CASS) software is owned and copyrighted by the WALMYR Publishing Company, all rights are reserved, and use of the software does not imply ownership in any manner or kind.

The WALMYR Publishing Company reserves the right to deny use and to refuse continued support of the software to any and all who do not abide by the terms and conditions of its use.

3. LEGAL NOTICE

Any attempt to install or use scale scoring credits without prior purchase of the appropriate assessment scales will constitute an injury to our company and a violation of copyright law. Such violations will result in immediate termination of all rights to use the CASS software and will expose the violator to the pursuit of legal damages through civil and criminal remedies.

4. SOFTWARE AND FILES LOCATIONS

An important feature of the CASS software is that you can use it on a free-standing personal computer and you can it use on a Local Area Network (LAN) system. This copy of the software is designed for use on a free-standing personal computer. Please call or write WALMYR Publishing Company if you wish to install and use the CASS software on a Local Area Network.

Where Things Are Stored

Once you install the CASS software, it is important for you to know where it will be stored on your computer. The CASS installation procedure will create a new directory on your hard disk, and it will be named \CASSWIN. All of the CASS software will be placed inside the \CASSWIN directory and any necessary subdirectories.

Although the installation program permits you to use a different directory, we strongly urge you to use \CASSWIN. It can lead to considerable additional work, errors, and frustration on your part if you do not use the defaults supplied by the publisher.

5. SETTING UP THE CASS SOFTWARE

Once you have installed the CASS software on your computer system, it is ready for use. However, there is some important setup work to be done for your agency or practice that should be performed before you begin using the software with your clients. Please call up the online CASS Help and be sure to read the first three or four help topics.

6. NEXT STEPS

If you have not yet installed the CASS software on your computer system, by all means do so now. Once you complete the installation of the software it will be ready for use by you and your colleagues. You will quickly discover how easy it is to use any of the major features of the system. However, every new software tool is a confrontation of new mysteries about how to best use it. We offer the following as suggestions for solving those mysteries.

7. TRAINING MATERIALS

The minimum training materials needed to learn how to use the CASS software are now available to you. They consist of this file and the CASS online Help system. However, if you or your employees are not familiar with our assessment scales or have not previously used standardized assessment tools in practice, your training needs will be much larger. We recommend that you acquire a copy of each of the following documents for yourself and your trainers. Once you and your trainers have read and evaluated them, you can decide which of them should be provided to each employee.

Hudson, W. W., & Faul, A. C. (1998). *The WALMYR Assessment System*. Tallahassee, FL: WALMYR Publishing Co. This text may be ordered directly from within the supplies option of the CASS Manager's Module.

Nugent, W. R., Sieppert, J. D., & Hudson, W. W. (2001). *Practice Evaluation for the 21st Century*. Belmont, CA: Brooks/Cole Publishing Co.

Nurius, P. S., & Hudson, W. W. (1993). *Human Services Practice, Evaluation and Computers: A Practical Guide For Today and Beyond*. Pacific Grove, CA: Brooks/Cole Publishing Co. This text may be acquired by calling (800) 354-0092 or (408) 373-0728.

The MPSI Technical Manual. (1990). Tempe, AZ: The WALMYR Publishing Co. This manual may be ordered directly from within the supplies option of the CASS Manager's Module.

The FASI Technical Manual. (1990). Tempe, AZ: The WALMYR Publishing Co. This manual may be ordered directly from within the supplies option of the CASS Manager's Module.

WALMYR Assessment Scale Scoring Manual. (1990). Tempe, AZ: The WALMYR Publishing Co. This manual may be ordered directly from within the supplies option of the CASS Manager's Module.

You should also know that the initial database that is provided when you install the CASS software contains two sample cases; their case numbers are SAMPLE1 and SAMPLE2. These two cases can be used for demonstrations and training and to test the performance of the software.

We suggest you call up the SAMPLE1 case, select the open service period (Period 3), and then explore that case. For example, if you graph the ICS scores for Susan-Test, you will see a nice single-system design graph.

8. YOUR LOGON PASSWORD

When you call up the CASS program you will be asked to enter your User ID and Password. These are "*walmyr*" and "*scales*," respectively (don't enter the quotes). The User ID and Password must be entered as *all lowercase* letters.

9. NETWORK INSTALLATION

Instructions for installing CASS on a local area network can be found in the file named CASSNET.TXT. Please read and print that file if you wish to install the software on your network.

BEHAVIORAL OBSERVATION

PURPOSE The purpose of this chapter is to teach you how to observe and record overt and covert behaviors using direct observation (i.e., observation by practitioners, relevant others, or independent observers) and self-monitoring (i.e., a person's observation of his or her own behavior). We describe some general guidelines and methods for both types of behavioral observation, and show you how to ensure that the observations are valid and reliable. We also discuss in detail methods of recording behavior—particularly frequency, duration, and interval recording. Because the observation of behavior is often the most direct and valid measure of a target, it should be given high priority as a measurement method.

Introduction
    Behavioral Observation
General Guidelines for Behavioral Observation
Sampling Behaviors
    Continuous Recording
    Recording Samples
        Time Samples
        Client Samples
        Situation Samples
    Rates
Instruments for Recording Behaviors
    Principles for Selecting Instruments
    Some Instruments for Your Use
Ensuring Accurate Observations
    Maximizing the Reliability and Validity of Observations
    Verifying Reliability
    Verifying Validity
Methods of Recording Behavior
    Frequency
        Establishing Reliability
    Duration
        Establishing Reliability
    Interval Recording
        Establishing Reliability
    Additional Considerations with Interobserver Reliability
Analogue Situations
Recording Behavior in Groups
Summary

From Chapter 5 of *Evaluating Practice: Guidelines for the Accountable Professional*, Sixth Edition. Martin Bloom, Joel Fischer, John G. Orme. Copyright © 2009 by Pearson Education, Inc. All rights reserved.

INTRODUCTION

Most practitioners in human services hope to achieve through their efforts a change in someone's behavior, either directly or indirectly. Few are satisfied if the changes achieved fail to include changes in the actual behavior of people or organizations.

The range of behaviors practitioners try to change in their diverse practices is immense. These include, for example, developmentally inappropriate and maladaptive inattention, impulsivity, and hyperactivity (ADHD); flashbacks, avoidance, and emotional restriction (PTSD); and maladaptive rituals and thoughts (OCD). They also include enuresis; binge eating; purging; self-injurious thoughts and behaviors; panic attacks; problematic avoidance of certain situations; difficulty sleeping or problems with sleeping too much; reciprocity of positive and negative behaviors exchanged between partners; expressions of criticism and contempt; bullying, fighting, and other forms of physical aggression; truancy; homework completion; property destruction; theft; excessive alcohol consumption; illegal drug use; and driving while intoxicated. Many practitioners also deal with spousal abuse, sexual abuse, animal abuse, and other forms of violence. Also, in many contexts, compliance with interventions is an important issue, and compliance behaviors include medication adherence, attendance at AA meetings, and attendance at parenting classes mandated for parents with children in foster care, to name just a few examples. The potential list of behaviors encountered by practitioners is almost endless.

Yet, many times when practitioners go about evaluating how successful their programs are, they fail to measure carefully whether the behaviors with which they are concerned actually do change. Sometimes this is because, while they hope for behavioral change, much of their practice is not focused on behaviors. They often don't specifically intervene with behaviors, so that behavioral change becomes more of a by-product of intervention than a direct focus of intervention. Other times, they don't measure behavioral change because it's too complicated, too time-consuming, or too difficult, or because they haven't been able to observe or record the behavior accurately. However, measuring behavior is one of the most important ways of monitoring and evaluating practice. It also can be one of the best indicators of success.

What we really are talking about here are validity, reliability, and directness of measures. The observation of behavior is often the most valid method you can use because behaviors typically are the most direct expression of a client's concerns. Once these target behaviors are changed and no other target behaviors emerge to take their place, the practitioner and client have the best, most direct way of assessing their success. It would be difficult indeed to consider a case successfully terminated if other dimensions of a target appear to be changed, but the problematic target behaviors still exist. Because behavioral observation ideally occurs in the setting in which change ultimately is desired, the client's natural environment, it is indeed a direct method.

Similarly, behaviors used as outcome measures have a particularly good chance of being recorded accurately because they lend themselves well to clear, precise, and specific definitions. Therefore, the use of behavioral observation ranks highly on a hierarchy of potential methods because behaviors can be our most *accurate* indicators of success (e.g., see Crosland et al., 2008, and Van Camp, et al., 2008, for good examples of defining parenting behaviors).

In addition to their value as potentially accurate indicators of outcome, the use of behaviors has special advantages for practice. Because behaviors lend themselves well to precise definition, they have particular advantages for assessment. Clearly pinpointing a behavior as a target for change allows easier determination of possible factors affecting the target. It becomes easier to pinpoint what occurs before and after the target problem occurs and to examine any controlling effects these occurrences have on the target. Once a behavior is specifically defined, it becomes easier to determine information about the who, what, when, and where, conditions of the occurrence of the target, all of which are necessary for a complete assessment.

To be sure, many types of changes are important, and there are other ways of measuring success besides behaviors. Four of the important guidelines for the selection of outcome measures are: (1) how direct an indicator of the target is the measure, (2) how reliably can it be measured, (3) how valid is it, and (4) can it contribute to a beneficial outcome? We believe that, in many instances, the use of behaviors can meet all of these criteria. Add to this some of the advantages for assessment, and we therefore would suggest that the first method you should consider in evaluating practice is the observation of behaviors.

If all of this sounds a little bit too "behavioral," read on. We think that the way we define behavior will ease some of the suspicions you may have that when we're talking about behaviors, we're being so concrete, narrow, or specific that we're ruling out a good deal of relevant human activity. Perhaps you might even feel that this perspective is linked to only certain theoretical orientations, such as behavior modification and therapy. This is not what we're trying to do. In fact, in the sense in which we use the term behavior, we believe that it is directly relevant to practitioners across the whole range of theoretical orientations and approaches to practice.

Behavioral Observation

Behavior refers to what people *do* (e.g., time spent with spouse), in contrast to what people *have* (e.g., depression). Behavior includes how people move and what they think and feel (Cooper, Heron, & Heward, 2007; Kennedy, 2005; Friman, 2009). This encompasses a wide range of human activities. These, of course, include *overt* events—events that can be observed by others (at least theoretically)—such as the amount of time a client spends with his or her spouse or children; the number of times a client has sexual intercourse; the number of completed intervention tasks; the amount of time nursing home residents spend interacting with one another; the number of times a parent compliments his or her child; or the number of office, home, or telephone contacts with clients. But behaviors also include *covert* events—events that occur within the individual and therefore cannot be observed by others, at least directly—such as the number of self-deprecating thoughts; the amount of time spent feeling anxious, under stress, or overwhelmed; or the amount of time spent ruminating about some concern. Therefore, *behavior* includes just about all human activities, which should provide a sufficiently broad range of behaviors to suit practitioners from just about every theoretical orientation. The key is, to be considered a behavior, it must be *observable and measurable by someone*, whether that be the client (e.g., with thoughts) or an external observer.

Another aspect of behavioral observation has to do with who observes and records the behavior. People can observe their own behavior whether it's overt or covert. When a person observes and records his or her own behavior it's called *self-monitoring* (Cooper, Heron, & Heward, 2007; Sigmon & LaMattina, 2006). Outside observers (e.g., independent observers, relevant others, practitioners) can only observe overt behaviors directly. Observation by outside observers usually is called *direct observation* (Cooper, Heron, & Heward, 2007; Friman, 2009). Many of the principles and practices of behavioral observation apply to both direct observation and self-monitoring, but some don't, and we'll draw distinctions between these two methods where applicable (for a comprehensive discussion of behavioral observation see Cooper, Heron, & Heward, 2007).

Whether a behavior is overt or covert, or whether direct observation or self-monitoring is used, behavioral observation most often relies on counting behaviors. Therefore, in this chapter we talk quite a bit about counting. By *counting* we mean simply adding up the total amount of behavior. Again, we prefer a broad definition of counting to include how often some behavior occurs (its *frequency*), or how long it occurs (its *duration*). These are two important ways of counting behaviors that we describe later in this chapter, along with a way of estimating the relative frequency and duration of behaviors (called *interval* recording).

For now, we hope you have the idea that the types of behavior to which we're referring and the ways of counting and recording them include a broad range of human functioning and practice interests. Behavioral observation need not be at all mechanistic or unduly restrictive. In fact, behavioral observation can be a fruitful strategy for monitoring and evaluating practice.

Behavioral observation is not without problems. A host of issues can arise when considering whether to observe behaviors, particularly when direct observation is used in the "natural environment" (as opposed to, say, a closed or controlled environment like a hospital ward). Some of these issues have been discussed by Cooper, Heron, and Heward (2007) and Friman (2009). First, it's possible that an outside observer's presence may affect the situation in some way, thereby producing an invalid sample of behavior (i.e., by changing the typical sequence of events). This is the reactive effect. For example, a parent is less likely to use harsh discipline with his or her child in the presence of a social worker.

Second, in an open setting, with clients moving about freely, it's often difficult to observe accurately, which has led some practitioners to resort to artificial restrictions on the behavior of the people they're observing. Third, observing behaviors in the natural environment may be both costly and impractical. Finally, because the observer (hypothetically) has no control over the environment, a whole host of temporary events may have some effect on the behavior so that the conditions of data collection could vary across observations. This would mean that it might be necessary to collect data many times to obtain clear, accurate, and consistent measures of the target.

Self-monitoring avoids some of the problems of direct observation (Cooper, Heron, & Heward, 2007; Sigmon & LaMattina, 2006). Like behavioral observation, but in contrast to self-report scales, observation occurs close in time to the occurrence of the behavior and in the context in which the behavior occurred. Also, self-monitoring is a relatively inexpensive and efficient way to measure behavior, and it can be used to measure a wide range of behaviors, including covert behaviors. Also, self-monitoring has the added benefit of increasing the client's awareness of his behaviors and the circumstances in which it occurs, and this in itself can change behavior in a beneficial direction.

However, self-monitoring is not without its own problems. Some of these issues have been discussed by Sigmon and LaMattina (2006) and Cooper, Heron, and Heward (2007). In particular, the act of self-monitoring can lead to changes in the behavior being monitored; that is, like behavior observation by others, self-monitoring also can be reactive. Although the reactive effects of self-monitoring tend to be short-lived, they can still make it difficult to evaluate change over time due to an intervention. Also, sometimes clients are unwilling or unable to monitor their own behaviors accurately. Finally, it's difficult to verify the reliability with which covert behaviors or private overt behaviors (e.g., sexual behaviors) are self-monitored. The direct observation of publicly observable overt behaviors makes it easier to determine the reliability of the observations (e.g., two or more observers can observe the behaviors and their agreement can be determined). However, we don't believe that targets should be selected only because they can be reliably measured, ignoring whether they're the most relevant targets for the client's functioning. As long as it can be observed somehow, any behavior can be considered a potential focus of intervention.

On the other hand, we believe that these problems can be minimized by taking the precautions we suggest in this chapter, by using the resources of the natural environment, and by keeping the observational process as simple as possible. Putting all these suggestions together, we believe that you should place a high priority on behavioral observation to evaluate your practice.

Finally, we encourage you to review some of the work on the use of technology in behavioral observation. Richard and Gloster (2006) provide an excellent overall discussion of the use of technology in behavioral observation, and a good list of Internet sites with behavioral assessment resources. Ice (2004) provides discussion of recent technological advances in observational data collection and some of the hardware and software available for behavioral observation. Finally, Dixon (2003) describes and illustrates how to create a customized portable data collection system with Microsoft Embedded Visual Tools for the Pocket PC.

GENERAL GUIDELINES FOR BEHAVIORAL OBSERVATION

Many of the general guidelines for observation and recording described in these chapters apply directly to behavioral observation, as well as to all the other methods of measurement. Briefly, as a review, there are several steps to follow in developing your behavioral observation plan:

1. *Conduct a preliminary assessment.* Review the client's concerns. Gather enough information to give you a feel for the range of targets with which the client may wish to work. Begin helping the client focus on a workable area.

2. *Specify targets.* This is a most crucial concern in observing behaviors. Select targets that are personally, interpersonally, organizationally, or socially significant and potentially changeable. Try to identify discrete indicators for the target. For example, if the client states a concern in terms of vague attributes, motives, or other conditions, try to translate this into discrete events (what is he doing when he is acting "strange"?). Think about each target in terms of pinpointing it into "units

of behavior" that can be observed and counted. In order to facilitate an accurate count, each of these behavioral units can be defined as a cycle that has a beginning and an end. Be as specific as possible. Each behavior unit can be defined in terms of either how often it occurs (its frequency) or how long it occurs (its duration). (We describe these types of recording methods in more detail later in this chapter.) Think about each target in terms of who is doing what, to what extent, and under what conditions. Remember, though, you're still defining the target. You may not develop the goal until much later in the process, for example, after baseline data are collected. However, generally, goals are closely related to targets; for example, feelings of depression might be the target, and the reduction of these feelings the goal.

3. *Decide how many behaviors to record.* Keep the procedure simple. You don't want to frustrate or confuse whoever is doing the recording. As a general guideline, don't expect people to record more than one or two behaviors, especially when the recorders are clients or relevant others. Of course, a person may record several aspects of some behavior. For example, a husband may record not only how many times he loses his temper, but also with whom he loses his temper, when, where, and so on.

4. *Decide who should collect the data.* Essentially, you have four choices here: the client, yourself, a relevant other, or an independent observer. Each of the choices has clear advantages and disadvantages. The primary guideline perhaps is that the observer must be *able* to record; he or she must be present when the behavior occurs and be able to observe it. Sometimes only one person meets this criterion (e.g., the client must record his or her own covert behaviors), and then your decision is clear.

5. *Decide when and where to record.* You have two choices here, continuous recording or sampling. Continuous recording involves observing each occurrence of a target every time it occurs. Sampling involves observing target behaviors for a sample of clients, situations, or times, depending on the information you need. The key principle of sampling is to try to get a representative picture of the occurrence of the behavior. What-

ever type of sample is collected, though, you should try to standardize the time, place, and method used to observe, or it will be difficult to evaluate change over time. Establish clear and consistent guidelines regarding who, what, when, and where behavior is observed. (We discuss sampling issues in more detail in the following sections.)

6. *Train the observer.* It would make little sense to go through all these elaborate preparations if the person who is to do the recording is not trained sufficiently. Make sure the behavior is clearly defined for the observer, and that the observer knows whose behavior is to be recorded, how it's to be recorded, when, where, and for how long. For example, a teacher who is recording a sample of disruptive behavior by a student should be certain to arrange to observe the child clearly (in order to ascertain who is shouting), what behaviors are considered disruptive (e.g., shouting, hitting other children), where to observe (in the classroom and halls only), and for how long (say, 9:00 AM to 10:00 AM).

If possible, try to role-play or practice making the observations until the observer is comfortable and accurate. Try to develop one or two trial observation sessions in which the observer attempts to record the actual behavior. Then the observer can discuss with you any necessary revisions in the observational system, and the necessary revisions can be made.

7. *View behavior broadly.* To make this a more systematic process, build into your recording system methods for recording when and where a target behavior occurs and what happens after it occurs. This will allow you to evaluate environmental factors that might be affecting the target. Similarly, on whatever form you do decide to use to record information, you can simply add extra columns

to record the behavior, what happened right before, and what happened right after, as in Figure 1. (This and all of the behavioral observation forms discussed and illustrated in this chapter are in the "Word Documents" folder on your CD-ROM. Feel free to use and modify these as needed.) Most word processing programs allow you to easily create such forms. Be sure you give clear instructions as to what is to be placed in those columns, especially that the recording be brief and that it include what happens immediately before and after the behavior occurs. Finally, increasingly, computer hardware (desktop and handheld computers and Personal Digital Assistants [PDAs]) and software are available for the direct observation of behaviors and their antecedents and consequences (Dixon, 2003; Ice, 2004; Hektner, Schmidt, & Csikszentmihalyi, 2007; Richard & Gloster, 2006; Sidener, Shabani, & Carr, 2004; Stone, Shiffman, Atienza, & Nebeling, 2007).

8. *Collect baseline data.* Once all of the prior steps have been completed, you're ready to begin collecting preintervention or baseline information. This will give you a basis for comparison with data collected during and after intervention to evaluate effectiveness. It will also be crucial for assessment because the actual level of occurrence of behavior, as well as where and when it occurs, will become clear. This will then allow you to develop a clear and specific goal statement.

SAMPLING BEHAVIORS

As we indicated in the previous section, it may not be possible to observe a behavior every time it occurs in every situation. This is especially true with direct observation, although it can be problematic with self-monitoring also. Therefore, you will have to modify your measurement plan to meet the demands of the target and situation. There are two general types of recording that focus on when to collect data:

Observer _____ Client _____

Behavior to Be Observed _____

Date _____	What Happened Before	Behavior	What Happened After
Time _____			

FIGURE 1 Form for recording behaviors, antecedents, and consequences.

continuous recording and recording involving *samples*. We discuss each of these briefly in this section, as well as what to do when the observation times or, more generally, the number of opportunities for a behavior to occur vary—the use of rates.

Continuous Recording

Continuous recording involves recording every occurrence of a *target* behavior every time it occurs. Continuous recording as we define it implies that you already have selected what behavior to observe. (We're using the term *continuous recording* in a way that's slightly different from the way it's used in some of the behavioral literature. In the behavioral literature, recording all instances of a *preselected* behavior often is called *event sampling*, and continuous recording in that literature actually means that literally *all* behaviors are observed, a difficult if not impossible task.) So, continuous recording can be used when the observer is willing and available to record every occurrence of a target behavior, and when the target doesn't occur so frequently that it would be impossible to record every occurrence.

It's virtually impossible not to preselect target behaviors for recording (the alternative would be to record everything a client did, problematic or not, all the time). Therefore, we assume that all methods of behavioral observation start with the selection of the behaviors to be observed. Thus, continuous recording requires the selection of specific target behaviors to observe. In essence, you are almost always either observing samples of the client's behaviors (e.g., just the communication aspect of a more complex marital problem and just certain times or types of communication at that) or taking samples of other events or targets that may be related to what you and the client identify as the primary target. In addition, examining only selected occurrences of targets may help you determine which target to focus on first. For example, if you're attempting to assess the program of an agency, you might start by observing a large number of different events, but eventually select only those that provide the most useful information.

A number of examples of continuous recording by clients, others in the environment, or practitioners have been collected by Gambrill (1977). Examples of continuously recorded behaviors, recorded by *clients*, include all pages of schoolwork, all times a bronchometer was used for asthmatic attacks, and all times clients failed to talk when they wished to. Examples of behaviors continuously recorded by *relevant others* include bed-wetting incidents, whines and shouts, and compliance with requests. Examples of behaviors continuously recorded by *practitioners* include who appeared at group meetings, aggressive statements, greeting responses, and verbal reinforcements between a man and a woman as counted from an audiotape.

Recording Samples

The second type of recording involves sampling times, people or clients, or situations. The key assumption here is that the sample of behavior will accurately represent all behavior that would have been recorded if the observations weren't limited. The two basic reasons to sample behavior are because (a) its more efficient than recording all behaviors, and (b) the observers, clients, or targets are not available or the behaviors don't occur all the time. However, it's important to remember that samples only provide estimates of the actual occurrence of a behavior, and these estimates are only as good as the samples.

Time Samples. The most frequently used type of sampling is time sampling. In time samples, the target is observed for only portions of time, at fixed or random times selected to collect representative information about the target (Cooper, Heron, & Heward, 2007). Time samples can be used when the observer doesn't have time to record all instances of a target, when continuous recording is simply too difficult (e.g., when the target occurs over a long period of time), when the target doesn't have a clear beginning or end (e.g., a good or bad mood), or when the target lasts for varying periods of time (e.g., panic attacks).

There are two types of time sampling. The first involves preselecting time periods and then observing whether the target is occurring at all. If it is, the observer simply records that the behavior occurred during that time period. The observer would not have to record all instances of the occurrence of the target, since this may be impractical or impossible. This type of time sampling sometimes is called *momentary time sampling* (Cooper, Heron, & Heward, 2007).

Some examples of *client-recorded* momentary time samples (from Gambrill, 1977), all of which occurred too frequently for continuous recording, are recording intensity of pain every half-hour, recording the occurrence of positive self-thoughts every 2 hours, and recording obsessive thoughts that occur regularly by noting their presence (or absence) every hour. With this method, only selected occurrences are reported (e.g., if any at all occur during a 2-hour period, a check could be placed on a piece of paper that is divided up into 2-hour time periods). An example of a *relevant other* momentary time sample would be a parent recording a child's studying during selected periods of time. An example of a *practitioner* momentary time sample involves making a certain number of observations on each patient in a hospital per day to see if some target or behavior is occurring at all, say, in a situation where the target occurred frequently enough that it would be impossible to count all instances of its occurrence. An example of a form for time-sample recording, on which a check is placed in the appropriate box if the behavior is occurring during each observation interval, is presented in Figure 2.

When momentary time sampling is used, the most desirable method is to preselect times during which the target will be observed and then simply check on a sheet of paper that is divided up into those time periods whether it was occurring during the observation. It might also be possible for the client to just jot down on a sheet of paper or 3" × 5" card the occurrence of a behavior when he or she remembers to do so, but this would pose a problem in determining just how representative such recollections would be. In such a case, an electronic beeper (a remote control device that signals its wearer when activated by a caller) might be useful, if one is available, to prompt a client to observe and record at specific times. If you, a relevant other, or an independent observer is observing a client, it's important that the observation schedule not be obvious to the client. This is important so that the client doesn't specifically perform or not perform the behavior only during the observation periods.

The second type of time sampling involves recording all instances of a target, but only for selected periods during each day. This actually combines time sampling with continuous recording. This form of continuous recording can be used when the target occurs

Client's Name _____   Recorder's Name _____

Behaviors to Be Observed:

    A. _____

    B. _____

    C. _____

Length of Observation Interval: _____

Time Period Between Observations: _____

Time Sample

Behavior	1	2	3	4	5	6	7	8	9	10
A										
B										
C										

FIGURE 2 Sample form for time-sample recording.

so frequently that it is possible to record only during selected periods of time (when the target occurs, or occurs with its greatest frequency), only during selected periods (e.g., only during the dinner hour, only in one classroom, only with one person), or when the observer is only available during selected periods.

The key issue in using only selected periods of time for recording is to try to ensure that the period of time will produce a *representative* picture of the target. If the target occurs often and regularly, then you would need fewer periods during the day in order to be reasonably certain that what you observe is indeed representative of the total occurrence of the behavior. However, if the target occurs in more than one situation, those situations should be included in the periods of time you select for recording. Try to make the periods you do select similar in subsequent observations (e.g., succeeding days) so that you will have consistent opportunities to observe the target as it occurs. You can imagine the difficulties in making a reasonable and reliable assessment of the occurrence of a target if, for example, a client haphazardly self-monitors his or her frequency of self-deprecating thoughts at breakfast the first day, for an hour at school the next day, and watching television at night the following day.

Similarly, being aware of the need for representativeness in the periods you select can be helpful when you use the baseline observations to develop your assessment of the target and relate it to the situations in which it occurs. For example, if a client self-monitored the frequency of his or her self-deprecating thoughts only at home, you would have information only about the frequency of these thoughts in one setting. If the client monitored these thoughts in more than one setting—say, at home, at work, and on the way home from work—you might discover that the thoughts are related to a particular setting, and this in turn might suggest strategies for intervention.

Client Samples. This type of sampling is used when you work with a large number of clients (e.g., a ward or classroom). Using client sampling, you would select only a sample of clients for direct observation or self-monitoring observation at any given time. This is particularly useful for efficiently assessing an environment or program that may affect many people. Also, sometimes such information about a group of clients can be used as a basis against which the behavior of an individual client can be compared (e.g., whether an individual child actually is out of his or her seat or off-task more than his or her classmates).

The assumption here is that the people you do select are representative of the others. You do this by randomly selecting certain people for observation across the entire period of the baseline and intervention periods, or by rotating the people whom you observe so that all people in the group are systematically observed at one period of time or another. Spreadsheet programs such as Microsoft Excel can be used for this and other types of randomization. Also, it's not difficult to find good web sites that let you do this (e.g., www.randomizer.org).

Situation Samples. The last type of sampling involves the location of sampling—observing clients only in those situations where a target behavior will most likely occur, and being sure that the major possible locations are included in the recording plan. This is more of an issue in direct observation than self-monitoring, but in either case, situation samples are more efficient for the observation of environmental factors that might be affecting targets, and changes in the occurrence of those targets once intervention occurs.

Thus, in assessing, monitoring, or evaluating the effects of intervention on a target, you would be observing only during those situations where the target could be expected to occur relatively frequently. Obviously, it would be highly inefficient to observe, say, targets in marital communication in a place where such communication is unlikely to take place (e.g., a movie). It would be much more efficient and useful to observe those targets in such situations as mealtimes, when a communication problem is more likely to occur.

On the other hand, you want to be sure to include the range of locations in which the target event might take place. Use of an ecological-systems approach to behavior would suggest the importance of examining the different settings and locations in which a target might occur. If you aren't careful to do this, a number of problems could result (Cooper, Heron, & Heward, 2007). First, focusing on only one location (we mentioned earlier the problem of having a client self-monitor self-deprecating thoughts only at home) could produce a sample of behavior that is unrepresentative. If you find that the behavior occurs differently in different situations, you may need to tailor your intervention strategies for each of those different situations. Second, characteristics of any given location could change over time, leading to changes in the target behavior. This could produce the mistaken

Table 1 Rate of put-downs per minute made by Alan and Laurie

Child	Number of Put-Downs	Period Covered	Number of Minutes	Rate per Minute
Laurie				
Monday	ⅢⅢ IIII (14)	6:30–9:30	180	0.08
Tuesday	ⅢⅢ II (12)	7:00–8:45	105	0.11
Wednesday	ⅢI III (8)	7:00–9:00	120	0.07
Thursday	II (2)	6:45–8:30	105	0.02
Friday	IIII (4)	7:00–9:30	150	0.03
Alan				
Monday	II (2)	6:30–9:30	180	0.01
Tuesday	ⅢI (5)	7:00–8:45	105	0.05
Wednesday	II (2)	7:00–9:00	120	0.01
Thursday	(0)	6:45–8:30	105	0
Friday	(0)	7:00–9:30	150	0

assumption that the intervention program was responsible for the changes. Third, because you know that a behavior can change simply as a function of changing the setting, sampling from several locations will provide evidence as to whether behavior change has really generalized when you compare the baseline data from multiple settings with the intervention phase data from multiple settings.

Rates

It may be that the logical period of time for observing a target varies from observation time to observation time. Let's say that a mother wants help with her son's uncontrolled behavior when riding in the family car. Such rides, of course, vary in length from day to day and even throughout the day. In such cases, you should compute the rate of occurrence of the target to ensure that you have equal bases for comparing the target's occurrence over time. For example, suppose that the mother drove her son for 2 hours the first day, 1 hour the next day, and 30 minutes the third day. If you plotted the raw data for each day—say, the number of times the son yelled during the car trip—the differences across time would be due in part to the differences in length of the car trips, not to actual changes in the behavior.

A rate is a count per some unit of time (e.g., minute, hour, day). Rates are computed simply by dividing the number of occurrences of the target by the period of time (hours or minutes) the target is observed. Thus, if the client records seven angry thoughts while driving during the rush hour for 70 minutes, the rate of occurrence per minute would be 7/70, or .10 (.10 could be multiplied by 60, the number of minutes in an hour, to get the rate per hour, which would be 6). Rates can be plotted on a chart to provide a common index for observing the daily occurrence of a target. Table 1 (redrawn from Fischer & Gochros, 1975) and Figure 3 provide examples of rates as they were collected, computed, and then charted.

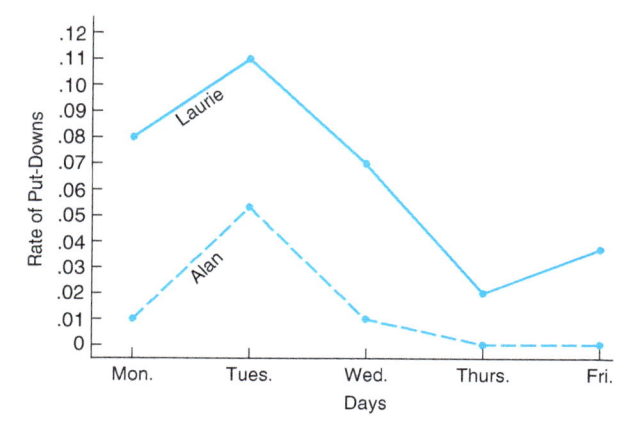

FIGURE 3 Rate of put-downs as plotted on a chart.

INSTRUMENTS FOR RECORDING BEHAVIORS

We strongly believe that recording shouldn't become an end in itself. It's crucial for you as the practitioner to try to come up with a recording system that is not aversive (perhaps it might even become pleasant) to those who will do the recording. Otherwise, your observer may balk at participating because of a complex or cumbersome recording system. Try to make sure the recording system is as uncomplicated as possible. Ultimately, you want recording to be a rather simple process that enhances the intervention program by increasing rather than decreasing the motivation of those involved.

Once the behavior is recorded, it will be placed on charts so that you can easily and clearly inspect progress visually. But before you put the data on the chart, you have to set up a system for collecting the information. Perhaps the simplest way is to use forms for recording the behavior. Forms are simple checklists that you give the observer or help the observer develop. They have spaces or boxes for checking off whether or how long a behavior occurs. We present some forms such as these for your use later in this chapter.

Sometimes forms cannot be used to record behavior, especially when the observer wishes to be unobtrusive. Imagine walking around carrying a form making check marks in front of an individual or group whose behavior you don't wish to disturb, or having a client do this at work while self-monitoring. In these situations, you want a less obtrusive or more accessible type of recording instrument. Data could be recorded on this instrument and then either placed on the checklist or form where it can be tallied up before being transferred onto the chart, or placed directly on the chart from the recording instrument.

Some interesting behavioral software can be found at the following web sites, but see Richard and Gloster (2006) for a more extensive list: Behavioral Evaluation Strategy and Taxonomy (www.skware.com), Multiple Option Observation System (http://kc.vanderbilt.edu/mooses/), The Observer (www.noldus.com/site/), and Systematic Observation Software (http://members.aol.com/Psychsoft/). Sidener, Shabani, and Carr (2004) provide a review and illustration of one particular system for collecting and analyzing observational data (Behavioral Evaluation Strategy and Taxonomy [BEST]). Finally, consider using Personal Digital Assistants (PDAs) for developing new and creative approaches to collecting data (Hektner, Schmidt, & Csikszentmihalyi, 2007; Ice, 2004; Richard & Gloster, 2006; Stone, Shiffman, Atienza, & Nebeling, 2007).

Principles for Selecting Instruments

Several principles should be considered when choosing an instrument to use (Fischer & Gochros, 1975). Selection depends on the nature of the target, the capabilities and motivation of the observer, and the complexity of the situation:

1. Is the method portable enough to be easily used where the behavior occurs? (Many times, a small 3" × 5" card will suffice, rather than a large clipboard or pad of paper.)

2. Is the method unobtrusive enough that it won't be distracting or embarrassing to those whose behavior is being recorded?

3. Is the method *likely* to be used? (No recording method is of much value if it won't be used.)

4. Is the method pleasant or enjoyable to use? (It's worth the time to sit down with the observer and try to come up with imaginative or pleasant ways of recording data.)

Some Instruments for Your Use

If you expect some exciting or mysterious instruments for recording, you may be disappointed. Just about all of the methods we mention are probably right at hand around your house or at work, and that's why we suggest them. Each has been used successfully to count behaviors. Most of these focus on simply determining whether behaviors do occur (frequency). If you plan to record duration, you'll also need a watch or clock.

There are a number of simple but quite effective instruments for recording behaviors (Cooper, Heron, & Heward, 2007; Fischer & Gochros, 1975):

1. Coins can be moved from one pocket to another or from one compartment in a purse to another every time a specified behavior occurs.

2. Poker chips can be used to keep track of behaviors around the house or in an institutional setting.

3. Inexpensive golf score counters worn on the wrist are useful for counting behaviors by inconspicuously "clicking off" behaviors on the knob.

4. Pedometers can be used to measure activity levels.

5. Knitting stitch counters also can be used to count behaviors; for example, a parent recording the number of times a child says or does something.

6. Small pieces of masking tape can be taped to the wrist, and checks can be made with a pen each time a behavior occurs. This inexpensive recording "device" can be used when other instruments are not practical.

7. Soap or a large pencil eraser can be kept in a pocket or purse and an indentation made using a fingernail each time a specified behavior occurs. Then, the indentations can simply be totaled up at a later time.

8. Necklaces or bracelets made of lanyards or rawhide with beads tightly strung on them can be used by simply moving one of the beads each time a behavior occurs.

9. Small cards kept in a pocket or purse can be used to collect data on a variety of behaviors. You can tuck one of these cards into the back of a pack of cigarettes to count the number of cigarettes smoked each day.

10. If you can afford it or your agency has one available, you might even use a small portable tape recorder or even a video camera to record incidents of behavior as they occur. One or more observers can then examine the tapes as often as necessary at convenient times, and determine the frequency or duration of selected behaviors.

As you can see, you're limited in your use of recording devices only by your imagination; most instruments are accessible, inexpensive, and easy to use. In addition to the simple instruments described previously, though, there also is an increasing array of powerful computer technology available for the direct observation and analysis of behavior. In some cases this technology is not all that expensive and not all that difficult to use (e.g., Richard & Gloster, 2006; Ice, 2004; and Sidener, Shabani, & Carr, 2004). Typically, this technology includes a specially designed hand-held keyboard, a small laptop computer, or a Personal Digital Assistant (PDA), and the observer simply presses different keys to record the observation of different behaviors. Usually the time the behavior is entered is recorded automatically, making it possible to examine the sequence of events, and often it's also possible to record the duration and frequency of the same behavior. The raw observational data can be printed or transferred to a personal computer to be charted and analyzed.

ENSURING ACCURATE OBSERVATIONS

Accuracy is really a combination of two factors: the reliability and validity of the data. Just as with any measurement method, there are a number of ways that the reliability and validity of behavioral observations can be enhanced or compromised (e.g., Baer, Harrison, Fradenburg, Petersen, & Milla, 2005). The definition of the behavior might be vague or incomplete, or perhaps even too complex. The behavior might be difficult to observe because of problems or distractions in the observational situation. A client's behavior might change as a result of being self-monitored or observed by someone else—the observations might be "reactive." The observer might be biased, perhaps expecting certain behaviors from the person being observed because of assumptions regarding how he or she "should" behave (this is especially likely when observers are asked to make global or subjective evaluations of behavior). The instruments for collecting data might be cumbersome or poorly designed. Observers may change over time in their understanding of just what should be observed.

When the reliability or validity of your observations is compromised, it's difficult or impossible to know just what the client's actual performance was, and whether any recorded change in behavior resulted from real change or from some change in the recording of the behavior (e.g., the observer's way of viewing the behavior). All of these things can affect not only the reliability and validity of your observations, but your entire intervention program. It's therefore crucial that you try to prevent these problems from occurring, to the extent possible, and that you attempt to evaluate whether the data are being recorded reliably and validly. The following guidelines will help to maximize the reliability and validity with which behavioral observations are made.

Maximizing the Reliability and Validity of Observations

From the beginning, you should try to maximize the reliability and validity of your observations. There's no foolproof method for doing this, but using some or all of the following strategies may go a long way toward helping you collect reliable and valid observations (Baer et al., 2005; Cooper, Heron, & Heward, 2007; Kennedy, 2005):

1. Make sure, in consultation with the client and other relevant parties, that the behavior appears to be the target of interest (i.e., it has face validity).

2. Make sure that the behaviors selected, and the times and situations selected for their observation, give a representative picture of the target (i.e., the content validity of the observations is sufficient). Don't select behaviors, times, and situations just because they are convenient.

3. Make sure the target behavior is clearly and specifically defined, and that the observer has clear cues regarding when or where the behavior is likely to occur.

4. Train and retrain the observers. Make sure the observers understand what behaviors to record and how to recognize them when and if they do and do not occur. Familiarize the observers with the recording instruments before they start using them. Set up trial periods, say, through role-playing, where the observers get a chance to practice. Give the observers continued training sessions, especially if the intervention program is a long one, to ensure a continuing understanding of the behaviors to be observed (to avoid "observer drift").

5. Monitor observers. Check the observers' data as soon as possible after they are recorded. Any disagreements or problems should be corrected as soon as possible. If you can (i.e., for publicly observable behaviors), conduct frequent unannounced reliability checks on a random basis by having a second person independently observe and record at the same time as your regular observer (e.g., both parents could collect data on a child's behavior; a student may be assigned to collect data along with a teacher; a nurse may make a reliability check to assess the consistency of a ward attendant's data; you as the practitioner may do a reliability probe, for example, by making a home visit and collecting data at the same time as the client). Such checks are important because evidence shows that they increase the reliability of observations. Observers who know that such unannounced checks can occur may be more vigilant.

6. If more than one observer is to be used, make sure the actions of one will not influence the other. If possible, place them in areas where they cannot view each other.

7. Make sure the recording procedure itself—the data-gathering instrument—is accessible, portable, and easy to use. If the system is too complex (e.g., too many different types of behaviors are observed), the reliability and validity of the observations can be affected. In general, try not to set up a recording procedure that will be aversive to the observer.

8. Make sure the observers don't have to work so hard or so long at collecting data that they become fatigued and begin collecting inaccurate data.

9. See that the behavior is recorded immediately after its occurrence. Delays can lead to incomplete or distorted data.

10. Try to make record-keeping a routine. Make sure the observer has incentives to record. Be encouraging and supportive, and offer a good deal of praise for recording efforts.

11. Make sure the data are used. Can you imagine the observer's frustration if some clear and specific use of the data is not made? If the data are not used, you can be sure your observer will lose interest in recording.

12. Try to make observers as inconspicuous as possible in order to minimize reactivity.

13. Don't inform relevant others or independent observers of expected changes in clients' behavior, if at all possible. This precaution will minimize the chances that observations will be distorted because of observers' expectations about change.

Verifying Reliability

In particular, when publicly observable events are targeted you will want to verify the consistency with which different observers observe the same behavior (i.e., interobserver reliability). In order to verify that behavior is being observed consistently, different observers should independently observe and record the same behaviors (e.g., as described in the last point previously) when practical. Then, once the behavior is recorded by each observer, the interobserver reliability is computed. Interobserver reliability is usually reported in terms of some type of percentage of agreement. There's some consensus that agreement of roughly 80% (or .80 if not converted to percentages) or more indicates good reliability, although 90% is preferred (Cooper, Heron, & Heward, 2007; Friman, 2009). A lower figure suggests that perhaps too much error may be influencing the observer, and suggests the need to clarify the definition of the behavior or to provide additional training.

The procedure for estimating reliability depends on the method used for recording. Later in this chapter we provide a specific method for estimating reliability for each type of recording. These methods provide a reasonable estimate of reliability without being unduly complex; they're quite simple and require no more skill than simple multiplication and division. Other methods of estimating reliability also are available (e.g., Cooper, Heron, & Heward, 2007; Kennedy, 2005).

Don't be too put off when you see the "numbers." We promise you that each computation is simple and that you'll be able to master it with very little practice. This all should become clear later in this chapter, where we give examples for use with each of the three key methods for recording behavior: frequency, duration, and interval recording.

Verifying Validity

You may recall several strategies verifying validity also were discussed in chapter 2 and it's possible to use some of these methods to verify the validity of behavioral observations. In general, this can be done by comparing the observations to some standard (i.e., criterion validity) or to other measured, predicted variables (construct validity). As an example of criterion validity, we cited the example of comparing a student's reported frequency of completed homework assignments with the teacher's records of completed homework. As an example of construct validity, you could compare a student's reported study time with changes in grades (assuming that study time and grades are positively related), or you could compare changes in study time and grades in response to an intervention designed to increase these outcomes. Figure 4 shows hypothetical results that support the

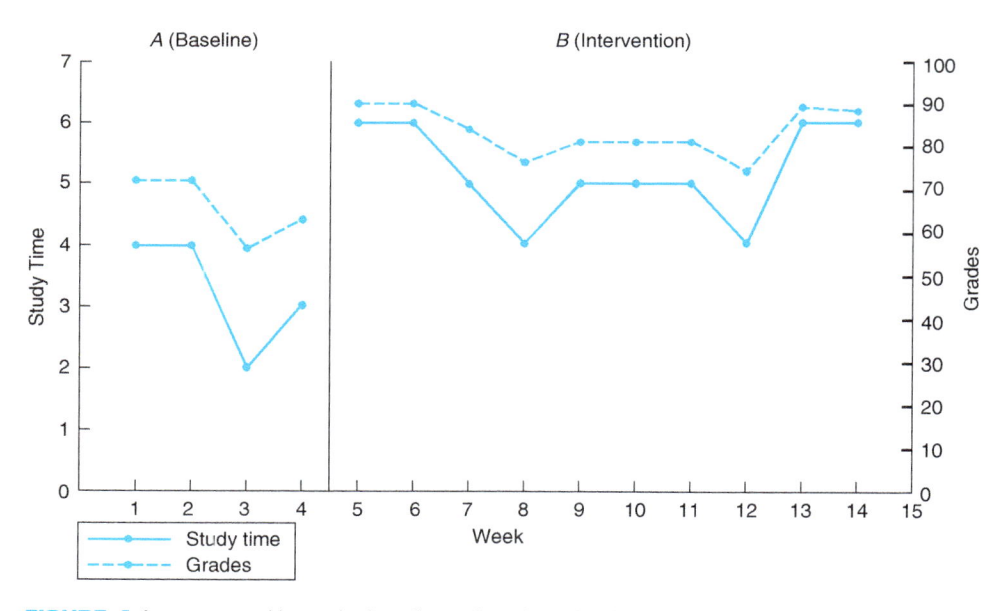

FIGURE 4 Average weekly study time (hours) and grades (percents).

construct validity of a student's weekly reported study time; as reported study time increases, average weekly grades increase (the two results converge). Moreover, in the intervention phase (*B*) you see that reported study time and grades increase following the implementation of an intervention designed to increase these outcomes (the outcome is sensitive to change).

The results shown in Figure 4 also provide another example of concomitant variation. When study time goes up, grades go up; when study time goes down, grades go down. This suggests the importance of study time in improving grades, although there might be other explanations for the relationship. For example, it might be that the quality of the student's relationships with his or her family, parents, or peers causes the changes in study time and grades. Therefore, this concomitant variation is useful for suggesting causal connections for intervention purposes, but you should think critically about alternative explanations for such concomitant variation before drawing conclusions about causes.

In sum, when you collect information about different, though related, outcomes from different observers, and when this information fits in a theoretically logical and predicted pattern, you are in a better position to conclude that the observations are valid. This is especially important when having someone self-monitor covert behaviors because of the impossibility of checking interobserver reliability. In any case, though, the measurement of multiple behaviors using multiple observers puts you in a better position to draw valid conclusions about events that influence client targets, and this information can be used to select, develop, and implement more effective intervention strategies. In this way, a good single-system design is a study in validity.

METHODS OF RECORDING BEHAVIOR

Behavior can be measured by counting the *frequency* with which it occurs (i.e., how often it occurs) and by measuring its *duration* (how long it lasts). Also, frequency and duration can be estimated using *interval recording*.

Behavior also can be measured in terms of its *magnitude* or *intensity*. Intensity is often evaluated by psychophysiological devices that are not readily available to most practitioners, or that are simply too expensive or too complicated or inappropriate for naturalistic observation. Bernston and Cacioppo (2006), Friman (2009), Larkin (2006), and Zald and Curtis (2006) provide information about these methods. In Chapter 6 we provide a discussion of individualized rating scales (IRSs), a simple and practical way to measure intensity. All practitioners can use individualized rating scales, and we suggest you review that chapter for a description of how to use them to evaluate the intensity of a behavior.

Whatever attribute of behavior you choose to record, many behavioral observations proceed by the use of *codes*. Codes are symbols or two- or three-letter phrases that are used to represent specific categories of frequently occurring behavior or events that are being observed (Haynes, 1978). Either these codes are entered on forms as the behavior occurs or the forms can be prepared in advance with code categories already on them, so that all the observer has to do is check off whether that category exists. Almost anything can be used as a code; for example, "+" for praise, "−" for punishment, "M" for mother, "E" for eating, and so on.

Codes are valuable for several reasons (Haynes, 1978): (a) They allow the analysis of a large number of behavior categories; (b) they're adaptable to many situations, populations, and behaviors; (c) they allow analysis of relationships among behaviors, and between behaviors and environmental events; (d) they make it easier to observe more people at the same time (e.g., in a group setting).

There are a variety of existing coding schemes for the observation of numerous different types of behaviors. For example, Johnston and Mah (2008) discuss coding systems for ADHD children; Frick and McMahon (2008) discuss coding systems for child and adolescent conduct problems; and Snyder, Heyman, and Haynes (2008) discuss coding systems for couple distress. However, sometimes preexisting coding systems require extensive training, they may not always be relevant to the idiosyncratic targets presented by clients, and they may be more appropriate for direct observation than for self-monitoring. Nevertheless, preexisting coding schemes might be relevant for your clients, and they might save you the time involved in developing a coding scheme from scratch. Also, when you use a coding system that has been used before, it might be possible to compare your evaluation with previous evaluations that used the same coding scheme.

Frequency

Frequency counts simply involve counting the number of times a behavior occurs during a given period of time, ignoring the duration of the behavior. Frequency recording is probably the most commonly used recording procedure because of its many advantages (Cooper, Heron, & Heward, 2007). It's relatively simple to use. Usually no special equipment is necessary, but when it is, it's easy to use (e.g., a wrist or golf counter). The number of times a behavior occurs often is especially sensitive to changes over time, so that such changes provide a clear and direct measure of change. In addition, the number of times a target occurs is often the most important characteristic to both clients and practitioners.

Frequency counts are used when a target behavior occurs too often and needs to be decreased (e.g., arguing), or doesn't occur often enough and needs to be increased (e.g., initiating communication). Therefore, if the goal of intervention is to change how often a behavior occurs, the obvious focus of measurement should be on recording its frequency.

A frequency count requires that the observed behavior has two characteristics. First, it should have a clear beginning and end so that separate occurrences of the behavior can be distinguished. It also should last for approximately the same amount of time each time it occurs, so that the units counted are roughly equal (Cooper, Heron, & Heward, 2007). If the behavior is ongoing (e.g., sleeping, studying, ruminative thoughts, interaction with a child), it would be inappropriate to use frequency recording. For example, if a person studied 1 hour one day and 5 minutes the next, each would be considered, using a frequency count, as only one occurrence, and a great deal of information would be lost. But if the behavior has a clear beginning and end and is fairly constant, frequency recording would probably be your best bet. Of course, the same category of behavior in different individuals may lend itself to frequency counts in some people and not in others. Crying that occurs frequently but lasts only 10 to 15 seconds may be appropriate for a frequency count, whereas crying that occurs infrequently and lasts for periods of 20 to 30 minutes would not be, and measuring its duration might be more appropriate.

Frequency counts can be taken as a simple tally of how many times a behavior occurs. Once the behavior is clearly defined, the observer merely checks (or clicks) off whether a behavior occurs using either a simple form for counting or any of the instruments described earlier. (A simple all-purpose form for recording the frequency of occurrence of a behavior is displayed in Figure 5.) A period of time is designated in advance, although this is more important for direct observation than self-monitoring because the client is always present to self-monitor (although self-monitoring may be more practical in some situations than in others). If the behavior occurs frequently, the time period would be shorter (imagine sitting for 4 hours recording every occurrence of a behavior that occurs 30 times per hour), while longer periods of observation are necessary for infrequently occurring behaviors to be sure you have an accurate picture of their occurrence. At the end of each observation period or at the end of the day, the total occurrences of the behavior are tallied and simply placed on a chart.

Frequency counts can be expressed in terms of the number of times a behavior occurs, or in terms of rates. A rate is just a count per some unit of time (e.g., minute, hour, day). If the length of the observation time is the same each time, the number of occurrences can be used. If the length of observation time varies from day to day, use rates. Rates are computed by dividing the number of times a behavior occurs by the total observation time. A form for frequency recording during varying periods of time (using rates) is displayed in Figure 6.

The number of times a behavior occurs also can be measured as a percentage of the time it occurs in response to some event or stimulus. For example, an adolescent client might record how often he or she uses a contraceptive during intercourse, and the number of times he or she has intercourse may vary each week. Therefore, you would calculate the number of times he or she uses a contraceptive per times he or she has intercourse. The client may have intercourse once the first week and use a contraceptive on that occasion, that is 100% of the time, and he or she may have intercourse twice the second week and only use a contraceptive one of those two times, that is 50% of the time. The percentages could be graphed rather than the actual number of target behaviors, since the latter could be purely a result of the number of opportunities for the behavior to be observed.

There are some circumstances under which frequency recording is difficult. One of these, as we already mentioned, is when the behavior has no clear beginning and ending. Another is when a behavior is occurring so quickly that it's difficult to count. Finally, if a behavior occurs infrequently, it might be difficult to have observers other than the client record it because they may become bored with the observation task and miss occurrences of the behavior.

Many behaviors have been assessed using frequency counts, including behavior by individuals,

Behavioral Observation

Client's Name: _____ Recorder's Name: _____

Behaviors to Be Observed: _____

_____

Time Period (Hours/Day): _____

Date	Number of Times Behavior Occurred	Additional Comments

FIGURE 5 Sample form for recording frequency of occurrence of behavior.

families, groups, and communities. Some of these behaviors include the following: number of practitioner–client contacts, number of "homework" tasks completed by a client, number of negative thoughts, number of positive self-statements, number of times a spouse initiates conversation, number of chores completed, number of times one child hits another, number of times a child gets out of his or her seat without permission, number of greetings to staff made by patients on a ward, number of aggressive phrases used, number of times an individual attends a meeting, number of fights during recess, number of times each group member speaks, and so on. The range of behaviors appropriate for frequency recording is immense.

Establishing Reliability. Interobserver reliability in measuring the frequency of covert behaviors (e.g., thoughts) cannot be established, but for publicly observable behaviors, two observers can be used to establish the reliability of frequency recording. Each observer records the number of times a behavior occurs during the same time period. At the end of this period, their observations are compared to see whether they recorded the same number of behaviors.

Behavioral Observation

Client's Name: _____   Recorder's Name: _____

Behaviors to Be Observed: _____

_____

Date	Frequency	Total	Time	Rate	Additional Comments
9/1	ⅢⅠ Ⅱ	7	20 minutes	.35	
9/1	Ⅲ	3	10 minutes	.30	

FIGURE 6 Form for frequency recording during varying periods of time (rates).

A percentage of agreement is determined—the interobserver reliability. We discussed the basic procedure of determining interobserver reliability earlier, and promised to show you a simple way of calculating it. Here's how to do it.

If both observers have exactly the same number of observations tallied, there's no problem. Their agreement (the reliability) is 100%. More typically, though, one will have more behaviors checked than the other. Simply divide the larger number of behaviors into the smaller and multiply by 100. The result will be the interobserver reliability.

Let's say in a 1-hour period, Observer 1 checks off 10 occurrences of behavior and Observer 2 checks off 12. Divide 10 by 12 and multiply by 100 ([10/12] × 100 = 83%). (Sometimes you might see the reliability reported as .83, which simply means the results of the division weren't multiplied by 100.) Simple, wasn't it? Looking for at least 80% agreement, you'd conclude that in this case the interobserver reliability of 83% was satisfactory.

There's a potential problem with this procedure for computing reliability. The 83% means that the two observers agree on total frequency, not that they necessarily agree 83% of the time on the *same* behaviors. It may be that one observer recorded 12 occurrences of the behavior and the other observer recorded 10 different occurrences. Thus, the reliability figure should be interpreted cautiously because the two observers might not be observing the same behavior. This problem can be overcome when observers record their observations using computers that are synchronized according to time, although typically such equipment is not available. Of course, the problem of recording different behaviors will be decreased in direct proportion to how clearly the problem is defined—the clearer the definition of the problem, the more likely it is that observers will record the same event.

Duration

For some behaviors the major concern is time—the behavior either lasts too long or not long enough, or it occurs too soon or not soon enough after some event or other behavior. In such situations, where the goal is to increase or decrease the *length of time* some behavior is performed, or the amount of time that elapses before a behavior occurs, duration recording can be used.

Duration recording usually involves recording the length of time some behavior occurs. For example, a father and mother might record the amount of time spent reading to or talking with their children, spouses might record the amount of enjoyable leisure time they spend together, a client with a sleep disorder might record the number of hours per day spent sleeping, a teacher might record the amount of time a student is academically engaged, a parent might record the amount of time per day a child spends crying, or a practitioner might record the amount of time spent with a client.

Another type of duration recording involves measuring how long it takes for a behavior to occur in relation to the occurrence of some stimulus (e.g., the amount of time that elapses between a parent asking a child to go to bed and the time the child gets in bed, the amount of time that elapses between a classroom bell ringing and a child being seated). This type of duration recording usually is referred to as *response latency*. Latency is useful when the goal is to increase or decrease the amount of time between the opportunity for a behavior to occur and the occurrence of the behavior.

Another variation of duration recording, *interresponse time*, is similar to latency recording. It involves recording the amount of time that elapses between the occurrence of two instances of the same response; for example, the amount of time between completing two different tasks or between having two different thoughts, or the amount of time between accidents for children with nocturnal enuresis. Interresponse time is useful when the goal is to increase or decrease the amount of time between instances of the same behavior.

Duration recording is relatively simple to use, since it involves determining only the length of time between the beginning and end of a behavior, or the amount of time between one event or response and the occurrence of a behavior. You will need some form of timepiece; stopwatches or inexpensive runners' chronographs are useful and practical because they're relatively precise, but any watch or clock, preferably with a second hand, can be used. The observer must note the time a behavior begins and the time it ends, or the amount of time between one event or response and the occurrence of a behavior. A simple, all-purpose form for recording duration counts is displayed in Figure 7.

As discussed previously, if different observation periods are of equal length, duration can be expressed in terms of the actual amount of time that a behavior lasts during an observation period. When observation periods are not equal, duration should be expressed as the proportion or percentage of time during an observation period that a behavior occurs. This is similar to the way that rates are determined for frequencies.

For latency or interresponse time recording, the average latency or interresponse time for an episode of behavior is computed. For example, suppose that the target involves reducing the amount of time between a father's request and the time the son complies with the request. On the first day of observation the father makes five requests and the elapsed times are 15, 10, 25, 5, and 10 minutes. The average latency for that day is computed by adding these times together and dividing by the number of episodes of behavior, which in this case is the number of requests by the father (i.e., $15 + 10 + 25 + 5 + 10 = 65/5 = 13$ minutes).

Duration recording, as well as frequency recording, requires that the beginning and end of the behavior be defined clearly. However, with duration recording be particularly careful that observers agree when a behavior begins and ends. For example, imagine trying to record the duration of a tantrum where a child may cry continuously for several minutes, whimper for short periods, stop all noise for a few seconds, begin intense crying again, and so on. Thus, with duration recording, one must be clear, and have agreement among observers, about how to handle these changes (e.g., periods of silence, changes from crying to whimpering) so that recording is consistent.

Any number of behaviors are appropriate for duration recording (Cooper, Heron, & Heward, 2007; Friman, 2009), such as studying, exercise, time spent in obsessive thinking, insomnia, asthma attacks, tension and migraine headaches, tantrums, crying, length of meetings, maintenance of penile erections, time spent cleaning up before dinner, periods of feeling depressed, and so on.

Establishing Reliability. Interobserver reliability is computed for duration recording in practically the same way as for frequency recording, but again, this

Behavioral Observation

Client's Name _____ Recorder's Name _____

Behaviors to Be Observed: _____

_____

Time Period for Observation: _____

Date	Length of Time Behavior Occurred (e.g., minutes)	Total Time (minutes)	Additional Comments

FIGURE 7 Form for recording duration of behavior.

is not applicable for covert behaviors. Two observers record the behavior during the same time period. Then, the smaller duration is divided by the larger duration, and the result is multiplied by 100.

Let's say Observer 1 recorded the behavior as occurring for 20 minutes and Observer 2 recorded the duration of the behavior as 25 minutes. Divide 20 by 25 and multiply by 100 ([20/25] × 100) and you get 80% as your percentage of agreement estimate of interobserver reliability. Our standard suggests that this is an acceptable figure, although just barely.

A key to ensuring observer agreement for duration recording is to be certain that both observers begin and end at the same time so that each will be observing for the same period of time. Also, as with frequency recording, you should interpret this type of reliability estimate with caution, because even with high agreement you cannot be absolutely certain that the same behaviors were being observed. However, as with frequency recording, this problem can be overcome by clear definition of the behavior to be observed or when observers record their observations using computers that are synchronized according to time.

Interval Recording

There are times when it may be difficult to use frequency or duration recording. For example, a behavior such as speaking might not only be difficult to break into discrete units for frequency recording, but may be ongoing for long periods, making duration recording (just sitting and watching from beginning to end) difficult and impractical. In these situations, where frequency or duration recording is not quite appropriate, a variation of time sampling called *interval recording* (or interval counts) can be used. For the most part, interval recording is used for direct observation, because of its complexity, and not for self-monitoring; interval recording is almost always used in a "controlled" setting, such as a school classroom.

In interval recording, a period of observation is selected (e.g., 30 minutes) and then divided into equal blocks of time (intervals), usually of rather short duration (e.g., 10–15 seconds). The behavior is then recorded as either occurring or not occurring for each interval. One way this is done is for the observer to have a miniature tape recorder with an earphone and a tape on which a tone has been recorded at preset intervals (e.g., 10 seconds). For longer intervals a simple kitchen timer or stopwatch could be used. In any case, the observer records whether the behavior was occurring at the sound of the tone. This allows the observer time to record whether the behavior occurred and then refocus attention on the person being observed. In any case, the outcome of interest is the percentage of intervals during which the target behavior occurs.

There are three slightly different ways to determine whether to record a behavior as having occurred during an interval. An observer can record a behavior as having occurred (a) if the behavior occurred at all, or during a specified portion of the interval (this is called *partial-interval sampling*); (b) if the behavior occurred throughout the entire interval (this is called *whole-interval sampling*); or (c) if the behavior occurred at a particular time during the interval, such as at the beginning or end of the interval (this is called *momentary-interval sampling,* and it is similar to time sampling, except that with time sampling the time between intervals is usually longer). In general, momentary-interval sampling provides the most accurate estimates (Kennedy, 2005).

The basic process of interval recording involves the observer watching the client for the interval (called the "observation interval"), then marking his or her observation sheet (the "recording interval" period), then observing for the next interval, and so on. This method can be used with individual clients, families, or groups. For example, Crosland et al. (2008) used a one-minute interval to record staff–child interactions in terms of three types of interactions: *positive*, *negative*, or *no interaction*. Staff members were observed one at a time for 20 minutes.

There are some distinct advantages to using interval recording (Kazdin, 1975). First, it's flexible, since the presence or absence of a behavior during some time period can be observed for almost any type of behavior. It doesn't matter whether the behavior is discrete or continuous.

Second, interval recording can be used to record a number of different behaviors at the same time, because you don't have to see every occurrence of the behavior, and you can alternate behaviors (e.g., watching behavior A for 10 seconds and then recording, watching behavior B for 10 seconds and then recording). Similarly, interval recording can be used to observe different people, because you don't have to see every occurrence of the behavior and you can alternate observing different people (e.g., watching the first person for 10 seconds and then recording, watching the second person for 10 seconds and then recording).

A third advantage of interval recording is that the results can be converted easily into rates. This is done by dividing the number of intervals during which the behavior occurred by the total number of intervals observed. For example, if a behavior occurs in 25 out of 100 intervals the resulting rate of .25 shows that the behavior occurs a specific proportion of time. As with frequency and duration, rates from interval recording are often expressed as percentages, but this just involves multiplying the proportion by 100 (i.e., .25 × 100 = 25%).

There are some problems with interval recording. First and foremost, it requires the undivided attention of the observer to both the time interval and whether the behavior occurs. Thus, it's a demanding form of recording. Therefore, interval recording is probably not suitable for most clients or relevant others. It requires higher levels of skill and training than frequency or duration recording.

Second, interval recording provides an *estimate* of the frequency or duration of behavior, not a direct determination of frequency or duration. That is, with interval recording, you can tell the number of intervals in which the behavior occurred, but you cannot tell how many times or for how long the behavior occurred overall. The reason for this is that you're only recording *whether* it occurred in each interval; the behavior actually might have occurred five times in one interval, but only is recorded as having occurred once. Furthermore, a review of research on the accuracy of interval recording in estimating the frequency and duration of behaviors indicates that in general it doesn't provide accurate estimates of frequency, although it provides better estimates of duration (Foster & Cone, 1986). Interval recording does, however, provide an indication of the relative changes in the frequency or duration of behavior over time (e.g., changes in the proportion of intervals the behavior was observed to occur), and this is probably how it's best used (Alessi, 1988).

Third, it's sometimes difficult to decide the duration of the interval. There is simply no unequivocal answer as to how long an interval should be, since intervals from 5 seconds to several minutes have been reported in the literature. As a general rule, research indicates that intervals longer than 10 seconds may produce inaccurate results, but intervals of 5 seconds or less are hard to score reliably (Foster & Cone, 1986). Therefore, as a general rule, 10-second intervals seem to provide fairly accurate results.

Once the behavior is clearly defined, the duration of the interval is established, and the length of the overall observation period is set, the observer simply jots down on a preset recording sheet whether a behavior occurs. There are several ways to do this. The observer can write yes or no in a blank box, or simply put a check or hash mark in the box if it occurs, or circle some preset symbol such as a plus sign if the behavior occurs, or a minus sign if it doesn't. We recommend the latter method because it demands less of the observer. We also recommend that the observer record something in each interval whether or not the behavior occurs (e.g., a "+" if it does and a "−" if it doesn't). In that way, there will be no question later whether blank intervals were left blank because the observer forgot to record.

Interval-recording forms should have the intervals represented across the top and the periods of observation down the side. If a group is to be observed, instead of having the observation periods down the left side of the sheet, each of these could represent a different individual in the group. Thus, the first individual could be observed for a 10-second interval, then the second individual for a 10-second interval, and so on. This would continue until each individual has been observed for one interval, and then the entire process is repeated. A basic form for use in interval recording is displayed in Figure 8. (An alternative form would be one in which the spaces are left blank and a check mark is simply placed in the box if the behavior occurs; see Figure 9.)

Any number of different behaviors have been measured using interval recording, including social responses of psychiatric patients; student behavior, such as paying attention, sitting in seats, and working quietly; appropriate mealtime behavior; behavior of withdrawn or uncooperative children; verbalizations of children; prosocial, antisocial, and nonsocial group behavior; and so on.

Establishing Reliability. The same basic principles described previously are followed for determining interobserver reliability, but there are a few differences. For interval recording, reliability is determined by comparing the proportion of intervals that two observers agree on the occurrence and nonoccurrence of the behavior. This is the most frequently used method for determining reliability for interval recording. In this method, each interval in which the observers agree that a behavior did or did not occur is termed an agreement, and each interval in which only one observer scored a behavior (i.e., where different events are recorded) is considered a disagreement. Then, reliability is determined by dividing the number of intervals in which the observers agreed by the number of agreements *plus* disagreements (i.e., the total number of observations) and multiplying by 100.

$$\frac{\text{Agreements}}{\text{Agreements} + \text{Disagreements}} \times 100$$

Let's say the observers recorded behavior for 60 ten-second intervals, and the observers agreed that the behavior did occur in 20 intervals and also agreed that the behavior *did not* occur in 30 intervals. In the remaining 10 intervals they disagreed, with only one or the other observer recording the behavior as having occurred. The interobserver reliability would be calculated, as in the equation, by adding the agreements (20 + 30) and dividing by the agreements plus the disagreements (20 + 30 + 10). The resulting figure would be multiplied by 100. The reliability figure then would be 83% ([50/60] × 100).

$$\frac{20 + 30}{20 + 30 + 10} = \frac{50}{60} \times 100 = 83\%$$

A critical consideration in determining the interobserver reliability of interval recording is whether

Behavioral Observation

Client's Name: _____   Recorder's Name: _____

Behaviors to Be Observed: _____
_____

Time Period (Length of Total Observation Period): _____

Duration of Each Interval: _____

Minutes	Interval									
	1	2	3	4	5	6	7	8	9	10
1	+ −	+ −	+ −	+ −	+ −	+ −	+ −	+ −	+ −	+ −
2	+ −	+ −	+ −	+ −	+ −	+ −	+ −	+ −	+ −	+ −
3	+ −	+ −	+ −	+ −	+ −	+ −	+ −	+ −	+ −	+ −
4	+ −	+ −	+ −	+ −	+ −	+ −	+ −	+ −	+ −	+ −
5	+ −	+ −	+ −	+ −	+ −	+ −	+ −	+ −	+ −	+ −
6	+ −	+ −	+ −	+ −	+ −	+ −	+ −	+ −	+ −	+ −
7	+ −	+ −	+ −	+ −	+ −	+ −	+ −	+ −	+ −	+ −
8	+ −	+ −	+ −	+ −	+ −	+ −	+ −	+ −	+ −	+ −
9	+ −	+ −	+ −	+ −	+ −	+ −	+ −	+ −	+ −	+ −
10	+ −	+ −	+ −	+ −	+ −	+ −	+ −	+ −	+ −	+ −

+ = Target behavior occurred

− = Target behavior did not occur

FIGURE 8 Form for interval recording.

the observers start and stop their intervals at the same time. If not, the results may be meaningless. This is usually accomplished by having some type of device that alerts the observers to the beginning and end of intervals (e.g., a tape-recorded tone, a flash of light on a video screen).

Additional Considerations with Interobserver Reliability

There are a couple of problems with using the percentage of agreement between observers, described earlier in this chapter, to measure interobserver

Behavioral Observation

Client's Name: _____ Recorder's Name: _____

Behaviors to Be Observed:

    A. _____

    B. _____

    C. _____

Time Period: _____

Duration of Each Interval: _____

Interval

Minute	Behavior	1	2	3	4	5	6	7	8	9	10
1	A										
	B										
	C										
2	A										
	B										
	C										
3	A										
	B										
	C										
4	A										
	B										
	C										
5	A										
	B										
	C										

FIGURE 9 Form for interval recording of more than one behaviour.

reliability. A major problem is that this method tends to be inflated by chance agreement between observers. But there are ways of computing reliability that are not subject to these limitations.

Kappa is a widely used measure of agreement that is useful for quantifying interobserver reliability in a way that corrects for chance agreements (e.g., Cohen, 1960; Fleiss, Levin, Paik, & Fleiss, 2003). Because you might see kappa discussed in the literature, we'll briefly describe it here. Kappa equals 1 when perfect agreement occurs, 0 when observed agreement equals chance agreement, and less than 0 when observed agreement is less than chance agreement. Most of the time kappa will be lower than the percentage of observed agreement because it subtracts out that part of agreement that is due to chance. Therefore, the standards for adequate reliability when kappa is used are lower than for percentage agreement. A kappa of .85 or greater is considered excellent, a kappa in the range from .75 to .84 is considered good, a kappa between .60 and .74 is adequate, and a kappa below .60 is poor (Mash & Hunsley, 2008) (see Fleiss et al., 2003, for somewhat less stringent standards). Kappa can be computed using a simple calculator.

Selecting and computing the most appropriate measure of interobserver reliability isn't the only problem in determining interobserver reliability. We also recognize that it's not always realistic for you to find two observers to do this reliability check. If the client and a relevant other are both available and willing to record (the secondary recorder only in certain situations), that would be great. But in other circumstances, no one else might be available. Then, the second recorder might be you. You might make home visits, once in the baseline period and once in the intervention, and do some recording yourself. Then your recording could form the basis for the reliability check. Or, you could set up an analogue situation in the office in which you and the client role-play and record (we discuss this in more detail in the next section).

Obviously, the more you remove the behavior from its real circumstances—you in the home, a role-play in your office—the more likely it is that the validity of the behavior will be affected, that is, what you are recording might not be the real target behaviors. Thus, you would interpret reliability figures from circumstances such as these with caution. On the other hand, no reliability information on the recorded behaviors may mean that you don't really know whether changes are real or due to measurement error. Thus, without any reliability checks, you must be even more cautious in your interpretations.

ANALOGUE SITUATIONS

Ideally, behavior should be observed in the environment in which it naturally occurs, because that is where you want behavior change to occur. However, sometimes it's not possible or practical to observe behavior in the natural environment, especially when using direct observation. The behavior might be too difficult to observe accurately in the natural environment, or observation by you, a relevant other, or an independent observer might be too time-consuming or otherwise costly. Often, the irrelevant and changing conditions in the natural environment are difficult to control, making it impossible to make observations under standardized conditions. Some behaviors occur so infrequently or at such unpredictable times that they are difficult if not impossible for you or an independent observer to measure (e.g., asthma attacks). In these situations we recommend that you consider the use of *analogue* situations.

Analogue situations are contrived situations designed to elicit a sample of behavior that ideally will be representative of behavior that occurs in the natural environment (Friman, 2009; Gold & Marx, 2006; Roszvist et al., 2006). That is, behaviors are observed in a simulated situation where efforts are made to have the situation approximate in some ways the real-life situation. For example, a child welfare worker may ask a parent and child to play in a room full of toys so that he or she can observe them through a two-way mirror. Another example would be you and the client role-playing a job interview to observe the client's skills. Frequency, duration, or interval recording can be used to measure different aspects of the behavior as it occurs in the analogue situation.

There are several types of analogues: paper-and-pencil, audiotape, videotape, role-playing, and enactment (Gold & Marx, 2006; Roszvist et al., 2006). Clients typically are asked to respond to these analogues as they ordinarily would in the natural environment, although sometimes, in order to determine the client's goals, a practitioner may ask the client to behave the way he or she would like to ideally. A basic assumption underlying the use of analogue situations is that the closer the analogue situation resembles the natural environment, the more likely it is that the observed behavior will be representative of that in the natural environment. These different types of analogues are reviewed briefly, in ascending order of their similarity to the natural environment, and we also provide some examples of their use.

With *paper-and-pencil* analogues a client is asked to respond orally or in writing to a situation that is presented in written form. (A variation of this type of analogue involves the use of a personal computer to present the analogue situation, and record, summarize, and store the client's responses.) For example, Rhodes and her colleagues developed 19 vignettes designed to assess foster parent applicants' skills and abilities to manage some of the unique challenges of fostering (Rhodes et al., 2006). Foster parents were asked what they would do if faced with each of a set of common dilemmas that foster parents often experience, and then trained raters rated the degree to which the desired responses were provided.

Audiotape and *videotape* analogues are similar to the paper-and-pencil analogue, except the client hears, or hears and sees, the stimulus situation. Then the client is asked either to describe or to actually act out how he or she would respond, and these responses are observed and recorded. For example, Berlin (1985) audiotaped descriptions of 12 different situations that were designed to elicit self-critical responses. For each audiotaped situation clients were instructed to listen to the description of the situation, imagine that it was really occurring, and orally describe their reaction to the situation. Clients' descriptions were audiotaped, and based on these audiotaped responses, observers recorded the frequency of "self-critical responses," and "positive coping responses," and the length of time between the end of the recorded situation and the beginning of the client's response (i.e., response latency).

In the *role-playing* analogue, the client is asked to visualize a situation in the natural environment and his or her response to it, or to act out situations with the practitioner, other staff, or other clients (e.g., in group therapy) portraying people relevant to the situation. For example, Van Camp, Vollmer, and Goh (2008) presented foster parents with nine role-play situations, one for each parenting skill taught. The practitioner introduced each situation and acted out the role of the child. The number of correct steps in a sequence of parenting behaviors was observed, divided by the total number of applicable steps, and multiplied by 100 to measure the percentage of steps performed accurately.

In the *enactment* analogue the client interacts in the agency or clinical setting with people or objects that he or she has difficulty interacting with in the natural environment. For example, husbands and wives are often asked to discuss problems of their own choosing (e.g., concerning finances, children, household tasks, sexual intimacy) in a clinic setting and different dimensions of their communication behavior are observed or recorded for later observation (expressions of criticism and contempt, as well as appreciation or respect). (Snyder, Heyman, & Haynes, 2008, summarize observational methods in this area.) Or, a parent might be asked to enact certain situations with a child (ask the child to do a certain task) and observations then are made of the interactions, either in a clinic setting or in the home. (Frick & McMahon, 2008, summarize observational methods in this area.)

Enactment and role-play also can be done using virtual reality technology, and this is the most recent development in the observation of behavior in analogue situations (Gold & Marx, 2006; Rosqvist et al., 2006). Virtual reality technology immerses a person in a three-dimensional computer-generated virtual world within which behavior can be measured. For example, a child might be placed in a "virtual classroom" in order to assess behaviors associated with ADHD, and environmental factors influencing these behaviors. However, although the use of virtual reality technology to create analogue situations in which behavior can be observed has a number of advantages, at the present it doesn't seem likely that most practitioners will have access to this technology.

In all of the analogue situations you will want to collect structured information on the observed behaviors. You can do this in at least two ways, particularly in the enactment and role-playing analogues. First, you can use a checklist (e.g., Crosland et al., 2008; Van Camp et al., 2008). Depending on the situation, you can develop a list of behaviors that you consider optimal in a given situation (for example, maintaining good eye contact). These behaviors can be transferred onto a checklist, and you simply check off whether or not the behavior occurred during an observation session. Second, you can develop a simple scale to rate the degree to which desired behaviors were performed, say from zero (none of the behaviors), to seven or higher, equaling all desired behaviors. Both the number of behaviors checked on the checklist and the scores on the scale can be plotted as points on the chart.

All of this makes analogue measures sound quite viable. You might even be wondering, *Why bother to measure behavior in the natural environment?* The problem is that it isn't always certain that behaviors elicited in analogue situations predict behaviors in the natural environment and, in fact, the research in this area is somewhat mixed, if not discouraging (Gold & Marx, 2006; Rosqvist et al., 2006). Therefore, when analogues are used, it's a good idea whenever possible to try to collect some information concerning the concurrent validity of the analogue data. This might involve having the client, a relevant other, or even an independent observer make periodic observations in the natural environment.

In addition to periodic checks on the concurrent validity of analogue observations, it also is important to determine interobserver reliability, just as it is when behaviors are observed in the natural environment. Similarly, just as in the natural environment, it's often useful to examine the construct validity of the behavioral observations by using different methods to measure the target, and by examining how different measures vary together over time in a predictable way for a given client.

RECORDING BEHAVIOR IN GROUPS

Because many practitioners spend a substantial part of their practice time with families and small groups, we'd like to discuss how some of the principles covered so far apply in those situations. In fact, just about all the methods described in this can be used in family and group situations. Thus, role-plays and analogues can be used (especially easily with groups), as can frequency, duration, and interval recording (e.g., see Rose, 1989, and the references cited in Rose, 1988, and see Macgowan, 2008, and Toseland & Rivas, 2009, for good discussions of the use of a broad range of measures suitable for practice evaluation with groups, including behavioral observation).

The key here, though, is distinguishing between recording an individual's target in the context of a group, and recording information on the group as a whole. For example, you might be working with a family and ask each family member to keep track of some behavior (or fill out some standardized scale like a measure evaluating the strength of family relationships). You would then have information from each individual for each measure. While under some circumstances, these can be pooled (e.g., the total number of times family members recorded feeling "put down" by other family members), often these are simply individual measures in the *context* of a group. And while they can provide very valuable information, they may not provide information on changes in the group as a whole.

Under some circumstances, you may very well wish to record behaviors of all members of a family or group at the same time. This might involve students in a class, members of a psychotherapy group, or residents of a nursing home interacting with one another. These behaviors can be recorded using frequency, duration, or interval methods as described earlier in this chapter. While there may be some advantages to using interval recording (every person doesn't have to be watched all the time), any of the methods can be used.

First, it's decided just who will do the recording. Relevant others, caretakers like teachers or nurses, other practitioners functioning as observers, or even designated members of the group could do the recording.

Then, a checklist of behaviors to be observed should be developed. This would allow the observer to simply note in columns next to each behavior who in the group engaged in that behavior. A variation of this method is to list the names of all members of the group in the left-hand column, and along the top of the form, note what behaviors will be observed. Then only a check needs to be placed in the relevant place if the behavior occurs (see Figure 10).

The last condition is to make sure that the observer(s) are well-trained, the behaviors clearly defined, and all observers know when they're to start and stop recording. If the recording times do vary, than rates of behavior can be used.

One widely used method of observing and recording group interactions is called SYMLOG (Systematic Multiple Level Observation of Groups) (Bales, Cohen, & Williamson, 1979) (see www.symlog.com). Though somewhat complicated to use, this approach can analyze both overt and covert behaviors and interactions of group participants. SYMLOG uses a three-dimensional diagram based on coded observations of group interactions; it can be used to evaluate change in a number of variables at the same time, including targets that range from emotional problems of group members to their behaviors in engaging in group tasks.

An interesting approach that seems especially useful with children is the "freeze technique" (Rose

Behavioral Observation

Name	Behavior to Be Observed				Date _____ Time _____
	Initiates Verbal Request	Responds Verbally to Question	Cries	Laughs
Harvey				
Rodney				
Irving				
Sam				
Duke				
Larry				

FIGURE 10 Form for group recording.

& Tolman, 1985), in which a timer is set off at irregular intervals and the group members are asked to "freeze" in place. Then, whatever behavior the group member is engaging in can be noted, and if this technique is used in an intervention phase, interventions such as reinforcement can be applied.

Results of group recording can be cumulated and placed on a chart using the same methods you would for individual clients. In fact, those charts can be placed in easily observed locations and can act as a real stimulus for development of group morale, and an aid to facilitative group and family processes. When the entire group sees changes (or lack of changes) in the chart, group processes can be utilized to examine this information and develop strategies to move the group more readily toward its goal.

These group data can be used to increase or decrease the frequency or duration of certain group behaviors ranging from social amenities to number of chores completed. They also can be used to determine which group members might be most or least likely to exhibit some specific behavior, as simple as whether (or how) they are participating in the group. This information can be particularly useful in highlighting the need for selective interventions within a group. (For an innovative approach to data visualization for the evaluation of group treatment, see Patterson & Basham, 2002).

Summary

Behavioral observation can be one of the most useful forms of measurement because of its potentially high validity and reliability, and because it can be especially useful for assessment purposes. We defined behaviors as relatively discrete events, including both overt and covert activities. We noted that self-observation is typically called "self-monitoring," and observation by an outside observer is often called "direct observation." We then presented some general guidelines for both types of behavioral observation. This was followed by a review of a number of different methods for observing behavior, as well as some principles for selecting those methods.

We emphasized methods for ensuring that your behavioral observations are accurate. We briefly reviewed the validity of behavioral observations, emphasizing their generally high face validity and the fact that behaviors often tend to be the most direct and clearest form of a target. We also discussed the importance of establishing the reliability of behavioral observations, and suggested a number of ways of preventing unreliable observations with an emphasis on the necessity for regularly checking interobserver reliability.

The last part of the chapter focused on three main methods of behavioral recording: frequency, duration, and interval recording. Each of these methods was defined and described in terms of how it can be used. We also gave examples of typical behaviors that might be measured by each, and a form for recording each type of measure. Some simple formulas for calculating interobserver reliability also were presented. Finally, this chapter looked at the way behaviors can be observed in analogue situations and in families and small groups.

In essence, selection of a method of behavioral observation depends on two key conditions. One is the type of behavior selected for observation. Frequency recording should be used when the goal is to increase or decrease the number of times a behavior occurs, and the behavior is relatively constant and has a clear beginning and end. Duration recording should be used when the goal is to increase or decrease the length of time a behavior occurs, or the length of time between events, and the behavior has a clear beginning and end. Interval recording should be used when the goal is to increase or decrease the relative frequency or duration of behavior and frequency or duration recording are impractical (e.g., when the beginning and end of the behavior are difficult to discern or when multiple clients or behaviors are observed simultaneously). A second consideration has to do with the practicality of the recording method and the resources available. If one recording method is not convenient, easy to use, accessible, and clear, then it is wiser to switch to another method or instrument that would more readily meet these criteria.

STANDARDIZED SCALES

PURPOSE This chapter describes standardized scales, how to locate them, how to select them, and how to use them for single-system evaluation. The chapter also describes a number of specific standardized scales for completion by clients, practitioners, relevant others, and independent observers, and it provides a list of references for locating information about additional standardized scales. The use of personal computers to administer, score, interpret, store, and manage standardized scales is discussed, and one such program—CAAP—is illustrated. Finally, the construction of standardized scales for particular agency needs is described briefly.

Introduction
What Are Standardized Scales?
    Advantages of Standardized Scales and Cautions in Their Selection
Selecting a Standardized Scale
    Purpose
    Directness
    Relevance to Intervention Planning
    Reliability
    Validity
    Ease of Use
    Accessibility
Administering a Standardized Scale
    Maximizing the Accuracy of the Information
    Selecting the Administration Setting
    Selecting the Timing and Frequency of Administration
Some Available Standardized Self-Report Scales
    WALMYR Assessment Scales (WAS)
        Scoring
        Interpretation
    Using Standardized Scales to Determine Clinically Significant Improvement
        Determining a Clinical Cutoff

Some Limitations of Standardized Self-Report Scales
Some Available Standardized Scales for Practitioners
Some Available Standardized Scales for Relevant Others
Some Available Standardized Scales for Independent Observers
Some Additional Standardized Self-Report Scales
Do-It-Yourself Scales
Using Standardized Scales in Groups
Computer Management of Standardized Scales
Summary
Appendix
    Reference Books for Tests and Measurements
Computer Assisted Assessment Package (CAAP): A User's Guide

From Chapter 7 of *Evaluating Practice: Guidelines for the Accountable Professional*, Sixth Edition. Martin Bloom, Joel Fischer, John G. Orme. Copyright © 2009 by Pearson Education, Inc. All rights reserved.

INTRODUCTION

Wouldn't it be nice to be able to meet a new client, get a preliminary understanding of his or her concerns, and then pull out of a drawer a questionnaire that you could easily use to measure repeatedly the targets identified for intervention? Wouldn't it be nice if you knew the reliability and validity of the questionnaire in advance?

Is it really possible to do all this? In fact, in many situations it is indeed possible to find a questionnaire that's already available, that does do all of these things, and that you know has been used successfully before.

There's a general term for such a tool— it's called a *standardized scale*. Because there are so many standardized scales available—literally thousands of them—the focus of this chapter is largely on helping you select one or more for your use. However, we also recommend and describe some specific standardized scales. But because your range of targets may be great, we want to enable you to be able to *select* scales that meet your own needs.

WHAT ARE STANDARDIZED SCALES?

Standardization refers to uniformity of procedures when administering and scoring a measure, and it implies the availability of existing data concerning the validity and reliability of the measure. Thus, a standardized scale is a measure that involves the administration of the same scale items (or other stimuli such as statements) to different people using the same administration and scoring procedures. It typically also involves the collection of information concerning the validity and reliability of the scale during its development. Suggested by the idea of standardization is the fact that standardized scales measure targets in terms of concepts with some general relevance to different clients (e.g., marital satisfaction, depression). This is in contrast to individualized rating scales and, in most cases, behavioral observations and logs, which are developed on a client-by-client basis and are designed to measure the unique aspects of an individual's experience.

Standardized scales, as we use the term, are often also called *standardized indexes*. In addition, what we have in mind is not the detailed, multipaged assessment scales that may be given once to a client at intake to collect data about life history, in-depth information about marital or family relations, and so on, but rather standardized scales that can be used for evaluation with single-system designs. Detailed, multipaged assessment scales definitely have their purpose in helping provide data on client functioning and for initial assessments, but they're not useful or practical for ongoing monitoring of client functioning. Rather, we're talking about briefer scales that can be used in single-system evaluation as repeated measures to monitor and evaluate client outcomes.

Standardized scales can be described in terms of six characteristics: (1) what they measure, (2) how well they measure it (i.e., their validity and reliability), (3) how they're structured, (4) how many dimensions they measure, (5) from whom they elicit information, and (6) their utility (i.e., how measures might be used to improve the decisions you make about your clients, the outcomes experienced by your clients, and the extent to which the measures are efficient, cost-effective, and acceptable to clients).

Standardized scales are available for measuring almost every conceivable area of human functioning. In general, standardized scales can be used to measure behaviors, feelings, cognitions, and attitudes. Also, there are standardized scales that measure almost every conceivable specific target area—ranging from alcoholism and anxiety to sexual satisfaction and suicide potential. In essence, scales dealing with almost any area in which you might be working have been designed and already are available. In the Appendix at the end of this chapter is a list of books that reference, describe, evaluate, and, in many cases, include copies of such standardized scales. You also might find the following Internet locations useful for locating information about standardized scales: Neurotransmitter.net (www.neurotransmitter.net/index.php); Health and Psychosocial Instruments (www.ovid.com/site/products/ovidguide/hapidb.htm#top); Harvey Cushing/John Hay Whitney Medical Library, Yale University School of Medicine (www.med.yale.edu/library/reference/publications/tests.html); Catholic University of America University Library (http://libraries.cua.edu/nurscoll/testmeas.html); University of Texas Library (www.lib.utexas.edu/subject/ss/psyc/test.html); and University of Washington Alcohol and Drug Abuse Institute (http://lib.adai.washington.edu/instruments/).

Standardized scales vary quite a bit in terms of their demonstrated validity and reliability. Extensive research evidence is available documenting different aspects of the validity and reliability of some standardized scales. For other standardized scales, only minimal evidence is available. All else being equal, it is best to select standardized scales that have a lengthy history of research and practice applications. (The absence of information on a topic—most commonly on validity, especially with newly developed instruments—does not mean the measure is not standardized. It does mean, though, that you interpret the results with more caution.) Fortunately, there are an increasing number of good reference books that you can use to get critical summaries of research concerning the validity and reliability of standardized scales (see the Appendix at the end of this chapter).

Standardized scales also differ in terms of their structure. Typically, though, standardized scales contain multiple questions, statements, or some other type of item rated along some dimension (e.g., a 7-point scale ranging from "strongly disagree" to "strongly agree"), items that require the selection of one option from several available options (e.g., multiple choice), or items that require some form of a "yes" or "no" response.

Standardized scales also differ in terms of the number of concepts they measure. Some standardized scales measure one concept, and the responses to all items are combined to provide a measure of that concept (e.g., marital satisfaction). Typically, these are called *unidimensional* measures. Other standardized scales measure more than one concept by combining responses from different subsets of items into separate measures of distinct concepts that often are related (e.g., satisfaction in relationships with co-workers, friends, and children). Typically, these are called *multidimensional* measures, and the measures of different concepts typically are called *subscales*. Multidimensional standardized scales often provide both measures of distinct but related concepts, and a measure of an overall concept thought to unify the distinct concepts measured by the subscales (e.g., overall satisfaction in interpersonal relationships).

Another dimension on which standardized scales differ is the perspective of the respondent. Standardized scales span the range of possible perspectives. A primary perspective is the client's (this is called a *client self-report scale*). Other perspectives around which numerous scales have been developed include those of the practitioner, relevant others, and independent observers.

Finally, standardized scales differ in terms of the time, effort, and training needed to administer, score, and interpret them. Many standardized scales are time-consuming, or require extensive specialized training. Many of these traditionally have been the province of clinical psychologists (e.g., the MMPI). This chapter, however, focuses on standardized scales that have been called *Rapid Assessment Instruments* (RAIs) (Levitt & Reid, 1981), the numerous standardized scales that are relatively brief; can be administered, scored, and interpreted without much time and effort; and can be used by professionals without extensive training in their use. In any case, the use of standardized scales can be simplified greatly by using personal computers, and so in a later section, we discuss the use of personal computers in the management of standardized scales.

Advantages of Standardized Scales and Cautions in Their Selection

Standardized scales have important advantages. A major advantage is that they are usually pretested for validity, reliability, or both. Therefore, you'll have some basis for judging the psychometric characteristics of a standardized scale, and often you'll have some basis for comparing the results you obtain with a client with the results obtained in previous research with relevant groups (i.e., norms might be available).

Another advantage of standardized scales, in contrast to an unstructured interview, for example, is that, at their best, standardized scales are structured to systematically and comprehensively elicit the information necessary to measure a target. This structure imposed by a standardized scale can increase the chance that the information necessary to measure a target will be collected.

Many standardized scales also have another advantage; that is, they can be used to compare the functioning of an individual client to the functioning of a normative population. This information then can be used to determine whether a client has a significant problem at the beginning of intervention, and whether the problem is no longer significant at some point during the course of the intervention, all relative to some normative population.

Another advantage of standardized scales is their efficiency. Many scales are rather simple to use. They're inexpensive, readily available, generally take very little time or energy on the part of either practitioner or client, and can be easy to administer and score. Further, they often provide a good deal of information about a variety of topics that are important to monitoring and evaluating practice.

Standardized scales have some compelling advantages, including the ease with which they can be used, the wide range of available scales to measure numerous concepts, and the increasing ease with which these measures can be located using reference texts, such as the ones listed in the Appendix to this chapter.

Despite their advantages, standardized scales should not be used to measure every target, nor should their results be accepted uncritically. One area for caution is that the name given to a standardized scale indicates the concept the author *intended* to measure, or otherwise believes the scale measures. Just because a measure is called a measure of "family functioning," "depression," "marital satisfaction," or "self-esteem" doesn't necessarily mean that that's what it measures. Also, just because two or more standardized scales claim to measure the same concept doesn't necessarily mean that they're interchangeable. Evidence of the reliability, and especially the validity, of a standardized scale is necessary to determine whether it measures what is intended, how well it does so, and the extent to which it measures the same concept as other measures.

Another issue is the fact that in many, if not most, cases you won't know all that you'd like to know about the reliability and validity of a particular standardized scale (or for that matter any measurement method). For example, you might find a standardized scale that seems perfect—designed exactly for the kind of target you're dealing with—with high test–retest (stability), and high internal consistency reliability. However, you might also find that only one or two types of validity issues have been dealt with, or perhaps that there is no validity information, or that the scale is fairly new, so research on its properties is not completed (e.g., its sensitivity to change, its utility with clients similar to your own). In such cases you should be cautious in your interpretation of the results you get with the scale, and your caution should be in proportion to the existing amount of information concerning validity and reliability.

Even if you find a standardized scale with comprehensive evidence of validity and reliability, remember that the research conducted on such scales is always done on large groups, under circumstances that are different in important ways from practice, and sometimes with people who are different from your clients in important ways (e.g., ethnicity, gender, age, education, etc.). Typically, participants involved in research on standardized scales don't have an ongoing relationship with the researcher; they don't complete the scale more than once or at most twice; and their scores don't have a bearing on their receipt of services (Rubin & Babbie, 2007). Indeed, as we mentioned earlier in the book, many, if not most, scales are initially studied (or "normed") on nonrepresentative groups. The more variation, say, cultural, ethnic, and so on, that your client has in comparison with the normative group, the greater the problem in using a given scale with your client. Thus, with an individual client there's always a chance for error—the group data may not apply. It may even be that on a particular day, something else that occurs distorts the client's or rater's perceptions so that the scores that day are off. Some of this may be overcome by the instructions you give in administering the scale and in conducting reliability checks, and so on. But the point is, no measure is foolproof. Don't uncritically accept the results of standardized scales; indeed, the validity of the results may vary from day to day and from client to client. So, as with all measures, remember that the score from a standardized scale is just one more piece of information that you can use in the context of all of the other quantitative and qualitative information that you have about your client, and only use and interpret this information in this broader context.

Another thing you should be cautious of is the fact that standardized scales measure targets in terms of general concepts that are assumed to be relevant to different clients, but they might not correspond to the unique realities of a particular client. (In a way they're like ready-to-wear clothing instead of custom-made clothing.) One apparent solution to this problem is for you to add or delete items from a standardized scale in an attempt to tailor it to a particular client. However, such *ad hoc* modifications in a standardized scale might compromise the validity and reliability of the scale in unknown ways and might compromise your ability to compare the results of the scale with results from previous research. Also, in some cases standardized scales are copyrighted with the provision that they be used intact without modifications, and to do otherwise would be a violation of copyright law. Therefore, in general we don't think it advisable to try to tailor standardized scales to particular clients. If you can't find a standardized scale suited to a particular client target, you should consider the direct observation or self-monitoring of client-specific behaviors, the construction and use of individualized rating scales, logs, or the use of nonreactive measures selected especially for a particular client target. You also might consider developing a new standardized scale, which we discuss later in this chapter. However, you're not required to use a standardized scale for each and every case (or any other measurement method for that matter). In some cases there might not be a suitable standardized scale available, or other methods of measurement might be more consistent with the conceptualization of the target. Remember, *the goal is to fit the measurement method to the client's target, not to fit the client's target to a convenient measurement method.*

Related to the fact that standardized scales measure targets in terms of concepts is the fact that some of these concepts are relatively general, and as such, are relatively indirect measures of targets. For example, measures of global impairment, such as the Global Assessment of Functioning scale, which we discuss later in this chapter, might be useful for providing an overall picture of changes, but such overall scores might be relatively insensitive to client change in delimited areas of social functioning targeted for intervention.

A final thing you should be cautious of in using standardized scales is the use of too many scales with a client. Because standardized scales tend to be easy to use, some practitioners combine them in a sort of test battery, and routinely administer them to all their clients. Of course, if the scales don't specifically apply to the client's target or situation, this is simply wasted effort. Also, the client may be overwhelmed or simply not take his or her responses seriously. In that case you may lose the client or lose meaningful results from the scales.

SELECTING A STANDARDIZED SCALE

The guidelines we've provided so far suggest only certain cautions in the selection of standardized scales. You still need more specific guidelines to judge the adequacy of individual scales and to make comparisons of different scales designed to measure the same target. For example, there are numerous standardized scales measuring alcohol use disorders (e.g., Rohsenow, 2008), depression (e.g., Dougherty, Klein, Olino, & Laptook, 2008; Persons & Fresco, 2008; Rush, First, & Blacker, 2008), and marital distress (e.g., Snyder, Heyman, & Haynes, 2008), to name just a few, and often you'll be faced with having to decide among different standardized scales designed to measure the same target. The purpose of this section is to help you make these judgments.

There are several guidelines that you can use to help you choose specific scales. These guidelines are based on the more general material regarding basic measurement principles, as well as on more practice-oriented criteria, all of which are applied here specifically to standardized scales. We should probably start by saying that it's unlikely that you will ever find "the perfect measure." Few measures will have all the characteristics or meet all the criteria described as follows. Thus, you will have to try to find measures that meet as many of these criteria as possible.

While we suggest caution in using and interpreting any standardized scale, for those that don't meet all the criteria, we urge that you be extra cautious. At the least, be clear about what criteria are not met, and try to estimate just how that might affect your use of the scale. For example, you might find that a standardized scale measure of alcohol abuse has been tested with men but not women. If your client is a woman and you suspect that women are more likely to underreport alcohol-related problems, you might take very seriously any hint of alcohol problems from a woman's responses. Following, then, is a brief description of several guidelines you can use to select specific standardized scales for your practice. Table 1 is a suggested outline for evaluating a standardized scale (see also AERA et al., 1999; Hunsley & Mash, 2008).

Purpose

The first and most obvious consideration in selecting a standardized scale is to determine its purpose. For what kinds of targets was it designed? For what kinds of client groups has it been used? Does the scale appear suitable to help you monitor and evaluate practice for your client with his or her unique background and experiences?

Find out if the previous research has been conducted on targets or clients like your own, and if norms for comparison purposes with your client's scores have been established. Often, norms for standardized scales are developed using white, middle-class college students as subjects. If your client differs substantially from the normative group (e.g., in ethnicity or income), the norms may not be applicable. If you still use the scale, you must interpret the results with due caution.

You may also find that a particular score serves as a "cutting point," a score that serves as a boundary

Table 1 Outline for evaluating standardized scales

A. General Information
   Title of questionnaire (including edition and forms if applicable)
   Author(s)
   Publisher, date of publication
   Time required to administer
   Format (booklets, answer sheets, other test materials, available scoring services)
B. Brief Description of Purpose, Nature of Scale
   General type of scale (e.g., individual or group, checklist)
   Population for which designed (age range, type of person)
   Nature of content (e.g., verbal, numerical)
   Subtests and separate scores
   Types of items
C. Directness
D. Relevance to Intervention Planning
   Utility for determining improvement or deterioration
   Utility for determining the presence of a condition
   Utility for determining conditions affecting or maintaining a condition
   Utility for selecting an effective intervention
E. Technical Evaluation
   1. Norms
      Type (e.g., percentiles, standard scores)
      Standardization sample: nature, size, representativeness, procedures followed in obtaining sample, availability of subgroup norms (e.g., age, sex, education, occupation, religion, ethnicity)
   2. Reliability
      Types and procedure (e.g., test–retest, alternate-form, internal consistency) including size and nature of samples employed
   3. Validity
      Types and validation procedures (content, criterion, construct) including size and nature of samples employed
   4. Sensitivity to change
F. Ease of Use
   Qualitative features of scale materials (e.g., design of scale booklet, editorial quality of content, attractiveness, durability, appropriateness for clients)
   Clarity of directions
   Scoring procedures
   Practicality
   Potential for repeated administration
G. Accessibility
   Practitioner qualifications and training
   Cost
   Copyright protection
H. Reviewer Comments
   Critical evaluation from formal reviews such as *The 17th Mental Measurements Yearbook* (Spies, Plake, Geisinger, & Carlson, 2007).
I. Summary Evaluation
   Major strengths and weaknesses of the measure cutting across all parts of the outline

Adapted from *Psychological Testing*, 4th ed. (pp. 676–677) by A. Anastasi, 1988, New York: Macmillan.

separating scores that indicate serious problems from scores that suggest the absence of such problems. Thus, a score on one side of the clinical cutting point suggests the existence of problems that may require professional services, while a score on the other side of the clinical cutting point suggests the absence of problems needing attention. (We'll have more to say about using a "cutting point" later in this chapter.)

Directness

In searching for a standardized scale to measure a target, try to select one that is as direct a measure of the target as possible. The more direct the measure, the more likely it is to register any changes that occur in the target, and the more likely it is to be meaningful and useful in general to you and your client. There are two ways in which standardized scales are sometimes used indirectly in place of more direct standardized scales, and you should be cautious of such uses.

One indirect use of a standardized scale is in measuring a general concept in place of using a measure of a specific dimension of that concept targeted for intervention. For example, if your intervention is designed to improve the quality of a parent's child-discipline skills, it would be better to use a measure of the quality of those particular skills instead of a general measure of parenting skills or knowledge. Or, if your intervention is designed to provide a client with tangible resources (e.g., food or clothing), it would be better to use a measure of the amount and quality of tangible resources instead of a general measure of social support. Finally, if your intervention is designed to eliminate a husband's physical abuse of his wife, it would be better to use a measure of physical abuse instead of a general measure of marital satisfaction.

Although, in general, standardized scales that provide direct measures of targets are preferable to those that are more general and less direct, more general multidimensional standardized scales do have a place in single-system evaluations. Such scales can be used for initial screening to determine the presence of specific targets for intervention, and they can be administered periodically to determine the generality of change, including a determination of improvement or deterioration in unanticipated areas. For example, the Multi-Problem Screening Inventory (MPSI) (Alvelo, Collazo, & Rosario, 2001; Hudson, 1990; Hudson & McMurtry, 1997; Nugent, 2003; Nurius & Hudson, 1993) includes 27 different subscales measuring a wide variety of targets (e.g., depression, alcohol abuse, school problems). In some cases the MPSI might be useful for screening and for determining the generality of change, but it would be inefficient to administer such a measure frequently in a case with a delimited number of targets. Finally, later in this chapter we describe several measures of overall impairment that you might find useful under some circumstances.

Relevance to Intervention Planning

In the selection of a standardized scale, or any measurement method for that matter, there should be reason to believe that it will enhance the intervention process in some way. Will it help determine whether a target is improving or deteriorating, so that any necessary modifications in the intervention plan can be undertaken? Will it help to determine whether a client is in need of intervention in a particular area? Will it help determine what may be affecting or maintaining the target? Will it help select the most effective intervention strategy? In most cases a single standardized scale won't help answer all of these questions, but if the answer to most or all of these questions is no, you should probably rethink the use of that particular scale.

Reliability

You should look to previous research to get an idea of the reliability of a standardized scale. You should look for evidence of the internal consistency of the scale items by looking for evidence of "split-half" or "odd-even" reliability or "coefficient alpha." If the scale is designed for use by practitioners, relevant others, or independent observers, or for obtaining information from clients about publicly observable events, you should look for evidence of interobserver reliability (the consistency with which information is provided by different observers). Finally, you should look for evidence of the test–retest reliability of the scale, the stability or consistency of the responses to the scale over time, a criterion that is particularly important in single-system designs because of repeated use of measurement tools over the course of baseline and intervention periods. In each case, the higher the reliability the better, and as a general rule, if the reliability is .80 or better, you have reasonably good reliability.

In addition to looking for existing evidence of the reliability of a standardized scale, there are some things that you can do to get some idea of the interobserver or

Standardized Scales

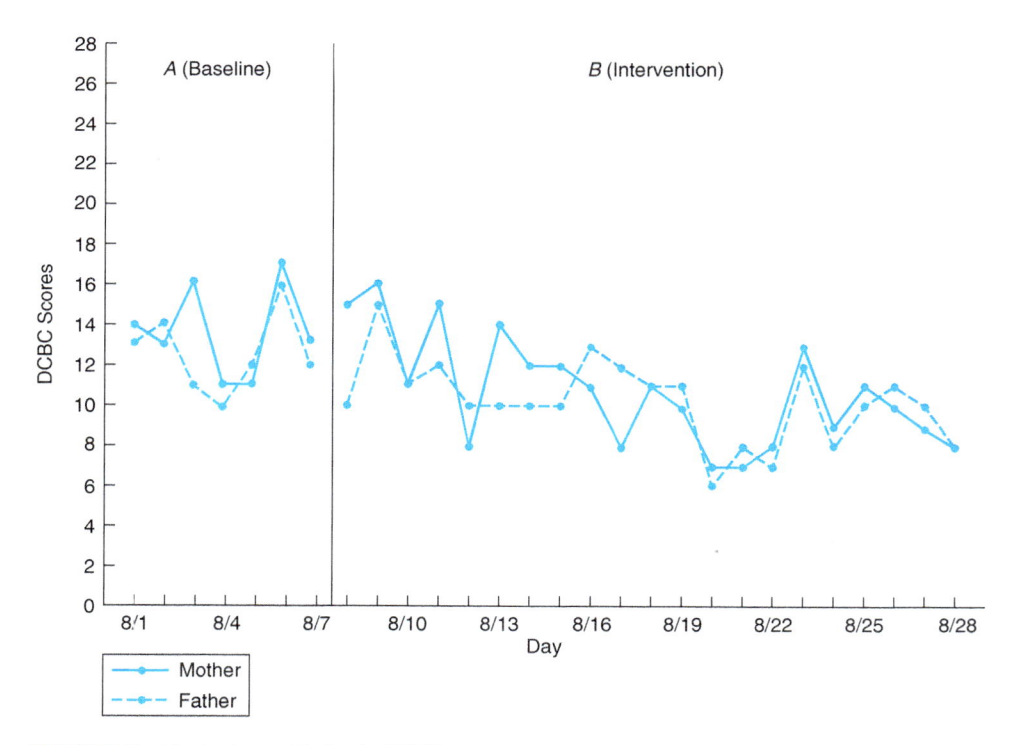

FIGURE 1a Mother's and father's DCBC scores.

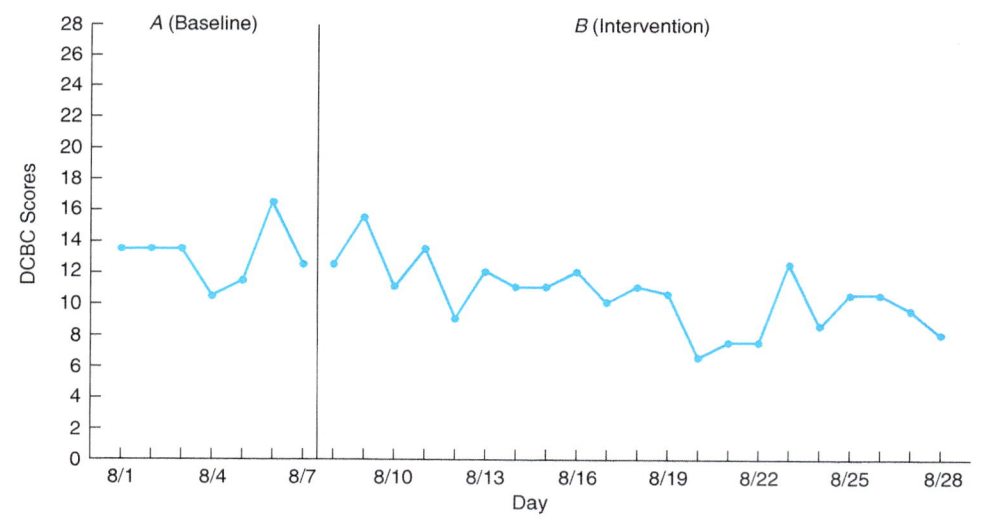

FIGURE 1b Average DCBC score.

test–retest reliability (but not internal consistency reliability) of a scale as used with a particular client. If relevant and practical, you can have two different people provide information about a client, even if only on a spot-check basis, and you can examine the agreement between observers (e.g., using visual examination of a graph, or some more precise statistical index such as kappa or a correlation coefficient. If two observers regularly complete the same standardized scale, the reports can be examined individually or they can be averaged and the average examined.

Suppose, for example, that in working with the parents of an 8-year-old girl one target for intervention is the child's behavior problems in the home. You decide to measure these problems using the subscale of the Daily Child Behavior Checklist (DAB), which is a 28-item parent-report checklist that measures displeasing child behaviors in the previous 24 hours (Fury & Forehand, 1983). This scale has a potential range of values from 0 to 28, and higher scores indicate more displeasing behaviors. Suppose that both parents completed the DAB and the results shown in Figure 1a were obtained. As shown in this figure, the observations are correlated over time but they're in less than perfect agreement. Figure 1b illustrates the average of these observers' scores. The advantage of such an average is that it will be more reliable than the observations of the individual observers (Fleiss, Levin, Paik, & Fleiss, 2003), and it will make it easier to discern trends. However, some information is lost in computing an average, and so it seems best to consider the scores of individual observers before averaging scores. It might be, for example, that one observer tends to have higher scores than the other, or that there are large differences between observers on some days that, when discussed with the observers, provides useful information for treatment.

You also can get some idea about the test–retest reliability of a standardized scale by examining the pattern of scores during baseline. If the scores are relatively stable during baseline you can be more confident of the test–retest reliability than if the responses are variable. In a way this is the single-system design version of test–retest reliability. Suppose, for example, that one target of intervention in working with a family is resolving problems around a fourth-grade boy's homework problems. You decide to measure these homework problems using the Homework Problem Checklist (HIP) (Anesko, Schick, Ramirez, & Levine, 1987), a 20-item parent-report measure of homework problems. The HIP has a potential range of scores from 0 to 60, with higher scores indicating greater problems; the average HIP score for fourth-grade boys is 11.84. You could be more confident of the test–retest reliability of the HIP if you obtained the stable HIP scores shown in Figure 2 than if you obtained the variable scores.

If the scores are variable, it might be due to inadequate test–retest reliability or to actual changes in homework problems. In either case, though, such variable scores can be transformed in an attempt to get a clearer picture of the pattern of results. One way to do this is to compute the average of the scores for the first and second time periods and plot this average for the first time period, average the scores for the second and third time periods, plot this average for the second time period, and so on. This is an example of a "moving average." The moving average for the variable HIP scores is shown in Figure 2. Notice that the moving average is much more stable than the untransformed, variable HIP scores. Also, such an average has the advantage of being more reliable than the separate data points, although it can obscure information. Thus, it's best to examine both untransformed and transformed scores (e.g., an unusually high score on one day and an unusually low score on another day might suggest important determinants of the target, but when scores from the 2 days are averaged they will produce a relatively typical score).

Most standardized scales haven't been developed for repeated administration over time, and they haven't been tested for stability under these conditions. Therefore, in selecting a standardized scale you should look for existing evidence of test–retest reliability, but you should also examine your data for particular clients for signs of stability or instability over time, especially during baseline phases when an intervention is not operating to produce change in whatever is being measured. You should also try to use baselines that are as long as practical.

Validity

Of course, you want to know whether a standardized scale really measures what its name implies. Does it appear valid "on its face"? That is, do the items on the scale appear to be "getting at" what they should? (Face validity is the least rigorous kind of validity, but a type that can be important in convincing a client of the relevance of the measure.) Check to see if other types of validity are addressed. Do the items in the scale seem to represent all the areas that should have been

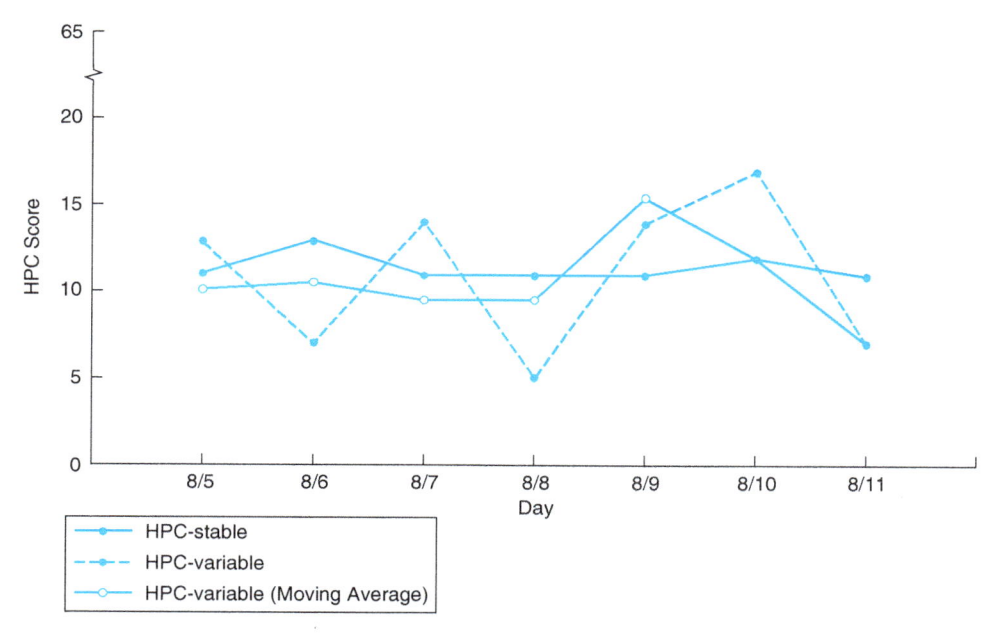

FIGURE 2 Stable, variable, and transformed HPC scores.

included (content validity)? Is there any mention of criterion (concurrent or predictive) validity? If so, you should be able to evaluate how well your scale compares or correlates with other measures that are considered to be valid measures of the target in question. The higher the correlation, the better. Further, you want to know whether your measure allows you to make predictions; for instance, to forecast whether people with certain scores on your scale are more or less likely to be a certain way or do a certain thing in the future. Similarly, you want to know whether your scale can distinguish between people who purportedly have a problem and those who don't. For example, if you're interested in a measure of depression, you would need to know whether a measure can distinguish between people who are and are not depressed.

You also would want to see whether a scale has construct validity. Has previous research on the scale shown that an interpretation of the instrument as a measure of a theoretical variable has been substantiated? If so, the scale you're reviewing should provide information on how many studies were conducted, how strong the associations were, and what studies might contradict this conclusion.

One aspect of construct validity for which you should be especially alert is evidence that a standardized scale is *sensitive to change* (i.e., when actual change occurs, the scale registers the change). If a scale hasn't demonstrated sensitivity to change in previous research, you can't be sure that it will show change even if your client really changes. This in itself is difficult to demonstrate, but if your scale has been used in previous research, and has shown sensitivity to change with those clients, then you do have some basis for concluding that it might pick up changes with your clients as well. A recent book by Hunsley and Mash (2008) addresses the issue of sensitivity across a wide range of measures.

Many scales don't provide information on all these forms of validity. But you would be on safer grounds using a scale that contains more information on validity (say, including criterion-related or construct validity) than less of it (say, just face validity). Many scales in early stages of development have little information on validity (e.g., studies relating this scale to others that already have established validity). In those situations, face validity (plus all the other criteria) might be all you have to go with. Then, you simply will have to be more cautious in interpreting results.

In addition to relying on existing evidence of the validity of standardized scales, your own evaluation of an individual client also can provide some evidence of the validity of standardized scales as used with your particular client (Proctor, 1990). Let's look at an example of this.

Suppose that a client seeks help because she feels overwhelmed with the burden of caring for her elderly mother, and she wants to improve her relationship with her adolescent daughter. She believes, and you agree, that a lack of support from her family in the care of her mother is a major cause of her feeling overwhelmed. You select the following measures for your evaluation:

1. The Caregiver Burden Scale (CBS) is selected to measure the client's feelings about her role as a caregiver to her elderly mother (Zarit, Reever, & Bach-Peterson, 1980). The CBS is a 29-item self-report scale that has a potential range of values from 0 to 84, and higher scores indicate more burdens.
2. The Perceived Social Support–Family Scale (PSS-Fa) is selected to measure family social support (Procidano & Heller, 1983). The PSS-Fa is a 20-item self-report scale with a potential range of values from 0 to 20, and *lower* scores indicate *more* support. (Actually, with the author's original scoring procedure, higher scores indicate more support, but the direction of the scores was reversed for this example to make it easier to interpret the relationship between this scale and the other two scales in the example.)
3. The Parent–Child Areas of Change Questionnaire (PC-ACQ) (Jacob & Seilhamer, 1985) is selected to measure the amount of change in the adolescent perceived as necessary by the mother. It's a 34-item self-report scale with a potential range of values from −102 to +102, and higher scores indicate that more change is seen as necessary.

Each scale is completed weekly. After a 3-week baseline, a 7-week intervention designed to increase family social support and decrease the mother's feelings of being burdened is implemented, and this is followed by a 7-week intervention designed to reduce the amount of change in the adolescent perceived as necessary by the mother. Results are shown in Figure 3 with scores on all scales ranging from 5 to 35, and the following patterns provide evidence of validity:

1. The week-to-week pattern of change in burden and social support is similar—when PSS-Fa scores go up (i.e., support decreases), CBS scores also rise (i.e., perceived burden increases), and when PSS-Fa scores go down, CBS scores also decrease. Therefore, the PSS-Fa and the CBS appear correlated over time, and this provides support for the construct validity of these two scales.

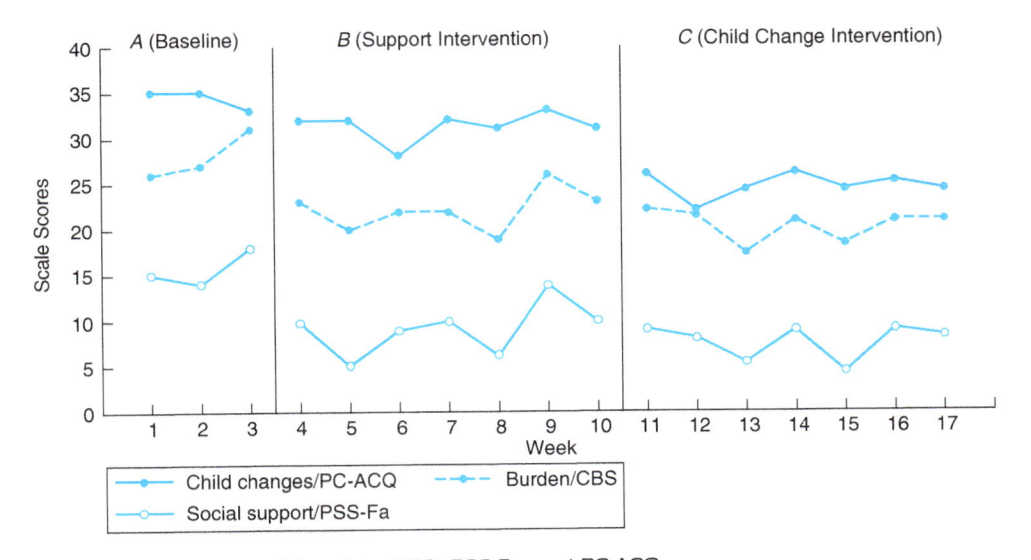

FIGURE 3 Construct validity of the CBS, PSS-Fa, and PC-ACQ.

2. The week-to-week pattern of change in PSS-Fa, CBS, and PC-ACQ scores are similar, but they don't follow exactly the same pattern (e.g., they're not perfectly correlated). The fact that these patterns are somewhat different suggests that to some extent the three scales measure different targets, and this provides further support for their construct validity. If the week-to-week pattern of change were the same for each scale, it would suggest that they all measure the same target (e.g., perhaps just generalized distress), instead of distinct targets.

3. The PSS-Fa, the CBS, and the PC-ACQ decrease when the intervention designed to enhance family social support is implemented (i.e., phase B), but the decrease in PSS-Fa and CBS scores is larger than the decrease in PC-ACQ scores. When the intervention designed to reduce the amount of change in the adolescent perceived as necessary by the mother is implemented (i.e., phase C), there's a further decrease in the PSS-Fa and the CBS, but the largest decrease occurs for the PC-ACQ scores. This pattern of change between phases suggests that the PSS-Fa, the CBS, and the PC-ACQ change in a theoretically predicted manner in response to intervention, which in turn suggests that they're sensitive to "real" change in the problems they attempt to measure.

Other measures also might be useful in the evaluation of this case, and these would let you further examine the validity of the measures. For example, the mother could be asked to self-monitor the amount of time spent caring for her elderly mother, and other family members might be asked to do the same. Individualized rating scales could be constructed to measure idiosyncratic caregiving responsibilities, mother–daughter conflicts, or aspects of family social supports of concern that weren't measured by the standardized scales. In any case, though, such information and the patterns of results among the different measures can provide evidence for the validity of the measures, or raise questions about their validity that might otherwise be overlooked.

Ease of Use

Single-system designs require the repeated measurement of client targets over time. Therefore, the ease with which a scale is used is an important consideration. A client or an observer might be "turned off," irritated, or bored when asked to fill out the same scale week after week. Although this is not just a problem of standardized scales (any measurement method may become aversive), the fact that a standardized scale never changes, requires some time and energy, and may not be all that interesting after the first few times one fills it out, add to the general problem. In part, this may be an issue regarding how much time the scale takes, how clearly it is written, and how much effort it requires. Try to find standardized scales that are reasonably brief, take no more than 5 to 15 minutes to complete, and don't require too much energy to fill out.

The time it takes to score and interpret a standardized scale is another consideration in determining the ease with which it can be used. Most standardized scales are relatively easy to score by hand or with an inexpensive calculator, and they're relatively easy to interpret. On the other hand, some standardized scales are complicated to score, some even requiring computer scoring, and their interpretation requires considerable time and training.

The characteristics of the person asked to complete a standardized scale also should be considered in determining ease of use. The person must be able to understand the scale. Reports of standardized scales increasingly include information about the reading level necessary to understand a standardized scale, and you should try to match this with what you know about your client's education and abilities.

Finally, if training in the use of the scale is necessary, the person must be able and willing to be trained. Don't select standardized scales that are beyond the ability of clients or observers asked to complete the scales.

Fortunately, there has been an increasing recognition of the importance of the ease with which measures can be used in practice. This recognition has led to the development and dissemination of a large number of standardized scales that can be used relatively easily on a repeated basis (e.g., Fischer & Corcoran, 2007a, b); see also the Appendix at the end of this chapter.

Accessibility

Accessibility is also an important consideration in the selection of a standardized scale. Some standardized scales are difficult to obtain. For example, some standardized scales need to be purchased from their authors or from companies that own the scales. In some cases these costs might be unacceptable. Some standardized scales are copyrighted, and you need permission to use the scale. Some standardized scales are not available for use by some professionals (e.g., some scales are available only to psychologists), or are not available to professionals without documentation of special training (e.g., courses in psychometrics and test interpretation).

ADMINISTERING A STANDARDIZED SCALE

Once you've selected your scale or scales for use with a particular client or target, you are still faced with the task of enabling someone to complete it. This may not be an easy matter. Whether you ask the client, a relevant other, or some other helping professional to fill out a scale, you may run into trouble. The way you involve someone in completing the scale is probably as important as selecting just the right scale for him or her to fill out.

It's likely that in your practice you mainly will be focusing on using standardized scales completed by your client, that is, self-reports. There are, of course, many instances when you may be using standardized scales completed by relevant others or other professionals, depending on the target or situation (e.g., a parent providing regular ratings of a child's behavior, a teacher filling out a checklist for a student, etc.). But the bulk of use of standardized scales appears to be directly with clients. For that reason, this section of the chapter focuses on the use of standardized scales directly with clients, though many of the principles (e.g., with regard to explaining the purpose of the instrument, etc.) apply no matter who is completing the scale. Actually, many of the principles on teaching clients or others to count behaviors (e.g., carefully defining the behavior, adequate training in observation, and achieving satisfactory interobserver reliability) apply here too. This is especially so when you're asking a relevant other to fill out a rating scale or behavior checklist.

Ideally, no single measurement method should be used to assess and monitor a client's targets, regardless of whether it's a standardized, self-report scale or some other type of measurement method. In general, we think you should use more than one measurement method, if possible, because no single measurement method will provide a comprehensive and completely accurate picture of a client. Different methods of measuring the same target will provide a more accurate picture of the target than a single method, although even multiple measures may not provide a completely accurate picture.

In some situations the sole use of a standardized, self-report scale is the only feasible option. For example, the client might refuse to use another measurement method, or information about the target of intervention is only directly available to the client (e.g., thoughts, feelings, or private behaviors).

Maximizing the Accuracy of the Information

Once you decide that a standardized scale is appropriate, it's crucial to attend to how you go about involving the client in its use. As we suggest for other measurement methods, present the scale with confidence and certainty about its usefulness. Sometimes practitioners with no experience in the use of measures in practice request this information in an uncertain, embarrassed, and apologetic fashion. This might suggest to the client that the task isn't important, or that it's indeed unreasonable to ask for the information, and the client might act accordingly and provide less than complete or accurate information. If you believe that the information you are requesting is important, convey this to the client; if you don't believe it's important, maybe you shouldn't ask for it!

Another way to increase the accuracy of the information collected using standardized, self-report scales is to give clients incentives for accuracy. A key incentive is the prospect of the successful resolution or prevention of target problems. After all, the information you are requesting is (or should be) for the client's benefit. It will be used to plan the intervention and to monitor its success so that any necessary modifications can be made to achieve a successful outcome. Often this point can be made by using the medical analogy (i.e., "just as a doctor uses a thermometer to monitor progress, we, too, have to have some method for checking our progress"), because most people have experience with "tests" used by physicians.

If the information you're asking for doesn't seem relevant to the client, it might be difficult to persuade the client that he or she will be better off to provide accurate reports. Therefore, the degree to which the requested information seems relevant to the client might also influence the accuracy of the client's reports. People will be more willing to provide complete and accurate reports if they understand the need for the information than if the information doesn't seem relevant. So, obviously you shouldn't ask for irrelevant information, but make sure the client understands the relevance of the information you do request.

Even if a client wants to provide complete and accurate information, ambiguous instructions can reduce the reliability of the reports because clients are left guessing about just what it is they are supposed to do or report. So, you can increase the chances of getting accurate information by giving the client clear instructions. Take the time to explain the task, and be sure that the client understands the instructions. When appropriate, you might ask clients to restate the instructions as a means of gauging whether they understand. In any case, encourage clients to ask questions whenever something is unclear, and be sure to give them the impression that you have the time to answer their questions, because this might encourage clients to ask much-needed questions. Also, make sure that you're knowledgeable about the measurement task and are prepared for questions.

Clients might want to provide complete and accurate information, but they might be reluctant because they don't know who has access to the potentially embarrassing information they're asked to provide. Therefore, another way to increase the accuracy of self-reports is by assuring the client of confidentiality. However, don't inadvertently deceive the client by implying that such information is completely confidential. Numerous exceptions exist to the privilege of confidentiality, and you need to be careful not to promise a greater degree of confidentiality than you can guarantee (Bloom & Orme, 1993; Kagle & Kopels, 2008).

Your reaction to the information provided by a client is another factor that can influence the accuracy of the information. For example, you might subtly show surprise or disapproval in response to a client's report, and consequently the client might subsequently provide less accurate information. For example, a practitioner might inadvertently encourage a client to report improvement even when it doesn't occur. You should be careful not to suggest possible responses.

Remember that self-reports are limited not only by what a client is *willing* to tell you, but also by what they're *able* to tell you. For example, under the right circumstances a client seeking help with alcohol abuse problems might be willing to tell you the average daily amount of alcohol consumed in the previous month, but unable to remember this information.

A parent might be willing to report, but unable to remember, the number of arguments with his or her adolescent in the previous 2 weeks. Therefore, the accuracy of self-report information depends upon whether the client has the information you request. You should ask yourself, and the client, whether the client is able to provide the needed information even if he or she is willing to do so. After all, you may get inaccurate information.

To ensure the accuracy of the information, try to be as sensitive as possible to the educational, social, and cultural background of the client, especially when there are differences between you and the client (such as age, gender, ethnicity, or sexual orientation). There is no substitute for cultural (and social) competence when requesting others to provide information. Some people may be so afraid of or uncomfortable with the scale for any number of reasons that, unless you give them an opportunity to express themselves, they may simply throw away the scale, not return it, or answer in an incorrect or distorted way. You may even want to read all of the questions aloud with clients just to make sure all of the terms are understood, and perhaps help them answer the first few questions to ensure that they do understand them. In fact, if clients have trouble reading or understanding the scale, one option may be to read the items aloud and have clients respond orally rather than in writing. However, many clients won't tell you directly that they can't read, so you need to look for signs of this and provide these clients with a face-saving "excuse" for your reading the questions to them (e.g., the scale is complicated). When you read items and ask the client to respond orally rather than in writing, interpret your results with caution since such changes may compromise the validity of the measure.

Sometimes self-report scales are subject to problems such as *response bias* (the client responds to each item on a scale in the same or a patterned way—for example, all 2s on a 5-point scale)—and *social desirability response set* (the client's responses to some items are based more on what the client thinks he or she "should" say than on what he or she actually thinks or feels). Some scales have built-in ways to solve these problems. For example, some try to control response bias by varying the directionality of items so that a 2 on one item might indicate something positive and a 2 on another something negative. Others may try to control social desirability by carefully wording items so that they don't obviously reflect social values. One of the most effective ways to control these problems is in how you present the scale to the client, urging the client to be completely honest because that is the only way you can plan the optimal intervention program. In addition, encourage the client to try to respond to each item independently, that is, not in a pattern. If you do find a patterned response, you should use the resulting data cautiously, if at all, and you should talk with the client (or observer) to try to determine the reason for the responses and to try to increase the accuracy of the responses to the scale.

Selecting the Administration Setting

You have at least two options for where your client completes the scale: in your office or elsewhere, for example, in the client's home. If the scale is relatively brief, you may have the client fill it out at the office just before coming in to see you or even during the first few minutes of the interview. The advantage is that you can be relatively sure it will be completed, it will be completed at about the same time on a regular basis, you will be available to answer questions, and you can give immediate feedback to the client.

On the other hand, if the client is able and willing to fill out the scale at home, it could serve as a sort of "homework" task that can help structure your at-home intervention program (if you're working on one). Similarly, if the client fills out the scale at home, he or she can do so without the potential pressure of feeling "watched," and perhaps the act of filling out the scale will provide more material for you and the client to work on in your next meeting.

Another thing to keep in mind about the setting is that the client should have a private, quiet, physically comfortable place to complete the scale. Privacy is important because asking a client to provide personal information when other people are around can be embarrassing and may lead to biased reports. For example, reports elicited from an adolescent might differ depending upon whether they're elicited in private or in the presence of parents. A quiet, comfortable environment is important because asking clients to report information under uncomfortable, chaotic, noisy, or otherwise distracting conditions also can reduce the accuracy of the report.

A final consideration is that the client should complete the scale at the same time and in the same place each time. For example, if the client is filling out the scale every week, try to see that he or she fills it out under generally the same conditions, for example, at the same time (say, after dinner) and in the same place (say, in the kitchen). The purpose of this is to try to minimize the chance that the client's responses will be determined or affected by the situation. If conditions do vary, try to take this into account when scoring and interpreting the results.

Selecting the Timing and Frequency of Administration

Finally, you have to make a decision about how often to fill out the scale. This depends on four things. The first is instructions accompanying the scale. If the scale has built-in requirements for how often it should be administered, you probably don't have to worry too much about this issue. Second, the length of the scale and the time and energy it takes probably are related to how often you have the client fill it out. A general rule would be the longer the scale and the more time it takes, the less often you would ask someone to fill it out. Third, the willingness or ability of the client to fill out your scale plays a key role in determining how often you ask him or her to fill it out. If the client indicates he or she is getting bored or annoyed with the scale, it's a good sign that you should ask him or her to fill it out less frequently. This is something that should be checked each time the client returns a scale to you. Finally, the reason for using the scale, as well as the type of scale, should have a bearing on how often you use it. As a general rule, the more you rely on a standardized scale as your primary measure for assessment and evaluation, the more often you should administer it.

We generally recommend that self-report scales be filled out approximately once a week, unless they are extremely brief (say, under 10 items) and have very good test–retest reliability that shows they will be stable when used repeatedly. This will give you some indication of changes in the target over time, as well as a sense of the extent or magnitude of the target at any given time. On the other hand, once-a-week administration does place some limitations on the utility of the information because it doesn't allow day-to-day tracking of changes. More precise behavior checklists and rating scales, for example, those filled out by relevant others, can be used more frequently, on an "as needed" basis, or daily if necessary. Of course, it's up to you to make adjustments if the scale is being used incorrectly. You may have to increase or decrease its use based on feedback from each person using it.

Once you begin to collect data from a scale, and assuming this can be translated into some quantity, such

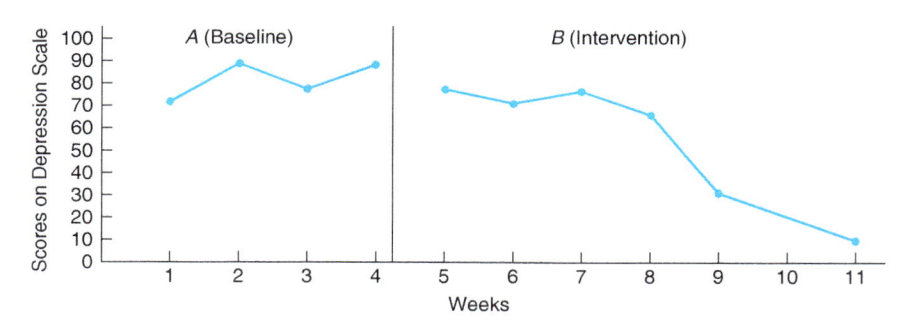

FIGURE 4 Scores on a depression scale for baseline and intervention periods.

as a total score or subscale scores, you can chart this information just as you would any other type of data you collect. This chart can serve as a clear source of feedback to the client about his or her scores on the scale and can also be used as a starting point for further work. For example, Figure 4 illustrates baseline and intervention information for a depression scale in which higher scores indicate greater or more depression.

SOME AVAILABLE STANDARDIZED SELF-REPORT SCALES

So far the thrust of this chapter has been to try to help you evaluate and select standardized scales. One of the primary reasons for this focus is that there are so many standardized scales (literally thousands, as we've mentioned), and such a huge range of practitioners, targets, and settings, that it would be extremely difficult if not impossible to identify standardized scales that would be suitable for all people in all settings at all times. Thus, we believe the more productive strategy is to provide guidelines for you to use to select your own scales.

However, we would like to take this one step further. There are some standardized scales that we can suggest just to illustrate the types and range of instruments that are available. In this and the following sections we provide some examples of standardized scales to be completed by: (a) clients (i.e., self-reports), (b) practitioners, (c) relevant others, and (d) independent observers. Of course, we are not trying to present all possible available instruments. For example, in the area of client self-report scales, two new books by Fischer and Corcoran (2007a, b) describe and reproduce hundreds of measures. In addition, journals such as *Psychological Assessment, Applied Psychological Measurement, Educational and Psychological Measurement, Research on Social Work Practice,* and *Assessment* frequently feature newly developed standardized scales. Thus, we are providing only a sample of available measures in each area. The Appendix to this chapter lists a number of references for locating other measures. Table 2 provides some examples of standardized self-report scales along with brief descriptions of each.

WALMYR Assessment Scales (WAS)

One of the encouraging innovations in measurement for single-system evaluation in clinical practice has been the development of a set of standardized scales by Hudson and his co-workers—the WALMYR Assessment Scales (WAS) (Hudson, 1997; Hudson & Faul, 1998). Most of these scales were designed specifically for single-system evaluation to monitor and evaluate the magnitude (extent, degree, intensity) of a client's problem through periodic administration of the same scales to the client.

To date, over 35 scales have been developed for the WAS package, based on an assessment of the types of personal, interpersonal, and social dysfunctions that appear to take up a large portion of practitioners' time. These scales are listed and described briefly in Table 3; one of the actual scales (Figure 5) is reprinted with permission of Dr. Walter Hudson.*

---

*The scales should not be reproduced directly from the book. Additional information about all of these scales and order forms for purchasing them can be obtained from WALMYR Publishing Co., PO Box 12217, Tallahassee, FL, 32317-2217. Voice: (850) 383-0045; Fax: (850) 383-0970; Email: walmyr@walmyr.com. Also, a web site is available to provide information about these scales: www.walmyr.com.

Table 2 Examples of standardized self-report scales

- *Children's Depression Inventory (CDI):* See Table 4.
- *Beck Depression Inventory-2nd ed. (BDI-II):* The BDI-II is a 21-item measure of depression. The BDI-II is copyrighted and can be obtained from:
  Pearson
  19500 Bulverde RD
  San Antonio, TX 78259
  Voice: (800) 211-8378
  Fax: (800) 232-1223
  Internet: http://pearsonassess.com
  Beck, A. T., Steer, R. A., & Brown, G. K. (1996). *Beck Depression Inventory-II Manual.* San Antonio, TX: Psychological Corporation.
- *Inventory of Depressive Symptomatology (IDS) and Quick Inventory of Depressive Symptomatology (QIDS):* See Table 4.
- *Center for Epidemiologic Studies Depression Scale (CES-D):* The CES-D is a 20-item measure of depressive symptoms. The CES-D is in the public domain.
  Radloff, L. S. (1977). The CES-D Scale: A self-report depression scale for research in the general population. *Applied Psychological Measurement, 1,* 385–401.
- *Outcome Questionnaire-45 (OQ-45):* The OQ-45 is a 45-item measure of subjective discomfort, interpersonal relations, social role performance, and positive aspects of satisfaction and functioning. The OQ-45 is copyrighted and can be obtained from:
  OQ Measures
  P. O. Box 521047
  Salt Lake City, UT 84152-1047
  Voice: (888) 647-2673
  Fax: (801) 747-6900
  Internet: www.oqmeasures.com
  Lambert, M. J., et al., (1996). The reliability and validity of the outcome questionnaire. *Clinical Psychology and Psychotherapy, 3,* 106-116.
- *Penn State Worry Questionnaire-Past Week (PSWQ-PW):* The PSWQ-PW is a 15-item measure of generalized anxiety. The PSWQ-PW is in the public domain and can be found in:
  Stober, J., & Bittencourt, J. (1998). Weekly assessment of worry: An adaptation of the Penn State Worry Questionnaire for monitoring changes during treatment. *Behavior Research and Therapy, 36,* 645-656.
- *Alcohol Use Disorders Identification Test (AUDIT):* See Table 5.
- *Drinker Inventory of Consequences (DrInC)*: The DrInC is a 50-item measure of five alcohol-related problem areas: Physical, Intrapersonal, Social Responsibility, Interpersonal, and Impulse Control over the respondent's lifetime (DrInC-2L) and since the last interview (DrInC-2R). The DrInC is in the public domain and it is available online or from:
  Center on Alcoholism, Substance Abuse, and Addictions (CASAA)
  The University of New Mexico
  2650 Yale SE MSC11-6280
  Albuquerque, NM 87106
  Voice: (505) 925-2300
  Fax: (505) 925-2301
  Internet: http://casaa.unm.edu/inst.html
  Miller, W. R., Tonigan, J. S., & Longabaugh, R. (1995). *The Drinker Inventory of Consequences (DrInC): An instrument for assessing adverse consequences of alcohol abuse* (Project MATCH Monograph Series, Vol. 4) (NIH Publication No 95-3911). Rockville, MD: National Institutes of Mental Health.
- *Stages of Change Readiness and Treatment Eagerness Scale (SOCRATES)*: The SOCRATES is a 19-item measure of readiness for change in alcohol and illicit drug users. The SOCRATES is in the public domain and it may be used without permission. The alcohol and drug use versions, scoring templates, and guidelines for interpretation are available free of charge from:
  Center on Alcoholism, Substance Abuse, and Addictions (CASAA)
  The University of New Mexico
  2650 Yale SE MSC11-6280
  Albuquerque, NM 87106

Table 2 (*continued*)

  Voice: (505) 925-2300
  Fax: (505) 925-2301
  Internet: http://casaa.unm.edu/inst.html
  Miller, W. R., & Tonigan, J. S. (1996). Assessing drinkers' motivation for change: The Stages of Change Readiness and Treatment Eagerness Scale (SOCRATES). *Psychology of Addictive Behaviors, 10,* 81-89.

- *Columbia Impairment Scale (CIS):* The CIS is a 13-item global measure of impairment in children and adolescents, and it measures four dimensions: interpersonal relations, psychopathology, job or schoolwork, and use of leisure time. There are two versions of the CIS, one administered to the child and another to the parent. The CIS can be used without permission, it can be found in Bird et al. (1996), and it can be obtained from:

  Hector R. Bird, M. D.
  Department of Child Psychiatry
  New York State Psychiatric Institute
  1051 Riverside Dr.
  New York, NY 10032
  Voice: (212) 543-2591
  Fax: (212) 543-5730
  Bird, H., et al. (1996). Global measures of impairment for epidemiologic and clinical use with children and adolescents. *International Journal of Methods in Psychiatric Research, 6,* 295–307.

Table 3 The WALMYR assessment scales package

Personal Adjustment Scales
Generalized Contentment Scale (GCS). The GCS is designed to measure the severity of nonpsychotic depression.
Index of Self-Esteem (ISE). The ISE is designed to measure the severity of problems with self-esteem.
Index of Clinical Stress (ICS). The ICS is designed to measure the severity of problems with personal stress.
Clinical Anxiety Scale (CAS). The CAS is designed to measure the severity of problems with phobic anxiety.
Index of Peer Relations (IPR). The IPR is designed to measure the severity of problems in peer relationships.
Index of Alcohol Involvement (IAI). The IAI is designed to measure the severity of problems with alcohol abuse.
Index of Drug Involvement (IDI). The IDI is designed to measure the severity of problems with drug abuse.
Sexual Attitude Scale (SAS). The SAS is designed to measure a liberal or conservative orientation toward human sexual expression.
Index of Homophobia (IHP). The IHP is designed to measure the level of homophobia.

Dyadic Adjustment Scales
Index of Marital Satisfaction (IMS). The IMS is designed to measure the severity of problems in a dyadic relationship.
Index of Sexual Satisfaction (ISS). The ISS is designed to measure the severity of problems in the sexual component of a dyadic relationship.
Partner Abuse Scale: Non-Physical (PASNP). The PASNP is completed by the abuse victim and is designed to measure the severity of problems with nonphysical abuse in a dyadic relationship.
Partner Abuse Scale: Physical (PASPH). The PASPH is completed by the abuse victim and is designed to measure the severity of problems with physical abuse in a dyadic relationship.
Non-Physical Abuse of Partner Scale (NPAPS). The NPAPS is completed by the abuser and is designed to measure the severity of problems with nonphysical abuse in a dyadic relationship.
Physical Abuse of Partner Scale (PAPS). The PAPS is completed by the abuser and is designed to measure the severity of problems with physical abuse in a dyadic relationship.

Family Adjustment Scales
Index of Family Relations (IFR). The IFR is designed to measure the severity of family relationship problems as seen by the respondent.
Index of Parental Attitudes (IPA). The IPA is designed to measure the severity of problems in a parent–child relationship as seen by the parent.

Table 3 (*continued*)

Child's Attitude toward Mother (CAM) and Child's Attitude toward Father (CAF). The CAM and CAF scales are designed to measure the severity of problems in a parent–child relationship as seen by the child.

Index of Brother Relations (IBR). The IBR is designed to measure the severity of problems with brother relationships as seen by a sibling.

Index of Sister Relations (ISR). The ISR is designed to measure the severity of problems with sister relationships as seen by a sibling.

Children's Behavior Rating Scale (CBRS). The CBRS is designed for use by a parent or guardian as a scaled checklist to reflect the type and degree of behavioral problems that are exhibited by a child.

Organizational Assessment Scales

Index of Sexual Harassment (ISH). The ISH is designed to measure the severity of sexual harassment as seen by the respondent.

Client Satisfaction Inventory (CSI). The CSI is designed to measure the degree of satisfaction experienced by clients with respect to services.

Index of Managerial Effectiveness (IME). The IME scale is designed to measure the severity of problems in managerial ability as seen by the respondent.

Index of Job Satisfaction (IJS). The IJS scale is designed to measure the degree of satisfaction an employee feels in relationship to her or his current employment situation.

Educational Assessment Scales

Classroom Teacher Evaluation Scale (CTES). The CTES is used to evaluate teacher performance in the classroom.

Practicum Instructors Evaluation Form (PIEF). The PIEF is used to evaluate field practicum instructor performance as a teacher.

Multidimensional Assessment Scales

Brief Adult Assessment Scale (BAAS). The BAAS is a self-report measure that helps you to better assess and understand the severity or magnitude of adult client problems across 16 different areas of personal and social functioning: depression, self-esteem problems, partner problems, sexual discord, problems with a child, personal stress, problems with friends, aggression, problems with work associates, family problems, suicide, nonphysical abuse, physical abuse, problems at work, alcohol abuse, and drug use.

Brief Family Assessment Scale (BFAS). The BFAS is a self-report measure that helps you to better assess and understand the severity or magnitude of seven different family problems: personal stress, family supports for members, familial economic stress, family member aggressive behavior, problems with children, drug use in the family, alcohol use in the family.

Family Assessment Screening Inventory (FASI). The FASI scale is a multidimensional self-report measure that helps you to better assess and understand the severity or magnitude of family problems across 25 different areas of personal and social functioning.

Gate Control Pain Management Scale (GC-PMI). The GC-PMI scale is a multidimensional self-report measure that is designed for use in the assessment and management of chronic pain.

Inner Interaction Scale of Social Functioning (IISSF). The IISSF scale is a multidimensional self-report measure that helps you to better assess and understand the severity or magnitude of social functioning problems across three different areas of social functioning, namely achievement, satisfaction, expectation, and three areas of social dysfunctioning, namely frustration, stress, and helplessness.

Multidimensional Adolescent Adjustment Scale (MAAS). The MAAS scale is a self-report measure that helps you to better assess and understand the severity or magnitude of adolescent client problems across 16 different areas of personal and social functioning: depression, self-esteem problems, problems with mother, problems with father, personal stress, problems with friends, problems with school, aggression, family problems, suicide, guilt, confused thinking, disturbing thoughts, memory loss, alcohol abuse, and drug use.

Multi-Problem Screening Inventory (MPSI). The MPSI scale is a multidimensional self-report measure that helps you to better assess and understand the severity or magnitude of client problems across 27 different areas of personal and social functioning.

Multi-Problem Screening Questionnaire (MPSQ). The MPSQ scale is a brief multidimensional self-report measure that gives you rapid client assessment across eight areas of personal and social functioning with the use of only 65 items.

Of course, there are hundreds of other self-report scales that are appropriate for use with single-system designs. We hope our description of the WAS package won't discourage you from using the references we provide in the Appendix and exploring and using other instruments.

The major reasons we are presenting this set of scales, as an example of available scales, is that it's one of the few—perhaps the only—package of scales designed to be used as repeated measures expressly with single-system designs. Most of the scales are short (usually 25 items), easy to administer, easy to interpret, and easy to complete and score. Each one takes about 3 to 5 minutes to complete and about the same time to score. Also, all of the WAS scales can be administered and scored using the CAAP computer program described later in this chapter.

In addition to being feasible for use with single-system designs, most of the scales in the WAS package have internal consistency reliabilities of .90 or better, which is very high. Similarly, for the scales for which test–retest reliability (stability) has been examined, these reliabilities have been very good. Further, these scales all have excellent face, concurrent, and construct validity. They have good ability to discriminate between people known or admitting to having problems and people who claim or are known not to have problems in each area. In other words, the scales appear to measure what they're intended to measure.

Scoring. For most of the WAS package clients are asked to rate each item on a 7-point scale ranging from 1, "none of the time," to 7, "all of the time." (For some of the scales a 5-point scale is used.) For each scale the lowest possible total score is 0, the highest is 100, and higher scores indicate greater magnitude of a problem.

A distinct advantage of these scales is that they are all scored in the same way. To minimize response set bias, all of the scales contain some "reverse-scored" items, and the first step in scoring each of these scales is to reverse-score these items (the particular item numbers to be reverse-scored are listed at the bottom of each scale). For example, for a questionnaire that uses a 7-point scale, a score of 7 is rescored as 1, a score of 6 is rescored as 2, a score of 5 is rescored as 3, a score of 4 is left unchanged, a score of 3 is rescored as 5, a score of 2 is rescored as 6, and a score of 1 is rescored as 7. The easiest way to do this is to first circle the reverse-scored item responses, cross out the original responses, and either use the rescoring method described earlier in this paragraph or use the following formula to get the reverse-scored item response (note that this formula produces the same results as the reverse-scoring process described previously and also can be used to reverse-score any items on any scales) (Hudson, 1997):

$$Y = K + 1 - X$$

where:
Y = the reverse-scored item response
K = the largest possible value for an item response (i.e., 5 or 7)
X = the original item response

Thus, if an item to be reverse-scored is given a 5 by a client and $K = 7$, then $Y = 7 + 1 - 5 = 3$.

After reverse-scoring the appropriate items for a scale, the total score for that scale is computed by using the following formula (Hudson & Faul, 1998):

$$S = \frac{(\text{Sum}[Y] - N)(100)}{(N)(K - 1)}$$

where:
S = the total score
Sum (Y) the sum of the item responses (i.e., add all item responses *after* reverse-scoring)
N = the number of items that were properly completed
K = the largest possible value for an item response (i.e., 5 or 7)

In other words, add up all scores after reverse-scoring, subtract the number of items properly completed, multiply that by 100, and divide that by the number of items properly completed multiplied by the largest possible value for an item response minus 1.

Any item that is left blank or given a score outside the scoring range is assigned a score of 0. Incidentally, if your client does happen to omit some items, you should check with the client to see why this happened. It may be that the client did not understand the item. It also could be that the client is particularly sensitive about, or has a problem dealing with, the issue raised by that question. Indeed, these omissions could serve as a clue to other problems that could help you in developing a more well-rounded intervention program. However, if the client completes fewer than 80% of the items for a scale, we suggest that particular scale not be used, since its validity might be affected.

Standardized Scales

Table 4 Example of Generalized Contentment Scale

Items	Score	Reverse Score (K − Y + 1)
1	3	
2	1	
3	3	
4	4	
⑤	6	2(7 − 6 + 1)
6	5	
7	1	
⑧	2	6(7 − 2 + 1)
⑨	3	5(7 − 3 + 1)
10	1	
⑪	1	7(7 − 1 + 1)
⑫	4	4(7 − 4 + 1)
⑬	6	2(7 − 6 + 1)
14	2	
⑮	5	3(7 − 5 + 1)
⑯	4	4(7 − 4 + 1)
17	2	
18	5	
19	2	
20	2	
㉑	7	1(7 − 7 + 1)
㉒	1	7(7 − 1 + 1)
㉓	5	3(7 − 5 + 1)
㉔	4	4(7 − 4 + 1)
25	2	
	33	48

As an example, suppose on the Generalized Contentment Scale (a measure of the degree of nonpsychotic depression, with higher scores indicating greater depression; see Figure 5) a client reports the scores listed in Table 4.

To score the scales, follow these steps:

1. *Reverse-score all the items noted at the bottom of each scale.* For this scale, reverse-score items 5, 8, 9, 11, 12, 13, 15, 16, 21, 22, 23, 24. This is done in the third column of the table.

2. *Add up all the items you reverse-scored.* The total at the bottom of the third column is 48.

3. *Add up all the items you did not reverse-score.* In the second column, these scores (with the items you reverse-scored deleted) total 33.

4. *Add these two sums together.* (48 + 33) = 81. This completes the first step, the sum of all scores after reverse-scoring.

5. *Subtract the number of properly completed items, which in this case is 25.*

    (81 − 25) = 56.

6. *Multiply this figure by 100*

    (100 × 56 = 5,600).

7. *Divide this number by the number of items completed times 6 (if the items are answered on a 7-point scale and 4 if they are answered on a 5-point scale.)*

    $$\frac{5{,}600}{(25)(6)} = \frac{5{,}600}{150} = 37.3, \text{ or } 37$$

8. *The final number, 37, is the client's score on the scale (in this case, the GCS or depression scale) developed to range from 0 to 100.*

Interpretation. On all scales of the WAS, the higher the score, the greater the magnitude of the problem. How high does a score have to be to indicate a significant problem, though? Most of the WAS scales have a "clinical cutting point" or "cutoff score" of approximately 30 (Hudson, 1997). The exact score varies a little depending on the particular scale. The idea here is that people who score over 30 generally have been found to have problems in the area being measured, while people who score below 30 have been found not to. Therefore, the cutting score provides a rough diagnostic indicator and a useful standard against which to judge the success of an intervention.

The cutting score should be used with caution and further research is needed to completely validate it. At present it's probably best to use a score of 30 as a rough guide to the presence or absence of problems. It would be better still to consider a range of values from 25 to 35 as a gray area that indicates the cutting point regarding the possible presence or absence of a problem. This particular gray area is based on the fact that the standard error of measurement for these scales is approximately 5. (The exact value varies depending on the particular scale.) If a score falls within this gray area of ±1 SEM, it's best to get additional supporting evidence before concluding that the client does or doesn't have a significant problem in the area being assessed. Scores below 25 probably indicate the absence

Name: _____ Today's Date: _____

This questionnaire is designed to measure the way you feel about your life and surroundings. It is not a test, so there are no right or wrong answers. Answer each item as carefully and as accurately as you can by placing a number beside each one as follows.

1 = None of the time
2 = Very rarely
3 = A little of the time
4 = Some of the time
5 = A good part of the time
6 = Most of the time
7 = All of the time

1. ____ I feel powerless to do anything about my life.
2. ____ I feel blue.
3. ____ I think about ending my life.
4. ____ I have crying spells.
5. ____ It is easy for me to enjoy myself.
6. ____ I have a hard time getting started on things that I need to do.
7. ____ I get very depressed.
8. ____ I feel there is always someone I can depend on when things get tough.
9. ____ I feel that the future looks bright for me.
10. ____ I feel downhearted.
11. ____ I feel that I am needed.
12. ____ I feel that I am appreciated by others.
13. ____ I enjoy being active and busy.
14. ____ I feel that others would be better off without me.
15. ____ I enjoy being with other people.
16. ____ I feel that it is easy for me to make decisions.
17. ____ I feel downtrodden.
18. ____ I feel terribly lonely.
19. ____ I get upset easily.
20. ____ I feel that nobody really cares about me.
21. ____ I have a full life.
22. ____ I feel that people really care about me.
23. ____ I have a great deal of fun.
24. ____ I feel great in the morning.
25. ____ I feel that my situation is hopeless.

Copyright © 1992, Walter W. Hudson   Illegal to Photocopy or Otherwise Reproduce
5, 8, 9, 11, 12, 13, 15, 16, 21, 22, 23, 24.

FIGURE 5 Generalized Contentment Scale (GCS).

of a problem, and scores above 35 probably indicate the presence of a problem. However, even a score of 24 doesn't absolutely indicate the absence of a problem, and a score of 36 doesn't absolutely indicate the presence of a problem. The point is that higher scores should be seen as deserving of attention, with the goal of intervention being to reduce those scores to at least below 30.

While these scales are intended to be used to measure the severity, intensity, degree, or magnitude of a problem, they were not designed to determine the source or origin of the client's problem. Thus, to that extent, they don't provide all the diagnostic or assessment information that is necessary prior to beginning an intervention program. Information about the nature, source, origin, or type of problem should be obtained from the client, relatives, co-workers, friends of the client, and your own assessment.

The periodic administration of the same scale to marital partners or family members can provide useful information for planning and evaluating an intervention. For example, the Index of Marital Satisfaction (another WAS measure) might be administered periodically and independently to a husband and wife. Each spouse might be asked to rate his or her own satisfaction, and to estimate the partner's satisfaction. This might enhance the detection of misperceptions and facilitate communication, in addition to providing a basis for monitoring change over time. Ideally, an intervention designed to enhance communication would reduce dissatisfaction, and would increase the extent to which the husband and wife understand each other's level of satisfaction.

Figure 6, for example, shows a husband's self-ratings of marital dissatisfaction as measured using the Index of Marital Satisfaction (IMS) (higher scores indicate greater dissatisfaction), and his wife's estimates of his dissatisfaction. Figure 7 shows comparable data for the wife. Figure 6 shows that during baseline and intervention the wife overestimated her husband's level of dissatisfaction, although after the onset of intervention the overestimation was gradually reduced. Figure 7 shows that during baseline there was no relationship between the wife's self-rating of satisfaction and her husband's estimates of her satisfaction, although after the onset of intervention there was a high degree of agreement between the self-ratings and the husband's estimates. Finally, both Figures 6 and 7 indicate that the degree of dissatisfaction for both partners was steadily reduced over the course of intervention.

There are some precautions in using the WAS scales. The scales are not recommended for children under the age of 12. Also, they should not be self-administered to clients with poor literacy skills. Similarly, all of the scales should be used with extreme caution with any clients who may need to demonstrate positive change in order to qualify for a change in legal status, for example, prison inmates or patients in mental hospitals seeking release. You have to discuss their use even more carefully with such clients and attempt to evaluate whether the data are reasonably accurate before you can be relatively certain of their clinical or evaluation value in such situations.

Using Standardized Scales to Determine Clinically Significant Improvement

Standardized scales can be used to determine whether *clinically significant* improvement occurred for a particular client. In this context clinically significant improvement typically means that a client's measured functioning on a standardized scale is in the dysfunctional score range before intervention (e.g., above a

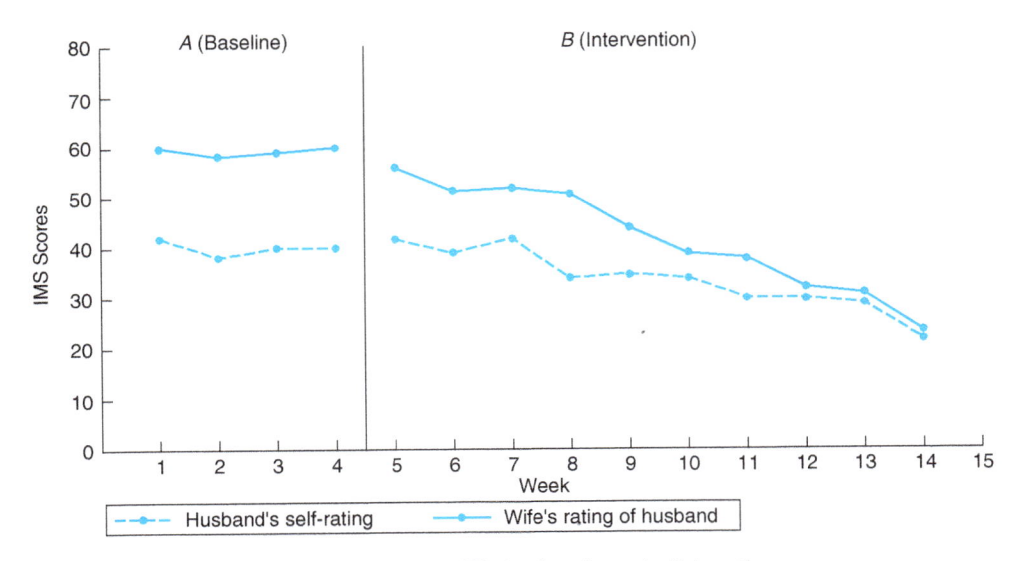

FIGURE 6 Index of Marital Satisfaction (IMS): husband's and wife's ratings.

Standardized Scales

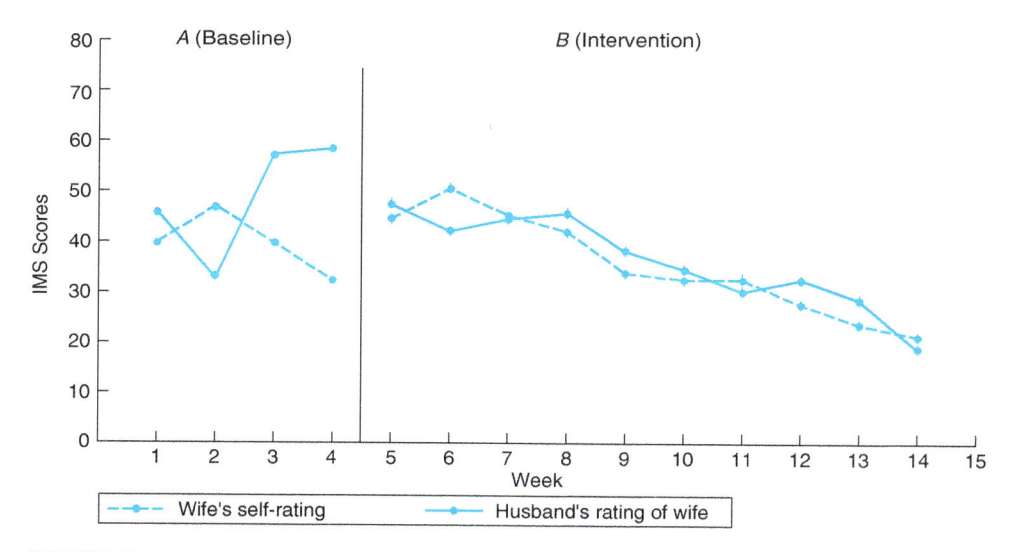

FIGURE 7 Index of Marital Satisfaction (IMS): wife's and husband's ratings.

clinical cutoff), in the functional range after intervention (e.g., below a clinical cutoff), and the change is reliable (Bauer, Lambert, & Nielsen, 2004).

The most widely used procedure for determining clinically significant improvement was developed by Jacobson and his colleagues (Jacobson, Follett, & Ravenstorf, 1984; Jacobson, Roberts, Berns, & McGlinchey, 1999; Jacobson & Truax, 1991). This procedure has been tested under a number of different conditions and it compares favorably to alternative methods. It is the most widely used method, and it is easy to compute (Atkins, Bedics, McGlinchey, & Beauchaine, 2005; Bauer, Lambert, & Nielsen, 2004; Harmon et al., 2007; Ogles, Lunnen, & Bonesteel, 2001; Ogles, Lambert, & Fields, 2002; Wise, 2004) (see Kellett, 2007, for an example of the use of this procedure with a single-system design and Morley, Williams, & Hussain, 2008, for a good example of the use of this in a practice setting.). The procedure involves determining whether a reliable change occurred, if the change was in the direction of improvement or deterioration, and whether the change was *clinically significant*.

Reliable change means that change in a client's scale score from one time to another is more than you would expect just from measurement error. The *Reliable Change Index* (RCI) lets you address this question. To compute the RCI you need the client's pretest and posttest scale scores (e.g., first baseline and last intervention data point). You also need two things from previous research: (1) the internal consistency reliability (coefficient alpha) of the scale from the normative sample used to test the scale; and (2) the standard deviation from the normative sample used to test the scale. Frequently, the latter two pieces of information can be found in the article(s) reporting the development of a scale, and often they are reported in books such as Fischer and Corcoran (2007a, b) and Rush, First, and Blacker (2008).

The RCI is simple to compute, but we won't detail the computations here (Bauer, 2004). An RCI greater than $+1.96$ or less than -1.96 indicates reliable change (Wise, 2004, and others suggest ± 1.65 or even lower values under some circumstances.). However, reliable change can be in the direction of improvement or deterioration, and you determine which based on whether higher scale scores indicate improvement or deterioration, and whether the pretest score was higher or lower than the posttest score.

For example, suppose you're using a scale to measure depression; higher scores indicate greater depression, and pretest and posttest scores are 40 and 25, respectively. Also, the normative sample standard deviation for the scale is 15, and coefficient alpha is .90. The RCI is 2.24, indicating reliable change. More specifically, *reliable improvement* occurred because higher scores indicate greater depression, and the posttest score was lower than the pretest score.

Instead of computing the RCI to determine whether reliable change occurred, it's possible to compute the minimum change in a scale score indicating reliable change (RC) for a particular scale. All you need to do this is the internal consistency reliability (coefficient alpha) and standard deviation from the normative sample used to test the scale. Or, instead of the standard deviation, you can use the standard error of measurement. RC is easy to compute, but to simplify things you can use the Microsoft Excel *Clinical Significance* workbook that calculates the RC automatically after you enter the reliability and standard deviation or standard error of measurement. (If you're interested, the formula for computing RC is shown in this workbook.) Let's continue our example to illustrate this. If the normative sample standard deviation is 15 and coefficient alpha is .90, the RC equals 13.15. That is, a change of 13.15 or larger indicates reliable change.

If reliable change occurred in the direction of improvement, the next step is to determine whether the improvement was clinically significant. If the client went from being in a dysfunctional score range (e.g., above a score of about 30 on the WALMYR scales) to a functional score range (e.g., below a score of about 30 on the WALMYR scales), clinically significant improvement occurred.

Let's continue our example. We determined that reliable change occurred and, more specifically, reliable improvement. Suppose the scale had a clinical cutoff of 30. Then, we could say that *clinically significant improvement* occurred because the pretest score (40) was in the dysfunctional range and the posttest score (25) in the functional range.

To summarize, *clinically significant improvement* occurs if the client's score shows reliable change in the direction of improvement and the score moves from the dysfunctional to functional range. *Reliable improvement*, but not clinically significant improvement, occurs if the client's score shows reliable change in the direction of improvement, but does not move from the dysfunctional to functional range. *No change* occurs if the client's score does not show reliable change and does not move from the dysfunctional to functional range (Change from the dysfunctional to functional range that is not reliable is, well, not reliable.). Finally, *reliable deterioration* occurs if the client's score shows reliable change in the direction of deterioration. (We are assuming that the client was in the dysfunctional range to begin with; otherwise, why would you intervene? So change from the dysfunctional to functional range isn't relevant here.)

Determining a Clinical Cutoff. What if a standardized scale does not have a reported cutoff score? In this case, there are different ways to determine if a client's score falls within a dysfunctional or functional range, depending on the information you have available (Bauer, Lambert, & Nielsen, 2004). If you have the mean and standard deviation of the scale for a normative functional population (e.g., those who neither seek nor need treatment for the problem), you can use two standard deviations from the mean as the cutoff. More specifically, use two standard deviations above the mean when higher scores are undesirable (e.g., depression), and two standard deviations below the mean when higher scores are desirable (e.g., self-esteem). For example, suppose you have a depression scale for which higher scores are undesirable, and a functional normative population with a mean of 40 and standard deviation of 10. The cutoff would be 60 (i.e., 40 + [2 × 10]). A score below 60 would put the client in the functional range, and a score above would not.

There's a better way to determine a cutoff if you have a mean (M) and standard deviation (SD) available from both a functional and dysfunctional normative population. In this case the cutoff score is calculated as follows:

$$\text{Cutoff} = \frac{(SD_{\text{dysfunctional}} \times M_{\text{functional}}) + (SD_{\text{functional}} \times M_{\text{dysfunctional}})}{(SD_{\text{dysfunctional}} + SD_{\text{functional}})}$$

This formula is not as difficult to compute by hand as it might look, but to simplify things you can use the Microsoft Excel *Clinical Significance* workbook that calculates this cutoff automatically after you enter the means and standard deviations. Let's look at an example. Suppose you have a functional normative population with a mean of 40 and standard deviation of 10, and a dysfunctional normative population (e.g., those seeking treatment for a problem) with a mean of 55 and standard deviation of 10. The cutoff is 47.5 and it is calculated as follows:

$$47.5 = \frac{(10 \times 40) + (10 \times 55)}{(10 + 10)}$$

So, a score below 47.5 would put the client in the functional range (i.e., closer to the mean of the functional population than the mean of the dysfunctional population), and a score above would not. This example is illustrated in Figure 8. As you can see from this figure, the combined group cutoff is the midpoint (actually weighted midpoint) between the means of the two populations. You also can see from this figure that the cutoff based only on the functional population is more lenient, and in general this will tend to be the case. However, the cutoff will be more accurate when you have information from both populations.

There are potential challenges involved in using these methods to determine clinically significant improvement, as there are with all methods (e.g., Blanton & Jaccard, 2006; Morley, William, & Hussain, 2008; Ogles, Lunnen, & Bonesteel, 2001; Wise, 2004). Consequently, you should remember that this is just one more piece of information that you can use in the context of all of the other quantitative and qualitative information that you have about your client, and you should only use and interpret information about clinically significant improvement in this broader context. Clinically significant improvement as defined above does not automatically guarantee a meaningful change in a client's real-world functioning or quality of life and it might or might not be meaningful to the client, significant others, or society at large. Also, this procedure is only as good as the available normative group(s), and in some cases the information from representative, relevant normative populations will not be available or will be difficult to select. In addition, remember that this method allows you to rule out measurement error as a plausible explanation for change, and to determine whether the change was clinically significant, but it does not speak to the question of whether it was your intervention or something else that caused the change—this is an issue of design. Finally, as with any method for determining change, the method is only as good as the measurement instrument used.

Finally, traditionally clinical significance involves comparing a pretest and posttest score. This provides some indication of change from start to finish, and certainly provides a benchmark for evaluating the success of an intervention. However, don't misunderstand us here; we are not suggesting that you only collect pretest and posttest scores. It's critical to monitor outcomes on an ongoing basis from baseline through intervention so that you can use this information to manage and modify your intervention as you go along (e.g., Lambert, 2007; Lambert et al., 2002, 2003; Harmon et al., 2007).

SOME LIMITATIONS OF STANDARDIZED SELF-REPORT SCALES

Standardized client self-report scales, whether administered by computer or done using paper and pencil, have some potential limitations and disadvantages. First, the client, perhaps out of a long-term habit, may not be aware of the occurrence of the target, and even your best efforts to help the client

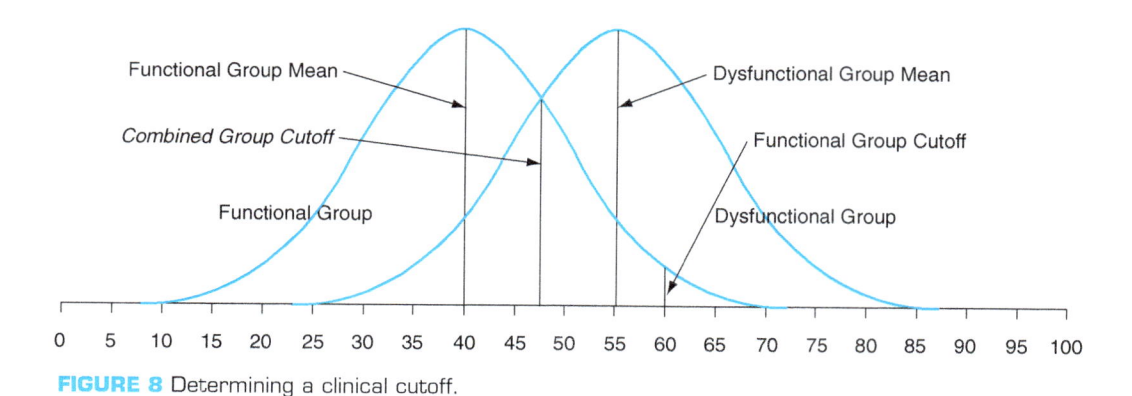

FIGURE 8 Determining a clinical cutoff.

become aware (perhaps through role-playing the target to increase awareness) may not succeed. Second, clients may not be able to provide the needed information because they are too disabled or too young. Third, the client may simply not want to provide information, or may wittingly or unwittingly provide inaccurate information. Clients might tell you what they think you want to hear, especially when you're in a position to give or withhold valued social sanctions and the client's reports might influence your decisions (e.g., a parent may not admit abusing a child to a child protective services worker, knowing that the worker is legally mandated to report this information). Clients might unwittingly report more change than actually occurred to justify their investment of time, money, and effort. You may do your best to motivate the client, but that also may fail.

Finally, a client's recording of his or her own target may have a reactive effect so that the target might change during the baseline simply due to the effects of recording. However, a study by Applegate (1992) showed no reactive effect (regarding outcome or dropout) from use of standardized scales. One way to handle any possible reactivity is to extend the period of time over which baseline data are collected, but this often may not be possible.

In some cases the client may be the only source of information about a target (e.g., if the target is a cognition or other private event), and the client may not want to systematically collect baseline information on the target. For example, the client may be under stress and might be impatient to initiate intervention and go about the business of changing the target. (This impatience is often shared by the practitioner.) Yet, ill-prepared interventions may be doomed to failure. Thus, as part of that preparation, recording in general, and baseline recording in particular, provide some of the foundation for enhancing your potential for more effective intervention.

SOME AVAILABLE STANDARDIZED SCALES FOR PRACTITIONERS

There are a number of standardized scales that can be completed by practitioners to assess client functioning. Examples are shown in Table 5, along with a brief description of each measure and the original reference for each measure (see Hunsley & Mash, 2008, and Rush, First, & Blacker, 2008, for more discussion of many of these measures.).

There are potential advantages and disadvantages to practitioner reports, just as there are with self-reports or any other type of reports (e.g., Bostwick & Bostwick, 1987; Lambert, Shapiro, & Bergin, 1986; Reid & Smith, 1989). Practitioner reports can be valuable because the practitioner is in a unique position to observe and understand clients because of his or her professional training and experience, familiarity with the clients, and the ease of recording unobtrusively. However, the validity of practitioner reports may vary with how the practitioner perceives that the information will be used (e.g., by the practitioner or for administrative use). The data may be biased because of the practitioner's desire to succeed, or because of the need to justify the time and effort expended with a client. In addition, the practitioner might not always be present when the problem occurs, since most problems obviously don't occur only or mainly during office or home visits. Finally, personal biases might influence a practitioner's assessment of some types of clients (e.g., clients of lower socioeconomic status, clients of a different ethnicity or cultural background, clients with a different sexual orientation).

Most standardized scales, whether they are used by clients, practitioners, or relevant others, contain multiple items that are combined into a total score or subscale scores to measure a particular concept. There are, though, several single-item standardized scales developed for practitioners or independent observers that are useful for the overall assessment of client functioning. These include, for example, (a) the Global Assessment of Functioning (GAF) scale, based on Axis V of the DSM-IV-TR (APA, 2000), shown in Figure 9, and reviewed in Rush, First, and Blacker, (2008); (b) the Children's Global Assessment Schedule (CGAS) (Bird, Canino, Rubio-Stipeo, & Ribera, 1987; Shaffer et al., 1983), shown in Figure 10 and reviewed in Rush, First, and Blacker, 2008; (c) the Social and Occupational Functioning Assessment Scale (SOFAS) (Goldman, Skodol, & Lave, 1992), reviewed and reproduced in Rush, First, and Blacker (2008) and contained in Appendix B of DSM-IV-TR; and (d) the Global Assessment of Relational Functioning (GARF) scale (Dausch, Miklowitz, & Richards, 1996) reproduced in Rush, First, and Blacker (2008).

Global ratings of the functioning of clients, such as those provided by the GAF, CGAS, SOFAS, and GARF have a number of advantages (e.g., Dougherty, Klein, Olino, & Laptook, 2008). They allow practitioners to use their professional judgment to measure

Standardized Scales

Table 5 Examples of standardized scales for practitioners

- *Brief Psychiatric Rating Scale (BPRS):* The BPRS is an 18-item measure of global psychiatric symptom severity. It was developed for use by an appropriately trained mental health professional upon completion of a clinical interview with a client. The BPRS is reviewed and reproduced in Rush, First, and Blacker (2008), and it is in the public domain and available without cost.
  Overall, J. E., & Gorham, D. R. (1988). The Brief Psychiatric Rating Scale (BPRS): Recent developments in ascertainment and scaling. *Psychopharmacological Bulletin, 24,* 97-99.
- *Children's Depression Rating Scale-Revised (CDRS-R):* The CDRS-R is a 17-item measure of depressive symptoms based on a semi-structured interview with the child (or an adult informant who knows the child well). The interviewer rates 17 symptom areas (including those that serve as DSM-IV criteria for a diagnosis of depression). The CDRS-R is copyrighted and can be obtained from:
  Western Psychological Services
  12031 Wilshire Blvd.
  Los Angeles, CA 90025-1251
  Voice: (800) 648-8857
  Fax: (310) 478-7838
  http://portal.wpspublish.com/
  Poznanski, E. O., & Mokros, H. G. (1999). *Children's Depression Rating Scale-Revised (CDRS-R).* Los Angeles, CA: Western Psychological Services.
- *Inventory of Depressive Symptomatology (IDS) and Quick Inventory of Depressive Symptomatology (QIDS):* The 30-item IDS and the 16-item QIDS measure the severity of depressive symptoms, both are available in clinician and self-report versions, and both are available free for download from www.ids-qids.org/index.html.
- *Working Alliance Inventory (WAI):* The WAI is a 36-item measure of the quality of the alliance between therapist and client. Client, therapist, and observer versions are available. The WAI is reviewed and reproduced in Rush, First, and Blacker (2008), reproduced in Fischer and Corcoran (2007b), and it is copyrighted but can be used with permission from:
  Adam O. Horvath, Ed.D.
  Department of Education
  Simon Fraser University
  8888 University Dr., 8556edb
  Burnaby, BC Canada V5A 1S6
  Voice: (778) 782-2160
  Email: horvath@sfu.ca
  Horvath, A. O., & Greenberg, L. S. (1989). Development and validation of the Working Alliance Inventory. *Journal of Consulting and Clinical Psychology, 36,* 223–233.

client functioning in a holistic fashion; and the practitioner can take all of the known relevant information into account, weigh it, and make a judgment about client functioning in its entirety. Also, they're easy to use, accessible, and relevant for use with a wide range of clients. Finally, they can provide an overall measure of the degree of impairment associated with a particular problem (e.g., substance use disorders, conduct disorders, depression).

Professional judgment and discretion and the measurement of global functioning do have potential disadvantages (e.g., Dougherty, Klein, Olino, & Laptook, 2008). Measures of global functioning don't provide a basis for determining the degree of change in specific areas targeted for intervention. Also, the exercise of professional judgment and discretion in the measurement of global concepts allows considerable room for the introduction of idiosyncratic practitioner biases. However, the detailed anchors that accompany the GAF, CGAS, SOFAS, and GARF do help to reduce this problem, relative to other global measures with less-detailed anchors, or those that are constructed on an individual basis, such as the individualized rating scales.

Single-item global measures of client functioning completed by practitioners can be efficient and useful in the repeated measurement of client functioning. However, they should not be used as the sole basis for measuring client outcome because of their potential for bias and the fact that they often don't provide information about specific areas targeted for intervention.

Standardized Scales

Global Assessment of Functioning (GAF) Scale
Consider psychological, social, and occupational functioning on a hypothetical continuum of mental health–illness. Do not include impairment in functioning due to physical (or environmental) limitations.

Code (Note: Use intermediate codes when appropriate, e.g., 45, 68, 72.)

Code	Description
100 – 91	Superior functioning in a wide range of activities; life's problems never seem to get out of hand; is sought out by others because of his or her many positive qualities. No symptoms.
90 – 81	Absent or minimal symptoms (e.g., mild anxiety before an exam), good functioning in all areas, interested and involved in a wide range of activities, socially effective, generally satisfied with life, no more than everyday problems or concerns (e.g., an occasional argument with family members).
80 – 71	If symptoms are present, they are transient and expectable reactions to psychosocial stressors (e.g., difficulty concentrating after family argument); no more than light impairment in social, occupational, or school functioning (e.g., temporarily falling behind in schoolwork.)
70 – 61	Some mild symptoms (e.g., depressed mood and mild insomnia) *or* some difficulty in social, occupational, or school functioning (e.g., occasional truancy or theft within the household), but generally functioning pretty well; has some meaningful interpersonal relationships.
60 – 51	Moderate symptoms (e.g., flat affect and circumstantial speech, occasional panic attacks) *or* moderate difficulty in social, occupational, or school functioning (e.g., few friends, conflicts with peers or co-workers).
50 – 41	Serious symptoms (e.g., suicidal ideation, severe obsessional rituals, frequent shoplifting) *or* any serious impairment in social, occupational, or school functioning (e.g., no friends, unable to keep a job).
40 – 31	Some impairment in reality testing or communication (e.g., speech is at times illogical, obscure, or irrelevant) *or* major impairment in several areas, such as work or school, family relations, judgment, thinking, or mood (e.g., depressed man avoids friends, neglects family, and is unable to work; child frequently beats up younger children, is defiant at home, and is failing at school).
30 – 21	Behavior is considerably influenced by delusions or hallucinations *or* serious impairment in communication or judgment (e.g., sometimes incoherent, acts grossly inappropriately, suicidal preoccupation) *or* inability to function in almost all areas (e.g., stays in bed all day; no job, home, or friends).
20 – 11	Some danger of hurting self or others (e.g., suicide attempts without clear expectation of death; frequently violent; manic excitement) *or* occasionally fails to maintain minimal personal hygiene (e.g., smears feces) *or* gross impairment in communication (e.g., largely incoherent or mute).
10 – 1	Persistent danger of severely hurting self or others (e.g., recurrent violence) *or* persistent inability to maintain minimal personal hygiene *or* serious suicide act with clear expectation of death.
0	Inadequate information.

FIGURE 9 Description of Global Assessment of Functioning (GAF) Scale.
[Reprinted with permission from the *Diagnostic and Statistical Manual of Disorders*, Fourth Edition, Text Revision. Copyright © 2000, American Psychiatric Association.]

SOME AVAILABLE STANDARDIZED SCALES FOR RELEVANT OTHERS

There are a number of standardized scales that can be completed by relevant others to assess client functioning. Examples are shown in Table 6, along with a brief description of each measure and the original reference for each measure (see Hunsley & Mash, 2008, and Rush, First, & Blacker, 2008, for more discussion of many of these measures.).

There are many advantages to having relevant others provide information about a client (e.g., Bostwick & Bostwick, 1987; Lambert, Shapiro, & Bergin, 1986; Reid & Smith, 1989). First, the

Children's Global Assessment Schedule (CGAS)

Rate the client's most impaired level of general functioning for the specified period by selecting the lowest level that describes his or her functioning on a hypothetical continuum of health–illness. Use intermediary levels (e.g., 35, 58, 62).

Rate actual functioning regardless of treatment or prognosis. The examples of behavior provided are only illustrative and are not required for a particular rating.

Specified Period: 1 mo

91–100   *Superior functioning in all areas* (at home, at school, and with peers); involved in a wide range of activities and has many interests (e.g., has hobbies or participates in extracurricular activities or belongs to an organized group such as Scouts, etc.); likeable; confident; "everyday" worries never get out of hand; doing well in school; no symptoms.

81–90   *Good functioning in all areas;* secure in family, school, and with peers; there may be transient difficulties and everyday worries that occasionally get out of hand (e.g., mild anxiety associated with an important examination, occasional "blowups" with siblings, parents, or peers).

71–80   *No more than slight impairment in functioning* at home, at school, or with peers; some disturbance of behavior or emotional distress may be present in response to life stresses (e.g., parental separations, deaths, birth of a sibling), but these are brief, and interference with functioning is transient; such children are only minimally disturbing to others and are not considered deviant by those who know them.

61–70   *Some difficulty in a single area, but generally functioning pretty well* (e.g., sporadic or isolated antisocial acts, such as occasional hooky or petty theft; consistent minor difficulties with school work; mood changes of brief duration; fears and anxieties that do not lead to gross avoidance behavior; self-doubts); has some meaningful interpersonal relationships; most people who do not know the child well would not consider him or her deviant, but those who do know him or her well might express concern.

51–60   *Variable functioning with sporadic difficulties or symptoms in several but not all social areas;* disturbance would be apparent to those who encounter the child in a dysfunctional setting or time but not to those who see the child in other settings.

41–50   *Moderate degree of interference in functioning in most social areas or severe impairment of functioning in one area,* such as might result from, for example, suicidal preoccupations and ruminations, school refusal and other forms of anxiety, obsessive rituals, major conversion symptoms, frequent anxiety attacks, poor or inappropriate social skills, frequent episodes of aggressive or other antisocial behavior, with some preservation of meaningful social relationships.

31–40   *Major impairment in functioning in several areas and unable to function in one of these areas,* i.e., disturbed at home, at school, with peers, or in society at large, e.g., persistent aggression without clear instigation; markedly withdrawn and isolated behavior due to either mood or thought disturbance; suicidal attempts with clear lethal intent; such children are likely to require special schooling and/or hospitalization or withdrawal from school (but this is not a sufficient criterion for inclusion in this category).

21–30   *Unable to function in almost all areas,* e.g., stays at home, in ward, or in bed all day without taking part in social activities or severe impairment in reality testing or serious impairment in communication (e.g., sometimes incoherent or inappropriate).

11–20   *Needs considerable supervision* to prevent hurting others or self (e.g., frequently violent, repeated suicide attempts) or to maintain personal hygiene or gross impairment in all forms of communication (e.g., severe abnormalities in verbal and gestural communication, marked social aloofness, stupor).

1–10   *Needs constant supervision* (24-hour care) due to severely aggressive or self-destructive behavior or gross impairment in reality testing, communication, cognition, affect, or personal hygiene.

FIGURE 10 Children's Global Assessment Schedule (CGAS). (Adapted from Bird et al., 1987.)

ultimate goal of our intervention efforts is to improve the way clients function in their day-to-day environment, and relevant others often are in a unique position to provide information about clients' real-world functioning. Second, some interventions are interpersonally based (e.g., treatment of couples and families), and so the perspective of other involved parties is necessary to judge the success of an intervention. Third, it may be possible for others to observe the target as it "naturally" occurs, unobtrusively, without producing a reactive effect. Finally, someone in the environment may be extremely motivated to collect data because the target is especially distressing to him or her.

Table 6 Examples of standardized scales for relevant others

- *Eyberg Child Behavior Inventory (ECBI) and Sutter-Eyberg Student Behavior Inventory-Revised (SESBI-R):* These 36-item ECBI and 38-item SESBI-R measure conduct problems in children ages 2–16, as observed by parents and teachers, respectively. The ECBI is reproduced in Fischer and Corcoran (2007a), and the ECBI and SESBI-R are copyrighted and can be obtained from:
  Psychological Assessment Resources
  16204 N. Florida Ave.
  Lutz, FL 33549
  Voice: (800) 331-8378
  Fax: (800) 727-9329
  Internet: www.parinc.com
  Eyberg, S. M., & Pincus, D. (1999). *The Eyberg Child Behavior Inventory and Sutter-Eyberg Student Behavior Inventory.* Professional manual. Lutz, FL: Psychological Assessment Resources (PAR).
- *Children's Depression Inventory (CDI):* The CDI is a 27-item measure of depressive symptoms in youth and it can be used with children ages 7–17. Self-report, parent, and teacher versions are available. The CDI is copyrighted and can be obtained from:
  Multi-Health Systems
  P.O. Box 950
  North Tonawanda, NY 14120-0950
  Voice: (800) 456-3003
  Fax: (888)-540-4484
  Internet: www.mhs.com
  Kovacs, M. (2003). Children's depression inventory manual. North Tonawanda, NY: Multi-Health Systems.
- *Alcohol Use Disorders Identification Test (AUDIT):* The AUDIT is a 10-item self-report measure of the quantity and frequency of alcohol use indicative of hazardous alcohol use, indicators of dependence, and adverse consequences suggesting harmful use of alcohol. The AUDIT also can be completed by a collateral source. The AUDIT is copyrighted but can be reproduced without permission. It can be obtained from www.who.int/publications, and it is reviewed and reproduced in Rush, First, and Blacker (2008).
  Babor, T. F., Biddle-Higgins, J. C., Saunders, J. B., & Montiero, M. G. (2001). *AUDIT: The alcohol use disorders identification test: Guidelines for use in primary health care.* Geneva, Switzerland: World Health Organization.

Information from relevant others can be valuable, but there are some potential problems and limitations with using relevant others to record. First, some clients simply don't have relevant others, or they may not want you to collect information from relevant others. Second, relevant others may be unwilling to cooperate at all, or they may "fudge" their recording depending on how they see its use. Third, the reason that makes relevant others so useful a data source—their day-to-day relationship with the client—also might bias their responses. Fourth, relevant others might not know enough about a particular client target to provide adequate information (e.g., a relevant other might know that an alcoholic client still drinks, but not how much). Fifth, sometimes it can be time-consuming and otherwise expensive to collect information from relevant others. Finally, if the client has access to information provided by relevant others it can prove embarrassing and even harmful to the client's relationship with relevant others (e.g., asking a person to assess the extent to which a neighbor maltreats his or her children).

SOME AVAILABLE STANDARDIZED SCALES FOR INDEPENDENT OBSERVERS

Many of the standardized scales listed in Table 5 can be used by independent observers and practitioners, as can the assessment measures described in Table 6. Independent observers, such as your colleagues, supervisor, or outside consultants, can provide valuable assessments of your clients (e.g., Bostwick & Bostwick, 1987; Lambert, Shapiro, & Bergin, 1986; Reid & Smith, 1989). For example, you might have a colleague review a random sample of audiotapes or videotapes of your sessions with a client, or even interview your client. Independent observers have the advantage that they're less personally invested in a client and so they might be able to provide a more accurate, less biased assessment. However, the fact that independent observers are less involved with a client also can be a disadvantage because they will be less familiar with the client. Also, in busy agencies it might not be possible to have your colleagues provide independent assessments of your clients except on a limited basis.

SOME ADDITIONAL STANDARDIZED SELF-REPORT SCALES

In addition to the WAS scales, there are many, many, self-report scales that you can use to monitor and evaluate your practice. Examples are shown in Table 6, along with a brief description of each measure and the original reference for each measure (see Hunsley & Mash, 2008, Fischer & Corcoran, 2007a, 2007b, and Rush, First, & Blacker, 2008, for more discussion of many of these measures.).

DO-IT-YOURSELF SCALES

There are so many standardized scales appropriate for practice that it hardly seems necessary to develop your own in most instances. However, if you can't find anything at all in your area of interest, you may feel you must devise your own. Developing your own standardized scale is no easy matter. It requires a good deal of time, effort, and energy. There are numerous good books devoted to the principles and practices of developing and using standardized scales (e.g., Aiken & Groth-Marnat, 2005; Anastasi & Urbina, 1997; DeVellis, 2003), and we recommend you use one or more of these to guide your efforts.

If you do take on the task of developing a standardized scale for your clients, you should try to determine its validity and reliability. Otherwise, you run the risk of collecting information that is of no use or that is misleading and possibly even harmful. Developing and testing a standardized scale are rather technical tasks, but not impossible. There are a variety of good books on this subject, as mentioned, and numerous examples of measurement development and testing for you to draw upon (see the Appendix at the end of this chapter). Also, you might try to (a) enlist a colleague with expertise in measurement if you don't have this expertise yourself, (b) collaborate with a university-based measurement expert, or (c) interest doctoral students with some expertise in such projects as part of their dissertation research. You might find collaborators more easily than you imagine because of your ready access to the client population on which to test the measure.

If your scale is administered repeatedly to clients, you might be able to examine its test–retest reliability. Also, you might be able to examine its internal consistency reliability (e.g., coefficient alpha) and the adequacy of specific questions or items (e.g., using item-analysis). In addition, you might be able to examine the criterion validity of your scale by examining the extent to which it: (a) predicts certain outcomes (e.g., premature termination of treatment, child abuse or neglect, placement of a child in foster care); (b) correlates with other known measures of the concept your scale was designed to measure; or (c) differentiates groups known to have more or less of the concept supposedly measured by your scale. Finally, if your agency routinely administers measures of other concepts along with your scale, you might be able to examine the extent to which these other measures relate to your scale in a theoretically predicted manner; that is, you could examine the construct validity of your scale.

USING STANDARDIZED SCALES IN GROUPS

Many of the standardized scales described in this chapter can be used to monitor and evaluate change in individual clients in groups (see Macgowan, 2008, and Toseland & Rivas, 2009, for good discussions of the use of a broad range of measures suitable for practice evaluation with groups, including standardized scales). However, there also are standardized scales developed specifically to be used with groups.

One of the most widely used self-report, standardized scales is the Yalom Curative Factors Scale (Lieberman, Yalom, & Miles, 1973; Stone, Lewis, & Beck, 1994). This scale is comprised of 14 items that evaluate 12 dimensions in therapeutic groups. These dimensions are: (1) altruism, (2) catharsis, (3) cohesiveness, (4) existentiality, (5) guidance, (6) hope, (7) identification, (8) family reenactment, (9) self-understanding, (10) interpersonal input, (11) interpersonal output, and (12) universality.

More recently, Macgowan developed the Group Engagement Measure (GEM) (Macgowan, 1997) to assess seven related areas of group engagement: attendance, contributing, relating to worker, relating with members, contracting, working on own problems, and working on other members' problems. The GEM is a 37-item leader-report measure of engagement for each group member, although it has been adopted for use as a self-report measure (Levenson & Macgowan, 2004). The psychometric properties of the GEM have been examined in a number of recent studies and results appear very promising (Macgowan, 1997, 2000, 2003; Macgowan & Levenson, 2003; Macgowan & Newman, 2005).

The Group Atmosphere Scale (GAS) (Silbergeld et al., 1975) and the Hemphill Index of Group Dimensions (Hemphill, 1956) examine different aspects of group functioning, though both measures are rather long. The GAS consists of 120 true-false items with 12 subscales examining such aspects of group environment as aggression, support, autonomy, and involvement. The Hemphill Index consists of 150 items on 5-point scales and measures 13 characteristics of groups including such dimensions as autonomy, control, participation, and stability.

Finally, the widely used Hill Interaction Matrix (HIM) (Hill, 1977) is a measure that uses group members, leaders, and/or observers to respond to 72 items on group process. This measure can be used to distinguish between group interactions that occur on two dimensions—the content that is discussed and levels and type of activity that take place in the group.

COMPUTER MANAGEMENT OF STANDARDIZED SCALES

Personal computers are being used increasingly in the administration, scoring, interpretation, storage, analysis, and general management of standardized scales (e.g., Berger, 2006; Butcher, Perry, & Hahn, 2004). However, just as there are too many standardized scales to describe here, it's also impossible to detail the many different computer programs for the management of standardized scales. This is a rapidly growing area, so you should look for current developments in journals such as *Journal of Technology in Human Services, Social Science Computer Review, Behavior and Information Technology*, and *Computers in Psychiatry/Psychology;* in software and book review sections of professional journals; and *The 17th Mental Measurements Yearbook* (Spies, Plake, Geisinger, & Carlson, 2007). You also should look on the Internet in such places as CUSSnet (www.uta.edu/cussn/cussn.html), Human Service Information Technology Applications (HUSITA) (www.husita.org), and the Buros Institute (http://buros.unl.edu/buros/jsp/search.jsp).

The CAAP User's Guide begins on page 208

CASS is a general-purpose personal computer program for, among other things, through CAAP, managing standardized scales. In addition to such general-purpose personal computer programs, there also are a variety of specialized programs available for the management of standardized scales (e.g., Berger, 2006; Butcher, Perry, & Hahn, 2004). There are programs available for the administration, scoring, and interpretation of particular measures and some of these programs not only score the scales, but also generate extensive narrative explanations of the scores. There also are programs known as "shells" into which you can enter existing standardized scales or scales developed by you or your agency, and these programs then will administer, score, and otherwise manage the measures. In addition to personal computer programs that operate solely on your on-site personal computer equipment, there also are a number of companies to which you can mail your scales for scoring and interpretation, or to which you can transmit your scale data by telephone via an on-site computer terminal and modem. Mail and teleprocessing are most likely to be useful to practitioners who administer lengthy standardized scales that require extensive interpretation, i.e., not RAIs.

There are some concerns raised by the use of personal computers to manage standardized scales and other types of measures (e.g., Berger, 2006; Butcher, Perry, & Hahn, 2004). They require start-up time in learning the operation of the computer and the particular software program, in addition to training in the proper use and interpretation of the measures. They also require a financial investment in the computer equipment and software. In addition, computer administration of measures may seem intimidating and impersonal to some clients, and there are some clients (e.g., those who can't read) who won't be able to use some of these systems. Extra care needs to be taken to ensure that clients understand the task at hand and are able to respond appropriately. Finally, computerized measures, just like their paper-and-pencil counterparts, shouldn't be accepted uncritically. They still must have demonstrated validity and reliability, in addition to being direct, relatively easy to use, accessible, and relevant to intervention planning. Just because such measures are computerized and seemingly "scientific" doesn't mean that they're accurate and useful.

The personal computer management of standardized scales and other measures does have some important benefits, as suggested by this brief description of CAAP and other related personal computer software (e.g., Berger, 2006; Butcher, Perry, & Hahn, 2004; Nurius & Hudson, 1993). They can increase the speed and efficiency with which standardized scales are managed, and this can free up time to deliver services. They also can increase the accuracy with which standardized scales and other measures are administered and scored. Even the most conscientious practitioner can make mistakes in scoring measures, and these mistakes can lead to incorrect practice and evaluation decisions; computers reduce the chances of making such errors if properly used. Also, some programs, including CAAP, check client responses to make sure that they fall in the range of requested values (e.g., a client might enter an "8" when the measure calls for a response that ranges from 1 to 7). We hope you will try and use the CAAP program to experience some of these advantages.

Summary

Standardized scales involve the uniform administration and the uniform scoring of items to provide a quantitative measure of some concept. A hallmark of standardized scales is that data usually exist concerning their validity and reliability, although standardized scales differ considerably in the amount and quality of such information. Standardized scales are available to elicit information from clients, practitioners, relevant others, and independent observers, although most are self-report measures. Examples of scales for eliciting information from different perspectives were provided, along with a list of references for locating information about additional standardized scales. Advantages as well as problems in using standardized scales were described. Essentially, these measures are efficient and readily available, but there's a danger in using them without appropriate cautions. Specific criteria were described to help you select a standardized scale from the many that are available, and some general guidelines for administering these scales were provided. The use of personal computers to administer, score, interpret, store, and in general manage standardized scales was discussed, and one such program, CAAP, was noted and is described in detail in the User's Guide at the end of this chapter. Finally, the construction of standardized scales for particular agency needs was described briefly.

APPENDIX

REFERENCE BOOKS FOR TESTS AND MEASUREMENTS

AIKEN, L. R., & GROTH-MARNAT, G. (2005). *Psychological testing and assessment* (12th ed.). Boston: Allyn & Bacon.

ANTONY, M. M., & BARLOW, D. H. (2001). *Handbook of assessment and treatment planning for psychological disorders.* New York: Guilford Press.

ANTONY, M. M., ORSILLO, S. M., & ROEMER, L. (EDS.). (2001). *Practitioner's guide to empirically based measures of anxiety.* New York: Kluwer Academic/Plenum.

BOLTON, B. F., & PARKER, R. M. (2008). *Handbook of measurement and evaluation in rehabilitation* (4th ed.). Austin, TX: Pro-Ed.

CHUN, K. M., ORGANISTA, P. B., & MARIN, G. (2003). *Acculturation: Advances in theory, measurement, and applied research.* Washington, DC: American Psychological Association.

CONE, J. D. (2001). *Evaluating outcomes: Empirical tools for effective practice.* Washington, DC: American Psychological Association.

DANA, R. H. (2005). *Multicultural assessment: Principles, applications, and examples.* Mahwah, NJ: Erlbaum.

DONOVAN, D. M., & MARLATT, G. A. (EDS.). (2005). *Assessment of addictive behaviors* (2nd ed.). New York: Guilford Press.

FEINDLER, E. L., RATHUS, J. H., & SILVER, L. B. (2003). *Assessment of family violence: A handbook for researchers and practitioners.* Washington, DC: American Psychological Association.

FISCHER, J., & CORCORAN K. (2007A). *Measures for clinical practice: Vol. 1. Couples, families, children* (4th ed.). New York: Oxford.

FISCHER, J., & CORCORAN, K. (2007B). *Measures for clinical practice: Vol. 2. Adults* (4th ed.). New York: Oxford.

GITLIN, L. N. (2006). *Physical function in older adults: A comprehensive guide to its meaning and measurement.* Austin, TX: Pro-Ed.

GOLDMAN, B. A., & MITCHELL, D. F. (2002). *Directory of unpublished experimental mental measures.* Washington, DC: American Psychological Association.

GRISSO, T., VINCENT, G., & SEAGROVE, D. (2005). *Mental health screening and assessment in juvenile justice.* New York: Guilford Press.

HERSEN, M. (2004). *Psychological assessment in clinical practice.* New York: Brunner-Routledge.

HERSEN, M. (ED.). (2006). *Clinician's handbook of adult behavioral assessment.* St. Louis, MO: Academic Press.

HERSEN, M. (ED.). (2006). *Clinician's handbook of child behavioral assessment.* St. Louis, MO: Academic Press.

HERSEN, M. (ED.). (2007). *Handbook of psychological assessment, case conceptualization, and treatment.* New York: Wiley.

HUNSLEY, J., & MASH, E. J. (EDS.) (2008). *A guide to assessments that work.* New York: Oxford University Press.

JORDAN, C., & FRANKLIN, C. (EDS.). (2003). *Clinical assessment for social workers: Quantitative and qualitative methods* (2nd ed.). Chicago: Lyceum.

KAMPHAS, R. W., & FRICK, P. J. (2005). *Clinical assessment of child and adolescent personality and behavior.* New York: Springer.

KELLERMAN, H., & BURRY, A. (2007). *Handbook of psychodiagnostic testing* (4th ed.). New York: Springer.

KEYSER, D. J., & SWEETLAND, R. C. (EDS.) (2005). *Test critiques: Volume XI.* Austin, TX: Pro-Ed.

LOPEZ, S. J., & SNYDER, C. R. (EDS.). (2003). *Positive psychological assessment: A handbook of models and measures.* Washington, DC: American Psychological Association.

MADDOX, T. (2008). *A comprehensive reference for assessments in psychology, education, and business* (6th ed.). Austin, TX: Pro-Ed.

MARUISH, M. E. (ED.). (2004). *The use of psychological testing for treatment planning and outcomes assessment: Vol. 2. Instruments for children and adolescents.* Hillsdale, NJ: Erlbaum.

MASH, E. J., & BARKLEY, R. A. (2007). *Assessment of childhood disorders* (4th ed.). New York: Guilford Press.

McDOWELL, I. (2006). *Measuring health: A guide to rating scales and questionnaires* (3rd ed.). New York: Oxford University Press.

MURPHY, L. L., PLAKE, B. S., & SPIES, R. A. (2006). *Tests in print VII.* Lincoln, NE: Buros Institute of Mental Measurements.

NADER, K. (2007). *Understanding and assessing trauma in children and adolescents: Measures, methods, and youth in context.* New York: Routledge.

NEZU, A. M., RONAN, G. F., MEADOWS, E. A., & McCLURE, K. S. (EDS.). (2000). *Practitioner's guide to empirically based measures of depression.* New York: Springer.

OGLES, B. M., LAMBERT, M. J., & FIELDS, S. A. (2002). *Essentials of outcome assessment.* New York: John Wiley & Sons.

PANIAGUA, F. A. (2005). *Assessing and treating culturally diverse clients: A practical guide* (3rd ed.). Thousand Oaks, CA: Sage.

RATHUS, J. H., & FEINDLER, E. L. (2004). *Assessment of partner violence: A handbook for researchers and practitioners.* Washington, DC: American Psychological Association.

REYNOLDS, C. R., KAMPHAUS, R. W., & HENDRY, C. N. (EDS.). (2003). *Handbook of psychological and educational assessment of children: Intelligence, aptitude, and achievement* (2nd ed.). New York: Guilford Press.

ROBERTS, A. R., & YEAGER, K. R. (EDS.). (2003). *Evidence-based practice manual: Research and outcome measures in health and human services.* Oxford: Oxford University Press.

RUSH, A. J., JR., FIRST, M. B., & BLACKER, D. (EDS.) (2008). *Handbook of psychiatric measures* (2nd ed.). Washington, DC: American Psychiatric Association.

SAJATOVIC, M., & RAMIREZ, L. F. (2003). *Rating scales in mental health* (2nd ed.). Cleveland: Lexi-Comp.

SATTLER, J. M., & HOGE, R. D. (2006). *Assessment of children: Behavioral, social, and clinical foundations* (5th ed.). Austin, TX: Pro-Ed.

SMITH, S. R., & HANDLER, L. (2006). *The clinical assessment of children and adolescents: A practitioner's handbook.* Hillsdale, NJ: Erlbaum.

SPIES, R. A., PLAKE, B. S., GEISINGER, K. F., & CARLSON, J. F. (2007). *The seventeenth mental measurements yearbook.* Lincoln, NE: Buros Institute, University of Nebraska.

SUZUKI, L. A., & PONTEROTTO, J. G. (EDS.). (2008). *Handbook of multicultural assessment: Clinical, psychological, and educational applications* (3rd ed.). San Francisco: Jossey-Bass.

TOULIATOS, J., PERLMUTTER, B. F., STRAUS, M. A., & HOLDEN, G. W. (2001). *Handbook of family measurement techniques.* Newbury Park, CA: Sage.

WALL, J. E., & WALZ, G. R. (2004). *Measuring up: Assessment issues for teachers, counselors, and administrators.* Austin, TX: Pro-Ed.

WILSON, J. P., & KEANE, T. M. (2004). *Assessing psychological trauma and PTSD.* New York: Guilford Press.

CAAP

COMPUTER ASSISTED ASSESSMENT PACKAGE (CAAP)

A User's Guide

CASS was developed for human service practitioners, and it provides a good example of a comprehensive, easy-to-use, personal computer program that simplifies and enhances the recording, storage, retrieval, and organization of client data. CASS is the general name of this program, but there is another program included with CASS named CAAP (Computer Assisted Assessment Package).

CAAP was developed to be used by clients and the resulting client information is available to you through your use of CASS. CAAP administers almost any type of standardized scale or test to your clients, and it automatically scores it, charts the results in a single-system design format, updates the information for a client each time a measure is completed so you can monitor client progress over time, and stores the information in the computer. In particular, CAAP will administer the WALMYR Assessment Scales (WAS) package (described earlier) to your clients, reverse-score the necessary items, compute the total score, graph the results in a single-system design format of your choice, and automatically update a client's file each time a scale is completed so you can monitor the client's progress over time.

An especially notable feature of CAAP is that although it comes with ready-to-use scales, you can add an almost unlimited number of additional scales, including ones constructed by you or your agency. Therefore, it's possible to use CASS to construct a tailor-made package of computer-administered instruments for use in your practice. In fact, you can add scales that focus on the practitioner's perspective as discribed earlier in this chapter, and fill then out yourself.

To use CAAP, a client needs to have some familiarity with your computer keyboard and must be able to read, but that's about all. However, before you use CASS with a client, you should use CAAP as if you were a client, and you should walk each client through CAAP at least once before you ask him or her to use it independently. For the most part, though, on-screen menus guide the client through CAAP. We'll walk you through what a client will see in this process. *(First, though, you need to create a client record.)* Finally, after we walk you through what a client will see when he or she completes a scale using CAAP, we will show you how to exit CAAP, return to CASS, and view and graph the resulting scale scores.

We assume that you know very little about computers, and we apologize in advance if this isn't the case. There are a few things that you need to know at the outset, but if you've used Windows before you probably already know these.

Before starting, first be sure to familiarize yourself with the basic operations of your computer (e.g., location of your A drive, "Enter" key, "Ctrl" key, and ← ↑ → ↓ keys). In particular, find out what version of Windows is installed on your computer.

Also, you'll need to know the following terms to install and use this software:

- **"Click"** means use your mouse to move the arrow you see on your screen to a certain word or place on the screen, and then click the *left* mouse button once.
- **"Right-click"** means use your mouse to move the arrow you see on your screen to a certain word or place on the screen, and then click the *right* mouse button once.
- **"Double-click"** means use your mouse to move the arrow you see on your screen to a certain word or place on the screen, and then click the *left* mouse button *twice quickly.*

WARNING If the program does not run according to the following instructions, as a last resort you might have to reinstall the program.

STARTING CAAP

▶ Double-click the CAAP icon (clasped hands) on your desktop.

▶ When the following window appears, enter the client case number, press the Tab key, and enter the client password (e.g., "charlie" for this case). *Remember, you cannot use CAAP without first creating a case in CASS.* When you type the password it will appear as ******. You need to enter the client case number and password exactly as you entered them when you created the case (i.e., the same combination of upper- and lowercase letters).

If you forget the case number or password you can use CASS to get them by clicking "Get a Client Record" from the "File" menu and then, after basic client information is established on the start screen, clicking "Displaying Current Case" from the "File" menu. (First, though, you'll need to exit CAAP, as shown in the following section.)

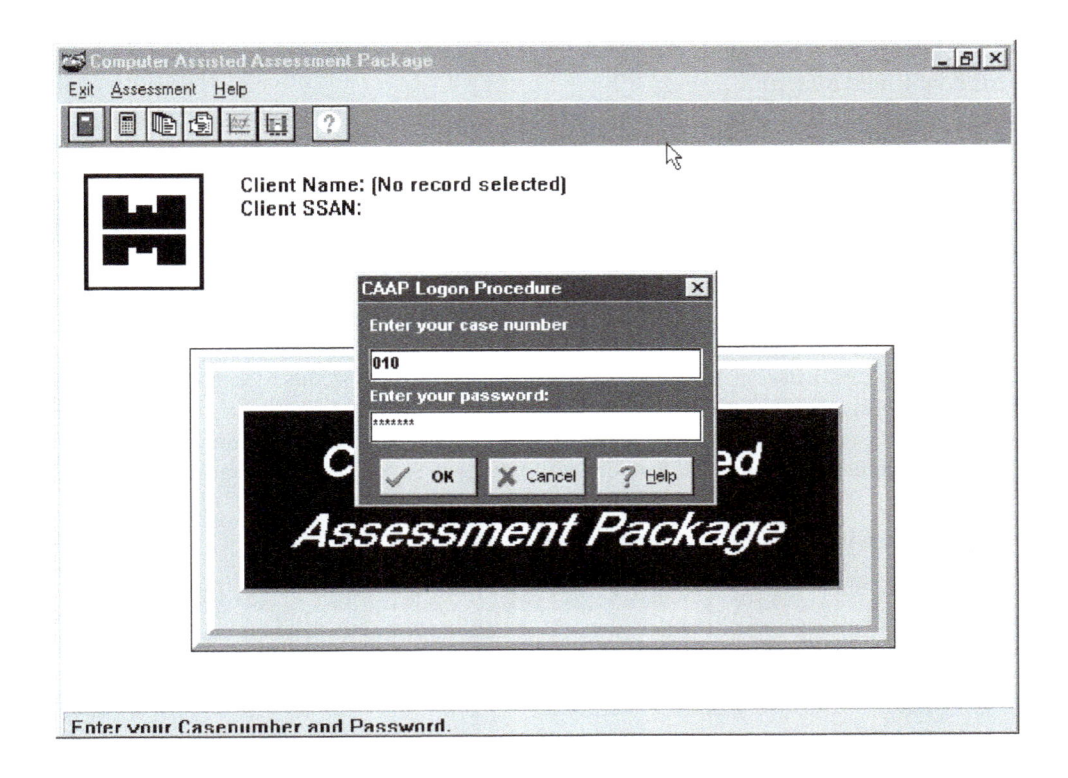

▶ After you've entered the case number and password, click "OK" and the "CAAP Logon" window will appear.

▶ Click "OK" and the window will disappear. We'll refer to the resulting screen (not shown) as the start screen.

Notice the menu bar items at the top of the screen shown (i.e., "Exit," "Assessment," and "Help"). You can click any of these items and menus will be displayed. We'll discuss these menu bar items and menus next. Also, note the buttons below the menu bar. These give you another way of doing the same things you can do with the menus. When you move the arrow to one of these buttons, after a short pause a note appears describing its purpose.

COMPLETING A SCALE

CAAP is used to administer scales to clients, score and graph these scale scores, and automatically transfer and update this information so you can access it using CASS. To see how this is done, pretend you are a client and work through the following exercise. Note that the version of CAAP you have only lets you administer a limited number of certain scales. (You can get a list of the available scales—over 100 of them—and determine the number of "scale credits" for each by selecting "Display Scale Scoring Credits" from the "Supplies" menu in the CASS "Management Module.")

▶ Click "Assessment," and move the arrow to "Complete An Assessment Scale" and "Unidimensional Client Record."

(Note that CASS also lets you score assessment scales. Click on "Assessment" in CASS, then on "Score Assessment Scale." This option lets you enter item scores for completed scales, e.g., those completed by hand, and CASS will then automatically score and store this information just as if the client had completed it using CAAP. You also can print the scores in the form of a graph from this location.)

▶ Click "Unidimensional Client Record." The list of available unidimensional scales appears.

(Unidimensional scales measure one concept, and multidimensional scales measure more than one concept. For example, the Generalized Contentment Scale [GCS], illustrated following, is a unidimensional scale measuring depression. A multidimensional measure of psychological disorders might measure depression, anxiety, and so on, and provide separate scores for each concept.)

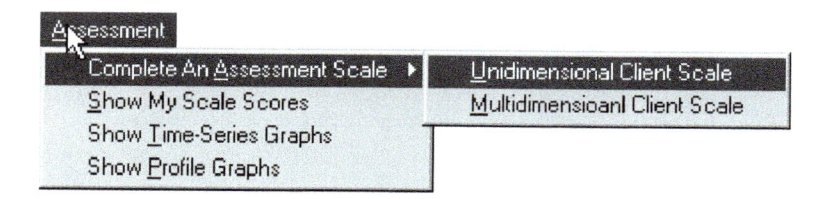

▶ Click the down (▼) and up (▲) arrows on the window to scroll through this list and view the available unidimensional scales.

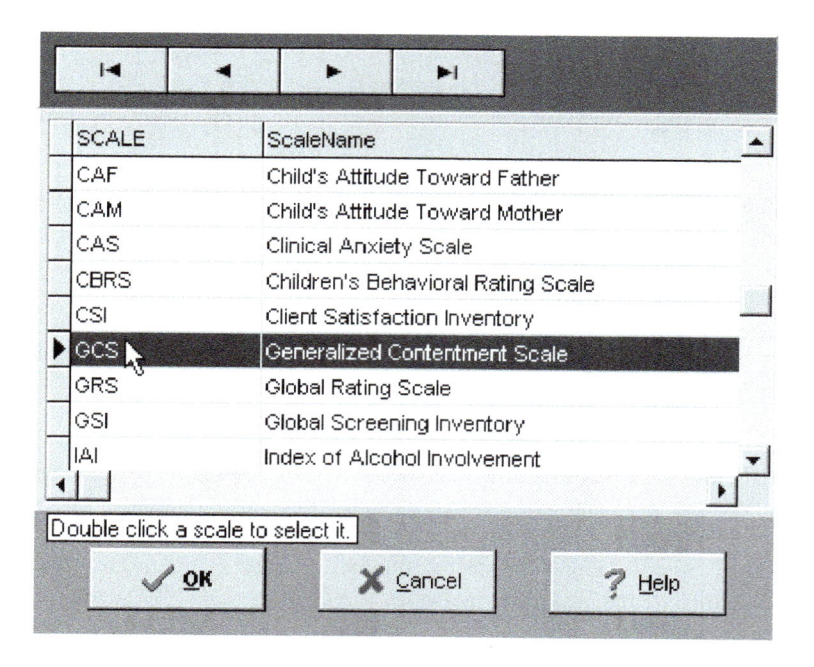

▸ Move the arrow to GCS and double-click, or click once and then click "OK." The following window appears.

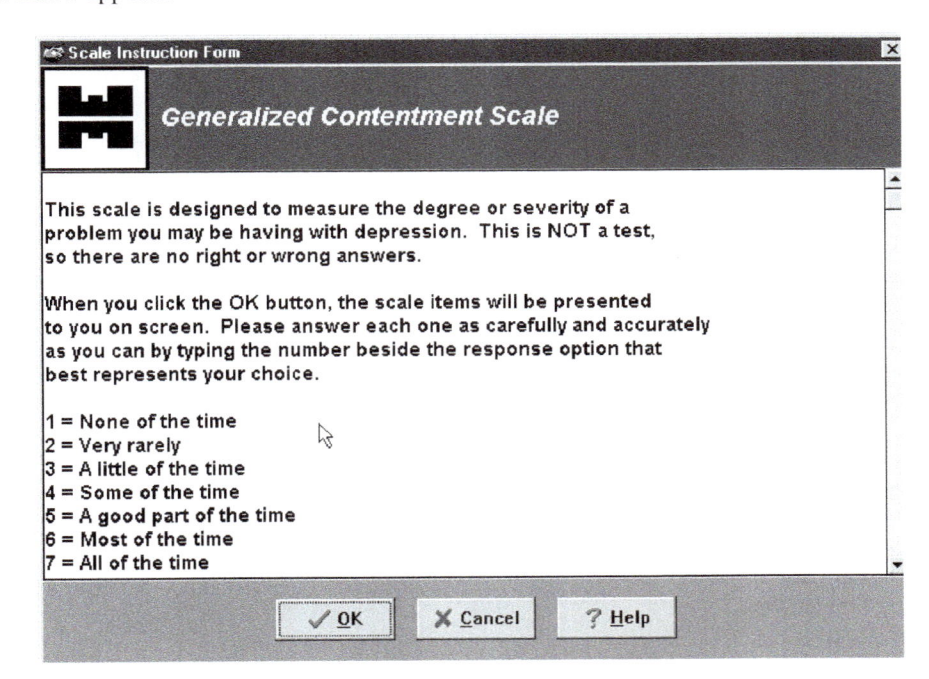

> **Scale Instruction Form**
>
> **Generalized Contentment Scale**
>
> This scale is designed to measure the degree or severity of a problem you may be having with depression. This is NOT a test, so there are no right or wrong answers.
>
> When you click the OK button, the scale items will be presented to you on screen. Please answer each one as carefully and accurately as you can by typing the number beside the response option that best represents your choice.
>
> 1 = None of the time
> 2 = Very rarely
> 3 = A little of the time
> 4 = Some of the time
> 5 = A good part of the time
> 6 = Most of the time
> 7 = All of the time
>
> [OK] [Cancel] [Help]

▸ Read the instructions, click "OK," and the "Please Answer All Items" window appears.

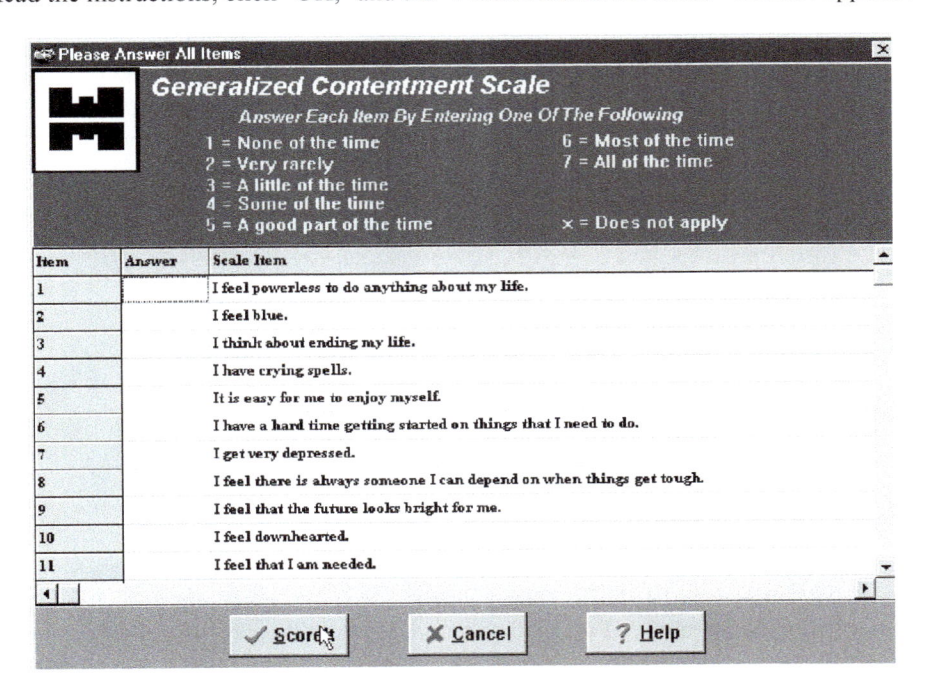

> **Please Answer All Items**
>
> **Generalized Contentment Scale**
> Answer Each Item By Entering One Of The Following
>
> 1 = None of the time
> 2 = Very rarely
> 3 = A little of the time
> 4 = Some of the time
> 5 = A good part of the time
> 6 = Most of the time
> 7 = All of the time
> x = Does not apply
>
> | Item | Answer | Scale Item |
> |------|--------|------------|
> | 1 | | I feel powerless to do anything about my life. |
> | 2 | | I feel blue. |
> | 3 | | I think about ending my life. |
> | 4 | | I have crying spells. |
> | 5 | | It is easy for me to enjoy myself. |
> | 6 | | I have a hard time getting started on things that I need to do. |
> | 7 | | I get very depressed. |
> | 8 | | I feel there is always someone I can depend on when things get tough. |
> | 9 | | I feel that the future looks bright for me. |
> | 10 | | I feel downhearted. |
> | 11 | | I feel that I am needed. |
>
> [Score] [Cancel] [Help]

▸ Complete the scale as if you were a client. Use the arrow keys on your keyboard (↑ ↓) to move up and down. If you make a mistake, move to it and type over it. When you are finished, click "Score It" and the following window appears. (The score will be different depending on your responses to the items.)

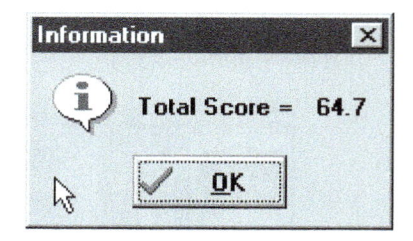

▸ Click "OK" and the "Save the Score?" window appears.

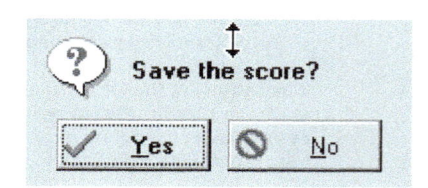

▸ Click "Yes" and the "Confirmation" window appears.
▸ Click "OK" and the start screen (not shown) appears.

VIEWING SCALE SCORES

It's possible for you and/or a client to view and graph the client's scale scores from within CAAP. (You can also do this in CASS by following roughly the same steps described here for graphing scale scores while in CAAP. While in CASS, you enter each of the client's scores individually to view and graph them.) Here's how to do it.

▸ Click "Assessment" and "Show My Scale Scores."

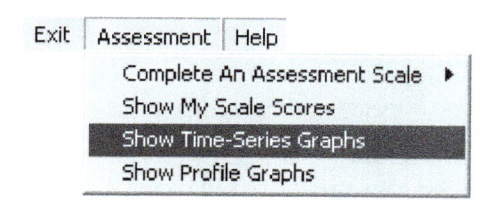

A table with client scale and item scores will appear. The client (you in this case) completed the Generalized Contentment Scale (GCS). This is a measure of nonpsychotic depression. Note that you can move your arrow to one of the arrows on this and similar screens, and click to see additional information.

▸ Click "Close" to return to the start screen.

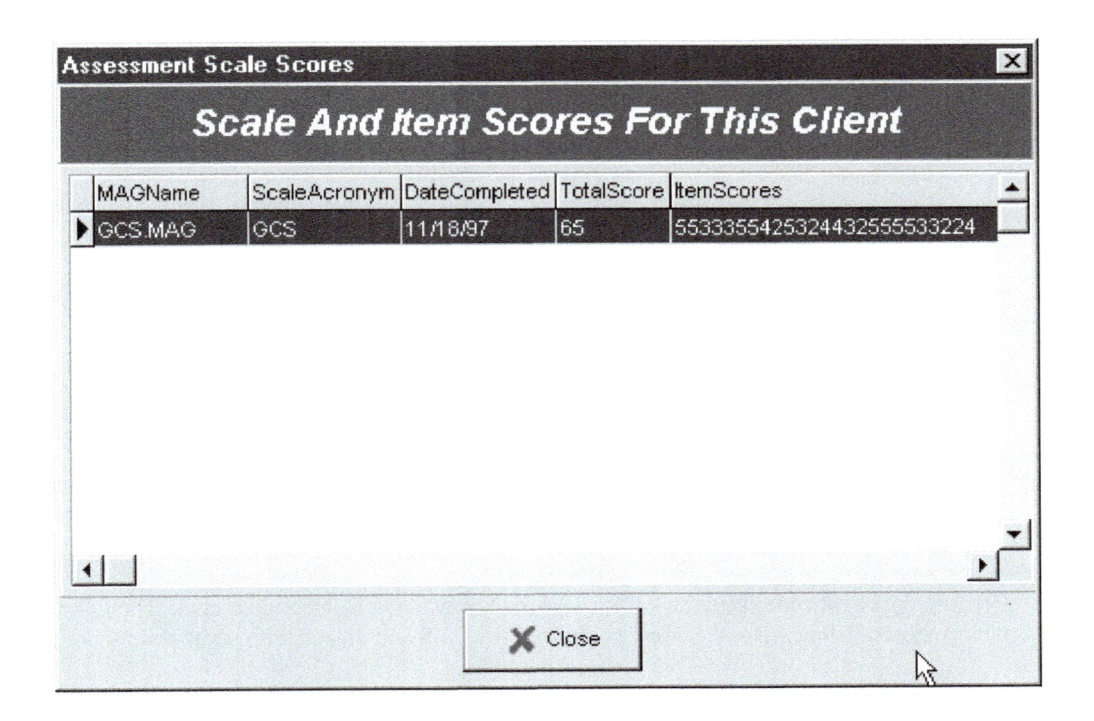

GRAPHING SCALE SCORES

CAAP creates single-system design graphs of scale scores that are updated automatically each time a client completes a scale. You can edit these graphs and print them.

▸ Click "Assessment" and "Show My Time-Series Graphs." A list of scales that can be graphed appears.

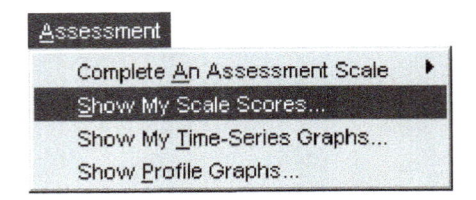

▸ Click the down (▼) and up (▲) arrows on the window to scroll through this list and view the available unidimensional scales.

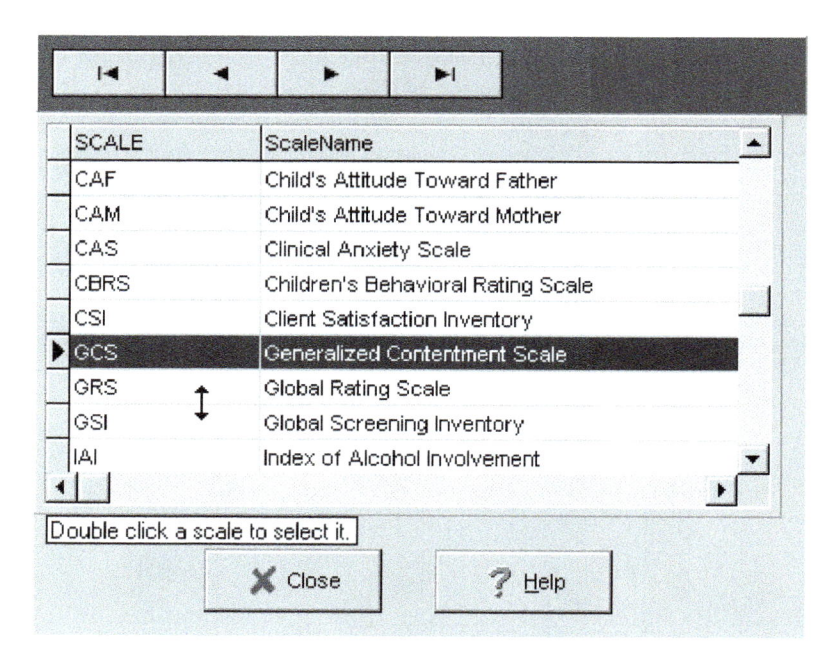

▶ Because the client completed the GCS, move the arrow to GCS and double-click. The following table appears, listing when the client completed the GCS and the resulting total scale score(s).

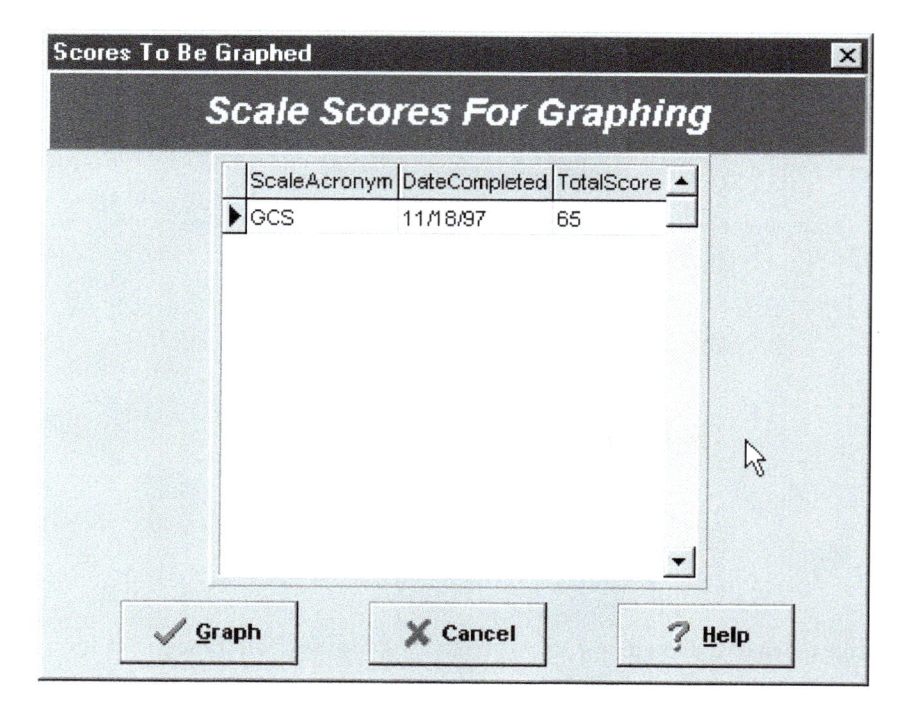

▸ Click the "GCS" line to highlight it, then click "Graph" to get the following graph. Of course, this isn't much of a graph because the scale was completed only once.

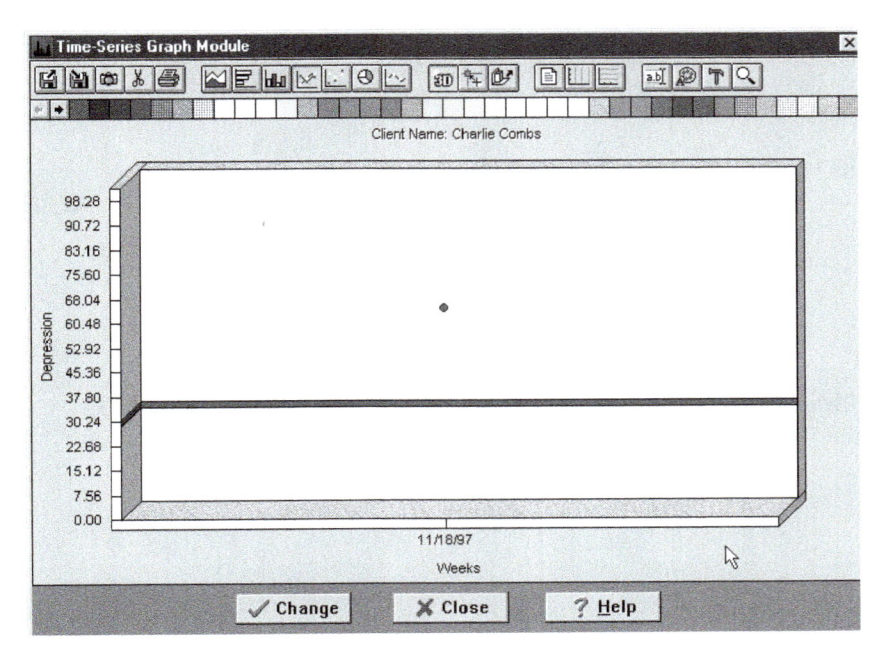

▸ If you don't like this three-dimensional graph, click the "3D" button and the following graph will appear.

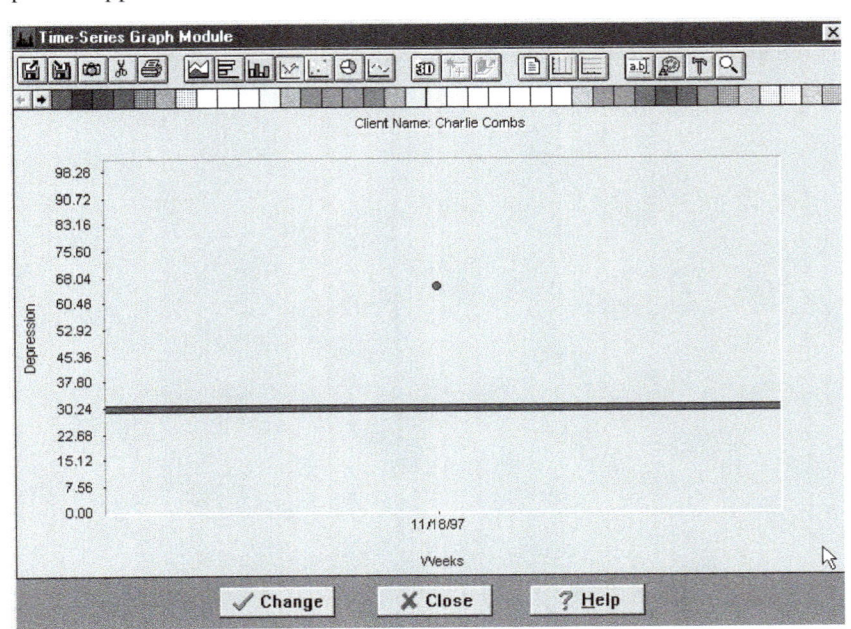

You can change this graph in a number of ways (e.g., edit titles). You can explore ways this graph can be changed by moving the arrow to any button on the tool bar line, and *holding the right mouse button.*

▶ Clicking the "Printer" button will print the graph. If you have trouble printing the graph from within CAAP, you also can reenter the data in CASS and print the results from there. And of course, you can always use the "Print Screen."

▶ Clicking the "Edit Titles" button will let you change the chart title and the X and Y axes titles.

▶ Click "Close" to return to the start screen.

ONLINE HELP

Online, context-sensitive help is available at many places in CAAP. Also, it's possible for the client to get help with a wide range of topics and to print this information. To do this use the CAAP "Help" menu in the same way as the CASS "Help" menu.

EXITING CAAP

▶ Click "Exit."

LOGS

PURPOSE This chapter describes the use of logs or structured diaries kept by a client to record the unique qualitative circumstances surrounding his or her problems, as well as quantitative dimensions of those problems, such as intensity and frequency. Logs provide a method for collecting information about the context and content of a client's daily experience as it happens in the environment in which it occurs. The use of logs to pinpoint and define targets, generate individualized hypotheses for intervention, and monitor and evaluate change over time in a client's problems is described. This chapter also describes the use of the practitioner log, an adaptation of the client log. The practitioner log can be used in much the same way as a clinical record to monitor the delivery of services and for the same purposes as the client log.

Introduction
Types of Client Logs
    Time Variations
        Preset Time Categories
        Open Time Categories
    Target-Category Variations
        Exploratory Log
        Target Problem Log
        Interaction Log
        Evaluation Log

Putting Qualitative and Quantitative Information Together
Introducing Clients to Logs
Practitioner Logs
Maximizing and Verifying the Reliability and Validity of Logs
Summary

From Chapter 8 of *Evaluating Practice: Guidelines for the Accountable Professional*, Sixth Edition. Martin Bloom, Joel Fischer, John G. Orme. Copyright © 2009 by Pearson Education, Inc. All rights reserved.

INTRODUCTION

One of the major tasks for practitioners is to secure enough information about the client's life to adequately develop, implement, monitor, and evaluate an intervention program. We've suggested in previous chapters a number of ways of doing this, ranging from charting information on graphs, to behavioral observation of specific behaviors, to using standardized and individualized scales. In addition to these methods, all of which have slightly different focal points and uses, most practitioners elicit and store for future use different types of qualitative information about the ongoing context in which a particular client's targets occur. The client log is a form of self-monitoring that will help you to obtain this type of information in a systematic, useful, and relevant manner, and it will help you with other assessment and evaluation tasks (Watson & Tharp, 2007).

Client logs (also called *client annotated records, critical incident recording, structured diaries, experience sampling, and ecological momentary assessment*) serve several functions. First, they can help *pinpoint and define client problems* in a way that is sensitive to the unique perceptions and circumstances of individual clients. Second, they provide a way to explore and clarify the dynamic and unique contexts in which a client's problems occur. This can help you and the client *generate contextually sensitive individualized targets and interventive hypotheses*. Third, logs can incorporate some of the methods discussed in earlier chapters (e.g., self-monitoring of the frequency or duration of behaviors or feelings or subjective ratings of individualized targets), and this information enhances the precision with which logs can be used to *monitor and evaluate change over time in a client's targets*. Fourth, logs are one of the primary ways we can connect qualitative data to our evaluations, as we involve the client in the process of providing feedback. Finally, client logs can serve a preventive/interventive function, that is, to teach the client to focus on his or her unique situation in an orderly way that can enhance client functioning and promote better functioning in the future (Avina, 2008; Cooper, Heron, & Heward, 2007; Watson & Tharp, 2007).

Client logs have been used in practice with a number of different targets. For example, they are often used in conjunction with cognitive behavior therapy for depression as a way to teach clients to identify, contextualize, monitor, and change automatic, unrealistic, maladaptive modes of thinking in order to change negative moods and maladaptive behaviors (e.g., Persons, Davidson, & Tompkins, 2001). Also, "sleep diaries" are often used in the treatment of sleep disorders to quantify, contextualize, and monitor different aspects of sleep problems (e.g., number of awakenings during the night, total time slept) (Rush, First, & Blacker, 2008). In addition, logs are used frequently in the treatment of eating disorders to quantify, contextualize, and monitor different aspects of eating disorders (e.g., purging and associated cognitions) (Sysko, 2008). Finally, "pain diaries" are used extensively in the treatment of pain to quantify, contextualize, and monitor different aspects of pain (e.g., severity) (Stone, Shiffman, Atienza, & Nebeling, 2007; Turk, Okifuji, & Skinner, 2008).

This chapter discusses different types of client logs and how they can be used to (a) pinpoint and define client problems, (b) generate contextually sensitive individualized intervention hypotheses, and (c) monitor and evaluate change over time in a client's targets. (We won't focus on the interventive function of logs because that is better left to a book on intervention strategies. Watson and Tharp, 2007, and Cooper, Heron, & Heward, 2007, provide excellent discussions of how to use client logs for self-directed behavior change.) In addition, we'll give numerous examples of client logs and provide forms for client logs that you can use in your own practice. Finally, we'll discuss practitioner logs, an adaptation of client logs to the collection of information by the practitioner.

TYPES OF CLIENT LOGS

The client log is a structured diary, kept by the client, of events that are relevant to the target situation, focusing on the client's perception of the events or situations. The use of the client log is an attempt to help the client systematically and objectively record those events in a way that is less susceptible to the pitfalls of recall and memory reconstruction (e.g., Hektner, Schmidt, & Csikszentmihalyi, 2007; Stone et al., 2007; Watson & Tharp, 2007). Thus, logs are helpful in getting ongoing feedback about targets, as well as the contextual factors that may be inhibiting client growth or maintaining client problems.

Client logs involve self-reports, but they are distinct from standardized self-report scales in that, for the most part, standardized scales involve reports of behaviors and feelings that

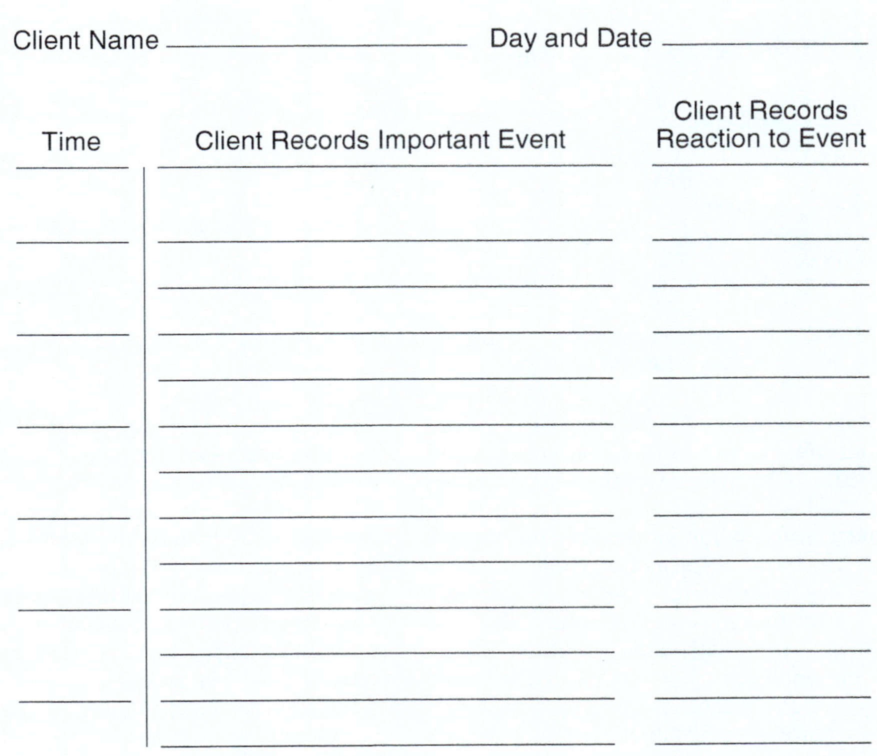

Logs

Client Name _____ **Day and Date** _____

Time	Client Records Important Event	Client Records Reaction to Event
_____	_____	_____
_____	_____	_____
_____	_____	_____
_____	_____	_____
_____	_____	_____
_____	_____	_____
_____	_____	_____

FIGURE 1 General format for client log.

occurred *at another time and in another place* (Sigmon & LaMattina, 2006, p. 146). Client logs, on the other hand, involve self-observations of behaviors and experiences made in the client's normal environment when they occur, or at least close to the time they occur. This is important because a client's reports about past behaviors and experiences might not be recalled accurately for any one of a number of reasons, or they might be influenced by the immediate circumstances in which they are obtained (e.g., the level of depression reported for the past week might be influenced by the level of depression at the moment). Logs can be used to reduce these potential biases and to better understand clients within the context of their normal environment (Hektner, Schmidt, & Csikszentmihalyi, 2007; Stone et al., 2007).

All client logs use basically the same format. They involve a prepared form, which has listed across the top the types of information you want collected. The type of information that you list there would vary with the nature of the target. At a minimum it involves recording whether some incident occurred, when it occurred, and how the client responded to it. Figure 1 illustrates a general format for a log. However, client logs do differ in terms of *when* information is recorded (i.e., sampled), or *what* is recorded, as illustrated in Figure 2.

Time Variations

When you set up your plan for the client to use a log, you have two basic choices: using preset time periods (sometimes called *interval-contingent* sampling), or letting the client establish the times to record, based on the client's assessment of what incidents are critical (sometimes called *event-driven* sampling). In addition, in some circumstances it might be desirable to use random sampling to select when the client should record (Hektner, Schmidt, & Csikszentmihalyi, 2007; Stone et al., 2007).

Logs

	Target Category	
Time Dimension	Open: Any important event may be noted in the log	Specifically defined by practitioner and/or client
Times for recording in the log are specifically set		
Open: Client should record in the log whenever the event occurs		

FIGURE 2 Variations in client logs—problem categories (defined in advance or open) and time dimensions (preset or open).

Preset Time Categories. Establishing in advance regular periods of time for recording can mean one of two things: (a) You have some idea about when the target will occur, and you can specify that the client collect as much information as possible during that time; or (b) you need information about a whole range of client activities spread out over the entire day, and you want that information collected, to the extent possible, over regularly scheduled intervals.

The first option, focusing on one particular period of time, might occur when the client has narrowed down the occurrence of some target event to a particular time period. Let's say a client complains about family arguments during dinner and immediately before and after dinner. The client log then may cover the time period from 5:00 PM to 7:00 PM every night. You might then ask the client to keep a record of family arguments during those 2 hours. This information could be used to generate hypotheses about strategies to reduce these arguments (e.g., suppose that the arguments all centered on family finances). Also, the act of recording the arguments provides a record of their frequency each day, and this could be charted to provide a more precise quantitative basis for monitoring and evaluating change (it might also be possible to record the duration of these arguments as part of this record).

The second option using preset time categories would be used to develop ideas about factors related to the client's target(s). You might ask the client to make an entry in his or her log about the events that occurred during that hour and his or her reaction to them. For example, a school teacher who wants to increase constructive student participation might be asked to record at the end of each class period the occurrences of satisfactory class participation and the events surrounding them. This record could be used to generate hypotheses about strategies to increase constructive class participation (e.g., suppose that most instances of constructive class participation occurred when the teacher asked students to think of examples of the material under discussion). The record also would indicate the frequency of constructive class participation, and this could be charted to provide a more precise quantitative basis for monitoring and evaluating change. (It also might be possible to have the teacher record the duration of each occurrence or estimate each duration later on.)

In some circumstances it might even be sufficient to have clients complete a log at the end of each day (Stone et al., 2007), although others argue against this (Hektner, Schmidt, & Csikszentmihalyi, 2007). In part, this depends on the target. A major argument with your child probably will be recalled accurately. Exact thoughts or feelings might be more difficult to recall accurately.

With both types of preset logs, as with any other logs, it's best for the client to record as soon as possible after the event occurs. This way, events may be less distorted by memory. To increase the chance that the client will be able to do this, naturally occurring time prompts might be used (e.g., the end of a class period for a teacher), or some type of artificial reminder might be used (e.g., the client might set the alarm on a personal digital assistant [PDA], or even program the alarm to occur randomly. Indeed it's also possible to record logged information directly on a PDA, which then can be uploaded to a personal computer [Hektner, Schmidt, & Csikszentmihalyi, 2007; Stone et al., 2007].). Of course, recording immediately is no guarantee that events will not be distorted. In any case, if the client does forget to record at a particular time, encourage the client to fill in that part at a later time, even at the risk of the event not being recorded as accurately as it might otherwise have been.

The main advantage of using preset time categories is that you probably will get a great deal of information. This is because the client is to record events that occur during those preset times even if he or she may not see them as critical. Thus, you and the client together will have the option of evaluating whether there may indeed have been something important related to the client's target during that period.

The disadvantage of preset categories is the flip side of the advantage. When the client records events every hour whether or not those events are "critical," you may get a good deal of material that is irrelevant, at least to the client's target.

Open Time Categories. The second time variation of a client log, using open time categories, is sometimes called *critical incident recording*. With this type of log, the client, with some advance guidance from you, makes a decision as events occur as to which events seem critical (i.e., are related to the problem). These events are then recorded as soon as possible after they occur. The period of time, of course, could vary between recording intervals. It may be once or twice a day, or it could be a dozen or more entries daily.

As an example of this type of log, a couple seeking help with their relationship could be asked to record events with each other that they found especially enjoyable and their responses to these events. This information then could be used to generate hypotheses about strategies to enhance the relationship (e.g., suppose that many of the enjoyable events involved their spending leisure time in mutually enjoyable activities). Such a record also would indicate the frequency of enjoyable events (per day or week), and this could be charted to provide a more precise quantitative basis for monitoring and evaluating change. It also would be simple to have each partner rate his or her degree of satisfaction with each interaction using a simple individualized rating scale. These ratings would indicate which of the enjoyable interactions were most satisfying, providing further clues about how to enhance the relationship, and providing additional information that could be used to monitor and evaluate change over time. These ratings also could be averaged for each day and charted to provide a quantitative indicator of progress. Figure 3 illustrates a general form that could be used to record this type of information.

The main advantage of critical incident recording is that it deals only with data the client perceives as significantly related to the target. Thus, a large amount of information that may be irrelevant is omitted, and it may be possible to pinpoint those events affecting the continuation of the target.

The disadvantage of critical incident recording is that, because the client is screening out many activities and the time guidelines for recording are not precise, the recorded events may be distorted. At the least, they may not really be representative of critical incidents in the client's life (e.g., in sampling fatigue in depressed clients, clients may select times when they are most tired. Or, they might not record times when they are extremely tired because they are too tired to record.). Of course, distortions or omissions could occur with any type of client log, but the lack of time guidelines may increase that problem. It could be especially important, then, for the practitioner and client to go over in advance those events that should be recorded and those that reasonably could be omitted.

Target-Category Variations

Several types of target categories could be used to increase the specificity of what the client records. Each of these depends on the specific purpose of the client log. The first category, of course, would be more or less open, corresponding to the critical incident record, in which the client records whatever he or she views as essential. More specific target-category variations were proposed by Schwartz and Goldiamond (1975), who discuss three types of problem categories for client logs—the exploratory log, target problem log, and interaction log. We also discuss a fourth type of log, the evaluation log. All of the different types of logs can be viewed as adaptations or extensions of the general model illustrated in Figure 1.

Exploratory Log. The purpose of the exploratory log is to help clarify and define the target and to collect detailed information on the target to aid in assessment (Schwartz & Goldiamond, 1975). This is a beginning log, which is especially useful for pinpointing and defining problems and the circumstances surrounding their occurrence. It's a descriptive (rather than precisely analytic) log that can change over time to a more precise log once you have a clearer idea of what events are affecting the target. The exploratory log can be set up to record critical incidents, or it can use preset time categories, which you would determine based on the nature of the problem.

Logs

Client Name _____ Day and Date _____

Time	Client Records Important Event (Include Frequency or Duration Count)	Client's Reaction	Individualized Rating Scale

FIGURE 3 Log illustrating open time categories with IRS.

As an example of an exploratory log, Rose (1989, p. 101) reports asking clients to keep a diary of situations and whether they're dissatisfied or satisfied with their responses, in order to identify problematic situations and client strengths. Such a record could be used to generate hypotheses about how to intervene with individual clients. It also would indicate the frequency of situations (per day or week) in which clients were satisfied and dissatisfied with their responses, and this could be charted to provide a more precise quantitative basis for monitoring and evaluating change. The client also could rate the degree of satisfaction with each recorded situation using a simple individualized rating scale. These ratings would indicate the situations in which the client was most satisfied, which might provide further clues about how to intervene, and these ratings also could be charted to provide a quantitative indicator of progress.

Forms for two types of exploratory logs are presented in Figures 4 and 5. Figure 4 presents a form for the most elementary exploratory log, the critical incident log. This log requires very little preset, specified information. Figure 5, suggested by Schwartz and Goldiamond (1975), presents a form for an exploratory log that has more preset categories. Of course, the time and event categories can be changed to fit the time and situation, and a column can be added for ratings from individualized rating

Logs

CRITICAL INCIDENT RECORDING FORM

Client Name _____   Day and Date _____

Time	Incident	Comment

FIGURE 4 Form for critical incident recording (without preset categories).

scales. Finally, Figure 6, from Schwartz and Goldiamond (1975, pp. 166–167), presents an example of an exploratory log that is filled out (for other examples, see Watson & Tharp, 2007).

Target Problem Log. The target problem log is used when the client and practitioner are unable to distinguish between the target, on the one hand, and other activities, situations, or events on the other. It's used when the conditions that are controlling or maintaining the target, say the antecedents and consequences, are not clear (Schwartz & Goldiamond, 1975; Watson & Tharp, 2007). The purpose here is to isolate those situations or events that occur at the same time as the target, before the target, and after the target. Figure 7 provides a form that can be used for a target problem log.

You might want to modify the categories of this form to be more explicit regarding a particular case. For example, in a case involving a client's anxiety about studying, instead of "events before problem," you might substitute "events that led you to think about studying," and so on. Thus, each form can be individualized to meet the unique needs of a particular client. For example, a client log for problems in developing effective social skills could include categories focusing on instances of effective and ineffective behaviors (as defined by you and the client). The "reaction" category also could be used to record behaviors or responses that might have been more effective in that situation.

Interaction Log. This is a variation on the target problem log. When the target is clearly an interpersonal one, you probably would want to obtain information on the activities of others that may be related to the client's target. This will allow you to examine interactions between the client and others that center on the identified target (Schwartz & Goldiamond, 1975). The interaction log will permit you to identify patterns or to develop an intervention plan focused on altering the dysfunctional elements in those patterns.

Figure 8 is a form that can be used for recording interaction information. The client should be

EXPLORATORY LOG

Client Name _____
Place _____ Day and Date _____

Time	Place	Activity	Who Was There?	What You Wanted	What Happened	Your Reaction

FIGURE 5 Form for exploratory (descriptive) log.

EXPLORATORY LOG

Client Name: Peter Kotten

Day and Date: April 22, 1994

Time	Place	Activity	Who Was There?	What You Wanted	What Happened	Your Reaction
8:00 AM	Home	Eating breakfast	Wife and I	Eat; feel reasonably pleasant	She kept trying to talk to me	I got irritated and yelled at her
8:45 AM	In car	Driving to work	Just myself	Wanted to get over feeling bad and get to work relaxed	Driver cut in on me	Started honking and yelling at her
10:00 AM	Work	Completing a letter	Secretary and I	Get work done	She was not finished	Gave her a nasty look, but did not say anything

FIGURE 6 Partially completed exploratory log.

TARGET PROBLEM LOG

Client's Name _____   Day and Date _____

Time	Place	Activity	Who Was There?	Problem Behavior (What Happened)	Events Before Problem	Events After Problem	Other Events During Problem	Your Reaction

FIGURE 7 Form for target problem (analytic) log.

INTERACTION LOG

Client Name _____ Day and Date _____

Time	Place	Who Was There?	What I Said	What They Said	What I Said	Other Events That Followed	Your Reaction

FIGURE 8 Form for interaction (analytic) log.

Logs

Client Name: Mrs. Olamana Day and Date: Thursday, May 7, 1998

Time	Incident	Depression Scale Rating	Your Reaction
8 AM	Couldn't get baby to eat.	7	Damn! This is frustrating.
9 AM	Baby asleep, I'm watching TV.	2	I feel fine, relaxed.
10:30 AM	She's up again; wet the bed.	9	I don't think there's any way out. It's hopeless.

FIGURE 9 Hypothetical critical incident journal combined with IRS.

instructed to fill in only those categories that are appropriate. For example, depending on who speaks first, one or another category might be left blank. If this does not apply, the client should just leave that space blank.

Evaluation Log. The types of logs discussed in this section can be extended to include frequency counts or individualized ratings of targets or other events, as illustrated earlier in this chapter. Other dimensions of target events, such as the duration of an event, also can be included. Extending logs in this way gives you a more precise quantitative basis for monitoring and evaluating client change, and thus the name "evaluation" log.

The simple act of logging target events gives a good count of those events. Thus, without any additional effort, the client log provides information about the frequency of a target's occurrence.

It's also a relatively simple matter to include individualized rating scales in a log to have a client rate his or her feelings or thoughts about the recorded event. You can do this by adding one more category to any of the forms presented earlier in this chapter, that category being the client's score on an individualized rating scale designed to measure the client's feelings about the recorded event. For example, suppose your client is a mother who complains that she can't accomplish anything during the day and that she "just feels depressed all day." She could keep a critical incident log and score each entry on a 9-point scale from 1 ("not at all depressed"; "I can accomplish all I want to") to 9 ("extremely depressed"; "I can't get anything done, I just sit and mope"). Figure 9 presents three hypothetical entries from her journal plus her own self-ratings. The ratings could be averaged each day and monitored over time, as could the daily frequency of critical incidents.

Figure 1 also can be used to illustrate a general model for an evaluation log. Frequency, duration, or ratings of target events from an evaluation log then can be dealt with and analyzed, including, for example, charting and comparing baseline and intervention periods.

PUTTING QUALITATIVE AND QUANTITATIVE INFORMATION TOGETHER

As we've mentioned earlier in this chapter, client logs can be combined with other measures to enhance the precision with which logs can be used to monitor and evaluate client change, and to generate contextually sensitive individualized interventive hypotheses. This can be done in different ways, but in each case it involves organizing the information in order to try to see the extent to which two events, behaviors, or targets go together (i.e., whether they're correlated over time). This is the idea of "concomitant variation." If the events consistently seem to increase or decrease at the same time (i.e., they're positively correlated), or one consistently increases while the other decreases (i.e., they're negatively correlated), this provides important information to you

Logs

Self-Ratings:

1–3	4–6	7–9

Journal Entries

1. Baby asleep; I'm watching TV.
2. _____
3. _____

1. _____
2. _____
3. _____

1. Couldn't get baby to eat.
2. She's up again; wet the bed.
3. _____

FIGURE 10 Categorizing events according to self-ratings.

about possible circumstances that influence a target. The fact that the two events are correlated doesn't necessarily mean one is causing the other, but it does give you enough information to suggest the need to examine the hypothesis that one *might* be causing the other.

Let's return to the example of your client, the mother who complains that she can't accomplish anything during the day and feels "depressed all day." As before, she could keep a critical incident log and rate each entry on a 9-point scale from 1 ("not at all depressed"; "I can accomplish all I want to") to 9 ("extremely depressed"; "I can't get anything done, I just sit and mope"). Figure 9 presents three hypothetical entries from her journal plus her own self-ratings. The incidents recorded in Figure 9 could be organized according to the ratings associated with the incidents, as illustrated in Figure 10, or they could be charted with notes about concomitant events, as illustrated in Figure 11 (this type of graph is sometimes called an *annotated chart*), to try to get some idea about just what it is that makes the client depressed. This method provides excellent systematic feedback that examines the relationships between the

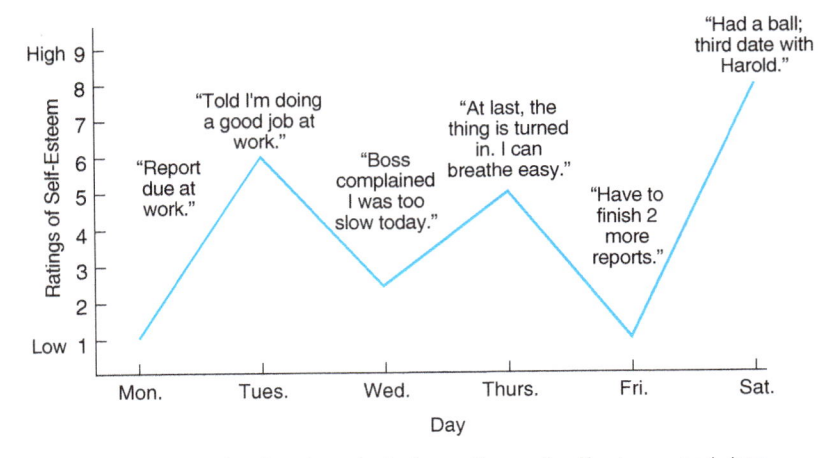

FIGURE 11 Example of a chart including ratings of self-esteem and data from a client log, as well as annotations of concomitant events.

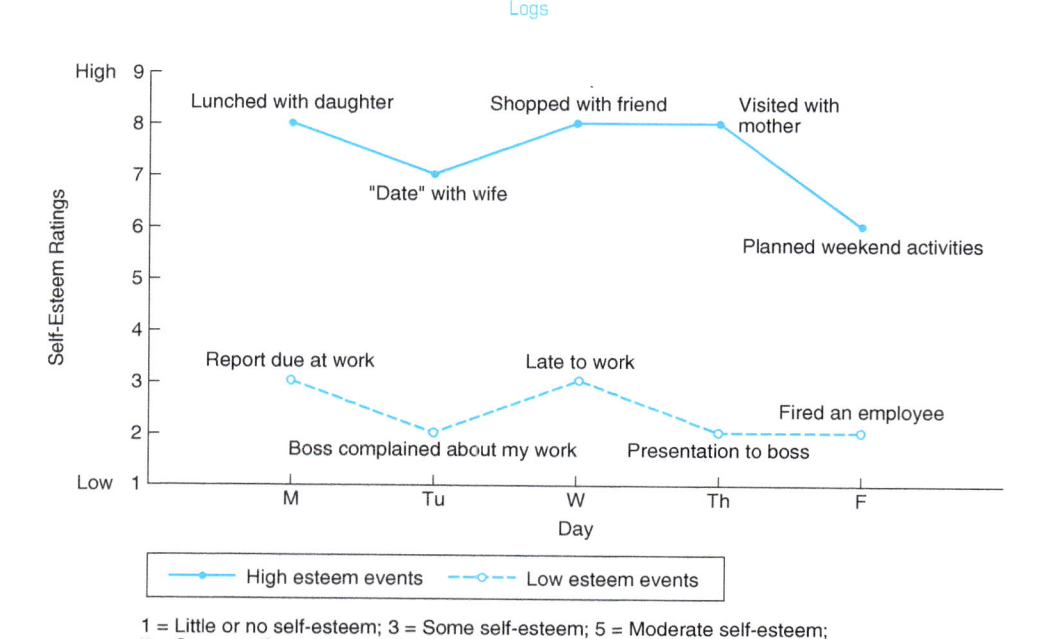

FIGURE 12 Self-esteem ratings of low and high self-esteem events.

occurrence of specific events, and problematic or positive changes in your client's way of thinking or feeling.

As another example, suppose that your client is a man who complains that he has very low feelings of self-esteem, but he can't pin down the things related to these feelings. Suppose that you ask the client to record one critical incident each day that makes him feel especially good about himself and one that makes him feel especially bad. Also, suppose you ask him to rate how each incident makes him feel on a 9-point scale ranging from 1 ("low" self-esteem) to 9 ("high" self-esteem).

The ratings for the two different types of incidents could be plotted, as illustrated in Figure 12. As the information on the chart suggests, the client's feelings of self-esteem appear to be related to on-the-job problems: either the pressure of work or the fear of criticism. To the extent that this possibility can be validated, it points to an important area of exploration for intervention. Conversely, his positive feelings of self-esteem seem to be associated with spending leisure time with friends and family, so the intervention might build on this as a way of increasing self-esteem. Therefore, the annotation or logging on the graph combines the best of the qualitative narrative with the quantitative graphing. We don't need to drop the qualitative information from a log when we develop graphs, and indeed such annotations can make graphs more meaningful.

Again, we'd like to emphasize that when examining the relationship between qualitative and quantitative events, or between any events for that matter, it's important to remember that it's risky to assume that one variable causes another. For example, in the case of the depressed mother it might be that her depression is making it difficult for her to deal with her child, rather than vice versa. Perhaps other data, from the client log or from other sources, could shed light on this and lead to further suggestions for interventions.

INTRODUCING CLIENTS TO LOGS

When you introduce the client to the use of written logs, it may be a good idea to explain the logs as a way of helping the client record what happens to him or her, so that you can use the information to help plan and evaluate the intervention program. You might want to use a physician's notes as an example of why the log is needed. A physician keeps notes on the patient's complaint and situation in order to have a clear record that will suggest the etiology of the complaint and the progress toward its resolution.

One advantage of the log—and it seems reasonable to say this to the client—is that it's a more or less formal record of events that occur, but may be forgotten or somehow overlooked when the client meets with the practitioner. Many clients will respond quite positively to the idea that they're to keep track of important events in their own lives (Watson & Tharp, 2007).

With most clients, you will have to go over the log carefully in advance, demonstrate how it's to be used, and even fill in some of the information on the log using your own experiences as examples. You might demonstrate the interaction log, for example, by role-playing its completion with the client using the previous portion of the interview session as data for the log (clients receiving treatment in groups could role-play with one another). This way you can see whether the client understands what to do. In any case, be certain that you don't make the log too complicated, either in the information to be collected, or in the terminology that you use for the categories.

A most important condition for using client logs is to have forms available for the client to use. You can modify these forms to fit the needs of each client, but we don't suggest just telling the client to go out and fill out a notebook or journal "free-style." The prepared forms will structure the activity and make it seem more focused and more relevant.

Even when you prepare the forms for a client log, written logs assume that clients are literate, capable of writing and willing to write, and sufficiently disciplined to record the necessary information. When one or more of these assumptions are unreasonable for a client, other methods can be used. For example, clients can tape-record the information, although with some clients it will be necessary for you to practice with the client before recording can begin. For some clients, personal digital assistants (PDAs) might be useful for self-monitoring (Hektner, Schmidt, & Csikszentmihalyi, 2007; Stone et al., 2007). For others, a simple small pocket notebook might be best.

You probably will have to guide the client in the amount to write (or, when a tape recorder is used, how much to record). That is, you want to tell the client, with tact, that you don't want a complete "blow-by-blow" description of every event during the day, nor do you want a complete autobiography. Rather, you want to be clear that the recorded events should be related to the client's target(s), and should be recorded as succinctly as possible. You might suggest that the client summarize each event using only a line or two. You might even practice this with the client, using hypothetical situations. On the other hand, on the forms you do use, be sure that there's enough room between the lines for the client to write. There's nothing more frustrating for the client than trying to use a form that simply doesn't provide enough room, even for succinct statements.

When the client brings the logs in to you, you would want to go over them with the client. Schwartz and Goldiamond (1975) recommend that the practitioner, at least initially, read them aloud to the client. This is done so that the practitioner can serve as a model for how to deal with the information on the log. This is done also, in part, to reduce misunderstandings due to illegible handwriting, and because it allows the client to fill in additional details regarding the recorded events. The client may read the logs aloud to the practitioner if the client desires to do so. The session may cover the entire log, or concentrate on parts of it that seem especially critical or problematic.

Client logs are not for everyone. Indeed, even very motivated clients may tire of their use over time. Thus, you may get far more information from some clients in the baseline period than you will over a long intervention period. Many people will just tire of filling out these logs.

This is one reason that we recommend modification of logs into evaluation logs. If you are keeping track of the frequency or duration of each incident (counts), or are collecting information on an individualized rating scale for each incident, the longer form of the log may be modified over time so that the client simply counts each incident and/or rates it on an IRS, and the continuity of the measure from baseline through intervention is thereby maintained.

PRACTITIONER LOGS

Many practitioners take notes during or after talking with clients, and some even tape-record some sessions with clients. Practitioners can use some of the same types of logs used by clients to make recordings more systematic and productive, and these can be called "practitioner logs." In a way this isn't anything new; what we're talking about is similar to the systematic practice of clinical records that are often kept by practitioners (Kagle & Kopels, 2008). However, using a structured log-type record provides more focused and succinct information that is more easily analyzed, and it provides some control over practitioner bias by providing a structure for the information recorded.

Practitioner logs can serve the same functions as client logs. They can be used to (a) pinpoint and define client targets; (b) generate contextually sensitive, individualized, intervention hypotheses; and (c) monitor and evaluate change over time in a client's targets. In addition, practitioner logs can be used to monitor the services provided to clients.

Let's look at an example of a practitioner log. Suppose that you are working to get the client to express his or her feelings to you. You might use the client's interaction log to identify circumstances that facilitate or impede achieving this objective. You could keep notes on your log indicating incidents when the client disclosed feelings and the context in which this occurred (e.g., in response to a direct question by you, in the discussion of a particular area of client concern). (Another way to approach this would be to record "critical incidents" that seemed to elicit the expression of feelings.) The log you are keeping might provide clues about how to increase the expression of feelings (e.g., you need to make a request that the client express feelings). This log also would provide a record of the frequency with which the client expresses his or her feelings, and this frequency could be charted in order to monitor progress toward this objective. You also could record the quality of each self-disclosure using a simple individualized rating scale. These ratings might suggest areas in which the client is more or less able to disclose feelings, which might provide further clues about how to increase self-disclosure. These ratings also could be charted to provide an additional quantitative indicator of progress toward this intermediate goal.

Let's look at another example of a practitioner log. Suppose that you're leading an adolescent pregnancy prevention group composed of both boys and girls. As part of your assessment of the skills needed by these adolescents, and as part of your evaluation plan, you have mixed-gender dyads role-play stressful dating situations (e.g., being asked to spend the night with a date, being asked whether or not you have a birth control device). You could keep a log of these role-plays for each adolescent (or perhaps audiotape or videotape and later record); on the logs you record the type of unreasonable request that is role-played and whether the adolescent is able to refuse the unreasonable request effectively. (A simple IRS also could be used to rate the effectiveness of the response.) This log could be used to generate individually tailored targets and intervention strategies. Also, a ratio of the number of effective refusals to the number of unreasonable requests could be constructed from the log for each client, and this quantitative index could be used to monitor progress for individual clients.

Practitioner logs also are useful for monitoring the delivery of services. In fact, this is a common use of logs (e.g., Kagle & Kopels, 2008). This is just a log with a column to enter the (a) date of service, (b) time of service, (c) service activity, (d) person receiving the service, and (e) purpose and content of the service. An example of a practitioner log is illustrated in Figure 13. The use of this general type of log is fairly widespread, and such information increasingly is being entered, stored, and organized using a computer.

As a practitioner, you have extensive training in human behavior and intervention strategies, and you're intimately involved in the helping process with clients. This puts you in a unique position to observe and record information about the unique circumstances of your clients and about the services provided to them. Therefore, the use of practitioner logs can provide valuable information. However, you need to remember that your stake in the outcome may color your view of this process and even more important, that the information available to you is limited to your firsthand observations of the client during a limited amount of time and in a restricted range of situations. Therefore, it's important to take steps with practitioner logs, as with all measures, to maximize the reliability and validity of the information collected.

One more way of conceiving the practitioner log is thorough annotation of graphs on client targets. Recall that the graph represents the ongoing series of collected data on the intensity or frequency for a given target. These data are posted on the graph at regular time intervals. So, you already have the amount or size of the target and the point in time in which it occurred. We had recommended annotating outliers, or extreme scores, so as to understand the unusual nature of these scores and make more sense of the ordinary pattern of target events. Now, we want to extend this idea of annotating for all data points, trying to characterize the context of each one (which is what logs are all about) while viewing them within the time series of target events. Annotating

Logs

Date	Time	Activity	With	Purpose/Content
7/29	9:00–9:15 a.m.	Phone call	Ms. M.	Scheduled a home visit and explained reason for visit.
7/30	3:00–5:00 p.m.	Home visit	Ms. M. and son	Discussed allegation of neglect with Ms. M. Talked with Ms. M. about her resources (food, employment). Assessed Ms. M.'s parenting knowledge, skills, and resources. Made arrangements for Ms. M. to apply for financial assistance. Scheduled another home visit.
8/6	3:00–5:00 p.m.	Home visit	Ms. M.	Followed up on financial assistance application. Worked with Ms. M. to enhance parenting skills. Worked with Ms. M. to increase social supports. Scheduled another home visit.

FIGURE 13 Example of a practitioner log.

every data point on the graph would get rather confusing, so instead we suggest having the graph constructed as before but have attached pages for each graph where you could add whatever log information you needed. The time points or dates would correspond to the lines on the additional pages. For example, 2/4 and 2/5 on the time line would link to lines 2/4 and 2/5 on the log sheets.

As we discussed previously, there could be various ways of recording systematically some log information. The general format for client logs (Figure 3) would suggest at least the notation of important events for the client and the client's reaction to those events. To add an individual rating scale component, we could also record for each datum how the client felt about it (positive, neutral, negative, etc.). The exploratory log might add information on the place and what happened—who was there, what the client wanted, what happened, and the client's reactions (Figure 6). And so on, with other types of logs.

What this approach offers is a holistic view of each datum so as to develop realistic patterns of happenings surrounding the client. We not only know the time and amount of each target event, but who and what was involved, how it happened, what the client reaction was, and anything else we care to note relevant to the case situation. From this rich lode of baseline information, we can construct an intervention plan sensitive to the nuances of the situation, while at the same time collecting relevant data on changes that occur during our intervention.

MAXIMIZING AND VERIFYING THE RELIABILITY AND VALIDITY OF LOGS

Different factors can influence the reliability and validity of client and practitioner reports of the frequency, duration, or intensity of client targets. We also discussed strategies for maximizing and verifying the reliability and validity of these reports. In particular, we emphasize the importance of obtaining and comparing information about client targets from multiple sources (e.g., clients, practitioners, relevant others, and independent observers), and using multiple measurement methods (e.g., observation of the frequency and duration of specific behaviors, ratings using individualized rating and standardized scales). These strategies also apply to client and practitioner logs, although logs do have some distinct features.

Client logs are useful because they capture a rich array of information about the client's perceptions of his or her targets and the unique circumstances under which these targets occur. Practitioner logs capture a rich array of information about a client from the unique perspective of a person who is highly trained and intimately involved in the helping process. However, the diversity and subjectivity of some of the information collected with logs has the potential to decrease the reliability and validity of the information. Therefore, it's especially important to use the strategies discussed to try to maximize the reliability and validity of the information collected with logs, and to verify the reliability and validity of this information by obtaining and comparing information from different sources and different measurement methods.

First and foremost, try at the outset to ensure that the information collected using logs is accurate. Explain to clients in a confident manner the importance of recording, and emphasize that accurate recording is essential to the success of the intervention. Gently impress on the client that the value of client logs depends almost completely on their accuracy, and be certain that the client doesn't think that he or she can "help" the program by being "overgenerous" in reporting progress. Ensure that the information collected is relevant, the data collection task is not too taxing, and the measurement tasks are defined clearly. Make sure that the proper tools are available for recording (e.g., forms, tape recorder), and that the tools are simple, inexpensive, easy-to-use, and unobtrusive. Train, monitor, and retrain the client in the proper recording procedures. Make sure recording is done as soon as possible after the event to be recorded. Be sure you use the information that is collected; be encouraging, supportive, praising, and empathic of the client's recording efforts, but be careful you don't inadvertently encourage the client to report improvement when it doesn't occur.

A variety of strategies for verifying the reliability and validity of the frequency, duration, or intensity of a target were discussed. These strategies also can be applied to the information collected by logs. Try to verify the consistency with which different people observe the same events (i.e., interobserver reliability). Use of other observers in the client's home, making telephone calls, interviewing others in the client's environment about the events the client reports, and even comparing two independently prepared logs, all have been suggested by Schwartz and Goldiamond (1975) as methods of verifying the interobserver reliability of client logs. The reliability of practitioner logs can be verified by audiotaping or videotaping sessions with clients and having a supervisor, colleague, or in some cases, a consultant, review all or randomly selected parts of the recorded information; they even could independently construct a log with which the original log can be compared.

In general, the validity of the information collected by logs can be verified by comparing the information from logs to some standard (i.e., criterion validity) or to other measured variables with which it theoretically should or should not be associated (construct validity). For example, a man receiving help for verbally and emotionally abusing his wife might be asked to keep a log of abusive incidents and the circumstances under which they occur. His wife may be asked to keep a parallel log against which the husband's log could be compared (assuming the relative accuracy of the wife's information, and that these reports would not put the wife at further risk). The husband and wife also might be asked to each complete a standardized index of marital satisfaction on a regular basis, and changes in marital satisfaction and abuse could be compared over time, on the assumption that when abuse decreases, satisfaction will increase. Finally, one way to verify the validity of an interventive hypothesis generated by a log might be to implement the intervention suggested by the log and examine whether the expected change occurs.

Verifying the reliability and validity of logs is important, but what the client chooses to report and how it's reported is as important as "objective reality." Thus, both what the client does and doesn't report are topics for discussion in interviews. You and the client can decide on the meaning and utility of such information. Even if the client's data can't be checked objectively, this doesn't mean that the information automatically should be excluded from consideration. Simply discussing the decisions the client made to include or exclude certain occurrences can provide fruitful information for assessment and intervention.

Summary

Client logs are structured diaries kept by the client to record the unique qualitative contextual circumstances surrounding his or her targets, and to record quantitative dimensions of these targets. These logs can be set up to include preset (e.g., every hour) or open (e.g., critical incident) time categories, and can include any number of categories of information. Four types of logs—exploratory, target, interaction, and evaluation—can be used, and forms were provided for your use in practice. These logs can be used to pinpoint and define problems, generate individualized hypotheses for intervention, and monitor and evaluate change over time in a client's targets. The practitioner log is a variation of the client log that can be used for much the same purposes, although it also can be used to monitor the delivery of services. Finally, we discussed strategies for maximizing and verifying the reliability and validity of client and practitioner logs.

REACTIVITY AND NONREACTIVE MEASURES

PURPOSE This chapter begins by describing reactivity as the way measurement procedures themselves can produce changes in what is being measured. Sometimes, the practitioner wants to increase reactivity to facilitate whatever goal the client is seeking. Other times, reactivity has a negative effect, interfering with whatever goal the client wants to obtain. From the perspective of practice evaluation reactivity is important because it can be difficult to distinguish the effect of an intervention from the effect of reactivity. We will present ways to increase positive reactivitiy, and to decrease negative reactivity. Then we will present an array of ways to minimize reactivity.

Introduction
Reactivity of Measures
    Minimizing Reactivity
    Reactivity in Self-Monitoring
    Guidelines for Using Reactivity in Self-Monitoring
Unobtrusive (Nonreactive) Measures
    Archival Records
    Public Records
    Private Records
    Behavior Products
    Unobtrusive Observations
    Types of Unobstrusive Observations
    Physical Traces
Summary

From Chapter 9 of *Evaluating Practice: Guidelines for the Accountable Professional*, Sixth Edition. Martin Bloom, Joel Fischer, John G. Orme. Copyright © 2009 by Pearson Education, Inc. All rights reserved.

INTRODUCTION

In any social situation, particularly a high stakes situation when one person is seeking help with a personal problem, what each person (client or practitioner) does—what they say, how they act, etc.—influences the other to some extent. This is equally true when one person (such as the practitioner, a spouse or parent, or an independent observer) measures or observes the client in some way. There will be some influence felt by the client, and this influence can be useful or harmful to attaining client goals, depending on circumstances. From the perspective of practice evaluation, reactivity is important because it can be difficult to distinguish the effect of an intervention from the effect of reactivity.

For instance, if a parent merely stands by without comment watching her child brushing his teeth according to the dentist's instructions, then this will probably increase the likelihood that the child will try to do it correctly. Or, when a practitioner informs a group of teenagers that she will be measuring their sexual experiences with a questionnaire at the end of the semester, some teens might become more circumspect and less sexually active, knowing that their behavior will be studied. We'll call this *positive reactivity,* when the act of observation by another person increases the pressure on the client to act so as to achieve a socially desired goal. Take, for example, a mother whose children are in foster care because of her cocaine use. Before she can regain custody of her children she must test negative for drugs for several months during which random drug tests will be administered.

On the other hand, *negative reactivity* occurs when an act of observation by another person increases the pressure on the client to act according to what the client believes is expected of him or her in this situation, in contrast to the client's true feelings or ordinary behavior. Continuing the toothbrushing example, the presence of the parent may simply lengthen the amount of time the child is moving the brush in his mouth without getting off placque effectively because hard brushing is painful to the child. Or, some sexually active teens may feel more pressure for increased sexual activity than ordinary, so they will live up to their self-defined reputations (and contrary to adult mores on teen sex).

There are times when a practitioner might want to increase the pressures toward positive reactivity, so as to achieve some socially desirable goal. As we will discuss, the literature contains many stratagems for doing this. Likewise, we know how to decrease the pressures toward negative reactivity, thereby gaining a more nearly true picture of the client's feelings and behaviors. We'll consider this topic shortly as well. But remember: whatever you are doing when you observe a client/situation may influence the outcomes of that observation. This is reactivity at work.

It is probably best to think about the degree to which measures used to evaluate practice are reactive, not just whether or not they are reactive (Fritsche & Linneweber, 2006; Webb et al., 1981). In this chapter we will discuss methods and measures designed to reduce reactivity.

Unobtrusive (nonreactive) measures are measures that can be used without the knowledge of the person being measured. If a person (or organization for that matter) is not aware of evaluation, or at least of a particular form of measurement, there's no reason to believe that reactivity will occur. The very question of unobtrusive measures is unnerving for some people, especially civil libertarians, because being evaluated without being aware one is being observed brings up some difficult ethical issues regarding the invasion of privacy and police state tactics, even when performed on behalf of voluntary clients. The dilemma is that if all clients were told that they were being observed, this would, as we discussed previously, change the target behaviors, which may be harmful to clients in the long run. If we do not tell clients that they are being observed, we may be violating their rights and liberty, which is unethical in a democracy. Is it worth the ethical risk to obtain sensitive information unobtrusively? We will discuss this issue at the conclusion of the chapter.

REACTIVITY OF MEASURES

Reactivity can occur for different reasons (Rosenthal & Rosnow, 1991; Webb et al., 1981). If you, as an evaluator, can understand these reasons, you can minimize reactivity and gain a more nearly true picture of the client's situation. First, reactivity can occur because the client adopts a role that is inconsistent to some extent with his or her actual beliefs, feelings, or behaviors. For example, the client might adopt a "good client" role, acting in a way consistent with the implicit goals or presumed expectations of important persons in the client's life. Or, the client might adopt a "bad client" role, acting contrary to his or her perceived understanding of what relevant others wish in this situation. Taking the "good client" role may make the intervention appear more successful than it actually is, while taking a "bad client" role can have the opposite effect.

Second, reactivity can occur because the client fears being judged unfavorably, and thus acts in a way that the client thinks will make him or her "look good," which will not reflect the real situation and thus, may lead the practitioner in wrong directions. Third, the frequency of measurement can be reactive, as increasing familiarity with the measurement process may lead to less interested or less motivated responses, or, on the other hand, familiarity may lead to better responses as the client becomes more skilled in giving "good" answers, rather than making real changes in behavior. This is the issue of *instrumentation*.

Fourth, practitioners may react to agency demands for successful outcomes and "see" what they hope to see. We can double-check this source of reactivity, as it is possible to have two independent observers looking at the same situation at the same time, and comparing answers—an interrater reliability check. Fifth, characteristics of the observers may also affect the behavior of those observed. For example, differences in gender, age, ethnicity, and so on may influence the client behavior to be different from what it ordinarily is. Likewise, characteristics of clients, including differences described previously, but also including religion, income level, and educational attainment, may influence observations made by practitioners or independent observers. Furthermore, characteristics of those who oversee data collection and make interpretive judgments (for instance, within secular or religious agencies) may influence observations.

Minimizing Reactivity

Given the omnipresence of reactive situations, you can understand the great effort practitioners and evaluators go through to minimize reactivity. One way to detect reactivity is to use multiple measures for the same target, because while each method may be reactive in its own way, other methods will be reactive in different ways, so that if a consistent picture of the client situation emerges among all the measures, it will strengthen our confidence in our overall understanding of the client (Eid & Diener, 2006). We'll return to this point when we suggest using both direct measures and indirect unobtrusive measures together for the same target.

One way to reduce reactivity is to use measures that are valid and reliable. For example, measures of clearly defined targets that have high interrater reliability, or high test–retest reliability, will increase our confidence that the changes that do occur are less likely due to changes in the measurement method, and more to do with the targeted events.

Likewise, client-related reactivity can be reduced by encouraging the client to be as honest as possible for his or her own benefit, for example, when filling out a questionnaire. This requires that the client be engaged fully as a participant in his or her own helping situation, and that a strong degree of trust exists between client and practitioner.

In addition to these general suggestions for overcoming reactivity, there are a number of ways to minimize reactivity when client behaviors are observed in natural environments, and when clients know they are being observed. (However, none of these guarantees nonreactivity; they merely minimize it, where possible.)

1. Overall, observers should try to be as inconspicuous and unobtrusive as possible, including avoiding interactions with those observed before, during, and after the intervention; avoid eye contact.

2. The observer's presence should be explained to those being observed in simple, matter-of-fact language that this is their job in this agency, and then proceed with the business at hand.

3. The observer should be positioned away from the ordinary flow of movement while still allowing an unobstructed view of the entire area.

4. The observer's clothing and behavior should not create any unusual attention.

5. The observer should follow all formal and informal rules and regulations of the setting in which he or she is observing.

6. The observer should enter the setting during the least disruptive time, such as before, rather than during, a session.

7. The observer should spend some time in the setting prior to data collection, so that everyone will be accustomed to the observer's presence.

Reactivity in Self-Monitoring

One of the most common measurement methods involves having clients observe and record their own behavior, including thoughts and feelings. This is called self-monitoring. Self-monitoring has been used as an intervention with the expectation that it will indeed lead to beneficial changes (Avina, 2008; Cooper, Heron, & Heward,

2007; Sigmon & LaMattina, 2006; Watson & Tharp, 2007). We prefer to be conservative on this issue of reactivity in self-monitoring—that it may have occurred unless we have reasonable eivdence that it did not.

Practitioners should be aware of the following factors that may increase reactivity in self-monitoring. These are only suggestions, since the research evidence is not yet all in:

1. *Motivation.* Higher motivation to change may lead to more reactive changes.

2. *Desired direction of the behavior.* Self-monitoring may contribute to an increase in positive behaviors and a decrease in negative ones.

3. *Practitioner instructions.* It may be that simply telling clients before intervention that their behaviors will or should change can produce reactive effects in self-monitoring (independent of real changes in the behaviors).

4. *Nature of the target.* Some studies have shown that verbal behavior is less reactive than motor behavior.

5. *Goals and feedback.* It appears that setting specific goals, being rewarded for progress, and receiving feedback on performance increase reactive effects.

6. *Timing.* Recording prior to engaging in a target behavior (like smoking or eating) seems to produce more reactivity than recording after engaging in the behavior. In general, reactivity is more likely to occur at the beginning of a recording program, and is likely to weaken over time. That is why we do not recommend self-monitoring as a sole intervention; the effects won't last.

7. *Nature of the recording instrument.* The more obtrusive the device used to record, the more reactivity seems to occur.

8. *Number of behaviors monitored.* The more behaviors that are self-monitored, the less likely it is that reactivity will occur.

9. *Scheduling of self-monitoring.* Recording behaviors intermittently seems to produce less reactivity than continuous recording.

Guidelines for Using Reactivity in Self-Monitoring

You may actually want to use reactive effects to enhance your intervention program; that is, reactivity can be used in the positive sense, to add to the force behind your intervention. For example, in helping a client reduce caloric intake while self-monitoring, you may try to motivate him to change by discussing the benefits of doing so, suggesting that this intervention has helped people like him, setting specific goals and setting up a reward system for progress toward those goals, placing a recording sheet in a prominent public location at his apartment, or focusing solely on caloric intake as a target. Each of these actions may amplify the reactive effect of your program to get him to reduce caloric intake.

On the other hand, you may wish to minimize reactivity in self-monitoring. For instance, you may have a client who is insecure and dependent on her parents. Your program involves assertiveness training, and you decide not to impose other demands on the client by emphasizing the fact that she is taking control into her own hands. So you focus on her verbal behavior; you ask her to monitor several aspects of the effects of her assertiveness training program; you unobtrusively measure the number of cigarettes she smokes at your office that you think reflect her insecurity and being ill at ease; and you ask a colleague to look into your office at each visit to estimate her security level by the posture she assumes. Each of these actions may reduce the reactivity of your multiple measures of her state of mind and give you a more nearly complete measure of her progress toward self-control.

The following summary of suggestions may allow you to increase or to minimize reactivity, as you think best with your particular client.

Increasing Reactivity in Self-Monitoring

1. Have the client focus on self-monitoring positive behaviors that are to be increased or negative behaviors to be reduced.

2. Focus on a very limited number of motor behaviors, and make these observations on a regular and systematic basis.

3. Set specific goals and make clear value statements about the desirability of these changes.

4. Give feedback on the client's performance moving toward the goal, and provide reinforcement for these changes.

5. Tell the client prior to intervention that his or her behavior will or should change, and use a very intrusive recording device to exhibit these changes.

Decreasing Reactivity in Self-Monitoring

1. Focus on verbal behavior and have client self-monitor multiple behaviors.

2. Use unobtrusive measures and an independent observer's reliability check of your measures.

3. Record on an intermittent basis, using a stable baseline.

4. Compare the client's initial retrospective reports about the occurrence of the target behavior with his or her score on an instrument designed to measure the target.

5. If reactivity still appears to be high, consider an independent program to teach the client to record more accurately, or reconsider your measurement package.

In many of these suggestions, the goal is to compare records obtained through self-monitoring with those obtained from some other measurement methods. Also, be patient; it is likely that the client will be more reactive at first when you begin your observations, and that this will weaken in time. Still, it is wise to be aware of the possible reactive effects and interpreting such data if self-monitoring is the only form of measurement used.

UNOBTRUSIVE (NONREACTIVE) MEASURES

Unfortunately, many unobtrusive methods are indirect ways of measuring targets. In these instances they probably should serve as secondary sources of information when there is more direct evidence of changes in the client's target. However, in some instances, when the unobtrusive measure is a direct record of the targets (e.g., school grades or number of math problems finished correctly), it can serve as a primary measure.

The validity, reliability, utility, and directness of these measures have to be estimated when you make your decision regarding whether to use them. As just one example, in deciding to use records that have been collected for other purposes as a measure of your target, it is important to determine that the records were collected consistently and in the same way across time, so that any changes in the records are not merely a result of changes in the way the records were being kept or some other irrelevant outside event.

Some unobtrusive measures have weaknesses that make their use as the sole or even primary data source open to question. We discuss some of these weaknesses in this chapter so that you can be aware of the pitfalls in some unobtrusive measures. Often, though, unobtrusive measures can be used in conjunction with other measures, and changes over time in the different measures can be charted and compared. For example, suppose that you're a school social worker charged with developing a schoolwide program to increase interaction among African American and white students. You might unobtrusively monitor the proportion of students sitting next to different-ethnicity students in the lunchroom or classroom. This measure would not capture the total amount of time spent together. Therefore, you might survey students weekly and ask them to report the total amount of time spent with different-ethnicity students. These self-reports would probably not be completely accurate, either. For example, on implementation of the intervention there might be increased social pressure to interact with students of a different ethnicity, and this might lead to overreports of the amount of time spent (i.e., the intervention would appear effective even if it was not). However, if the changes in the different measures are comparable, for example, as shown in Figure 1, support is provided for the accuracy of the observed pattern of change.

The types of unobtrusive measures we describe, in large part using the Webb et al. (1981) categories, are archival records, behavior products, unobtrusive observation, and physical traces.

Archival Records

If there's anything with which most helping professionals are familiar, it is records. Yet, while records are sometimes considered to be the professional's number one enemy, they can be extremely useful in helping measure the client's target. Archival records essentially refer to records that are kept for various purposes not necessarily related to your intervention program. But because these records are available from a variety of sources and can be useful, they comprise perhaps the most important form of unobtrusive measure. There are two basic types of archival records—public and private (Webb et al., 1981).

Public Records. There is a whole range of public records that could be considered as measures for evaluating the success of your interventions. For

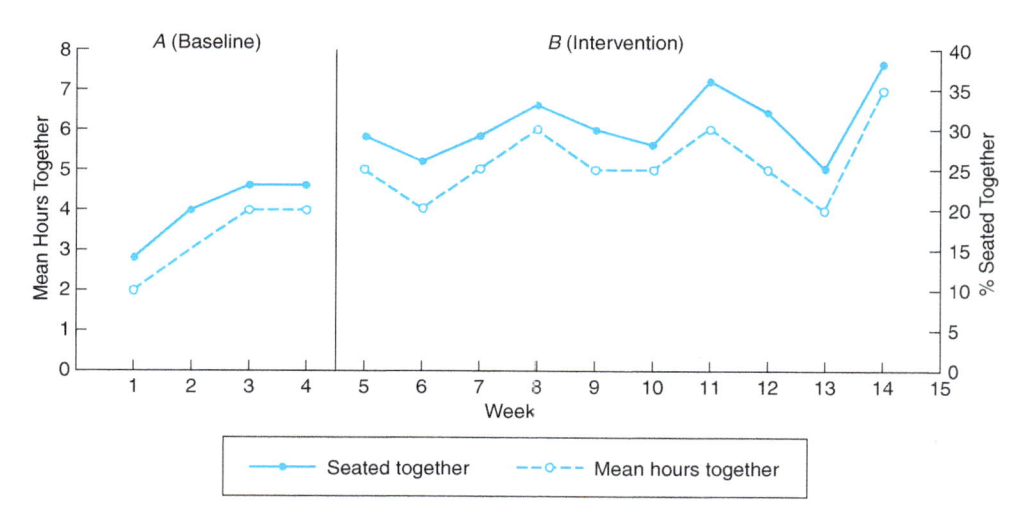

FIGURE 1 Interaction between white and African American students.

example, Webb et al. (1981) describe categories of records such as actuarial records (e.g., demographic records such as births, deaths, divorces, marriages), political and judicial records, government documents, and the mass media.

To some extent, we use a bit of license in calling all of these records "public." Not all may be available to everyone. Yet, in the broadest sense, we refer to those measures that are truly public (open and available to every citizen), plus those that are collected by organizations and agencies that may not be widely available to all citizens, but are available to you as a helping professional (e.g., a school record). In essence, we define public records as those that are usually maintained by organizations over periods of time for a variety of their own purposes, but may be used by you to measure the success of your intervention.

Many of these records are of particular value in analyzing changes over time in organizations, policies, or interventions aimed at groups or large collectives. Thus, if your intervention efforts involve an attempt to change an agency's program policies, you have immediately available to you a whole range of data tapping important dimensions of possible interest; these include, for example, measures of staff turnover, number of complaints, number or types of referral sources, productivity, characteristics of clients, time on the waiting list, number of premature terminations, case records, process recordings, and so on.

Let's say you design a program to increase the number of low-income clients coming to your agency. By simply inspecting the intake sheets of your agency, you will have excellent feedback regarding whether any changes did in fact take place. A chart documenting these changes might look like the one in Figure 2. Similarly, you might want to use the functioning of the participants in your agency's programs as an overall outcome measure. You can do this by simply adding up individual data and using averages.

Perhaps your goal is to decrease the occurrence of criminal acts among juvenile gang members who participate in your agency's program. You could use measures such as the average number of offenses per program participant; the proportion or number of those who are arrested or convicted, or who become recidivists; or the average length of stay in a correctional facility over some specified time period. With all of these measures, though, it's important to be sure that the data are both valid and reliable. For example, program participants might simply be going into other neighborhoods to commit crimes. Or police, notified that a program is under way, may be more reluctant (or more willing) to arrest program participants. But if these obstacles can be overcome, your chart might look like Figure 3.

There are a host of other potential uses of public records, especially in the institutions and organizations

Reactivity and Nonreactive Measures

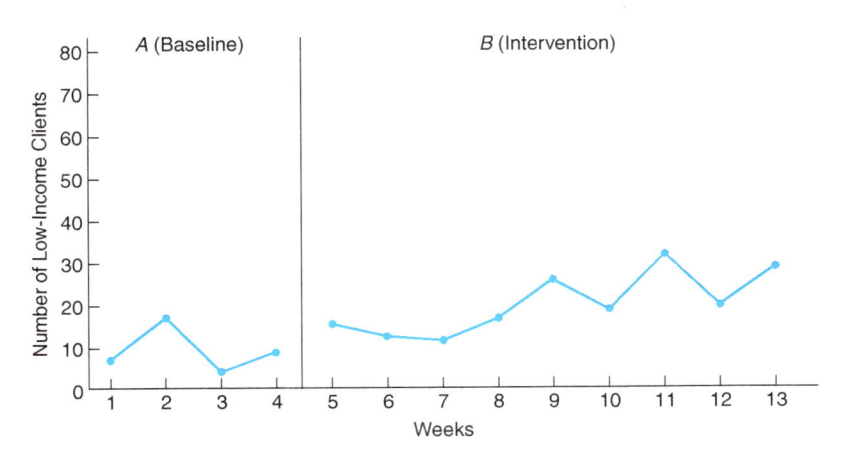

FIGURE 2 Number of low-income clients being seen at intake.

in which most helping professionals work—hospitals, schools, clinics. These records can be used for evaluating not only the effects of programs aimed at changing agency policies, but also the effects of intervention programs on individuals.

Perhaps the best example of data available for other purposes that can be used to evaluate individual and program effect is school records. A whole range of data typically is collected in schools: academic grades, scores on standardized tests (IQ, achievement tests), attendance records, number of problems or pages finished correctly (don't forget the *correctly* part; it may be of little value to have 10 problems finished with the wrong answers, unless you're only building the client's motivation to spend time on the work). Of course, with data such as homework assignments, it's important to evaluate whether your client had roughly similar amounts and type of work over the days of the program so that any changes won't be purely a result of the teacher changing the assignment. (The teacher's cooperation might also be elicited to ensure consistency.)

You can use such data to evaluate changes in either groups or individuals. For example, Figure 4 depicts the progress of a program intended to improve a student's attendance at school, while at the same time enhancing the learning conditions for the student at

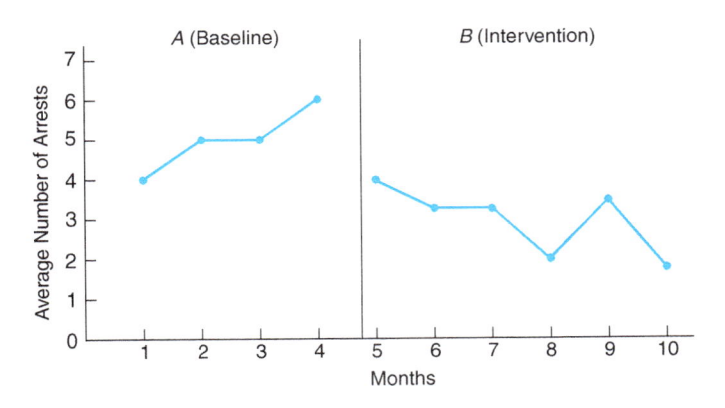

FIGURE 3 Average number of arrests per month of program participants.

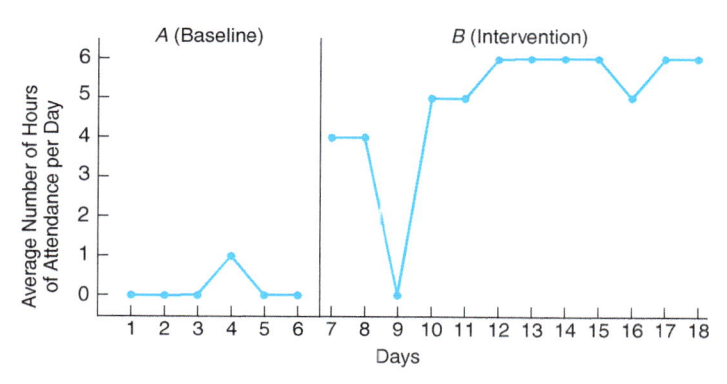

FIGURE 4 Average number of hours of attendance per day for Wilma.

school. Figure 5 describes the results of a program intended to evaluate the practitioner's success in helping a whole class of low-income children turn in completed homework assignments every day. On the other hand, these records might be highly reactive if the student is aware that they are being used for purposes of evaluation.

A number of potential problems could arise with the use of public records. First, there is the uncertainty involved in any data collection that you did not personally collect. There may have been extenuating circumstances in their collection that are harmful to your client, perhaps because of biases in gender, ethnicity, age, or whatever, that you are not aware of.

These data may be incomplete, and thus give a slanted picture of prior events. At the most practical level, it is often difficult to determine what is available in the realm of public records. Once you do, you may have difficulty in obtaining access to the data; this could require a long process of negotiation with the organization. Then, if you do get access, you might be shocked to find that all the data weren't on hand in the first place, or that they were collected on a sloppy basis. Finally, archival data are generally rather inflexible. You might want information by the week and it's only available by the month. You might need it broken down by age or other characteristics and it's not.

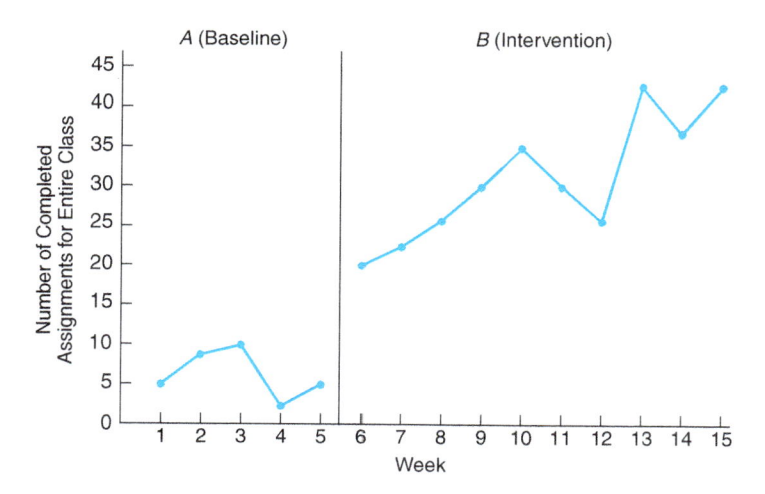

FIGURE 5 Number of assignments turned in per week in Ms. Jones's class of 25 students.

But, if you are to use archival data, you will have to be content with what you do find. The data are unobtrusive and can avoid many reactive effects. They particularly avoid the "guinea pig effect" of people knowing they're being evaluated; often, the data are collected well before a study or intervention program is undertaken, or they may have been collected for other purposes. Finally, records offer the advantage of allowing the evaluation of activities that otherwise might be lost. This is particularly so when evaluation was not perceived as necessary until after the fact. Sometimes, archival data are easy to obtain, and worth squeezing out as much information as they hold for your present and independent purposes.

Private Records. Private records generally are much less available than public records, but they can be helpful to you in planning and evaluating intervention programs. Two key principles in the use of private records, of course, are (a) obtaining the client's permission to examine them, and (b) maintaining confidentiality about what you find.

Let's say you're helping a family deal with a variety of stressful events including managing their finances. If this family is keeping a record of expenditures—credit or debit card records, checking account, budget book, shopping lists, and so on—you may be able to not only see how much money is spent over a given period of time, but also understand how the money is allocated (i.e., what proportion goes to food, activities, clothing). If the family is willing to keep ongoing records, you would have a good indication of changes from the baseline to intervention periods.

Of course, using private records poses a problem in ascertaining their validity. (Political events reveal that this may be as much or more of a problem with public records.) Such records may be deliberately misrepresented or mistakenly distorted. Thus, one task for the practitioner is to try to evaluate whether the documents report accurate information and can be used as a measure for evaluating changes. In the event that they're unintentionally distorted, the practitioner can also help the client develop a more accurate system of keeping records.

Behavior Products

Behavior products are an important source of unobtrusive measures. Behavior products essentially refer to the effects or results of behaviors rather than the behaviors themselves. That is, rather than directly monitoring the actual behavior of the client, you would monitor any temporary or permanent effect that can be seen as the result of a specifiable behavior. Ayllon and Azrin (1968) note that behavior products can be used when a more direct measure of the behavior might interfere with the behavior being observed, when it takes too much time to observe the behavior directly, or when the actual behavior itself is not available for measurement. Because the observer is not ordinarily present when behavior products are used (unless, of course, the observer happens to be the client), there's less chance for the measurement process to interfere with the natural occurrence of the behavior.

There are a number of advantages to using behavior products. First, a product readily lends itself to precise quantification. For example, the number of cigarettes smoked can be assessed by counting cigarette butts left in an ashtray. Second, the observer doesn't have to be present when a behavior is performed. For example, instead of watching a child litter his or her room, the observer can simply count how many articles weren't put away after the play period. Or, stealing could be measured by leaving a child alone in a room and then measuring the number of missing objects. Third, using behavior products generally doesn't disturb or interrupt the flow of the client's behavior. Even when the client is recording, he or she can carry out daily activities in an uninterrupted fashion, counting the product only at certain predefined times during the day (e.g., before going to bed). Finally, recording behavior products is relatively easy to implement, requires little or no special equipment, and can easily be taught to the client or relevant others.

There are some problems with the use of behavior products, however. First, the information is generally limited to "how many" or "how much," and controlling conditions cannot easily be evaluated. Second, many behaviors, as we define them (e.g., feelings and thoughts), don't leave products. Third, you have to be sure that the product really is a direct reflection of the behavior of concern and not other factors. This is especially true when more than one person is in the area where a product was left. For example, just because several toys are left out doesn't mean that Johnny left them out (watch out for his older brother). Finally, it may be that some behavior products are not sensitive to slight changes in the actual target behavior, so that these changes may not be noticed when only products are being monitored.

There are a number of behavior products that you could consider using. The number of cigarette butts in

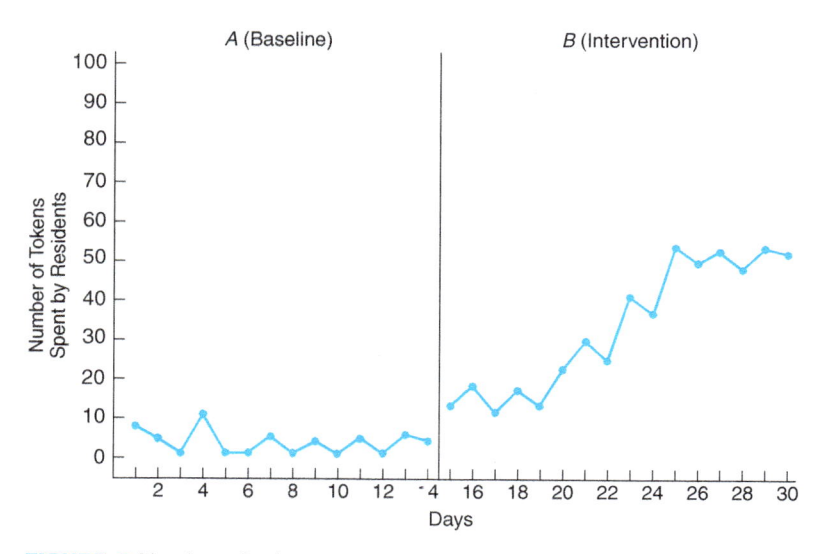

FIGURE 6 Number of tokens spent per day.

an ashtray is a good sign of the frequency of smoking. In a program to increase home safety practices for preschoolers you might unobtrusively observe the number of safety risks on a home visit (e.g., uncovered electrical outlets, accessible medicines, and dangerous cleaning products). In a weight reduction program, the number of actual behaviors might be measured (e.g., how much or how fast one eats). But because this might prove not only inefficient but reactive, you might simply choose to monitor actual weight changes, the key product of eating behavior. (Of course, to the extent the client is aware of this monitoring, this would not be a totally unobtrusive measure.)

School settings and other settings involving children, including the home, provide a number of opportunities to use product measures. Completed assignments, children's workbooks, crayon writing on the wall, results on quizzes (a measure perhaps of studying behavior), and items not put away are examples of the range of behavior products available.

Other behavior products that could be considered relatively unobtrusive might be those involved in helping a family or a group on a ward in a hospital care for their own rooms; for example, you could measure items left on a floor, beds that are made, or other products of self-management programs. Similarly, if you were setting up a program to diminish litter in a low-income housing project, you might use a measure of the amount of litter in selected yards of the project.

Let's assume you develop a token economy program on the psychiatric ward of a medical hospital. Rather than measuring the actual behaviors for which the tokens are earned, you might measure the behavior product—the number of tokens that the residents spend. This could be displayed as in Figure 6.

Unobtrusive Observations

The next category of unobtrusive measures—unobtrusive observation—is a variation on and an elaboration of several of the themes presented in earlier chapters. (Typically, this is called *simple observation*, but we think that the term *unobtrusive observation* is more descriptive.) Specifically, unobtrusive observation refers to situations "in which the observer has no control over the behavior or sign in question, and plays an unobserved, passive and nonintrusive role in the research situation" (Webb et al., 1981, p. 197). For example, it is now possible to attach a global positioning device to a car in order to monitor the location of the car; it would be possible for a parent to track where a child drives, without the child's knowledge. (We're not suggesting that this is a good idea!) In other words, the observer observes without the client being aware of it. Of course, once the target is observed, the remainder of the measurement procedure takes on all of the characteristics. That is, the key difference here is who observes and how that person does it. A frequency count is treated as a frequency count no matter who does the counting.

Although unobtrusive observations do have the obvious advantage that while the practitioner or observer is observing, the client is not aware of it (e.g., through a transparent mirror or when students in a classroom or patients on a ward are engaged in some activity and don't notice the observer), there are problems inherent in this approach. The first one concerns problems arising from changes in the observer—either from growing bored with or becoming increasingly expert at the observations. (This is the issue of *instrumentation*.) Regular reliability checks would help to minimize that problem.

A second concern with unobtrusive observations is that they're limited to certain phenomena. Because the observer should generally be unnoticed (or, at least, should be observing in unnoticed ways), many of the observations may have to take place in public locations or private locations with special arrangements (one-way viewing mirrors, tape recorders, etc.).

Finally, there's a question of validity with regard to unobtrusive observations. Because sometimes one is looking for observable indicators that may be suggestive of other events (e.g., attitudes), it's important to be cautious in making interpretations. Unobtrusive observations are often best used as secondary sources of data or, perhaps, data that can be used to cross-validate other observations.

Types of Unobtrusive Observations. The types of unobtrusive observations that you can use seem limited only by your imagination and creativity, not to mention the more practical consideration of having someone available to make the unobtrusive observations. But, in addition to just a count of some behavior or activity, four other types of unobtrusive observations have been described (Webb et al., 1981).

The first type is the observation of physical signs that might be used to make inferences about attitudes or behaviors. Illustrations of these include changes in hairstyle or makeup, or wearing certain clothes or jewelry, exemplifying changes in style. An example of this would involve the client who complains about being unattractive to those of the other sex. The practitioner might set up a program to help the client learn to dress or groom more attractively, and use "physical signs" to evaluate success.

A second type of unobtrusive observation would be the analysis of expressive movements, including smiles, frowns, and gestures. Of course, when one is trying to infer attitudes, feelings, or behaviors from expressions and gestures, an obvious difficulty is in verifying the meaning of what is observed. This might be done by using other signs or other unobtrusive measures to validate the observations. In some circumstances, for example, with use of videotapes for feedback to clients, the practitioner might ask the client the meaning of some gestures that had been observed (but not necessarily the ones being measured to evaluate the program) to check the overall accuracy of inferences about the client's expressions or gestures. Because nonverbal communications tend to play a large part in interpersonal communications anyhow, their analysis for use as an unobtrusive observation simply means being more systematic in observing them. But analyzing and making inferences about others' nonverbal communication require understanding of the context and situation of gestures, and also the possible meaning for the sender and receiver.

A third category of unobtrusive observation is physical location analysis, examining the way the client uses his or her body in a given social space. This type of measure is commonly used in social psychological research on attitudes, for example, examining seating patterns as an index of interethnic relations. But this type of measure also has promise as a secondary or proxy measure for therapeutic purposes. For example, the proximity of members of a family or group in their seating arrangements during sessions with the practitioner might be used to measure changes in their feelings about one another over time.

The fourth category of unobtrusive observation is the analysis of language behavior. The purpose of this is to analyze both the content and the expressiveness of the content in relation to time of day, presence of others, and location of the conversation. Thus, you might use tape recordings of interviews to keep track of changes in clients' feelings about themselves and/or others. Then, by noting changes in both the frequency of the use of certain words (e.g., positive references to oneself), as well as qualitative or expressive changes in the use of those words, you would have a built-in measure of change over the course of the intervention program. Another example would be to structure family problem-solving activities and then to record these on videotape or observe them through a transparent mirror to be used as ongoing assessment and/or evaluation information.

Physical Traces

The last type of unobtrusive measure involves physical traces. Although there's considerable overlap between physical traces and behavior products, there are some differences. Physical traces refer to evidence left by an individual or group with no knowledge that it may be used for other (e.g., evaluation or research) purposes. Webb et al. (1981) distinguishes between two types of trace measures—*erosion,* where the degree of wear on some object produces the measure, and *accretion,* measures of the deposit of some material. The distinction here is between materials *worn away* and materials *deposited,* with emphasis on the physical aspects of those effects. Physical trace measures generally require some degree of inference about the behaviors that produced them. Moreover, a good deal of rummaging around is often involved in order to discover trace measures. They, therefore, tend to be among the least-used measures, especially for single-system evaluation.

Erosion measures refer to the natural remnants of some individual's or group's activity that has selectively worn down certain objects. For example, if you're working in a nursing home, you might determine what the most popular activity in that home is by observing where the rugs were most worn. It might be in front of the television set or in front of the windows where people spend time looking out at the street. This could give you a possible measure for evaluating changes in the group's activities.

Other erosion measures might include decay and breakage. Active or aggressive physical activity can be inferred from the number of broken items (e.g., windows) in a school or on a ward. The frequency of repair, replacement, or cleaning of certain objects in a setting may be used as an indicator of frequency of usage.

One must be careful in using erosion measures to be sure that unrelated factors are not the reasons for observed changes. For example, a new janitor's zeal in cleaning may be responsible for changes in the patterns of use as detected by wear and tear on the floor. Similarly, it would help to know the amount of ordinary wear and tear on objects so that any excessive erosion or wear and tear can be related to target behaviors with more assurance.

The second category of physical traces is accretion measures. These are objects deposited by clients in a given setting or the ordinary debris left by client interaction with or consumption of material. In addition to some of the behavior products mentioned in an earlier section that may be viewed as accretion measures, such as cigarette butts, these measures often focus on analysis of remains or even rubbish. For example, one could ask a spouse to count the number of beer bottles in the trash as a way of measuring the extent of the spouse's drinking problem.

Of course, reliability and validity concerns are as important in using physical traces as they are with other measures, and especially important when being used to make inferences about behaviors. For example, if you were to use the changing number of beer bottles in the trash per day as an indicator of the episodic nature of stress in the client's life, you would have to be certain that changes in the number of bottles simply don't reflect different patterns of throwing out the garbage, and represent only the client's drinking behavior.

Summary

This chapter reviewed the nature of reactivity, changes that come about in a target due to the act of measurement. We discussed different sources of reactivity, and we suggested a number of ways of overcoming reactivity in general. We then focused on reactivity in self-monitoring and offered several guidelines for how to increase or decrease reactivity depending upon what is desirable in a given case.

The remainder of the chapter dealt with unobtrusive measures. Unobtrusive measures are measures that can be used to evaluate changes over time without interfering with or affecting the observed target simply by the act of measurement. In large part, these measures are most suited as secondary sources of data, although in certain instances, where they comprise direct evidence of changes, they may be suitable as primary measures. Four types of unobtrusive measures were described and examples presented of their potential use for practice: archival records (both public and private), physical traces (evidence left behind by the client), behavior products (rather than the actual behaviors themselves), and unobtrusive observations, where the observer doesn't play an active part in the client's interactions on the dimension being observed.

SELECTING A MEASURE

PURPOSE This chapter briefly reviews all of the types of measures we've discussed in this book and then presents a framework to help you select measures in your practice. The use of multiple measures is strongly recommended, and guidelines for the selection and use of multiple measures are provided.

Introduction
    Summary of Available Measurement Methods
Considerations in Deciding on a Measure
    Characteristics of the Measure
    Characteristics of the Target
    Characteristics of the Practitioner and Practice Approach
    Characteristics of the Client and Resources Available
    An Exercise in Selecting Measures

Use of Multiple Measures
    Why Multiple Measures?
        Changes Are Often Multidimensional
        Measures Often Do Not Correlate
        Multiple Measures Increase Confidence
    Problems with Using Multiple Measures
    The Measurement Package
    Guidelines for Using Multiple Measures
Selecting a Measure
Summary

From Chapter 10 of *Evaluating Practice: Guidelines for the Accountable Professional*, Sixth Edition. Martin Bloom, Joel Fischer, John G. Orme. Copyright © 2009 by Pearson Education, Inc. All rights reserved.

INTRODUCTION

We hope the chapters in this part have convinced you that there are ways to measure just about any target that you might encounter in practice. We hope also that we haven't overwhelmed you by offering so many options. Life would be so much easier if we could just point to one method and say: "Use it for everything; it always works." Unfortunately, both life and measurement just aren't that simple. Given that fact, and the fact that you probably would like to remain flexible about what you measure, while at the same time having something other than guesswork to use in selecting measures, we'd like to present in this chapter some ideas on selecting appropriate measures for any given situation. These guidelines may not be as clear-cut as, say, a statistical test of significance, and they do require some creativity (the art of practice?) in evaluating the range of available measures and making a selection for each situation, but they also should provide some basis for helping you in that selection by describing some of the issues and criteria you would want to consider.

Summary of Available Measurement Methods

Before we get into the actual issues and guidelines, take a look at Table 1, which summarizes the measurement methods we've discussed and the guidelines for their use. (It might be a good idea for you to keep this summary handy as you contemplate which ones to choose.) The actual criteria for using each of these methods and the guidelines for using them were discussed in the chapter devoted to each.

CONSIDERATIONS IN DECIDING ON A MEASURE

Once you're familiar with the range of measures that are available and the indications for their use, there are still some other factors you would want to consider before you make your selection. We're going to describe several of these in the hope that it will help you be even more precise in your selections. These characteristics are not listed here in order of importance. In any given situation, any one of these characteristics might play the key role in your selection.

Characteristics of the Measure

You may recall a number of basic principles of measurement that are directly applicable in considering what measure to use. In essence, we noted that no measure is perfect or error free. But to the extent that a measure is intended to measure a certain characteristic, it should be influenced mainly by that characteristic and as little as possible by other factors. Thus, to briefly review some of the criteria we discussed, you want measures that are:

1. *Reliable.* Your measure must be consistent, giving similar results when it's used under similar conditions.

2. *Valid.* To the extent that it's possible to know this, you want to try to ensure that your measure measures what it's supposed to.

3. *Sensitive to change.* If changes do occur in a target, you want to be sure that your measure will be able to pick them up. An insensitive measure, by definition, is one that won't indicate change even though actual changes have come about. Although we discussed this criterion largely in relation to standardized scales, it pertains to the use of any measure.

4. *Nonreactive.* Try to use measures that will do as little as possible to change the target simply by the act of measurement. If it seems your measure may produce some reactivity, use the reactivity to the benefit of the client.

5. *Direct.* To the extent possible, try to select a measure that most accurately represents (or actually is) the real target. The closer the measure approximates the real target, the more useful it will be. Indirect measures have their place. But the more direct your measure, the more accurately you will be able to assess a situation.

6. *Easy to use.* Try to use measures that are easy enough to administer, score, and interpret so that they can be administered repeatedly.

7. *Accessible.* Try to use measures that are easy to obtain (e.g., not restricted to certain professions, not expensive).

Table 1 Summary of available measurement methods

Measure	Situations Where Best Used
Behavioral Observation	Use to measure overt or covert discrete target behaviors. Use direct observation to measure overt behaviors, and self-monitoring to measure overt or covert behaviors. • Use frequency recording when the goal is to increase or decrease the number of times a behavior occurs, and when the duration of the behavior is relatively constant and has a clear beginning and end. • Use duration recording when the goal is to increase or decrease the length of time a behavior occurs, or the length of time between events, and the behavior has a clear beginning and end. • Use interval recording when the goal is to increase or decrease the relative frequency or duration of behavior and frequency or duration recording is impractical (e.g., when the beginning and end of the behavior are difficult to discern or multiple clients or behaviors are observed simultaneously).
Individualized Rating Scales	Use to measure targets defined specifically for a given client, along relatively subjective dimensions (e.g., intensity, satisfaction, severity, importance). Use individualized self-report rating scales to elicit information from clients, and individualized observer rating scales to elicit information from practitioners, relevant others, or independent evaluators.
Standardized Scales	Use to measure targets in terms of concepts with some general relevance to different clients, using a method that is standardized across clients, that often has demonstrated validity and reliability, and that lets you compare a client's data with relevant group norms. Use standardized self-report scales to elicit information from clients, and standardized observer scales to elicit information from practitioners, relevant others, or independent evaluators.
Logs	Use client logs to pinpoint and define client targets; to assemble a qualitative picture of events prior to, during, and after a target event; or to evaluate change in the frequency, duration, or intensity of self-monitored targets. • Use logs with preset time categories when you have some idea when a target occurs and you want data collected at regular intervals. • Use logs with open time categories when you need information about "critical incidents." • Use an exploratory log to pinpoint and define a target and to get information about the circumstances surrounding the target. • Use a target problem log when the target is defined, but information about the circumstances surrounding the target is unclear. • Use an interaction log to examine interactions between the client and others that centered on an identified target. • Use an evaluation log to measure change in the frequency, duration, or intensity of self-monitored targets. Use practitioner logs to pinpoint and define client targets; to assemble a qualitative picture of events prior to, during, and after a target event; to evaluate change in the frequency, duration, or intensity of client targets; and to monitor the provision of services.
Unobtrusive (Nonreactive) Measures	Use to measure change in client targets in a way that avoids changing the targets by measuring them. • Use archival records when relevant existing data are available and accessible. • Use behavior products or physical traces when a behavior has an observable temporary or permanent effect on the environment. • Use simple observations when unobtrusive observations are possible.

8. *Relevant to intervention planning.* To the extent possible, use measures that will facilitate decisions about the presence of client targets, the factors affecting or maintaining the targets, the most effective intervention strategies for the targets, and, most important, the degree of improvement or deterioration in the target.

Characteristics of the Target

The nature of the target should be a major factor in deciding what measures to use. In Table 1, we review the wide range of measures available so that you can fit one or more of these to a given target. It would make little sense under most conditions to select a measure that is valid and reliable but that doesn't accurately represent the desired outcome. This is perhaps the key—your measure should be a direct representation of the outcomes you hope to attain. If your goal is a change in a behavior, observe the behavior. If the goal is a change in perceptions, use a self-report measure of perceptions. *Make sure the measure you select is directly relevant to what you hope to accomplish.*

Characteristics of the Practitioner and Practice Approach

We haven't forgotten the important role that you play in selecting a measure. By this we mean not only your own preferences and choices, but also the intervention approaches you use.

First, we hope that your own comfort with a given measure won't be a major factor in selecting a measure. Not that comfort isn't important, but we believe that the main way of achieving comfort is by practice and experience. If your personal comfort was your only guideline, you'd stick only with what you already know and never try something new.

On the other hand, if everything else is equal, and you have a choice between two measures, each of which has similar characteristics and is equally relevant to the target, then go ahead and select whichever one you're more comfortable using. Indeed, the more comfortable you are with a given measure, the more you may induce confidence in others to use it.

Second, each measure you use should correspond to at least one component of your intervention, in the sense that the measured outcome is the direct target of at least one intervention. However, in considering the correspondence between measured targets and interventions, the entire configuration of targets and interventions for a case also should be considered. For example, intensive family preservation services designed to prevent the removal of a child from his or her home use multiple interrelated interventions (e.g., the provision of tangible, social, and emotional parenting resources and parent training), targeted at multiple interrelated short- and long-term outcomes (e.g., enhanced social supports, improved parenting skills, better parent–child relationships, elimination of maltreatment, continued parental custody) (e.g., Fraser, 1990; Pearson, 1990). Therefore, a measured target may be linked to more than one intervention (e.g., maltreatment may be reduced by the provision of resources and by parent training), and change in some targets may depend on change in other targets (e.g., continued parental custody may depend on reduced maltreatment and reduced maltreatment may depend on better social supports and parenting skills). Nevertheless, whenever possible, each target should be measured, and the measure of one target shouldn't be substituted for the measure of another target, because it's unlikely that one will represent perfectly the other (e.g., it's unlikely that a measure of parenting skills could substitute for a measure of the quality of parent–child relationships).

Finally, your theoretical orientation or approach to practice might play a part in your selection of measures. Suppose that an adult comes to you with depression, and your practice approach suggests that to affect depression you have to change automatic, unrealistic, maladaptive modes of thinking in order to change negative moods and maladaptive behaviors. In this case it might be reasonable to ask the client to keep a log to track such thoughts and the context in which they occur, and to complete a standardized self-report measure of depression (Persons & Fresco, 2008).

Characteristics of the Client and Resources Available

When it comes right down to it, you must select a measure that somebody is willing to *use*. In essence, our point is you have to consider who will be doing the observation and recording, and select measures that person will be willing to use. The measures should not be burdensome or irrelevant to the person(s) who will use them. (This may require a good deal of preparation of those persons on your part.) They should be convenient and easy to use. Everything else being equal, try to select the easiest, most pleasant, least time-consuming measure. Make sure the rationale for and importance of the measure are clearly understood by the people who will use them. Select a measure that the person won't regard as silly or childish, or a waste of time.

An Exercise in Selecting Measures

If you're still having a problem with selecting measures, try the following exercise. Select a target that seems difficult to measure, and enumerate as many different practical methods for measuring it as possible. Suppose, for example, that you decide that the quality of the relationship between a parent and child would be difficult to capture. More specifically, suppose that you're faced with trying to enhance the quality of the relationship between a single mother and her adolescent son. Your task for this exercise is to devise as many practical ways as possible of measuring the quality of this relationship. Write them down before you read the rest of this section.

There are, in fact, a number of ways that the quality of the relationship between a parent and child can be measured, although of course no single measure can capture all aspects of the relationship that are of concern. The one or ones you choose may be determined by a combination of your negotiations with the client, that which appears most relevant to the case, or your theoretical orientation. Following are several ways that you can measure this target, corresponding to the chapters on measurement in this section of the book, and that also can serve as a focus for your intervention.

1. *Behavioral observations.* There are any number of different indicators that you, the client, or some other person (e.g., another family member, a teacher) could observe to measure the quality of the relationship. These might include, for example, the amount of time spent together, the amount of time necessary to resolve a disagreement, the number of arguments, the number of negative statements the parent makes about the child, or vice versa. Furthermore, these observations could take place in the natural environment or in an analogue setting.

2. *Individualized rating scales.* You could work with the mother and the son to enumerate separate, individually tailored sets of targets relevant to the quality of the relationship, and to develop the most appropriate dimensions on which to rate the targets. Also, you could construct a scale for your own use that would include the targets you perceived as most important and the dimensions on which to rate these targets.

3. *Standardized scales.* There are numerous standardized scales devised specifically for measuring different aspects of the quality of the relationship between a parent and child and the quality of family relationships (e.g., Fischer & Corcoran, 2007a; Touliatos, Perlmutter, & Holden, 2001). Moreover, the available measures include ones that are designed to obtain information from the perspective of parents, children, and practitioners.

4. *Logs.* The mother and son each could keep a log to record the unique qualitative circumstances surrounding aspects of their relationship, and to record quantitative dimensions of targets selected for intervention, such as intensity and frequency. These could be used to pinpoint and define targets, generate individualized hypotheses for intervention, and quantify change over time in each client's targets. In addition, you could use a log in much the same way as a clinical record to monitor the delivery of your services and for the same purposes as the client log.

5. *Nonreactive measure(s).* You could use public records (e.g., school records of the number of times the school contacted the mother about discipline problems with the son), or you could use simple observation and select some specific physical signs (e.g., proximity of the mother and son), expressive gestures (e.g., smiles or frowns), or language patterns (e.g., use of certain words). Other types of simple observations also could be used. For example, if one point of contention between the mother and son was the "messiness" of the son's room, when making home visits the practitioner could unobtrusively look into the son's room. If the room is too neat (e.g., everything perfectly in its place, etc.), then the mother may be putting too much stress on her son to behave. If the room is too messy (e.g., nothing in

place, what the son might do if he didn't exercise any control whatsoever), then parental guidance may have broken down, which is a concern in this context. If the room is somewhat messy (e.g., what mother–son negotiate to be an acceptable degree of private sloppiness), then that is a positive in this context.

As mentioned before, in real practice, targets are rarely clearly defined and measures so obvious that you don't have to go through a process of creative thought to come up with measures. On the other hand, we believe it can be done. This is not an academic exercise with few real-world implications. Every time you're faced with a new problem or client, you have to go through a process such as the one we just described where you rule in or out one or more of the types of measures we described. Just for the sake of gaining experience, following the exercise on selecting measures you just completed, try to see how many of the measures described in this book really can be adapted to measure each of the targets on your list.

USE OF MULTIPLE MEASURES

Instead of seeking the best single measure to monitor and evaluate your practice, select the best *set* of measures with *best* defined as the set that lets you rule out the most important and likely threats to the validity of the results (e.g., observer's expectations, client's socially desirable responses) without requiring an unreasonable expenditure of resources. This can include the collection of information from multiple sources (e.g., a client's assessment of his or her depression and a relevant other's assessment of the client's depression), the use of multiple methods to measure the same target (e.g., a standardized self-report measure of depression and self-monitored depressive behaviors), and the measurement of multiple targets you suspect might be related (e.g., depression and marital satisfaction). There are important reasons for using more than one measure with each client.

Why Multiple Measures?

At several points we have hinted at reasons for using multiple measures, for example, to provide a check on the reliability and validity of your measures, to balance and offset possible weaknesses inherent in individual measures, to provide information about internal and external changes, and so on. However, there are three other reasons that we haven't discussed.

Changes Are Often Multidimensional. There often are unanticipated changes in different areas of functioning because of the complexity of human beings, organizations, and communities. Different dimensions of the same target might respond differently to an intervention. For example, a client's self-reported feelings of depression might show improvement, but not the client's self-monitored depressive behavior. In addition, it's possible that an intervention program focused on one area may produce changes in other, related areas as well. For example, changing a parent's excessive drinking habits could easily affect the family atmosphere, communication, and activities. Therefore, the measurement of different areas of functioning can provide information about the breadth and generality of change and provide a more sensitive gauge of change.

Measures Often Do Not Correlate. In general, the same information collected from different sources (e.g., parents, children, and teachers) are, at best, moderately correlated and there are any number of possible reasons for this (e.g., De Los Reyes & Kazdin, 2005; Eid & Diener, 2006; Kraemer et al., 2003; Neyer, 2006; Smith, 2007). Inconsistencies among observers might result from the fact that behavior is different in different circumstances (a child's behavior might be different at school, at home, and in a recreational or therapeutic setting). Inconsistencies among observers also might result from legitimate differences of opinion (e.g., different members of a family can have legitimate differences of opinion about the degree of existing family cohesion, family conflict, or other dimensions of family functioning; social workers and clients can have legitimate differences of opinion about the adequacy of a client's parenting).

It's also true that often the same targets measured using different methods (e.g., self-reports and behavioral observations) are, at best, moderately correlated and there are a number of possible reasons for this also (e.g., Eid & Diener, 2006). For example, different methods may measure different aspects of the same target (e.g., behavioral observations focus on behaviors, and many self-report measures of depression focus on more subjective aspects of depression).

In essence, you can't assume that the degree of change registered by a single measure of a target, or as reported by a single person, gives you the whole picture. Often, different measures place emphasis on different aspects of a target, and different people have access either to different samples of a client's behavior or to legitimate differences of opinion. The use of multiple measures and information collected from different sources is necessary to provide a comprehensive picture of a target and to ensure that if one measure is not sensitive to important areas of change, other measures will detect them.

Multiple Measures Increase Confidence. When you measure targets with multiple measures, and you measure multiple targets, you can get some idea about the validity of your measures by examining the interrelationships among the different measures. To explore the validity of your measures, first formulate hypotheses about how the different measures should be related (or correlated) over time and how individual measures fit in with the entire case situation. Next, begin your evaluation, and as you're going along, examine the emerging patterns among the measures to see if they support your hypotheses.

If the bulk of your hypothesized relationships are supported by your evaluation results, you can be more confident that you have an accurate picture of the actual change than if you measure a single target or if you measure given targets using a single method. If a measure doesn't change in a predicted fashion, then you can't be certain whether the measure is invalid or your hypotheses or theory about the measure are wrong, but you do know that you should be cautious about the interpretation of the results from the measure. However, the confidence placed in a particular measure should be judged in relation to the entire case situation (i.e., the results obtained with a single measure should be compared to the pattern of results obtained with all other relevant measures). Indeed, you always should remember that the information you get from any one measure is just one piece of information that you should interpret in the context of all of the other quantitative and qualitative information that you have about your client.

Problems with Using Multiple Measures

We want to be perfectly clear about this. We're not suggesting the use of multiple measures as a sort of "what the heck" approach ("What the heck, I might as well throw in more than one measure and see what I come up with"). Obviously, the more measures you use the greater your chance of finding "something." Instead, we hope your selection of measures will be grounded to the extent possible in a careful evaluation of possible relevant and important outcomes. In particular, it's important to select measures having different strengths and weaknesses (e.g., the use of several standardized self-report scales designed to measure the same target wouldn't provide much balance, because they probably would share many of the same potential biases). That is, try to select measurement methods and sources of information such that the imperfections of the different measurement methods and sources of information are counterbalanced.

Our recommendations to use multiple measures do contain some problems. One of these was alluded to previously—the fact that changes are often inconsistent across measures and therefore difficult to evaluate coherently. Related to this is another major problem—trying to decide weightings for the measures (i.e., which are most important). If change doesn't occur in one, but does in another, is it possible to conclude that intervention was effective? How do you interpret and integrate conflicting information (e.g., Kraemer et al., 2003; Smith, 2007)?

Perhaps a partial solution to this problem lies primarily in the way clients rank their priorities. Change in measures of a client's major concerns might be weighted most heavily in evaluating success. Of course, if a client is involuntarily receiving some form of court-mandated intervention (e.g., for child maltreatment), measures of the court-mandated outcomes should be given a high priority, although client concerns also should be given important consideration. Second, you might apply the principle that we discussed earlier about direct measurement: Changes that most directly represent changes in actual functioning should be given priority, and those that appear most removed from actual functioning receive lower priority in evaluating success. Third, you might consider the nature of the target. For example, a child's self-report of depression (an "internalizing problem") might be given more weight than his or her teacher's report that the child isn't depressed. Or, a teacher's report that a child has trouble interacting with peers (an "externalizing problem") might be given more weight than the child's report that peer relationships are not a problem. Finally, consider characteristics and circumstances of the informant. For example, a parent who is severely depressed might have trouble accurately reporting information about a child; a teacher who has 30 children in class might have trouble focusing on the child sufficiently to obtain accurate information; or a divorced, noncustodial parent simply might not be around the child often enough to know what is going on with the child. In the end, you'll have to weigh all of the available relevant information and use your best judgment to integrate and resolve discrepant information.

Another problem with use of multiple measures is perhaps obvious—if you use more than one measure, it will probably take more time and energy. Somebody has to do the measuring. We believe that the added time and energy involved in using multiple measures necessitate evaluating each circumstance individually. In some situations this might not be a problem. For example, you may use data that are already being collected for other purposes, say, from archival records. In other situations, the value of getting information using different methods or sources may outweigh any possible problems. At the least, to the extent that multiple measures are used, try to select those that don't overburden one person, whether it would be because the tasks become tedious or boring, or simply are too time-consuming. Thus, it might be wise to have the client collect data using one measure, and someone else collect data using another.

Finally, sometimes with complex multidimensional interventions (e.g., the family preservation example discussed previously) the correspondence between outcome measures and interventions can be relaxed. Remember, specific outcome measures should be linked directly to at least one intervention, although these links should be viewed within the entire configuration of interventions and outcomes.

The Measurement Package

One way of viewing everything we've been discussing is the need for developing a *measurement package* for every client and situation. The measurement package would be those measures that would be best suited to the specific target(s) involved in a given case, that would most adequately measure the changes expected to occur, and that would evaluate those changes from the points of view of those who are involved.

In this context, it might be helpful to distinguish between primary and secondary measures. The *primary* measure is the one closest to or the most direct expression of the target. It's also the one on which you would most expect change to occur. When use of more than one measure is not possible, this is the one measure you would select.

The *secondary* measure (or measures) would be less directly related to the specific target. It might be less direct, more general, or more subjective. The secondary measure would be used to complement or supplement the primary measure. It would probably not be used as your sole source of data collection.

The measurement package, in addition to attempting to measure more than one dimension of a target, might also be constructed from the point of view of different people concerned with the target. To the extent possible and practical, obtain information from different knowledgeable sources, including clients, relevant others, and independent evaluators, and, of course, your own perspective.

We would suggest, when possible, to include at least two of these perspectives when selecting a measurement package. This will provide a broader perspective on the target, tap dimensions that might otherwise go unnoticed, add to the information that you will use in determining whether to change or terminate a program, and increase the validity of any observed changes, especially when independent reports agree.

Finally, it's important to select a measurement package in which the potential weaknesses inherent in individual measures are offset and balanced by other measures in the package (e.g., Eid & Diener, 2006). For example, nonreactive measures might be selected to counterbalance reactive measures, information might be collected from relevant others to counterbalance the limited direct information available to you as the practitioner, general measures might be used to counterbalance the limited information elicited by specific measures, or individualized rating scales might be constructed and used to counterbalance the more general information elicited by standardized scales.

Numerous examples highlight the importance of using different measurement methods, collecting information from different sources, and measuring multiple targets in order to best monitor and evaluate your practice (e.g., Hersen, 2006a, b; Hunsley & Mash, 2008; Rush, First, & Blacker, 2008). For example, standardized scales and direct behavioral observation, and parent-, teacher-, and self-reports (under some circumstances, when age appropriate) are important for monitoring and evaluating interventions for children and adolescents with conduct problems and attention-deficit/hyperactivity disorders

(Johnston & Mah, 2008; Frick & McMahon, 2008). Standardized self-report scales measuring alcohol consumption patterns, consequences of drinking, and motivation to change, are important for monitoring and evaluating interventions for alcohol use disorders (Green, Worden, Menges, & McCrady, 2008). Behavioral observation, standardized self-report scales completed by both partners, and individualized measures, such as goal attainment scaling, are useful for monitoring and evaluating interventions with couples (Snyder, Heyman, & Haynes, 2008). Standardized scales and sleep diaries (i.e., logs) are useful for monitoring and evaluating interventions for sleep disorders (Rush, First, & Blacker, 2008).

Guidelines for Using Multiple Measures

Given the previous considerations, we recommend the following guidelines for the construction of a measurement package:

1. Try to use more than one measure.

2. Try not to duplicate measures (e.g., two different self-report measures of depression) just for the sake of having multiple measures; select measures that use different measurement methods, that measure different targets, that measure different dimensions of the same target, or that are based on information obtained from different sources.

3. Try to include at least one direct measure, especially if an indirect measure is being used.

4. Try to select the most direct measures.

5. Try to include the observation of overt behaviors (actual functioning)—whether in the natural environment or in a contrived setting—whenever applicable.

6. Try to give priority to situation-specific measures rather than global measures (e.g., a measure of social anxiety related to a problem in heterosexual relationships, rather than a measure of general anxiety).

7. Try to include at least one nonreactive measure, especially if a reactive measure is being used.

8. Try not to overburden one person with all the measurement responsibilities.

9. Try to obtain measurement information from more than one person (e.g., client and relevant other).

10. Try to assess what type of change is more crucial in a given case, so that measurement can be geared toward assessing the most appropriate change.

11. Try to select measures that are tailored to the specific client, situation, and target.

12. Try to focus measurement resources on measuring the primary target(s) that brought the client to your attention.

SELECTING A MEASURE

Although we've covered numerous measures for numerous uses, you still need some way to begin to narrow down the field to help you make a selection for a given client. In Figure 1, we've provided a framework to help you begin that selection process.

The first thing you can do is evaluate a variety of characteristics that will help to provide some preliminary directions. These include, as we discussed earlier in this chapter, the nature of the target, your own preferences and practice orientation, the nature of the client, and the types of resources available. All these can be evaluated regarding the ways in which they can aid or impede the collection of information on the target(s).

Next you can decide on the source or sources of information. As we discussed in this chapter, the source can be the client, you (the practitioner), a relevant other (such as a parent, spouse, teacher, or other caretaker), or an independent evaluator (e.g., a trained observer or a colleague of yours, such as another staff member).

Next, review the available measures. Based on your earlier decision about what sources of information would be most useful and feasible, you will begin to be able to narrow down the field. The client can provide information using self-monitoring of behaviors, individualized rating scales, standardized questionnaires, and logs. The practitioner, relevant others, and independent evaluators can use behavior observation, individualized rating scales, standardized questionnaires, logs, and nonreactive measures.

The next step is to evaluate the characteristics of the available measures: reliability, validity, directness, ease of use, accessibility, and relevance to intervention planning.

Finally, all that's left is for you to select your measurement package—not always a simple process,

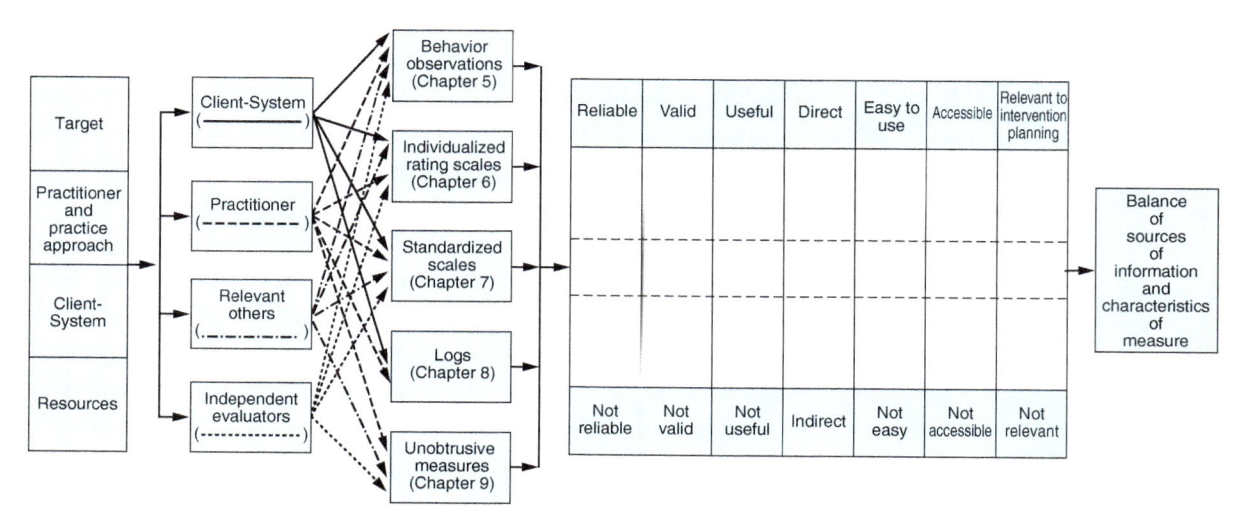

FIGURE 1 Framework for selecting a measure.

we admit, but a necessary one. Use the guidelines we presented in the previous section on use of multiple measures. Consider a primary and secondary source of information. Consider also collecting information from two sources and using two or more different types of measurement methods. Counterbalance the strengths and limitations of each measure so that you have measures that have different potential biases (e.g., biases likely to make a client look "good," and biases likely to make a client look "bad"). Putting this all together, we believe you will have a good chance of selecting a particularly useful measurement package to help you monitor and evaluate your practice.

Summary

This chapter focused on helping you select the most appropriate measures to be used in any given case or situation. We first briefly reviewed the types of measures that we've discussed in this section of the book. Then we discussed the factors you should consider in deciding on a measure: characteristics of the measure itself, characteristics of the target, characteristics of the practitioner and practice approach, and characteristics of the client and available resources. The last section of the chapter recommended the use of more than one measure whenever possible, in essence, building the idea of a "measurement package" into your practice. The chapter concluded with a set of guidelines for using multiple measures and a framework for selecting a measure.

BASIC PRINCIPLES OF SINGLE-SYSTEM DESIGNS

PURPOSE This chapter presents an overview of single-system designs by describing the basic principles underlying all of these evaluation approaches. These basic principles will help you to understand what single-system designs are and how they work; this is especially important if you have to construct new evaluation designs to fit the unique circumstances of your client situation. We also discuss some limitations of each design to help you assess what design would be best given what you are trying to accomplish with the design. We end with an overview of the single-system designs that are discussed in following chapters in greater detail.

Introduction
An Example Connecting Practice and
    Evaluation Designs
Purposes of Single-System Designs
Unique Characteristics of
    Single-System Designs
    Interventions That Are Clearly Defined
    Comparison of Baseline and Intervention
        Periods
    Phases
        Length of Phases
        Adjacent–Nonadjacent Phases
    Changes in Intervention
    Complicating Factors
        Carryover
        Contrast
        Order of Presentation
        Incomplete Data
    Training Phase
    Maintenance Phase and Follow-Up Plans
    Collaborative and Team Efforts

Causality in Single-System Designs
    Criteria for Inferring Causality in
        Single-System Designs
        Design Validity
        Statistical Conclusion Validity: Did Change
            Occur?
        Internal Validity: Was Change Caused by Your
            Intervention?
        Construct Validity: Did You Implement Your
            Intervention and Measure Your Outcomes
            Accurately?
External Validity and Generalizability
    External Validity: Does Your Intervention
        Have the Same Effect with Different Clients
        and Under Different Circumstances?
    Enhancing Generalizability
        Replication
        Probabilities
        Meta-Analysis
Overview of Single-System Designs
Summary

From Chapter 11 of *Evaluating Practice: Guidelines for the Accountable Professional*, Sixth Edition. Martin Bloom, Joel Fischer, John G. Orme. Copyright © 2009 by Pearson Education, Inc. All rights reserved.

INTRODUCTION

All practitioners design their practice; that is, they plan how they are going to establish a good working rapport with the client, how they will act in regard to the client's problems and challenges so as to facilitate positive client change, and the like. All of these plans can be described as a *practice design,* a design for practice that would reflect your use of evidence-based practice. Similarly, we use the term *evaluation design* to describe how practitioners plan to monitor the progress and evaluate the outcome of the practice design; this, of course, is what evaluation-informed practice is all about. Evaluation designs involve a plan to collect baseline information on targets in a given case that will be compared, according to logical rules, with the same target events after the intervention has been initiated. All single-system designs answer a first question: (1) Did the target problem change after the intervention began? Some single-system designs—the more sophisticated or powerful ones—answer a second question: (2) What evidence is there that the intervention may have caused that change?

Understanding the logical rules underlying single-system designs will provide a foundation about the various designs that are commonly used, both the basic single-system designs, and the more powerful ones. Sometimes we employ an evaluation design directly with our clients, but much of the time we have to customize these designs to fit our client's particular situation. To do this customizing, we have to know the logical rules and to what degree we are violating them, so as to get as much helpful feedback as possible on our practice with this client. We also have to recognize that in bending logical rules, we reduce the confidence we can place in our conclusions about our results.

In addition, all single-system designs are approximate evaluation procedures, easy to use, brief and straightforward, but frequently they are limited in what they can tell us. They face complicating factors and threats to their validity, and thus place limits on how much we can generalize from these results to a new case situation. We will discuss these limitations, so that you can use single-system designs in an optimal way for your practice evaluation.

We will conclude this chapter with a brief overview of the evaluation designs.

AN EXAMPLE CONNECTING PRACTICE AND EVALUATION DESIGNS

Imagine a conventional case recording in which a practitioner summarizes the events in a case as they transpire, along with planning notes. The top half of Table 1 represents this practice design. Let's say that a person comes to a social service agency as a result of feeling depressed; the practitioner takes a case history, collecting pertinent demographic and background information surrounding what appears to be the problem. These events are summarized in the first column of Table 1.

After the practitioner has made an initial assessment of the situation, he arranges to collect some more specific information to determine the scope and depth of the problem by asking the client to keep track in a log of her happy and sad feelings and the events surrounding them. The practitioner also asks her permission to obtain information from her employer on her job performance, and from her husband on whether she is eating adequately to maintain her health. This information will illuminate the context of her depressed and nondepressed feelings, as noted in the second column of Table 1.

The third and fourth columns represent the first intervention, which consists of trying, through rational conversation, to support (reinforce) client strengths while ignoring (extinguishing) client limitations so as to counteract her depressed state of mind. The practitioner continues to collect ongoing information from the client, the client's employer, and the client's husband throughout this time. He does not observe any important change in her feeling state, and so he decides to change his tactics.

In the fifth column, the practitioner begins a new intervention, trying to impart social skills to the client through assertiveness training so she will be able to solve her problems more directly. He begins to observe strong positive changes, as recorded on her logs, her employer worksheets, and her husband's reports, which appear to be resolving her presenting problem. So, after discussing this with the couple, he closes the case (sixth column).

Not many cases are as obliging as this one, but as an example, it serves to make our point on the parallels between practice and its evaluation. The bottom half of Table 1 represents an evaluation chart or graph, indicating how each of the practitioner's actions can be translated into evaluation design notations. These translations refer to the baseline or intervention periods, and

Basic Principles of Single-System Designs

Table 1 Hypothetical example connecting practice and evaluation designs*

	1	2	3	4	5	6
PRACTICE	The practitioner takes a case history.	He then arranges for the client to keep a log about her feelings when she is depressed, what came before and what were the consequences. Records of her work absences were also obtained, and her spouse rated her eating patterns.	Based on the initial information, the practitioner discusses the client's strengths and resources during the next session.	He continues this discussion into the next session as well. (The intention is to support the client's strengths by his focused attention.)	Not satisfied with client progress, the practitioner begins to train the client in assertiveness skills.	Assertiveness training continues until client data show it is having its desired effects on depression, job, and eating patterns. After consultation with the couple, the case is closed.
			(Information-gathering on the client's depressed feelings, work record, and eating patterns continues throughout these intervention periods.)
EVALUATION	(Subjective frame of reference) Subjective reconstruction is made to establish a frame of reference for baseline data.	A (baseline)	B (first intervention)		C (second intervention)	
		Baseline data are collected, concurrent, and/or reconstructed. Objective and systematic observations including self-reports, observer reports, and records that permit some tests of validity and reliability.	The first intervention period.	The first intervention period continued.	The second intervention period.	The second intervention period continued until termination. (The practitioner may decide to collect some follow-up data after a period of time to ensure that the desired goals have been maintained outside of treatment.)
			(The same observations, self-reports, and data from records from the baseline are collected throughout the intervention periods.)

*The upper half describes a *practice* design; the lower half describes an *evaluation* design. Reading the same segment of each half of the table shows the parallels between practice and evaluation.

to their initiation, removal, and reinstatement. The notations *A*, *B*, *C*, and so on represent the symbols for different phases from which logical predictions may be made; these will be discussed in this chapter.

The verbal case history is a subjective reconstruction of life events that simply establishes a frame of reference for the more objective baseline data, which will be used as the reference point against which new data from the intervention period are to be compared. The data collection continues throughout the service program in order for the client and practitioner to benefit from the logical comparisons that may be made with the information. Whatever the practitioner chooses to do first about the client problem is the first intervention, and when it does not appear to be making any difference in the client's problem, the practitioner chooses to change the intervention. The data now inform the practitioner and client that the problem has been significantly reduced, not merely in statistical ways, but in real-life behaviors as well, and so, the case is terminated.

This "textbook-perfect" case answers only the first question: Has some real improvement occurred in the client's problems? It cannot answer the second question: Did the practitioner's efforts help to cause that positive change? An answer to this latter question requires a more complex design. Our main point is that *whatever the practitioner does* can be summarized as notation in an evaluation design and subjected to logical analysis to answer the two fundamental questions on (1) the presence of change, and (2) the causes of that change. These answers constitute a scientific evaluation of practice, and are a critical aspect of accountability, especially in these times of managed care (Bolen & Hall, 2007).

PURPOSES OF SINGLE-SYSTEM DESIGNS

There are four main reasons for using single-system designs—as one of the hallmarks of evaluation-informed practice—in every practice situation. These reasons constitute the linkages between practice and evaluation that make them one integral activity for the helping professions (Proctor, 1990). First, these designs encourage practitioners to *assess* the case as objectively as possible, and to *monitor* changes in the client targets and/or situation over time. With the ongoing monitoring, you can make informed decisions that may help move events toward client goals—including changes in the intervention if this is indicated by the monitoring. *Assessing, monitoring, and adapting to change over time are the essence of sensitive evidence-based practice and sensible evaluation-informed practice.*

The second purpose of single-system designs is to *evaluate* whether changes actually have occurred in targeted events. This will involve some comparison of the initial status of the client and situation with some later status. This comparison depends on some more or less objective measurement of the targets over time, which is why we emphasize clear measurement procedures along with clearly defined targets. It is important to distinguish the evaluation of change from the next purpose of designs, inferring causality.

The third purpose of single-system designs builds on the second, but adds that the evaluation now concerns whether the practitioner's intervention could be *causally linked* to these observed changes. This added interest requires that the designs be logically strong enough to support the inferences of causality. Some single-system designs—generally the more rigorous or sophisticated ones—are logically capable of permitting causal inferences while others lack this quality. They all have to do with the principle of concomitant variation or, more specifically, the *principle of unlikely successive coincidences* (Jayaratne & Levy, 1979).

Briefly stated, these principles suggest that causation may be reasonably inferred the more observations we obtain on their joint appearances and/or their joint absences, given that one (application or removal of the planned intervention or cause) precedes the other (the observed effect or change in the target). One such joint occurrence (e.g., introducing an intervention followed by a change in the problem) could perhaps happen by chance, but the more times these jointly occur, the less likely is their pairing to have occurred by accident. Rather, such a set of occurrences provides the basis for inferring causality (Jayaratne & Levy, 1979, p. 139), especially when the practitioner introduces a planned change and predicts the outcomes. For making causal inferences about whether the intervention produced the observed change, the practitioner generally needs a design more rigorous than the *A-B* design, which is not able to rule out the possibility that other events may have affected the problem.

The fourth major purpose of single-system designs is to enable practitioners to *compare the effectiveness* of different interventions. All practitioners want to develop a repertoire of effective strategies but often find it difficult to do so because of the great variety of individual factors involved, such as client characteristics, the nature of an idiosyncratic problem in unique contexts, and chance happenings during the time spent with each client. However, by employing the more powerful evaluation designs, it becomes possible under some circumstances to compare specific intervention techniques with one another in one client/situation. Thus, the practitioner can begin to develop a base of intervention methods that appear to be demonstrably more effective than other interventions he or she used. This gives a new meaning to "practice wisdom," where the practitioner learns from objectively measured experiences what techniques work in what situations with what kinds of clients. This strategy of building knowledge is derived directly from evaluation-informed practice and also contributes to the evidence-based practice base. Of course, these are still tentative understandings so that when the practitioner uses the same effective technique with new clients, he or she should still evaluate these new situations. However, knowing that a technique has been shown to be effective with a given case gives the practitioner a head start toward a successful outcome for the new case situation. Sometimes a practitioner will contribute to helping translate an evaluation hypothesis that received confirmation with a single client into a full-blown experimental/control group design so as to provide solid confirmation of the new technique that, when published, becomes part of the evidence-based practice that other practitioners might also use in their work.

UNIQUE CHARACTERISTICS OF SINGLE-SYSTEM DESIGNS

There are a number of characteristics that make single-system designs different from other evaluation and research designs. We discuss these characteristics here. Many of these distinctive characteristics of single-system designs enable you to look at causal relationships between the techniques you have used in practice and the changes you have observed in the client's problems or challenges.

We recognize that actual practice is often very complicated, where you may only see the client a few times, or where heavy caseloads make it difficult to devote as much time as one might like to any one case. Thus, many of the more sophisticated single-system designs may not be employed consistently. In such cases, we believe that the basic *A-B* design should be used as a minimal attempt at evaluation. Yet, it is important to understand these design characteristics, not only to recognize them when you run across them in your reading, but to have them available when you do find you are able to evaluate your practice. Knowing these basic characteristics will help you to understand the strengths and weaknesses of whatever design you use. Following, then, are the key characteristics of single-system designs.

Interventions That Are Clearly Defined

Since the intervention is crucial in distinguishing the baseline (nonintervention) period and the intervention period, per se, we need to clarify exactly what we mean by the word "intervention." We reject the definition that suggests that whatever the practitioner does constitutes the intervention, from greeting the client initially, asking what brings the client to the agency, listening actively to what the client says, and all the other good things that practitioners do to build rapport and to assess the presenting situation. Rather, we go beyond these standard conditions for good practice to the specific planned actions that practitioners take to affect or change the target problems or challenges.

By our definition of intervention, we would also reject those statements that say we did "psychotherapy," or "family therapy," or "counseling," or that we engaged in "community action or development." These statements are so general as to be meaningless when it comes time to try to replicate our actions with new clients in new situations, or to tell colleagues what we did that proved to be so successful. *Intervention techniques are defined as specific planned actions in which we can clearly describe who did what to whom under what conditions.* This means clearly identifying the steps that should be taken in order to implement the intervention as planned. For examples of clearly operationalized intervention techniques that can be implemented on a step-by-step basis see Fischer (2009, Appendix), Cormier et al. (2009), and Van Hasselt and Hersen (1996).

In evaluating practice, we also attach symbols to these specific planned actions, one symbol to each unique action. However, sometimes several planned actions exist at the same time, so we have to devise a way of describing these various combinations of interventions. Look at Figure 1, where three levels of intervention techniques are indicated. At the top of that figure (row 1), we present a distinct, single intervention technique with the symbol *B*. (The symbol *A* is reserved for baseline or nonintervention periods.) For example, a practitioner might intentionally nod encouragingly at each attempt by a shy teenager to tell his story.

However, nodding is also combined with other distinct intentional actions by the practitioner, such as taking an attentive posture (bending slightly forward to indicate interest) and asking some questions to bring out other aspects of the boy's situation. These are distinctive techniques used to encourage this youth, but they are also commonly combined into a *package* of techniques known as *active listening*. We have two choices on

Basic Principles of Single-System Designs

1. [Intervention technique B] = One operationally definable type of intervention technique or action. Notation: B

2. [Intervention technique B] [Intervention technique C] [Intervention technique D] / B = One *package* (or integrated set of distinct intervention techniques) used at the same time. Notation: B (representing the three techniques) or BCD.

3. [B [Intervention technique B] C D] [C [E] [F]] = One program (or integrated set of distinct packages and/or techniques) used with the same client/system at the same time.

(representing the two distinct packages), $BCDEF$ (the separate techniques), or B alone if what is included is clearly specified. Notation: BC

4. [Baseline A] [Intervention technique B] [Intervention technique C] = *Changing of phases:* from A to B to C. Notation: $A\text{-}B\text{-}C$.

5. [Baseline A] [Intervention BC] [Intervention BCD] = *Changing of phases and intervention:* from A to BC to BCD. Notation: $A\text{-}BC\text{-}BCD$.

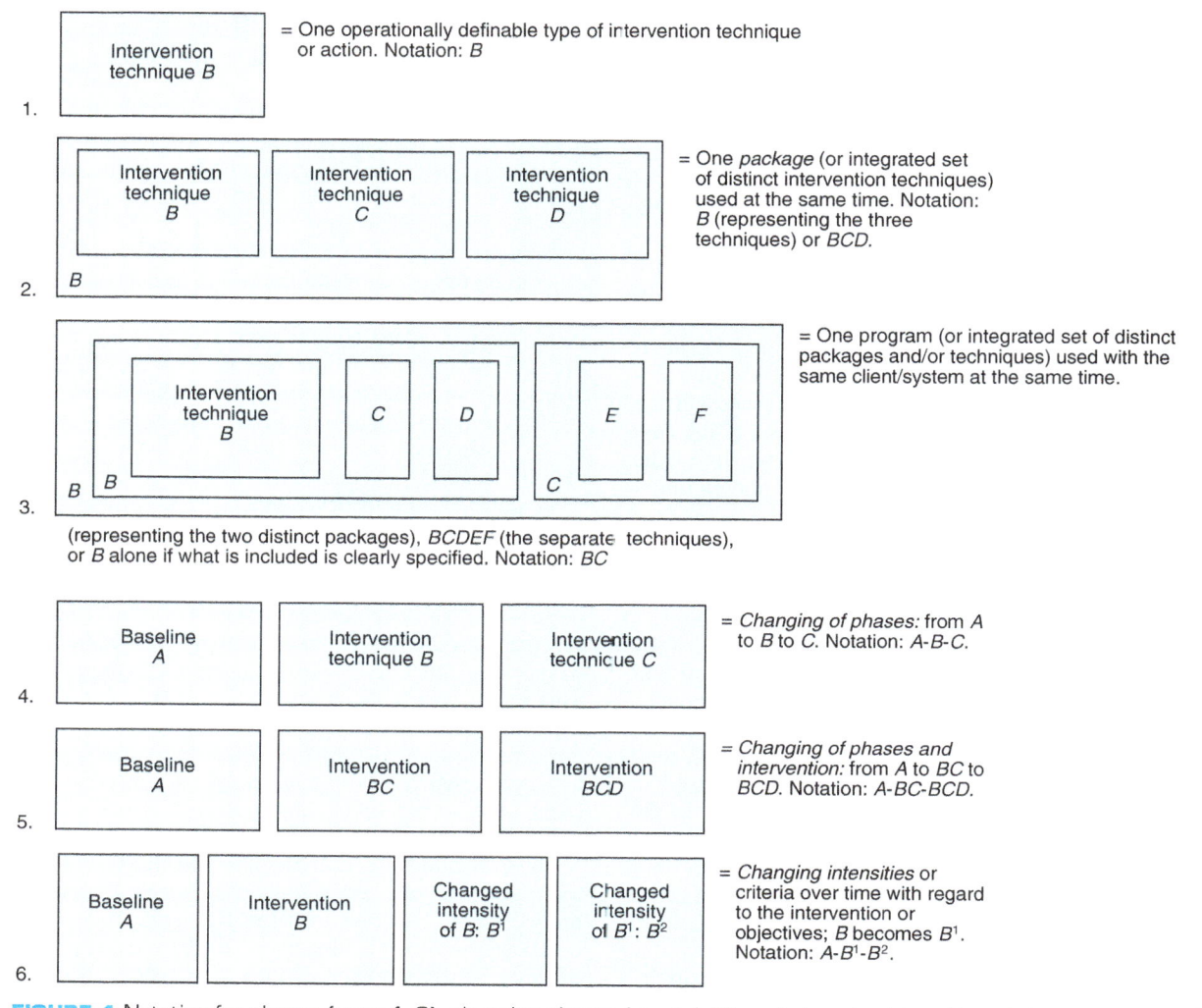

6. [Baseline A] [Intervention B] [Changed intensity of B: B^1] [Changed intensity of B^1: B^2] = *Changing intensities* or criteria over time with regard to the intervention or objectives; B becomes B^1. Notation: $A\text{-}B^1\text{-}B^2$.

FIGURE 1 Notation for phases (rows 1–3), changing phases (rows 4–5), and changing intensities of the same intervention (row 6).

---

annotating this package: either we simply list each technique by its own symbol but in combination with others, as in *BCD* (row 2), or, we can label the whole package as one coordinated intervention, with the symbol *B*, recognizing that it has three distinct components.

In addition, this package of active listening might itself be combined with other packages or techniques, into a *program* of service. For example, a practitioner might combine the active listening package with a cognitive-behavioral approach in which the client is aided to challenge his irrational beliefs that are causing his emotional distress. If this cognitive-behavioral approach is symbolized as *E*, then we would have a program containing specific defined techniques *BCDE*. Or it could be symbolized by the separate packages within that program, namely *BCD* and *E*. Or it could be symbolized by *B* alone, recognizing all the other specifically defined techniques that were involved in the program (row 3).

The remaining rows in Figure 1 show how we can indicate a change in phases, as when we go from one technique *B*, to a distinct new technique *C*.

Beginning with a baseline, *A*, this would be symbolized as *A-B-C* (row 4). We could also change combined techniques, such as from *A* to *BC* to *BCD* (row 5), or from *A* to *BCD* to *BC*.

Likewise, we can change the intensities of the intervention, or the criteria for what constitutes a successful performance by the client. These would be symbolized by changes in superscript of the existing intervention from *B* to B^1 to B^2 (row 6).

The point of all this is to be able to know exactly what went into the intervention that was (or was not) successful in dealing with client concerns; this way we can begin to build a repertoire of effective interventions and help provide information for broader research efforts to help inform evidence-based practices.

When you begin to chart your evaluation design, use whatever symbols you wish, but indicate on the legend of the chart exactly what is included in that symbol used for the intervention. Of course, all those good practitioner actions that set the client at ease and gain good assessment of the situation are important to practice (see Bohart & Greenberg, 1997, for reviews of research on the effectiveness of empathy as a crucial element in interpersonal helping). However, intervention is the formal, planned *addition* a practitioner makes to ongoing interviewing and relationship skills that will facilitate changes in the client situation. These are the formal techniques of evidence-based practice, and clearly, they build on the relationship the practitioner has constructed with the client.

Even if you believe (with Carl Rogers and others) that the practitioner/client relationship is the core of practice, then you still might be able to distinguish a basic level of empathy during assessment from a higher level of empathy during the intervention phase. In one classic study, Truax and Carkhuff (1965) experimentally raised and lowered levels of empathy and warmth, confirming predictions that stronger empathy led to more positive outcomes than weaker empathy (see also Nugent, 1992a.).

In all interventions, especially those employing relationship as the core of practice, we need to verify that the intervention actually occurred as planned, to ensure *intervention fidelity*; that is, was the intervention actually implemented as planned and as the intervention was designed to be used (Perepletchikova, Treat, & Kazdin, 2007). (This is also referred to as *treatment integrity*.) That is why we recommended earlier use of intervention techniques that are clearly operationalized.

There are several factors to consider in specifying your intervention to ensure fidelity (Blythe, Tripodi, & Briar, 1994; Gresham, 1997). Practitioners have to be clear about their individualized intervention (by noting in the case record specifically what was done) or if a standard method was used (also to be noted in the case record). This record should include information about dosage (how much and how often was the intervention applied); context (what factors helped or hindered the delivery of the intervention); and involvement (what did key actors do in participating in this intervention). In this way, the intervention itself might be monitored to help to know as precisely as possible what was in fact done in this particular situation. As we monitor changes in the target, so too can we monitor the *intervention* to ensure that it is carried out in the way intended (Gresham, 1997).

Likewise, we need to ensure that the intervention clearly deals with the appropriate, intended targets, so as to justify any logical assertions we make as to outcomes. For example, if your goal is to improve your client's self-esteem, then the interventions should be focused as directly as possible on changing her self-esteem, such as helping her challenge her self-defeating attitudes, rather than using possibly more accessible targets merely because they *are* accessible, like "increasing number of dates per month"—unless dates can be clearly linked with the primary target (self-esteem).

Finally, we want to remind you that all interventions should be evidence-based, to the extent possible. To that end, we have provided numerous references that can help guide you in your search for the most effective techniques of intervention.

Comparison of Baseline and Intervention Periods

The key distinguishing characteristic of single-system designs involves the planned comparison of an intervention period with a nonintervention period. Usually the nonintervention or baseline comes first, as part of the assessment of the presenting situation. (Sometimes, in emergencies, the intervention might have to come first, perhaps along with a single, perhaps retrospective, baseline assessment of the client's situation for which emergency services are needed.) The exact same observations in baseline are continued during the intervention period, so as to be able to monitor the progress of the case, comparing the current intervention status with the stable pattern of baseline conditions. This comparison can lead to: (1) continuation of the intervention that seems to be going in the right direction; (2) modification of the intervention to increase the speed of its effect;

(3) change of the intervention, either as something new or something added to the existing intervention; or (4) cancellation of the intervention, either because it is not doing what it was intended to do, or because it was successful and this part of the service is being ended.

As we will discuss later in this chapter, there are times when observations are occasionally made after the service has been terminated in order to *follow up* on the longer term effects of service. These follow-up times usually occur at random times to see if the target has maintained its successful outcome, and may take place weeks or even months after termination. If the desired behaviors have continued beyond the service period, this adds to the confidence about the effectiveness of the intervention; the longer lasting the positive changes, the more confidence we have in the intervention. If the target returned to pre-intervention levels, it signals the need for a booster shot, that is, a new application of the intervention, or possibly an entirely different intervention, to obtain staying power.

Unlike classical experimental/control group designs in which the comparison is between groups, in single-system designs the comparison is between different time periods for the same client or system. *The underlying assumption is that if the intervention had not occurred, the pattern of untoward events observed during the baseline would likely have continued to occur as before.*

However, after the baseline, a planned intervention is implemented and, one hopes, appears to have had some impact on the target. The basic evaluation questions now are: (1) has a change actually occurred, and (2) can we infer that the intervention may have caused that change? The single-system design used in this situation has arranged events so that you can logically deduce answers to the first question, and possibly to the second question (if your design is logically powerful enough).

Phases

Phases are the periods of time when distinctive evaluation activities occur. The baseline is one phase in which, by definition, no planned intervention occurs, only planned observations of targeted problems and events. It is given a distinct symbol, *A*, to represent the period of time in which baseline information is collected without an intervention. Sometimes, a practitioner will return to a baseline after an intervention period as logically directed by some evaluation design; this is usually indicated by the symbol *A* with a subscript (A_2) meaning return to baseline after some intervention. Or, shorthand symbols may be used, such as *A-B-A*, when it is understood that the second *A* (A_2) is a return to the initial baseline, while continuing to collect observations as before.

As discussed earlier, it is possible to combine intervention techniques at the same time, like the three activities mentioned in *active listening*. Figure 1 showed ways of presenting this, either by a summary symbol, *B*, or by having all three elements combined in *BCD* as representing the practitioner's actions during one intervention period. During this intervention period, the same observations continue as before.

By combining these ways to symbolize distinct interventions and baselines as combinations of phases, we can choose evaluation designs that are logically constructed to tell us whether the target changes, and if powerful enough, whether the intervention is a cause of that change.

Length of Phases. The basic principle in deciding on the length of any phase, baseline, or intervention, is to continue as long as needed to get a relatively stable picture of the target in that phase, so we can go on to another phase with this target (or to another target entirely). In the initial baseline, we would like to have a clear and distinct understanding of the presenting problem, so we can know when there is a change during intervention. Sometimes the baseline target will not stand still, even in a reasonably long baseline period; this erratic or unpredictable state represents the initial state of the problem and we can use it to compare to a more stable, desired level of target behavior during intervention. At other times, there are larger social and/or biological cycles affecting events in the short time periods in which the practitioner is collecting information, such as seasonal unemployment or periods of wakefulness and sleeping. There often is not a way to change these kinds of contextual factors, and the practitioner must simply be aware of how they may affect all observations and the intervention program itself. Try to provide the opportunity for stable patterns to appear, if they are going to do so. Just remember that there will be at least some variability in the data, just as there is in life itself.

In addition to allowing phases to be sufficiently long to permit the natural variability to appear as relatively stable patterns of events, the length of *adjacent* phases should be approximately equal whenever possible to allow external and internal factors to influence the target behavior in the same way in both periods. Thus, when differences between phases do occur, it will be more likely that these were due to the planned intervention, rather than external events.

Unfortunately, there is often a conflict between two characteristics of phases—attaining stability of the target event and the equal length of adjacent phases. Moreover, the intervention phase often lasts much longer than the baseline phase, because some targets change slowly. And sometimes practitioners feel pressure to cut the baseline period short in order to start the intervention. Or, the case may be prematurely terminated, making the intervention period shorter than the baseline.

We have no perfect solution for these kinds of conflicts, except to recommend that you gather reasonably clear and stable baseline data so your plans for helping will be as clearly directed as possible, and your ongoing monitoring of the helping situation will be as useful as possible, should changes in intervention be necessary. A clear and stable picture of change in the intervention period is probably more important for practice than having equal lengths of phases, even though this leaves the door open to alternative explanations about factors producing this outcome. In general, we recommend taking the option more useful for practice than for evaluation where there is a conflict.

And finally, you will not be struck down by lightning if you have to cut short the baseline to a few observations, and if the intervention lasts only a few more meetings as well. This is often the nature of short counseling situations; continue to collect objective information as best you can, but be aware that what sense you can make of these data will be limited by the small number of baseline and/or intervention observations.

Adjacent–Nonadjacent Phases. Consider an *A-B-C* design in which an initial baseline period, *A*, is followed by two distinct intervention periods, *B* and *C*. For the most accurate logical comparisons, two phases to be compared should be adjacent—for example, *A-B* or *B-C*—rather than separated by an intervening phase, as in *A-C*. This is because with separated phases, the effects of events occurring in the intervening time, or the order among events, could affect or produce the changes observed. If you want to compare the baseline with an intervention, *C*, then you would have to design a situation with this arrangement: *A-B-A-C*. In such a design, a baseline is adjacent to each of the distinct interventions, *B* and *C*. However, additional logical problems could exist if you were to compare the two interventions to *each other* because in the *A-B-A-C* design they are no longer adjacent. Obviously, the greater the separation between phases, the less clear their relationship becomes. With more complicated designs, however, it becomes possible to compare individual interventions with baselines and with other interventions.

Having said that, the guideline regarding the comparison of adjacent phases is just that: a guideline. All visual comparisons in single-system designs are approximate to some extent, for numerous reasons. Basically, though, we use the variations of designs that we will be discussing to take some of the guesswork out of the process. Therefore, for example, an *A-B-A-B-A-B* design will give us far greater confidence in our conclusions about the effectiveness of an intervention than a simple *A-B* design. This is true mainly if the pattern of results is in the expected direction each time, where the *B* phases show improvement and the *A* phases continue to resemble the initial *A* pattern (A_1).

The adjacent-phase guideline is not intended to suggest that we *not* look at patterns unless those patterns achieve "perfection," since all visual analysis is analysis of patterns. Indeed, even comparison of *adjacent* phases is not a perfect process. Our argument here, simply, is that, for purposes of establishing causality, it is safer to not *directly* compare nonadjacent phases, but we certainly form guesses (hypotheses) from such comparisons (analysis of patterns).

The issue then is that it's not so much that you *can't* compare nonadjacent phases, as that there are potential problems that might occur when doing so. These potential problems need to be considered and explored to the extent possible (e.g., by replication of an *A-B-A-C-D* design using a different order of interventions or use of an interaction design). Replication of results usually is the key in any case, as we will emphasize later in this chapter, but perhaps here it's important to point out the wisdom of varying the design in conducting the replication.

The basic point about adjacent–nonadjacent phases is that for the clearest, logical comparison, phases should be adjacent. This means that the practitioner seeking a reasonably rigorous evaluation of several interventions employed with one client will have to arrange interventions and baseline periods carefully in order to make these determinations.

Nonadjacent phases can, however, provide you with some hypotheses for future testing even though these phases don't offer the basis for direct logical comparison. That is, what *appears* to be true in a comparison of nonadjacent phases may in fact turn out to be true when two interventions are compared with a more appropriate design.

Changes in Intervention

One of the major strengths of single-system designs comes in the information they provide regarding the ongoing course of events related to the target. With such information, the practitioner and the client are in a position to take knowledgeable action in maintaining, changing, or terminating the intervention.

Changes in intervention require clearly defined interventions, and to the extent that interventions themselves change—due to practitioner fatigue, pressures from agency or client to hasten change or do things differently, etc.—the practitioner needs to use a distinctive symbol for each new or changed intervention. Then, the practitioner can tell if the target problem is getting worse and the intervention needs to be changed; or whether the problem is changing too slowly, and a change in the intensity of the intervention needs to be made or an entirely new intervention needs to be tried; or whether the target is changing appropriately in the desired direction, so the practitioner should continue as before.

Let's take the basic single-system design, the *A-B* design, and work through all of the logically possible changes that can occur, with their specific notations.

1. The first intervention may be continued without any change. The *A-B* notation continues.

2. The first intervention may be changed in intensity; that is, either more or less of it may be used, as appropriate. Or the criterion of what is acceptable performance may be changed; that is, more or less of a client's performance is now required to obtain the same intervention (such as positive reinforcement). The notation for changing intensity is $A-B^1-B^2$.

3. An entirely new intervention may be implemented and added to the old intervention. The notation would be *A-B-BC*.

4. An entirely new intervention may be implemented, in place of the old intervention, which is now terminated. The notation would be *A-B-C*.

5. One intervention may be removed altogether with or without a substitution of another intervention. These notations would be *A-BC-B* or *A-BC-BD*.

6. A training phase may be introduced to train the client to make use of the full intervention. Sometimes notations of training phases are added; sometimes the training is included in the intervention itself so no special notation is used. These notations could be: $A-B^1$ (training)-B^2 (intervention); *A-T* (training)-*B*; or *A-B* (when the intervention includes a training phase). (See the discussion of Training Phases below.)

7. Sometimes a phase is added to help the client maintain the gains from the intervention when the practitioner is about to terminate the service. The maintenance phase is distinct from the intervention itself, since it focuses on teaching the client to perform the whole intervention himself or herself without the practitioner. Notations of the maintenance phase could include: *A-B-M* (maintenance); *A-B-C* (where *C* is a new intervention used as a maintenance program); $A-B^1-B^2$ (if the intervention's intensity is modified to focus on maintenance); or *A-B* (if *B* somehow includes helping the client learn to maintain the gains made during the intervention). (See the discussion of Maintenance Phase and Follow-Up Plans, later in this chapter.)

8. There are many other more powerful designs to be discussed at the end of this chapter, and later in this part, in which interventions are removed and added back, or are introduced in a step-wise fashion, and the like. All build on the logic that is present in the basic *A-B* design.

Changes in intervention are the name of the game in single-system design; we often change or modify interventions over the course of a case, and we need to know how to evaluate the effects of these changes. In this section, we'll deal with a number of issues on changing interventions. We mentioned removing interventions on occasion to make use of the power of logical designs. Let's clarify how we are going to use several similar terms because they are frequently confused in the literature:

1. *Removal*—our generic term to apply to any situation in which the original intervention is taken away for any reason.

2. *Withdrawal*—a complete removal of the first intervention while continuing to collect data (given that a successful change in the target had occurred during that first intervention)
3. *Reversal*—a removal of the first intervention and then applying that intervention to another target during the removal phase, while continuing to collect data on the original target.

Next, let's distinguish *reversible* and *irreversible* changes. Reversible changes are those that may disappear when the intervention is removed. For example, when you stop paying your teenager to clean his room, you may see that cleaning behavior disappear. The behavior was reversible. Irreversible changes are those that do not go away when the intervention is removed. For instance, your client takes a set of lessons in assertiveness training, and once the training has ended, the client retains the skills for future use since it has been incorporated into her or his thinking and acting.

If you want to determine which of several intervention techniques is really affecting the problem, it is important to *change only one intervention at a time,* when possible. Then, you can determine what factor is influencing what change and to what degree. If you change two interventions at once, then it is difficult to determine how each of them influenced the resulting change. There are some powerful evaluation designs that can help you to sort out individual effects.

Complicating Factors

As single-system designs are used to evaluate changes from one intervention back to baseline or to other interventions, certain logical problems emerge that complicate their analysis. These complications all share the same effect of confusing any causal analysis because artifacts from the design itself might be involved in producing the effects. In fact, much of the discussion in this chapter—everything from length of phases to changes in intervention—also could be interpreted as presenting threats to the internal validity of the evaluation. We return to this topic later on in this chapter. Following are some of these complicating factors and how one might attempt to overcome their effects.

Carryover. *Carryover* refers to a situation where the effects obtained in one phase appear to "carry over" into the next phase. The term *carryover* is generally used in the context of removal designs. Thus, if you attempted to remove a successful intervention to create a second baseline to determine whether your intervention was actually affecting the problem, and the problem stayed at that level despite the removal, carryover effects would pertain. In technical terms, it could be said that you were not able to retrieve the first baseline during the second baseline phase. Although this may indicate that the learning that was produced in the first intervention really was solid, or that it was irreversible, it does limit your ability to interpret whether or not your interventions were related to that positive outcome because you can't isolate the effects of the intervention you used. Indeed, carryover effects might also be produced by extraneous outside influences having some impact on the target problem. For example, a seasonal change—say, from cold to warm weather—might coincide with the end of a first intervention phase. Even with removal of the intervention, one could still not "retrieve the baseline" because positive changes might be related to, or reinforced by, the seasonal changes. Thus, carryover effects complicate your interpretation of your data.

Contrast. Even if you do return to a stable baseline condition before implementing a new intervention, it is possible that the client will observe a difference between the two interventions and react to this *contrast* rather than to the second intervention itself (Jayaratne & Levy, 1979, p. 228). For example, if a municipal judge was experimenting with the most appropriate level of traffic fines, first beginning with a $5 fine and then trying a $50 fine in a subsequent month, there might be a public outcry about the contrast and not about the need to have some system of fines. Perhaps reducing the contrast between interventions (amount of traffic fines) might minimize this type of problem.

Order of Presentation. Another inevitable consequence of using several interventions is that one must come before the other, so the *order of presentation* of these interventions may itself be part of the causal impact. For example, if you implement an *A-B-C* or even an *A-B-A-C-A-D* design, you will not be able to detect whether part of the outcome was due to the order of the interventions, in that the effects of one intervention actually may build on the effects of a prior one. Nor will you be able to tell whether it would have been different had you implemented the interventions in a different order, for example *A-C-B* or *A-B-A-D-A-C*. Solutions to this problem are complex, but they could involve a randomized order of presentation so that no known bias in the order of presentations of the interventions will be acting on the client. On the other hand, a more sophisticated design may be used in which interventions are presented in deliberately counterbalanced sequences.

Incomplete Data. There will be many occasions on which you will not have a continuous run of information in baseline and/or intervention periods. Unfortunately, some textbooks imply that clients always fit nicely into a neat 10-day baseline, followed immediately on the next day with the full-blown intervention. If so, fine. You have a nice *A-B* design. But some period of time often intrudes between the baseline and the intervention phases as well as within those phases.

There are two types of situations in which this is likely to occur: when the data are incomplete for any reason—we take up this topic in this section—and when there is a training phase in the intervention period—discussed in the following section.

There are many possible reasons that the data may be incomplete. Examples would be if the client left town on a business trip; if the practitioner got sick; or if relatives came to visit the client, changing the context temporarily. In these kinds of situations we recommend that recording be continued, if possible. Depending on the situation, it may be necessary only to add a few more observations to make sure the former baseline pattern is continuing (see Figure 2a); or it may be necessary to do an entirely new baseline period if the gap in recording is lengthy (see Figure 2b). On some occasions, there may be stop-and-start baselining, in which case the practitioner must decide whether any of the baseline data are acceptable as a frame of reference (see Figure 2c). The overriding issue is to obtain some semblance of stable and typical data about the client's target situation.

When only a few data points need to be added to the baseline (as in Figure 2a), then follow the instructions for presenting missing data on a chart by indicating the missing time units on the chart with dots rather than a solid line. When many data points are missed, then indicate that a new baseline has been established (A_2) with a new vertical construction line in dashes (as in Figure 2b). (A_2, with the "2" in subscript, simply means the second baseline period, with no other changes implied.)

The most important point about incomplete data is how to use them in the analysis that compares baseline with intervention data. Some analyses require that lines for analysis be drawn using all of the data. If there are only a few gaps as indicated by dotted connecting lines, then use the entire period as that frame of reference. If there are many gaps, say in the baseline, and a new baseline period is taken, then use only the new baseline as the frame of reference for what happens during the intervention period. Or, you can analyze the data by using only the actual collected data points, as in the case of Figure 2c, using 11 out of 18 baseline points.

Training Phase

The second very common situation in practice occurs when baseline data cannot be connected immediately with the intervention data because of a *training phase*. The practitioner wants to initiate some plan of action (intervention) after a stable baseline emerges, but because of the nature of that intervention, it is not likely to begin immediately due to the need to train someone (the client, a relevant other) in how to conduct the intervention. For example, the client may have to learn assertiveness skills over several workshop sessions before beginning to apply these skills in a work context. During the time that the client is learning these skills, there may be some effect on his or her behavior but not likely the full effect of this intervention. So, recording likely will reflect this with no change in the target (Figure 3a), gradual changes in the target (see Figure 3b), or possibly irregular changes, as when some threshold must be reached before an effect occurs (see Figure 3c). For extra clarity, you could simply add a *T* in parentheses following the notation you chose (e.g., $A-B^1(T)-B^2$).

The basic question is how to analyze these training-phase data relative to the comparison between baseline and intervention. The training phase forces a separation between baseline and intervention, and thus violates the guideline involving the importance of having adjacent phases for analysis. We propose two solutions. The first is to continue to compare baseline against the combined training and intervention phases (as in Figures 3a, b, and c), and expect the obvious, that there may not be any major change during the training portion, although there may be some trend in a positive direction. If no change appears in an intervention phase that doesn't contain a training component, then the practitioner has to question whether this is due to the incomplete learning of the intervention or the intervention itself being ineffective. With a training phase, however, the practitioner

Basic Principles of Single-System Designs

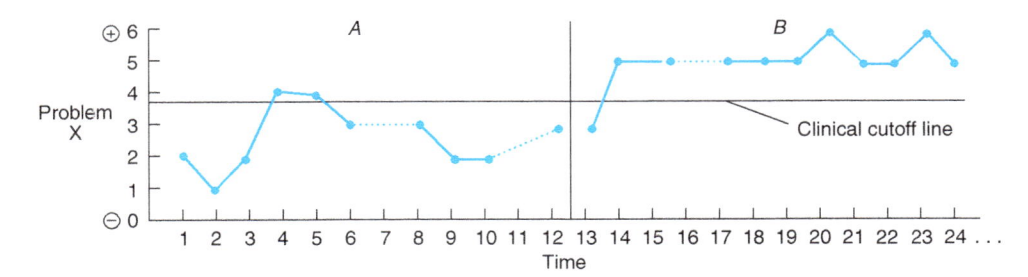

FIGURE 2A Hypothetical data showing a few missing data points in baseline and intervention. Analyze these data as if there were 12 baseline observations of which 2 are above a clinical cutoff line and 8 are below. Likewise, count 12 intervention observations of which 10 are above and 1 is below the cutoff line.

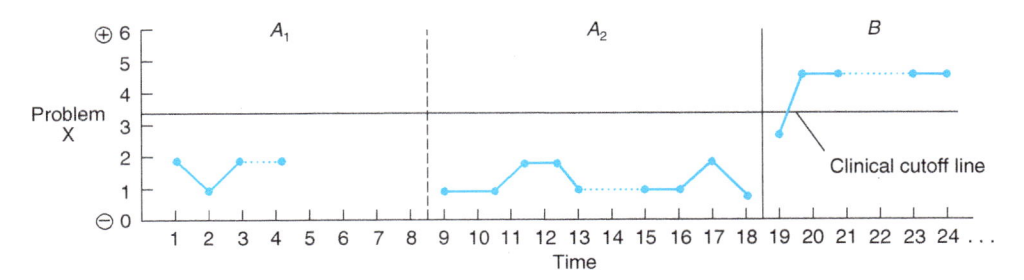

FIGURE 2B Hypothetical data showing a large gap in baseline A_1, requiring the establishment of a new baseline, A_2.

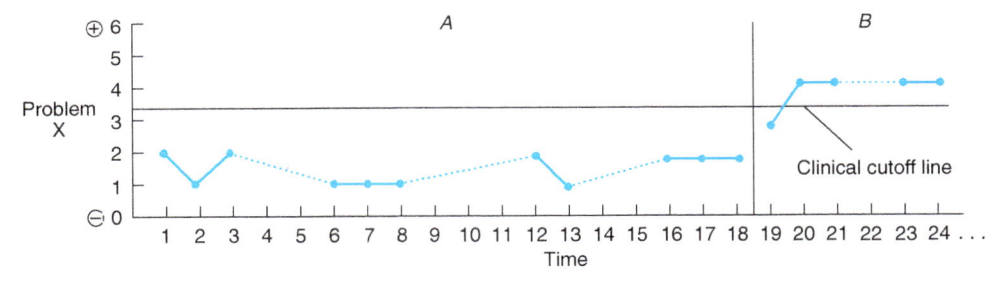

FIGURE 2C Hypothetical data showing stop and start baseline data that require the practitioner to decide if and when enough information is available to begin the intervention. The data can be analyzed using only the 11 actual data points in calculations of the proportion below the cutoff line (11/18); see Part IV.

probably should be willing to tolerate no change for a longer time than if the full intervention is applied and should have taken effect immediately. The danger of interpreting data with training phases is that the combined training and intervention phases may exhibit some carryover effects. That is, it may be the special qualities of the training rather than the intervention itself that are, in part, causing the apparent changes in target behavior. For instance, being in a workshop on assertiveness training may itself be a stimulus for action.

The second possibility is to label separately the training and the intervention phases as B^1 and B^2 (as in Figure 4). An example would be when the

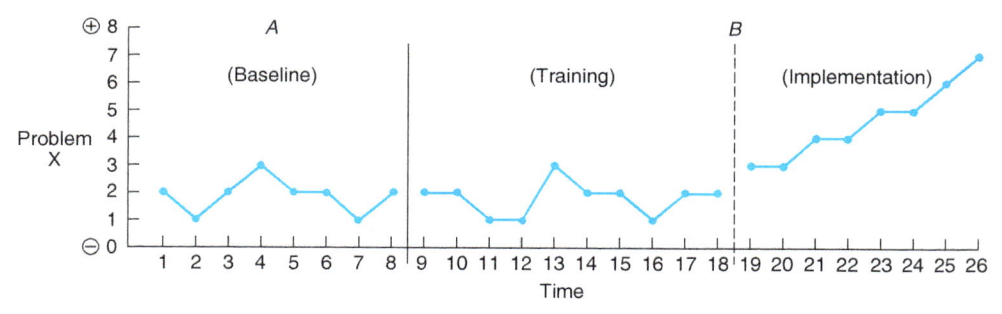

FIGURE 3A Hypothetical data showing no change in target behavior during the training phase.

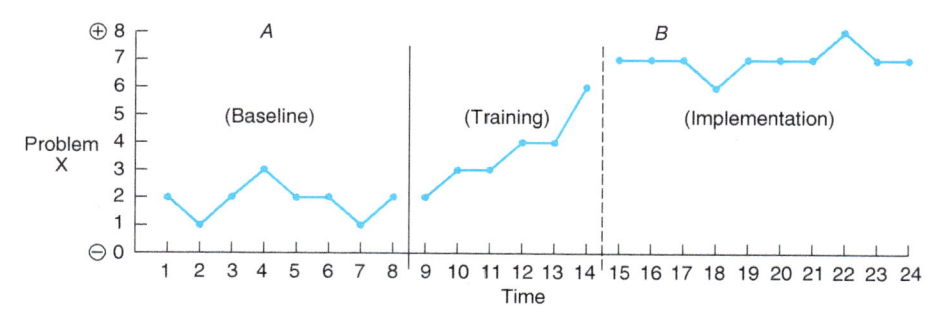

FIGURE 3B Hypothetical data showing gradual changes in target behavior during a 6-week assertiveness training phase.

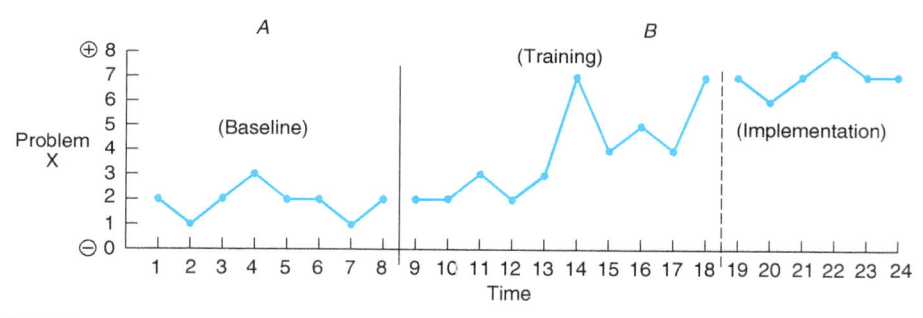

FIGURE 3C Hypothetical data showing irregular changes in target behavior during a 10-week assertiveness training phase.

practitioner has to train a parent in a child management program for 2 weeks before the parent actually uses it in an effort to change the child's behavior. In situations like this, one possibility is to use the following notation: A stands for baseline, B^1 for the training period, and B^2 for the period when the program is actually implemented. The rationale is that implementation period B^2 is largely a modification of B^1. This also allows you to determine whether any changes come about during the training period itself, and also whether the changes that occur during the implementation period exceed the changes in the training period. Presumably, in this illustration (Figure 4), because the training is a prior event necessary for the implementation of the program, whatever changes occur in B^2 could be a result of a combination of the

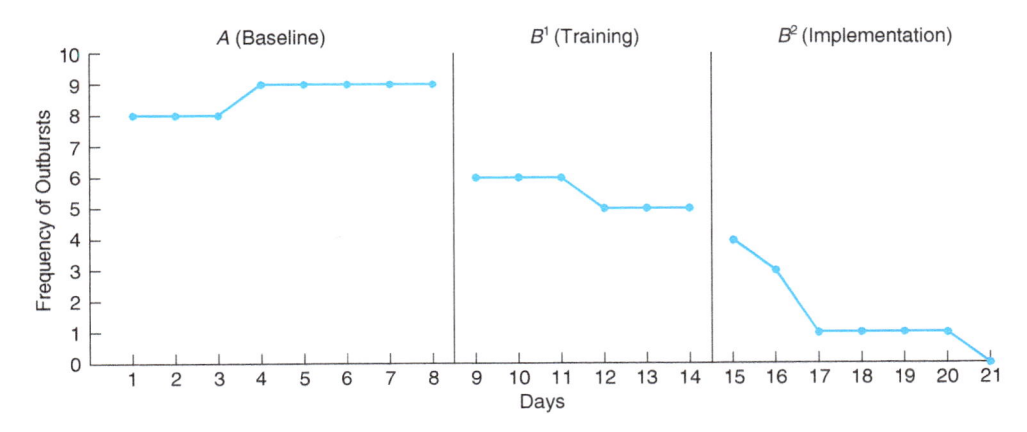

FIGURE 4 Chart illustrating phases for training and implementation as distinguished by changes in intensity.

training and the implementation. That is, the results from B^2 may be confounded because of possible carryover (or order of presentation effects) from B^1. However, if no changes had occurred in the B^1 phase, there would be more evidence that the changes may more likely be due to the intervention itself.

Of course, training phases (as well as missing data) can affect the conclusions you draw about the impact of your intervention (causality). There are no perfect solutions for this problem. You, of course, will have to be more cautious in your conclusions. You might even consider combining the training phase with an adjacent phase for your analysis and then subtract the training phase in a second analysis so that you can compare the results of the two analyses.

Maintenance Phase and Follow-Up Plans

Implicit in many single-system designs published in the literature is the apparent assumption that simply ending on an intervention phase will be sufficient to guarantee that the positive effects of intervention will last forever. Of course, there is no guarantee of lasting effects of any service program. Thus, we strongly recommend the development of a *maintenance* or generalization plan to be added to all intervention plans in an attempt to ensure that the changes produced by your intervention program are lasting changes. Assuming just for the purposes of illustration that the B phase is the last intervention phase, we recommend several things for you to do to help ensure continuity of positive outcome. First, extend the B period to ensure that the target has been changed to a satisfactory level. Second, conduct follow-ups on a periodic basis to ascertain how well this satisfaction level has been maintained. If it has not, or if it shows signs of slipping, then a "booster shot" of reinstituted intervention may help. Third, and most importantly, the last phase in your *practice design*, following the successful completion of the intervention proper, should include a program to maintain and to transfer the changes to the client's natural environment after the intervention is completed (see Goldstein & Kanfer, 1979; Karoly & Steffen, 1980; Rzepnicki, 1991, for numerous examples of successful maintenance programs). Building in such a maintenance program is the essence of both good practice and good evaluation.

When you are developing a program to maintain and to transfer the effects of your intervention program to the natural environment, you actually have three options regarding your *evaluation design* so that it will reflect what you are doing in your practice design. The first is to simply modify the intervention phase—B, for example— by fading out or changing the schedule of reinforcement or by seeing the client less frequently. You could then consider this maintenance phase as a B^2 phase with the original B phase becoming B^1; this is because you are modifying the intensity of the intervention.

The second option is to continue your B-phase intervention and to add a new intervention to enhance the transfer process—for example, adding homework assignments to in-office role-playing. This would then be considered a new BC phase.

The third option is to drop the B-phase intervention altogether after it has been successful and to add

Basic Principles of Single-System Designs

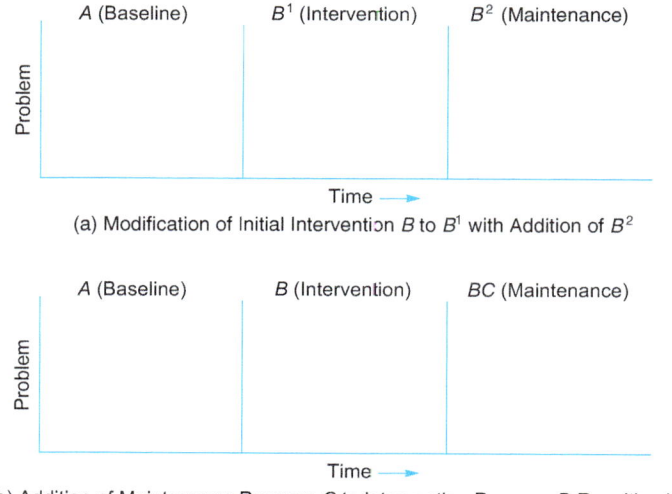

(a) Modification of Initial Intervention B to B¹ with Addition of B²
Phases: A (Baseline), B^1 (Intervention), B^2 (Maintenance)

(b) Addition of Maintenance Program C to Intervention Program B Resulting in BC
Phases: A (Baseline), B (Intervention), BC (Maintenance)

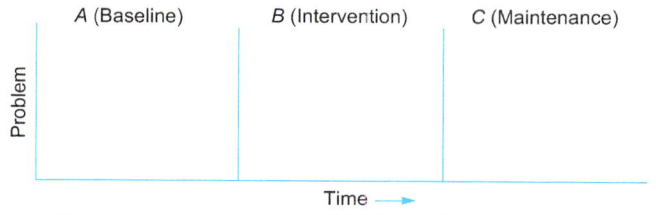

(c) Dropping of Intervention B and Addition of Maintenance Program C
Phases: A (Baseline), B (Intervention), C (Maintenance)

FIGURE 5 Three options for notation of maintenance and transfer programs.

---

a completely new maintenance phase—for example, discontinuing your work with a client being discharged from a hospital and beginning work with the family to maintain the changes. This would then add a separate C phase indicating a new intervention resulting in an A-B-C design.

These three variations of maintenance and transfer programs are illustrated in Figure 5. For extra clarity on your chart, you could add an M in parentheses following your notation (e.g., A-B-$C(M)$).

There remains no substitute for the good old-fashioned *follow-up* evaluation. Whether this is a single "probe" conducted once at some point following termination, or a series of reevaluations conducted at regular, predetermined intervals, we urge that you conduct follow-ups, preferably using the same measures that were used to evaluate change during the baseline and intervention periods. But even if this is not possible, we suggest, at the least, maintaining contact with the client—whether by telephone, mailed questionnaires, or in-person interviews—to inquire about whether changes have been maintained.

We believe that only after follow-up evaluation reveals that change has been maintained can the overall practice and evaluation designs be considered complete. Not only that, maintaining contact with the client after termination, however minimal, is essential for practice purposes. It allows you to make yourself available in the event old problems reassert themselves or new problems arise, and, above all else, it shows that you *care*.

This discussion of maintaining intervention effects and transferring them to the client's natural environment is applicable to all single-system designs, especially those that end on an intervention phase. It is also, we believe, an essential condition of good practice. Thus, we see another example of the integration between evidence-based and evaluation-informed practice. We will refer to this point on many subsequent occasions.

Collaborative and Team Efforts

Practitioners in agencies frequently find themselves in collaborative efforts with colleagues on behalf of a given client. In other circumstances, such team efforts are the rule, not the exception. Is there any way of teasing out the contributions of separate practitioners in these collaborative efforts, or is the collective intervention what is to be measured? There might be ways of conducting separate evaluations, but it may not be worth the time and effort to do so.

First, there is nothing wrong with measuring a collective effort. The intervention (*B*) can be viewed as a package of interventions taken as one. However, instead of there being several types of interventions conducted by one practitioner, in the team effort there may be one or more interventions conducted by two or more practitioners all during the same time period. Thus, one chart with one *A-B* design signifies results from the joint efforts of all concerned. For example, a client at a drug abuse center may undergo a number of experiences over the course of a 2-week period, such as a detoxification phase administered by one set of practitioners, an individual counseling procedure delivered by another practitioner, another intervention involving group counseling, possibly some job skills training, and so on. Different practitioners are involved in each of these interventions.

The client's time is sorted carefully into a sequence of planned interventions to address the problems of addiction: (a) to be detoxified from the present state of addictiveness; (b) to gain understanding of the personal, family, and peer group factors that may have led to addiction in the past; and (c) to gain skills in resisting these pressures in the present and future. With reference to goal (c), there are a set of specific targets the client is learning, and measurement indicates the extent of that learning. However, what contributes to learning how to resist peer pressures to join in group drug use? Probably all of the experiences at the drug rehabilitation center contribute in part. Is it possible to sort out the distinctive contribution of each? It may be, but only in very special circumstances. For example, if several interventions are being conducted concurrently—individual counseling, group counseling, and so on—then it would be difficult to sort out the unique contributions unless they are conducted at random times and, after each occasion, some measurement is taken of relevant outcome variables. Then, this approximates the alternating intervention design.

On the other hand, if the interventions are applied sequentially, then it might be possible to sort out the differential effects of each stage of the intervention, using one of the variations of successive intervention or changing intensity designs.

Another exploratory method might be to use a "reverse log" approach, where the *practitioners* each add a critical incident to a log on the client, indicating for a given class of problems—for example, "dealing with authority figures"—what happened before, during, and after a given episode. Then, in a team meeting, individual practitioners might attach numbers to the qualitative information, indicating whether the client was making very good or good progress, no change, or regression or strong regression, with regard to that target. By talking together when making these ratings, the practitioners could come to some understanding on a common frame of reference in assigning scores. Then, one could average the amount of progress made on a given target when the client was with one practitioner/situation, as contrasted with another practitioner/situation. These, admittedly, would be rough indicators, but if two practitioners were in one situation, there would be the possibility of a reliability check. However, whether changes in the client are due to the method being used or to the practitioners' different personality fit with the client, or both, could not be distinguished.

Another exploratory device would be to ask clients, at the end of each day, how much progress they felt they made during that day in each of the service situations. If the ratings are comparable to the reverse log, then one could compare how much constructive/destructive change the client and specific practitioners observed in given situations. Averages for these changes also could be computed and compared with practitioner averages. Overall ratings of practitioner contributions to the client's problem solving also could be obtained from the client and compared to average ratings.

CAUSALITY IN SINGLE-SYSTEM DESIGNS

In addition to being able to provide information about whether changes in the target have occurred between baseline and intervention, single-system designs also offer the possibility of making causal inferences—did the intervention produce the observed outcome? In this section we discuss some of the general principles related to these causal inferences, followed by a discussion of some of the threats to a conclusion that the intervention produced the changes; these "threats" are actually *alternative explanations* for a given set of results that must be carefully considered in planning an evaluation. Following the discussion of causal inferences, the subsequent section discusses issues regarding generalizing the causal information obtained in one situation to other situations or clients.

Criteria for Inferring Causality in Single-System Designs

Discussions of causality have occupied philosophers of science from the beginnings of speculative thinking. We offer the following brief discussion of causation with this background in mind in an attempt to aid you in making reasonable inferences regarding the connection of your intervention to the observed changes in target problems. Several criteria that can be used to evaluate causal relationships in single-system designs follow.

The first criterion for inferring causality is *temporal arrangement*, which means that the changes in the target problem must occur after the application of the intervention, not before. The charting of baseline and intervention data will quickly reveal whether this criterion is upheld. There probably will be some natural fluctuation during baseline in which the target problem may even move in a desired direction. However, over time, the typical pattern of the target probably will be portrayed by the baseline data pattern. With intervention, that pattern should change. If baseline data appear to be improving in the absence of planned intervention, the impact of the service program might be hard to interpret. Therefore, you may want to wait to see if improvement continues without any intervention.

The second criterion is the *co-presence of the application of the intervention and the desired change of target problems*. This does not necessarily mean instantaneous change, since not all social-interpersonal behaviors and situations are that responsive. However, given a reasonable period of time (about the same length of time as the baseline period in many cases), changes should begin if you are to draw conclusions about the causal efficacy of the intervention. Sometimes, the literature on a particular intervention will provide you with information on the time period you can expect before a given problem starts to change.

A third criterion is that *if target problems change for the better in the absence of the intervention, something else is causally related to the outcome*. If an intervention is removed before learning becomes irreversible, the target problem should show a decrease in desired performance. This is the basis for planned removal of an intervention and investigation of the concomitant change in the target problem. But ultimately, we are seeking irreversible positive changes.

The fourth criterion for making logical inferences about the causality of the intervention concerns the *repeated co-presence of the intervention and the observations of the desired change*. Each time the first occurs, the second also should be present. Given the natural variability of human events, we do not mean that this criterion demands perfect correlation, but rather that a clear pattern of continuing co-presence is exhibited.

The fifth criterion brings in *other possible influences to test whether they may be the actual cause of a given change in the target behavior*. This criterion suggests the importance of attempting to determine whether there is any other continuously co-present factor that could be causally related to the outcome. If the desired change of the target event occurs only in the presence of the intervention and with no other known influence, this becomes an additional source of information regarding causal inference.

The sixth criterion deals with *consistency over time*. The relationship of events—intervention and change in the target—should be maintained over time with no unexpected or unexplained fluctuation in that pattern.

The seventh and final criterion to be discussed here involves the *conceptual and practical plausibility that the inference is grounded in scientific/professional knowledge*—or at least isn't contrary to it—as well as being consistent with practical experience. This is a very broad criterion and perhaps is the starting point of the entire causal investigation; this is because you formulate your causal hypothesis on the basis of a review of the literature and conceptual-practical analysis of the situation when intervention plans are being made.

Having offered these seven criteria for making logical inferences about causality using single-system designs, we hasten to add that these do not provide absolute or certain grounds for making a causal inference. Social causality is a complex affair in which many apparently distant events may be intricately related in diverse ways. However, we offer these pragmatic criteria in the hope that you will be a little more prepared to back up your statements of effectiveness using single-system designs.

In summary, a way of viewing this discussion on criteria for inferring causality is to look for persistent *concomitant variation* between the intervention and the desired change in the target events. When these two—and only these two—events persistently covary (change together), you may have some basis for inferring causality, with other things being equal. As mentioned previously, we might also think of these causal relationships in the context of the *principle of unlikely successive coincidences* (Jayaratne & Levy, 1979) in which a set of events, for example, baseline and intervention phases, occurs repeatedly, and while the first set might have happened by chance alone, with each succeeding pair of occurrences, it is increasingly unlikely that they are happening by coincidence, particularly if they were predicted to occur. This "unlikeliness" is another way of thinking about probability: The more unlikely some set of events is to happen by chance, the more likely it is to have occurred by design, specifically, by practice design. However, there are many other factors that have to be taken into consideration before excluding alternative explanations for why given outcomes occurred as they did, or before we can logically generalize from one situation to others. The next portion of this chapter covers these topics.

Design Validity. You may recall we discussed the term *validity*—or more accurately, measurement validity—as determining whether a measure actually was measuring what it was supposed to measure. But there are other uses of the word *validity* that refer to the *design*, and the way the design facilitates conclusions about causality. (The design also may facilitate conclusions about generalizability. This is called *external validity* and is discussed in the subsequent section.)

In this section, we focus on *design validity*: several ways in which characteristics of the design can affect conclusions that the intervention may have caused changes in the target. This is a key question for single-system designs. Indeed, the planned arrangements that comprise the designs are planned precisely to help us understand the effect of our interventions on target problems.

However, a number of factors affect our ability to draw conclusions about causality with single-system designs. We already have reviewed several of them in this chapter—differences among phases, differences in interventions, changing one variable at a time, and several complicating factors. In a sense, all these can raise questions about the validity of our causal inferences—are there other reasons than our intervention that could account for the results we obtained? Traditionally, these questions are called "threats to the validity of a design" because they can confound the conclusions about causality that we infer from our designs (Shadish et al., 2002).

There are a number of other questions about alternative explanations for a given set of results, that is, other threats to the validity of research and evaluation designs in general, and single-system designs in particular (Kratochwill & Levin, 1992; Shadish et al., 2002). One such question, or threat to the validity of a conclusion that involves the causality of our intervention, is that the observed change may have been caused by factors other than the intervention; these factors are the alternative explanations for the findings, which thus become *threats* to our presumed cause, the intervention.

As context for the discussion that follows, we emphasize the point that these threats basically raise *questions* about how we designed the evaluation that produced our outcomes; that is, did our evaluation design really rule out other possibilities about causality. The presence of a *possible* threat doesn't mean that there necessarily is an *actual* threat to our conclusions. When we think through the answers to these questions, we may discover that there is no threat to our conclusions because the design was strong enough to withstand the possible logical alternative answers for the results we obtained. In this case, we should look at these threats as questions to be answered so as to gain more confidence in our findings. But if we find that a threat is possible, given the design that we used, then we have to be less confident in our conclusion that the intervention caused the changes.

The most comprehensive discussion of these threats to the validity of designs is available in Shadish et al. (2002), building on the classical statement by Campbell and Stanley (1963). Shadish et al. distinguish among three classes of threats affecting conclusions about causality: statistical conclusion validity (as well as external validity, discussed later in this chapter), internal validity, and construct validity. Since much of this material is concerned with classical research and not single-system designs, we will focus only on the threats that are pertinent to single-system designs, modifying the original concepts to fit this evaluation model wherever necessary. As you will see, there is some overlap among the threats in each area, although this categorization is probably more helpful than condensing all these threats into one category (e.g., simply considering them all threats to internal validity). We pose these validity issues as a series of questions.

Statistical Conclusion Validity: Did Change Occur?
Threats to statistical conclusion validity essentially refer to questions involving *covariation* between the independent variable (intervention) and the dependent variable (the target problem). Before knowing whether an independent variable caused changes in a dependent variable, it is important to know whether there are sufficient grounds to believe that the independent and dependent variables vary together as we discussed in the previous section on criteria for determining causality. Indeed, knowing whether two variables covary logically precedes decisions about causality. Threats to statistical conclusion validity also tend to make it more difficult to determine effectiveness by presenting obstacles that make it more difficult to detect change.

While some of the threats to statistical conclusion validity are related to the use of statistical tests (e.g., violations of assumptions underlying statistical tests), some of the threats can be controlled by design (Orme, 1991). These threats to statistical conclusion validity are listed below, along with examples of each threat, all of which can make an intervention appear less effective. Essentially these all boil down to two types of errors, whether or not you use statistics to determine whether there is a systematic difference between phases: concluding that there is a difference between phases when there isn't (called a Type I error) and concluding that there isn't a difference between phases when there is (called a Type II error). Another way to think about this is to design your evaluation so that if there *is* a difference between phases, you will be able to detect it (called statistical power).

Threats to Statistical Conclusion Validity

1. *Reliability of measures.* Measures that have low reliability make it difficult to detect true changes and may make an effective intervention appear ineffective.

    Example: Ryan used a measure of self-esteem with test–retest reliability of only .40. Although the client's self-esteem actually changed over time, Ryan couldn't tell with his measure whether the change was real or merely a reflection of an unstable measure.

2. *Reliability of intervention implementation.* The intervention may be implemented in different ways from occasion to occasion, or, if different practitioners are involved, from practitioner to practitioner. This decreases the chances of obtaining true differences and may make an effective intervention appear ineffective.

    Example: An agency administrator noticed that an intervention used widely in her agency did not appear effective when the results of the intervention were pooled for all practitioners using the intervention. She suspected that the reason for this was that practitioners were implementing the intervention in a variety of ways. In order to promote standardization, she and the practitioners produced a manual to describe specific steps of the intervention that all could follow.

3. *Random irrelevancies in the intervention setting.* Any random changes in the setting of the intervention, including location, climate, time, and so on, may affect scores on the outcome measure and make an effective intervention appear ineffective.

    Example: Because the agency was being refurbished, David was forced to change offices several times during the course of his intervention with the Trask family. These changes made the intervention appear less effective than before the disruptions.

4. *Number of observations.* The smaller the number of observations, the more difficult it is to detect the effect of an intervention.

    Example: Terri was able to collect only two baseline observations and three intervention observations for her client. The small number of observations made it unclear as to whether substantial changes actually had occurred so that it was difficult to determine whether the intervention was effective.

Internal Validity: Was Change Caused by Your Intervention? The best known of the major threats to design validity is internal validity. Of the four (external validity is the fourth) types of design validity, internal validity most specifically relates to questions about ascertaining whether the intervention caused the changes in the target problem. That is, once covariation can be assumed, the next task is to determine whether *extraneous variables*—those outside of the intervention proper—could have influenced or produced observed changes.

In the list below, we review several common threats to the internal validity of single-system designs. The importance of these threats is that they pose certain risks in drawing conclusions about whether your intervention caused any observed changes, and we want to be sure you understand how their presence can affect those conclusions. It is important to point out that different designs contain different threats to internal validity; indeed, some of the more sophisticated designs actually can control many of these threats so that conclusions about causality can be made. We describe the way certain designs can control or minimize many of these threats.

Threats to Internal Validity

1. *History.* Did any other events occur outside of the practice setting during the time of the practitioner–client contacts that may be responsible for the particular outcome? Since single-system designs by definition extend over time, there is ample opportunity for such extraneous events to occur.

    Example: During the course of marital therapy, Andrew loses his job while Ann obtains a better position than she had before. Such events, though independent of the therapy, may have as much or more to do with the outcome than did the therapy.

2. *Maturation.* Did any psychological or physiological change occur within the client that might have affected the outcome during the time he or she was in a treatment situation?

    Example: Bobby was in a treatment program from the ages of 13 to 16, but when the program ended, it was impossible to tell if Bobby had simply matured as a teenager or if the program was effective.

3. *Testing.* Taking a test or filling out a questionnaire the first time may sensitize the client so that subsequent scores are influenced. This is particularly important with single-system designs because of reliance on repeated measures.

    Example: The staff of the agency filled out the evaluation questionnaire the first week, but most staff members couldn't help remembering what they said that first time so that subsequent evaluations were biased by the first set of responses.

4. *Instrumentation.* Do changes in the measurement devices themselves or changes in the observers or in the way the measurement devices are used have an impact on the outcome?

    Example: Phyllis, a public health nurse, was involved in evaluating a home health program in which she interviewed elderly clients every 4 months for a 3-year period. About halfway through, Phyllis made plans to be married and was preoccupied with this coming event. She thought she had memorized the questionnaire, but in fact she forgot to ask blocks of questions, and coders of the data complained to her that they couldn't always make out which response she had circled on the sheets.

5. *Dropout.* Are the results of an intervention program distorted because clients drop out of treatment, leaving a different sample of persons being measured?

    Example: While studying the impact of relocation on nursing home patients, a researcher noticed that some patients were refusing to continue to participate in the research interview because they said that the questions made them very anxious and upset. This left the overall results dependent on only the remaining patients.

6. *Statistical regression or regression to the mean.* Statistically, extreme scores on an original test will tend to become less extreme upon retesting.

    Example: Hank was tested in the vocational rehabilitation office and received one of the lowest scores ever recorded there, a fact that attracted some attention from the counselors who worked with him. However, because of a bus strike, Hank couldn't get to the center very often, and yet, upon retesting, he scored much better than he had before. Had Hank been receiving counseling during that period, it might have appeared as though the counseling produced the changes in score.

7. *Diffusion or imitation of intervention (contrast effects).* When intervention involves some type of informational program and when clients from different interventions or different practitioners communicate with each other about the

program, clients may learn about information intended for others.

Example: Harvey was seeing a practitioner for help with his depression at the same time his wife Jean was seeing a practitioner for help with anger management. Although their intervention programs were different, their discussions with each other led each of them to try aspects of each other's program.

Construct Validity: Did You Implement Your Intervention and Measure Your Outcomes Accurately? In this case, we are discussing construct validity as it affects *designs*. Issues related to the construct validity of designs occur when the procedures intended to represent a particular cause or effect construct can be interpreted as other constructs. Thus, what one practitioner thinks is a causal relationship between two specific constructs is interpreted by another practitioner as a causal relationship between other constructs. So, intervention efforts (e.g., systemic family therapy) that seem to produce changes in a target could be confounded with other variables (e.g., the practitioner's warmth or attention). Ensuring construct validity means attempting to ensure that how you operationalized your construct accurately reflects what you intended the construct to mean.

The following list describes several of the key threats to construct validity as they affect conclusions about causality:

Threats to Construct Validity

1. *Mono-operation and mono-method bias.* Use of only one measure per target and/or one method of recording (especially when there is more than one target) decreases the ability to draw conclusions. Using more than one would enhance conclusions by examining the extent to which multiple measures or multiple recording methods coincide.

    Example: Gye used only one self-report scale to measure outcome, and even though it showed improvement, it was hard to tell if the changes would have shown up using other methods of measurement.

2. *Hypothesis guessing.* When clients try to "figure out" what the practitioner appears to want above and beyond what the practitioner has said, the client may change partly as a result of wanting to conform to this hypothesis rather than because of the actual intervention.

    Example: Even though the practitioner tried to clearly describe what he was trying to accomplish, Kyle kept thinking there was "something more" going on and his behavior began to change due to his own guessing and not the actual intervention program.

3. *Evaluation apprehension.* Many people are apprehensive about being evaluated and therefore present themselves to practitioners in ways that are not totally accurate.

    Example: Thelma was so concerned about filling out the questionnaire that she scored all her responses in ways that made her seem much less depressed than she actually was.

4. *Practitioner expectations.* When the client is able to perceive the practitioner's expectations, it is difficult to know whether observed changes are due to the actual intervention or the expectations of the practitioner.

    Example: The entire staff knew that the agency director's expectations were that the staff would work especially hard during the agency's evaluation, so many of the practitioners began to put in extra time at the agency.

5. *Interaction of interventions.* Whenever more than one intervention is used with the same client, it is difficult or impossible to tell which intervention affected the target.

    Example: Kevin and Vickki, young parents of an abused child, were being aided by a series of parent skills training classes, followed by assertiveness training, and later by social effectiveness skills training. Communication between them seemed to have improved, and they were caring for their daughter more consistently. But at the end of intervention, the counselor wasn't able to pinpoint which of these treatments was most useful.

We discuss a number of single-system designs and will refer back to some of these threats to design validity in single-system designs with regard to what threats are especially relevant to what designs. At that time we will consider ways of overcoming these threats to the degree that this is possible. Often, the more complex designs attempt to reduce certain threats that the simpler ones cannot avoid. For example, the simple *A-B* design is always subject to the threat of history—something else occurring in the client's life that is external to the intervention but could affect the target problem. But with various experimental designs, when an intervention is removed and then later repeated, if the target problem also shows change (concomitant variation), then it is less likely that external events could be producing such a pattern.

EXTERNAL VALIDITY AND GENERALIZABILITY

One of the important services that classical research provides is the potential of cumulating its results and generalizing about one set of findings for application to new situations. However, with single-system designs, it is hard to prove that what may be true of work with one client is likely to be true for some other clients, problems, or settings. Therefore, the issue of external validity and generalizability is a vital one for both professional and practical reasons. Professionally, evaluation procedures such as single-system designs will not be adopted widely unless they can be shown to have the necessary practical and scientific credentials, including the capability of aiding in generalizing results across clients and situations. In practice, professionals would find an intervention of little interest unless the efforts devoted to evaluating that intervention in one situation could demonstrate that the intervention was potentially useful in other situations.

External Validity: Does Your Intervention Have the Same Effect with Different Clients and Under Different Circumstances?

External validity refers to the extent to which an effect of an intervention, and, therefore, the use of the intervention itself, can be generalized; that is, will an intervention work the same way with different clients and practitioners, in different settings, and over time. These are crucial issues because if your interventions can be designed to be applicable to other clients and settings as revealed through your evaluations, it would make your practice more meaningful. Similarly, understanding principles of external validity will help you draw conclusions about generalizing the results of *others'* work to your own practice.

A key precondition for understanding external validity is to determine whether the intervention that was used really produced the changes—the key issue for design validity—before one considers the possibility of generalizing results. This is because what we usually try to generalize is the *intervention* used in one or more instances to other clients or situations. Thus, it is important to be clear about whether it really was the intervention producing the changes—the key issue for design validity—before one begins considering the possibility of generalizing results.

The main issue for external validity (generalizability) is the extent to which the clients, settings, problems, or practitioners are representative. If it can be said, for example, that the clients in study 2 are exactly like the clients in study 1, it would be reasonable to assume the results from study 1 could be generalized to some extent to the clients in study 2. In classical research, the method for dealing with representativeness is through the selection of a random sample from a population. This tends to ensure representativeness and hence generalizability. In most intervention research, however, generalizability is based more on replication and extension of results than on probability sampling.

But the situation is different with single-system designs. Unfortunately, the issue of external validity is perhaps the most difficult issue of all for single-system designs. Here we typically are dealing with individuals, families, or small groups, none of which are selected randomly from some defined population. Even when a community is the focus of single-system design evaluation, it can rarely, if ever, be viewed as representative of some other community. Thus, the main threat to external validity with use of single-system designs is lack of *representativeness* of the client(s), situation(s), and/or problem(s) in a given evaluation, thereby placing restrictions on generalizing results to other people, situations, or problems.

There are several other types of specific threats related to external validity or generalizability. Based on the work of Shadish et al. (2002), Kratochwill (1978), and Cook and Campbell (1979), we describe a variety of threats to external validity. These threats are contained in the following list and concern the general question: *Can the results from a given single-system design be generalized to apply to different clients in different settings and/or different practitioners?* Even more specifically, the concept of external validity poses the question: If you did the same thing under different circumstances, would you get the same results? In other words, each of the problems below limits generalizability from one single-system evaluation to another.

Threats to External Validity or Generalizability in Single-System Designs

1. *Interaction under different conditions.* It is possible that every intervention works somewhat differently with different clients in different settings by different practitioners, thus reducing the likelihood of identical results.

   Example: Esther's friend Louise was much taken with her tales of using self-monitoring with adolescent outpatients, so she tried to adapt the technique to youngsters in her school who were having problems related to hyperactivity. Even though she followed Esther's suggestions as closely as possible, the results did not come out as well as they did in the other setting.

2. *Practitioner effect.* The practitioner's style of practice influences outcomes, so different practitioners applying the same intervention may have different effects to some degree.

   Example: Arnold had been substitute teaching on many occasions over several years in Marie's class and knew her course materials quite well. However, when he had to take over her class on a permanent basis because she resigned with a serious illness, he was surprised that he wasn't as effective in teaching her class as Marie had been.

3. *Different dependent (target or outcome) variables.* There may be differences in how the target variables are conceptualized and operationalized in different studies, thus reducing the likelihood of identical results.

   Example: Ernesto's community action group defined "neighborhood solidarity" in terms of its effectiveness in obtaining municipal services, defined as trash removal, rat control, and the expansion of bus service during early morning hours. While Juan used the same term, neighborhood solidarity, with a similar ethnic group in a different neighborhood, the meaning of the term had to do with the neighbors presenting a united front in the face of the school board's arbitrary removal of a locally popular principal.

4. *Interaction of history and intervention.* If extraneous events occur concurrently during the intervention, they may not be present at other times, thus reducing the generalizability of the results of the original study.

   Example: The first community mental health center opened amid the shock of recent suicides of several young, unemployed men. It was forced to respond to the needs of persons facing socioeconomic pressures. However, when a new center opened in a nearby area, there was no similar popular recognition of this type of counseling, and considerably fewer persons went to the second center than to the first.

5. *Measurement differences.* The more that differences exist between two evaluations regarding how the same process and outcome variables are measured, so too are the results likely to be different.

   Example: The standardized scales used by Lee with his majority group clients were viewed by the several minority group members as being too offensive and asking questions that were too personal, so he had to devise ways of obtaining the same information in less obvious or offensive ways. The results continued to show considerable differences between majority and minority group clients.

6. *Differences in clients.* The characteristics of the client—age, sex, ethnicity, socio-economic status, and so on—can affect the extent to which results can be generalized. Since clients in single-system designs are almost never randomly selected from a population, one can never be sure the clients in a single-system design are representative of any other group.

   Example: Nick devised a counseling program that was very successful in decreasing dropouts in one school with mainly middle-class students. But when Nick tried to implement his program in a different school, one with largely low-income students, he found the dropout rate was hardly affected.

7. *Interaction between testing and intervention.* The effects of the early testing—for example, the baseline observations—could sensitize the client

to the intervention so that generalization could be expected to occur only when subsequent clients are given the same tests prior to intervention.

Example: All members of an assertion training group met for 3 weeks and role-played several situations in which they were not being assertive. The formal intervention of assertion training started the fourth week, but by then all group members were highly sensitized to what to expect.

8. *Reactive effects to evaluation.* Simple awareness by clients that they are in a study could lead to changes in client performance.

Example: All employees at a public agency providing services to the elderly were participants in a study comparing their work with work performed by practitioners in a private agency. Knowing they were in the study, and knowing they had to do their best, the public agency practitioners put in extra time, clouding the issue as to whether their typical intervention efforts would produce similar results.

Enhancing Generalizability

The threats to external validity we described above are some of the major ones you should watch in thinking about the problems involved in generalizing results from one single-system evaluation to another.

On the other hand, there are some possibilities for generalizing results from single-system evaluations, such as when negative results in one case are enough to make you reject that intervention in another case, or when the behavior you studied is so unique that there isn't any other basis for thinking about a new instance of that type. In general, we would recommend thinking about generalizing results from one single-system evaluation to a new one whenever the earlier work will lead to a good beginning of the new intervention, so long as you continue to evaluate your practice to see whether it worked the second time or needed to be changed.

Thomas (1975), for example, suggests a number of these possibilities for generalizing results from single-system evaluations:

1. When the variability between clients is known to be negligible so that replication would be redundant.

2. When one case in depth clearly exemplifies many.

3. When negative results from one case are sufficient to suggest the need for at least revision, and possibly even rejection, of the principles that generated the particular intervention.

4. When the behavior studied is very unusual and there is limited opportunity to study it.

5. When the practitioner wants to focus on a problem by defining questions and variables that may lead to more refined approaches.

Similarly, from a commonsense perspective, you might try to generalize findings from one client to another based on how much alike their essential characteristics are, including the particular target problems that would be operationally defined and empirically measured in the course of collecting baseline data. They also include other relevant features of the client that would be likely to influence how clients would respond to the same intervention by the same practitioner in the same setting, such as age, gender, ethnicity, and the like—as well as pertinent individualizing factors—experiences with prior professional practitioners, level of self-esteem, and so on. In general, the more similar two clients are, the more likely the findings from one will apply to the intervention of the other.

Indeed, even though use of different interventions from one case to another is inevitable to some degree, practitioners seeking to extend results from one situation to another should attempt to make the interventions as similar as possible. This is equally true with the practitioner's style of practice, the target variables, and the measurement processes. Similarly, one should be sure that the client population and problems are similar—or differences accounted for—before attempting to generalize. However, differences will always remain, and thus, threats to external validity are a continuing problem for all research, including single-system evaluations.

Several other approaches to generalization of single-system designs have been developed. We briefly describe three of them here: replication, use of probabilities, and meta-analysis.

Replication. Even though representativeness is at the heart of generalizability, the main path to generalizability with single-system designs, as well as with classical evaluation designs, is in the *replication* of results. Replication essentially refers to successful repetition of results from one case, problem, setting, or situation to another. Replication as a method of generalizing results is especially pertinent because you may want to consider applying what you read in the literature to your own practice, or you may be thinking about generalizing your own work from one case to another.

Three types of replication that can lead to generalization of results in single-system evaluation have been described in the classic works by Sidman (1960) and Barlow, Nock, and Hersen (2009). The first method is called *direct replication*—the most basic form of generalizing by replication in single-system design. Direct replication is the repetition of a given intervention by the same practitioner. This is probably the most common form of replication (as we will see in our discussions of the other types—clinical and systematic replication), and therefore is a basic way of generalizing data from single-system designs.

Barlow, Nock, and Hersen (2009) present several guidelines for direct replication that are ways in which a practitioner interested in extending results from one client to another may do so with greater confidence. First, the same practitioner working in the same setting should work with problems that are similar across clients, such as a specific phobia. Second, client background characteristics should be as similar as possible to the case from which findings are to be generalized. A third guideline is that the intervention should be uniformly applied across clients until failure occurs.

If an intervention fails at any stage of the process, it is not necessarily a troublesome event in single-system designs. It can be observed quickly during ongoing monitoring of data, and it prompts the practitioner to make rapid adjustments in the intervention and to test these adjustments for appropriate client change. If the additional interventions lead to success, they can be replicated further for their transferability. If they are not successful, the distinctive characteristics of that client can be studied to try to find out what elements may have caused these results, information that likewise can be used in replication studies.

The second, more sophisticated, form of replication discussed by Barlow, Nock, and Hersen (2009) is *clinical replication*—the repeating of an intervention *package* containing two or more distinct techniques that is applied by the same practitioner or group of practitioners to a series of clients in the same setting with multiple problems that generally cluster together. (Usually this problem cluster is given a label, such as "autism" or "hyperactivity," but opinions differ about the usefulness of such labels.) The guidelines for clinical replication are similar to the guidelines for direct replication given above.

A series of common problems and interventions may be difficult to come by in some agencies because of the general heterogeneity of clients. Under these circumstances, it would be hard to develop a programmatic series of replications as required by this approach. On the other hand, where client problems remain fairly consistent, clinical replication—sometimes called field testing—is possible. A classic example of field testing for clinical replication is the work of Lovaas, Koegel, Simmons, and Long (1973). These practitioners illustrate clinical replication in their work with autistic children, a problem composed of at least eight distinct factors that contribute to the syndrome, including mutism, deficiencies in social and self-help behavior, and severe affect isolation. Over a period of years and through direct replication, they tested treatments for each separate component, and the treatment package constructed from these early studies was administered to subsequent autistic children. Results and follow-up data that indicate the general utility of the treatment package, even though improvement wasn't even for all children, are presented by Lovaas, Koegel, Simmons, and Long (1973). This fact prompted these researchers to continue looking for individual differences that impeded the treatment package. In field testing, the several intervention components dealing with some syndrome like autistic behavior are studied individually or are grouped in small packages in single-system designs, and over time, the general utility of these components are confirmed, leading practitioners to continue using the whole intervention program with clients exhibiting this same syndrome.

Systematic replication is the third and most far-reaching approach discussed by Barlow, Nock, and Hersen (2009). This is the attempt to replicate findings from a direct replication series, varying the setting, the practitioners, the problems, or any combination of these factors. This is obviously a more complex task and not one that a single practitioner is likely to undertake. However, we discuss this topic because collaborative efforts toward generalizing results of single-system designs may become more common.

Suppose that a practitioner working with a given client in a particular setting discovers that a technique called *differential attention*—briefly, reinforcing desired behaviors while ignoring others—appears to produce significant improvement. The practitioner successfully repeats his or her results with other similar clients; this constitutes direct replication.

Possibly, several colleagues of the practitioner learn about the technique and try it with their clients in the same institution with similar successful results (clinical replication). Suppose that the results of these separate studies are published, and other practitioners working with different clients in different settings become intrigued and try it with similar successful results. This would constitute an example of systematic replication.

In fact, this is approximately what did happen in a series of studies on differential attention. Barlow, Nock, and Hersen (2009) document a large number of studies of differential attention with different clients, settings, and practitioners, with initial results showing generally successful outcomes. In addition, equally useful negative results began to be reported with certain types of client problems (such as self-injurious behavior in children), thus setting limits on the usefulness of the technique. While Barlow, Nock, and Hersen emphasize that practitioners should proceed with caution when applying differential attention to new situations, they also note that a solid beginning was made in establishing the generalizability of this technique. This is one way in which the helping professions grow.

For all replication attempts, the question obviously arises: How many replications are sufficient to produce a reasonable hypothesis that the series of replications was successful, that is, can be trusted to show reliable results? When roughly 80% of replications are successful, one probably can conclude that the results are consistent enough to be treated as reliable. While this is an approximate guideline, it does appear to be a useful one in applying consistent standards across arenas of both evaluation and practice.

Probabilities. A different approach to generalization in single-system evaluations was proposed by Tripodi (1980). As opposed to the rough guideline of 80% discussed above, Tripodi suggests that statistical significance, using the binomial distribution, the two category probability distribution that is discussed in any standard text on statistics, can be used to determine the number of successful replications needed for evidence of generalization.

Tripodi (1980) discusses a number of assumptions that apply in using probabilities to assess generalizations, including similarity and specification of the following: clients, interventions, administration of intervention, problems, a consistent criterion of success, and an expected probability of success with each client (e.g., a .50 probability of success; lower or higher probabilities can be used given the difficulty of the problem or the record of success with that problem based on previous research).

Assuming, then, with no other evidence being available, an equal probability of success and failure (.50) for a given intervention, and using the standard .05 level of statistical significance, Tripodi (1980, p. 35) suggests that the estimated number of successes needed to achieve statistical significance can be determined by referring to a table of calculated probabilities such as can be found in many statistical texts. Thus, as just one example, 10 successes out of 12 tries at replication would be statistically significant. With low numbers of replication attempts, 6 or fewer at the .05 level, all of the attempts would have to be successful to be statistically significant. Further, the greater the probability of success, that is, more than .50, the higher the number of successful replications needed for statistical significance. (For example, based on a review of the literature, the practitioner might be able to expect a higher probability of success for the intervention, say .75.) Thus, if any given proportion of successes meets or exceeds the critical value in the probability table and is statistically significant, it is likely that with a given margin of error (say, 5 out of 100 at the .05 level), the effect of chance can be ruled out and the replication and generalization can be considered successful.

In the past, it may have been rather difficult to find available data that would let you calculate the percentage of successes over a number of studies. But evidence-based practice is predicated on the assumption that such evidence *is* available, and is likely to increase over time. Thus, Tripodi's approach may become increasingly useful as these evidence-based data accumulate.

Meta-Analysis. The last possibility for examining generalizability is through use of meta-analysis. Meta-analyses are especially important because they "reside at the top of the evidentiary hierarchy for answering evidence-based practice (EBP) questions as to which intervention, program, or policy has the best effects" (Rubin, 2008, p. 151).

Meta-analysis is a method for *quantitatively* aggregating, comparing, and analyzing the results of several studies (see Littell, Corcoran, & Pillai, 2008, for a recent introduction to meta-analysis for group research). The data in the individual studies are converted to a common metric, allowing easy comparison across studies. This common metric, called an *effect size* (typically using Cohen's *d*), allows an overall interpretation of whether the intervention periods of several single-system designs seem to have produced an effect on target problems beyond that which has occurred during several baseline periods. If so, this can be viewed as a kind of affirmation of generalizability.

While the literature of meta-analysis in general has exploded, with literally hundreds of studies and reviews available, there are relatively few meta-analyses of single-system designs though the numbers are increasing (e.g., Erion, 2006; Jenson et al., 2007; Moss & Nicholas, 2006; Nye & Schwartz, 2007; Shadish & Rindskopf, 2007; Wehmeyer et al., 2006; Xin, Grasso, Dipipi-Hoy, & Jitendra, 2005). Other examples of single-system design meta-analyses can be found at http://faculty.ucmerced.edu/wshadish/SSD%20Meta Analysis.htm.

Unfortunately, there are a number of very serious issues regarding the use of meta-analysis, both in classical research and in single-system designs. Most of these issues are beyond the scope of this book (Horner et al., 2005; Jenson et al., 2007; Littell et al., 2008; Logan, Hickman, Harris, & Heriza, 2008; Shadish & Rindskopf, 2007). In particular, measures of effect size are necessary to aggregate and analyze results, and there is considerable debate about how best to quantify effect size for single-system data. However, there have been promising developments in this area since the last edition of this book, most notably the work of Parker and his colleagues (e.g., Parker & Hagan-Burke, 2007a, 2007b; Parker & Vannest, in press; Parker et al., in press). Because the use of meta-analysis is increasing, and it has been recommended by some authors as a way of examining generalization in single-system designs, we provide a brief introduction to the way meta-analysis can be used to examine generalizability of results of single-system evaluations.

Among several ways for quantifying results of studies for meta-analysis, the most widely used is called the *effect size* (ES). The effect size is simply a way of examining the magnitude of the effect of an intervention (how large it is) of one study or across a number of studies.

There are two commonly used methods for calculating ES in group research (a number of other, more complicated formulas are described in Faith et al., 1997). The first (Glass, McGaw, & Smith, 1981) takes the mean of the control group (or in single-system design terms, the baseline period, *A*) and subtracts it from the mean of the experimental group (in single-system design terms, the intervention period, *B*), and the results are divided by the standard deviation of the control group (baseline):

$$ES = \frac{M_B - M_A}{S_A}$$

where

B = intervention period

and

A = baseline period

The second formula is almost identical to the first except that the standard deviation in the denominator is actually the pooled standard deviation of both the baseline and intervention (or control and experimental group) periods.

We're not going to trouble you with too many of the technicalities of the calculations now. For now, we just illustrate how the process—and a conclusion about generalizability—works.

First, all the single-system design studies that focus on a particular intervention (that which you want to examine for generalization) are collected. Most types of single-system designs—from *A-B*s to *A-B-A-B*s to multiple baselines—can be used (White et al., 1989).

Second, using one of the two ES formulas described above, the overall ES for the set of studies is calculated. (If the number of studies is relatively small, say 10 or fewer, a correction factor, called *K*, devised by Hedges, 1981, can be used to correct for bias due to the small sample.) This ES hypothetically could run the gamut from −3.70 to +3.70, although the most commonly reported effect sizes are in the 0 to 1.5 range. Third, one should do as good a job as possible in evaluating the methodological adequacy of the included studies. For example, if it can be shown that the studies with the strongest designs support one conclusion about the overall impact of some intervention and the poorest studies support another, the meta-analytic reviewer might change his or her overall conclusion.

The final step in meta-analysis is to interpret the findings. This is done in two ways. First, the overall ES is interpreted. Since the ES is in effect a standardized score, it can be interpreted like a Z score as the mean difference between groups (baseline and intervention periods) in standard deviation units. Thus, an ES of +1.0 suggests that the average client score in the intervention period was about one standard deviation above scores in the baseline period; an ES of .50 suggests the average client in the intervention period scored about one-half of a standard deviation above the scores in the baseline period; an ES of 0 suggests no difference in the scores of the average client between baseline and intervention; and a negative ES suggests scores in the intervention period actually deteriorated.

The second way of interpreting ES is to use any Z table to determine the percentile rank of the average client's intervention period scores above the baseline period. Thus, an ES of 1.0 (using the ES as a substitute for the Z score in the Z table) means the scores of the average client during the intervention period were above 84% of the scores in the baseline, while an ES of .50 means the intervention period scores were above 69% of baseline scores. (An ES of 0 means there was no difference between the baseline and intervention phase means. A negative ES and a percentage below 50% again suggest deterioration.)

So, what does this actually tell you about the generalizability of a given intervention? What results of meta-analysis purport to show is that a given intervention may produce a certain magnitude of effect across several single-system designs. The larger the effect size, the greater the magnitude of the effect. Thus, one way of looking at this information is that the larger the effect size, the more that the intervention under study may be producing an effect across several studies. In other words, the effect size may be one way of looking at the possible generalization of an intervention across different situations, clients, and perhaps problems. Of course, as we mentioned earlier, deciding whether an intervention actually caused an observed outcome is a design issue rather than a statistical one. Nevertheless, meta-analysis is an important, additional way of examining whether there is even some effect across studies before we decide whether it was our interventions that caused it.

As with all the guidelines for generalization discussed in this section, we urge extreme caution in interpreting the results of a meta-analysis. Apart from the fact that there are a number of issues regarding meta-analysis itself, there simply is no convincing (or at least agreed upon throughout the field) way to evaluate the significance (statistical, clinical, or social) of a given result. Knowing that, overall, a given intervention in several studies may have moved average scores in the intervention period to a point above 69% of the scores in a baseline may be interesting, and may indeed suggest some degree of generalizability of findings, but it has to be evaluated against a number of variables, including the time, effort, energy, and resources required to achieve such results.

In all, meta-analysis, along with the other methods described here, provides some ideas that can help in addressing the issue of generalizability in single-system designs. Used as rough guides, we believe all of these approaches help to advance the careful use of single-system designs to inform practice.

OVERVIEW OF SINGLE-SYSTEM DESIGNS

There are many ways to collect and analyze data in order to judge changes in target behavior and in order to decide whether the intervention can be inferred to be causally related to these changes. In this section, we preview the detailed discussions dealing with single-system designs. Each design is simply a systematic variation in observations and interventions with one or more targets. However, there are definable groupings among these designs that stem from the logical relationships among their components. In Figure 6 we illustrate the major features of the designs.

The top row of Figure 6 includes case studies that involve only interventions—no formal baselines. There is, of course, careful observation going on during professional intervention, but there may or may not be systematic recording of changes. The missing baseline phase is indicated by dashed lines. The point is that there is no solid prior information with which to evaluate changes in targets. Even though you may add a new intervention, C, which can be compared to

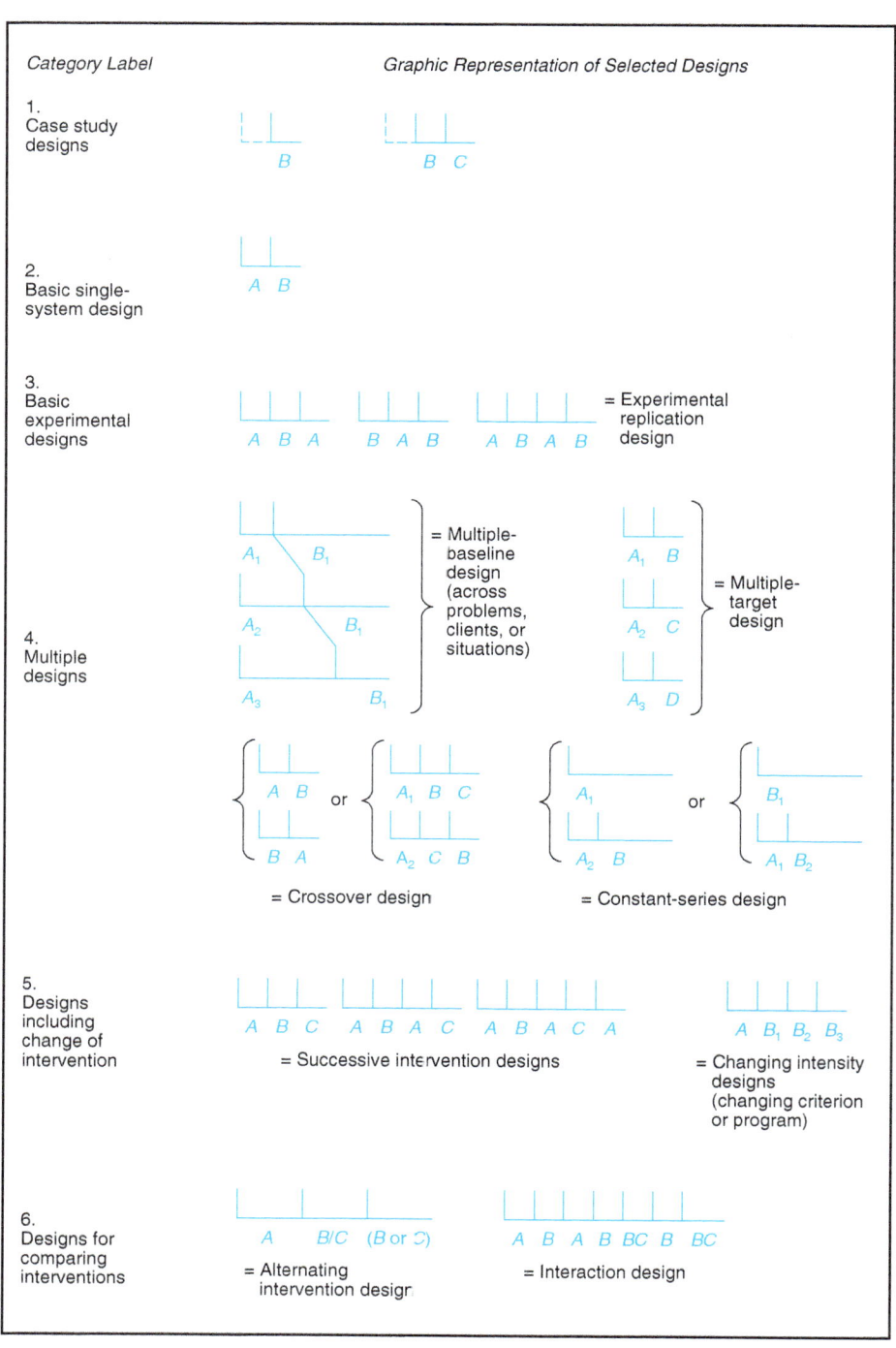

Category Label	Graphic Representation of Selected Designs
1. Case study designs	B B C
2. Basic single-system design	A B
3. Basic experimental designs	A B A B A B A B A B = Experimental replication design
4. Multiple designs	A_1 B_1 / A_2 B_1 / A_3 B_1 = Multiple-baseline design (across problems, clients, or situations); A_1 B / A_2 C / A_3 D = Multiple-target design; { A B / B A } or { A_1 B C / A_2 C B } = Crossover design; { A_1 / A_2 B } or { B_1 / A_1 B_2 } = Constant-series design
5. Designs including change of intervention	A B C A B A C A B A C A = Successive intervention designs; A B_1 B_2 B_3 = Changing intensity designs (changing criterion or program)
6. Designs for comparing interventions	A B/C (B or C) = Alternating intervention design; A B A B BC B BC = Interaction design

A = Baseline; A_1, A_2 = Baselines for different target behaviors.
B = Discrete intervention plus observation; B^1, B^2 = Variations of same intervention.
BC, BCD = Concurrent presence of discrete interventions B, C, D.
L = Observation phase present; ⌐⌐ = Observation phase absent.

FIGURE 6 Overview of categories of single-system designs.

data collected during intervention phase *B*, we still lack a baseline for true comparison.

The second row illustrates the basic single-system design, termed the *A-B* design, *A* for baseline, *B* for intervention. This is the simplest design that provides relatively objective information on changes in the target. However, this basic design is subject to many alternative explanations for why the changes emerged as they did—these are the internal validity threats described earlier in this chapter. There are some steps one can take to reduce these alternative explanations.

The third row of Figure 6 shows the experimental designs. They are experimental in the sense that you remove a successful intervention in order to study the effect of this manipulation on the target problem. If there is a concomitant variation with the presence and the absence of the intervention, then this provides the logical basis for inferring a causal link—that the intervention is likely causing some portion of the observed change. The *A-B-A, B-A-B,* and *A-B-A-B* designs are variations of experimental designs that involve removal of a successful intervention; all are powerful designs for drawing causal inferences.

The next four designs, in row 4, all involve multiple targets analyzed at the same time. The first of these designs is called the *multiple-baseline design*. It is important to note that you can compare the same intervention across different clients with the same problem and in the same setting, or, with different problems in the same client in one setting, or different settings with the same client involving the same problem. This is a versatile format. The multiple baseline design is especially useful examining the extent to which the effect of an intervention generalizes across clients, problems, or settings.

Likewise, *multiple-target designs* deal with different interventions addressed to different targets, but are viewed together so as to detect patterns of change among them. The multiple-target design is just as susceptible to threats from alternative explanations as the basic single-system design, the *A-B,* but the multiple-*baseline* design is able to remove some of these threats.

In the first case (constant baseline observations), if change occurs only on the target receiving the intervention, then this strengthens the inference that extraneous events may not be causally related to target changes. It does not directly show that *B* is causally related, however. In the second case (constant intervention), if change occurs only when the different targets receive the same intervention, and not during the baseline in the *A-B* design, then this also strengthens the inference that extraneous factors may not be causally related to the target changes.

The fifth row describes designs that involve changes in the intervention in which there is a true baseline. *Successive intervention designs* include any number of comparisons among baseline(s) and interventions in an attempt to enhance client outcome and perhaps begin to tease out just which intervention appears more effective. Logically, these are weak designs for comparing the effectiveness of specific interventions, but the practitioner can get some valuable hints that might be tested with stronger designs.

In the bottom row, we present complex designs, those involving combined interventions (either *alternating* or *simultaneous*) for the tentative information they provide on which is the stronger or preferred intervention. We also discuss the *interaction design* as the minimal logical form necessary to tease out directly the separate effects of two different interventions.

We will present an "ideal type" example, and then we'll present one or more recent evaluations that will inevitably have some modifications and compromises with the ideal model. This is what happens in the real world where conditions typically impose some constraints on the design, but these can still be very useful examples.

We hope that these examples will provide you with sufficient information to understand how deviations from the models affect your ability to draw conclusions. However, we do not want to discourage you from using your own variations.

Summary

This chapter presented an overview of the characteristics of single-system designs, and some of the complications and threats to their design validity and their generalizability. Designs are used for one or both of two major purposes: to describe change in target problems, and possibly, to infer that intervention was causally related to that observed change. Some designs also can be used to compare two interventions with each other. Designs are the arrangements of observations made before, during, and/or after interventions through which these questions may be logically addressed.

This chapter also discussed the complex issues surrounding causality, the various alternative explanations that may be given for any evaluation outcome, and the issues regarding generalization of outcomes. Some single-system designs are stronger than others in reducing alternative explanations. We concluded the chapter with an overview of single-system designs. However, we want to emphasize that the designs presented are basically "ideal types" that are described to help you understand the variety of uses and conclusions that are available from single-system designs. In real practice, you may use some of these designs exactly as described, or variations of them that specifically fit the needs of a particular case.

Essentially, all single-system designs begin with recording and then simply reflecting the changes you make in your interventions in subsequent phases. This is in line with our emphasis in this book that practice guides evaluation, rather than the other way around.

BASELINING

Collecting Information Before Intervention

PURPOSE This chapter describes the key first phase of almost every single-system design—the baseline. We discuss the importance of baselines, types of baselines, and how to decide how long to continue collecting information for baselines. We also discuss several issues related to collection of baseline information, including when baselines may not be necessary.

Introduction
Purposes of the Baseline
Types of Baselines
How Long Should Baselining Continue?
    Utility
    Stability
    Time
    Summary of Length of Baselining
When Are Baselines Not Necessary?
Issues Regarding Baselining
    Does Baselining Delay Intervention and Is Delay Detrimental?
    Does Baselining Actually Delay Intervention?
    Is Delaying Intervention Detrimental?
    There Are Times When Baselines Are Impossible
    Targets Often Shift During the Course of Intervention
    People Won't Cooperate in Collecting Baseline Information
    What If the Problem Improves During the Baseline?
Summary

From Chapter 12 of *Evaluating Practice: Guidelines for the Accountable Professional*, Sixth Edition. Martin Bloom, Joel Fischer, John G. Orme. Copyright © 2009 by Pearson Education, Inc. All rights reserved.

INTRODUCTION

One of the most distinctive and helpful features of single-system evaluation involves collecting information on the target problem/situation before formal intervention actually begins. This is called *baselining*. The period of time over which this information is collected is called the *baseline*. The information or data you collect is called the *baserate*, which involves systematic collection of data on the client's problem prior to the implementation of your formal intervention program. *The data you collect during baseline continue to be collected on the same target and in the same way throughout your intervention program.* They provide an important basis for monitoring and evaluating your effectiveness, since the baseline is almost always the first phase of your design. However, since baselining technically also could be defined as systematic collection of information on the target during *any* nonintervention period, a baseline phase could occur at any point in the overall process of contact with the client/system.

This chapter discusses the purposes of collecting baseline data, describes how you actually go about doing it, discusses when you need baseline data and when you don't, gives several examples of baselines, and also discusses many of the issues involved in collecting baselines.

PURPOSES OF THE BASELINE

Why bother to collect baseline information? There is one basic reason why recording—the systematic measurement of target problems and the keeping of records on those observations—is necessary. It ultimately will help to enhance your effectiveness by its critical function in evaluating your practice. Determining the baserate of the target problem gives you vital information about the magnitude of that problem (or even if it occurs at all) in its "natural" state before you begin intervention. Then you continue to get vital information as you monitor progress on that target during the intervention, whether progress is being made, or whether you had better rethink how you ought to handle this situation of no-change, slow-change, or negative change (deterioration). Baseline information can facilitate the selection of appropriate interventions because understanding the nature of the problem should help you connect to appropriate interventions related to the potential causes of the target condition. Knowing about these matters can help to move toward a more satisfactory outcome, although evaluation feedback cannot guarantee you success.

In many situations, having baseline information can be invaluable. Consider this example. Suppose that the problem you are working on involves a conflict between a parent and child about the child cleaning up his or her room. You ask the parent to collect baseline data, for instance, the number of articles left out each night. Your baseline data reveal this to be an average of about 18 articles per day. You put that information on a chart such as that shown in Figure 1.

Let's say that you start an intervention program and, after 1 week, the parent concludes that it is not working and therefore not worth the effort. At least this might be the parent's conclusion without data available to compare the intervention program with the preintervention state of affairs. Once the parent tabulated the data collected, and plotted them on a chart, the pattern could look like the one in Figure 2. There were so many articles left out each day that a drop of only a few didn't look like much. However, there was in fact a drop—an average of about five articles less a day during the first week of intervention compared to the baseline. Encouraged by this and aided by the practitioner, the parent might continue or modify the program and look forward to an even greater drop in subsequent weeks.

Let's consider baselining in relation to assessment of the client situation. Baselines are not a substitute for a comprehensive assessment, but they can provide important information as *part* of the assessment. When you are collecting baseline information, you are discovering a number of relevant facts about the client, problem, and situation. You may be finding out how often or for how long a problem occurs. You also may be discovering how often or for how long a positive behavior, thought, or feeling occurs so that your intervention program can build on that. You may be discovering where and when a problem occurs. Your baseline data might give you information on environmental factors that may be affecting a problem (e.g., events that precede it and perhaps elicit it or events that follow it and may reinforce it). Your baseline also may tell you how intensely the problem occurs (e.g., a client's self-evaluation of the intensity of his or her anxiety or the intensity of negative or positive thoughts).

Baselining

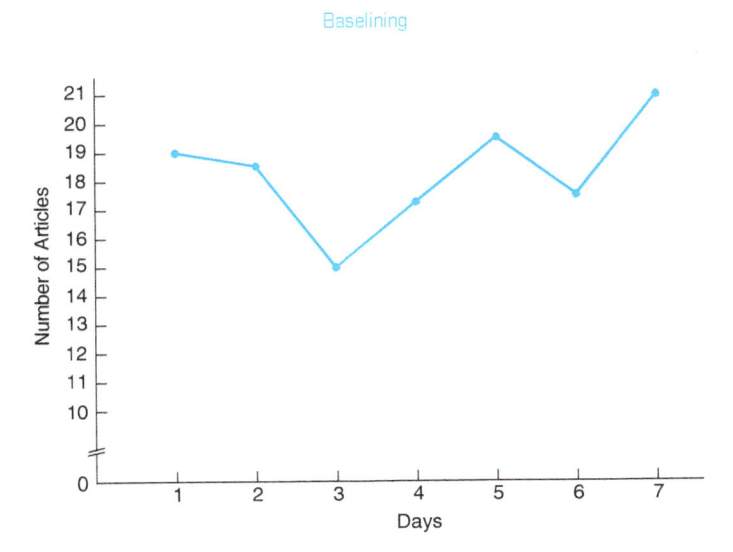

FIGURE 1 Number of articles left out each day during baseline.

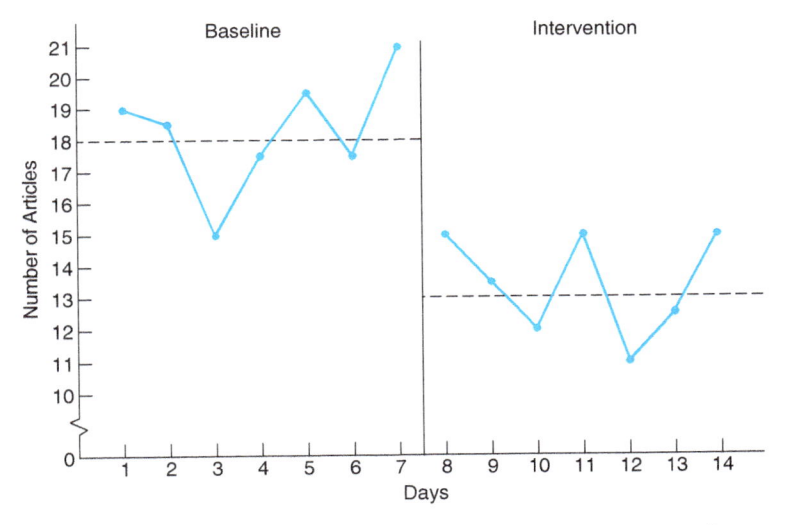

FIGURE 2 Number of articles left out each day during baseline and intervention.

Baseline information may help you pinpoint the targets of concern; their controlling conditions (e.g., location and situation); and their frequency, duration, and extent. You will use this kind of information, along with the evidence base of practice to select an intervention program and specific techniques of intervention, which potentially enhances your effectiveness by focusing on the client's precise needs at this time.

The baseline data, as part of the total assessment, help you to develop a *problem hypothesis,* a working hypothesis about factors that may be currently affecting or maintaining the problem. This hypothesis about the nature of the problem should be stated in terms relevant to developing your intervention program. Collecting baseline data makes this particularly feasible because the essence of baselining is observation or measurement of a problem as it occurs, as well as observation of the personal, interpersonal, and environmental factors affecting it.

As an example, let's say you are working in a school and a boy is referred to you for "disruptive behavior" in one of his classes—getting out of his seat without permission and talking out of turn. Without baselining the problem, you might have proceeded to begin an intervention program geared toward decreasing this behavior directly by, say, reinforcing him for sitting in his seat and not talking without permission. But a systematic period of baseline observations may have led to a totally different problem hypothesis. The baseline might have revealed that the problem really may have been a result of the child being bored in class, thereby leading to a totally different intervention, say, working with the teacher on developing more stimulating activities for the child.

Sometimes the baseline data may provide assessment information that suggests an intervention program may not be necessary at all. Sometimes a client with a complaint about himself or herself or about someone else will realize after baselining that the problem is of less concern than was thought to be the case. The problem may not occur nearly as often as the client thought or may not be nearly as extensive. In some situations this may allow the practitioner and client to actually terminate their work, to lower the priority for that particular problem, or to free up time and energy for working on another problem.

TYPES OF BASELINES

There are basically two types of baselines. The first is the *concurrent* or *prospective baseline*. This is the type most frequently discussed in the literature. These data are gathered in a planned, systematic way over time and are an attempt to identify the naturally occurring level of the problem/situation during the time period prior to intervention. Much of the discussion in this book assumes use of a concurrent baseline.

The second type of baseline is the *reconstructed* or *retrospective baseline*. The symbol used is (*A*), to differentiate it from the concurrent baseline symbol, *A*. Essentially, the reconstructed baseline is an attempt to *approximate* the naturally occurring level of the problem/situation by using the client's (or others') memories or recollections of the event or by using specific records of past events when they are available. This type of baseline can be used to supplement a concurrent baseline by presenting a "ball park" understanding of the problem in the recent past, or it can serve as a substitute when concurrent baseline data cannot be gathered.

When you are using a reconstructed baseline as your only baseline, it will serve as a primary source of both assessment data and data for evaluating effectiveness. For example, you may be able to use agency records to develop a reconstructed baseline regarding the number of cases on the waiting list over the past few months with one type of agency program compared to the number of cases on the waiting list after you implement a new type of program.

There are two primary guidelines for use of a reconstructed or retrospective baseline when you are relying primarily on memory. The first is that a reconstructed baseline is best used when the problematic events represent relatively specific, identifiable events. This is because of the obvious difficulties in reproducing events from memory and the possible distortions this may produce. Therefore, events such as number of instances of physical abuse over the past 2 weeks, number of letters received, number of conversations initiated, number of dates, and so on, would be far more desirable to use in reconstructed baselines than events such as "feelings of inadequacy" over the past few months or "affectionate feelings I had last January."

The second guideline is that if the reconstructed baseline is based on memories, the memories used should be from the immediate past—the 2 weeks to a month immediately preceding the beginning of intervention. This presumably would be most helpful not only for assessment purposes, but also when comparing baseline with intervention periods for evaluation purposes. However, try to assess how comfortable the client is in providing this information from memory, maybe confirming some memories by looking at the client's daily calendar. This will help you know how much weight to place on the client's memory and the reconstructed baseline. As a check, you might ask yourself, "Would I be able to remember that?"

Although the reconstructed baseline may not have the precision, nor the accuracy, of the concurrent baseline, when used judiciously and with the awareness of the possibility of distortions due to memory, it can serve as an important aid to practice. In agencies in which brief, crisis-oriented intervention is the norm, and/or in agencies in which contact with clients is limited to one or two instances, the reconstructed baseline might be the baseline of choice.

When a reconstructed baseline is based on archival records, the previous guidelines need not

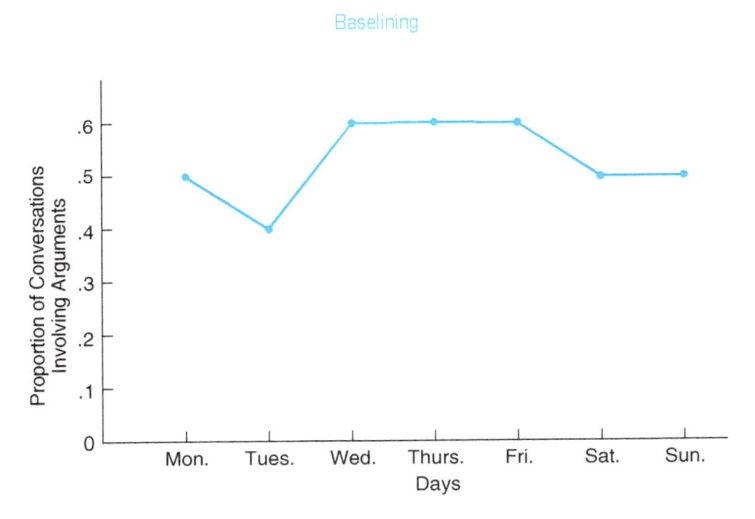

FIGURE 3 Concurrent (prospective) baseline: proportion of conversations involving arguments over 1 week.

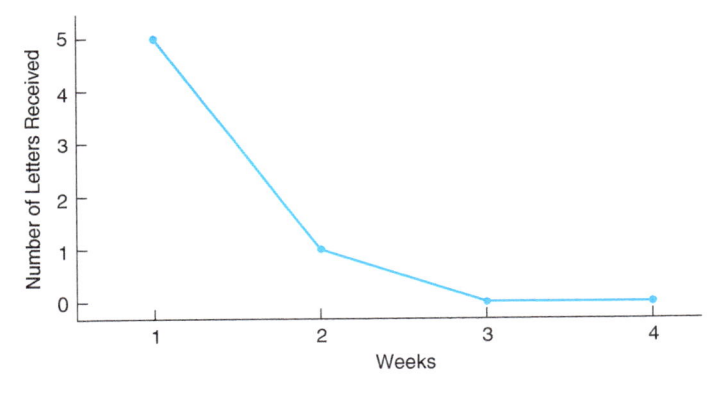

FIGURE 4 Reconstructed (retrospective) baseline based on memory: number of letters received over last month.

apply. This is because those data already have been collected, and memory does not play any part in considerations of accuracy.

Figures 3 through 5 give examples of baselines. Figure 3 is a concurrent baseline collected over time while other assessment activities were being simultaneously conducted. Figure 4 is a reconstructed baseline based on the client's memories, and Figure 5 is a reconstructed baseline using archival records.

HOW LONG SHOULD BASELINING CONTINUE?

One of the most obvious issues you will have to face when collecting the initial concurrent baseline data is how long you (or the client or another party) should continue baselining. That is, when should you stop baselining and begin the intervention period? There are no hard and fast rules on this. However, we can suggest some rough guidelines.

Utility

The principal guideline is derived from the purposes of baselining—helping with both the assessment and the evaluation of progress. Hence, the first guideline is that the baseline should be collected for a period of time long enough to be *useful* in both of these endeavors. The baseline period shouldn't be so brief that it won't be of much help in assessing and evaluating your case/situation. Nor should the baseline period

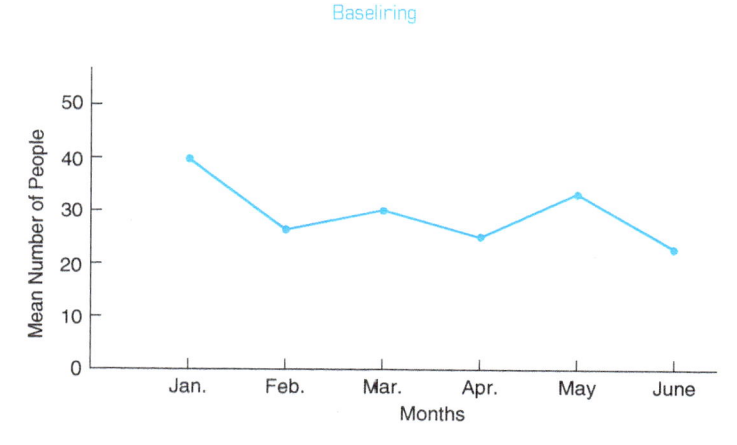

FIGURE 5 Reconstructed (retrospective) baseline using archival records: mean number of people kept on waiting list for more than a week.

continue for too long to the point that additional data are not needed or become irrelevant. If you're thinking that this does not provide a very precise outline of exactly how much data are needed to be useful, you're right. But the principle of utility does help in the development of clearer guidelines. Look at the baseline data you have collected to make the decision on when enough is enough: Do you have a clear and stable picture of the target concern?

Stability

The basic idea of a stable baseline is that once it is graphed, it does not contain any obvious (or unpredictable) cycles or wide fluctuations. Rather, looking at the baseline data allows you to be able to estimate what might happen to the target event in the future. So, look at the baseline data continually, and make a guess as to what will be happening the next time data are collected. If you begin to be regularly close to what you predicted, probably your data are stable enough to proceed with the intervention.

On the other hand, if the baseline data continue to be fluctuating, even after you have spent enough time for them to settle down, it may be that fluctuation is the exact nature of the baseline on this target. Then, you might begin and continue the intervention for a reasonable time, to see if this fluctuation begins to diminish. If it does, good; if not, then reconsider what is going on and whether you have a clear enough picture of the target problem.

Of course, stability in baseline data is preferable to wild fluctuations, so as to be clear about the client problem assessment, and also, to detect changes in that presenting problem during your intervention. The reason for this, as we said before, is that if the baseline is stable, you should be able to predict what is likely to happen to the target over time *without* the intervention. Then the change that does occur will be more obvious and useful in your decisions on next steps for this case. With unstable baseline data, you can't easily predict the future trend and would not be able to tell whether the problem changed on its own, without any effect of your intervention.

Barlow, Nock, and Hersen (2009, pp. 68–72) have presented several baseline patterns that could occur in any set of data, along with suggestions for how to handle those patterns. Figure 6 presents a few of the more basic patterns you are likely to encounter, along with some suggestions on how to handle them in analyzing baseline data.

Figure 6a illustrates a stable baseline that is flat; that is, a baseline in which there are no apparent upward or downward directions in the data. This is the most desirable pattern for a baseline, not only because it is easy to predict the future pattern (the dotted lines) of the problem, but because it shows a relatively constant rate of occurrence of the problem. Therefore, any departure from this flat pattern would stand out, and a positive or negative change would be clear. Furthermore, if there is an absence of effects following introduction of intervention, this should also be clear; the steady state would just continue.

We should point out here that Figure 6a represents what might be called the "classic" stable baseline. Some writers on the subject refer to this (the flat baseline with no upward or downward trend) as the only real stable baseline. However, we have added

Baselining

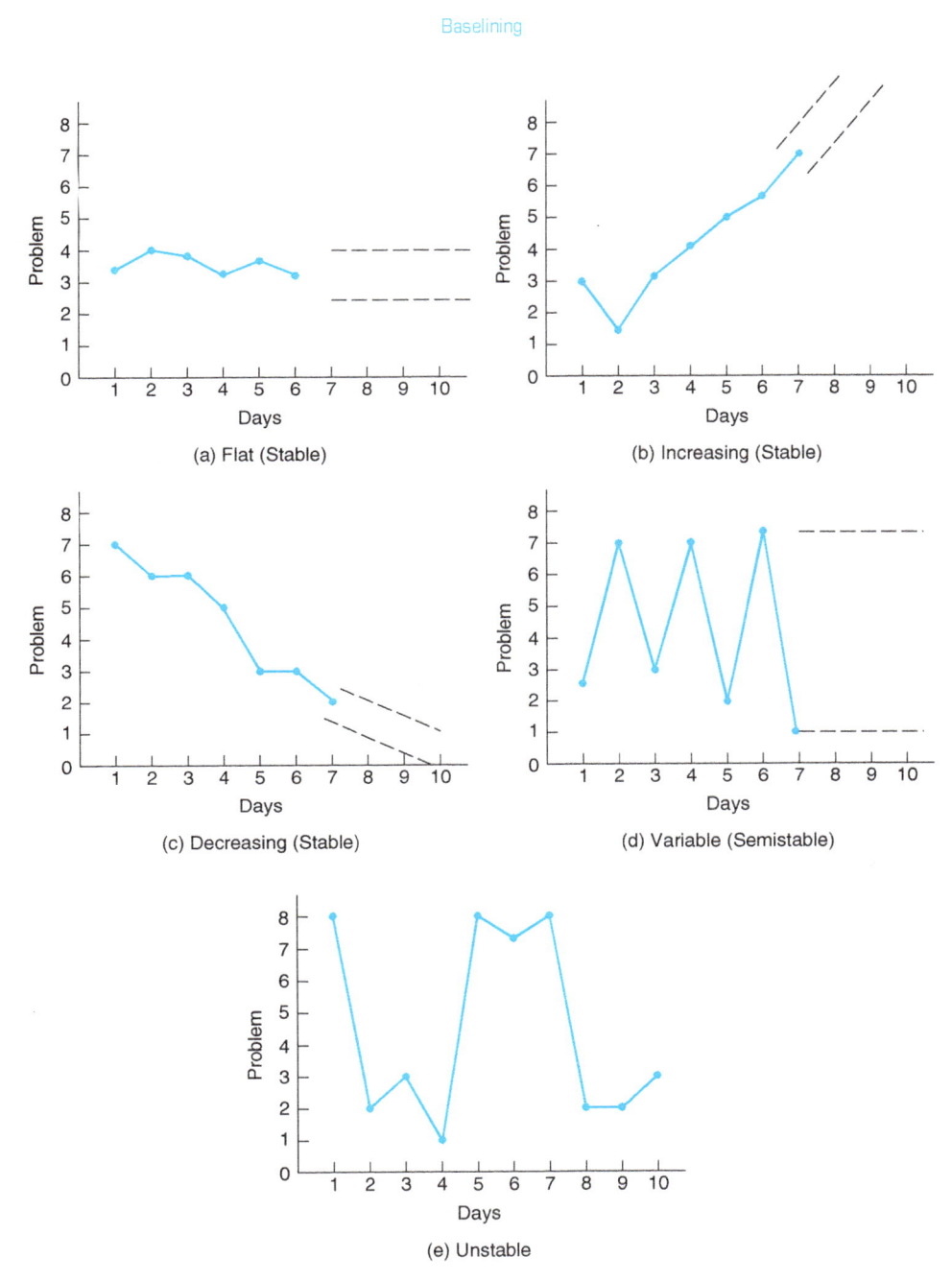

FIGURE 6 Patterns of stability in baseline data.

another dimension to the term stability—the notion of *predictability*. Thus, we maintain that several other baseline patterns (e.g., Figure 6b through 6d) also are stable or at least semi-stable because you still can predict what would happen if the trend detected in the baseline phase continued unchanged. Not everyone would accept our point of view on this point.

The charts in Figures 6b and 6c also show stable baselines because future trends can be predicted (dotted lines). However, these are also baselines with clear patterns or directions (trends) in them, one increasing and one decreasing. If the goal of intervention is to change the direction of the problem (e.g., to decrease the occurrence of a problem when the problem is increasing in the baseline, or vice versa), these baseline patterns are acceptable because any change in the direction of the problem can be noted easily. However, if the pattern in the baseline is already in the direction of improvement, an obvious problem of interpretation is involved. One possibility is to continue to collect baseline data and if the problem is resolved without any intervention, then fine. Or we could continue to collect baseline data until a flatter pattern (with less upward or downward direction) emerges. Another possibility is to implement intervention and then watch to see if the pattern continues at the same rate or decreases (suggesting possibly negative effects of intervention) or increases at an even higher rate, thus suggesting that intervention may have enhanced an effect that might have been occurring anyway.

Incidentally, any dramatic changes in the baseline pattern, especially in the desired direction, could indicate a reactive effect of recording. In such instances it would be desirable to extend the baseline, if possible, to see if this levels out with time, or whether the problem seems to be resolving itself.

A fourth pattern, the variable baseline, is commonly encountered in practice and is illustrated in Figure 6d. We consider this to be a semi-stable baseline because future direction of the problem can be plotted to some extent. But the variability (alternating high and low points) makes it difficult to draw any conclusions with a great deal of certainty. Thus, it might be best to attempt to extend this baseline also until a more stable pattern occurs. It would be even more desirable to try to assess the sources of variability; that is, to try to see if there are patterns in the target problem that can be related to identifiable factors. In this way the intervention plan can focus on those factors apparently associated with the higher occurrence of the problem on certain days or at certain times.

The final baseline pattern, the unstable baseline, is shown in Figure 6e. This pattern is unstable because not only are the data extremely variable, but no patterns can be detected in the data and the future trend of the data is difficult to predict. Again, perhaps the best strategy for dealing with this kind of baseline information is to attempt to collect more data until the pattern somewhat stabilizes, although the strategies described previously also would be possible. Or else, as we noted previously, accept this extreme variability if you have given it ample baseline time to change, then go into the intervention and see if the pattern changes.

In several of the problematic situations described previously we have suggested extending the baseline until stability is achieved; however, there are other strategies for dealing with this problem. The two main ones involve (1) making alterations in the evaluation design at subsequent phases in an attempt to evaluate the effects of the program (e.g., implementing intervention, withdrawing it, and reintroducing it), and (2) using some statistics to try to increase the stability in the baseline data, a technical point that we will discuss later on the topic of transformation of autocorrelated data.

We discussed the desirability of attaining a stable baseline almost as though it is possible to do so every time. However, there are a number of problems that may prevent you from extending a baseline to achieve stability. Two of the most common problems are: (1) You simply may not have the time to extend the baseline (for example, the client may not be able or willing to stay involved in the program or if you are working in an institution, there may even be pressure to discharge the client); and (2) Even more importantly, there may be an ethical problem involved in withholding intervention for an extended period of time just to achieve a stable baseline. This second problem is especially true when the problem results in serious discomfort to the client or others.

In summary, you probably would be best off in trying to develop your own guidelines regarding a decision about how long a baseline should be extended to achieve stability, using the common experiences of other practitioners dealing with similar clients in your agency. In other situations you may not be able to find any satisfactory method of dealing with the instability, and you will just have to learn to live with it. In these situations, any interpretation of changes found once intervention has begun should be done with due caution given your awareness of the instability in the baseline pattern in that you cannot interpret changes between phases with as much clarity as with a stable baseline.

Time

Another way of viewing the problem of how long to collect baseline data is to try to establish a basic guideline regarding the number of baseline observations necessary for the analysis comparing baseline and intervention data, then to try to follow that guideline across most case situations. To that end we offer the following suggestions.

First, the more baseline data, the better to detect change in intervention, up to a point. You can collect baseline data too long, and the target may change naturally, which may mean you have to collect more baseline data. So, try to find a happy medium of a stable or regular pattern at baseline and go onto intervention. We would recommend at least 10 baseline points because with more information, you are less likely to make a mistake, such as concluding that the intervention works when it does not, or concluding that it does not work, when in fact it does. Ten or more baseline points also would be useful for statistical purposes compared to a fewer number of baseline points. However, we are not suggesting that you collect 10 baseline points no matter what the situation in a given case. You must always watch what is ethically and practically possible, taking your cues from the practice situation as the case develops.

Second, if collecting 10 baseline points isn't possible, then try to fit data collection into weekly appointments or meetings, aiming at seven data points. A weekly schedule also gives a picture of the typical pattern of events in the client's week, when some days, maybe the weekend, are more difficult than other days.

Third, collecting information even for 7 days may not be possible. Then we suggest that you aim for at least three baseline points, especially when a clear pattern presents itself among these three. Three points probably is the minimum necessary to establish a trend or directionality, in any set of data. (See Figure 7 as an illustration.) Understand that this is not a desirable number, but it may be a practical or necessary number so as to get on with the intervention. In Figure 7a the problem seems to be occurring at a constant level, so a dramatic change, upward or downward, in the occurrence of the problem once intervention has begun might suggest that the three observations during baseline were sufficient. In Figure 7b the pattern is in the direction of the problem getting worse (e.g., an adolescent's rate of fighting increasing), so if intervention is begun after three observations and it reverses the direction, this would once again suggest that the three observations were sufficient.

Fourth, get whatever baseline information you can, including spending a few moments of your time reconstructing the recent past in terms of the targets, while getting one good example during this interview with your client. There probably will be at least one data point by which you can establish a target to deal with in intervention. You should understand that this is risky, but if you simply cannot get more data, go on to the intervention as necessary. It is possible to come back to a baseline situation after your intervention, a complex topic we'll discuss later.

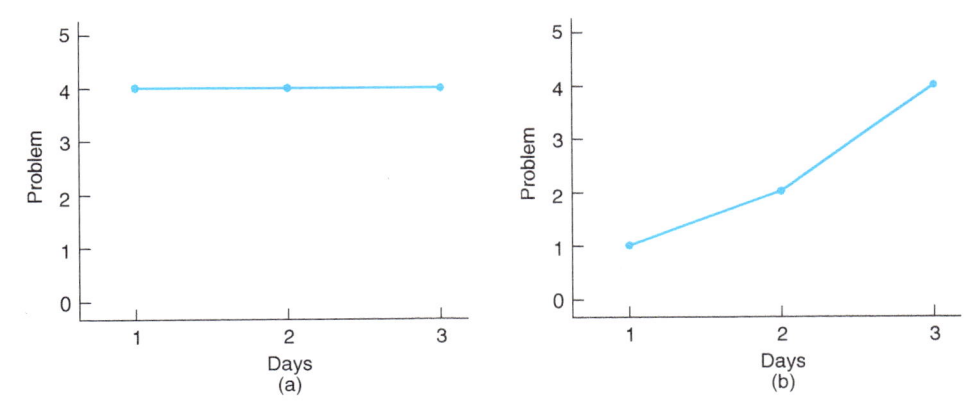

FIGURE 7 Two charts establishing a baseline pattern with only three observations.

Summary of Length of Baselining

There are several ways to determine how long to collect baseline data. All of them should be guided by the principle of utility, plus whatever realistic or ethical concerns may be present in a given case. Most important, it is desirable when possible to collect data until the baseline is relatively stable. Also, if possible, try to collect data for about 10 baseline points. However, what is most desirable may not always be possible, and in some situations it may be necessary to use even fewer baseline points, say, from 3 to 7. It is likely that the number of points necessary and possible will vary from case to case and situation to situation. If one concurrent baseline data point is all that is possible, so be it; try to reconstruct baseline information if that is at all possible. Also, the type of recording method you use may affect the length of baseline. Some methods, such as behavioral observations and individualized rating scales, allow daily observations, thus facilitating relatively brief baselines. Others, such as standardized scales, usually are given to the client only once per week. Do not change your data collection methods from baseline to intervention, such as a daily collection in one and a weekly collection in the other, as this will give you an artificial and incorrect view of the target, especially when you try to compare baseline data against intervention data.

We hope the guidelines we have suggested will help you in making a decision about how long to collect baseline data in each case and situation.

WHEN ARE BASELINES NOT NECESSARY?

Remember, we have always emphasized that the purpose of collecting baseline data and the entire evaluation process is to facilitate practice, not to hinder it. This means there are some fairly common situations in which it may not be necessary to collect baseline data. First, there may not be any time to collect concurrent baseline data. In times of crisis, intervention has to be given as soon as possible. But note, even in emergencies, practitioners need to know what it is they are addressing in order to provide sensible services. Then, after the emergency has passed and the practitioner is writing up casenotes, this would be the time to indicate whether a reconstructed baseline is possible.

A second situation in which no baseline is necessary is one in which the problem situation presents an obvious danger to the client and/or his or her environment. Delaying intervention and collecting baseline data would therefore pose a clear threat to health and safety. Intervention in such a case must be begun immediately to attempt to avoid any further (or impending) harm to anyone involved. In situations such as these a reconstructed baseline might be possible. For example, if the problem involves a mother's complaint that her child doesn't pay attention to her warnings and dashes out into streets with heavy traffic, it might be possible to get the mother's estimate of how often the child does this. However, imagine how ridiculous (not to mention dangerous) it would be to delay intervention so that you could collect a concurrent baseline of how many times the child runs into the street over the next week.

In both of these situations, the assumption that intervention can begin immediately, without the baseline, is based on the idea that the practitioner is, in fact, well prepared to do so. That is, he or she is familiar enough with the case/situation and effective techniques for dealing with it that little assessment time is necessary.

The final situation in which a baseline may not be necessary is when the problem with which you are concerned never occurs. Thus, your goal is to develop and then to increase the occurrence of some behavior, feeling, thought, organizational activity, or what have you. Obviously, if the problem never occurs (and your goal is to get it to occur presumably at some predetermined level), then a baseline would be a waste of time. If Marty, an aged Alzheimer's victim, never speaks, or if the organization seeking funding never admits African Americans, there is no need to spend time collecting information on rate of occurrence during baseline. However, if the client is not quite sure about how often or even whether a problem occurs, conducting a baseline might provide important information for both the practitioner and the client.

ISSUES REGARDING BASELINING

Baselining can be a particularly valuable tool for helping to assess the client/situation and for helping to evaluate your effectiveness. Baseline data can be gathered, with few exceptions, no matter what method of intervention you are using and regardless of the level of intervention (i.e., whether you are dealing with individuals, families, groups, organizations, or communities). However, despite the importance of the baseline period and in addition to some of the problems, there are some issues regarding baselining that bear discussion. Following, drawing especially on the work of Thomas (1978), are some of these issues.

Does Baselining Delay Intervention and Is Delay Detrimental?

Does Baselining Actually Delay Intervention? It seems that in most cases baselining should not delay the intervention program. First, baselining is not conducted outside of the context of the regular assessment. Baselining is conducted, at least in part, to help the assessment and to enhance the decision-making process regarding what intervention techniques to use. While assessment involves more than baselining, assessment and baselining are ordinarily concurrent events. The data collected are considered part of the general assessment data. Hence, under most conditions it is difficult to actually begin the intervention program before the baseline is completed, since a primary basis for selecting the intervention is the baserate information.

A second reason why baselining ordinarily should not delay intervention is that baselining usually does not take very long. As noted earlier in this chapter, usable baseline data points may be as low as one time (combined with a reconstructed baseline derived from that meeting), or even three to seven baseline points, if this is all that can be collected, but 10 baseline points is a more useful number in many case situations.

It is important to note that in most instances the "points" for data collection refer to days. Thus, a typical baseline period might run from 3 to 12 days (i.e., 3 to 12 baseline points), and in many instances it might run approximately 1 week (7 baseline points). It can be assumed that most practitioners have contact with their clients once or twice a week (in some instances, the contacts may be more frequent), and that in most cases at least 1 or 2 weeks are necessary before a systematic intervention program can be selected on the basis of the complete assessment. Moreover, it may be possible to collect information two or more times a day, building up the total number of baseline points. Therefore, not only is this period of time generally necessary for adequate intervention planning, but the period of time required for the baseline is often so short that the baseline per se hardly can be viewed as a major factor delaying the beginning of intervention.

Is Delaying Intervention Detrimental? There are two conditions under which intervention *might* be delayed. Both of these in large part should be decisions that the practitioner and client make on the basis of the assessment. Both of these conditions might actually enhance the outcome of the case rather than harm it. The first condition has to do with lack of stability in the baseline. If, as noted previously, the baseline data are extremely variable, the practitioner and client might want to negotiate an extension of the baseline so that they will be better able to evaluate intervention effects. In this situation the decision to delay intervention is a deliberate one, since the delay will allow for a clearer evaluation of change. A decision such as this is made in the context of the total assessment, and if it is deemed that it would be more important to begin intervention immediately because of the needs of the case, then the decision should be to implement the intervention.

The second instance in which intervention might be delayed also involves a deliberate decision on the part of the practitioner and client. This is a situation in which more assessment information is necessary in order to select the appropriate intervention. As one example, it might be that the first week of baseline *hints* at a pattern that only another week of baseline data could uncover. The success of any intervention obviously depends on selecting the right intervention program. This selection must be grounded in and related to a thorough assessment. It would seem, therefore, that once again a delay caused by the need for better or clearer assessment information can only result in more, rather than less, effective intervention.

There Are Times When Baselines Are Impossible

This statement certainly is often true, and situations in which baselines may be impossible were described earlier in this chapter. However, baseline information may be gathered and may be very useful in many situations in which it *appears* as though no baseline is necessary. The most common area in which this problem may occur is in emergency and crisis situations. For these we have recommended the reconstructed or retrospective baseline. While this is generally a cruder measure than the concurrent baseline, it can help both assessment and evaluation. Furthermore, the reconstructed baseline adds some degree of standardization to your practice so that comparable formats for all cases or situations are available as an aid to demonstrating your accountability.

Targets Often Shift During the Course of Intervention

A client's targets might change in important ways over time (Sorenson, Gorsuch, & Mintz, 1985). New targets might emerge; targets that were important initially might become less important; or targets might become more specific in nature. These changes might occur for different reasons (e.g., increased rapport between you and the client or relevant others, increased knowledge and awareness on the part of the client), but these changes need to be considered to get a complete and accurate picture of a client's targets. Therefore, just as assessment never really ends (you always are collecting information), you shouldn't just determine a client's targets once and then have the same ones measured over time no matter what else happens. You should periodically determine whether the targets have changed, and you should take such changes into account in the measurement of the targets. For example, if new targets emerge, these new targets should be measured and monitored over time.

For evaluation, it would be ideal if the initial set of targets identified for a client stayed the same. When different targets emerge over the course of a single-system evaluation, it becomes more difficult to determine change in targets and the reasons for any changes. For example, suppose that you use a design with a baseline phase followed by an intervention phase, using a specific set of targets elicited from the client at the beginning of baseline. You plan to have the client rate this set of targets on a regular basis during baseline and intervention, and then you'll compare the baseline and intervention ratings to determine change in the targets. If any new targets emerged during the course of intervention, you obviously wouldn't have ratings for them; this would make it difficult to determine the impact of the intervention on the new targets. Nevertheless, you shouldn't just ignore new targets, because you would end up with an incomplete and inaccurate picture of the client's targets.

Often in practice it is discovered that the original target is not appropriate for further work, that new or more urgent targets have emerged, or that the client is more willing to follow an intervention program focused on a problem that is different from the problem on which you currently are working (Thomas, 1978).

With any of these conditions, unless the assumption is that intervention can begin on the day the shifts (or desired shifts) are noted and that a period of adequate assessment and planning is not needed, it would seem the procedural guidelines would be the same as previously described. Under most conditions, effective intervention requires thorough assessment and planning. In such situations, several strategies are possible: (a) you could continue to monitor the old target, continue that intervention, and begin baseline observations on the new problem; (b) you could continue to monitor the old target, but stop or delay the intervention while refocusing most of your attention on the new target (both recording and intervention); (c) you could stop monitoring the old target, but continue the intervention if resources are not stretched too thin; or (d) you could stop monitoring and stop the intervention with the old target because the new one seems a much higher priority, and refocus complete attention on the new problem, including recording and intervention.

People Won't Cooperate in Collecting Baseline Information

It is easy to see why some clients might be reluctant to collect baseline data. It might be seen as delaying efforts to resolve the problem, as being silly or childish, or as being busywork. In large part we view reluctance to baseline—or, actually, to participate in any recording—as a function of how you present it to the people whom you want to record. If you present baselining with confidence and clarity, if you explain that it is built into the overall assessment process as regularly as a medical person builds in the need to monitor blood pressure, and if you emphasize the overall importance of baselining to intervention planning and evaluation, then we believe that most of the battle already will be won. As you probably can tell, we believe that the recorder's commitment to collecting baseline data may largely be a reflection of your own commitment.

We don't mean to suggest that it is always a simple task to get people to cooperate. In all cases, we urge you to use the guidelines for increasing the client's cooperation to record. We firmly believe that when baselining is explained to clients as not necessitating any particular delay in problem solving, and when you carefully select one of the measures so the recorder will see its relevance and be willing to use it, baselining will become as common and comfortable in your practice as any other aspect of your approach.

What If the Problem Improves During the Baseline?

There are some circumstances during which you might either see some improvement in the problem during the baseline, or where the client claims there is improvement (even though the baseline data don't show it). Related to this is a more subtle issue: the concern among many practitioners that the very fact that they have made contact with the client and perhaps developed some rapport during the baseline may improve the problem compared to the prebaseline period, making it less likely to produce clear changes in the intervention period, since those changes already took place during the baseline.

It is important to acknowledge at the outset that there may indeed be observable changes during the baseline period, and/or changes between the prebaseline and baseline periods. Of course, the possibility always exists that the changes are due to reactivity. We offered several suggestions for dealing with this problem there, including possibly extending the baseline (since the effects of reactivity often are short-lived).

Another way to evaluate this situation is to develop a reconstructed baseline for a period of a few weeks prior to the concurrent baseline as a way of comparing any differences between the two periods. This will produce at least a rough idea of the nature of those changes and what the practitioner has to do to enhance them during the actual intervention period.

But the essence of this whole issue as we see it lies in our definition of what intervention really means. We defined intervention as a formal, systematic, clearly defined, and planned activity geared toward improving the problem/situation. At the heart of the definition is the distinction between accountable professional practice and what nonprofessionals may do to alleviate problems. It is our belief that, even if the problem does improve during the baseline due to rapport, effects of the relationship, or other nonspecific factors of professional–client contact, the professional can and must go beyond these effects in producing changes due to his or her formal intervention program. In other words, the very nature of professional intervention—its identification as a formal program to change a problem/situation—means that it generally should build on and go beyond the relationship between the practitioner and client. We know that in some cases, the relationship may be all we can offer to the client, and it may even be sufficient (see Bohart & Greenberg, 1997, for a recent review of research on empathy). But the huge array of intervention technologies available to the helping professions and the considerable research on this topic strongly suggest that we, as professionals, should be able to demonstrate that our interventions have a clear effect over and above that which might be accomplished during an assessment/baseline and even rapport-building phase of contact with the client.

Summary

This chapter has presented basic principles and procedures of baselining. We first described the two basic purposes of baselining as helping you in your assessment of the case/situation and aiding you in evaluating the outcome. We briefly discussed the two major types of baselines, concurrent/prospective and reconstructed/retrospective, and the differences in their use. The next section discussed issues regarding how long baselining should be continued and the principles for deciding this, which involve utility, stability, and selecting a period of time using several guidelines. We also discussed the situations in which baselines may not be necessary. The chapter concluded with a review of some of the basic issues involving baselining.

FROM THE CASE STUDY TO THE BASIC SINGLE-SYSTEM DESIGN: *A-B*

PURPOSE This chapter discusses basic designs, from the traditional case study, which draws its subjective conclusions from simultaneous observation and intervention, to the first, basic single-system design, the *A-B* design. The *A-B* design has a clear baseline and intervention phase to make a more or less objective determination as to whether a change has occurred in the target problem. We recommend that, at a minimum, this basic *A-B* design be used with every case/situation.

Introduction
Case Studies or Predesigns
    Design *A*: Observation Only |A|
    Design (*B*): Intervention Only ||(B)
    Design *B*: The Case Study (Simultaneous Intervention and Observation) ||(B)
    Design *B-C*: Changes in the Case Study ||B|C
    Strengths of the Case Study Method
    Limitations of the Case Study Method
    Recommendations Regarding Case Study Methods
    Case Illustrations
    Introducing the Client to the Case Study

Design *A-B*: The Basic Single-System Design |A|B
    Strengths of the *A-B* Design
    Limitations of the *A-B* Design
    Recommendations Regarding the *A-B* Design
    Case Illustrations
    Aggregating *A-B* Designs
    Introducing the Client to the Basic Single-System Design
Summary

From Chapter 13 of *Evaluating Practice: Guidelines for the Accountable Professional*, Sixth Edition. Martin Bloom, Joel Fischer, John G. Orme. Copyright © 2009 by Pearson Education, Inc. All rights reserved.

INTRODUCTION

All single-system designs are constructed from two basic elements arranged in different ways for different purposes. One or more intervention periods are usually combined with one or more baselines (nonintervention periods) in order to develop conclusions about changes in the target problem and, possibly, the effects of the intervention on that problem. In this, we describe a number of designs and the strengths and limitations they exhibit. We also give our recommendations for the use of each design, as well as some suggestions for presenting them to clients.

This chapter discusses three topics, the first of which is case studies. These are not formal evaluation designs. They do not permit planned comparisons among phases of service. We discuss them because they are both historically important as precursors to true evaluation designs, and because they are still commonly used as if they provided objective information. We call these case studies "predesigns," meaning that they may contain one or another of the basic elements of a true evaluation design, but they do not integrate all of the vital elements.

The second topic in this chapter involves the basic single-system design, the A-B design, which we believe is a major evaluation tool for helping professionals because it permits a logical comparison of an intervention with a nonintervention period for the same client or client-system. This is the minimal arrangement of components that allows for a more or less objective assessment of the client situation before and during (or after) intervention. With the A-B design we can determine whether there was a difference between the A and the B sets of data.

A third topic of this chapter deals with elaborations of the A-B design as can be seen in the case studies we present. Our reason for introducing these designs is to emphasize that the A-B design is very flexible and can be extended or combined in creative ways to meet the needs of practice situations.

One last introductory word: We describe a large number of cases, adapted from the literature and also from our practice and students' practice, using various designs to illustrate the basic principles. Almost none of them will be "textbook perfect" because they are taken from real practice. These cases serve an important function, showing how these principles may be creatively adapted to fit particular practice circumstances. Where possible, we note the ways in which deviations from some of the principles could affect conclusions or interpretations of the data.

CASE STUDIES OR PREDESIGNS

Design A: Observation Only |A|

Design (B): Intervention Only | |(B)

Within the category of case study designs, we can distinguish those observations only [A –] and immediate interventions [– B] from true designs that offer planned comparisons needed to make logical deductions about changes in target problems. Let's begin with the situation in which only observations are made; we label this predesign A, meaning that only measurement or observation has taken place, with no intervention as such following. For example, a person may be admitted to a psychiatric hospital simply for observation. A child may be monitored after a traumatic event (e.g., the death of a parent). Therefore, this predesign may provide useful information about the need for intervention, especially if careful measurement procedures are used.

In addition, helping professionals may come in contact with persons seeking information. The intake interview may clarify enough for the would-be client to enable him or her to carry on without further services, even though the practitioner thought additional services might be useful. What is essentially information collection for the practitioner may be the stimulus for personal action on the part of the client, a point to which we will return shortly.

We can identify another variation of case study designs in which only intervention occurs. We will describe this as predesign (B), meaning an intervention or (B) phase that did not include concurrent observation or measurement as a planned concomitant to the intervention. The parentheses around (B) indicate a reconstruction of the observation or measurement aspect, together with the action. The most typical occasion for this would be in an emergency situation in which, for example, a bleeding person prompts a passerby to deliver first aid. This is not a pure case, for first aid properly given involves a quick survey of the entire situation, first, so as not to hurt the victim in one place while trying to help in another, and second, so as not to overlook other needs. However, this can be done very quickly, so the major emphasis is on immediate, temporary relief until medical help can be summoned.

Some forms of clinical intervention may also involve immediate assessment and immediate action, such as when a shy, unassertive client, who is having difficulty getting deserved promotions, tries to tell the therapist what she sees as the substantive problem, and the therapist begins to address her problem as expressed in metacommunication terms, that is, the way she sounds—too unassertive, too passive in a situation calling for more assertive behavior. Again, as with good first aid, there is some quick assessment of the situation, although it may be based more on what the theory says people *should* be like than on relevant background characteristics. For example, some regional ways of speaking involve slow, soft speech that might easily be interpreted as unassertive behavior upon first hearing them.

We want to emphasize the limitations of these *A*-only and (*B*)-only formats, since they tend to underlie a natural inclination of beginners to ask questions without real purpose or to "do something" without understanding what needs to be done, in what order, and by whom. The examples used for predesign *A* do not involve simply asking questions for the sake of asking questions; such questioning ordinarily is well-planned, although the plan is not necessarily visible to the persons being questioned. Likewise, taking immediate action against some visible wound may divert attention from more lethal problems that are less visible. For these parallel reasons we will take a strong stand that the basic single-system design, the *A-B*, with its planned attention both to systematic observations and intervention is the minimum basis of scientific practice. A careful baseline and a clear intervention are the minimum components of good service.

Basically, these observation-only and intervention-only formats quickly merge into the next type of design, the case study, labeled *B*, in which there is some degree of simultaneous intervention and observational assessment.

Design *B*: The Case Study (Simultaneous Intervention and Observation) |B

By case study we mean the simultaneous intervention and observation (recording) performed by a helping professional. This is labeled *B* and should be distinguished from the (*B*) situation in which, in principle, intervention occurs without formal, systematic observations. An important variation occurs when the practitioner uses two or more interventions at the same time, *BC*, each with its own distinctive intervention but sharing a common observational assessment.

Barlow, Nock, and Hersen (2009) suggest that historically the case study was a means by which practitioners communicated their successes on a case to their colleagues. From these communications, "schools" of practice were formed in a tradition that dates back at least as far as the days of Hippocrates, who first described his cases—successes as well as failures. Freud, for example, presented cases to illustrate his theory, although he went far beyond these cases to conceptually reconstruct the dynamics involved. The case study method dominated clinical practice for the first half of the last century and is still widely used in agencies as tools for continuing development of staff.

The core of the case study method is a careful study of the presenting condition viewed within whatever context is deemed appropriate. For the psychoanalyst, the context is the client's symbolic reconstruction of perceived relationships and events. For some social workers and community psychologists, the context may be the relationship of the individual client to his or her physical and social environments. Whatever standardization emerges through study of the case comes from the theoretical perspective under which it is constructed.

However, this has sometimes led to the parochial reasoning that practitioners are obliged to see and to treat the kinds of factors that a given theory considers important to the relative exclusion of those to which the theory does not attribute causal force. In short, the case study method could be an invitation to biased perceptions if the practitioner is not absolutely scrupulous about the openness with which he or she views clients and their problems. This is a difficult balancing act. Further, the case study does not allow systematic comparison between a nonintervention and intervention period. Thus, the case study method has a mixed reputation among practitioners and researchers.

Design B-C: Changes in the Case Study |B|C

One important extension of the case study is the addition of other interventions in a separate phase. Because the case study (in contrast to the intervention-only format) includes observational assessments, the B-C "design" has two consecutive sets of observational data. This permits the practitioner to make some additional judgments about changes in the client from phase to phase beyond those possible in the more limited case study, since he or she has two sets of data points. This still does not permit the practitioner to have a baseline or nonintervention comparison, although if, after the first intervention, there doesn't appear to be much change in the client, the B period is sometimes used as if it were a baseline period. However, if the client seems to have made progress (or has deteriorated), it is difficult to use a B-C format to make judgments about change or factors possibly affecting that change in the target problem because of possible order effects because there is no baseline or nonintervention period.

Sometimes practitioners use, in effect, a B-C-D-E-F . . . format, changing the intervention program during each contact with the client. The more changes that appear, the more difficult it is to sort out what is happening, since not enough time is usually given for the problem to stabilize during any one phase, and the more difficult it is to know what are possible causal factors. At this point, applying design principles to practice may not benefit the practitioner, because the picture becomes somewhat confused. On the other hand, there are situations where the practitioner tries one intervention to see how it works, and then turns to another intervention if the first one does not seem to have any effect. This may continue through several interventions.

Strengths of the Case Study Method. On the positive side, writers such as Barlow, Nock, and Hersen (2009), Stiles (2006), Browning and Stover (1971), Lazarus and Davison (1971), and Kazdin (1992), although in slightly different contexts, make the following types of observations. First, the case study "method" can foster clinical speculation and innovation because it is easily administered in just about any situation. Second, this method can cast light (or doubt) on a theoretical or empirical assumption or prediction by giving immediate feedback through testing that idea in practice. Third, the case study method can help to develop or to refine technical skills by close connection between practice techniques and their evaluation. Fourth, case studies permit the investigation of rare phenomena without having to collect large amounts of data from many persons. Fifth, case studies may be transitional experiences for some practitioners; the subjective information purposely collected in these approaches represents an introduction and perhaps a stimulus to use of more rigorous single-system designs. The hunches they generate and subjectively test are the same hunches that may be put to more exacting investigation.

Limitations of the Case Study Method. The case study method has a number of weaknesses and limitations. First, frequently several techniques are administered at the same time, making it difficult for the practitioner to tease out the active ingredients so as to benefit the next phase of intervention—using just the most effective intervention—and to be of use for future case situations. Second, the practitioner is often casual in specifying problems and in measuring those problems to see if changes occur. This leads to a strong bias in favor of interpreting events in terms of how a theory predicts the events will turn out as opposed to more empirically-based observations. Third, there is typically little validity or reliability-checking in case studies, making it difficult for others to use the same procedures in the same way. The case study method doesn't provide any impetus to challenge desired outcomes for alternative explanations as to why they turned out as they did. Fourth, case studies rarely are systematic, nor do they follow clear guidelines regarding measurement, design, or analysis. From the point of view of the canons of logic, case study methods are grossly lacking in power to make appropriate empirical observations, let alone causal inferences, and there are few solid benchmarks even to indicate whether change actually occurred. Primarily, this is because baseline/intervention comparisons are not used in case studies.

Recommendations Regarding Case Study Methods. There is no question that the case study method is a weak evaluation design if one considers it an evaluation design at all. As a *practice* design it may be fruitfully used in developing testable ideas in clinical as well as community practice. However, testable ideas also can be developed in the designs we will soon describe, so we suggest that if the case study method is used at all, it should be used as a temporary device until you are able to identify specific problems and set up clear measurement procedures for them. By making use of the suggestions offered in this book, we think that it is fully possible to do the specifying and measuring almost immediately. Therefore, we recommend leaving the case study approaches as methods of last resort (as during an emergency situation) or as very temporary approaches.

Case Illustrations. The first illustration is adapted from the case records of a family service agency dealing with people in the armed services and their families.

Mrs. D. came into the office greatly upset because she hadn't heard from her son in over 2 months. He is in the army, stationed in Germany for the past 9 months. He had established a pattern of writing a letter home each week until about 2 months ago when letters stopped. Mrs. D. has written a dozen letters imploring her son to write to her. She has not called him due to the expense (and also because she is intimidated by the thought of long-distance overseas calls). Her medical problems (ulcers) are acting up because of this situation, and she was told by a friend that we might do something to help. I told her that I would look into the situation and call her back soon. After Mrs. D. left, I confirmed her information about her son's location in Germany and sent an email to the base commander. I received a return email from the chief medical officer informing me that Private D. was injured in a serious auto accident 2 months ago. The medical officer requested that I inform the family that their son was now out of danger and was recuperating. I emailed back to set up a long-distance telephone call between mother and son and then called Mrs. D. with this information.

In this type of situation, one in which there would likely be contact with the client (Mrs. D.) only once or twice, there is little time to collect much information. The practitioner's task is quite clear: to find out the information and then to transmit it sensitively to the mother while helping her to make further contact with the son. These activities and goals are quite specific; either they were achieved or not. The measured target behavior—numbers of letters written for a period of time—initially could only be reconstructed from the conversation with the client. This target behavior was later reconfirmed by the medical officer, a reliability check of sorts. Thus, even with a case study with very limited information, it is possible to make certain types of evaluations (Bloom, Butch, & Walker, 1979). Figure 1 presents these data as an example of a reconstructed baseline, turning this basically simple case study into a somewhat more developed *A-B* design. This case is also an illustration of one way of dealing with limited-contact cases.

A second example of a case study illustrates a common practice phenomenon, *changing the intervention* (design *B-C*). Tenants in a public housing project organized an informal committee to appeal to the city to repair the apartment complex and to have better garbage pickup and pest control. A social work student was interning at this housing project and aided the neighbors in organizing their thoughts and presenting them to the Department of Housing at City Hall (phase *B*). Individual tenants made brief speeches about the conditions of their apartments or the problems they faced with garbage and pests. These presentations did not appreciably affect services, so after a period of time the committee met to consider stronger measures. At the suggestion of the student, they took pictures of the apartments and the grounds and invited the mayor and his deputies to join them at a press conference they were going to call, in which they would display the pictures and have the tenants tell their stories to the local television station and newspapers

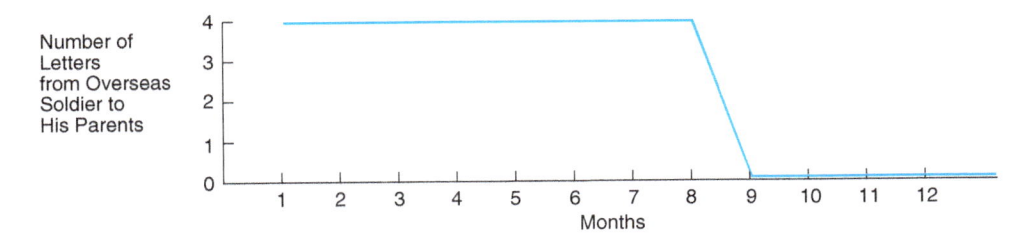

FIGURE 1 Reconstructed baseline data for the Mrs. D case.

[Adapted from "Evaluation of Single Interventions" by M. Bloom, P. Butch, & D. Walker, 1979, *Journal of Social Service Research, 2*, pp. 301–310.]

(phase *C*). The mayor called the Department of Housing, and they met with the committee in a special meeting *before* the scheduled press conference. Concrete actions that met many of the tenants' demands followed from that session.

In this situation the action component took priority over any formal measurement process. However, one might argue that the photographs constitute a "before" picture that could have been compared with photographs of the same places "after" the city took action. Note that there were two relatively discrete actions, a *B* and a *C* intervention, to use our formal terms. The first was the tenant groups making individual presentations to the Department of Housing, and the second was a concerted effort to influence the city services by a tenant group going through the mass media. It apparently seemed superfluous at first to the tenants and the student to collect objective information for evaluation. Yet, it was apparently the existence of this information (such as the pictures) together with the ability to act collectively on this information (through the mass media) that started some reaction to their requests. Clear information is needed for effective and accountable services.

Introducing the Client to the Case Study. How might you tell the client or another participant in a case study that you are going to make simultaneous observational assessments along with the intervention? The question is raised at this early stage of discussion about evaluation designs because the ethical implications are fully present throughout our discussions of single-system designs (as well as throughout all of research). Clients have the right to know what is going to happen to them, whether information is going to be collected, and how it is going to be used. As soon as observational assessments or measurements are made and records are kept, the client has a right to know about it.

In addition to the ethical reasons, most clients expect that what they say and the context of their lives will be carefully examined in order to enable the practitioner to help. Clients may not know the exact form of these data, nor how they are collected, but they generally recognize that effective service requires good information. They may also know that such information possibly could be used against them in situations in which case records may be used by public officials under certain legal conditions. So it is important for you to clarify the existence of information collection and its specific use. How can this be done?

We make some recommendations here for introducing the case study to the client that also will be useful in presenting other designs, but each design will require some special discussion concerning its particular format. We add to these recommendations at each stage. To begin with, we suggest four types of statements that could be made, each with its own individual expression for the particular circumstances of the client or situation, including when the client-system is a family, a group, a neighborhood, or any of the various receivers of professional services. Sometimes persons other than clients are involved in collecting data. These other persons—say, relevant others—also could be called "mediators" or "recorders" (any person other than the client who collects data on the problem).

1. *"I want to understand your situation so I can be helpful to you.* You (the client or the mediator) know the situation very well, but I have to ask questions until I understand what is happening and how you feel about it."

2. *"I need clear facts in order to be most helpful.* Even though the situation may be clear to you (the client or the mediator), it may not be clear to others who are involved. So I am going to be asking factual questions, such as how many or how often, in order to get as clear a picture of the situation as possible. It is similar to a medical person using a thermometer to get the facts about your temperature, even though you are sure you have a fever. Some of the questions I will be asking will be like a social thermometer in order to get the facts about your personal or social situation."

3. *"I will share these facts with you continuously,* both to check them with you and to keep you informed about the basis of my suggestions for you. Please tell me if I am wrong about anything."

4. *"I will build my plans for helping you based on these facts, and I will also modify these plans as the factual information changes over time.* I will be gathering information throughout the time we are together because this is how I'll know if we are moving in the right directions. It will also help us in knowing when our work together isn't needed anymore, that is, when you have resolved the problems that brought you here."

DESIGN *A-B*: THE BASIC SINGLE-SYSTEM DESIGN A|B

The *A-B* design is often seen as the foundation of single-system designs because of the basic distinction between, and the combining of, a baseline observation period, *A*, and an intervention period, *B*. The *A-B* design and single-system designs in general are fundamentally different from the case study in a number of important ways. Single-system designs involve planned use of a formal evaluation design, clear measurement rules, explicit analytic procedures, and clear identification of an intervention program, including when intervention starts and when it is completed. Single-system designs, in contrast to case studies, are generally more systematic and rigorous in the observation of events and in the analysis of the resulting data. Intervention is ordinarily not undertaken in single-system designs until baseline observations are made, and then this information is used as part of the ongoing process of selecting and planning the intervention and evaluating the practice.

The assumption underlying the *A-B* design is that the problems observed during baseline will likely continue in the same pattern if no changes are made in the system of forces acting on these problems. However, the intervention is a planned change seeking to modify the problematic events in a desired direction. Thus, the practitioner can compare the extent to which the problem occurs after the intervention with the pattern of problematic events existing before the intervention. The *A-B* design can clearly indicate whether any changes in problematic behaviors occurred. Certain analyses can determine whether such changes in patterns of events could have happened by chance alone. This becomes important information in practice decisions on whether to continue or to modify the intervention, as we will discuss later.

The *A* phase of the *A-B* design refers to the nonintervention/observation period. This *A* phase can take many forms, depending on the theory of or approach to practice being used and the nature of the events being observed, using the measures described in Part II of this book. All of the study or assessment methods used in this phase share one attribute: they seek to obtain information without changing the events in the process, that is, without being reactive. This goal is attained only to a degree as we discuss near the end of this chapter. However, in principle, just about all theories of practice attempt to obtain accurate information about the client and problem—the assessment proper—in order to take knowledgeable action.

The *B* phase of the *A-B* design refers to an intervention period along with the continued collection of data. These data are collected on the same targets, using the same time intervals, and with the same measures as used in the *A* phase. We have stated previously that the single-system design is theory-independent, in the sense that any intervention may be evaluated within the workings of single-system designs. Also, the more specific the intervention, the more clearly it can be evaluated. That is why we urge practitioners to be clear and specific about defining what interventions are employed. However, we are not suggesting that you get so minutely quantitative as to lose sight of the conceptual entity you are seeking to influence. "Family therapy" is awfully broad and nebulous as an intervention when the target is, say, communication problems between a teenager and a stepparent. Both the nature of the target and more specific interventions must be identified in order to really affect the specific target as well as to have an evaluation of the process that makes any sense to the practitioner. For example, persisting arguments over expenditures of money might be one target under consideration, and hours stayed out on weekends might be another. The intervention method might be limited to Functional Family Therapy (Sexton, Gilman, & Johnson-Erickson, 2005, pp. 116–119) in this case, or more specific kinds of communication training in others. In short, be as specific in stating what the evidence-based intervention is as you are in defining the problem.

Interventions may differ in scope and still be encompassed by the single-system design. It may be that one specific event has to be altered, such as training the nursing home staff to refer to Mrs. Willowby by her last name (and not by her first name) and to have discussions with her about the setting and current events as subtle reality prompters for an elderly person showing signs of memory loss. Or, the intervention can involve rearranging an entire social context, such as when Mr. Axton was admitted to the long-term care facility after a stroke left him paralyzed on the right side.

The process of helping involves the development of an intervention plan based on sound information about the client. Plans for measurement related to the success or failure of that intervention plan should be closely related to it. There must be agreement between the intervention plan and the outcomes selected for measurement; the various types of observations and measures taken must relate to the targeted conditions in the case and to the interventions used to modify those targets; that is, there should be a logical and reasonable relationship among the target problem, the measures, and the intervention. The *A-B* design provides time for the practitioner to think through carefully what the problems appear to be and what specific interventions may be selected to deal with them.

Strengths of the *A-B* Design

This basic single-system design is widely applicable to most types of problems and settings, as well as to all levels of intervention (i.e., from individuals to communities). It is the "work horse" of practice evaluation for reasons that are not hard to identify. Foremost among these is that *A-B* designs can reveal clearly whether there has been an actual change in target events, providing both monitoring and evaluation information. This is vital information that can lead to a number of practitioner reactions; *monitoring* of ongoing events lets the practitioner know whether to continue a given intervention, or whether to modify it one way or another, or whether to completely change it to another intervention. As an *evaluation* device, the *A-B* design provides information to the practitioner and to the client about outcome, and also provides information to the agency and to society at large. This evaluation function has some limitations, as we shall see, but any more rigorous evaluation design begins with these *A-B* characteristics.

As part of its systematic observations, the *A-B* design also can be helpful in the study or assessment phase of interacting with clients. One impetus that evaluation has on practice may be to seek more operational understanding of the presenting problems, not only to be able to measure them, but because greater specificity means greater clarity in developing relevant intervention plans. Further, we strongly recommend that the basic *A-B* design be elaborated upon by adding maintenance and follow-up phases and that are illustrated in some of the subsequent case studies, to be certain the improvements obtained in the *B* phase do not disappear over time.

The *A-B* design is the simplest logical structure permitting a planned comparison between the two key elements of the evaluation, the nonintervention period and the intervention period. Differences that emerge between the baseline and the events during and after intervention provide a very tentative look at possible causal factors. A key question is whether the intervention caused the observed change. Unfortunately, most of the time, this basic design cannot exclude a number of logical alternatives that could account for the observed results. These alternative explanations, such as the internal validity threat of history, but the point here is that obtaining such empirical results may prompt you to ask other questions that can be answered better by more rigorous designs. Not only can the practitioner using the *A-B* design flexibly adapt to new events emerging during intervention, but he or she can use other designs that consist of additions to the *A-B* arrangement that will begin to answer causal questions. Whether you add a whole new interventive phase, *C*, to the *A-B* design, or whether you begin another set of observations and interventions on a different problem to see whether this problem might be a controlling influence on the first problem, the comparison between baseline and intervention is the underlying theme.

Limitations of the *A-B* Design

In some ways the limitations of this basic single-system design are the converse of its strengths. Most important is that the *A-B* design can provide clear information only on whether there are changes in the problem between baseline and intervention. The *A-B* design *appears* to, but does not necessarily, provide strong evidence about whether the intervention *caused* the observed change. This is an important point, so let's examine it more closely. It is easy to assume that if there is one different event (the intervention) introduced into a stable set of events (the baseline condition of the target problem), then the different event caused the observed change. This, in fact, may very well be so, particularly when that different event was part of a planned program and when all other alternative explanations can absolutely be ruled out. However, to twist an old saying, people tend to accept any apparent cause in the hand rather than look for alternative causes in the bush. Scientists tend to beat the bushes for alternative explanations to be certain that they possess valid causal information. The *A-B* design does not let you rule out many alternative explanations for why the results occurred as they did. If Mrs. Willowby begins to regain her memory for persons, places, and time, we would like to infer that this was caused by the reality orientation program the staff engaged in. However, the *A-B* design doesn't exclude the fact that there may also have been a simultaneous change in her diet or other activities that may have had something to do with her improved cognitive functioning. With any *A-B* design, an event outside the intervention, even a change in season, which occurs at the same time as the intervention, could be responsible for observed changes.

Thus, we can't automatically assume the changes were due to our efforts. The *A-B* design is very simple. In essence, all that it clearly reveals is that there has been a change in a given problem. If the intervention program is complex, that is, if it contains several techniques at the same time, the *A-B* design also doesn't permit us to know which one or which combinations were more influential. Also, when focused only on a single problem, this design may not provide enough information on the event in question or on the related events that may be changing to provide a clear picture of the client/problem configuration. This is the reason we suggested multiple measures of problems so as to capture a broad or holistic view of the significant dimensions of the client/situation. Neither one evaluation nor any finite set of evaluations can fully express the complexity of human lives. However, obtaining meaningful data on one event can lead the practitioner to think that he or she has a strong hold on the full picture, which may lead to a false sense of security.

A fundamental limitation on any design that has a baseline concerns the question of whether intervention has already begun once the practitioner begins to ask questions of the client. Hasn't there been an effect on the client already by his or her simply being seen by someone for help? Won't the client think he or she is being "treated" when the practitioner asks pertinent questions? And won't the relationship inevitably have some effect on client functioning?

It is true that there may be detectable differences in the client's feelings, thoughts, or behaviors when he or she first comes to the practitioner. However, if we keep our focus on the client's specific problems rather than on nonrelated or nonspecific factors, then we may have another picture. The most important consideration is whether the target problem changes and this requires a baseline perspective that may or may not be independent of talking with the practitioner. The client may feel better or more relieved to be in contact with a professional helper, and this may even be reflected in other situations, but whether this contact has fundamentally affected the target problem is the real issue. Moreover, the nonspecific, possibly reactive, effects of the baseline contacts probably will diminish over time as the novelty wears off and the hard work of solving problems emerges as the main task. Thus, the main issue is not whether there has been a change in the problem when comparing the reconstructed level of the problem prior to baseline with the baseline data. Rather, the key question is whether the level of the problem that *is* occurring during the baseline can be reduced *further* in the intervention period after a formal intervention plan is implemented. In other words, has the goal been attained and the problem removed?

A final issue with the *A-B* design is that it ends, obviously, on a *B* phase. Technically, this means that it is impossible to know whether the changes that occurred in the *B* phase actually endured beyond your contact with the client. (This is exactly the same problem that occurs with *any* design that ends with a *B* phase.) Many times the *A-B* design appears to be incomplete as a record of change. Of course, a solution is obvious, and that is to add both maintenance and follow-up phases, using the notation for those phases; you will then have as complete a record of each case as you could have when using the *A-B* design.

Recommendations Regarding the *A-B* Design

There is a tendency among some practitioners and researchers to play down the *A-B* design because it doesn't permit the functional analyses about causality that more complex designs do permit. However, we take a strong stand with this key single-system design because it is basic, it is fully within the reach of every practitioner with every client and problem, and it provides a great deal of vital information to the practitioner.

In particular, the *A-B* design is most adaptable to the almost infinite variety of circumstances in which practitioners find themselves as a way of clearly indicating whether change in target problems has occurred. If used in addition to stimulate use of more rigorous designs that can tease out causal relationships, then the *A-B* design will have made a very important contribution to our clients *and* our professions. In comparison to the case study methods that easily fall into self-fulfilling prophecies, this key single-system design provides the basic foundation and the fundamental building block for a large array of logical ways of inferring causal efficacy of the intervention. We strongly urge you to consider adding maintenance and follow-up phases to the basic *A-B* design to facilitate better understanding of whether positive changes were enduring or not. However, because of its practicality and flexibility for use with all theoretical orientations, *we recommend the use of the A-B design—particularly with maintenance and follow-up phases—as the basic single-system design for practice.*

Case Illustrations

The first illustration of an *A-B* design is adapted from a study by Engel, Jensen, and Schwartz (2004). We will make these first examples of each evaluation design as clear as possible—what we call textbook "perfect"—and then other case examples will introduce bits and pieces of reality that require adaptations in order to achieve something like the "pure" design.

Chronic pain is one of the most difficult conditions for humans to bear, so when a new technology emerges that may offer some relief, it is worth exploring the possibilities. Engels, Jensen, and Schwartz (2004) examined the outcome of a biofeedback-assisted relaxation for chronic pain in three adults with cerebral palsy. The first participant got little relief from the procedure, while the second two indicated on their pain ratings that they found some relief. We have chosen to present only one case (participant 2) to illustrate the *A-B* design, even though the authors represented their study as a multiple-baseline design.

Participant 2 was a 35-year-old female who experienced constant mild-to-severe low back pain. She was employed 20 hours a week in a desk job, but needed assistance for routine activities of daily living. Her pain was aggravated by ordinary activities. All participants received thorough medical examinations before the study began. The baseline (*A*) for this study involved use of an individualized rating scale involving the collection of information in a "pain diary" in which the client recorded once at the end of the day using a scale ranging from 0 (no pain) to 10 (pain as bad as it could be). Baseline data were collected for 25 days, and while there are fluctuations in these data, the basic pattern is clear: pain levels mainly were between 4 and 7.

The intervention (*B*) involved seven 1-hour sessions of biofeedback-assisted relaxation training in an outpatient setting. The authors describe in detail what procedures they used and how this material was introduced to the participant. Briefly, they used a standard autogenic training procedure teaching the participant to rehearse standard verbal formulas for physiological and mental relaxation, such as "my arms are heavy and warm with relaxation." Then, the client was monitored with a biofeedback device at her indicated pain sites, and was encouraged to do "whatever was necessary to decrease the pitch of the feedback tone," such as practicing autogenic relaxation. The participant was asked to practice with training tapes at home. Intervention lasted for 60 days, and a follow-up continued another 55 days.

As indicated in Figure 2, there was a sharp decline in the daily record of pain intensity over the first 15 days of intervention, and then a pattern of fluctuations occurred, none of which reached the levels of pain in baseline. Follow-up data show less fluctuation at about the same, lowered level of pain intensity.

Discussion of this case situation suggests positive changes occurred in reduction of pain intensity, although there was still some fluctuation in level. But we do not know, given this design, whether it was the biofeedback or the practice or something else that accounts for this positive outcome. Certainly it did not work uniformly, as participant 1 attained no relief from his chronic pain, and participant 3 attained less than participant 2. So, what we ultimately learn is that this specific intervention *may* be beneficial for at least some adults with pain associated with cerebral palsy. This becomes important information for the next steps in practice and in evaluation.

It is also important to note that this is one of many case examples we provide in this book of the usefulness of single-system designs involving interventions from a variety of different theoretical orientations. Just a few of many interesting examples in the literature supporting this broad utility and refuting the myth that single-system designs are useful only in behavior modification include Broxmeyer's (1978) psychodynamic analysis of an acting-out youth; Dean and Reinherz's (1986) student cases using psychoanalytic theory with a dying patient and her family; Nelsen's (1978) use of an *A-B* design with a communication theory perspective; and Haynes's (1977) use of single-system designs within an ego psychology

From the Case Study to the Basic Single-System Design: *A-B*

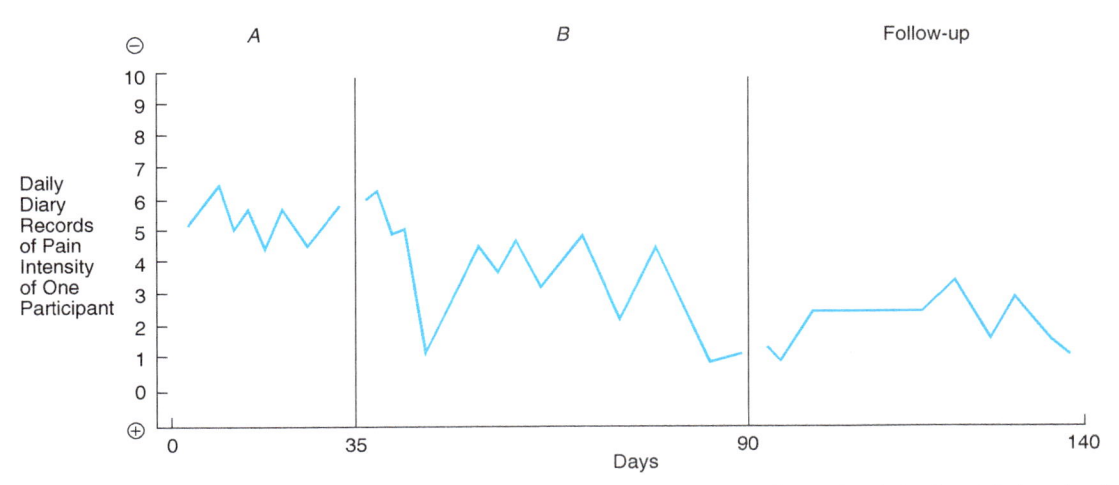

FIGURE 2 An example of an *A-B* design adapted from a study on "Outcome of Biofeedback-Assisted Relaxation for Pain in Adults with Cerebral Palsy: Preliminary Findings."
(J. M. Engel, M. P. Jensen, & L. Schwartz, 2004, *Applied Psychophysiology and Biofeedback, 29* (2), pp. 135–140.)

model. Tolson (1977) also describes single-system designs using the task-centered casework perspective; McCullough (1984) presents plans for the use of single-system designs in applied cognitive psychology; while Kolko and Milan (1983) use the existential approach in a study of paradoxical instructions. Bradshaw and Roseborough (2004) used this evaluation approach with cognitive behavioral interventions with persons with schizophrenia, and Briggs et al. (2005) used a behavioral parent-training group with a single-system design. These examples support our claim that single-system designs are theory-independent—that is, that this evaluation methodology can be employed by practitioners using virtually all intervention approaches.

A most creative use of single-system designs was reported by Vera (1990). In this report, Vera used single-system designs to evaluate changes resulting from two divorce adjustment groups. A total of 11 clients in two groups were provided 10 weeks of semi-structured treatment involving three components: (a) education, (b) support, and (c) therapy. A number of measures were utilized, including the Generalized Contentment Scale, the Index of Self-Esteem, and the Index of Peer Relations. (All of these standardized measures were developed by Hudson, 1997, and each has excellent reliability and validity.) The author defined improvement in divorce adjustment as a positive change in the Index of Well-Being, a composite score obtained by averaging the scores of each client on the three scales noted above, with lower scores equaling greater improvement. (This combining of scores is not a practice we can necessarily recommend, since this combination is of unknown reliability and validity.)

Although Vera states that she conducted a multiple-baseline design in comparing the two groups, data in the article are presented on each of the 7 clients in a separate chart; we choose to use some of these data as examples of the *A-B* design. Two of these charts were selected and adapted for presentation here, one for a client described as improved (Figure 3a) and one for a client described as having little or no improvement (Figure 3b).

As can be seen in Figure 3a, this client appeared to show a dramatic change from the baseline in which the client obviously was deteriorating to a turnaround and improvement during the intervention period. This improvement was generally maintained in the follow-up, although there is a slight trend in a negative direction. The second client, as shown in Figure 3b, shows almost no improvement, with data in both the intervention and follow-up phases closely paralleling the baseline.

A very interesting addition to this study was the fact that Vera also collected qualitative data from the screening interview and from information elicited in the group meetings. These data mainly focused on factors that could delay adjustment to divorce, such as presence or absence of support, multiple losses, other

From the Case Study to the Basic Single-System Design: A-B

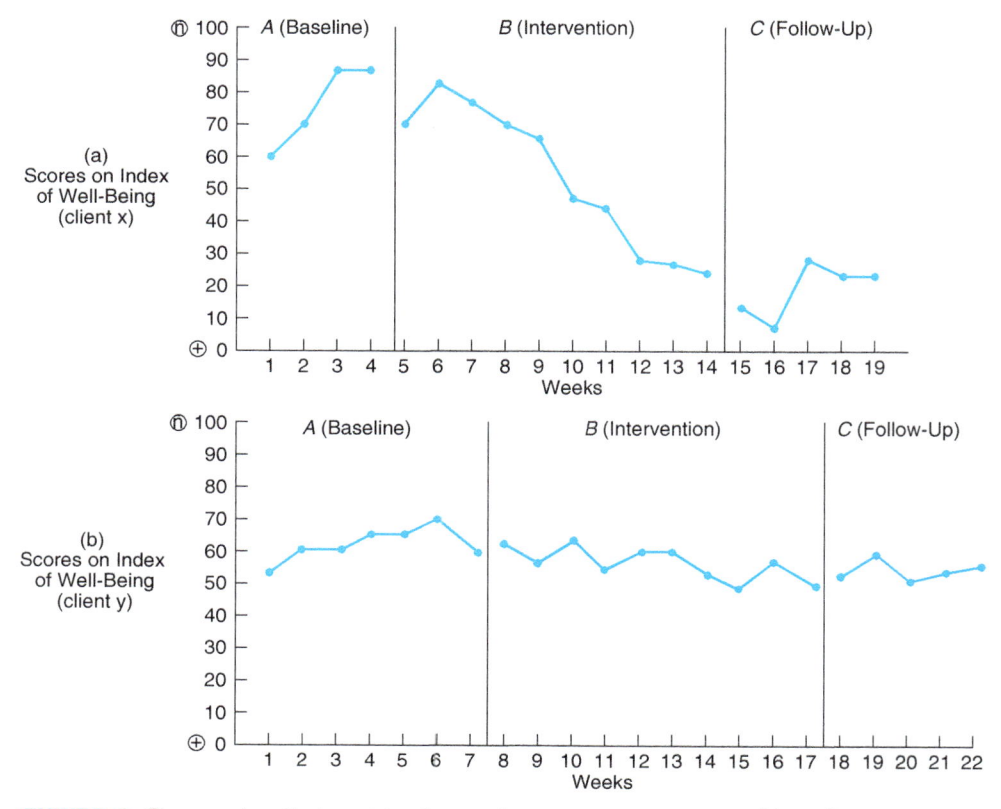

FIGURE 3 Changes in adjustment to divorce. Lower scores = more positive adjustment.
[Adapted from "Effects of Divorce Groups on Individual Adjustment: A Multiple Methodology Approach" by M. I. Vera, 1990, *Social Work Research and Abstracts, 26*, pp. 10–20.]

life events, and so on. When these data were applied to these two cases, it was found that the client who improved had only one of these factors, while the client who did not improve had five, the most of all 11 clients. The addition of these qualitative data is an excellent example of concomitant variation, the idea that we can use single-system designs to compare changes in the measures we are using with changes that occur at the same time outside of the intervention proper to examine their potential effects on overall change.

The inclusion of the follow-up period and the use of standardized measures, a group intervention program, and qualitative measures make this an excellent example for showing the potentials of single-system design. The relatively short length of the baseline for at least the first client (4 data points or 4 weeks) does impose some limitations on conclusions that can be drawn. But it should be pointed out that when using standardized measures as the only measure, there are some built-in limitations, since they typically are administered only once per week. Thus, it is reasonable to assume that Vera did not think it wise or practical to delay beginning her intervention period only because of the use of standardized measures.

King, Winett, and Lovett (1986) combine a classical research design with a single-system design to measure the effect of training in coping skills among women from dual-earner families. Two interventions were used to aid coping skills in a study involving four groups in which the scores of all of the members of a group were averaged together in the data we see in Figure 4: (a) a time-management training program and (b) a social support group, as well as (c) a combined intervention of 1 and 2, along with (d) a fourth group acting as a delayed treatment control. That is, this fourth group waited for 4 weeks after the study was finished, and then they were offered the combined

From the Case Study to the Basic Single-System Design: A-B

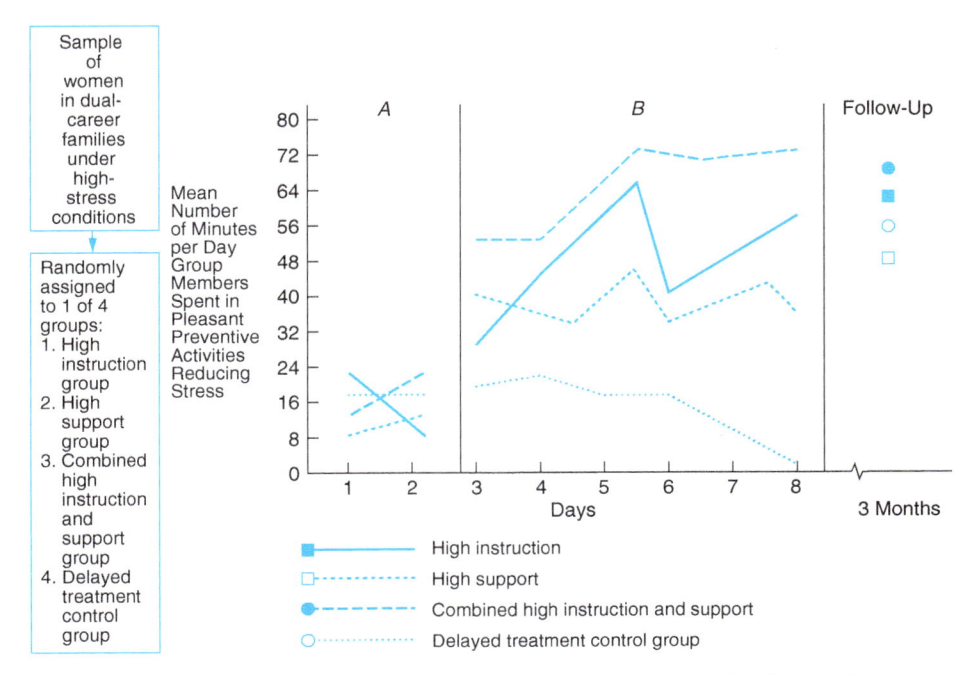

FIGURE 4 Combined experimental/control group design using an A-B-Follow-Up design.
[Adapted from "Enhancing Coping Behaviors in At-Risk Populations: The Effects of Time-Management Instruction and Social Support in Women from Dual-Earner Families" by A. C. King, R. A. Winett, and S. B. Lovett, 1986, *Behavior Therapy, 17*, pp. 57–66.]

program. Three months after the conclusion of the study, there was a telephone follow-up interview.

At baseline, there was no significant difference among the four groups on the target behavior, the mean number of minutes members of the group spent in high-priority activities (i.e., whatever was pleasing to the individuals involved, averaged over all of the individuals in a group). King et al. (1986) are mainly concerned with the experimental/control group design, but because they also use an *A-B* design, we can use this case to illustrate the integration of both classical and single-system designs.

Figure 4 shows data adapted from the King et al. (1986) study. Notice the pattern of changes in the four groups during the intervention, *B*, and what happens at follow-up. The control group continues its poor baseline pattern during the *B* phase, but after receiving the delayed intervention, it does well at follow-up, comparing favorably with the other three groups. If the control group had continued to do poorly, this would have cast doubt on the intervention program. It is unfortunate that the baseline was so short in the study, since that adds severe limitations to the analysis of change. On the other hand, the addition of the control group, the lack of change for that group in the intervention period, and then the dramatic improvement in the follow-up period after the control group received the delayed intervention, add considerable weight to the notion that the intervention produced the observed change in the four groups. Still, if this were only an *A-B* design, we would not have logical proof of causation.

Another example of an *A-B* design is provided by McSweeny's (1978) study of the effects of charging 20 cents for local directory assistance for the 1 million telephone callers in the Cincinnati area. This study has several interesting variations that we wish to call to your attention. First, the time span extended over a 14-year period. Second, 1 million callers were involved in this *A-B* study, in which the whole million were considered as a single system of persons involved in using or not using directory assistance. Third, parallel data were presented on long-distance directory-assistance calls for which additional charges were not made. McSweeny's chart of these data indicate a remarkable drop—some 60,000 fewer calls per day after the charge was introduced. Because the long-distance directory-assistance calls continued on their preintervention level, while the local directory-assistance dropped, the authors have, in effect, two *A-B* designs whose joint pattern provides a tentative logical basis for making a causal inference.

In each of these examples of *A-B* designs, a baseline period was identified using various types of measures. Then an intervention period was begun, again varying in the number and type of specific actions taken to affect the behavior, feelings, activities, or thoughts of the clients or target persons. Data ranging from one person to a large aggregated group of persons were used in making comparisons between baseline and intervention. Even large scale surveys rarely reach a million persons, and experimental/control group studies basically never do. Changes were observed in each example, and some observations were made about presumed causality. However, to be more conservative in the use of these evaluation tools, we would have to caution that the safest interpretation is that changes clearly did occur, but that conclusions about causality (*why* did the changes occur?) cannot be made without use of more powerful designs. Yet, for practitioners and decision makers these kinds of data are often used as the basis for policy or program changes. This is a risk that should be understood clearly. However, if such data are used as the basis of continuing hypotheses that will be tested in further action, then this may be a satisfactory solution until stronger tests may be conducted.

Aggregating *A-B* Designs

As we have seen previously, it is possible to develop causal clues by aggregating the results of several *A-B* designs. One illustration that expands on the basic *A-B* design is shown by the work of Levy and Bavendam (1995) in the field of women's health issues, a woefully neglected area of study (see also Bradshaw & Roseborough, 2004, which we interpret as being on the borderline between aggregated *A-B* designs and a multiple-baseline design.) They present five individual cases concerning theory-guided pamphlets developed to enable women's self-care regarding urologic problems (a frequent-urgency syndrome). All cases involve an *A-B* design, and thus no causal inferences on the individual cases can be made with regard to the effectiveness of the treatment. Three of the five cases appear to have successful results, while two showed no change, although one of these showed a reduction in feelings of urgency.

What can we learn from the aggregate of cases, as contrasted to individual cases? Levy and Bavendam (1995, p. 436) suggest that we have "... useful clues for further intervention design and development. In particular, this type of intensive research permits the investigation of possible factors operating for subjects for whom change was not as evident." It turns out that two women who reported no change in frequency stated in the exit interview that they did not follow the major recommendation in the pamphlet. So, while pamphlets may be useful for some clients, others may need a more intense intervention. The next step would be to tease out who needs intensive discussions and who will benefit fully by a well-written pamphlet.

Introducing the Client to the Basic Single-System Design

In addition to what we had proposed earlier in this chapter, we now want to add to the discussion the unique aspects of the *A-B* design that clients and others should understand. In addition to stating that you want to understand the client's situation clearly, that you need clear facts to be most helpful, and that you will share your understanding of these facts with the client, we suggested that you indicate that fact-gathering helps the practitioner to build a plan of action and modify it as needed.

Beginning with that last point, we recommend that for the *A-B* design, you add that "*some portion of the fact gathering will continue throughout our contact together*, not only when we are trying to assess the situation, but even during the intervention period when we work together to *change* the problem, in order to have a continuing record of any changes in your situation." Telling the participant that knowing exactly how much progress is being made or is not being made helps you decide what steps to take and when steps may need to be changed over time.

In addition, depending on how you practice, it may be useful to *train the client* to be aware of these clear indicators of the problem or of goal attainment so that he or she can continue to monitor after intervention is terminated: "*If you (the client or mediator) are aware of an emerging problem*, you might be able to handle it before it gets too serious. So part of my (the practitioner) job will be to help you monitor your own situation so as to be on the lookout for growing problems, as well as growing improvements."

On all occasions, be ready, willing, and able to share progress reports and answer questions about how you are using these data for monitoring and evaluation.

Summary

This chapter introduced several arrangements for evaluating work with clients, from observation only, *A*, to intervention only, (*B*), to the case study, *B*, in which intervention and observational assessment occur simultaneously. We also discussed variations on the case study, as when additional interventions are joined to the first intervention, *B-C*. The strengths, limitations, and recommendations regarding case studies were presented, along with some guidelines for introducing the idea of evaluation to clients.

The focus of this chapter was on the *A-B* design, the basic single-system design, with its many potentials for service to nearly all practitioners in almost all conceivable situations. This design, the first of the planned arrangement of baseline and intervention phases, clearly provides information on whether the client's target problems changed. This design does not provide causal answers. However, it can lead to formulations of hypotheses regarding causation that can be tested in logically stronger designs. We noted the strengths and limitations of the *A-B* design, and concluded with our strong recommendation that this be the minimum design used with every case or situation. We also presented some ideas of extending the *A-B* design.

THE EXPERIMENTAL SINGLE-SYSTEM DESIGNS: *A-B-A, A-B-A-B, B-A-B*

PURPOSE This chapter introduces a set of single-system designs that add a form of experimental control to the evaluation, in which an intervention is introduced and then removed and then introduced once again in order to examine whether the intervention seems causally related to changes in the target. These designs are among the most powerful of the single-system approaches, but they raise difficult ethical and practical issues, such as should we remove a successful intervention for the sake of learning about its causal nature? Thus, the aim of this chapter is to provide an understanding of the purposes, strengths, and limitations of these designs so that you can make wise choices regarding their use.

Introduction
Why Would a Practitioner Use an Experimental Design?
When Should an Intervention Be Removed?
Basic Experimental Designs
Experimental Removal of Intervention Design: *A-B-A* |*A*|*B*|*A*|
Strengths of the A-B-A Design
Limitations of the A-B-A Design
Recommendations Regarding the A-B-A Design
Case Illustrations
Introducing the Client to the A-B-A Design
Experimental Replication Design: *A-B-A-B* |*A*|*B*|*A*|*B*|
Strengths of the A-B-A-B Design
Limitations of the A-B-A-B Design
Recommendations Regarding the A-B-A-B Design
Case Illustrations
Introducing the Client to the A-B-A-B Design
Experimental Repeat of Intervention Design: *B-A-B* |*B*|*A*|*B*|
Strengths of the B-A-B Design
Limitations of the B-A-B Design
Recommendations Regarding the B-A-B Design
Case Illustration
Introducing the Client to the B-A-B Design
Summary

From Chapter 14 of *Evaluating Practice: Guidelines for the Accountable Professional*, Sixth Edition. Martin Bloom, Joel Fischer, John G. Orme. Copyright © 2009 by Pearson Education, Inc. All rights reserved.

INTRODUCTION

The notation of evaluation designs used in this book illustrates how complex designs are additive versions of more elementary ones. We discussed the basic components of evaluation designs—the *A* phase, involving data collection only, and the *B* phase, introducing some intervention while continuing the data collection. We then combined these phases in a certain order, *A-B*, so as to benefit from the logical possibility of comparing a before picture with the events during and after the intervention. In the present chapter, we continue to add *A* phases and *B* phases (or other interventions—*C*, *D*, etc.) in various orders and arrangements to benefit from other logical possibilities in understanding causal relationships. Such understanding is at the heart of effective practice because it contributes to our knowledge about what interventions work with what problems.

We suggested earlier that practitioners interacting with clients generate designs naturally in the course of assessing the problems and strengths in the clients' situations, making plans aimed at helping clients attain their goals, and then observing during the intervention period what effects the services seem to be having on them. By abstracting and generalizing from these common experiences it is possible to construct types of evaluation designs with various logical strengths and limitations derived from the properties of the designs themselves.

However, the group of designs discussed in this chapter appears to have a somewhat different origin from some of the other designs, stemming more from the experimental laboratory than from the clinic or the community action center. The emphasis of the laboratory is on experimental control over as many factors as possible in determining causal relationships among events. In the everyday world the practitioner often does not have such control over clients or events, and indeed, this control may be counterproductive when the practitioner seeks to have clients assert effective control over their own lives. However, if we are to understand causal relationships in order to make effective practice decisions, at times we may need to use some of the evaluation designs that provide this relatively rigorous information.

Consider this commonplace situation: A client has come for assistance, receives it, and the service is terminated when the problem apparently is resolved. Occasionally, the practitioner makes a further contact to ask how things are going. If all is well, that's fine; if not, perhaps a social or psychological booster shot (more *B*) is given, or possibly a new intervention (*C*) is implemented, until the practitioner and client are once again content with a stable problem resolution. We submit that this informal follow-up, with or without booster shots, is the basis of the following evaluation designs insofar as they ask the question: What happens after the (first) intervention is terminated? This question implies not only an interest in whether target events change, but whether the intervention produced *stable* changes, and, ultimately and most critically, what caused those changes. Causal knowledge is fundamentally useful in effective practice with a given client and also when working with other, similar clients.

We have labeled each of the designs in this chapter as "experimental." But don't emphasize this label too strongly, as all designs imply some degree of experimental arrangement of events in nature. What we wish to stress here is that by design a practitioner may wish to terminate an intervention *and* return to the nonintervention/observation period as a planned way of understanding the causal efficacy of the intervention. The underlying assumption is that starting from the baseline, if that problem event significantly improves with the introduction of a new condition (the intervention) and then changes back to its original state upon removal of that condition, and then improves *again* after the intervention is reintroduced, then that intervention logically may be inferred to be causally related to that change.

As a whole, these designs are called *experimental removal* designs. The essence of experimental removal designs is the search for patterns in the data that correspond to changes in the phases of the design. Once the data are collected and charted, you can examine them to see if there are changes that are related to the implementation and removal of intervention, and conversely, to the beginning and end of nonintervention (the baseline periods). The fact that changes in these patterns of data do correspond to the specific phases of the design provides the basic evidence for inferring causality. You can actually examine the data to see the ways in which your intervention did or did not affect the problem all along the way, from the initial contact with the client to the very last contact. We call this the "principle of unlikely successive coincidences," in that if the problem is consistently seen to change in a positive direction only during the intervention periods, and reassert itself only during the nonintervention periods, this covariation is unlikely to be a coincidence; hence, a causal inference seems reasonable.

The question is, under what conditions is it appropriate to purchase the causal knowledge at the price of having to remove a successful intervention? Answers to this question are presented in the following section, as well as in the form of a series of designs, together with a discussion of their strengths and limitations.

Why Would a Practitioner Use an Experimental Design?

The introduction of an intervention and then its removal after it has achieved some level of desired change are not typical procedures among practitioners, although these are widely used in published evaluation studies. Why then would you ever want to remove a successful intervention, and is it ethical to do so? The major answer to this question is that you would remove an intervention when it becomes important to know whether what you did appeared to cause the target problem to change, and when such removal would not have a serious negative effect on overall problem resolution and client feelings, behaviors, and interactions with others. And, as always, in all practice situations, when you believe a procedure violates your professional ethics, or you or your client's personal moral values, we urge you to consider other options.

There are a number of occasions when causal information would be most helpful, and possibly essential to obtain. For example, if you worked in a large institution that had numerous clients with the same set of presenting problems, it would be useful to develop the technology, that is, the techniques of practice, that would reliably produce effective outcomes. What technology is used for this institutional setting is also useful information for the professions at large; it clarifies the scope and limitations of given techniques with certain classes of clients. Helping professions develop skills and show themselves accountable to the extent that effective technology is generated.

Another reason for needing causal information is that individual practitioners learn an array of approaches and techniques in their educational programs. While they can perform these intervention methods, they may not know with which methods they are most adept. Therefore, by demonstrating the functional link between interventions and outcomes in specific cases, you can learn how you can serve many clients more effectively—by using tools with which you are most skilled and by learning more about those with which you are not.

An additional reason for wanting to provide causal information has to do with the motivations of the users of the design. Let's say you have trained a rather dubious nursing staff to implement a particular intervention with their patients on their ward. They go along with the program but don't really feel committed to participating. What could be more motivating to a person than to show through the power of one of these designs the causal relationships between their intervention and positive changes in the problem? Once we can clearly establish for people—clients or relevant others—that what they are doing really *is* having a desired effect, we will have gone a long way toward encouraging their participation in the program.

When Should an Intervention Be Removed?

Some of the terms are particularly applicable to experimental designs. These are *withdrawal* and *reversal,* the two types of removal procedures. With both types the removal procedures constitute a new phase following the intervention phase; the new phase is labeled *A* (remember, we are trying to "reconstitute" the baseline) or A_2 to distinguish it from A_1, the first baseline. *Withdrawal* refers simply to removing the intervention altogether, in the hope of returning to the original baseline (nonintervention) conditions. *Reversal* refers to removing the intervention from the original target problem (e.g., crying), but applying it to another target problem. The second target problem can be either a polar opposite of the original (e.g., laughing—one can't laugh and cry at the same time), or it could be any other target problem. At the same time, except for continuing to record any instance of crying, the original target problem (the crying) is ignored. The advantage of the reversal design is that intervention can be continued, but is simply applied to a different problem. With both removal designs, though, the goal is to see whether the target problem changes toward its preintervention state when intervention is removed; if it does, then you are demonstrating "experimental control" over the problem, that is, providing evidence of a causal relationship between application and removal of the intervention and changes in the problem.

There are some intervention procedures that are obviously more difficult to remove than others. We described these as *irreversible*. For those that are impossible to remove (e.g., instructions to the client that cannot be reversed) you will have to consider a design other than an experimental design (e.g., multiple-baseline designs). For other interventions (e.g., techniques where the client already has been given instructions on what to do and/or already has begun practicing) you may, first, just ask the client not to practice what he or she has been taught, and/or second, discontinue your instruction, help, and support with regard to that specific technique. In these situations, even though the client may remember the instructions, simply not practicing them *may be* a sufficient removal. In fact, treating all cases as a practice "experiment" allows you to explore the potential and limitations of any practice and evaluation procedures. What doesn't work need not be used again.

Of course, the mere fact that you remove and then reinstate your intervention, obtaining clear sequential changes across the problem, does not *prove* that it was your specific techniques affecting the problem. It is still possible that some subtle (or not so subtle) alteration in other influences (e.g., the differential way you or others, such as family members, relate to the client in each phase) also may be producing the change. That is, sequential changes in the problem according to whether you apply or remove your intervention does not prove that the actual techniques themselves are causing the change. This is so even though it may be, in fact, some part of the intervention proper that is producing the changes. However, we are speaking here about inferences and degree of inferences. When your clear and specific interventions are chosen for the very reason that they are likely to affect the problem, then the probability that the causal inference is correct is increased. In the final result, however, the conclusion about ultimate causality may have to await the results of several replications, thereby increasing both internal and external validity.

Actually, there are two types of removal *designs* just as there are two types of *removals* that we discussed earlier. The first, and the one we've discussed most extensively, is the *planned* removal. This is where the practitioner *plans* to remove and then reimplement intervention in order to look for a causal relationship. The second type of removal design might be called accidental or *unplanned* removal. In cases such as these, for one reason or another (e.g., illness or vacation), the intervention plan cannot be implemented for a brief period. If you are lucky, or if you have informed participants in advance, the recorder will continue to collect data. This will give you a built-in removal period in that you will be able to have a fairly systematic look at what happens to the problem during this unplanned removal period. Then, the intervention can be reimplemented, if needed. However, even if data are not being collected during the removal period, you may be able to get some notion of changes in the target when the intervention is not being applied. This can be through feedback from the client (reconstructing his or her impressions of what happened) or by continuing to use archival data from records other professionals are collecting.

In both of these cases, we recommend that you use this information as though it were a removal, but with caution, because the unplanned nature of the removal may make the information difficult to compare with earlier phases. At any rate, the unplanned removal may give you not only information that allows you very tentatively to infer causality (did the problem change during the unplanned removal and change again once intervention was reimplemented?), but also information about what may be helpful in planning subsequent phases of intervention and termination. Ultimately, you want a successful positive change in the target event to be continued, even after termination.

But the question remains: When should an intervention be removed? Actually such removal is multi-determined, by environmental factors such as time limitations imposed by the setting; the limits of resources available; the finite patience and cooperation of the staff (especially those in institutional settings); predictions from the literature as to when an intervention would be likely to have an effect on a given problem; and most importantly, the degree of harm that may befall a client or others in such a setting (Barlow, Nock, & Hersen, 2009). In particular, *if it seems likely that some degree of harm may come to the client or to others by removing an intervention program, this would be a major reason that the intervention should not be removed,* and that other designs should be substituted.

Additional considerations regarding removal of an intervention are related to the design itself. We have discussed some of these issues on phases and length of phases, but it bears repeating that the major factor regarding determining when to change phases (including intervention phases) is the semblance of stability in the data. There is no easy formula for what constitutes stability of data. However, when it appears as though some stability in the data in the intervention phase suggests the intervention has begun to have a positive effect, say for at least three consecutive data points, then you might consider the possibility of removing the intervention to examine causal effects. It's also a good idea to try to remember to keep the first intervention period as short as possible when you are considering a removal. This will give the changes less time to become irreversible, a point to which we will return later in this chapter in the discussion of carryover effects. Finally, we also recommend using some simple methods of analysis to get an approximation of when the set of intervention data are different, visually and/or statistically, from the baseline data and to determine that the pattern of data points in the intervention phase does not vary irregularly. Then, at that point, you can make the decision about removing the intervention.

BASIC EXPERIMENTAL DESIGNS

Experimental Removal of Intervention Design: *A-B-A* |A|B|A

The first two phases of the *A-B-A* design are exactly like those of the *A-B* design. The logical comparison that is possible in the *A-B* design is possible also between these two phases (*A* and *B*) in the *A-B-A* design. In the *A-B-A* design, however, the practitioner decides to return to baseline conditions, the second *A* phase in the *A-B-A*. Now two adjacent comparisons are possible—between the first baseline and the intervention, and between the intervention and the second baseline. The underlying assumption is that if the intervention is really the causal ingredient, and change brought about by the intervention is reversible, then by removing it the target should return to the way it was before that intervention. An ideal example is a dark room (baseline condition), the turning on of a light switch (intervention creating light), followed by the turning off of the light switch (return to a dark room). Of course, it is not as simple as this to "turn off" human behaviors following an intervention, a point to which we return shortly.

The critical feature of the *A-B-A* design is the second *A* (A_2), which changes a basic *A-B* design into an experiment. The experiment consists of testing whether the introduction of the intervention is likely to have caused changes in the observed target behavior. The clearest way to test this idea with a given set of client and environmental factors is to take away the successful intervention and to see whether the target changes as it would if the cause of the improved behavior (the intervention) were removed. The second *A* is, in a sense, analogous to a follow-up, but differs in that the second *A* is obtained while the practitioner still has contact with the client, while follow-up occurs after termination. The practitioner then can choose to terminate or go into a second intervention phase, which then constitutes another experimental design which will be discussed shortly, since we don't want to end service when the client has gone back to the initial problematic phase.

As always, it may be necessary to move into a maintenance phase (often termed M) with the successful *A-B-A* design. This is a halfway stage between an *A-B-A-B* and the *A-B-A* design. It requires the practitioner to return to a service phase in the sense of teaching the client new skills, namely, to maintain the successful activities identified in the *B* phase.

An example of the withdrawal *A-B-A* is given in the classic experiment by Ayllon (1963) in which a psychiatric patient hospitalized 9 years had collected large numbers of towels and stored them in her room. There had been several unsuccessful attempts to change this behavior, which was viewed by many staff members as reflecting an unconscious need for love and security. Ayllon began his work by taking a baseline count of the number of towels in the patient's room when she wasn't there. Then, the intervention was to have the staff people give her towels—between 7 and 60 a day—to reach a satiation point. This was achieved in several weeks when she had 625 towels hoarded in her room. At that point in the intervention period she herself started to take towels out of her room. The researcher returned to baseline conditions—the usual allotment of towels dispensed in the regular way was reinstituted—and data showed that the patient went to an average of 1.5 towels in her room per week. This rate was maintained during a year of follow-up observations, contrary to predictions from the psychiatric staff at the hospital.

The *A-B-A* design raises an important question, that of the continuation of interventive effect. Presumably, the *B* phase of this design saw the client attain some stable and desired form of behavior. (In the case of the satiated patient the turning point was when she began to remove towels herself rather than hoarding them as she had for 9 years.) Therefore, removing the intervention can show whether the client's performance was learned (i.e., whether it became a relatively stable part of the client's behaviors). With the hoarding patient, the learning appears to have been effective and long-lasting.

Strengths of the A-B-A Design. The added comparisons derived from the removal of the intervention offer stronger bases of inferring causality than in the basic single-system design, the *A-B*. The practitioner now has two points of logical comparison as contrasted to one in the *A-B* design. Given the fact that the successful intervention is purposely removed in order to observe its effects—namely, whether the target problems also change in the direction they were before intervention—this provides an experimental manipulation of the independent variable in order to identify causal factors.

Moreover, if the practitioner replicates this design with other client problems, the effect is cumulative with regard to causal inferences. To clarify this point, suppose that the towel-hoarding client also hoarded food (A_1). Then the intervention might consist of the staff giving her more food and more towels (*B*). Assume that the same outcome occurred, that the hoarder eventually resisted taking more towels and food from the staff. And further assume that she stopped these hoarding behaviors for more than a year (A_2). We have two *A-B-A* experiments with the hoarder with essentially the same results of the effect of satiation. For each separate target event the intervention appears to be causally involved. However, this inference receives added weight when the set of interrelated predictions are supported, since it is increasingly unlikely that each target in the set would have changed in that same direction by chance alone. A network or system of results provides more information than the sum of its constituent results, since new predictions can be derived more readily from a network of events than from a single event.

Limitations of the A-B-A Design. The major limitation of the *A-B-A* design stems from the practice concern about ending contact on a nonintervention phase, having removed the successful intervention. If the intervention is in fact a causal factor and it is thought to be reversible, then presumably the target problem has returned to near the preintervention level (the baseline phase), which is to say, to some problematic level that led the client to seek help (or receive it) in the first place. (The exception to this statement occurs with techniques such as satiation, as discussed above, or when the intervention produces irreversible changes.) Regardless of how much information is obtained about causality, helping professionals would have a very difficult time accepting this design if it violated the most basic axiom of ethical helping: Help if you can, but do no harm. Returning a client to a problematic state after having resolved that state may appear to practitioners to be doing harm.

However, all interventions end (and one might consider the termination period of intervention in general to be a type of *A* phase, as long as follow-up observations are made). Therefore, one approach to having an *A-B-A* design without this ethical and practice concern is to use an *A-B* design and have an extended follow-up analogous to the second *A* phase. That is, the second *A* phase can be viewed as simply follow-up with continual monitoring of the problem. Then, intervention can be reimplemented if the positive change seen at *B* does not return.

There are also alternative explanations that are especially pertinent to this design. For example, consider sequential confounding—events in the final observation period may not be the same as in the first observation period, since there may be carryover from the intervening period. Carryover is an important problem for all multistage intervention programs. As we discussed previously, it is difficult to reinstate any given set of social forces, and in the case of irreversible events such as new learned behaviors, it may be impossible to reinstate even a similar set of forces. Generally speaking, what people learn cannot always be removed simply by ceasing to teach that piece of information or skill. Solutions to this dilemma require use of more sophisticated designs, wherein variations of intervention are deliberately counterbalanced so that carryover effects of particular arrangements are controlled in the design. (We will discuss further effects of carryover in relation to the next design, the *A-B-A-B*.)

Another practical limitation of the *A-B-A* design is in communicating it to the client. How do you tell a client that you are removing the intervention after attaining the desired goal? We will discuss this issue in the section on introducing the client to this design, but we note it here because use of this design could take on the flavor of having a client as a "guinea pig" in an experiment. Moreover, the recipient of services, at least on the surface, may not understand how he or she benefits directly or obviously from the removal of the intervention.

Recommendations Regarding the A-B-A Design. We do not recommend this design for most practice situations and suggest use of any of the other single-system designs discussed in this that can accomplish the same logical analysis as this one but that do not have such a steep price to pay for attaining this logical advantage. If this design were used with a client on one part of his or her problems while maintaining contact because of others, then the *A-B-A* design might be used within a cluster of other designs (see Kirchner et al., 1980, who employ an *A-B-A* design within an overall multiple-baseline design).

Also, for situations in which the case terminates after an *A-B* design, it would be good practice (and good evaluation) to have follow-up observations on a planned basis to assess whether the intervention was sustained after contact with the practitioner. However, in general, since there are other ways of obtaining the kind of information the *A-B-A* design offers, we cannot recommend it under ordinary circumstances.

Case Illustrations. Ludwig and Geller (1999) present one study from the literature on organizational behavior in a series of investigations on the promotion of safe driving among pizza deliverers, using a rare *A-B-A* design with a nonequivalent control group. As these authors note, the pizza delivery business is a dangerous occupation, with a driving accident rate three times the national average. This is probably due to the fact that the majority of pizza drivers are inexperienced drivers (ages 16 to 25), driving at the riskiest time periods (between 5:00 PM and 2:00 AM), who are compensated with commissions based on the frequency of pizzas delivered.

Ludwig and Geller (1999) distinguished between the target of an intervention and the agent of change. Most of the time, researchers are the intervention agents, but in this study, the agents of change were the pizza deliverers themselves, and they also were the targets of change. Prior research by these authors showed that the driving behavior of pizza deliverers could be dramatically improved by a driving safety awareness program, using seat belts, and making a personal commitment to buckle-up. Other research suggested that response generalization could occur, that is, an improvement in another area would occur similar to the targeted behavior.

In the current study, the pizza deliverers were involved in promoting a community safe-driving practice (i.e., the use of seat belts) being sponsored by their store. In fact, the pizza drivers were the actual target of intervention, and in addition, their use of turn signals also was studied as a nontargeted but related safe-driving practice. Using two stores in one community, one experimental, the other a control, the experimental group was enlisted as agents in a community-wide safety belt program, while the control group did not participate in the community program. Trained observers unobtrusively watched pizza deliverers in both groups, with a 10-week baseline period (*A*), followed by 6 weeks of training at one store (*B*) A, and then 6 more weeks of follow-up observation. There was a 5-week break, and another 7 weeks of follow-up observation (*A*).

Although the pizza deliverers were the main target of intervention, there was also a community intervention program, such as radio announcements, safety belt reminder cards on the top of each box of pizza sold, with a system of vouchers good for a free pizza for those customers spotted with the safety belt reminder card in their cars.

The results on 7,843 vehicular observations collected during this study show several important outcomes. First, there was a very high (approximately 92% average) interrater reliability on checks for use of seat belts and turn signals by pizza deliverers. These observations noted a substantial increase in seat belt use for the experimental group (from 57% to 75%, with a follow-up measure of 74% usage), while the control group did not show such a change. Second, data on the response generalization to use of turn signals was interesting. Again, the experimental group increased from 41% at baseline to 76% after intervention (and 73% at follow-up). The control group showed a slight decrease in turn signal usage during the same time period, supporting the response generalization hypothesis. There was also a telephone survey of people using pizza services—this was a university town—and there was a slightly favorable response to the community project and the involvement of the pizza store in it, which gives rise to some statements about the cost-effectiveness of such preventive programs.

The Experimental Single-System Designs: *A-B-A, A-B-A-B, B-A-B*

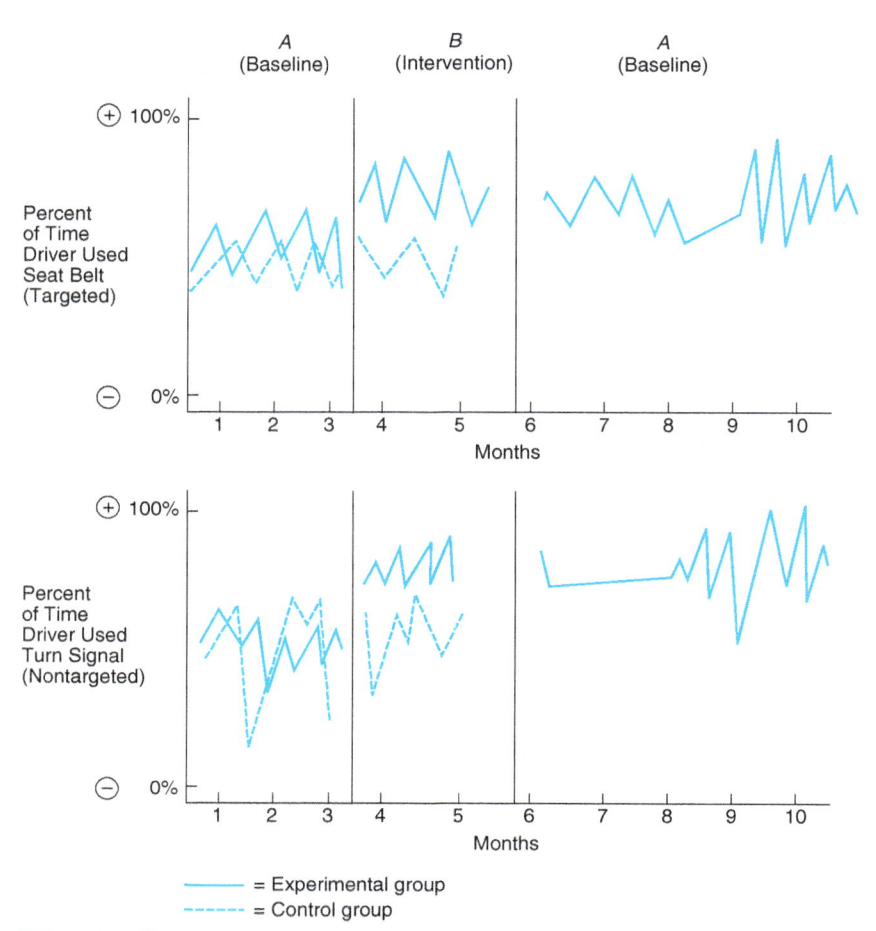

FIGURE 1 Percent of time pizza drivers in experimental and control groups used seat belts (targeted) and turn signals (nontargeted) during a safe driving campaign.

(Adapted from Ludwig & Geller, 1999.)

Figure 1 shows a simplified version of both *A-B-A* designs, on seat belt use and use of turn signals, for experimental and control groups, over a 10-month period. Since the targets did not return to original baseline (*A*) levels in the second baseline period (A_2) (carryover), these designs also can be viewed as *A-B* designs with follow-up. These designs offer an example of an intervention on one target that appears to have generalized to a related target, while at the same time showing continuation of the improvement. This study also illustrates the ways in which single-system designs and classical research—the nonequivalent control group design—can work together to develop answers to socially significant problems.

Another report of a practical application of the *A-B-A* design by Altus, Welsh, Miller, and Merrill (1993), focused on the effect of contingent reinforcement on an educational program for new members of a consumer cooperative. These new participants in a university housing cooperative were required to complete a standard 14-week educational program, consisting of lessons on the history of cooperatives, and on local co-op rules and procedures. A baseline of 4 weeks indicated low levels of new members completing the lesson's study guides. So, a 5-week dual intervention was introduced, in which members received a $2.00 rent reduction for completing the study guide at 90% or greater accuracy, and lesser reductions for 80% to 89%, and 70% to 79%. They also received a $2.00 fine for failing to complete the lesson or scoring below 70%. This intervention was removed on the tenth week for 5 weeks.

The results are clear: With no contingencies provided (A_1 and A_2), the percentage of new members completing the lesson study guides is very low; with an intervention (B) of credits and fines that is managed by the researcher, the rate of completion of the study guides is very high. New members scored slightly higher on the current period's study lesson than old members did on the same test, suggesting that new members were rapidly prepared to the level of old members in a short time period (see Figure 2).

In the real world, typically, researchers do not impose experimental conditions beyond the life of the study. So the question arises, can a member-managed intervention of the same credits and fines continue to motivate new members of the cooperative to attain high levels of study of its philosophy, history, and procedures? The data show that such a member-managed intervention was successful in producing a highly informed membership, even 9 years after the conclusion of this study. As Altus, Welsh, Miller, and Merrill (1993) note, this educational program is a simple, inexpensive, and sustainable way of providing cooperative members with the tools they need to maintain a democratic setting. In terms of this book, we note that this *A-B-A* evaluation supplied the experimental results sufficient for members to base their own continuation of the intervention program indefinitely.

A fascinating case showed the creative use of single-system designs with four clients infected with AIDS (Orgnero & Rodway, 1991). The intervention approach was based on Heimler's Social Functioning (HSF) method. HSF is a psychosocial approach that is particularly useful with AIDS patients. It is used in crisis interventions, in caring for the terminally ill, and in teaching stress management. It focuses on both internal and external sources of distress and addresses the major aspects of a person's being (social, physical, emotional, and spiritual). All clients were in great physical, mental, and emotional distress.

Two measures were used. The first was the Heimler Scale of Social Functioning, a standardized measure that produces a Coping Index that ranges from 0.0 to 2.5, with higher scores indicating poorer coping. The scores for each client were charted and tests of statistical significance, all of which are described in Part IV of this book, were used. In all cases, the results showed statistically significant (positive)

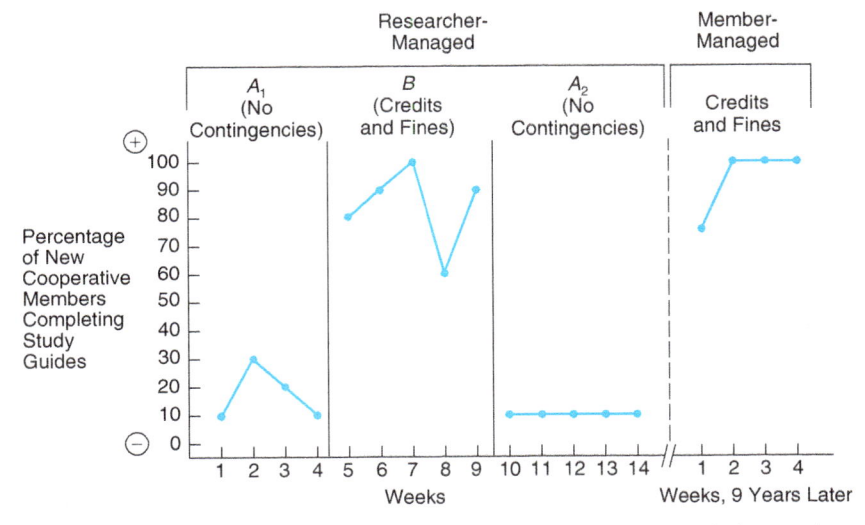

FIGURE 2 Percentage of new housing cooperative members completing study guides on the philosophy and procedures of cooperatives.
(Adapted from Altus, Welsh, Miller, & Merrill, 1993.)

changes in the clients' coping scores. One of these charts shows a statistical test called the two-standard-deviation band approach, which has been adapted in Figure 3 (with this approach, two consecutive points outside of the band indicate statistical significance; a better alternative to this two-standard deviation approach; see also, Callahan & Barisa, 2005 and Orme & Cox, 2001). The second measure was an individualized self-rating scale adapted for each client. The scores on those scales generally supported the results on the Heimler Scale of Social Functioning. With all clients, an A-B-A design was used. In every case, the intervention effects were maintained in the second A phase, suggesting that the changes had stabilized or become irreversible, and that the second A phase was serving best as a follow-up period (rather than an experimental manipulation).

This report is of particular interest for many reasons: First, it deals with AIDS, an enormous social and health problem that is still currently underserved; second, it illustrates single-system designs used with a broad-based psychosocial intervention (HFS); third, it is one of the few published reports using an A-B-A

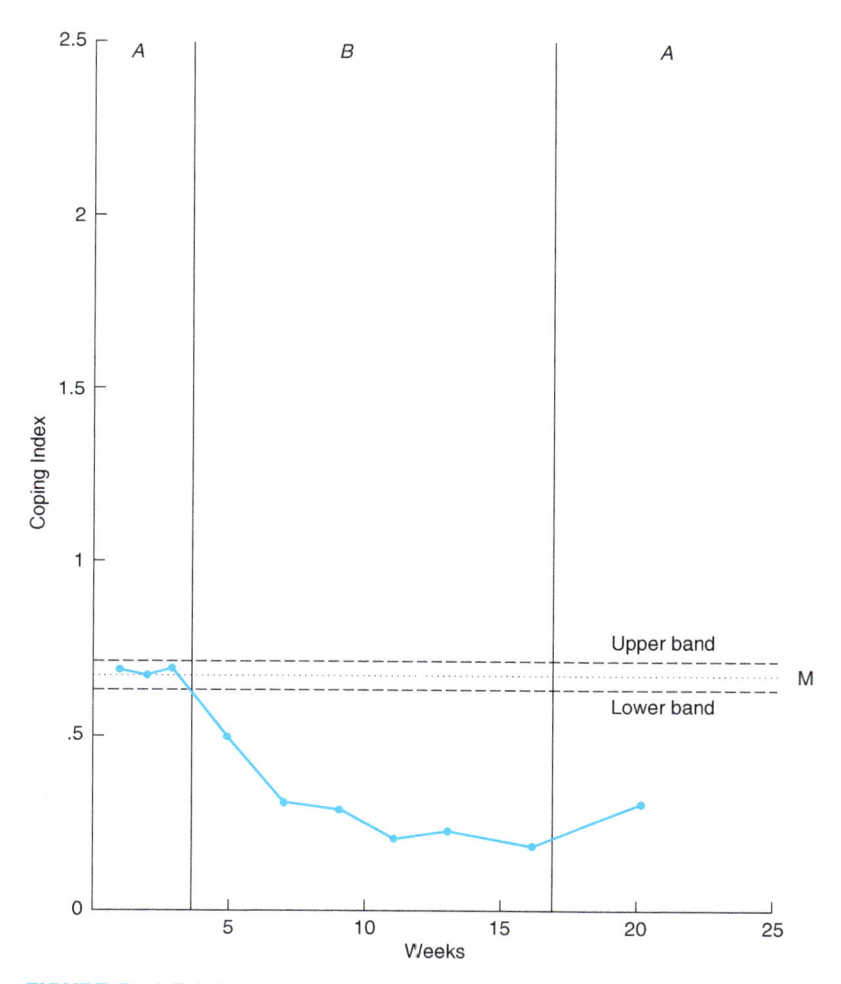

FIGURE 3 *A-B-A* design showing impact of HFS intervention with an AIDS patient using an analysis called the "two-standard-deviation band approach."

[Adapted from "AIDS and Social Work Treatment: A Single-System Analysis" by M. I. Orgnero & M. R. Rodway, 1991, *Health and Social Work, 16,* pp. 123–141.]

design; and fourth, this report in one article illustrates use of several of the procedures discussed in this book.

Introducing the Client to the A-B-A Design.
Frankly, introducing clients to an experimental procedure is one of the major challenges of these designs. It is difficult to explain to a client or relevant other who expects help why successful service is being removed. There are several basic approaches to this problem. First, if someone other than the client is collecting data, or if the data are collected routinely apart from the service program (such as school grades, etc.), then the practitioner can simply not tell the client. While this is a pure form of experimental procedure in which the reactive effects of data collection are minimized, you may have to make a judgment as to how ethical and/or suitable this strategy would be with each case or situation. For example, this may be most suitable with clients who may not be active participants in planning (such as very young infants or institutionalized persons with limited capacities) when approval of guardians can be secured.

The second approach involves telling participants. For example, you could say, "*You have been doing well so far* (in achieving your goals). *Let's keep recording to see how it continues to go, but let's not do x* (the intervention or service program). *This way we'll be able to see how you do without x* (the service program)."

A third approach combines the first two approaches. For example, if parents are involved in helping their child perform some desired activity, then the parents can be informed about the change in phases (such as the withdrawal of reinforcement). The child is not told, and the parents continue to collect data as before.

A fourth approach is linked to the next design (one that ends on an intervention phase). That is, you can introduce the idea of removal of intervention, but raise the possibility of returning to intervention if needed. "*This part of the service plan is a trial run* in preparation for the time when we end treatment. However, we need to know whether you're ready for stopping treatment by seeing how you handle problems on your own. We will keep track of events just as we did before in order to determine how well the treatment has worked."

Experimental Replication Design: *A-B-A-B* |A|B|A|B

The *A-B-A-B* design is a very important single-system design, for excellent reasons as we shall see. Each adjacent comparison can reveal differences in the data, which then may be related to the differences in the experiences involved. In the first comparison, between initial baseline and initial intervention, as in an *A-B* design, the practitioner observes the changes occurring. A clear and apparently stable difference between A_1 and B_1 sets the stage for asking the causality question: What part did the intervention play in these results? This also would apply, by the way, to deterioration as well as improvement effects. (The *subscripts* indicate which of the phases is being considered; for example A_1 refers to the first baseline, A_2 to the second baseline, and so forth; other than the order of presentation, there are no differences between A_1 and A_2 or B_1 and B_2 phases.) If B_1 is determined to be stable, a third change, removal of the intervention, provides the first experimentally manipulated source of evidence that the intervention may be causally related to observed changes. Assuming the second baseline data return to, or nearly return to, their initial state, this lends logical support to the experimental evidence that the intervention was indeed functionally linked with the change. Thus far we have an *A-B-A* design. Now, by adding a final intervention period (B_2), we add a second experimentally manipulated source of evidence regarding the causal nature of the intervention. By purposely manipulating the intervention, we have provided a strong basis for the inference of causality. By planning and observing these three instances of concomitant variation—A_1-B_1, B_1-A_2, A_2-B_2—we see the distinction between a change in target behaviors that happened by planned intervention in contrast to nature's random ways. In a word, we see evidence that the practitioner probably has helped cause the resulting change in target events.

We discussed previously the point that single-system designs are often additive; that is, that the strengths and characteristics of simpler designs such as *A-B* and *A-B-A* appear in the more complex designs, although their drawbacks (which may be overcome by the more complex designs) do not necessarily reappear. This fact will simplify the discussion here, but we want to remind you of these previous discussions.

One of the more important additions of the *A-B-A-B* design is that it terminates on an intervention phase that is professionally more acceptable than the *A-B-A* design, even though both involve removal of intervention in the course of service. Positive changes are supposed to occur from A_1 to B_1 and from A_2 to B_2, while changes from B_1 to A_2 should show deterioration. This pattern of expected changes is part of the logical pattern that gives this design its strength.

The *A-B-A-B* design is powerful because the experimental replications control for several threats to internal validity. Specifically, we believe that the *A-B-A-B* designs (and to a lesser extent the *A-B-A* and the *B-A-B* designs) are usually relatively safe from alternative explanations due to changing events occurring outside the immediate practice context ("history"), events occurring within the client ("maturation"), extreme scores naturally becoming less extreme over time ("regression to the mean"), and changes brought about by measurement of the outcome (reactivity). In each case it appears that the alternation of interventions and removal of interventions (and the parallel changes in target behaviors) lessen the possibility that these other extraneous factors could have influenced the data, particularly in short time periods.

Strengths of the A-B-A-B Design. Replication is a very strong source of support with regard to causal efficacy of the intervention. It is as if one were generalizing through replication what happened in the first part of the intervention to apply to what happened in the second part, although there might be differences expected because of the accumulation of influences and the more easily learned behaviors the second time around.

By ending on a service phase this design meets some practice and social criteria of ethical suitability and sensitivity lacking in the *A-B-A* design. Empirically, the practitioner–client relationship terminates at a point at which it has attained its goals twice, suggesting that learning has occurred. Logically, the removal and reintroduction of the intervention provides a strong basis for asserting control over the target problem when the predicted pattern of data emerges. Of course, as with all other designs, we recommend use of maintenance and follow-up phases once the changes in the final *B* phase are well-established and stable.

The *A-B-A-B* design also begins to provide the kind of information about functional relationships between variables that is at the heart of classical experimental/control group designs. This is a knowledge-*building* function rather than simply a knowledge-*using* function. Practitioners using this type of design are in a good position to report their findings to the profession in order to help others choose specific interventions for specific types of clients so that they will be likely to obtain defined classes of outcomes. This is a very strong scientific contribution to the knowledge base of all professions, stemming from the work of practitioners in the field, sometimes under ordinary practice conditions. This is where evidence-based and evaluation-informed practice join to contribute to a profession's knowledge base.

Moreover, for the practitioner himself or herself, this experimental design will help to build a repertoire of effective intervention techniques. We believe it is of major value for practitioners to know what interventions produce what types of effects with their own cases, given the background and skills of the unique practitioner.

For others involved in the experimental situation, such as parents or staff persons who are mediators participating in the intervention programs, there is the added benefit that they can see how their specific efforts are contributing to the client's behavior. This reinforces the mediator's behavior and thus ensures more cooperation with the intervention program. Designs such as this one, that can reinforce the all-important direct implementers of an intervention program, are very important considerations in planning interventions.

Limitations of the A-B-A-B Design. There are several problems involved in using this design. First, it is somewhat more cumbersome and more time-consuming than the basic *A-B* design. There has to be more control over the situation than many practitioners may have in order to be able to institute the replication part of the design. In addition, the issue of removing a successful intervention (B_1) once it has been attained is a problem here, as it was with the *A-B-A* design, although less so, since the intention clearly is to return to intervention after A_2. Should the client drop out before the B_2 phase is started, the practitioner would be left with an *A-B-A* design with its attendant problems.

It also is difficult to juggle the length of phases of the *A-B-A-B* design. In an ideal situation each phase should be of equal length, but in practice this is rarely possible. We recommend in such cases—in which other things are equal and in which phases cannot all be the same length—that B_2 be the longest phase and A_2 be the shortest. This means that the removal period would be minimized and the last intervention period extended for as long as possible to ensure that the problem stays changed.

But what if the B_1 phase doesn't show any change? Does this destroy the whole design? In effect, it makes the pattern in the B_1 phase similar to A_1. It would not be wise simply to repeat the B intervention again, so a new intervention, C, could be implemented to form a new design, A-B-C. The fact that B does not seem to have an impact is important information so that the practitioner does not lose for having tried it and moved to a modified design. One could go on and have an A-B-C-A-C design in which the B intervention is, in effect, removed from consideration in the logical arrangement to test for causality. Single-system designs are very flexible and take into account such occurrences; this is a great plus in the overall aim of being sensitive to the unique ongoing events in a case.

Another problem that experimental designs such as the A-B-A-B are subject to is carryover effects. Carryover effects simply are the inability to retrieve the original baseline (A_1) levels of the problem in a subsequent baseline (A_2). Thus, as an example, if a problem is occurring, say, at a rate of 14 occurrences per hour in the first baseline (A_1), and your intervention reduces this to a rate of 5 occurrences during B_1, carryover effects would be present if, in the second baseline phase (A_2), when the intervention is removed, the problem does not return to, or is not close to, its original level (say, staying in A_2 at a level of five to eight occurrences per hour). Figure 4 describes two hypothetical A-B-A-B designs, one with and one without carryover effects.

It is not always clear why carryover effects appear. It may be that instructions were irreversible, that the changes in phases just happened to coincide with some external factor, that the absence of changes (carryover) is only temporary, or other reasons that you simply may not know at the time. It also may be that the problem simply has been resolved, or is well on the way toward being resolved, and the new behavior is simply well-learned. To the extent that this is true (e.g., the problem has reached some stable, desired level), this may be an obvious advantage for the practitioner who then could turn the second baseline phase (A_2) into a maintenance and termination phase. Thus, from a practical point of view, presence of carryover effects may be advantageous.

On the other hand, carryover effects can pose problems. It is not always clear when we do or do not have carryover effects. There is a fuzzy area in which the problem does not quite reach its original level, but clearly does move in that direction. In our example (Figure 4a), this fuzzy area would be roughly between three to five occurrences per day. In situations like this, your guide should be both *stability* (does the problem stabilize at a given level with the absence of intervention?) and *directionality* (is there a clear trend away from the intervention phase level and toward the original baseline level?). If these two conditions do not pertain and you cannot make a relatively clear judgment as to whether the problem really has moved in the direction of the first baseline, then carryover effects probably have occurred.

But why should you care? Given the obvious practice advantages of carryover effects, do they really make a difference? The answer to this question depends on the purpose of your design. If you are really attempting to establish *why* the problem changed and whether your techniques affected it, these carryover effects make it unclear as to the extent to which you can claim the intervention program produced the changes that were observed.

One way of preventing carryover effects is to keep the phases, especially B_1, relatively short. This way, carryover effects have less opportunity to appear; that is, it is easier to retrieve the first baseline in phase A_2 if the first intervention phase (B_1) is relatively short. This is because the newly learned behaviors have less time to become irreversible or be part of a permanent change in the target. If they do appear and you want to maintain your A-B-A-B design, you could extend the second A phase (removal) to see whether the problem eventually does move toward its original level without intervention. In situations in which you are not certain how to interpret the data (the fuzzy area), be sure to interpret with caution. Finally, you can always turn the second A phase into a maintenance and termination phase as we suggested above and be very happy with the fact that the target *has* changed for the better.

Another possible limitation of the A-B-A-B design is the effect on colleagues or other workers of removing a successful intervention. As we mentioned before, it can be highly motivating when people see how their efforts are affecting a problem. However, you may run into the problem of other staff persons complaining about bearing the brunt of a client's problematic behavior. Thus, when the second baseline is implemented, all they see is that they have to go back to dealing with a problem that already has been reduced. Our suggestion is to prepare the staff for the removal

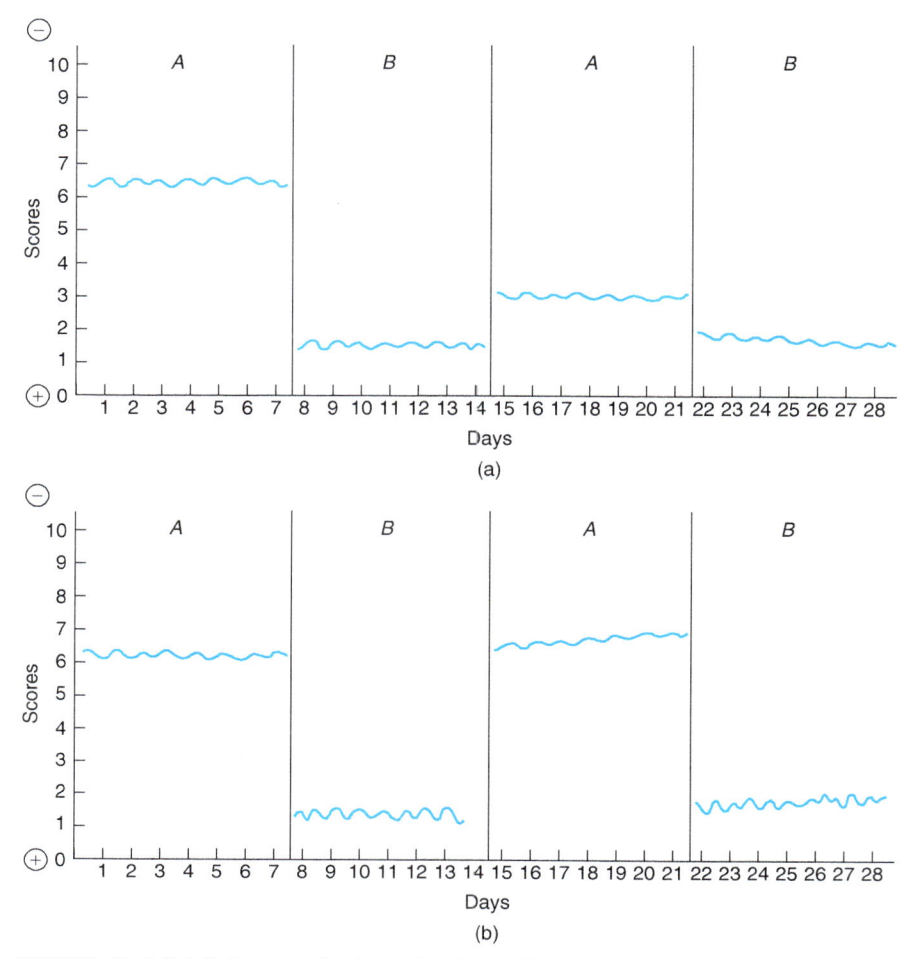

FIGURE 4 A-B-A-B designs with (a) and without (b) carryover effects.

period, explaining its purpose and eliciting their cooperation in advance. Of course, as we noted previously, due to possible carryover effects, the problem in the A_2 phase often doesn't attain the same level as in the A_1 phase, presenting staff with a less difficult task than they had to cope with during the preintervention period.

A final problem with the *A-B-A-B* design is analogous to problems in classical experimental designs. In single-system *and* group experimental designs, the problem may change when intervention is applied and removed (or, in a group design, in comparison with a control group), but there is no guarantee that your specific intervention techniques brought about the changes. They very well may have. But change also could be due to different ways of relating to clients during intervention and nonintervention periods, to different amounts of attention or enthusiasm, and so on. In classical experiments, this problem is addressed by adding more groups to the experiment, for example, an attention-placebo group, and/or an alternative intervention group, and/or by comparing practitioners' levels of interpersonal skills across groups. The problem is much trickier with single-system designs. It can be addressed somewhat by the designs that can compare alternative approaches. But the problem of not being clear about what part of the intervention was responsible for the changes is perhaps best addressed in single-system designs by replication.

When a similar intervention produces similar results across numerous instances with different practitioners and clients, you can have more confidence in a conclusion that the formal intervention itself (i.e., the techniques) was responsible for the observed changes.

As with other single-system designs, we are concerned that successful intervention effects are maintained and transferred to the client's natural environment. Sufficient time and energy should be devoted to this task by being sure to build in a maintenance phase at the end of the B_2 phase (Rzepnicki, 1991).

Recommendations Regarding the A-B-A-B Design. The experimental replication design is a very strong tool that makes many demands on the client as well as on the practitioner. If it is necessary to know or to demonstrate to others whether an intervention is in fact a controlling influence before further interventions are carried out, then this design would be very useful. It also has many secondary benefits, such as seeing whether a client has attained a stable, desired level of the problem while a relationship still exists with the helping professional. If the client maintains the desired level of the problem during the second *B* period, then this can be the basis for terminating work on that target event. If not, then the practice structure is already set up to continue working on that target event until it can be stably and independently maintained. Likewise, mediators and other service staff can see evidence of the impact of their work, a strong reinforcing factor.

Thus, we view the *A-B-A-B* design as a very powerful method, perhaps too powerful for some practice purposes, but useful in many contexts. Where there is need for causal information, this is a highly recommended design. You must decide whether it is worth the extra effort and time—from both your client and yourself—to use the *A-B-A-B* design.

Case Illustrations. Farrimond and Leland (2006) used a basic *A-B-A-B* design (with follow-up) that we offer as an illustration of both this single-system design method and as an example of what students might replicate as a kind of social action at the neighborhood level. These authors tried to increase donations to a supermarket's Food for the Poor Program using signs ("How about buying one for the Food Bank Bin?", followed by "Thank you") in front of the nonperishable food items on sale. At the bottom of the sign were four Food Bank sponsors (such as the Salvation Army). Another sign ("Food Bank Bin") was placed nearby at the collection site. The staff at the grocery store moved the signs around to new sale items each week.

Each of the phases in the *A-B-A-B* design and follow-up (2 months after the study ended) lasted for 2 weeks. Measurements included both the number of items donated and their value (in New Zealand dollars, where this study took place). The same vertical axis could accommodate both the number of items and the number of dollars. Figure 5 is adapted from their data.

Following the time line, we observe a very small number of items and an equally low dollar value during the baseline (A_1) in which there were no signs regarding making a donation. The authors did not use a longer baseline because no one was systematically counting the donations. Then, in B_1, the signs were placed as described above, and we see an immediate jump in donations and dollar value of these donations. When we discuss data analysis, we will see why these results are significantly different from baseline, but even commonsense suggests that the data indicate positive change. However, this change could have happened by chance or for some unknown reason. So, the authors returned to the baseline (A_2), that is, the signs were removed, and immediately, donations returned to their initial level.

At the second intervention (B_2), we again see a sharp rise in number and value of the donations, more erratic than in B_1, but of a similar level. The follow-up period, 2 months later, shows a continuing higher level of donations than initially, and especially, an increase in the value of items donated. Farrimond and Leland (2006, p. 250) note that the number of donations in both intervention phases was significantly greater than during the baseline phases ($p < .005$). With regard to costs, the author deducted the costs of the materials from the dollar value of the donations, and found an overall benefit of $NZ3,422.12 for the year, making this a cost-effective way for increasing donations to the Food Bank. Moreover, these signs were still in use 4 years after the initial study ended.

We make the point throughout these examples that real-life illustrations are more complex than hypothetical illustrations that might be constructed to clarify the principles of evaluation. Thus, in this case, as in many of our examples, such as length of baseline, stability of target event, and unequal length of phases, were not implemented in an optimal way. This is part

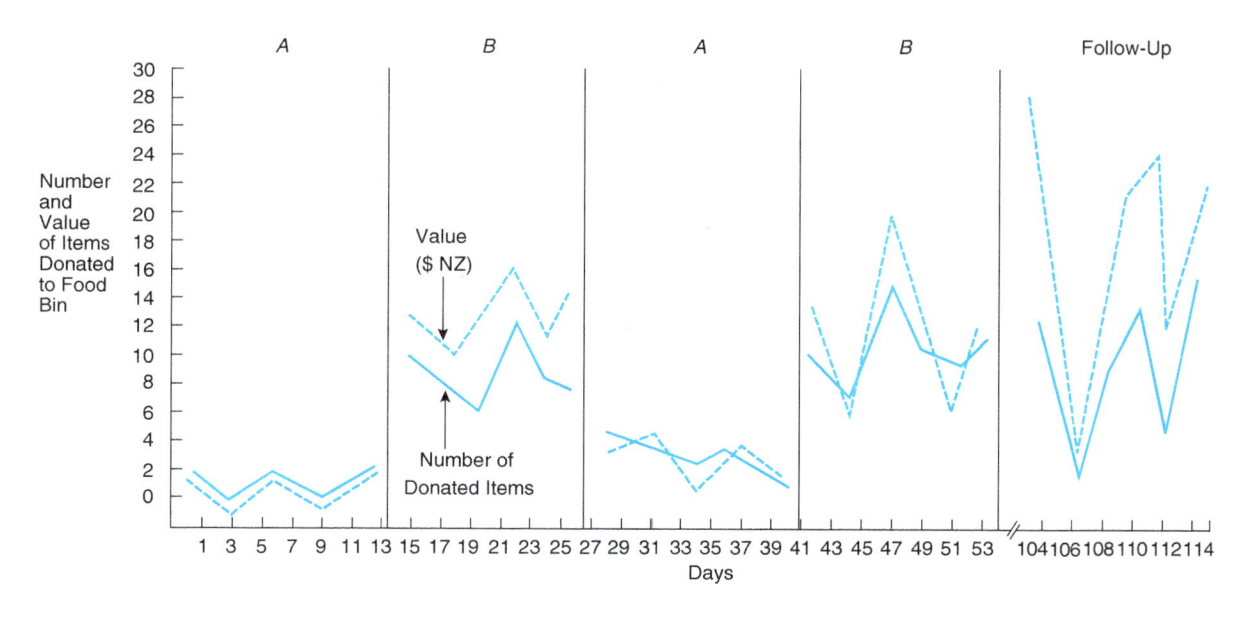

FIGURE 5 An *A-B-A-B* and follow-up design showing the number and value of items donated to a food bin in New Zealand.

(Adapted from "Increasing Donations to Supermarket Food-Bank Bins Using Proximal Prompts", by S. J. Farrimond and L. S. Leland, Sr., *Journal of Applied Behavior Analysis*, 2006, *39*, pp. 249–251.)

of the reality of practice. Rather than negate the value of each evaluation, it does present limitations regarding the certainty one can use in interpreting causal relationships. Thus, as a general guideline, we suggest that with each variation from the "ideal design," you simply use more caution in interpreting results.

A report by Brigham, Meier, and Goodner (1995) used the *A-B-A-B* design in a primary prevention effort to determine whether it was possible to increase designated drivers (DDs) so as to reduce alcohol-related accidents, a significant social and public health problem. Young drivers (and probably relatively recent drinkers) are disproportionately represented among persons driving while intoxicated (DWI). So, Brigham, Meier, and Goodner (1995) conducted an informal survey of local drinking establishments and found that few people participated in designating one member of their party who would not drink with the others so as to be able to drive them home safely. A local bar agreed to participate in the study; this bar had a long-standing designated driver program in which a person identified himself or herself as the DD and could get free coffee or soft drinks.

First, a team of observers sitting by the bar would be signaled by the bartender that someone had come forward as a designated driver. Two observers had to agree on the identity of this person—an interobserver reliability check—especially when this DD left the bar with his or her friends, in order to verify that this person was in fact the designated driver. These observations were made for three consecutive weekends (Friday and Saturday nights, from 8:30 PM to 1:00 AM) to represent the baseline rate of DDs.

The intervention consisted of three large wall posters and placards placed on the tables announcing the program: "Designated drivers, tell your server who you are, your drinks are on us! Free [brand name drinks X, Y, Z] or other nonalcoholic beers & wines, mixed drinks & coffee." The intervention lasted four weekends until the authors saw considerable improvement and some stability in the data.

Then the second baseline period began by the removal of the posters and placards, at which time the number of self-identified designated drivers returned to baseline levels. A second intervention period repeated the conditions of the first, and a similar increase in DDs occurred, but with somewhat less stability over seven weekends. The results, shown in Figure 6, indicate the success of the intervention. However, the question might be raised as to whether

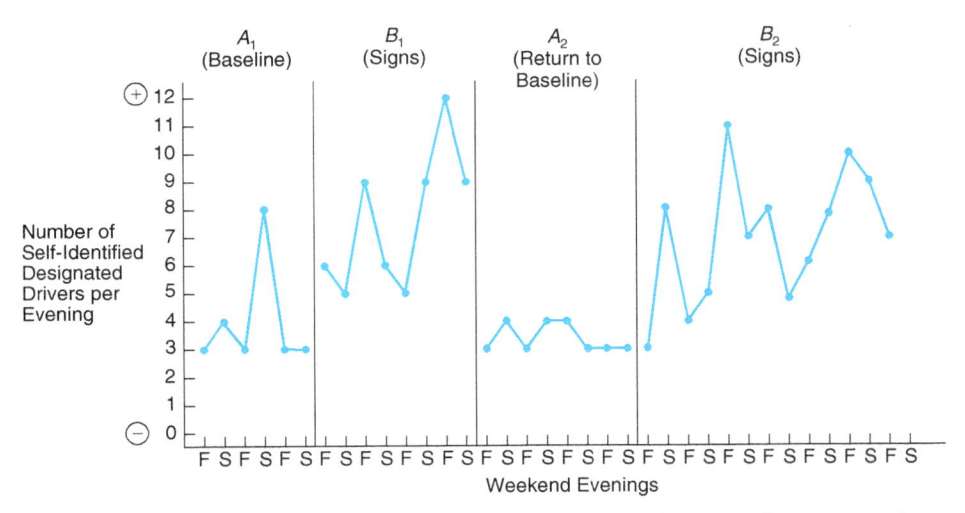

The Experimental Single-System Designs: *A-B-A, A-B-A-B, B-A-B*

FIGURE 6 Number of self-identified designated drivers per evening at a college campus bar. (Adapted from Brigham, Meier, and Goodner, 1995.)

having a designated driver encourages the others to drink more heavily than they might otherwise have done. The authors present a brief report suggesting that increased drinking occurs in less than 5% of respondents from another study. In general, this study illustrates the very practical advantages of a fairly sophisticated single-system design applied to a common problem using a simple, everyday intervention.

Our next example of an *A-B-A-B* design involves a combined experimental and qualitative analysis of a cognitive-behavioral intervention for anger (Nugent, 1991a). The client, Diane, a 28-year-old married woman, was concerned about her own severe angry "blow-ups" in which she verbally abused her husband and children. In the initial interview, the therapist developed a reconstructed baseline over the past week; the client expressed so much distress that a concurrent baseline was deemed unwise. The intervention consisted primarily of a "triple-column technique," in which the client, whenever she feels angry, lists in a notebook her automatic thoughts, evaluates them for distorted patterns, and substitutes rational responses. The first intervention phase (B_1) lasted 10 days. Following this, a removal phase was initiated, but the client became concerned over an increase in the frequency and intensity of her outbursts. Thus, the removal phase was limited to only 4 days. The removal phase (A_2) was followed by a 7-week B_2 phase. At the end of it, the client and her husband were referred to a marriage therapist for additional work focusing on their relationship.

At the same time as these procedures were occurring, the practitioner obtained qualitative results including open-ended interviews with the client, an open-ended telephone interview with the client's husband, plus a follow-up telephone interview and questionnaire 5 months after the treatment was completed.

As can be seen from Figure 7, there appears to have been a clear diminishing in angry outbursts over time. The author also applied a sophisticated statistical analysis (a time-series regression model) to these data that showed the changes also were statistically significant. The qualitative information provided by the client and her husband supported the quantitative results reported on the chart. The qualitative report also revealed that the client had substantially changed the intervention to be more suitable to her own style. Thus, while both qualitative and quantitative information supported the success of the overall process, some question remains as to the mechanisms by which the intervention, as modified by the client, affected the change.

The Nugent (1991a) report illustrates a number of the points made in this. First, quantitative and qualitative analyses can work hand in hand. Second, single-system designs can be very flexible. In this case, the design and intervention were modified to meet this client's needs. Third, even

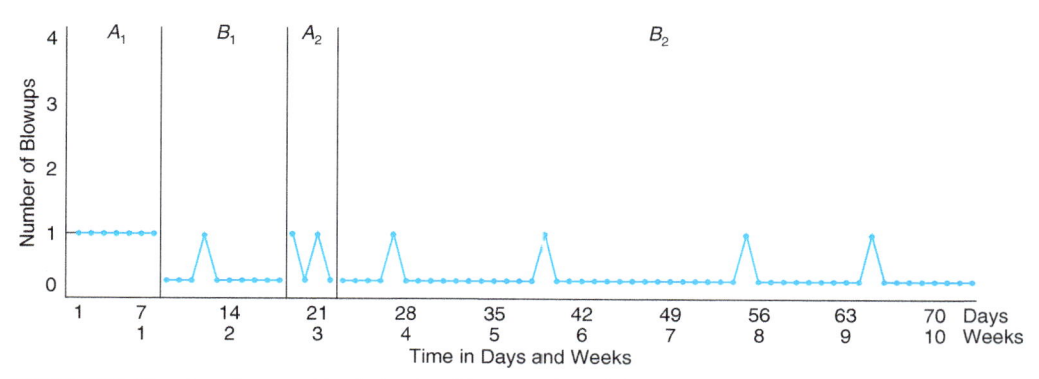

The Experimental Single-System Designs: A-B-A, A-B-A-B, B-A-B

FIGURE 7 Results of a cognitive-behavioral intervention with anger.
[Data adapted from "An Experimental and Qualitative Analysis of a Cognitive-Behavioral Intervention for Anger" by W. R. Nugent, 1991, *Social Work Research & Abstracts, 27*, pp. 3–8.]

without optimal conditions (in this case, a retrospective baseline and unequal length of phases), conclusions about effectiveness, and some inferences about causality, still can be made. In this case, the conclusions are bolstered by the use of a wide variety of information, plus application of statistical analysis to the results to confirm that results likely were not due to chance.

Shabini et al. (2002) describe some research conducted with three children with autism, ages 6 and 7, in which they were seeking to increase the initiation of social behavior with peers during school time free-play activities. The authors used a vibrating pager in the pockets of the children as their unobtrusive intervention, so as to prompt the child to initiate a conversation with, or respond to, the comments of their peers. Thus, social communication was the dependent variable. Interobserver reliability averaged 86% to 94% over the three subjects (see Figure 8).

Shabini et al. (2002) used an *A-B-A-B* design to evaluate the effectiveness of this tactile prompt on verbal initiation and verbal responses to peer initiation.

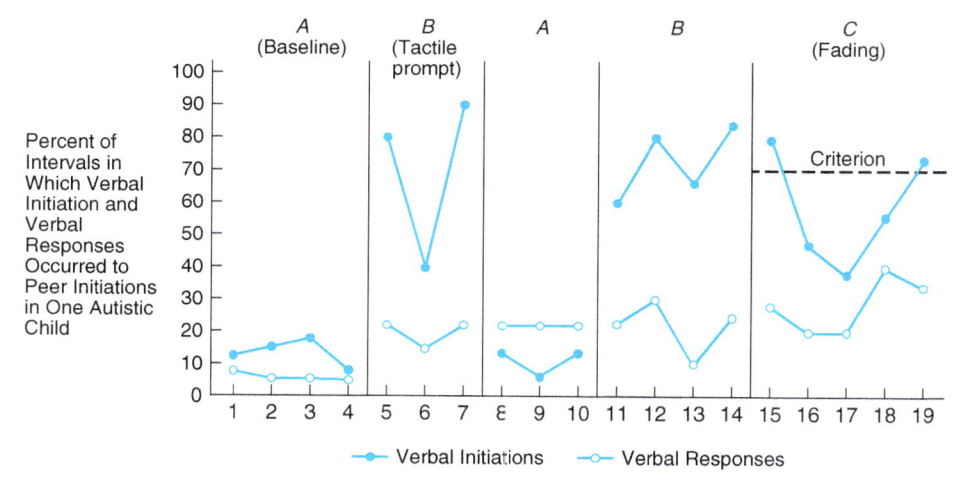

FIGURE 8 The pattern of verbal initiations and verbal responses by an autistic child in response to an unobtrusive intervention (vibrating pager in pocket of autistic child) that prompted the child to communicate with his peers.
[Adapted from Shabini, Katz, Wilder, Beauchamp, Taylor, & Fischer, 2002.]

The 19 sessions were divided differently for each of the three children, so we will be concerned with the general pattern among the three graphs. Figure 8 shows the patterns with one child, followed by a fading technique, in which the vibrating pager was used on a reduced basis; the level of fading was related to the child's initial baseline pattern as it was for the other two children.

Results show that when and only when the vibrating pager is used at a consistent level (i.e., before fading) is there a significant improvement in this child's initiating conversations with peers, and to a lesser degree, responding to peer-initiated remarks. The authors point out some limitations of their study, including too few phases where the tactile prompt was used, an undetermined effect of the device on peers' rate of initiation of conversation, and the fact that some prompts remained needed by the three children even after the intervention phase was terminated, suggesting the need for a more effective way to eliminate the vibrating pager or the need to extend the intervention phase to enhance the intervention's effects.

Introducing the Client to the A-B-A-B Design. This design is complicated and sometimes difficult to explain to clients or others involved in the service program. Some of the approaches that we recommend for use with the *A-B-A* design apply here, except that you can emphasize that the client will end up on an intervention phase so as to make sure that the service program has been an overall success. We also recommend that you alert the client that part of the final intervention phase may be used to help the client maintain improved behavior after the intervention is over. This is a service required in any intervention, but the repetitive nature of the *A-B-A-B* design provides ideal conditions for making plans for the maintenance phase. Following are some comments you could use to introduce these ideas:

"*An important part of service is to discover whether what we have done together is sufficient to last when you are on your own. Therefore, we are going to stop the treatment part of our contacts for a short period of time (A_2) during which we will continue to collect information about y (the target). Then we will return to the treatment* (or some variation of it) *until we are certain that you can handle these types of problems on your own.*

"*This means that as part of our final services to you, we will talk about* (and practice) *how you can continue to solve the types of problems we have been discussing on your own*" (producing an *A-B-A-B-M* design).

EXPERIMENTAL REPEAT OF INTERVENTION DESIGN: *B-A-B* |B|A|B

Because of the unusual characteristics of the *B-A-B* design it might be helpful to begin with an example that comes from the field of preventive dentistry (McDonald & Budd, 1983). A community dental unit (instructors and students) went to a local grade school to instruct young children in proper ways to brush their teeth. At the same time, they used red-dye disclosing tablets to measure how effective a given brushing had been in removing plaque. A period of months intervened during which time the school children were left to their natural environment regarding dental health. The parents of the children were given disclosing tablets to be used on randomly assigned days. A second instructional session was then held to clarify and reinforce earlier instruction, as well as to obtain another set of data on how well children were following the brushing instructions. Figure 9 presents data collected in this project.

It can be observed from the data that most children attained the dental health criterion level during the first instructional phase, suggesting that they understood how to brush their teeth properly. The long middle period of the study showed that, initially, students were strongly influenced by the presence of the disclosing tablets, but over time they became less aware of or less pressured by them and their scores dropped. Finally, the second intervention showed that these students could easily regain their criterion performance. This suggests the usefulness of an ongoing reminder, or booster shot.

An interesting example of the *B-A-B* design as part of a larger design is drawn from a study by Stock and Milan (1993). They were seeking to improve the dietary practices of three elderly clients at an independent living facility, each of whom had a strong medical need to eat healthful foods. We will focus on the first part of their study because it uses the *B-A-B* design, even though they continue with several other interventions. At the beginning of the study, the resident staff told the researchers that none of these three clients seemed to be eating wisely, even though the dining room was decorated like a fine restaurant, with linen table cloths, fresh flowers, and a menu with four choices in each of the

The Experimental Single-System Designs: *A-B-A, A-B-A-B, B-A-B*

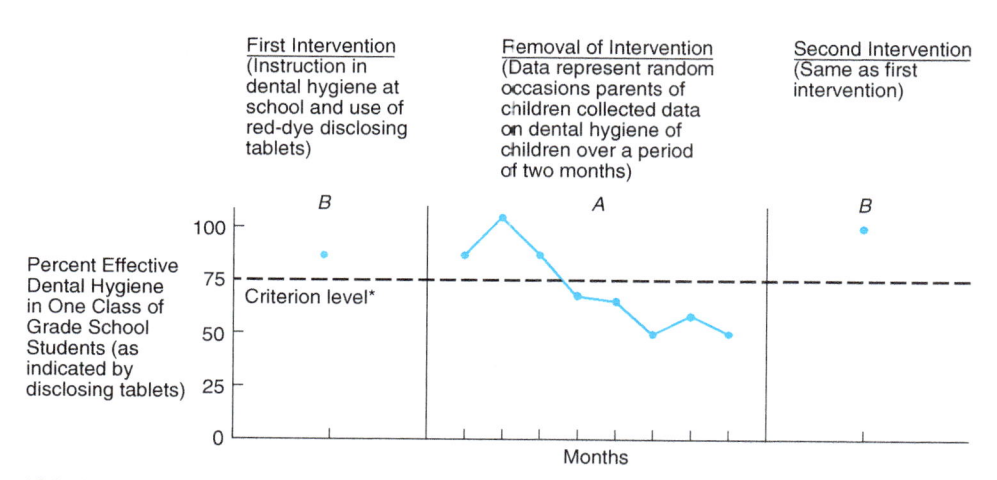

First Intervention (Instruction in dental hygiene at school and use of red-dye disclosing tablets)

Removal of Intervention (Data represent random occasions parents of children collected data on dental hygiene of children over a period of two months)

Second Intervention (Same as first intervention)

Percent Effective Dental Hygiene in One Class of Grade School Students (as indicated by disclosing tablets)

Criterion level*

Months

*Criterion level normatively defined as the lowest acceptable level of effective dental hygiene that promotes desired incidences of dental health.

FIGURE 9 Illustration of a *B-A-B* design in preventive dentistry.
[Adapted from McDonald & Budd, 1983.]

---

four courses—appetizers, entrees, vegetables, and desserts (see Figure 10)).

Stock and Milan chose to begin the intervention (B_1) immediately by using the existing system of menus on which prompts were placed for the healthful foods. A heart was placed by those items that were low-cholesterol and calorie-modified, and the names of these dishes were intended to sound appealing. Despite these efforts, data showed low percentages of healthy choices by the three clients in B_1, which validates what the resident staff had said.

The A_1 condition, a true baseline, involved removal of the prompts on the menus. There was no deterioration in healthy choices at this time, and indeed, one client (#2) seemed to improve her healthy choices. The B_2 condition was briefly reinstated, and again the data show little change from B_1 or A. Data like these are the nightmare visions of practitioners and evaluators alike. However, these authors were not discouraged, and instituted a cluster of other interventions—enhanced prompts, social reinforcements, a lottery that could be won by making healthy food choices, and co-opting residents (including the targeted three clients) to promote healthy food choices in fellow residents. This cluster of activities did indeed produce positive changes in client scores (phases C_1-CD_1-CDE-CD_2-C_2), but upon return to B_3 (the initial menu intervention with hearts prompting healthy choices), there was a return to nonhealthy eating.

It may seem surprising that we use an unsuccessful *B-A-B* example, but, in fact, we all have to be prepared for real-life events, and not every brilliant intervention seems to have the effects we predict it would. Remember the ethical advice from Hippocrates: Help if you can, but do no harm. We wonder why some of the relatively inexpensive interventions that were used and appeared to be helpful were not continued in place of the interventions that were rather clearly shown to be working.

While the absence of a true preintervention baseline means that the practitioner loses his or her opportunity for systematic comparisons with an initial baseline, as is possible in the *A-B-A-B* design, there are still a number of important comparisons that can be made, at least in theory. The first intervention may be compared with the baseline period, and the baseline period may be compared with the second intervention period. We offer the label of this design—the experimental repeat of intervention (there is no general agreement about how it should be identified other than by the letters *B-A-B*)—to emphasize the point that the intervention has been, in theory, conducted successfully when the practitioner decides to remove the intervention, establish a baseline period, and then reimplement the intervention to determine whether the intervention is really affecting the problem. This is like having a basic single-system design, *A-B*, but with prior knowledge of how the client may

The Experimental Single-System Designs: *A-B-A, A-B-A-B, B-A-B*

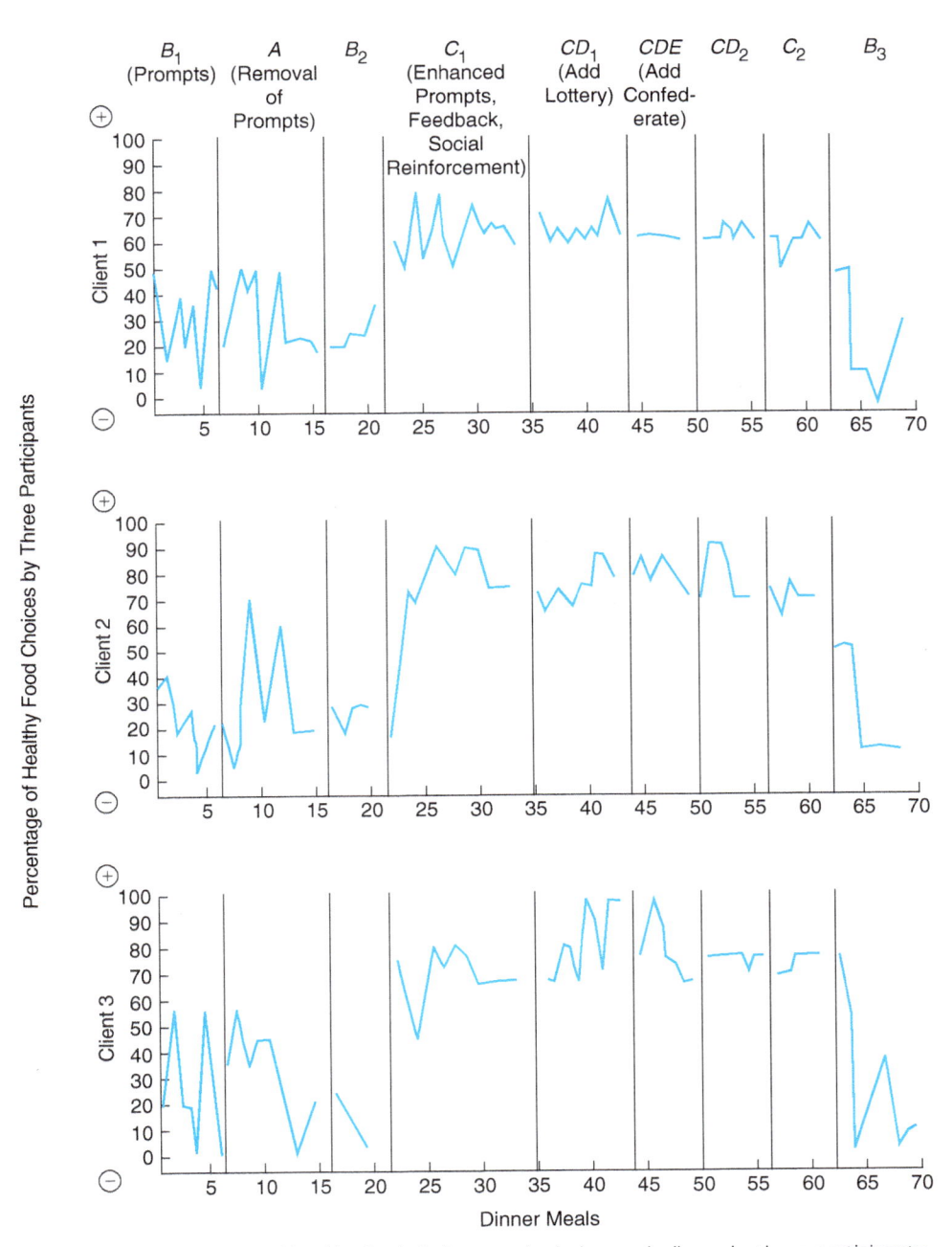

FIGURE 10 Percentage of healthy food choices made during each dinner by three participants (Amy, Beth, Carl) at an independent living facility during nine experimental conditions of the study.

(Adapted from Stock & Milan, 1993.)

react to the intervention that will be introduced. If the problem occurs again during the *A* phase, but the client returns to the same level of the target event in the second intervention phase that was exhibited in the first intervention phase, then you can assume, other things being equal, that the planned interventions are likely related to the observed changes in the problem.

As mentioned in earlier sections, it would be wise in any design that ends in a service phase to include, or add as a separate phase, a program that will maintain the gains achieved through intervention.

Strengths of the B-A-B Design. The major strength of this design stems from your ability to use it when you must begin intervention without a preliminary baseline phase, for example, in crisis situations or when delaying intervention might be harmful, and still establish whether the intervention appears to be affecting the problem. As with other experimental designs, you purposely remove a successful intervention to observe the changes in target behaviors and then reinstate the intervention according to plan. If the data vary in accordance with that practice hypothesis, then there is a stronger basis for causal inference. If data stubbornly refuse to behave as intended by the theory, you may need a different theory.

The other strength of the *B-A-B* design, in contrast to the *A-B-A* design, which has the same number of logical comparisons, is that the *B-A-B* design ends on a service phase, thus fulfilling professional demands that work with the client be sensitively terminated when the target problems have been resolved. This design permits crisis intervention to begin immediately while still not losing the opportunity for an experimental design in the sense that we have been using this term for single-system designs.

Limitations of the B-A-B Design. A major limitation of this design, which is shared with the other removal designs, is the question of ethical suitability of removing a successful intervention—unless it is an accidental or unplanned removal—in order to test the functional connection between the intervention itself and the outcome. Such a design requires considerable control over the situation and the cooperation of others in accepting the removal of a successful intervention while some nonintervention (and likely problematic) condition ensues.

Another limitation, at least in terms of logical inferences, is that the lack of the initial baseline sharply reduces the logical comparisons that can be made. Lacking an initial baseline, this design may disguise an initial training phase with its partial or incomplete achievement of desired behavior change.

Recommendations Regarding the B-A-B Design. We recommend this design almost to the degree that we would recommend the more powerful *A-B-A-B* design. When no initial baseline can be conducted and situations occur permitting and benefiting from the logical analysis that removal designs can offer, then this design can be quite useful. It also is useful in contexts such as crisis intervention or other dangerous situations for clients when there isn't time for a full-blown initial baseline. Thus, while the *B-A-B* design has its limitations stemming from lack of the initial baseline, it is a strong design and well worth considering on a selective basis. It might also be worth considering a *B-A-B-A* design where the second baseline permits the planned observation of the staying power of the *B* intervention. Finally, it may be possible, even in crisis situations, to add a reconstructed baseline as a first phase, thereby allowing an additional baseline/intervention comparison to enhance causal inferences.

Case Illustration. The final example of a *B-A-B* design involves an actual case in which one of the authors was involved. The case started with the unfortunate suicide of a popular high school student one weekend, which was the stimulus for a crisis intervention team to come to the student's high school the following Monday morning. The crisis team led discussions about the event among students and teachers, in both large and small groups. Participants voiced feelings of distress, sadness, and anger over the suicide, and asked what could have been done to prevent it. The crisis team recommended that everyone at the school learn the danger signs of suicide—such as suicide talk or previous attempts, personality or behavior changes for no apparent reason, and various forms of depressed behavior that occur nearly every day for at least 2 weeks. The team instituted an early-warning system whereby a student or teacher could turn in a confidential note to the school health team describing a person's danger signs. The notes had to be signed in order to be considered valid—that is, not practical jokes—but were to be kept confidential by the health team who would follow up on the leads individually and privately.

Records were kept of the numbers of signed notes received and acted upon. The notes were taken as a sign of shared concern for fellow students, and were thus encouraged by the crisis team in the first week they were at the school. They had intended to spend at least 2 weeks there, but another emergency occurred—a fire in a nursing home that required relocation of survivors and meetings with them and their families—that took the team away for 2 weeks. This constituted an unplanned removal phase. When they returned to the school, they resumed their group discussions. The early-warning note system was maintained throughout this time, and continued throughout the school year. Figure 11 presents the data from this project.

As part of their service program, the crisis team set up support groups among students and teachers that became the main thrust of the maintenance phase (C) of this report—where the clients (students and teachers) were trained to help themselves after the crisis team left. Figure 11 shows the initial crisis intervention phase, B_1, then a baseline phase when they were suddenly called to serve another group, and a return to the intervention phase, B_2, plus a maintenance phase.

Introducing the Client to the B-A-B Design. First, we suggest you review previous introductions (in this chapter). In addition, there are some aspects directly related to the unique features of this design. On the one hand, it may be easier to discuss the evaluation component of a project in which the practitioner has already achieved a successful intervention. If the entire project is described before the first intervention, then the same directions applicable to the other experimental designs hold here too. On the other hand, clients may raise questions regarding the *B-A-B* design, such as, why change anything? Or why rock the boat? Our suggested responses to these types of statements are as follows: "*I am as pleased as you are about the positive changes in the problem* (or the positive steps toward achievement of the goal), *and I want to make sure that we can keep this level of achievement going after the service program is over. Therefore, I would like to have a trial run by removing the treatment and still continuing to collect information about how well you are doing with these types of problems. If the problem returns to bothersome levels, we can start the treatment once again and that will be the last part of the service program. We want to make sure you can handle these problems on your own in the future.*"

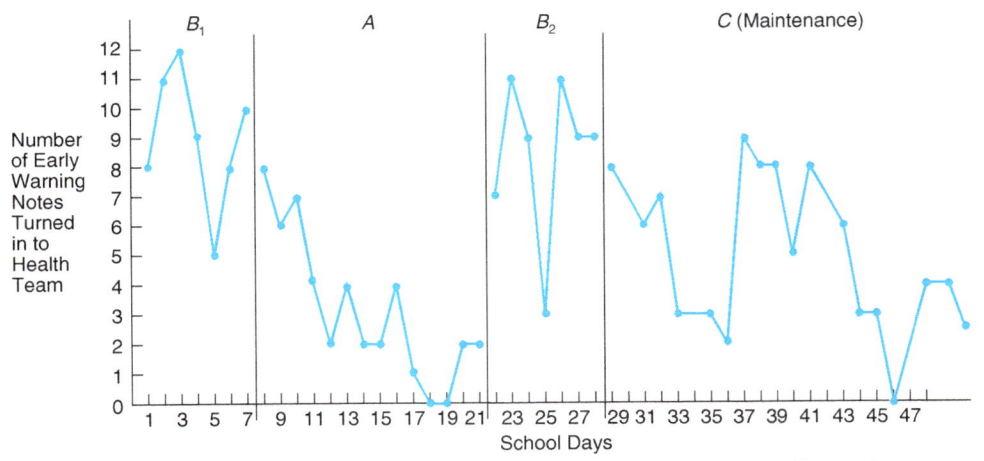

FIGURE 11 Crisis intervention at a high school regarding a student suicide, illustrating a B-A-B design plus maintenance phase.

Summary

We have described three experimental designs, all of which involve the removal of a successful intervention (i.e., one in which observations of target behaviors appear to be clearly moving toward desired levels) followed by a baseline period in order to test the potential causal effects of the intervention's impact on the target behavior. Variations on this return to baseline make up the three designs: *A-B-A*, *A-B-A-B*, and *B-A-B*. Because of the successively unlikely occurrence that such variations in the target problem could have happened by chance, we have the basis for inferring a causal influence on the part of the planned intervention. This means that not only is the pattern of change documented, but control over that change is to some extent documented as well. This is the basis for a logical analysis of the events in question. This is a very powerful set of designs that you should consider carefully, evaluating each design for its own strengths and limitations.

We also discussed the difficulties in using such designs, such as practical problems (there could be carryover effects from one phase to the next phase), ethical considerations (is it right to stop a successful intervention in order to attempt to understand causality?), and collegial problems (who wants to work with a troublesome client, especially after the problem appears to be resolved?). Thus, with logical power comes social dilemmas regarding practicality.

MULTIPLE DESIGNS FOR SINGLE SYSTEMS

Baselines, Targets, Crossovers, and Series

PURPOSE This chapter deals with single-system designs that involve multiple elements, specifically multiple baselines and multiple targets, and certain variations of these two. Multiple-baseline designs can be used with more than one problem, client, or setting, which makes them very versatile. Multiple-baseline designs also can be used as an alternative to the experimental designs when there are practical limitations (such as carryover effects), or ethical concerns (such as removing a successful intervention for a serious problem), or problems in staff cooperation (who would have to handle the return to the problematic behavior phase). Multiple-target designs are helpful in generating meaningful patterns among behaviors. Crossover and constant-series designs offer some interesting and practical variations on the other multiple designs. Overall, the four designs discussed in this chapter are very accessible for ordinary use by practitioners.

Introduction
Multiple-Baseline Designs: Across Problems, Clients, or Settings

$x\ |\ A\ |\ B$
$y\ |\ A\ |\ B$
$z\ |\ A\ |\ B$

Strengths of the Multiple-Baseline Design
Limitations of the Multiple-Baseline Design
Recommendations Regarding the Multiple-Baseline Design
Case Illustrations
  Across Problems
  Across Clients
  Across Settings

Introducing the Client to the Multiple-Baseline Design
Multiple-Target Designs

$x\ |\ A\ |\ B$
$y\ |\ A\ |\ C$
$z\ |\ A\ |\ D$

Case Illustration
Strengths of the Multiple-Target Design
Limitations of the Multiple-Target Design
Recommendations Regarding the Multiple-Target Design
Introducing the Client to the Multiple-Target Design

From Chapter 15 of *Evaluating Practice: Guidelines for the Accountable Professional*, Sixth Edition. Martin Bloom, Joel Fischer, John G. Orme. Copyright © 2009 by Pearson Education, Inc. All rights reserved.

Variations on Multiple Designs
Crossover Designs

x | A | B | x | A | B | C |
y | B | A | or y | A | C | B |

Constant-Series Designs

x | A | x | B |
             or
y | A | B | y | A | B |

Baseline-Only Control   *Intervention-Only Control*

Summary

INTRODUCTION

There are several relatively powerful single-system designs that involve working with several target problems, several clients, or several settings at the same time, while holding the other two of the three elements constant. (For example, if we work with several problems, then we work with only one client in one setting.) With the multiple-baseline design in particular, the practitioner can make some logical inferences about possible causal effects of the intervention without removing the intervention. Thus, the multiple-baseline design can serve as an alternative to the experimental designs; they also have advantages in their own right in that they can provide information about *generalizability* of results across clients, targets, and settings. Moreover, the designs discussed in this chapter emphasize a fact that practitioners have always faced, that client problems and goals often come in multiples. One way to represent this practical state of affairs in design terms is by way of multiple-baseline designs, so as to identify patterns of change and the possible causal relationship between interventions and outcomes, and to examine the generalizability of intervention effects across clients, targets, and settings.

The designs discussed in this chapter may appear in some ways more complicated than those discussed earlier. However, we want to emphasize that this complexity exists mainly in the initial presentation of the designs because they are different from the ones we've already examined. Once you understand the underlying arrangement of baselines and interventions, we hope you will recognize that these are quite easy to use in ordinary practice.

MULTIPLE-BASELINE DESIGNS: ACROSS PROBLEMS, CLIENTS, OR SETTINGS

x | A | B |
y | A | B |
z | A | B |

Multiple-baseline designs have three elements that may be varied: target problems, clients, and the settings in which the client(s) and problem(s) exist. When one element (say, two or more of a client's problems) is studied, the other elements have to be kept constant (one client in one setting). These three patterns are illustrated in Figure 1. While there are different elements examined in each of the three cases, the same basic logical pattern of analysis is used. In this section, we introduce this basic pattern.

Multiple-baseline designs exhibit the following characteristics: There are two or more different target problems, clients, or settings on which baseline information is collected (indicated by the x, y, and z in the figure at the beginning of this section). As soon as a stable pattern of baseline data is obtained in the baselines on all the targets, then an intervention (B) is introduced only to the first target. The second and third baselines are continued. If a desired change occurs in the first target while no obvious change occurs in the second and third, then the same intervention, B, is applied to the second target, while the third baseline is continued. Again, if a desired change occurs in the second target (and the first target continues to maintain its desired changes), then the same intervention, B, is applied to the third target. If a desired change occurs in the third target, while the first and second targets maintain their desired changes, then we have the basic multiple-baseline pattern that permits us to note that desired changes occurred when, and only

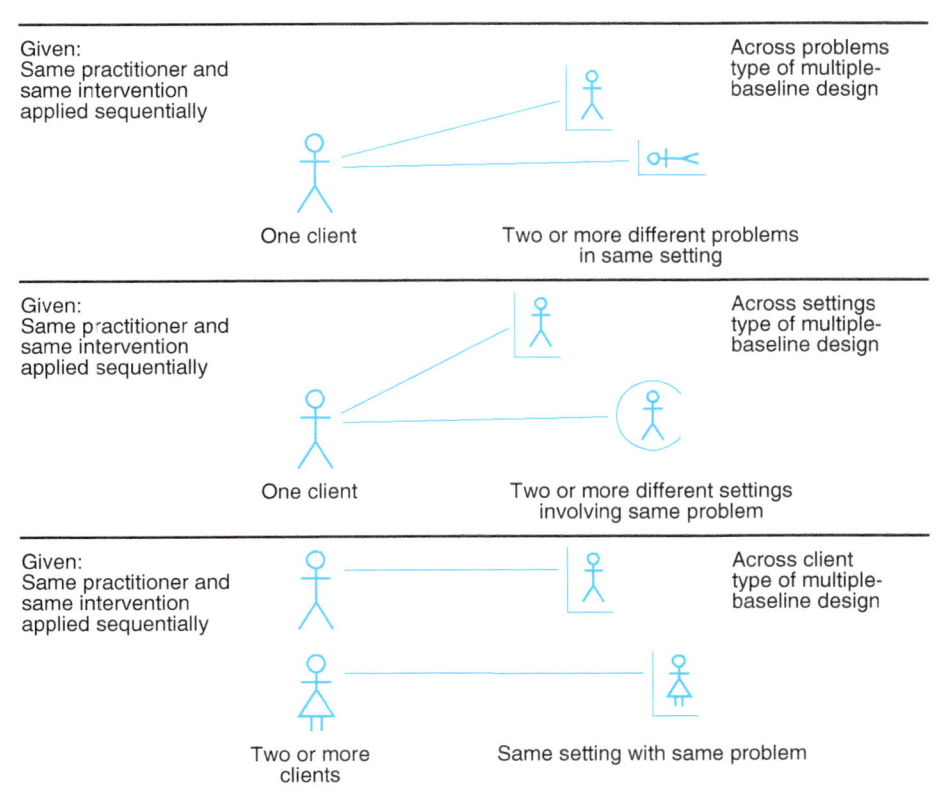

FIGURE 1 Patterns of multiple-baseline design components across problems/goals, client/systems, and situations.

when, the specific intervention occurred *on a sequential basis*. This becomes the basis for inferring causality, that the intervention likely was a primary cause related to the observed outcomes in the several targets, viewed sequentially. This basic pattern holds whether the targets are two or more client problems, two or more different clients, or two or more different settings, as indicated in Figure 1. The essence of the inference of causality is that the *changes occurred in sequence,* only after introduction of the intervention. Thus, once again, the "principle of unlikely successive coincidences" would permit the argument that there may be a causal relationship between implementation of the intervention and changes in the target.

Some special issues affect the different types of multiple-baseline designs. One concerns the number of targets used. Opinions differ. Hypothetically, two targets would be sufficient to demonstrate sequential change involving the same intervention. However, some writers recommend three targets at a minimum (Barlow, Nock, & Hersen, 2009), while others suggest four or more (Kazdin & Kopel, 1975). Greater numbers of targets, each changing when and only when an intervention is applied to it, make it increasingly unlikely that these planned changes are happening by chance alone.

Obviously, the more targets that are required for the use of a multiple-baseline design, the less likely it is that some practitioners will use the design. So, we offer our standard caution: The consensus on minimum numbers of target problems is three. If you use only two targets, then consider the findings merely suggestive. If you can handle more than three, then you have much stronger evidence of causality.

It is important to add that any two targets may be treated in sequence as the basis of a multiple-baseline design. For example, consider a practitioner with four targets. If targets 2 and 3 changed when an intervention was applied to target 1, there would be a serious problem if only the first three targets were being observed. However, as long as target 4 did not change, the practitioner can still try for a multiple baseline with the first and fourth targets only. The second and third targets become simple *A-B* designs where change can be evaluated, without causal implications of the multiple baseline design from targets 1 and 4.

Another topic with regard to multiple-baseline designs concerns how long a successful intervention should be continued on the first target before applying that same intervention to a second target. Again, opinions differ, but a consensus suggests that at least three sessions or observations are needed to indicate a stable improvement in the first target and no major change in the second. A larger number would be preferable on length of baseline.

The versatility of multiple-baseline designs is remarkable. The logic of the design states that two or more targets in the same system and context are needed for sequential treatment as the basis of inferring causality for that intervention. Thus, we may use two or more different clients as targets, or two or more different problems from the same client as targets, or two or more different settings involving the same client and problem. We illustrate each of these variations briefly now, and then go into greater detail later.

The first type of multiple-baseline design is *across problems*, and involves one client (or client/system) with two or more problems (the different baselines) in one setting. As an example of a multiple-baseline design across problems, Jacobson (1979) used this design in work with couples showing severely distressed marital relationships. Taking one couple as an example (Jacobson discusses six cases), the process first involved a 2-week baseline period consisting of an assessment and use of a modified version of the Spouse Observation Checklist (Weiss, Hops, & Patterson, 1973), data on which were phoned in at the end of each day. (Figure 2 summarizes about 14 baseline data points by averaging each week's data and recording these average points.) At the initial intervention session (the third week), the couple was presented with an analysis of their marital problems and a rationale for the treatment they were about to receive. Each session began with an analysis of the data the clients had supplied during the previous meetings.

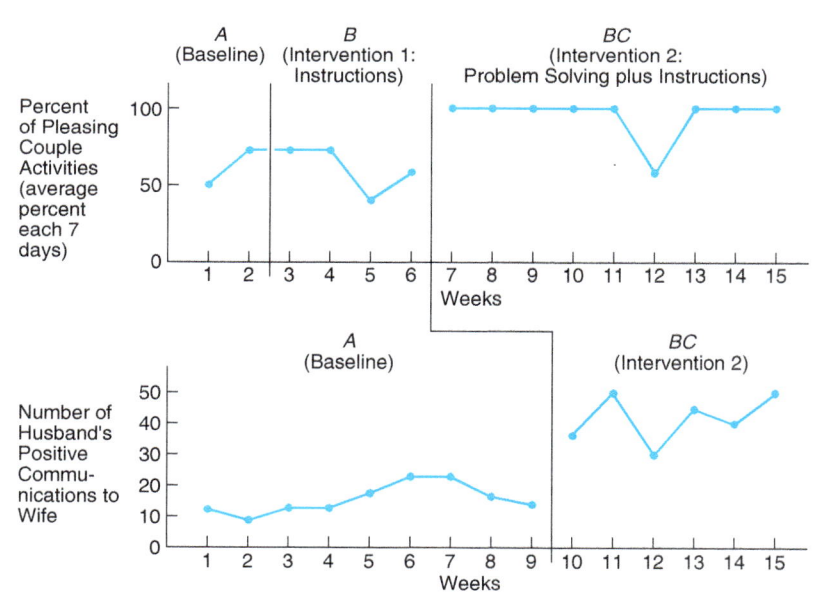

FIGURE 2 Case illustration of a multiple-baseline design across problem behaviors for a married couple.

(Data adapted from "Increasing Positive Behavior in Severely Distressed Marital Relationships: The Effects of Problem-Solving Training" by N. S. Jacobson, 1979, *Behavior Therapy*, *10*, p. 318.)

The first intervention consisted of instructing the clients to increase the intimate behaviors desired by the spouses and to decrease those activities designated as undesirable. Four weeks of this intervention did not produce any desired changes, so the practitioner added a second intervention (problem-solving training) on the seventh week, at which time substantial improvements were made. After 3 weeks of stable, desired behavior on the first target problem, with no significant change in the baseline of the second target problem, the practitioner introduced the problem-solving training plus instructions for the second problem (husband's lack of positive communications to his wife). A major improvement is recorded, while the first target problem continues at a generally high level of performance. Jacobson notes that this design cannot tease out the influences of problem solving alone because it may be confounded (at least in the first baseline) with the first intervention (instructions) and in both baselines with relationship skills and other communications. However, this is an interesting example of the variations possible in the multiple baseline across problems. First, it involves couples as the system for analysis; it recognizes that sometimes new interventions may be necessary (for the first target), and that this experience can be used immediately with the second target. Yet, you can see its classic multiple-baseline form within these variations.

The second type of multiple baseline is *across settings*, in which one client (or client/system) has one problem exhibited in two or more settings. Cushing and Kennedy (1997) provide evidence regarding the effectiveness of peer tutoring for the tutor, while other studies have looked at the effects on the person tutored. They show, using a multiple-baseline design across settings, that academic engagement, assignment completion, grading, and perceived classroom participation all are improved in students without disabilities who provided peer support for students with moderate to severe disabilities. In Figure 3, adapted from Cushing and Kennedy (1997), one tutor (Louie) is followed over a period of 25 days in three different academic settings as he tutors another student (Leila). As the first part of the multiple baseline demands, a baseline condition (Louie working alone) is observed in English class for 12 days, while this same baseline continues in both science and social studies classes at about the same level as before. There is a drop in performance when the intervention is applied in another setting, but there is an immediate improvement back to the typical baseline level of engagement for Louie. Then a slight increase in Louie's participation is observed during the intervention phase in the first setting, as he is tutoring Leila in the same class. Then the same intervention is introduced in the second setting (a science class), followed by an immediate strong improvement in Louie's performance in that same class, as he tutors Leila. Finally, the same intervention is introduced in the third setting (social studies class), and again, Louie's performance sharply improves, as he is tutoring Leila in that class.

This study is a good approximation of the logical rules for the multiple-baseline design across settings. Louie's baseline performance in each of the three setting is reasonably good but not perfect (good enough to be selected as tutor). However, when he sequentially tutors the other student in three settings, he himself improves in that same setting. This study shows the creative use of a sophisticated single-system design applied to a very common, everyday situation in many schools. Tutoring helps the tutored student, but also the tutor makes improvements in performance as well.

The third type of multiple baseline is *across clients* or *client-systems*, in which the same practitioner applies the same intervention sequentially to two or more persons/groups who exhibit the same problems in the same setting. Let us illustrate this design with an example drawn from Miltenberger and his colleagues (2004) who have explored the difficult question of children playing with guns—and getting injured or killed. The goal is to train young children not to play with guns should they find them in their houses. So, let's imagine this scenario. Six children, ages 6 and 7, are recruited from a summer day care program, and with permission from their parents, they receive safety training about guns: (1) don't touch, (2) get away, and (3) tell an adult about the gun. The training is clear and simple and directly related to the issue of gun safety. Each child has to pass a qualifying test to make sure he or she understand the rules. They receive the training, and sequentially, the children are tested in a simulated gun situation at school and at home. Note that this across-clients design incorporates some across settings as well. A perfect multiple-baseline design across clients would look like this: each child would show a problematic baseline (they were all curious and touched the gun, etc.). Then, after individual training, each child in sequence would show the correct behavior in the simulated gun situation in each setting.

Needless to say, the reality that Miltenberger and his colleagues found was nothing like this ideal model. Some of the six children could not learn to a criterion

Multiple Designs for Single Systems

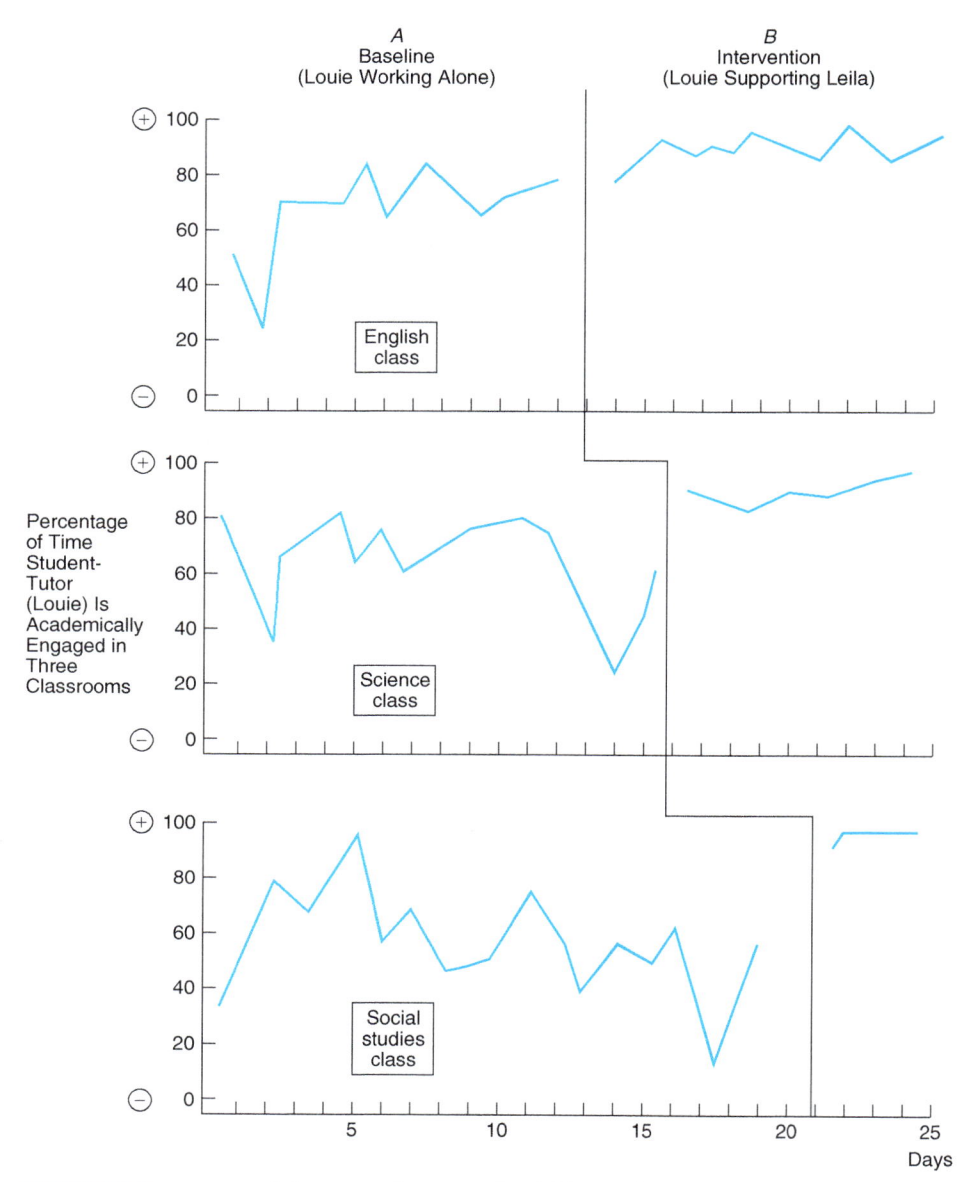

FIGURE 3 Percentage of time a student-tutor (Louie) is academically engaged in three classrooms when working alone or supporting (tutoring) another student (Leila).
(Adapted from Cushing & Kennedy, 1997.)

level the three simple rules of gun safety, so they received extra training including *in situ* training, and even extra reinforcements for successful performance. Even then, not all children showed consistent learned behavior. Are these extra efforts at training different interventions or one broadly defined intervention? The authors chose to use the broad definition, where training may take a variety of forms (the social context and the type of reinforcers being two of them), and that all were to be used to achieve gun safety. As shown in Figure 4, there was anything but continuous improvement toward the gun safety goal. And to their credit, the authors note other limitations of the study, such as having only two home assessments in baseline, and in one case the whole intervention appeared to stimulate one young bandit to gun play, not gun safety. The overall conclusion the authors reached is that behavioral skills training together with

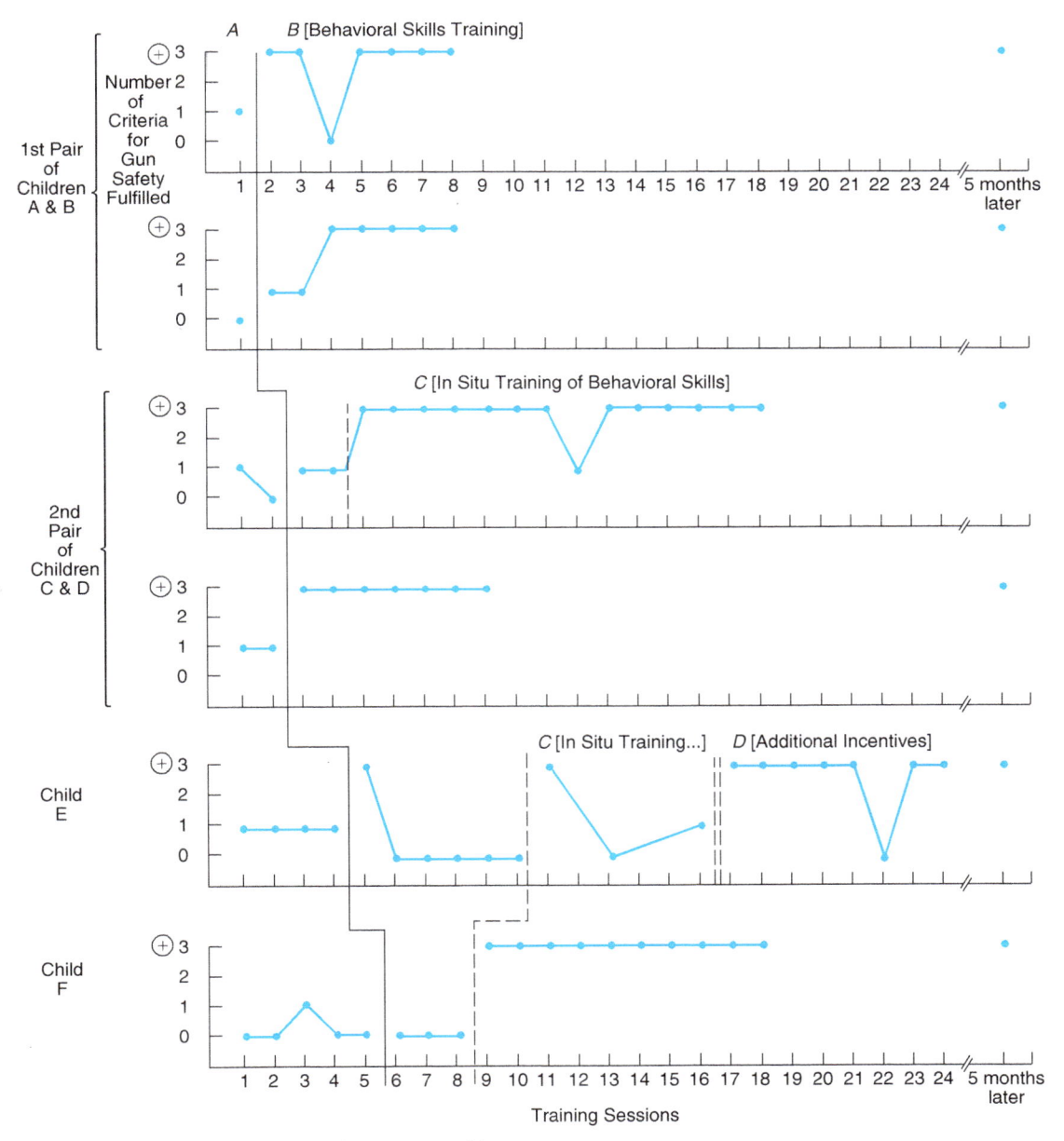

FIGURE 4 A multiple-baseline design across subjects.

(Adapted from "Evaluation of Behavioral Skills Training to Prevent Gun Play in Children" by R. G. Miltenberger, C. Flessner, B. Gatheridge, B. Johnson, M. Satterlund, & K. Egemo, 2004, *Journal of Applied Behavior Analysis, 37*, pp. 513–516.)

boosters and add-ons can be successful, although children will vary in their responses to this mix of interventions. Our conclusion is more limited, that these data do not show any one simple intervention will help all young children achieve gun safety, although the overall results are encouraging, especially because a 5-month follow-up showed continuing positive results.

These three cases illustrate the three types of multiple-baseline designs. We next consider the strengths and limitations of these designs and our recommendations regarding their use. Then we present a number of case examples to illustrate the underlying patterns as well as the variations these designs can include.

Strengths of the Multiple-Baseline Design

It is clear that this design is quite adaptable to changes in problems/goals, clients/systems, or settings. Indeed, when clients present multiple problems, this design represents one way of dealing with them in a planned fashion whereby you might cluster those with high priority for immediate action, and then in sequence deal with others later, and still obtain considerable insight into whether your interventions appeared to be responsible for the changes observed. This assumes that the *same* intervention can be applied to different problems, or in different settings, or to different clients (with the same problem).

Likewise, there are few designs in the single-system spectrum that permit practitioners to compare interventions across settings such as is possible with the multiple-baseline design. This has important implications if you wish to note that the baseline condition (e.g., unassertiveness) is exhibited consistently across different situations. Then we can study whether the intervention deals with that target successively in different settings.

The multiple-baseline design may be the design of choice when problems of carryover or irreversibility of effects are present or when the first intervention cannot be removed so that you can't use experimental (removal) designs. This is because with removal designs you stay with the same problem, client, and setting so that carryover or irreversibility may limit any conclusions that could be drawn from the removal. On the other hand, since multiple-baseline designs use *different* problems, clients, or settings, standard carryover or irreversibility effects are not as germane; this is because you are switching domains (problems, clients, settings) rather than removing the intervention and staying with the same domain. (However, it is also possible to have carryover effects over clients, problems, and/or settings, a point to which we return below.)

We also have suggested the utility of this design *in place of* the experimental designs that remove a successful intervention in order to test whether that intervention is causally linked to observed changes. With the multiple-baseline design, if the first target changes while the others remain more or less unchanged, then this tells you that not only has the first target changed, but the change is limited to that target even when other events are present and are part of the total intervention effort. This focused demonstration of control over desired targets is at the heart of the multiple-baseline design. That is, the controlled application of the intervention and the predicted sequential effect become the basis for an inference that the practitioner's efforts are causally related to the observed change.

It may be argued that using the multiple-baseline procedure also is a way of testing the generalizability of the intervention. If the problems are similar and the settings are similar, then sequential application of the same intervention to different clients offers some basis for inferring that the intervention is generalizable, assuming there is no contact among recipients of the service that would constitute contamination of the data. In a similar way, it is possible to generalize an intervention across problems and situations as well.

Limitations of the Multiple-Baseline Design

Many times it is hard to arrange life in neat packages such as are required in principle by the multiple-baseline designs. Yet, practitioners have to develop a set of priorities because they cannot work on every problem at the same time. Therefore, while practice is complex, the multiple-baseline design seems ready-made for such complexity because it allows you to sort out targets and deal with them one at a time while collecting baseline data on the others—again, assuming that you are using the *same* intervention with all of these targets.

Within the design itself, some special problems emerge. You are required to obtain stable baselines from two or more targets. It is easily conceivable that one or another of those targets may resist presenting a nice, neat, stable baseline. What should you do with the other problems in the meantime? We suggest that you go to work on those targets that have stabilized using the multiple-baseline design. Just put the charts for these targets that have these stable baselines together with the chart of your first intervention target, so you can compare them in the standard multiple-baseline manner. For the unstable ones, you can continue to search for a stable baseline and, if one does eventually occur, do a simple *A–B* design on this one. Linking these "unruly" targets with the overall multiple-baseline design might provide other insights as to the relationships among the several target events. (We will discuss more of this with regard to the next design.)

There is yet another problem when several targets are identified and one is dealt with in sequence before the others: the issue of *order of intervention*. This is more of a problem with multiple baselines across problems, because there may be an unknown effect of the order of intervention on the overall outcome of the service program. One answer would be to deal with target problems in some random order, but that would be unsatisfying to most practitioners. The other option is to vary the order across different clients and to try to compare differences among outcomes. However, this is very tenuous, since so many other considerations affect outcomes. When the problems in a set are all of equal difficulty, a random selection (or just flipping a coin) among targets would be quite possible.

A third problem with use of multiple-baseline designs is that the same intervention is required to be used across all problems, clients, and situations. This is because the main purpose of the multiple-baseline design is to produce a causal statement about the effects of a specific intervention. Sometimes this presents a problem for the practitioner who would like to study the causal effects with one client who has two different problems calling for two separate interventions, say, decided upon by reviewing the literature to see what intervention is evidence-based for what problem.

In cases such as these, practice standards demand that you use the appropriate interventions for each problem. You still could consider using a multiple-baseline design in cases such as this; let's face it, the designs we illustrated earlier were not perfect, and there even was some question about whether the same intervention *was* applied. However, in such a case, you would have to recognize the limitations on drawing statements about causality that ensue from using different interventions. You probably would be able to conclude correctly in such designs that *something* about your planned interventions *was* related to the change, but you would not be able to conclude that it was a specific intervention technique or package. In fact, when different interventions are applied to problems in this manner, we would be more comfortable in calling this a *quasi-multiple-baseline design* than an actual one.

A fourth problem with multiple baselines, and perhaps the key problem, has to do with the possibility that changes associated with introduction of the first intervention with the first baseline may show up in the other baselines as well. This is another variation on the theme of carryover effects. On the one hand, if you have an impact on two different targets with one intervention, don't complain too much. It just means that this one intervention causes differences in two or more targets; you're getting two for the price of one.

On the other hand, if you really want to use a multiple-baseline design, then we have two recommendations for this situation (Kazdin & Kopel, 1975). First, try your best to use problems, clients, or settings that are as independent as possible. Try to select problems, clients, or settings that appear to be relatively distinct from each other so that changes in one don't produce changes in the other. This is less of a concern when dealing with multiple baselines across clients because the problems of two or more clients would be less likely to affect each other than two problems of the same client (with some exceptions such as spouses, siblings, etc.).

Second, try to use as many baselines as possible—three or four rather than just two. The more baselines you use, the greater the chance you have of finding at least two in which the changes introduced into the first don't generalize to the second. If at least two targets show the predicted effects of sequential changes, then the logic of the multiple baseline is applicable to those targets.

Recommendations Regarding the Multiple-Baseline Design

If given the choice of removing a successful intervention or applying the same interventions to several targets in sequence as in multiple-baseline designs, then the choice may be dictated by ethical and/or practical considerations. The multiple-baseline design provides a relatively strong basis for logical inference of causality and is highly flexible in its use in field settings. It would be possible to incorporate other designs within the multiple-baseline design; for example, one might remove a successful intervention that was established in a multiple-baseline design and return to baseline (like an *A-B-A* design to see if the problem returns (see Kirchner et al., 1980.) The multiple-baseline design does require considerable advance planning and control of the situation. This suggests that if you specifically consider the alternative of multiple-baseline designs as you are specifying goals and formulating intervention plans, you will increase your chances of using this strong and ethically sound method of evaluating practice. We urge its careful consideration for both practice and ethical reasons, but also because of its potential contribution to conceptualization and empirical knowledge building as you attempt to grasp the whole picture of a given client/system.

Case Illustrations

Across Problems. A clinical case illustrates the use of a multiple-baseline design across three problems. The case involved a woman who was being seen for pervasive ritualistic behavior that interfered with all aspects of her functioning (Cooper, 1990). The practitioner had seen the client for three years, once or twice a week, using psychodynamic psychotherapy. While the practitioner saw a number of gains from this treatment, she was having no impact on the client's ritualizing behavior. The practitioner, therefore, decided to implement a behavioral treatment that included modeling, exposure, and response prevention techniques.

The practitioner asked the client to do self-monitoring of the frequency of three of the ritualized behaviors: number of twists, presses, and clicks of her makeup case each morning; minutes spent rinsing in the shower; and percentage of time counting her belongings.

We have adapted the author's findings, as seen in Figure 5. The intervention program on these three rituals was completed in eight weeks. With the three problems, the changes occurred only after the intervention began on each. (Note that because the baselines were started at different times and at different intervals, the standard chart was not possible. However, by examining the dates of each chart, you can still see that the changes in the targets occurred in sequence.) This sequencing of effects lends credence to Cooper's (1990) conclusion that the intervention appears related to the change in each behavior.

Although the author does not provide data on what happens to the problem in each baseline after intervention begins with the subsequent problem, she does state that by the 6-month follow-up, 46 of 54 rituals were gone, apparently including the three in this report.

This case had two other interesting dimensions. First, in addition to visually analyzing the data on the clients, the author used the celeration line to statistically analyze the results. With all three problems, the results were statistically significant.

The second fascinating aspect was the impact this case apparently had on the author. Being able to help her client reclaim her life in only two months, after three years of unsuccessful psychotherapy, profoundly affected the author, opening up new treatment possibilities for all clients. The author states that her practice is now far more innovative and eclectic.

Across Clients. Mottram et al. (2002) present results of their study of a classroom-based intervention to reduce disruptive behaviors in three especially problematic second grade boys. What is interesting about their design, a multiple-baseline across clients, is that they also add a "control group" composed of the composite scores of five classmates identified as using appropriate behavior in class. The results may surprise you, as they did the researchers.

The three boys with problems were all seven years old. One was African American, one Filipino, and one Chinese, all with IQs within the "normal" ranges, all from middle-class families, and all performing academically at a satisfactory level. However, their disruptive behavior included not following the teacher's instructions, calling out in class and making noises at inappropriate times, and not staying in their seats. The intervention was a package of posting classroom rules, a token economy (positive reinforcement) used when the child was obeying rules, a response cost when he was not, and a mystery prize given at the end of the day if the child had earned enough tokens. Interobserver reliability averaged 91% agreement, and a rating of teacher acceptability of the intervention package was high (4.5 on a 5-point scale).

Figure 6 shows the four graphs in this study. In typical multiple-baseline fashion, the baseline was conducted for a suitable period of time to establish a stable picture of undesired behaviors on all three boys, whereas the composite score of the five control group children

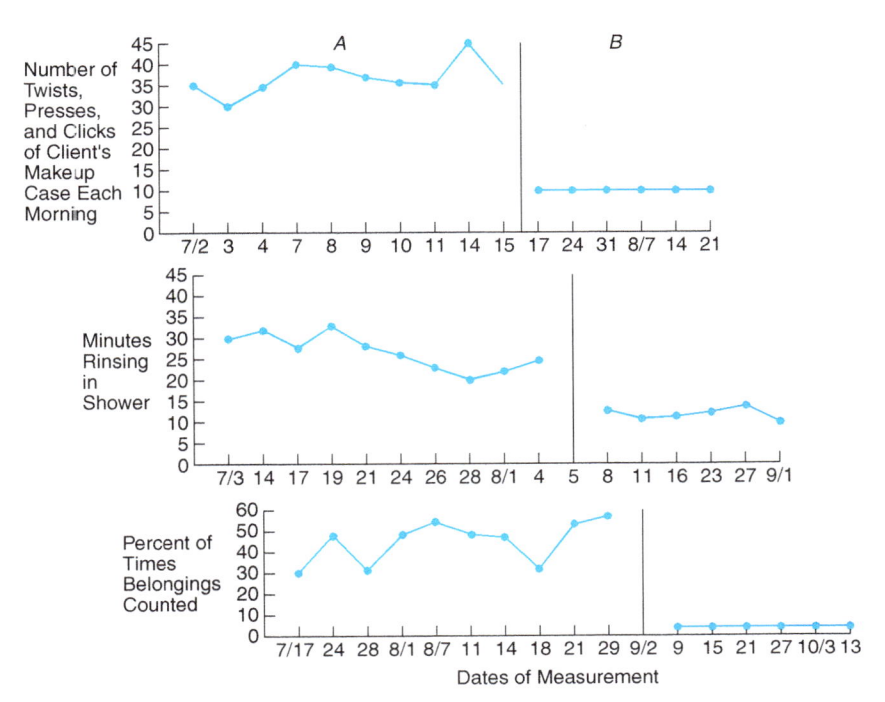

FIGURE 5 Multiple-baseline design across problems: Treatment of an obsessive-compulsive disorder with modeling, exposure, and response prevention. (Note time intervals are not drawn equally.)

(Adapted from "Treatment of a Client with Obsessive-Compulsive Disorder" by M. Cooper, 1990, *Social Work Research & Abstracts, 26*, pp. 26–32.)

showed a relatively low and relatively stable pattern of disruptive behaviors. Note that the vertical axes have their positive end at the bottom, and the negative or problem end at the top. When the intervention was given to the first disruptive boy, the changes in his disruptive behavior were rapid and positive, while there was no change in the disruptive behavior of the other two boys. Then the same intervention package was introduced to the second boy, again with rapid and positive changes, with no lasting effect on the disruptive behavior of the third boy, although he made some improvements for a few days, before returning to his disruptive ways. The control group showed little change in their low levels of disruptive behavior. Finally, the same intervention was introduced to the third boy, and results were similar to the first two boys, rapid change showing much less disruptive behavior. The study concluded with a follow-up for three weeks after all experimental interventions were removed; stable positive scores were maintained.

The surprise was that the scores of the three formerly disruptive boys were *lower* than the composite scores of the nondisruptive boys at the end of the study. The strong effect of the intervention package and its continuation in follow-up was credited to the natural contingencies of the classroom environment that helped maintain the newly acquired behavior by the experimental subjects. The ease of use of this intervention package suggests that it could well be used with the entire class.

Jung and Jason (1998) used a multiple-baseline design to present a culturally sensitive promotive intervention. This intervention involved training Asian-American immigrants in interviewing skills that would increase their probability of success in job hunting, while not changing their ethnic values. These authors point out that there are a number of incompatible values in self-presentation between the Asian and American perspectives, such as demonstrating deference as a sign of respect for others (versus being appropriately assertive on one's own behalf). Such courteous behavior may be interpreted as passive or unmotivated in Western culture, while assertiveness in a first meeting situation may be seen as impolite in Asian culture. So,

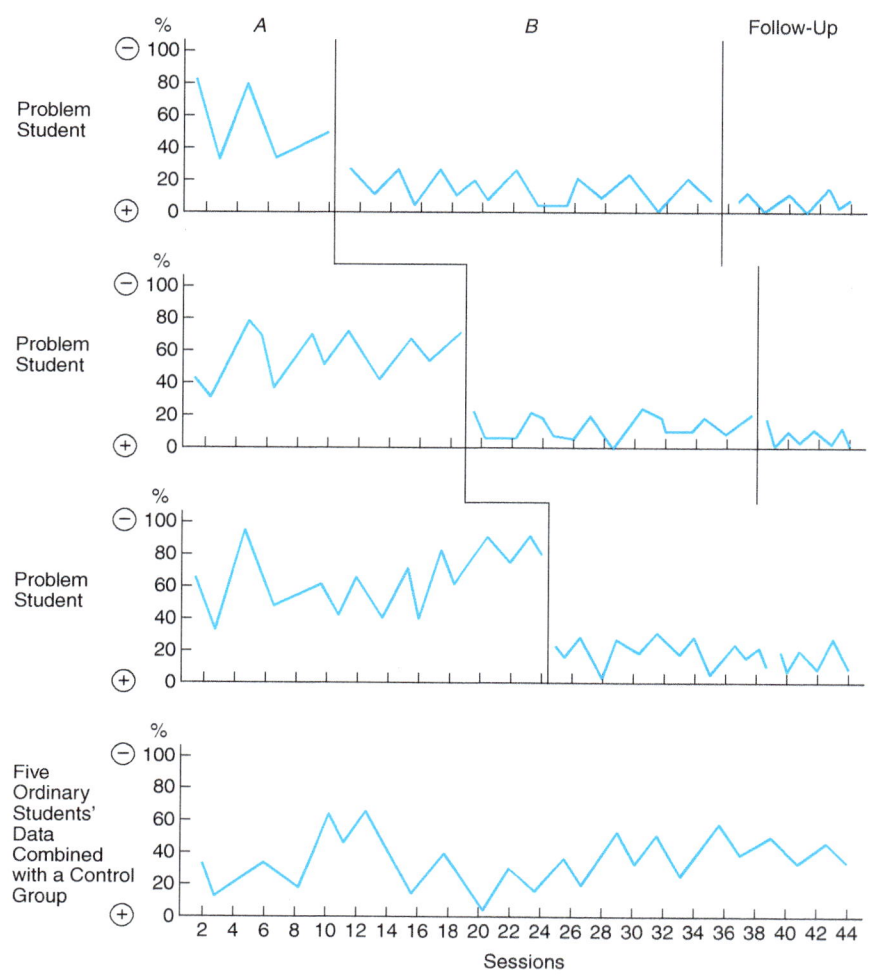

FIGURE 6 Percentage of disruptive intervals observed across three problematic students and a composite average among five ordinary students.

(Adapted from "A Classroom-Based Intervention to Reduce Disruptive Behaviors" by L. M. Mottram, M. A. Bray, T. J. Kehle, M. Broudy, & W. R. Jenson, 2002, *Journal of Applied School Psychology*, *19* (1), pp. 65–74.)

the training task was to emphasize that Asian values should not be abandoned in many settings (home, ethnic community), but could be modified in Western job application settings so as to optimize chances of getting a job for which the individual was well qualified.

Three Asian-American volunteers participated in the study, which consisted of sequential training on: (1) social greeting skills, (2) verbal assertiveness, (3) work independence but also social compatibility with team members, and (4) determination to be successful based on previous accomplishments. Data were collected during twelve simulated interviews over a 6-day period to assess the baseline and postintervention skills on these four skills. The interviews were videotaped and evaluated by four trained volunteer observers. There was 75% agreement on videotape ratings and 95% agreement between two observers of the actual four interview skill dimensions. (There were also other ratings, but we will focus on the taped interviews, except for the important note that several social validity measures were used, including one in which household members were also interviewed with regard to possible adverse effects of this training in Westernized customs. No adverse effects at home were noted.)

Figure 7 presents an approximation of one participant's experience in the job training, as representative of the others as well. The results are typical of multiple-baseline designs, with three exceptions. First, instead of one client with multiple problems, this design used a small group of clients with multiple target problems. Second, the initial target on two of four behaviors showed some improvement during baseline, but after intervention, there was an abrupt increase in performance for all behaviors and participants. Third, there was some improvement in the second skill—verbal assertiveness—at the time when the first intervention was introduced, although this mainly was a continuation of an earlier trend in the baseline of verbal assertiveness. However, on average, there was a clear improvement with the group of three clients on all behaviors.

The data show clear improvement in the four behavioral aspects of Westernized job interviewing skills. Some of the four proved more difficult to attain high levels of expression than others. Expressing social skills reached nearly 100% levels, and verbal

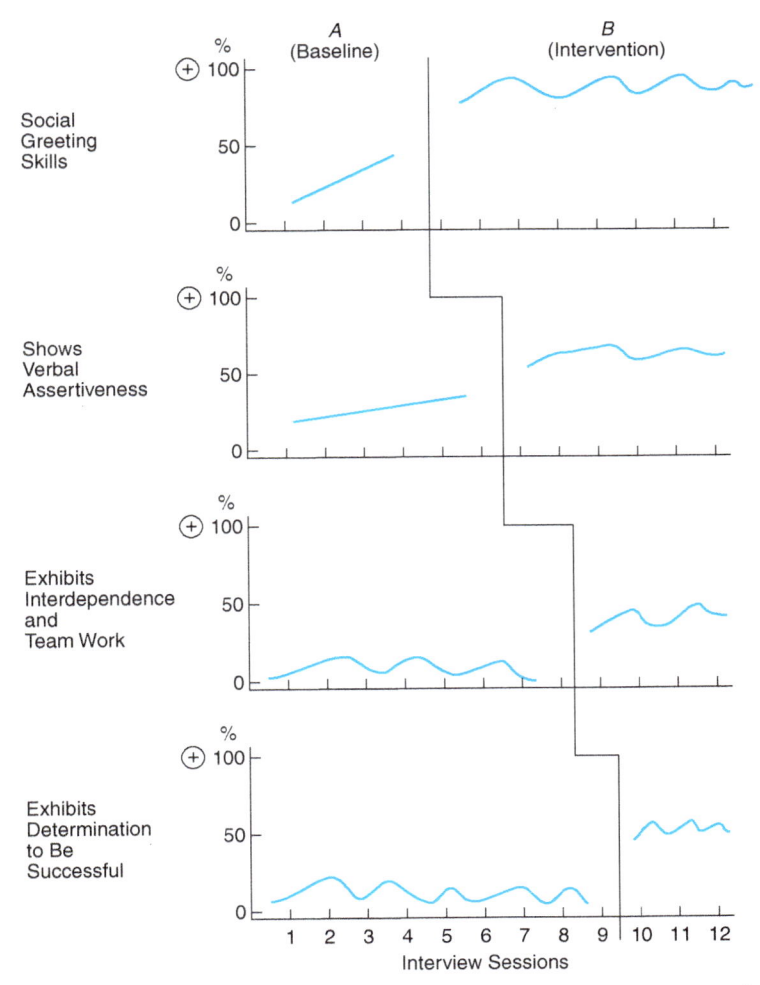

FIGURE 7 Percent of occurrences of four types of interview skills used by Asian-American job seekers as part of a job-training program.

(Adapted from Jung & Jason, 1998.)

assertiveness reached about 75% expression. However, working independently, yet being a team player and expressing determination to be successful based on previous work accomplished, did improve as compared to baseline, but were still at about only the 50% level of expression. In addition, because all targets showed improvement, mainly after intervention was begun, and because the intervention was the same across all targets, this multiple-baseline design allows the inference that the intervention, social skills training, probably was responsible for the changes.

A 1-month follow-up indicated that all of the trainees had looked for jobs, and one had a job offer, while another was forming a family business with relatives. One limitation of this study is that the follow-up was too brief a time period for adequate assessment of the overall effects. However, the implications of this study are important for helping professionals in dealing with diversity and adaptation, without damaging either the individual's culture or his or her opportunities within the dominant culture.

A very interesting example of the use of a multiple-baseline design with three clients with similar problems in a single setting was described by Kolko and Milan (1983). The clients were one female and two male adolescents referred to a private counseling center by a county juvenile court. All three had school-related problems in common, including tardiness and academic problems. The problems were conceptualized by the practitioner as a type of "resistance," and for the intervention, the practitioner selected the techniques of reframing combined with paradoxical instruction. The reframing component was designed to induce or maximize opposition, while the paradoxical instruction—sometimes called "prescribing the symptom"—directed the clients to maintain their truancy and tardiness problem behaviors. The primary outcome measures were archival records—class attendance and academic grades—thus minimizing reactivity. The reliability for observing class attendance/absence was over .89 for all clients.

Figure 8 is an adaptation of the original multiple-baseline report of Kolko and Milan (1983). As can be seen from the data, in all three cases attendance improved only after the introduction of the intervention and appears to be relatively well-maintained at

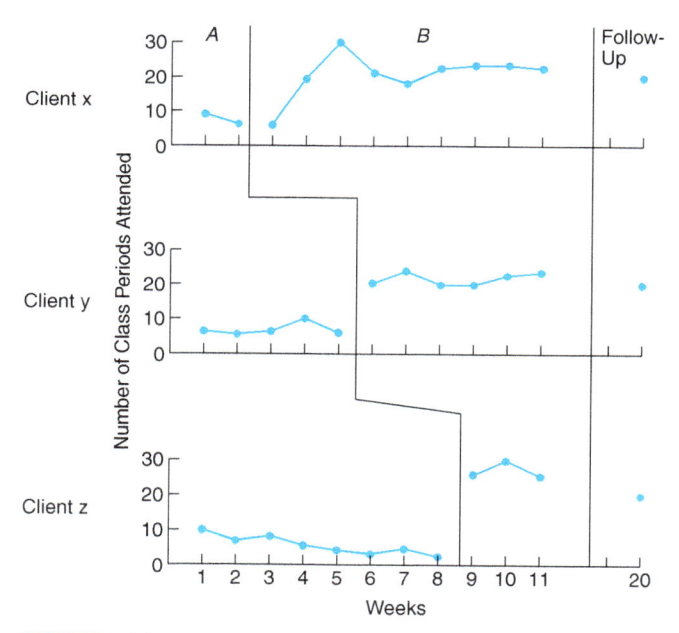

FIGURE 8 Multiple-baseline design across clients: Application of reframing and paradoxical instruction to academic problems.

(Adapted from "Reframing and Paradoxical Instruction to Overcome 'Resistance' in the Treatment of Delinquent Youths: A Multiple Baseline Analysis" by D. J. Kolko & M. A. Milan, 1983, *Journal of Consulting and Clinical Psychology, 51*, pp. 655–660.)

follow-up. Although the first baseline was rather short (two points), the length of the second and third baselines was adequate. This and the clear sequencing of effects all support the causal relationship between application of the intervention and change in the problem. In all three cases, grades also improved following the implementation of intervention, and parents and teachers indicated that there was improvement in other areas as well.

Perhaps the most interesting part of this case is that single-system design procedures were used with an intervention from a phenomenological perspective, one that is often viewed as, if not unresearchable, difficult to study. This case, along with many others in this book, provides additional validation of our notion that single-system designs can be used with interventions from any theoretical system.

Barone, Greene, and Lutzker (1986) present a report on home safety with families being treated for child abuse and neglect. Their study involves a multiple-baseline design across families. They note that over 90% of all injuries, and more than half of the fatalities among children under 5 years of age, occur in the home. There are approximately 4 million home accidents a year involving children. Because children who are abused or neglected are at high risk, the authors experimented with a Home Safety Education package to help in reducing hazards in the home. (An audio slide show was presented on several occasions at the beginning of the intervention period indicating the hazards and how to control them.) The results of their work are shown in Figure 9, adapted from their report to emphasize two of the three reported cases.

After the baseline (8 days for one family and 18 days for the other), the intervention was administered, the Home Safety Education package, which involved the slide show, instruction, and check-ups. As soon as a stable and acceptable level of target behavior was observed in the first family, intervention was begun

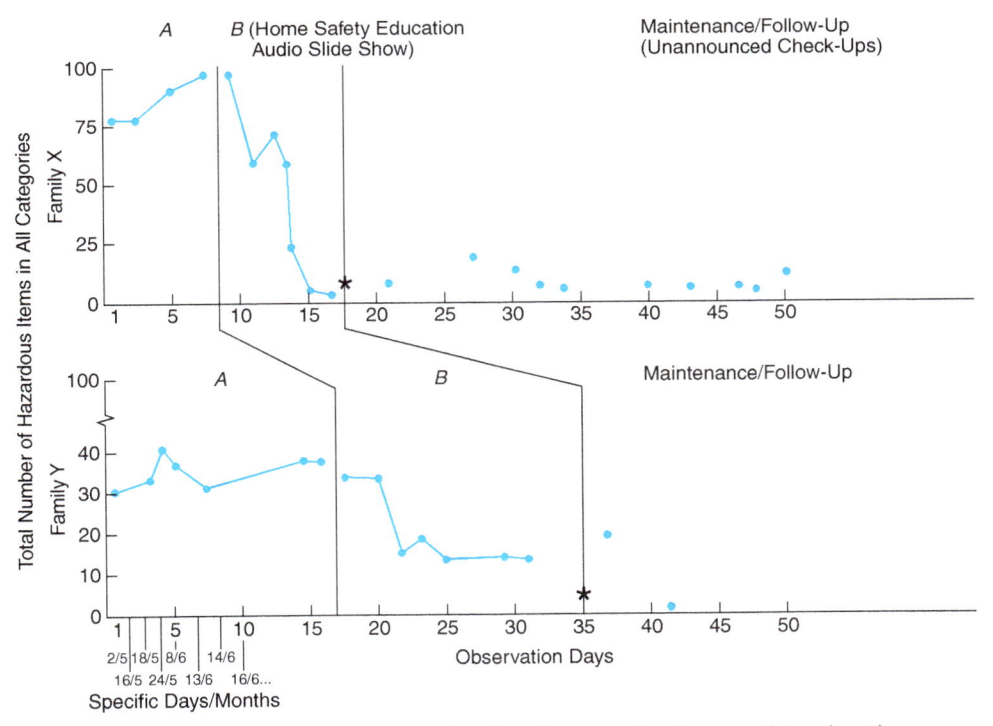

FIGURE 9 Multiple-baseline design across family units to study a home safety education program for abusive/neglectful families.

[Data adapted from "Home Safety with Families Being Treated for Child Abuse and Neglect" by V. J. Barone, B. F. Greene, & J. R. Lutzker, 1986, *Behavior Modification, 10*, pp. 93–114.]

with the second. With both families, a kind of maintenance phase, involving unannounced follow-up checks, also was implemented. We describe this as a maintenance function, rather than a simple follow-up, because the service team was still in a treatment relationship with the clients. The data indicate a concomitant reduction of hazardous household conditions with the presence of the Home Safety Education package, although family Y reduced fewer hazardous materials than did family X (see Figure 9).

Several points can be made about the clients in this case. First, the scale of total hazardous items differs between the two charts because the Y family always had a much lower rate than the X family; this is indicated on the chart by the break marks above 40 items for the Y family. Second, notice that there is an asterisk on each chart, indicating the point in the service process when unannounced check-ups were instituted (at about 17 days for family X and 35 days for family Y). These check-up data represent discrete probes—that is, they are not linked together as are the baseline and intervention data points, as in the ordinary presentation of follow-up data. However, these data also might be considered a kind of maintenance phase, since the presence of the practitioners at these unannounced check-ups involved an intervention. Note, too, how the time line is indicated, using both the days and months, and the number of observations. Both are useful; the days might indicate some cycles related to social patterns, while the numbers of observations will be used in the analysis of these data.

We want to raise one ethical point in connection with the study by Barone, Greene, and Lutzker (1986) regarding the length of baseline in connection with cases of suspected child abuse and neglect. Presumably the families involved in this study were known to the child protective services practitioners so that baselines of 8 and 18 days were not an immediate risk to the children involved. However, in some cases, a baseline may need to be greatly shortened or eliminated altogether if the events of the case involve risk to participants.

Across Settings. Knapczyk (1988) used a multiple-baseline design across settings in his work with two young teenagers who were exhibiting aggressive behaviors in several school settings. The teenagers were in special education programs, but were mainstreamed in several classes as well. Analysis of their aggressive behaviors showed that these behaviors tended to occur when the youngsters tried to initiate social interactions but were rebuffed in various ways by their classmates. Knapczyk carefully operationalized the interactional event that led to aggression and then worked out alternative social behaviors that could be used to replace the aggressive ones.

Baseline data consisted of the same observations that had been used to identify when aggressive behaviors occurred. The intervention involved modeling and rehearsal of social skills relevant to each of the three specified settings—the special class, the shop class, and a gym class. As indicated in Figure 10, displaying these data for one of these youngsters, in textbook-perfect fashion, problematic behaviors continued in a given setting until the intervention was administered specific to that setting. After the intervention, a clear reduction in the problem behavior was seen and generally was maintained during the follow-up period. The author noted that these findings support other research reports about the need for social skills training for special-education students to fulfill the purpose of mainstreaming these youths. In many instances, improved social performance is necessary to have them effectively integrated into the regular educational setting.

Brothers, Krantz, and McClannahan (1994) use an *A-B-C* with follow-up design within a multiple-baseline design across settings to study how to increase participation in recycling waste paper at a child development institute. This study is set against a backdrop of efforts to preserve the environment, rather than continuing to burden landfills with paper products that do not biodegrade (even after 25 years of burial).

A baseline period of 10 working days established the weight of paper trash in three settings: the administrative, office, and instructional areas of the institute. Then, the first intervention for staff in all three settings began with the announcement (in their paychecks) that a centrally located recycling container would be available (in approximately the center of the building) the next work day. Because this information was available to all staff, it constitutes a common intervention, *B*. The results showed some increase in recycling at levels that became reasonably stable.

A third intervention, *C*, was introduced 10 working days later in the *administrative* area by means of another memo in the paychecks of these workers (privacy and exclusiveness of intervention *C*) informing them that there would be local (desktop) containers in their area for recycling. This produced a stronger increase in recycling in the administrative area, while

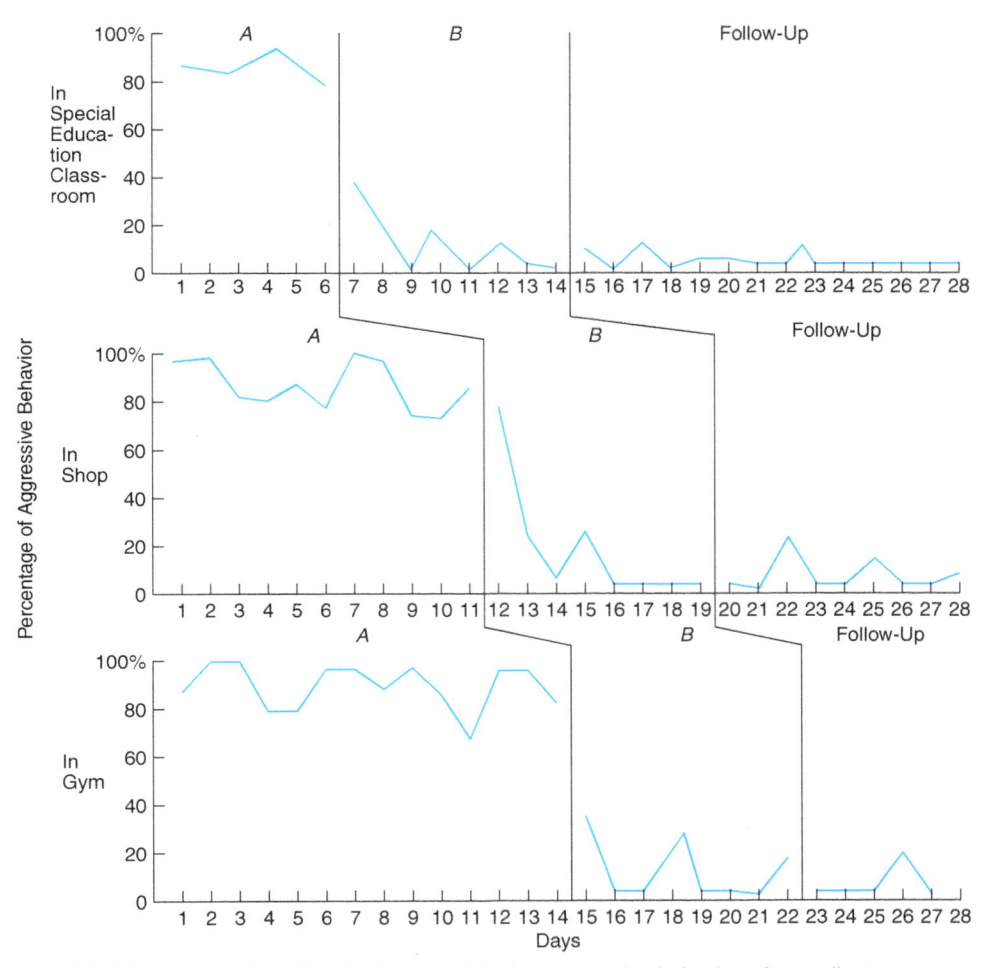

FIGURE 10 A multiple-baseline design in which the aggressive behavior of one client was modified in three different school settings.

[Adapted from "Reducing Aggressive Behaviors in Special and Regular Class Settings by Training Alternative Social Responses" by D. R. Knapczyck, 1988, *Behavior Disorders, 14*, pp. 27–39.]

recycling levels remained more or less constant in the other two areas. Another 10 days later, a memo was sent to workers in the *office* area informing them that a local container would be available in their area (another C intervention); again, the data show an increase in recycling among office workers, while the same level of recycling continued as before with workers in the instructional area. In yet another 10 working days, a memo was sent to workers in the *instructional* area informing them that local containers would be available, and again, increased rates of recycling appear. The changes in recycling occurred in sequential fashion, only after intervention C was applied (see Figure 11).

Four follow-ups were conducted at 1-, 2-, 3-, and 7-month periods, which indicated that recycling was continuing at very high levels (between 84% and 98%) among all three work settings. This study provides the logical basis for asserting that desktop containers are a low-cost, highly successful way to attain recycling objectives and to maintain them over the long run. Thus, the multiple-baseline design provided a fairly objective basis for making office decisions that are environment-friendly.

Multiple Designs for Single Systems

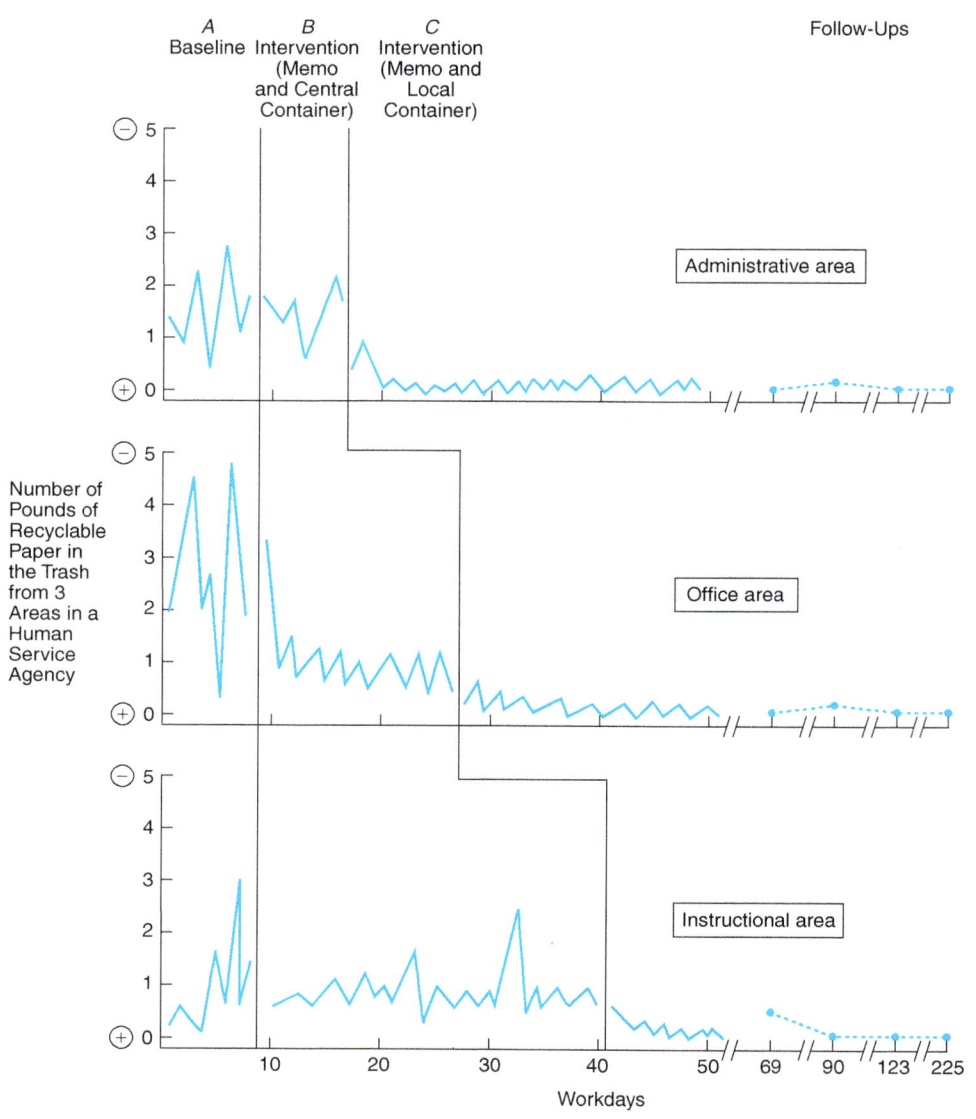

FIGURE 11 Number of pounds of recyclable paper in the trash from three areas in a human service agency.

[Adapted from Brothers, Krantz, & McClannahan, 1994.]

Introducing the Client to the Multiple-Baseline Design

We are happy to report that introductions to this design are often easier than introductions to experimental designs. In the case of multiple-baseline designs, you say what you would ordinarily say in "partializing" a problem—setting priorities among a set of tasks to be accomplished: *"In looking over the set of problems you have presented and as we have discussed them, it seems the best strategy is to work on the problem of x first, and see how we're doing before we start on the next problem. Once the first problem seems to be doing okay, then we'll start work on y, since this seems to be the order of their importance to you."*

Then, in describing the baseline (as in earlier "introduction" sections), you would go on to discuss the intervention and achieving some stability in this phase before going on to the next problem: *"We'll be using a B approach to deal with the first problem, and I would like you to help collect information about that problem both before we start working on it and during the time that intervention is going on. This way we'll know the extent of the changes in the problem. Also, continuing to collect information until we have finished with all of the problems will tell us whether a problem stayed fixed once we completed work on it."*

For each of the tasks in sequence, you can use these words, or words to this effect. If you plan on using other designs, such as the experimental removal design within the multiple-baseline procedure, then these variations can be introduced to the client.

MULTIPLE-TARGET DESIGNS

$x \mid A \mid B$
$y \mid A \mid C$
$z \mid A \mid D$

Multiple-target designs are sets of two or more *simultaneous A-B* designs involving different targets (*x, y, z*) and, usually, but not necessarily, different interventions that are presumed to be dealing with conceptually related problems. By viewing the patterns of changes between or among the *A-B* designs, you may be able to generate some practice hypotheses. For example, does the pattern of events in the baseline periods suggest priorities for intervention plans? Let's see what this might look like in practice.

Case Illustration

It will be useful to begin with an example of this design, which we believe to be widely used in practice, although not with sufficient awareness of how useful a tool is at hand. In this illustration the practitioner was a psychiatric social worker employed at an outpatient department of a university medical school's psychiatric clinic. Each chart on the client, shown in Figure 12, can be interpreted independently as an *A-B* design—the pedophiliac fantasies, the feelings of depression, and the frequency of social contacts with peers (Bloom & Block, 1977). Each has its own unique intervention.

Notice some important patterns among these three charts, which are arranged so that the same time units appear in parallel. The one time during the baseline when the client had contacts with peers her own age was in or near the major low points of the other two charts when viewed together. When one chart was low (problematic behavior) and the other high (nonproblematic behavior), no social contact was made. Let's look at the intervention period to test this pattern hypothesis. Again, the lowest points of both the other charts (the pedophiliac fantasies and the feelings of depression charts) occur first before a period of time begins when the patient has frequent contacts with her peers. Is this a meaningful pattern or just an accident?

We suggest that this type of multiple-target analysis can generate meaningful patterns, but not as logical bases for establishing causal relationships. Rather, these patterns of concomitant variation among two or more different baselines generate *practice hypotheses* to be tested in the next steps of practice. For example, the data from these three charts suggest that the order of practice would be to reduce the psychological distress (pedophiliac fantasies and feelings of depression) before the desired social behavior can be expected to occur. This is counter to another hypothesis that the practitioner might have followed: If the client could only make social contacts, then her self-defeating thoughts and feelings might be reduced. However, the patterns of baseline data among the three charts do not appear to support this order of events nor the practice strategy based on it.

Should you depend on these patterns to make critical practice decisions? Probably not on an unequivocal or sole basis. But as tentative empirical evidence, it is a first approximation for a practice strategy. Certainly, conceptual or theoretical practice guides also may be used. However, if they run counter to the immediate empirical evidence, then you should be very cautious about adopting either the theory or the tentative empirical patterns.

Strengths of the Multiple-Target Design

The simplicity of this design is appealing. As a set of *A-B* designs applied to different targets, typically with different interventions, each separate design can stand by itself. In addition, by positioning the charts of the several *A-B* designs so that the data for the same time points are matching (as in Figure 11), you might be able to observe patterns across different

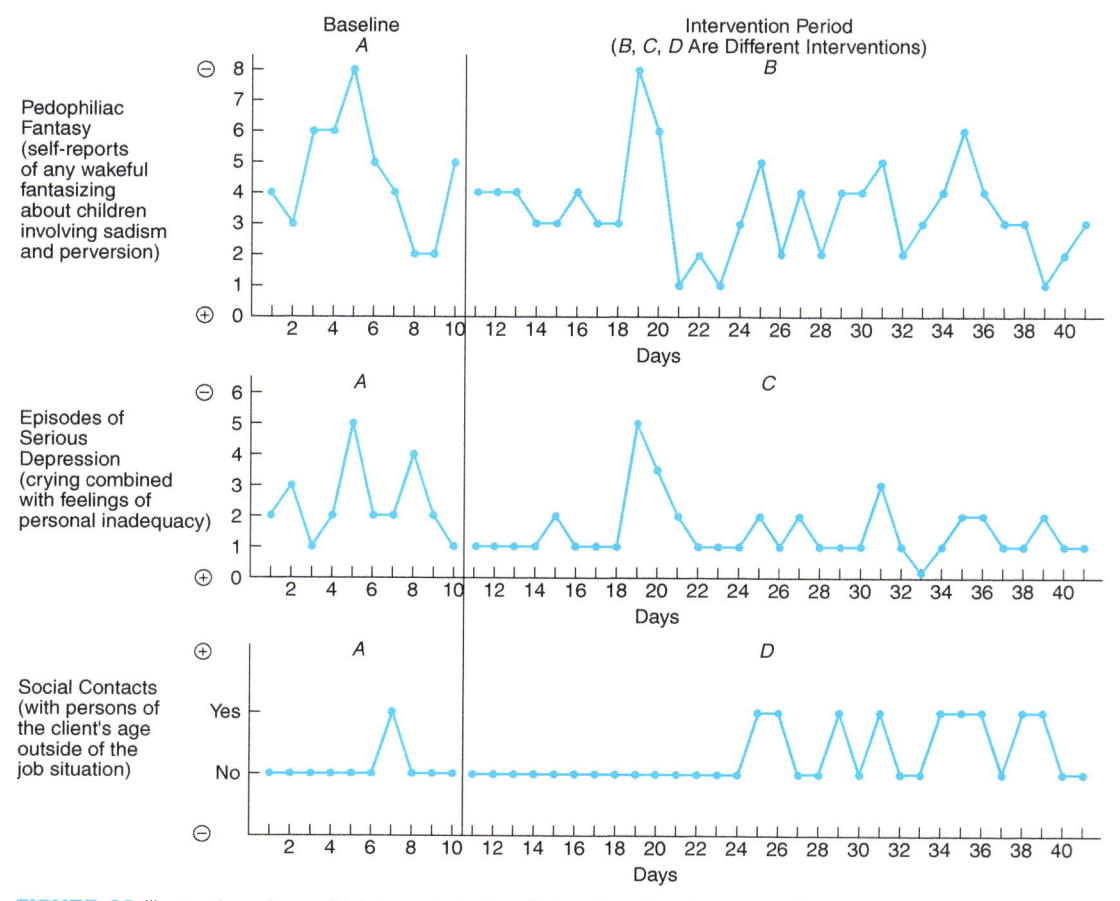

FIGURE 12 Illustration of a multiple-target design. (Note that the charts are drawn so events occurring in the same time periods can be compared.)

(Adapted from "Evaluating One's Own Effectiveness and Efficiency" by M. Bloom & S. R. Block, 1977, *Social Work, 22*, pp. 130–136.)

events as well as within each given event. Sometimes a theory might predict a configuration of events in advance, in which case you are aided in looking for that configuration. But even when no conceptual pattern has been predicted, visually inspecting the several charts at the same time may unearth patterns not previously suspected. These patterns are to be taken as hypotheses for further testing, not as established facts. This approach may be one operational definition of "practice insight"; that is, it is an intuitive grasping of diverse pieces of information to form one integrated view of the client. This also may be the way concepts are formed—abstractions from varied instances of behavior.

Limitations of the Multiple-Target Design

There are many logical, sound designs that can provide clear information not only on change, but also on the basis for causal inference, so that the choice to use the multiple-target design, which lacks these strengths—because the changes are not planned to occur on a sequential or staggered basis as with the multiple-baseline design—must be well-founded. In fact, use of the multiple-target design typically really implies less a decision in advance than a comparison of patterns of data from three *A-B* designs after the fact. We make some recommendations shortly about when the best use of this design might be made.

In addition to problems regarding causality, there are some other issues regarding the use of the multiple-target design. What if, for example, there is progress on one target event and not on the others? This breaks down the predicted pattern about what causal factors were involved. We do not necessarily view this as a limitation. It is as important to know what is *not* the case (what doesn't work) as it is to know what *is* the case (what appears to work). Such a state of affairs (when no patterns of events appear to make sense) is sufficient to drive the practitioner back to the beginning to seek to understand the situation. However, it is far better to learn what you do not know than to be deceived (by yourself) into thinking you have some understanding when you have little.

Recommendations Regarding the Multiple-Target Design

We recommend that those who make use of only the basic single-system design (*A-B*) as their approach to evaluation also consider using this additive design. It requires no more effort than goes into monitoring each separate component and may offer some good opportunities to form and test some systematic hunches about the nature of the entire case or sets of cases. Until the logic of the pattern of changes is explicated, we don't recommend reliance on this design as a tool of ultimate evaluation. However, it can be useful as an initial tool that will lead to more rigorous testing. Because so many clients are troubled by multiple problems, this multiple-target design can be recommended as one method of grappling with complex situations.

As an exploratory tool with *rare* cases, it might be very useful to try to find some patterns that are linked with available knowledge bases. The common features of an uncommon circumstance might suggest ways to approach finding these patterns. Also, for common problems in which you believe you know the likely course of events, the multiple-target design may be a useful shorthand for keeping track of events without getting into a more elaborate design.

Introducing the Client to the Multiple-Target Design

Simply use the suggestions given for the *A-B* design; the added advantages of looking for patterns is "free," although you may wish to share these insights with your clients to check them out. For example, you might say, "*I notice that just before you do* (some problematic act), *from the charts it looks like* X *and* Y *occur*—for example, low levels of X and high levels of Y. *This suggests a pattern to be on the lookout for. What do you think?*"

Depending on your guiding theory of practice, it may be possible to give the observed pattern a label. For instance, feeling depressed and frustrated may be preceded by an exchange with a client's boss and spouse, both of whom make unfair demands on the client's time. A label for this pattern might be unassertiveness and might be helpful in focusing practice activities

VARIATIONS ON MULTIPLE DESIGNS

Two types of designs could be viewed as variations of the "multiple" designs we have discussed. These are crossover and constant-series designs. Each type of design offers some unique advantages, although neither has the explanatory capacity of the multiple-baseline design.

Crossover Designs

$$\begin{array}{c|c|c} x & A & B \\ \hline y & B & A \end{array} \text{ or } \begin{array}{c|c|c|c} x & A & B & C \\ \hline y & A & C & B \end{array}$$

Every basic design in the single-system universe can be modified to fit different practice contexts. These modifications will change the logical basis for inferring causality, but may be necessary because of the nature of the presenting circumstances. In this section and the following section, we discuss some variations partly for their own sake, but also in part to stimulate creative thinking about single-system designs.

Some important variations on the multiple-target designs have been suggested by Barlow, Nock, and Hersen (2009) (see also Hayes et al., 1999). They are called crossover designs, in which two concurrent interventions (typically, the same intervention for both targets) take place, each on a separate target but in reverse order for one client. One type of crossover design would involve two *A-B* designs for one client, performed concurrently, but in an *A-B* order for one target and a *B-A* order for the other. Then, if changes occur when and only when the intervention is applied, we have some, though quite limited, basis for inferring causality. For the *A-B* designs, it is necessary to replicate the interventions on these targets, or to add more targets, as a basis for inferring causality, since clients may respond to some intervention because of its novelty in spite of the varied order of presentation (Barlow, Nock, & Hersen, 2009).

Suppose that a neighborhood association is trying to cut down on litter in the streets, while at the same time trying to encourage recycling of paper, glass, and metals. Because of limited personnel, the officers of the association propose to take one problem at a time, beginning with the litter problem. They devise an information package that identifies the scope of the problem, indicates the costs in managing the problem, and propose some simple steps in reducing the problem. They decide to measure the amount of litter on the neighborhood streets and also the number of people sorting their trash for recycling on garbage pickup days. Near the time when the litter campaign was to get under way, the neighborhood association received a small grant enabling them to develop materials for the recycling campaign. Therefore, they begin their measurement of both problems, but intervened immediately on littering. They noticed some sizable reductions in littering, while there was no effect on recycling. Then they shifted their personnel to the recycling project, while continuing to collect information on littering. Thus, they have used an *A-B* design for the recycling problem and a *B-A* design for the littering problem. If positive change is observed when and only when the same intervention is applied to each target, then there is somewhat stronger evidence of causality than with two separate *A-B* as in, say, a multiple-target design.

The logic of crossover designs requires that two concurrent interventions take place, each on a separate target but in the reverse order, within the same larger setting, and for the same length of time, so as to hold these factors constant during the evaluation period. Medical clinical trials often have additional features, such as a double-blind arrangement where neither the participants nor the research staff know who is getting what intervention at any given time, to prevent any biasing of the outcomes. An example of such a medical trial is the work of Feingold, Oliveto, Schottenfeld, and Kosten (2002) in which a specific drug (Desipramine), known to reduce craving for cocaine, is compared with a placebo drug containing inert ingredients in the same container as the actual medication. Clinical drug trials often require what we would term a training, or warm-up, period until the medications can have their full effect. In the Feingold et al. study, all 109 drug-using participants received a liquid to swallow containing an active maintenance medication and a set of three capsules, which may or may not have contained the active drug under study. Only the pharmacist preparing the capsules was not "blind" as to their true ingredients.

All participants received placebos in the first 2 weeks of the 26-week study. Group I received the drug first, starting with smaller doses and getting larger doses within a week's time. Group I tapered off the drug for 1 week before going on the placebo. Group II started the drug test in the second half of the study, going from smaller doses to larger ones over a week's time.

The order in which the drug or placebo is presented might also be studied to observe any carryover effects, by randomizing what participants go into what group, as these authors did. The critical outcome measure of current addictive drug use was through urine samples that were either cocaine-free or not. Feingold et al. (2002) used several methods to present their data, such as mean proportion of cocaine-free samples, and a hierarchical linear model indicating presence or absence of cocaine-free urine. We will adapt one of their graphs for present purposes (see Figure 13).

From this pattern of crossover effects, the authors drew the following conclusions. First, those participants who received the drug made improvements (more cocaine-free urine samples) whenever the drug was taken, as compared with the periods of time when the placebo was taken. Second, the authors observed that when the drug was administered for the first 13 weeks, the effect was carried over into the second period when only placebos were given. This carryover effect did not occur when the placebo was administered during the first period; indeed, Group II showed rapid improvement when the drug was given in the second time period. The authors also studied these effects on opiates, with yet other effects of the crossover design. They concluded that drugs used, order of presentation, and type of addictive problems are all relevant to decision making regarding drug control.

Another type of crossover design involves two different interventions presented concurrently but in reverse order, such as in an *A-B-C* and an *A-C-B* order. When consistent changes occur, such as improvements associated with *B* and no changes with *C*, then, "the likelihood of that effect is increased beyond that of the component simple phase changes were they not synchronized" (Barlow, Nock, & Hersen, 2009). These authors provide an example drawn from the educational research field. A school

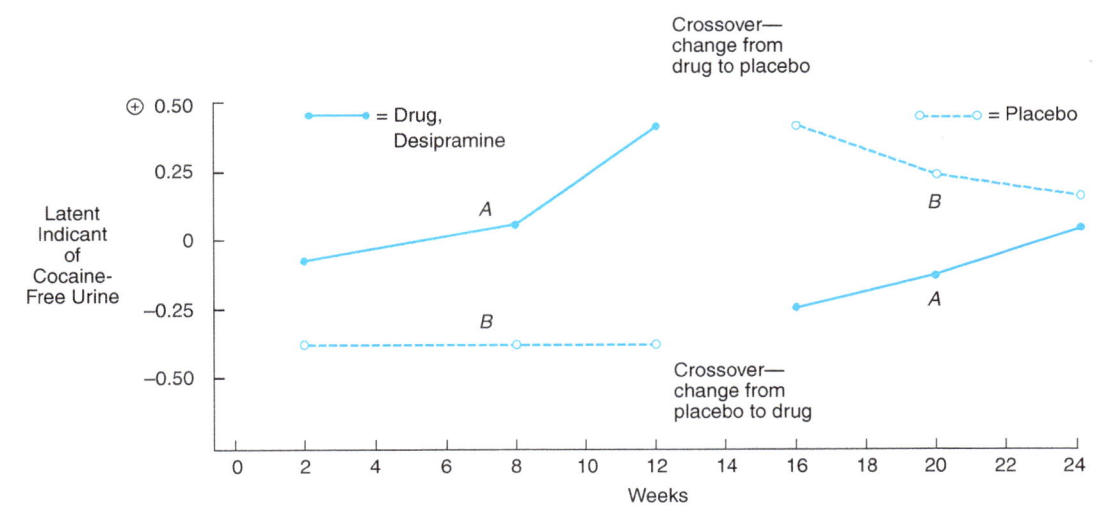

FIGURE 13 A crossover design showing the effects of changing from a placebo to a drug to reduce craving for cocaine, or vice versa.

(Data and charting adapted from "Utility of Crossover Designs in Clinical Trials: Efficacy of Desipramine vs. Placebo in Opioid-Dependent Cocaine Abusers" by A. Feingold, A. Oliveto, R. Schottenfeld, & T. R. Kosten, 2002, *American Journal of Addictions, 11*, pp. 111–123.)

wishes to test the differences between two methods of teaching, one using programmed texts, the other employing conventional texts. The programmed text comes in two versions, for math and for English, and so by random choice, the programmed text in English is used for a month while the regular text in math is used. Then the next month, the process is reversed, and the regular text is used in English, while a programmed text is used in math. The students are tested frequently on what they are learning in these courses. If the programmed text proves superior to the regular texts in both math and English, regardless of when they were introduced to the same set of students, then there is greater likelihood of establishing the effectiveness of this intervention than would have been attainable by two separate *B-C* comparisons.

The major requirements of the crossover designs are having two concurrent phase changes with the same interventions presented in reverse order (*A* to *B*, *B* to *A*; or *B* to *C*, *C* to *B*; etc.). These phases must be in the same setting, with the same length of phases. In this way, various threats to the internal validity of the findings are kept equivalent for each target of intervention.

Crossovers like this can be added to any situation involving two targets when the same intervention can be used with each. It is a way of strengthening the *A-B* comparisons with no extra effort except careful planning of when each phase is to occur.

Constant-Series Designs

x | A | or   x | B |
y | A | B   y | A | B

**Baseline-Only   Intervention-Only
Control   Control**

This variation of the multiple-target design also was suggested by Barlow, Nock, and Hersen (2009). One form of the constant-series design involves the fact that practitioners frequently assess or measure target problems without taking corrective action. Rather than waste this information, the practitioner can combine this situation with a simple *A-B* design to demonstrate that while the *A-B* shows predicted changes, the other target (*A*-only) remains about the same. This is termed a *baseline-only control*.

Another form of the constant-series design involves the situation in which intervention (*B*-only) is required immediately and continuously on one target, while another target permits the regular *A-B* design. Rather than waste this information, the practitioner can combine this situation with a simple *A-B* design to demonstrate that while the constant intervention shows continuous improvement, the *A-B* design (with the same intervention) shows variations in the target depending on whether the intervention is being applied. This is termed an *intervention-only control*.

In general, the constant-series designs provide some evidence about the causal efficacy of the intervention by observing it to be associated with changes in the target when present, and with no changes in the target when it is not present. They are not logically strong designs but provide enhanced confidence for using the results from the basic *A-B* design, with little additional effort. As Barlow, Nock, and Hersen (2009) point out, if a practitioner were to do a baseline-only control on one target, an intervention-only control on another target, and a basic *A-B* design on the third, all with equivalent results (such as positive change occurring *when and only when* the *B* was presented), then a set of separate weak (but nonintrusive) designs are combined into a single pattern that adds to the meaningfulness of the overall results. It is difficult to indicate precisely how strong such a composite would be, but this combination would exhibit a kind of concomitant variation that is the basis for the logical strength of multiple-baseline designs.

Summary

Several types of relatively powerful designs seem to parallel practice activities very closely, and thus provide you a relatively easy way to evaluate your own practice. This chapter presented several of these designs, all of which include multiple elements: multiple baselines across problems, clients, or situations; multiple-target designs that involve two or more different targets and their different interventions; and two variations of these designs, the crossover and the constant-series designs. Common to them all is the emphasis on *patterns* of outcomes.

Multiple baselines involve obtaining a stable baseline on two or preferably more targets with one client, or with one target with several clients, or with one target with one client in several settings. An intervention is then introduced to the first target (or client or setting) while recording baseline information on the others. After a desired level of change has stabilized in the first target, the same intervention is applied to the second problem or client or setting, and so on. This logically demonstrates control over the targets and shows that change occurs only when the intervention is employed. This is a powerful single-system design with the added advantage that no removal of intervention is necessary. It also is possible to use a variety of other single-system designs within the multiple-baseline design, increasing its flexibility and utility.

Multiple-target designs are several *A-B* designs that are analyzed for patterns among them that can serve as the basis for practice hypotheses, but not logical inferences of causality as such. This is a vital service for practitioners and can be employed in a wide variety of situations.

Crossover and constant-series designs are variations of multiple-target designs that, through different arrangements and comparison of phases, allow slightly stronger causal inferences than do multiple-target designs.

Any design beyond the basic *A-B* adds activities and/or phases that are more complicated than the basic *A-B* design, and the designs described in this chapter are no exception. However, we have stressed how close these designs are to what practitioners actually do, and thus recommend their use whenever possible.

CHANGING INTENSITY DESIGNS AND SUCCESSIVE INTERVENTION DESIGNS

PURPOSE This chapter presents several designs that involve successive changes in the interventions, in the intensity of the interventions, or in the intensity of the outcomes. These designs build upon those discussed previously, but they have some distinctive features relevant to a wide variety of practice situations, and they require separate explanation for their appropriate use. These designs include changing intensity designs, in which the objectives or intervention programs are varied in intensity, and successive intervention designs, in which multiple interventions are used one after another, with important logical implications regarding causality.

Introduction
Changing Intensity Designs:
   $A\text{-}B^1\text{-}B^2\text{-}B^3$ $|A|B^1|B^2|B^3$
  Changing Criterion Design
  Changing Program Design
  Characteristics of Changing Intensity Designs
    Strengths of Changing Intensity Designs
    Limitations of Changing Intensity Designs
    Recommendations Regarding
      Changing Intensity Designs
    Case Illustrations
    Introducing the Client to Changing
      Intensity Designs

Successive Intervention Designs: *A-B-C, A-B-A-C, A-B-A-C-A* $|A|B|C$ $|A|B|A|C$ $|A|B|A|C|A$
  The *A-B-C* Design $|A|B|C$
  The *A-B-A-C* Design $|A|B|A|C$
  The *A-B-A-C-A* Design $|A|B|A|C|A$
    Strengths of the A-B-A-C-A *Design*
    Limitations of the A-B-A-C-A *Design*
    Recommendations Regarding the A-B-A-C-A
      Design
    Case Illustrations
    Introducing the Client to the A-B-A-C-A *Design*
  Extensions of the Successive Intervention Design
Summary

From Chapter 16 of *Evaluating Practice: Guidelines for the Accountable Professional*, Sixth Edition. Martin Bloom, Joel Fischer, John G. Orme. Copyright © 2009 by Pearson Education, Inc. All rights reserved.

INTRODUCTION

Practitioners often use different interventions over the course of a case. These different interventions may reflect new problems that have arisen since the last contact or may reflect new ideas that occurred to the practitioner about the case/situation. It is important that single-system designs capture these changes in intervention or in the intensity of intervention.

Yet, these changes also may present a problem because changes in interventions are difficult to assess logically. Was it the last intervention that caused the change, or the cumulative impact of the past several sessions, or the order of presentation, or what? The designs discussed in this chapter may help to provide some guidelines for changing interventions, as well as some bases for drawing conclusions about changes in target problems.

CHANGING INTENSITY DESIGNS: A-B^1-B^2-B^3 $\quad |A|B^1|B^2|B^3|$

An important extension of the *A-B* design is the *changing intensity design*. In these designs, either the *criterion* (i.e., trying to attain either more or less of the target condition while holding the intervention constant) or *intervention* (i.e., applying more or less of the intervention in order to attain the same goal) is varied in intensity over time in response to information you are receiving about change (or lack of change) in the target. There are two types of changing intensity designs—the *changing criterion* design and the *changing program* design. We describe each of these separately in the following sections.

Changing Criterion Design

The first type of changing intensity design is the changing criterion design in which the *criteria* or requirements of the client's performance are increased (but also could be decreased, hypothetically) in a stepwise progression in order to attain a given objective. The reason we use this design is to portray the results of your planned shaping program, a step-by-step attainment of increasingly complex goals. First, a baseline period, *A*, is followed by an intervention period, *B*. Presumably, some change occurs in the desired direction; however, the change is not at the desired level of the final goal. To achieve that goal, the practitioner moves to the next objective using the changing criterion design, retaining the same intervention, but requiring a higher level of performance (the next objective) for a given consequence to occur. These second and subsequent intervention periods would be distinguished from the first by *superscripts*: The first *B* period becomes B^1, followed by B^2, B^3, and so on. (Remember, superscripts are different from subscripts: The former denote change in intensity, the latter denote only what order a given phase has in a sequence of phases.) The changing criterion design thus permits the practitioner to move in graduated steps toward a terminal goal, for example, setting a series of sequential, intermediate objectives that the client can attain at progressively higher performance levels on the way toward achieving the final goal.

Let's use as an illustration of this procedure the efforts of a small human service agency to document its effectiveness, a necessary effort to maintain its status in receiving United Fund moneys. The United Fund adopted a policy that member agencies had to document a certain minimum level of verified successful case outcomes, and gave each agency a year's time in which to provide this documentation. Quarterly installments of funds were made contingent on showing progress over preceding quarters. Figure 1 shows that the agency in question made satisfactory progress, with an increase in percentage of successful case outcomes each quarter, thereby qualifying them for funds each quarter.

Changing Program Design

The second type of changing intensity design involves changing the intervention *program* (rather than the criterion or client's performance) by increasing or decreasing in a stepwise progression the intensity or amount of intervention activities required to produce a given outcome. We use such a design to reflect the results when we have to *increase* the intensity of an intervention because we are not achieving the desired results or when we gradually *decrease* the intervention as we *fade out* (gradually decrease) a successful intervention. First, a baseline period, *A*, is followed by an intervention period, *B*. Some change may occur in the desired direction; however, the change does not reach the desired level. The practitioner then decides to change the intensity of the intervention in progressive steps. That is, in subsequent phases, you would modify the original intervention by providing progressively more (or less) of it, although the objectives and goals remain the same.

Changing Intensity Designs and Successive Intervention Designs

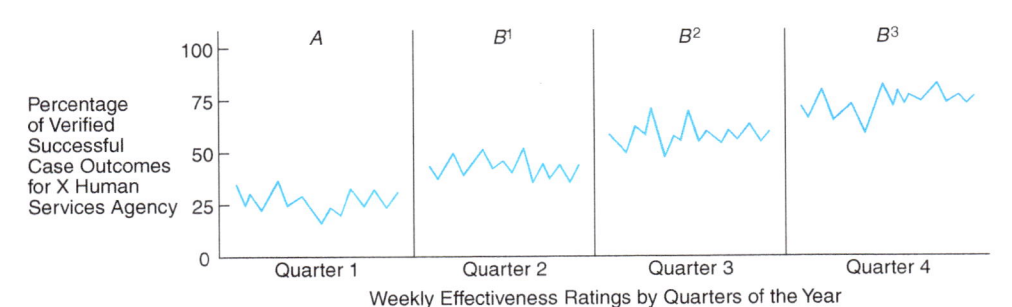

FIGURE 1 Changing criterion design illustrated by rising levels of agency performance required in order that it receive a quarterly allotment of United Fund support.

More of the intervention would be offered if the terminal goal had not been reached (e.g., more varied or more intense reinforcement, increasing the number of sessions or meetings per week, etc.). Less of the intervention would be offered if the goal *had* been reached and you wanted to reduce your participation gradually (i.e., fade out) before termination (e.g., changing to an intermittent reinforcement schedule, reducing the number of practitioner–client contacts, etc.). Just as in the changing criterion design, these second and subsequent intervention periods would be distinguished from the first by superscripts, with the first intervention period becoming B^1, followed by B^2, B^3, and so on.

For example, consider this situation, which actually was one of the first cases in which one of the authors used the changing program design (the name of the child, of course, is disguised): Wes, a 7-year-old boy, was giving his parents such a hard time that they were at their wits' end. Among several complaints, the author and the parents agreed to focus first on what appeared to be the most disturbing of his behaviors: tantrums. The author thought that a time-out procedure might be the fastest way of eliminating the tantrums. A measurement plan was established using both frequency and duration of tantrums as the target. Unfortunately, the first intervention phase—using 10-minute time-outs in the parents' bedroom—had only a negligible impact on Wes, as can be seen in Figure 2. The second intervention (B^2) used 15-minute time-outs, and progress was clearly evident; but the tantrum behavior appeared to stabilize at an unacceptable level. The author and the parents then decided to intensify the intervention (B^3) to 20-minute time-outs, and within the week, the problem had receded to an acceptable level and Wes himself seemed more cheery and upbeat.

Characteristics of Changing Intensity Designs

Strengths of Changing Intensity Designs. Both the changing criterion and the changing program designs reflect the controlling impact of the practitioner's work on the target problem by the successive progression of changes toward a desired outcome, linked with stepwise changes in either the criterion of performance expected of the client (in the changing criterion design) or changes in the intervention program in response to the client's performance (in the changing program design). Both types of changing intensity designs are flexible; such changes can be planned, or they can be made on an ad hoc basis as the situation warrants. Changing intensity designs are simpler than multiple-baseline designs in that they do not require two or more independent targets in order to study change and causality; however, the sequential changes in one target present similar—though less powerful—types of information. Unlike experimental designs, changing intensity designs do not remove interventions in demonstrating change. Thus, they are not subject to some of the ethical and practical problems that the more powerful experimental designs produce.

The changing criterion design sets intermediate objectives on the way toward some terminal goal, and, therefore, each step on the way may be viewed as the client reaching a subgoal. This may be very motivating for some clients.

The changing program design is relatively easy to use and offers precise control over the intervention program, making successive changes in the intensity of the intervention in response to feedback from monitoring the target. This design simply reflects the necessary changes (in intensity) in an intervention

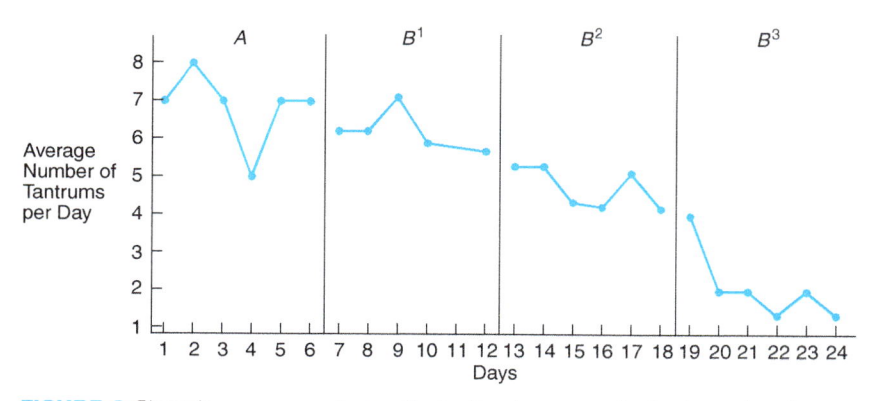

FIGURE 2 Changing program design illustrating increases in the intensity of the intervention (time out: B^1 = 10 minutes, B^2 = 15 minutes, B^3 = 20 minutes).

program that practitioners make in response to the data they collect. This information is useful in the cost/benefit sense of knowing the optimal balance of obtaining some desired outcome for a given amount of intervention.

Overall, the core idea of changing intensity designs is that a stepwise progression of either objectives or interventions is simply reflected in the design. This contributes considerable structure and direction to practice, and yet may be very motivating for the client as well.

Limitations of Changing Intensity Designs. Both the changing criterion and the changing program designs are limited to situations in which you can more or less shape behaviors and events gradually over time to produce desired results. You must make sure that the initial baseline is sufficiently stable so that changes are not already occurring. Moreover, for the most precise information, each step should be restabilized before going on to the next step; this requires close monitoring, and thus makes this design relatively labor-intensive. However, the idea here is not that the design per se is so difficult, since the design only reflects what the practitioner is doing in the intervention program. We also realize that this "restabilization" may not always be possible, because the changes reflected in these designs are a response to changes, or lack of sufficient changes, in the target.

Changing intensity designs are not necessarily good designs for establishing causality. Despite the fact that you can assess change as occurring at the same time as the program or the criterion is changing, factors such as carryover and order effects across the phases or even history (changes in the target problem as a result of some other event in the client's situation) make it difficult to interpret causal effects clearly.

In addition, it is not clear how much change should be required between each step. Too big a change may produce problems in attaining the goal, while too small a change may have little meaning to the client. You have to experiment with changes during the course of the intervention. The best guide is probably to examine the stability of the change. If you have not reached the terminal goal and the intermediate change or lack of change seems stable, then this would be the point at which you would change the criterion or the program.

Recommendations Regarding Changing Intensity Designs. Overall, the limitations of this design probably reflect its relatively recent addition to the family of evaluation designs. We expect that its flexibility and versatility will commend it to practitioners, and that their experiences will further clarify the strengths and limitations of these designs.

Using these designs, you are required to be able to control graded sequences of the program or the performance criteria needed to obtain a given goal. However, being able to specify intermediate steps simplifies practice when the terminal goal is difficult to reach.

Changing intensity designs are to be used under the same conditions as *A-B* designs, but they reflect the realities of practice in which practitioners wish (or need) to make changes in program or performance criteria as they go along. In addition, changing program designs, in particular, can be used to keep track systematically of changes in the client as you gradually reduce or fade out your participation prior to termination. These designs are therefore highly practical and practice oriented, even though they are not powerful tools for causal analysis. They require minimal sophistication and rigor and can be used in a wide variety of settings and circumstances. We recommend that you consider these designs as practice-friendly extensions of the basic single-system design.

Case Illustrations. The first illustration shows a changing criterion design used with chronic back pain as the target. Chronic back pain is a persistent problem for large numbers of people, many of whom typically react to the posttreatment pain with self-disabling behaviors, such as slow, guarded walking, which they believe (incorrectly) will be helpful in reducing the pain. Geiger et al. (1992) conducted a rigorously controlled study on the use of feedback and contingent reinforcement to improve walking behavior in persons with chronic back pain. The dependent variable was rate of walking, chosen because it "(a) is incompatible with common self-protective debilitating pain behavior . . . , (b) can be accurately measured, (c) has been used by a number of researchers . . . , and (d) is of obvious importance in everyday activities" (Geiger et al., 1992, p. 180).

Geiger et al. (1992) also used a self-rating scale on pain and recording of medications taken. (Most of the clients came to the hospital on medications, but all medications were eventually eliminated as part of the general treatment, independent of the study.) Fifteen participants at a chronic pain clinic agreed to take part in the study in which a clever reinforcement system was constructed (involving tokens that could be exchanged for a state-operated lottery ticket, a relaxation tape, biofeedback cards, or a gourmet dinner). Points would be rewarded for given walking speeds relative to each client's starting rate. "The initial criterion for each client was the average of his/her two highest baseline rates plus 5%. Criteria for successive steps in the changing criterion design were similarly determined" (Geiger et al., 1992, p. 180). Some of these experimental clients used only contingent reinforcement, while others began with either no reinforcement, or noncontingent reinforcement, but later moved to contingent reinforcement. Each of these experimental participants showed generally the same pattern of results when the contingent reinforcement was applied (see Figure 3).

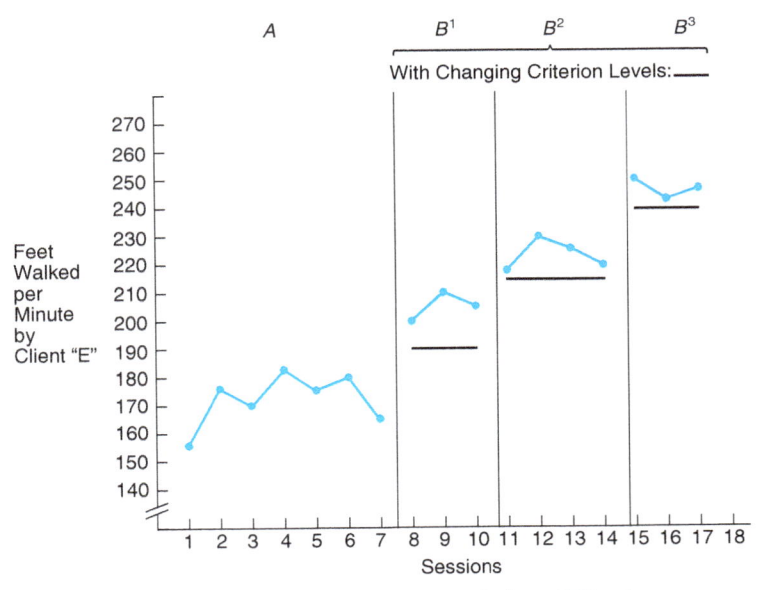

FIGURE 3 Walking rates for one experimental client ("E") using no-reinforcement baseline in a changing criterion design.
(Adapted from Geiger, Todd, Clark, Muller, & Kori, 1992.)

A five-person comparison group involving no reinforcements and noncontingent reinforcements also was used, thus combining a classical research design with a single-system design. Reliability checks were taken (interobserver ratings of walking speed), which produced agreements between 99% and 100%.

Baseline was established for each client, beginning with either a no-reinforcement condition, or a noncontingent condition. The pattern shown in Figure 3 is typical of all of the experimental clients. The baseline showed the characteristic guarded pace, with contingent reinforcements leading to increased rates. The overall results showed a positive direct correlation between walking speed and contingent reinforcement plus feedback. Each new criterion was met, except for the last criterion in one experimental client. Average self-ratings on pain were collected over a baseline of four sessions, and a final treatment pattern over the last four sessions. Geiger et al. (1992, p. 184) report the average decrease in reported pain was 36% for experimental clients, and 13% for comparison clients.

Overall, this study shows that it is possible to rigorously control a study of chronic lower back pain and walking, using a relatively simple, practical, and inexpensive method of providing contingent reinforcement (and the feedback on how well one is doing). The changing criteria were reasonable steps; that is, clients were medically able to meet them if they counteracted their (falsely) self-protecting behaviors and walked more rapidly. And the method of arriving at the new criterion is clear and applicable across clients.

We introduced a case example on chronic back pain, using an *A-B* design as its evaluation method (Engel, Jensen, & Schwartz, 2004). And here, we introduce a second chronic pain study by Geiger et al. (1992), using a changing criterion design. This provides an interesting opportunity to compare the studies, their methods, and what decisions you would make based on their findings. You may recall that the Engel, Jensen, and Schwartz (2004) study employed biofeedback training as its intervention against chronic back pain, while the Geiger et al. (1992) study provided feedback contingent with the participants walking a little further each time for tokens that could be spent in ways that each person found reinforcing. Both were "successful" in producing positive results—that is, chronic pain was controlled in some clients with relatively small investments in interventions in an area (chronic pain) that has been difficult to address. So, what would you do, M. Practitioner, if you found these two pieces of evidence for identifying the basis for your practice? While there are many differences between the two studies, which provides the stronger logical evidence? Which is easier to perform, especially without a lot of money or time and effort involved? Which would be easier for your clients with chronic pain to accept and to use? These are important types of questions to ask, because you will be forced into making similar decisions when you use evidence-based practice.

Clinical cases can be exceedingly complex, and the evaluation designs should attempt to capture as much of the complexity without losing the central focus on the client's improvement. Kahng, Boscoe, and Byrne (2003) present a difficult case of a 4-year-old girl who would not eat food at meal times; she continued to use the bottle for her entire nutrition, and so she was brought to a hospital where the following procedures were used to get her to accept food. We have adapted their discussion for use in this book.

Using negative reinforcement—that is, the removal of some unpleasant stimulus when the client performs some desired behavior—the treatment staff was able to let the child "escape" (i.e., have a short time away from) the unpleasant task (of eating a whole meal) if she would swallow a spoonful of food (applesauce at first, other foods later). For this acceptance of the spoonful of applesauce, she was given a blue chip (a token that could be exchanged for something she desired, namely, not eating a whole meal). That is, the child was required to "buy" her escape by accumulating blue chips. Once this pattern was established, the treatment staff required the child to swallow more spoonfuls of food in order to get her blue chip, thus raising the criterion for the child to buy her desired escape from eating a whole meal.

As we can see in Figure 4, a simplified version of this study, there were two baselines, each 15 meals long, the first simply using positive reinforcement (verbal praise) if she swallowed the spoonful of food. The second baseline used the same positive reinforcement, plus physically guiding the spoon toward the child's mouth. Neither of these succeeded in getting the child to swallow anything. When the negative reinforcement was used in the intervention period, we can see a small amount of movement at first, and then an increasing improvement as the criterion was increased for getting blue chips to escape the eating of the meal. Eventually, the little girl was regularly eating 14 spoonfuls of applesauce, and later, other foods as well, by following the same method.

There are several interesting points, even in this simplified adaptation. First, two baselines were used, presumably to make sure that two basic attempts to get the child to eat had been tried, with no desired behavior

Changing Intensity Designs and Successive Intervention Designs

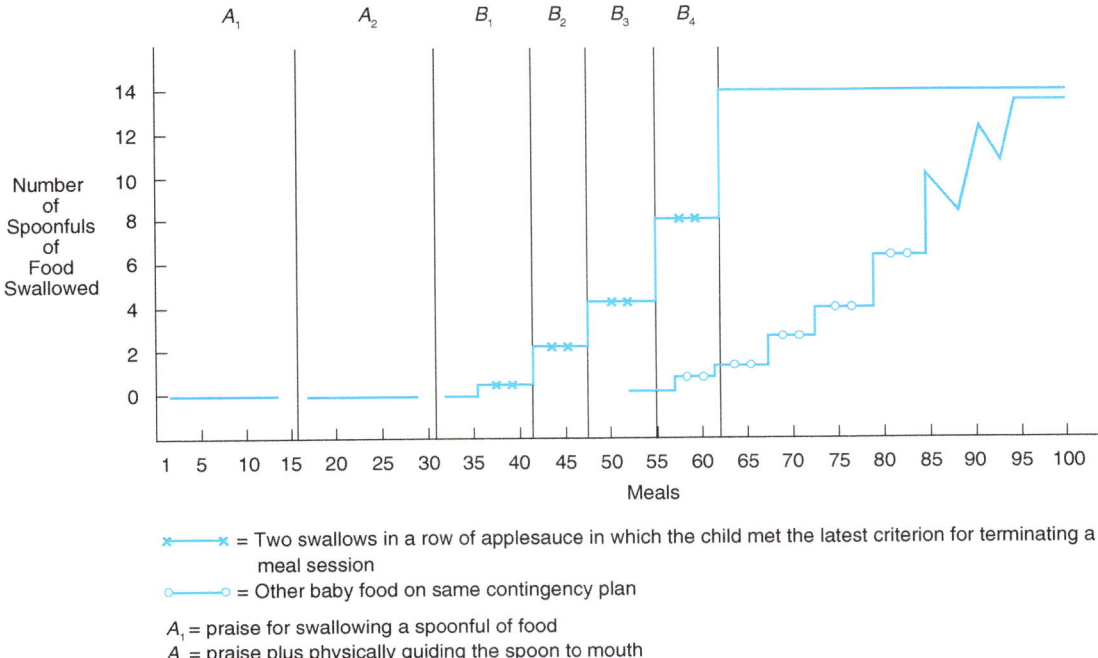

x—x = Two swallows in a row of applesauce in which the child met the latest criterion for terminating a meal session
o—o = Other baby food on same contingency plan

A_1 = praise for swallowing a spoonful of food
A_2 = praise plus physically guiding the spoon to mouth
B = negative reinforcement = swallowing the criterion number of spoonfuls of food to get token to end meal session

FIGURE 4 A changing criterion design, in which a child who would not eat solid foods had to "buy" her escape from eating a meal by swallowing spoonfuls of applesauce (and later, other baby foods) in increasing numbers of spoonfuls at each "buy out."

[Data and chart adapted from "The Use of an Escape Contingency and a Token Economy to Increase Food Acceptance" by S. Kahng, J. H. Boscoe, & S. Byrne, 2003, *Journal of Applied Behavior Analysis*, *36* (3). pp. 349–353.]

observed in either baseline. This means that a standard intervention (praise for eating) was the ethical condition that served as baseline, against which a new intervention could be compared. The child was probably being fed by bottle as well. Second, the intervention (feeding the child spoonfuls of food) was really two interventions, because only the applesauce was accepted, while harder, chewing foods took longer to be accepted, reflecting, the authors note, the child's natural preference among foods. All foods used in this study were eventually accepted on a regular basis, but this study needed a follow-up to see whether this clinical intervention was sustained over time after the study ended. The intensity of effort in getting the child to eat could only occur in closed settings at considerable expense, but the idea of this changing criterion design could be adapted for other service settings.

Watson-Perczel, Lutzker, Greene, and McGimpsey (1988) present what we consider a changing program design involving families adjudicated for child neglect. The focus of their study was an attempt to help the families clean up their homes, which were extremely and dangerously cluttered and dirty. The homes were often infested with freely roaming bugs; excrement and rubbish were frequently present in various rooms; and the children were invariably poorly clothed and sent to school unclean.

Into these difficult circumstances ventured the practitioners, who (among many other activities and goals) attempted to instruct the clients on how to clean their homes. First, the practitioners established rapport with the families, including identifying private areas with the clients that would not be measured. Then the team used a data-collection system referred to as the Checklist for Living Environments to Assess Neglect (CLEAN). Each room that was to be cleaned was assessed by areas and functions, thus establishing a reliable tool to measure cleanliness across clients.

The intervention was the teaching in stages of effective cleaning methods. The sequentially increasing activities and responsibilities were publicly assigned,

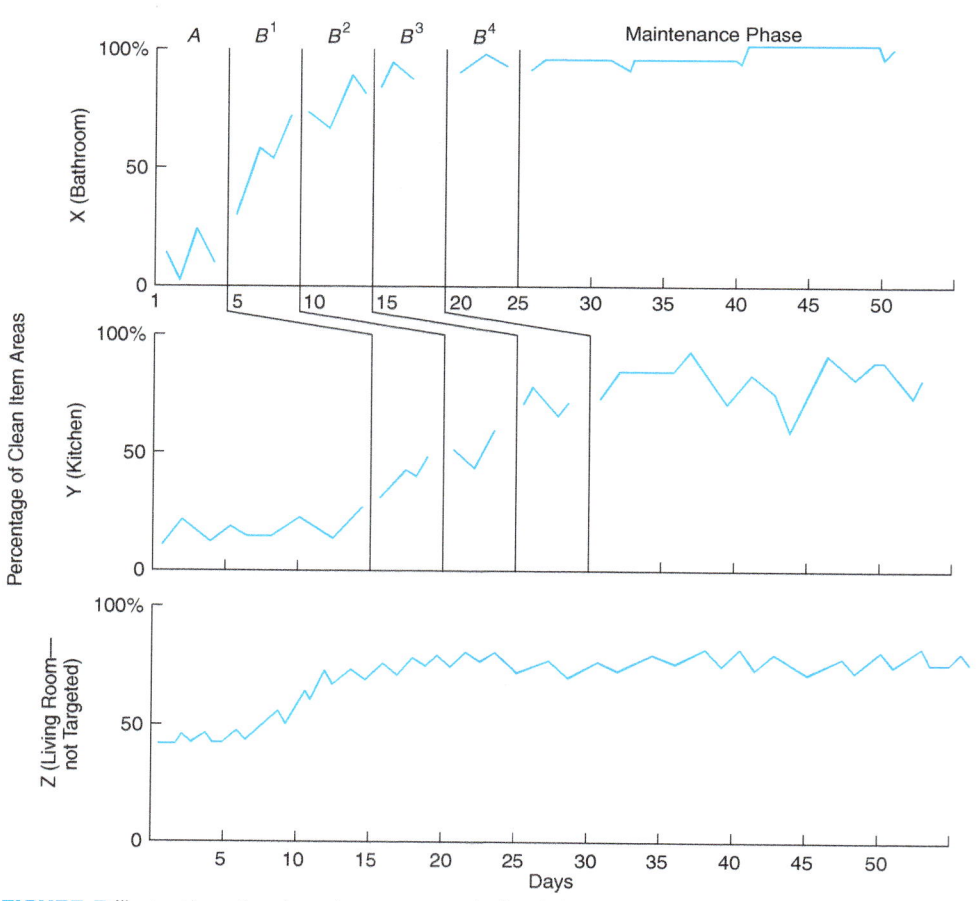

FIGURE 5 Illustration of a changing program design (with a multiple-baseline design superimposed) with each *B* phase involving a change in cleaning methods.

(Adapted from "Assessment and Modification of Home Cleanliness among Families Adjudicated for Child Neglect" by M. Watson-Perczel, J. R. Lutzker, R. Greene, and B. J. McGimpsey, 1988, *Behavior Modification*, 12, pp. 57–81.)

along with training on how to perform them. In terms of this text, we would describe these increasing training elements as changing intensities of the intervention program, that is, a changing program design.

Figure 5 is adapted from data presented by Watson-Perczel, Lutzker, Greene, and McGimpsey (1988). Note that two rooms in one client's home are identified for cleaning and receive the same intervention staggered over an 11-day period. This constitutes a multiple-baseline design on top of the changing intensity design. A third room (representing several others not subject to this same cleaning effort) shows somewhat less change over the period of the study (although the initial levels were higher so that there was less room for improvement), suggesting that generalization to other parts of the house may not be taking place.

Introducing the Client to Changing Intensity Designs.
In addition to the previously described introductions to each design, the present design requires further explanation about the changing intensities of the program or criteria for acceptable performance. (In interpreting results of these designs, we must keep in mind that it is possible that the clients' knowledge of their own performance will aid them in surpassing their record, or perhaps knowledge of their nearness to the goal also could be a stimulus.) However, it is

conceivable that there are situations in which the client cannot be told about the changing intensities. For example, a severely disturbed youth (diagnosed with schizophrenic behaviors) was being aided in stretching out the intervals between outbursts in his classroom by means of a token reward given to him if he was able to control himself until a preset alarm clock rang. Unknown to him, the practitioner was increasing the intervals between rings.

Assuming that it is possible to inform clients about the changes in program or performance criteria level in the changing criterion design, we suggest the following wording: *"Helping you solve your problem will be like climbing the steps of a ladder; each rung will move you closer to your goal. Your goal is G, and so we will arrange that if you accomplish O (the objective or a portion of that goal), then you can have R (the client's preferred reinforcement). Each time you move closer to that goal, we will provide this reward, and then we'll talk about what it will take to get that reward the next time."*

Similar introductions can be made for the changing program design. We suggest the following wording: *"Helping you solve your problem will be like climbing the steps of a ladder; each rung will move you closer to your goal. I (the practitioner) will change the intervention (increasing it or decreasing it according to the goal that the client and practitioner are seeking) at each step of the way to your goal."*

SUCCESSIVE INTERVENTION DESIGNS: *A-B-C, A-B-A-C, A-B-A-C-A*
|A|B|C|A|B|A|C|A|B|A|C|A

The successive intervention designs consist of a series of designs that employ different intervention methods, each applied one after the other in separate phases. Some of these are among the most commonly used of all designs, because in actual practice, it is often very difficult to apply just one intervention method or program and achieve effectiveness. Usually there is some need for changes in or additions to the intervention, either in new interventions or introduction of a maintenance program. Another reason why successive intervention designs are frequently used is that feedback from the data may indicate that a given intervention program is not working satisfactorily. Thus, changes in intervention programs are frequent, and our discussion of these successive intervention designs attempts to point out some of the logical possibilities and limitations of such formats.

Successive intervention designs can be planned in advance for more systematic comparisons between phases and to test the effects of a maintenance program. A much more common use in everyday practice is when immediate feedback suggests the need for modifications in an intervention. The changes are made and you simply note on the chart with a new phase when the changes began. There is a wide variety of successive intervention designs you might construct, some involving removals (return to baseline) between phases and others involving additions or complete changes in intervention, all depending on the needs of the particular case or situation. We will briefly introduce you to some of the major representatives of this group of designs and to the logical possibilities for conclusions drawn from each design. Remember, though, that these *are* merely examples, models that will help you understand just what you can conclude about the effectiveness of the interventions (causality) from these designs, because successive intervention designs can be any combination of phases that is necessary for a given case.

With all successive intervention designs, there is a temptation to look at the differences across phases and to compare results from an early phase with those from a later phase.

The problem is that one of the main reasons we use successive intervention designs is that the target doesn't change to a sufficient degree in the earlier phases. Thus, we add newer, better (more powerful, more specific) interventions in subsequent phases until we reach our terminal goal. Then, when we look back at our progress, it's easy to say, "Wow, intervention *E* did much better than intervention *B*. Just look at the differences in the target."

But, of course, a good deal has transpired between the time of implementation of interventions *B* and *E*, not only several different interventions that could have "prepared" the client for intervention *E*, but numerous external events that also could have affected the results. And especially if there's been no experimental manipulation to isolate and compare the causal effects of intervention *E* and intervention *B* (or *C* or *D*), we are left with some degree of uncertainty.

Having said all that, though, we will argue this: Because so much of single-system designs involves *approximate* comparisons, do feel free to compare results from nonadjacent phases. Just remember that there is a logical problem if you were to make a *causal* comparison. But, regarding the issue of nonadjacent phases, there is no logical problem with using such comparisons as the basis for *hypotheses* about subsequent use of those interventions with other clients. It may be that intervention E is indeed the most effective intervention in that successive intervention design. Then, it may be that intervention E is the most "logical" intervention to try first with the next client with similar problems.

We begin with the most simple, most commonly used successive intervention design, the *A-B-C* design.

The *A-B-C* Design |A|B|C|

The *A-B-C* design can be described as an extension of the *A-B* design, but with the addition of a new intervention, *C*. (The last phase could just as well be called *BC* if intervention *B* was continued and intervention *C* is added to it.) Comparisons can be made between the baseline and the first intervention. However, there is some logical difficulty in comparing the baseline with the second intervention, since an intervening event, *B*, has occurred, and we cannot distinguish the effects of *C* from the cumulative and ordered effects of *B* and *C*. If data from the *B* phase indicate a stable, positive change as compared to *A*, then observing clear changes after *C* provides a hint of causal factors but does not offer a clear basis for making a claim about causality because the phases are nonadjacent. We will soon describe more completely why the apparent change in the target from phases *B* to *C* is not an adequate basis for detecting causal relationships.

Of course, this design could be continued with subsequent phases, each designating a new intervention; for example, *A-B-C-D-E*. Similarly, this design or variations of it could be used both to add and combine phases, for example, when one does not want to completely eliminate a prior intervention. An example of this might be an *A-B-C-CD* design. However, while these designs might show clearly that a target has changed, these additions and combinations make it difficult to draw conclusions about causality because of order and carryover effects.

Practitioners might consider using the *A-B-C* design or elaborations of it as an economic way to test some practice ideas, recognizing that it does not provide the basis for inferring causality. If time and conditions do not permit the removal of one intervention and a return to baseline before the introduction of another, and if circumstances do not permit changing the intensity of the intervention as discussed earlier in this chapter, then it may be appropriate to employ the *A-B-C* design. But this design is most commonly used in practice to simply reflect changes in interventions based on monitoring changes in the client's progress (or lack of progress) toward a goal.

Another common situation in which the *A-B-C* design may be used is when *C* is a maintenance phase. That is, when the intervention *B* has been successful but a completely new intervention is needed to teach the client to use *B* without the aid of the practitioner, then phase *C* is properly employed to develop maintenance of the successful effects from phase *B*. Phase *C* tests the impact and the stability of maintenance training. A maintenance phase is a very useful and important addition to any *A-B* design; you will sometimes see it indicated by the letter M on the chart.

The *A-B-A-C* Design |A|B|A|C|

The *A-B-A-C* design represents a large improvement over the *A-B-C* design in interpreting results because of the return to baseline before moving to the second intervention, *C*. This is a special form of an experimental design, but rather than give it this label, we prefer to emphasize its limitations in providing causal knowledge of the C intervention by describing it, and the next design, as an experimental, successive intervention design. With an *A-B-A-C* design we can determine the full effects of the *B* phase by comparing it with the first and second baseline periods, since the second *A* phase is implemented because the *B* phase shows positive change. This first part of the *A-B-A-C* design is our old friend, the *A-B-A* design, which is powerful in itself. But we would need a third baseline to determine the full effect of intervention *C*, as we illustrate in the next section. It is important to note that because of the economy of an *A-B-A-C* design (two interventions are tested with one baseline before each intervention), you may think, as we said earlier, that you are *comparing* two different interventions, *B* and *C*, when in fact you are *experimentally* examining only one, the *B* phase; but you *are* raising some questions about the other, the *C* phase, that cannot logically or fully be answered within the context of this design. In short, we must carefully distinguish between what is required for determining the effects of one intervention and what is required for comparing the effects of two different interventions with a particular degree of certainty. We will return to this point shortly, as the next successive intervention design is introduced.

The *A-B-A-C* design may be employed in situations similar to those discussed in connection with the *A-B-C* design, but when you also want to have a stronger picture of the effects of the *B* phase. This is a very economical way of looking at two interventions, even though we emphasize that this design doesn't provide the logical basis for comparing the two interventions for their relative effect on the target problem.

A very appropriate use of the *A-B-A-C* design would be to have *C* be a maintenance phase to teach the client how to maintain the level of effect reached in the *B* phase. In such situations the last phase also could include a reinstatement of the *B* phase, plus the additional training for a maintenance phase, *C* (or as it is sometimes indicated, *M*). It would be more appropriate to use the notation *A-B-A-BC* to indicate this particular form of the design.

The *A-B-A-C-A* Design | A | B | A | C | A |

This form of the successive intervention design builds on the preceding designs but adds some important factors due to the return to the baseline after the second intervention. Let's examine it in detail. After the initial baseline, an intervention, *B*, is introduced, presumably to the point at which the problem is showing a positive change from the baseline, although the terminal goal will not have been reached. The first intervention is then removed, employing the same logic as discussed in the experimental designs chapter which is to have a basis for determining whether the intervention was likely causally linked with the observed change. Let's presume that the second baseline shows a return to near the original level, thus supporting the inference that *B* was causally linked with the observed change in the target. Next, a new intervention, *C*, is introduced, and after its positive and stable effects have been observed, it too is removed to produce a third baseline in order to provide a basis for determining the causal linkage of *C* to the outcome. This part of the *A-B-A-C-A* design is another old friend, *A-C-A*. Because of its rigor, this is not a commonly used design. But we use it here as a model to help you understand the causal implications of various design arrangements. Apart from the need to evaluate the effects of two separate interventions, a major reason for implementing a *new* intervention in the *C* phase is that, although changes in the *B* phase were positive, they had not achieved the terminal goal—hence, the need to employ a new intervention.

With this design, you would know about the effects of two separate interventions, *B* and *C*, each with its first and second baselines. The temptation again is to view such an *A-B-A-C-A* design as a direct comparison between the *B* and the *C* interventions; however, it is not totally appropriate to make this comparison. With the *A-B-A-C-A* design, you cannot really compare the contrasting or relative effects of *B* and *C*, because *B* and *C* are not adjacent to each other, as is required for such a comparison. Other reasons for this limitation on comparing the relative effects of *B* and *C* are that there may be some additive impact of the two interventions or the order of presentation may have something to do with the outcome. If you want to clarify the relative effects of the interventions, you might consider using an interaction design or alternating intervention design.

However, the *A-B-A-C-A* design does provide some important hints about the two different interventions that can be followed up later with another client, because it is useful to be able to study the separate effects of two interventions on a given target but in a different order. We discuss the *A-B-A-C-A* design more fully below as a model and representative of successive intervention designs.

Strengths of the A-B-A-C-A *Design.* As with other experimental designs, this design presents a basis for making some causal inferences. However, it goes beyond some of the previously described experimental designs by providing information on two different interventions for one client. By returning to the baseline on each occasion after each intervention has been conducted, you have a clear, logical picture of their separate effects. This is an economic feature of this design, enabling you to do a test of two interventions (individual techniques, packages, or programs) with the same client.

This design presents you with other important information, namely, two apparently successful interventions in connection with the one client. It also presents some choices as to what to do with this information with subsequent clients. For example, you may wish to combine interventions, *BC*, to observe their joint effect. Or, based on your observations, you may wish to return to the apparently more successful intervention of the two first before moving into a termination and maintenance phase.

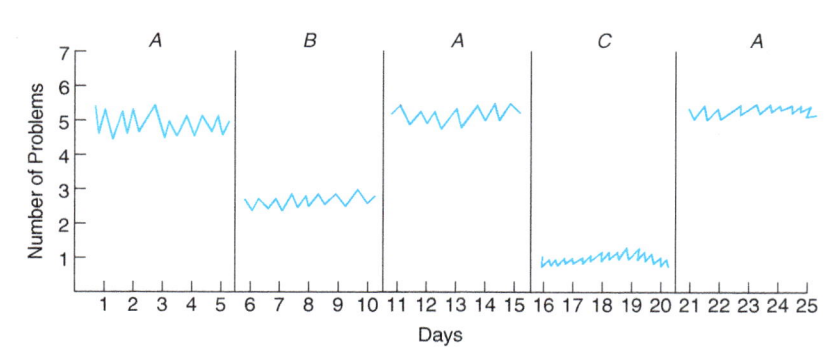

FIGURE 6 Hypothetical data to illustrate problem of order effects.

There is another general value in the use of the *A-B-A-C-A* design: You are aided in developing knowledge of effective intervention techniques for your repertoire. Also, with the *A-B-A-C-A* design, other persons who are involved in the different interventions can observe the impact of their contributions, and thereby be reinforced and encouraged to continue their contributions.

Limitations of the A-B-A-C-A *Design.* As we have stressed, the temptation with this design is to compare results obtained from the *B* and *C* interventions. However, logically this may not lead to accurate conclusions, as explained previously, because of other influences such as carryover effects, lack of adjacent phases of the two interventions, and order-of-presentation effects that may confound the picture. This design is not fully capable of sorting out these influences.

It may be difficult to convince a client to change from one already established, successful intervention to another intervention, although you can point out that the problem has not been completely resolved yet, nor the final goal attained, and that you would like to try a new intervention to achieve better results. If the client asks why you didn't try the new intervention first, you may say that you had to test out the more simple approach before considering the more complicated one. You also may point out that the intervention previously tried may be the more efficient one.

The last phase is based on observation alone rather than on intervention. This presents some practical problems should undesirable patterns of data appear (if the pattern remains positive, the final *A* phase can function as a follow-up phase). Presumably you could continue with another intervention—this is the point of successive intervention designs—but it will require additional explanations to the client as to why you changed from a successful *B* phase to another intervention that ended with less successful data appearing in the third baseline phase. You have to expect some of these negative turns of events in real-life practice, and they will always require explanation to a client who may be less than pleased.

While order effects tend to be a problem with the successive intervention design, some of the principles of the *A-B-A-C-A* design, combined with the principles underlying the experimental removal designs can be used to study, and rule out, order effects.

Let's say, in the development of a successful technique or technique package, you were to conduct an evaluation resulting in the pattern shown in Figure 6. The way to check out the possibility of order effects is simply to reverse the order of the two interventions *B* and *C* with a different client with a similar problem. This could produce results such as those in Figure 7, tentatively validating the notion of the greater effectiveness of *C* over *B*. Thus, an *A-B-A-C-A* design becomes an *A-C-A-B-A* design with the second and different client. This is similar to the rearrangement of phases regarding crossover designs. The main difference is that the rearrangement of phases in crossover designs occurs simultaneously, while the suggestion here is to reverse the order of the interventions with a subsequent client.

Recommendations Regarding the A-B-A-C-A *Design.* When the final observation phase (third baseline) of this design is analogous to a follow-up phase in which the client simply is watched carefully after two successful intervention phases, there is much to

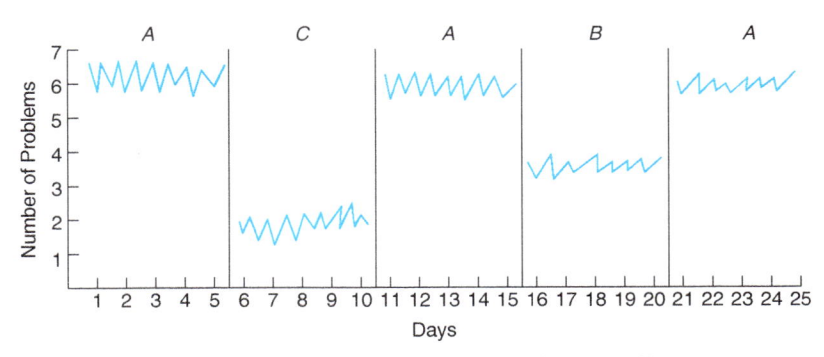

FIGURE 7 Hypothetical data illustrating how to study order effects (in comparison with Figure 6).

commend in the *A-B-A-C-A* design. It is an extension of the *A-B-A-B* type of experimental design, which offers economy and power in looking for possible causal effects, even though it has limits on comparing the *relative* effects of the interventions involved. We recommend this design in the same way we recommend the other experimental designs, particularly the *A-B-A-B* design, with the additional value that it allows the fairly common practice situation of use of two separate interventions with one client. It should be used when information on the functional relationships between interventions and outcomes is required. The *A-B-A-C-A* design is particularly useful when the first intervention, *B*, has not produced a strong enough change and the second intervention, *C*, is introduced in an attempt to reach the client's goal. The design requires a fair amount of control over the situation, and this may present difficulties in some settings.

Case Illustrations. Lloyd, Eberhardt, and Drake (1996) conducted a series of studies on cooperative learning with eighth- to eleventh-graders, using at one point, an *A-B-C-B-C* design—a kind of successive intervention design with removal of some interventions—so as to compare the effects of group and individual reinforcement contingencies in the context of group study. There has been a good deal of study of cooperative learning situations, where small groups of students work together to learn some topic. However, Lloyd et al. extended this type of study further by also comparing individual and group contingent reinforcements on average scores. (They also examined low-scoring individuals to study the effect of group study, but we will not discuss this part of their work.)

The particulars of the study that we feature here are these: Seventeen students in a first-year Spanish class in high school were given daily 10-item vocabulary quizzes. Baseline data (*A*) were plotted on the number of correct answers under the condition of individual study (in any way the individual chooses) with no contingencies for however they performed. Then, group study was introduced; this consisted of two groups composed of equal numbers of high- to low-scoring students, all of whom studied together one day for the quiz on the next day, for the same amount of time (7 minutes) as in the individual study condition.

The *B* intervention consisted of two factors: (1) group study and (2) individual reinforcements for nine or 10 correct answers; individual students would receive small tangible rewards, a pencil or candy, and public recognition. The *C* intervention consisted of a different set of factors: (1) group study, and (2) group reinforcements, in which all members of a group would receive some reward based on the average performance of the group of 9 correct answers or higher, or else to members of both groups if both mean scores were 9 or 10.

Independently, Lloyd et al. also collected anonymous survey information from participating students that served as social validation for the main part of the study. Students were asked about their preferences regarding both the individual and group contingencies, or none at all.

Figure 8 shows 31 successive quizzes and the average number of correct answers. Not shown here are the ranges of scores for each quiz, but they generally followed the average group scores. Overall, the results suggest that group study improved average spelling scores, but that average spelling scores improved the most under group study and group contingencies. However, Lloyd et al. (1996, p. 198) note that students with low baseline rates appear to be

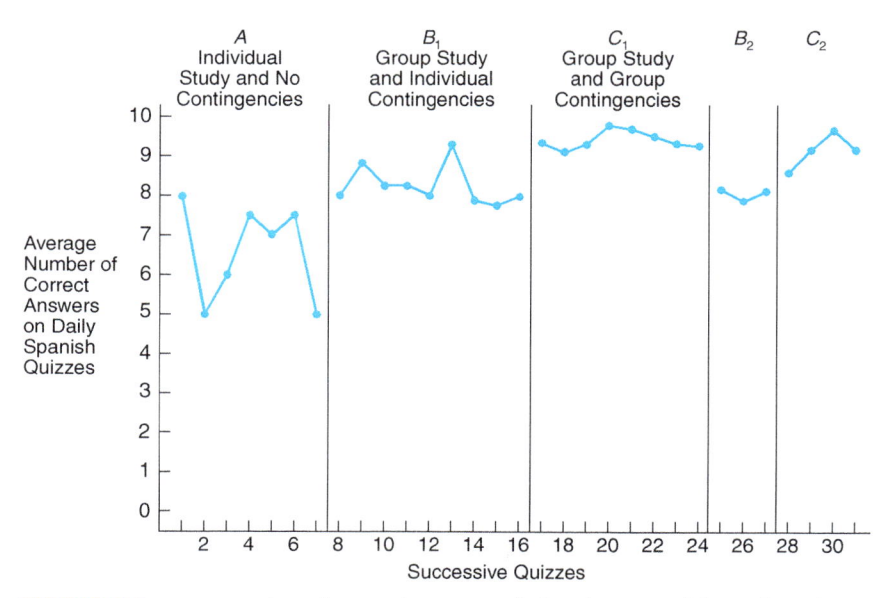

FIGURE 8 Average number of correct answers during three conditions of study plus reinforcement.
(Adapted from Lloyd, Eberhardt, & Drake, 1996.)

least likely to benefit from group study. These findings support the general trends in the literature.

We note that this design is a successive intervention design, except that instead of a return to baseline, there is experimental manipulation of two interventions. Thus, this design provides a strong hint about the differential effects of the *B* and *C* interventions, but it does not provide a full logical determination of their separate effects. For a full logical analysis, we would need an interaction design. Yet, important information was obtained in this classroom procedure where there were limits on how many removals might be ethically employed. In this case, the removal phase actually was just a change to another intervention to allow the opportunity for the experimental study of the effects of group versus individual reinforcement.

Maag, Rutherford, and DiGangi (1992) conducted what they called a multiple-treatment design related to on-task and academic productivity of learning-disabled students. However, because they were explicitly testing a theory and added components as directed by the theory, we would like to interpret this as a theory-guided variation on the successive intervention designs. Instead of the conventional addition of distinctive interventions, the Maag et al. study examines the effects of a theory-directed addition of components for one group of participants.

Learning theory applied to education has led to consideration of self-management training (Watson & Tharp, 2007). Self-monitoring has been identified as the major component of self-management training. Self-monitoring is itself composed of two elements—self-observation and self-recording; that is, a student must first become aware of his or her own behavior, and then be able to record the presence or absence of the targeted response (Maag, Rutherford, & DiGangi, 1992, p. 157). In addition, contingent reinforcement, well-established as able to increase performance, may be connected to self-management training. The authors point out that there has been little research on the differential efficacy of self-observation and self-recording as they influence reactivity, that is, how self-observing and self-recording influence self-monitoring, particularly with regard to educational goals such as having learning disabled students be on-task and solving math problems. Thus, this study involves three separate interventions: self-observation (*B*), self-recording (*C*), and contingent reinforcement (*D*).

In addition, behavior change studies often ignore the social context. So, a question of the *social validity* of the change (Kazdin, 1977) is raised: Do the changes in behavior make any difference in how the person functions in society? To answer this question, Maag et al. (1992) obtained information on the performance of nonlearning-disabled peers' functioning on the target variables, which thus provides a measure of ordinary student functioning in that school society. Then, the performance of learning-disabled students can be compared against this norm of performance to assess the social validity of the intervention, as well as the sheer amount of observed change.

Six learning disabled children in elementary school were studied, along with random nondisabled students from the same grades who were observed at the same time as the target children. Reliability checks (interobserver reports) were conducted and found to be at high levels. With regard to self-observation, a teacher's aide, who ordinarily circulated around the room, would touch the students on the shoulder as a relatively unobtrusive cue to have the students ask themselves, "Am I working on the assignment?" With regard to a unit of self-observing and self-recording, the children were prompted to indicate their behavior in an age-appropriate manner (the younger children checked off a smiling face if on-task, or a frowning face if not; older children checked in columns labeled on-task and off-task). Contingent reinforcement came in the form of praise when the students had improved over the previous session's performance or (in phase 2 of contingent reinforcement) if the students had improved in successively increasing rates over the previous session's level—a kind of changing intensity design feature—of the goals they and their teacher set collaboratively. Follow-up observations were also collected 1 week after the last intervention terminated.

Illustrative results are presented in Figure 9. Maag et al. (1992, p. 161) report "Distinct and substantial changes in both on-task behavior and academic productivity occurred for each student with the implementation of three out of the four experimental conditions: self-observing and self-recording (as one unit), and the two phases of self-observation, self-recording, and contingent reinforcement." When self-observation alone was used, it did not influence either on-task or academic behavior. Maag et al. (1992, p. 168) note that the largest gains in academic productivity occurred during the phase of contingent reinforcement plus goal setting. There were individual variations in response to these progressive interventions, depending in part on the level at which students began, and their cognitive characteristics. Of course, as with all successive intervention designs, it is difficult to conclude just what was the most relevant factor in producing the results due to order and carryover effects, and the simple cumulative effects of multiple interventions.

Introducing the Client to the A-B-A-C-A Design. The A-B-A-C-A design and the variations of the successive intervention designs presented here are perhaps a little more difficult to present than some of the earlier designs because of their two or more different interventions. Presumably, the first intervention was partially successful, and therefore you are in the position of saying something like the following:

"I am pleased that this (first) intervention has worked as well as it has, but I believe that there is more to be accomplished, and so I am suggesting another intervention that will approach the problem from a different angle. My hope is that we can make even more gains using this second approach, which, based on how you handled the first intervention, now offers greater promise of being more effective.

"To do this I will remove the first intervention but continue to collect information about how you are handling the problem/situation. Then, shortly, we can put the new information into effect and watch the very same behaviors as we have before to see whether they improve more than they did in the previous effort. If by chance they do not, then we can always go back and pick up on that first intervention again. However, in the long run it will be better, I believe, to try this second intervention. How does that sound to you?"

Extensions of the Successive Intervention Design

There are three designs that we want to call to your attention that extend the principles of these successive intervention designs while permitting you to isolate the most effective component of an intervention package. The first is the *multiple-component design* that contrasts two or more interventions with or without a formal baseline. The second is an *additive* or *construction design* that adds components to an initial intervention. The third is a *differentiating* or *strip design* that subtracts components from an initial intervention package (see Jayaratne & Levy, 1979; Thomas, 1975). The eventual result of this additive or differentiating process is to end up with what *appears* to be the most effective intervention for a given client. We emphasize the word *appears* because all of these methods are in

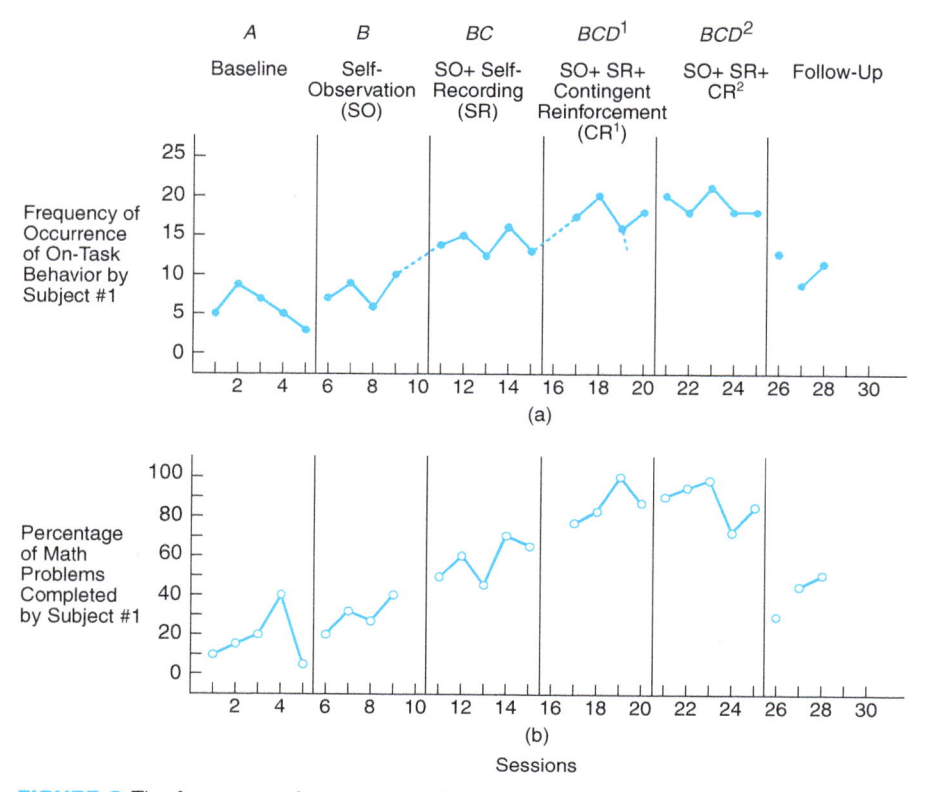

FIGURE 9 The frequency of occurrence of on-task behavior and the percentage of math problems completed by subject #1, a learning-disabled student (missed sessions are indicated simply by not recording on a particular day).

[Adapted from Maag, Rutherford, & DiGangi, 1992.]

fact shortcuts to a logically more rigorous design. The major value of these shortcut methods is their immediate feedback to the practitioner because they permit a rapid and approximate testing of the relative effectiveness of two interventions with a given client. In addition, these designs are useful in the general process of technique building and knowledge development for professional practice as they are used to identify components of practice that lead to more effective results.

The *multiple-component design* (Thyer, 1993) combines elements of the experimental replication and successive intervention designs. It can be used with or without baseline phases, although eliminating baseline phases, of course, limits its potential for logical inferences regarding causality. The purpose of this design is to attempt to compare the relative effectiveness of two different interventions.

The basic approach to the multiple-component design is to use the basic model of the experimental replication design (A-B-A-B), but to substitute different interventions instead of baselines for a "quick and dirty" comparison.

Use of such a design was described by Underwood et al. (as cited in Thyer, 1993). This design involved intervention with a severely developmentally disabled youth who engaged in high levels of self-injurious behavior during which he would strike his hand or face with his fist. The practitioner, a graduate student in social work, found two promising interventions in the literature, and he implemented them in a way that is similar to an experimental replication design. However, because of the severe level of the target problem, the practitioner chose not to use a baseline period.

The first intervention, called *interruption*, B_1, was implemented as a first phase. After five sessions and little change in the problem (frequency of actual or attempted self-injurious behavior), the second intervention, *interruption plus differential reinforcement*, BC_1, was implemented with a gradual decrease in the target. The second phase lasted 15 sessions. The third phase consisted of removal of *BC* and reimplementation of the original intervention, B_2. This lasted eight sessions with very little change in the frequency of self-injurious behaviors. The fourth phase was a reimplementation of the combined intervention, BC_2; during this phase, the problem dropped to its lowest frequency. These data are presented in Figure 10.

In this example, the two *B* phases functioned almost as baseline phases in the experimental replication design, suggesting the possibility that the *BC* intervention had more potential in reducing the frequency of the target problem. Of course, the absence of real baseline phases, the problem of order effects, and the presence of carryover effects in the third phase all present complicating factors. But this design is a good example of creative use of single-system designs to deal quickly, and through use of literature-based interventions, with a very serious problem.

The *additive* or *construction design* can be described by the following notation *A-B-A-C-A-BC-( )*. In this design, intervention *B* is attempted first, followed by a removal (A_2). Presumably, the practitioner is not satisfied with results obtained with *B*, so he or she tries a new intervention, *C*. Following a third removal, A_3, the practitioner then combines the *B* and *C* phases to see if this combination appears to be more effective than the previous interventions. The final phase, indicated by the parentheses, ( ), indicates selection of the apparently most effective combination, *B, C,* or *BC*. (Of course, because all of these phases are not adjacent, these comparisons must be approximate.) Follow-up would be necessary to test empirically whether the choice among *B, C,* or *BC* did indeed lead to successful change. A much less rigorous variation of this design, with conclusions therefore more speculative, would be to drop the removal phases. This results in an *A-B-C-BC-( )* design, a perhaps more realistic attempt to develop hypotheses for future testing.

The *differentiating* or *strip design* is described by the following notation: *A-BC-A-B-A-C-( )*. In the strip design, the practitioner begins with a combined intervention, *BC,* but then attempts to ferret out the apparently most effective component of the intervention. He or she does this by applying each of the components (*B* and *C*) separately, and by then ending up with the apparently most effective component (*B, C,* or *BC*). Again, because intervention phases are not adjacent, comparison across all interventions can only be approximate. It should be noted that by beginning with the combined intervention, *BC,* there might be a cumulative impact of an initially strong program that could exceed the impact of the separate ingredients. A follow-up should be conducted to test whether the choice among *B, C,* or *BC* did result in successful change. Of course, with these designs,

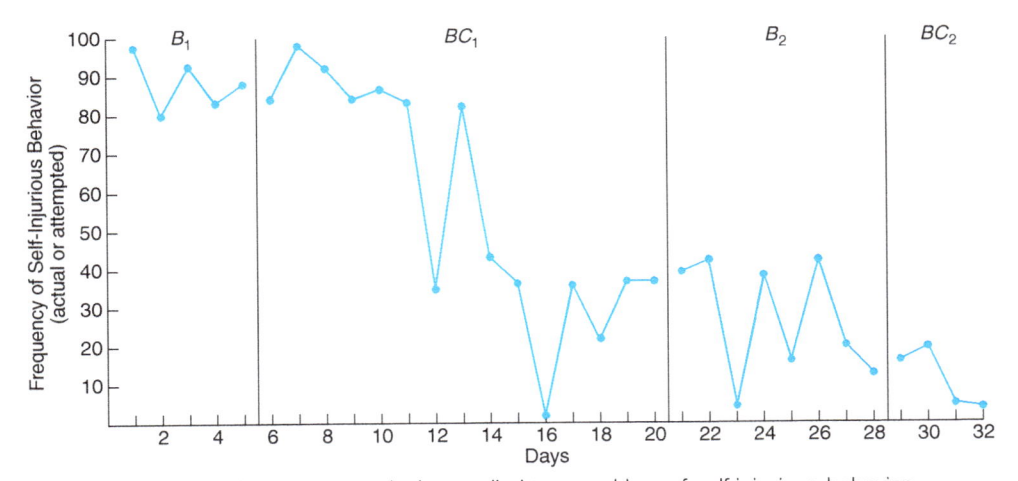

FIGURE 10 A multiple-component design applied to a problem of self-injurious behavior.

[Adapted from "Single-System Research Designs" by B. A. Thyer, 1993, in R. M. Grinell, Ed., *Social Work Research and Evaluation* [4th ed., 94–117], Itaska, IL: Peacock.]

because of the successive administration of several interventions or components of interventions, order effects cannot be ruled out. As with the construction design, it also would be possible to drop the removal phases, resulting in a design that is more realistic for practice but less rigorous, *A-BC-B-C-( )*.

By adding or subtracting intervention components within the context of returning to baseline, you can tentatively consider the impact of these separate actions in relation to one another. It is important to note that these shortcut designs do not provide a fully rigorous analysis of the relative effectiveness of components in an intervention package.

Summary

This chapter presented two major types of designs as illustrations of the numerous possibilities of designs that involve change, either in the intensity of the service program or the client's goals, or in having successive, discrete interventions introduced. Although they are extensions of the basic *A-B* design, they make important contributions in their own right.

Changing intensity designs vary in two ways. First, they may involve increasing (or decreasing) the criterion level of desired performance, and second, they may involve changing the intensity of the program itself. In either case the same intervention program is being used, but either the programs or the objectives are modified by degrees in order to move the client by successive approximation toward his or her goal.

Successive intervention designs come in many forms, from the simple *A-B-C* design to the more elaborate *A-B-A-C-A* design and extensions of the *A-B-A-C-A* design, such as the multiple-component, additive, and differentiating designs. These designs reflect the very common occurrence of using more than one intervention (technique, package, or program) in practice. While appearing to test two (or more) interventions, in fact these designs generally only offer hints as to their differential impact. For this, more complex designs are required.

DESIGNS FOR COMPARING INTERVENTIONS

PURPOSE This chapter considers several ways of trying to sort out the differential effects of specific interventions. The complex designs considered here are extensions of previously discussed designs; these designs enable you to compare or distinguish between the effects of two interventions. They are among the most rigorous of single-system designs, and, correspondingly, are more difficult to undertake than the designs considered previously.

Introduction
Alternating Intervention Design:
A-B/C-(B or C)

| A | B/C (randomized alternation of B and C) | B or C (apparently most effective intervention) |

Strengths of the Alternating Intervention Design
Limitations of the Alternating Intervention Design
Recommendations Regarding the Alternating Intervention Design

Case Illustrations
Introducing the Client to the Alternating Intervention Design
Interaction Design: A-B-A-B-BC-B-BC

| A_1 | B_1 | A_2 | B_2 | BC_1 | B_3 | BC_2 |

Strengths of the Interaction Design
Limitations of the Interaction Design
Recommendations Regarding the Interaction Design
Case Illustrations
Introducing the Client to the Interaction Design
Summary

From Chapter 17 of *Evaluating Practice: Guidelines for the Accountable Professional*, Sixth Edition. Martin Bloom, Joel Fischer, John G. Orme. Copyright © 2009 by Pearson Education, Inc. All rights reserved.

INTRODUCTION

The task of this chapter is to provide some basic information about designs to help you parcel out, or compare, the effects of distinct interventions. We present two designs (and variations on their themes) that will move you to the point of being able to make these determinations, at first approximately, and then with stronger evidence.

We speak of variations on the theme of the designs presented previously, even though each variation is fully a design in its own right. We call them variations to emphasize certain characteristics shared with other designs previously discussed and to illustrate how the designs discussed in this chapter basically are extensions of those discussed earlier. Because one of the designs described in this chapter, the interaction design, requires a large degree of control that is absent from most practice situations, that design is rarely used in everyday practice. However, there are specific indications for the appropriate use of this design, and each does illustrate a *model* for understanding how to interpret causal effects. Therefore, we provide an introduction to the basic principles related to these complex formats—the alternating intervention and the interaction designs.

ALTERNATING INTERVENTION DESIGN: A-B/C-(B OR C)

A	B/C (Randomized alternation of B and C)	B OR C (Apparently most effective intervention)

What do you do when you have two or more interventions that might work with a given problem, when you want to compare them relatively quickly, and when you are unable or unwilling to use a removal design? There actually are a number of designs that can accomplish this task. At the most general level, these can be called *multi-element designs* (Ulman & Sulzer-Azarof, 1975). Multi-element designs compare the effects of two or more interventions and/or other variables (e.g., two or more practitioners or locations for applying the interventions) on one target problem.

There are a variety of types of multi-element designs, but they are rather complicated and not much reported in the literature, so we won't pursue them.

One multi-element design, however, the *alternating intervention design* (Barlow, Nock, & Hersen, 2009), though similar in many respects to other multi-element designs, does appear to be both feasible for use in practice, and relevant to a common but critical practice problem. That problem involves trying to decide what intervention to use with a given problem when two or more interventions (or two variations of one intervention) appear equally feasible. When you are faced with this situation, the alternating intervention design is the design of choice.

The essence of the alternating intervention design is the fairly rapid alternation of two (and sometimes three) interventions so that their effects can be compared quickly with each other. Based on this comparison, the apparently most effective intervention is selected for continuing use.

There generally are three phases in the alternating intervention design (plus a maintenance and follow-up phase). The first phase is the baseline period during which preintervention observations of the target problems are taken as usual. Let's assume that based on these observations, you decide that there are two interventions that would be good choices for working with that problem, but that it is not clear just which one would be better, given the particular client and situation.

In the second phase of this design, you implement both of these interventions, rapidly alternating them in a *counterbalanced* fashion. Counterbalancing refers to presenting each a roughly equal number of times, but in such a way that the effects of the order of presentation are ruled out. (We describe how to do this below.) The results of this alternation of interventions are appraised, and the intervention that appears to be more effective in the second phase is then selected and applied by itself to the problem in the third phase, we hope to a successful conclusion. This results in an *A-B/C-(B or C)* design with the last phase comprised of the *B* or *C* intervention that appears more effective.

The only real trick in using the alternating intervention design is to counterbalance the two interventions, and, actually, this does not have to be too big a chore. The goal here is to present the interventions an approximately equal number of times, but varying the order in such a way that the order of presentation does not affect the results. In other words, if you were

Designs for Comparing Interventions

Table 1 Counterbalanced order of desensitization with and without coping statements

			Alternation Phase (Determined by flipping a coin)						
Day 8	9	10	11	12	13	14	15	16	17
With coping	Without coping	Without coping	With coping	Without coping	Without coping	Without coping	Without coping	Without coping	Without coping

applying two interventions, you would not want to apply one for 3 weeks, and the other one for the following 3 weeks. Obviously, the overall results would be confounded by such an ordering. What you are trying to accomplish is for intervention 1 to be followed as often as possible by intervention 2, *and* vice versa.

So, how do you do this? Simple. Just flip a coin! Consider intervention 1 as heads and intervention 2 as tails and then flip a coin to see which comes first each time you plan to administer an intervention. All you have to add to that is the restriction that no intervention will be applied more than a certain number of times in a row. That is, if heads comes up three times in a row, then you might automatically apply the "tails" intervention next. As a general guideline (there are no real, scientifically derived standards as of yet), we would suggest three times as the maximum for each intervention to be applied consecutively before the next intervention is applied. (Spreadsheet programs such as Microsoft Excel can be used for this and other types of randomization. Also, it's not difficult to find good web sites that let you do this such as www.randomizer.org.)

Just as an illustration of this design, let's say that an unemployed client comes to see you complaining that she has tremendous anxiety about job interviews. She is so worried about them that she is unwilling to undertake any. Let's say that you determine that she does have adequate skills for the interviews but that the anxiety keeps her from exercising those skills. Assume you develop an 11-point individualized rating scale to measure the anxiety, do a 1-week baseline, and decide to try the technique of systematic desensitization, a technique for overcoming maladaptive anxiety. But assume also you are not sure whether to do traditional desensitization or to add a new variation, coping self-statements (e.g., "I can make it"; "This interview won't be so bad") to the relaxation procedure. You decide to use an alternating intervention design in which in one session you would use desensitization *without* coping skills and in one session you would use desensitization *with* coping skills. By flipping a coin, you get the pattern displayed in Table 1. The application of these interventions produces the results illustrated in Figure 1. Based on these results, in the final phase you implement desensitization *with* coping self-statements.

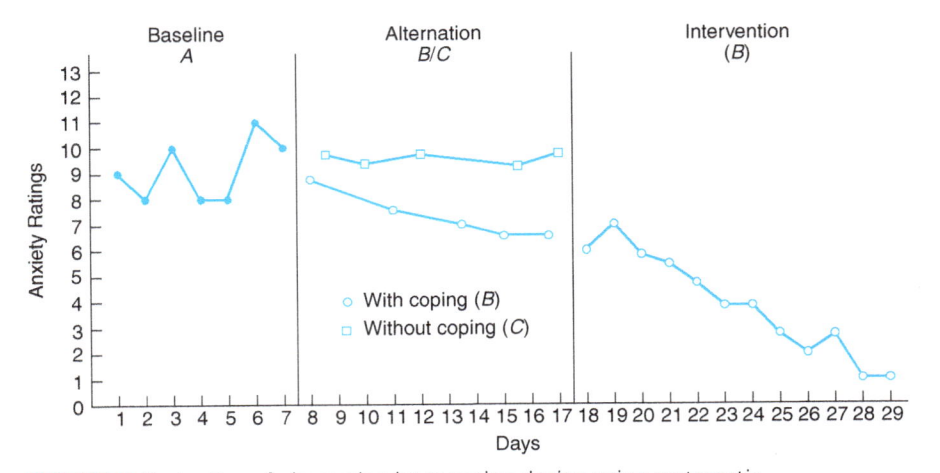

FIGURE 1 Illustration of alternating intervention design using systematic desensitization with and without coping self-statements.

Strengths of the Alternating Intervention Design

The alternating intervention design actually allows two sets of comparisons. The first, and the most important because of its uniqueness with this design, is the comparison between two interventions. The second comparison is between baseline and intervention periods. While the conclusions that can be generated from this comparison are probably no stronger logically than one can conclude from an *A-B* design, the alternating intervention design does allow this baseline-to-intervention comparison. In this case, the comparison is between the *A* phase and the *B/C* phase, and then the *B/C* phase with the final phase, since they are adjacent.

Another major advantage of this design is its flexibility. Not only can two interventions be compared, but several other types of comparisons are possible. As the case example illustrated, it is possible to examine two variations of one technique to determine which variation would be best for a particular client or even two completely different techniques. It is also possible to examine time variations in application of an intervention (three sessions a week versus one session a week, or morning applications of a technique versus afternoon applications), or to examine the use of more than one practitioner applying the same intervention. For example, a teacher at a university elementary school was having trouble with the child of a visiting professor from overseas. The young child simply did not follow her instructions. The principal was sensitive to cultural differences and suggested asking a second teacher (a male) to alternate with the first teacher (a female) in order to test out the idea that the child might do better with a male teacher. For a week the two teachers alternated including the child in their classes, and they recorded the number of "following instructions" behaviors. In this way they were able to determine in which class the child seemed to exhibit better self-control, enabling him to gain greater benefits from the year at the foreign school.

Of course, the more variations that are examined, the more complicated the counterbalancing. For example, we could compare two interventions and two practitioners by counterbalancing the various combinations of intervention and practitioner. You can see in Table 2 an example of counterbalancing involving two interventions, two practitioners, and two time periods.

Finally, a major advantage of the alternating intervention design is that it does not require a removal, and therefore might be more acceptable than experimental removal designs in many settings. Indeed, many practitioners often attempt to compare interventions to determine which is most effective, but may do so in a haphazard and unsystematic way. The alternating intervention design simply allows a feasible structure and overall plan for making such comparisons so that results are more reliable. In fact, because the interventions are counterbalanced, order effects (sequential confounding), which could be expected to show up in nonsystematic comparisons, can to some extent be ruled out.

Limitations of the Alternating Intervention Design

The alternating intervention design does not clearly rule out contrast effects—that is, differences arising due to the client's awareness of two different conditions being applied. Indeed, in the alternating intervention design, it is crucial for the client to be *able* to discriminate between the two applications of the interventions. To the extent that differential results are produced, this is all well and good. But if the results are produced *because* of the client's awareness of the differences rather than the interventions themselves, the conclusions are obviously confounded.

Table 2 Administration of the two interventions (I_1 and I_2), balanced across practitioners (P_1 and P_2) and time periods (T_1 and T_2)

Time Period	1	2	3	4	5	6	...n
T_1	$I_1 P_1$	$I_1 P_2$	$I_2 P_1$	$I_2 P_2$	$I_1 P_2$	$I_1 P_1$	
T_2	$I_2 P_2$	$I_2 P_1$	$I_1 P_2$	$I_1 P_1$	$I_2 P_1$	$I_2 P_2$	

Days column header spans days 1–6.

(Adapted from "The Simultaneous Treatment Design" by A. E. Kazdin & D. P. Hartmann, 1978, *Behavior Therapy, 9*, p. 915.)

Similarly, there may be a possibility of both order and carryover effects using an alternating intervention design. Although this is to some extent limited by the rapid alternation and counterbalancing as we mentioned previously, one cannot be completely sure that order and carryover effects are not present.

Another problem relates to external validity. This refers to the extent to which the intervention that is eventually selected in one alternating intervention design can be applied *by itself* (without the alternating process or the other intervention) to other, even similar problems needs to be evaluated on an empirical basis each time.

Another problem with the alternating intervention design is that if the practitioner is not able or willing to continue to alternate interventions or other conditions until the differences become clear, this design is not feasible. In fact, even more importantly, if the interventions you plan to evaluate are not likely to produce fairly rapid, observable changes under such alternating conditions, then the alternating intervention design should not be used.

Finally, there is some problem with the visual interpretation of these data. How much of a difference (in the *B/C* phase) is "enough" to warrant use of one or the other interventions? There really are no clear answers for that question. It is possible for some of the statistics to shed some light on this issue by doing a separate, simple statistical analysis on each intervention in the second phase in comparison to the baseline to see if one reaches statistical significance. In addition, it is possible to use more sophisticated data analysis techniques such as randomization tests, although typically these require advanced statistical skills and computers (Onghena & Edington, 2005; Todman & Dugard, 2001).

Recommendations Regarding the Alternating Intervention Design

When the practice task is to compare two or more interventions or intervention variations, and removal phases are impractical or impossible, the alternating intervention design is the design of choice. Moreover, this design may be used when there is difficulty in achieving a good or stable baseline, since the main comparison is between interventions. Further, we recommend this design for comparing two interventions involving two different practitioners. However, the limitations just described do suggest that this design be used with caution. For example, it may be hard to distinguish the effects of one intervention from another, leaving you unsure of what to do next. Further, if causal linkages are to be examined, we suggest that removal or multiple-baseline designs be utilized, or the more complicated designs described in the next section. Of course, if a quick, approximate answer to the question "Which of the following interventions seems to be most effective with this client?" is needed, the alternating intervention design can be quite useful.

Case Illustrations

Saville et al. (2006) compared two different teaching methods at the university level, first with graduate students in special education, and second with an undergraduate research class, using a form of the alternating intervention design. They established a baseline for each of the eight units being taught in the classes. This consisted of a pretest over content to be covered in class; scores on the pretests were not recorded as part of grades, but let students know what they were about to learn.

The interventions involved classical lectures over content and what the authors call "interteaching," which follows some traditions of behavioral principles of learning, but with more flexibility in their delivery. For interteaching, the instructor would prepare questions to guide students' reading and thinking through each of the eight specific units of the courses. Students would be divided into small groups that would have a different composition of students at each unit to discuss the guiding questions and come up with answers. The instructor moves around the class answering questions and monitoring comprehension of content. At the end of each class, students fill out questionnaires on issues with which they had difficulty. These issues would be the content of the brief lectures at the next session, after which new sets of small groups would discuss new questions for this next unit.

There was a quiz at the end of each unit. In the first study, lectures were used in sessions 1, 2, 5, and 8, while interteaching was used in sessions 3, 4, 6, and 7. On all occasions, students who obtained their knowledge from interteaching scored higher than when they learned through lectures. However, both methods of instruction showed improvement over baseline pretest scores.

In the first study, the authors alternated teaching methods on a random basis, and in the second study, they again alternated teaching methods, but counterbalanced the interventions (lectures and interteaching) with two sections of the class. Both sections took the same weekly tests. Again, the results favored interteaching over classical methods, and both were superior to baseline pretests (see Figure 2, a nontraditional alternating intervention chart).

The authors concluded that interteaching is a promising method that needs more study, but for our purposes, this study provides a nice alternating intervention design that went on to use the one (of two) interventions in the succeeding intervention period that appeared during the first intervention to be the more successful. We wonder how much the novelty of the interteaching method had to do with the students' reactions, which is another reason for further study including long-term follow-ups of the performance of each study group.

Kastner, Tingstrom, and Edwards (2000) studied the effects of Ritalin delivered to six fourth- and fifth-grade boys diagnosed with Attention Deficit-Hyperactivity Disorder, Combined Type (ADHD-CT). While the use of Ritalin for this disorder is controversial, the question posed by this study is a focused one: whether Ritalin given 45 minutes to 1 hour before testing the boys' reading skills was better or worse than giving it 3 to 4 hours before the testing. To determine the probable most effective time scheduling of the drug in a relatively short period of time (number of testing sessions), an alternating intervention design was used.

All of the tests of the 1-hour versus the 3- or 4-hour sequencing were done in a random sequence, with the provision that a maximum of three continuous occurrences of any particular condition would be allowed (as suggested earlier in this chapter). The basis for making an alternation was mastery of the reading passage by a given youngster. The passages to be read were also sequenced from easier to more difficult. The next randomly ordered condition (either the 1-hour or the 3- or 4-hour interval after administration of the drug) began at the next intervention session. (The fewer trials needed to master the material, the better.)

As seen in Figure 3. the graph portrays a reconstructed version of one of the six graphs for the subjects in this study. Note that the data points indicate *cumulatively* the number of trials it took the boys to master the reading passage. On the bottom line we observe the number of passages mastered (rather than time units per se). The two conditions, identified here as short interval and extended interval, are presented as two conditions compared in the same phase against each other. In all six cases, the short interval had better effects than the extended interval. In the one representative example we present here, the pattern shows that it takes more trials to master a passage when the drug is given 3 to 4 hours before the testing than when the drug is given 1 hour before the testing period.

An important part of this study was the independent verification of the more efficacious condition.

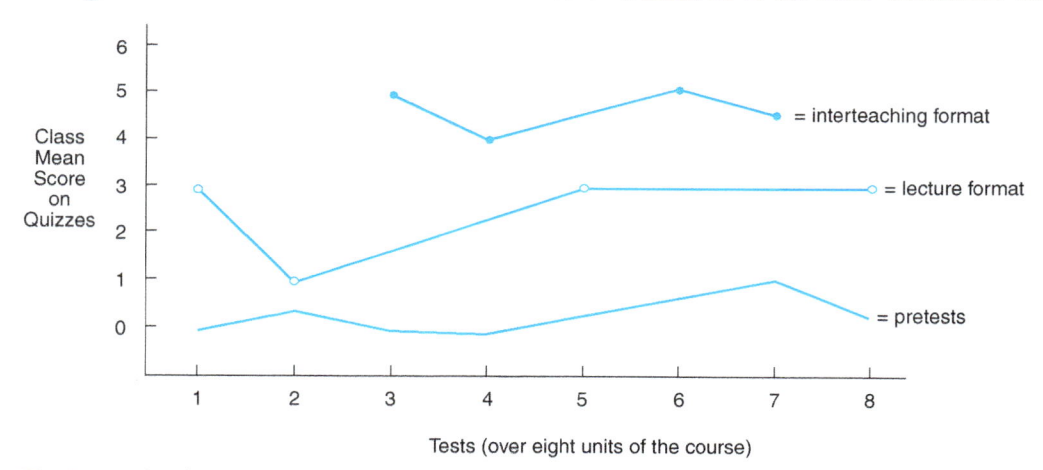

FIGURE 2 An alternating intervention design in which two teaching methods were randomly alternated, with test results compared to pretest scores at the beginning of each unit of the course.

(Data and chart adapted from "A Comparison of Interteaching and Lecture in the College Classroom" by B. K. Saville, T. E. Zinn, N. A. Neef, R. Van Norman, & S. J. Ferreri, 2006, *Journal of Behavior Analysis, 39*(1), pp. 49–61.)

Designs for Comparing Interventions

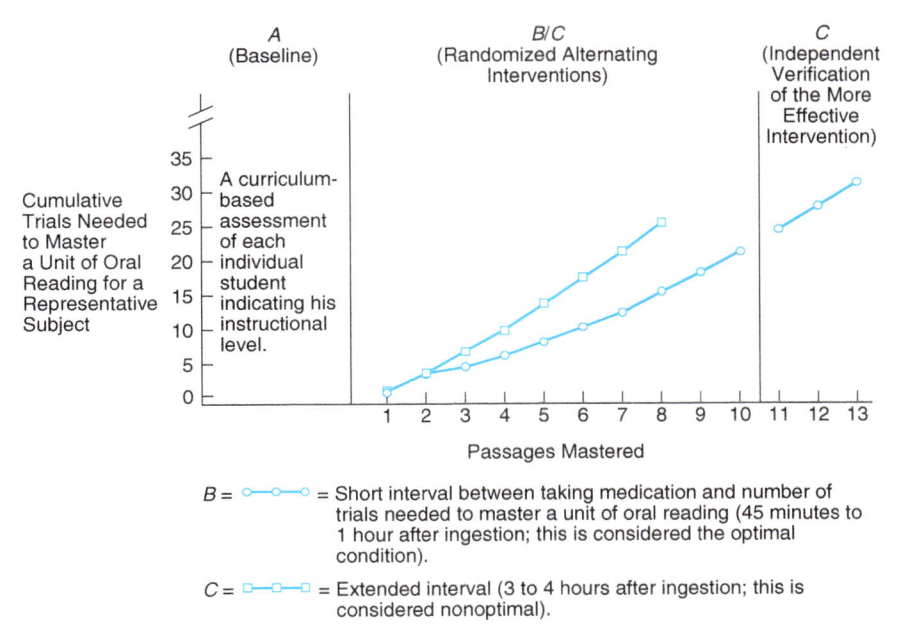

FIGURE 3 An alternating intervention design involving randomized short or extended intervals of time after ingestion of Ritalin before a child is able to master a unit of oral reading. (Adapted from Kastner et al., 2000.)

The six boys differed by degree in this independent verification, but in general, even with an independent observer verifying the number of trials to mastery, the short interval had lower cumulative trials to mastery than did the extended trials conducted during the main part of the evaluation.

Linton and Singh (1984) reported on the effects of two training procedures for teaching sign language to hearing-impaired developmentally disabled adults. Using the alternating intervention design, they combined a technique called positive practice overcorrection (repeating the right answer five times) with positive reinforcement, or used the overcorrection procedure alone. (The authors used a no-training control technique as well, but we will adapt their data to illustrate the alternating intervention part of their study.) Reliability of ratings of accuracy of the clients' signs was acceptable for two independent raters.

Figure 4. presents some data adapted from the Linton and Singh study on one client. A training phase is visible the first 5 days of the intervention period (B/C), although not identified as such by the authors; learning to sign takes practice. However, once the client caught on, he first showed more successful signing with the overcorrection technique alone. Overcorrection plus positive reinforcement appear to have confused the client at first. However, in time, the combined overcorrection technique plus positive reinforcement clearly became the stronger condition, producing more words signed correctly. Thus, this combination was the method of choice in the second intervention period, labeled B in the chart.

While it might appear obvious that the combination of methods would be better than the one alone, this was not the case immediately. There was a training period in which the client had to learn the skill and perhaps another training period in which the client came to appreciate the additional reinforcement given on top of producing a correct sign.

The following example of a variation of an alternating intervention design illustrates that practitioners may combine evaluation and research in one project, to the advantage of both. Maheady, Mallette, Harper, and Sacca (1991) tested a teaching innovation (called Heads Together [HT]) against the common instructional approach (the whole group approach [WG]) with a difficult, unruly class. The common whole

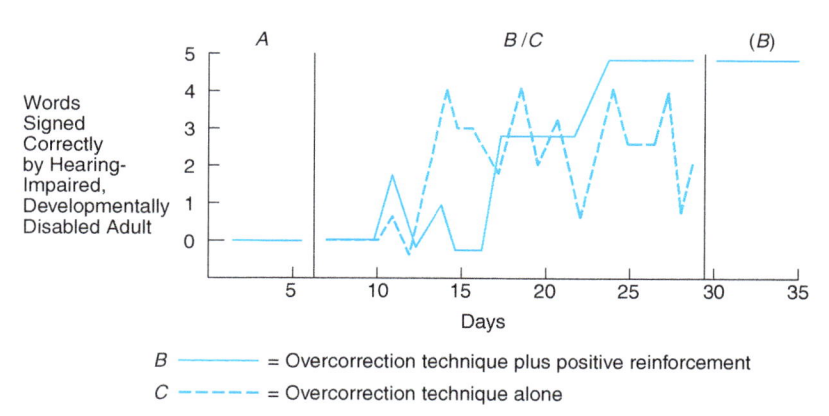

FIGURE 4 Alternating intervention design using positive practice overcorrection and overcorrection alone.

(Adapted from "Acquisition of Sign Language Using Positive Practice Overcorrection" by J. M. Linton and N. N. Singh, 1984, *Behavior Modification, 8*, pp. 553–566.)

group approach involves the teacher asking a general question to the class, and then calling on volunteers to answer, which tends to encourage the high-achieving students and discourage the low-achieving ones. The Heads Together approach involves arranging students in heterogeneous groups of four, with one high-achieving student, two average-achieving students, and one low-achieving student, who number themselves 1 to 4 and sit together. The teacher asks a question and allows a short time for the four-member groups to put their heads together to come up with the best answer—thus ensuring that everyone on the team knows the answer. Thus, when the teacher asks, "How many Number ____s (1, 2, 3, or 4) know the answer?" that member of the team, who can be high-, average-, or low-achieving, raises his or her hand. The teacher also asks other teams with the same number if they agree with that answer or want to correct it. Each team earns points for correct answers, and individual scores are also recorded. Team membership remained the same throughout the project.

Ordinarily, the teacher would conduct a social studies unit four times a week of about 30 minutes in length. For this study, she conducted this unit twice a week, once in the morning and once in the afternoon, so that the randomized alternation between the whole group and the Heads Together methods could be compared. Baseline measures were taken during the ordinary whole group method, and then the alternating interventions were used.

Figure 5 presents the results on the percentage of correct answers on social studies quizzes. Maheady et al. (1991, p. 29) point out that, in the baseline condition, about one-third of the class had failing averages, while two students earned A grades. In the alternating phase (*B/C*), the class averages were plotted separately, with students always performing better in the Heads Together method. In the last phase (*B*), the HT method is used all of the time, with similar results. Maheady, Mallette, Harper, and Sacca (1991, p. 29) point to the important fact that no student had a failing grade under the HT conditions, and six students earned A grades. These practitioners also studied on-task behavior with the alternating intervention format and found a similar pattern favoring the HT conditions, except that when HT was used alone in the third phase, there was no improvement in on-task behaviors. The experimenters suggest that team enthusiasm (congratulating one another) may have accounted for the off-task behavior; they propose to reconsider their measurement procedure to take account of this side effect of the HT method. The results are encouraging in the face of current educational challenges—changing demographics of the schools, rapidly enlarging knowledge base, and exhortations to improve learning for everyone. By forming heterogeneous learning groups and encouraging peer-teaching of teammates who then respond in a teacher-questioning format, Maheady, Mallette, Harper, and Sacca (1991) seem to be moving toward a very useful innovation.

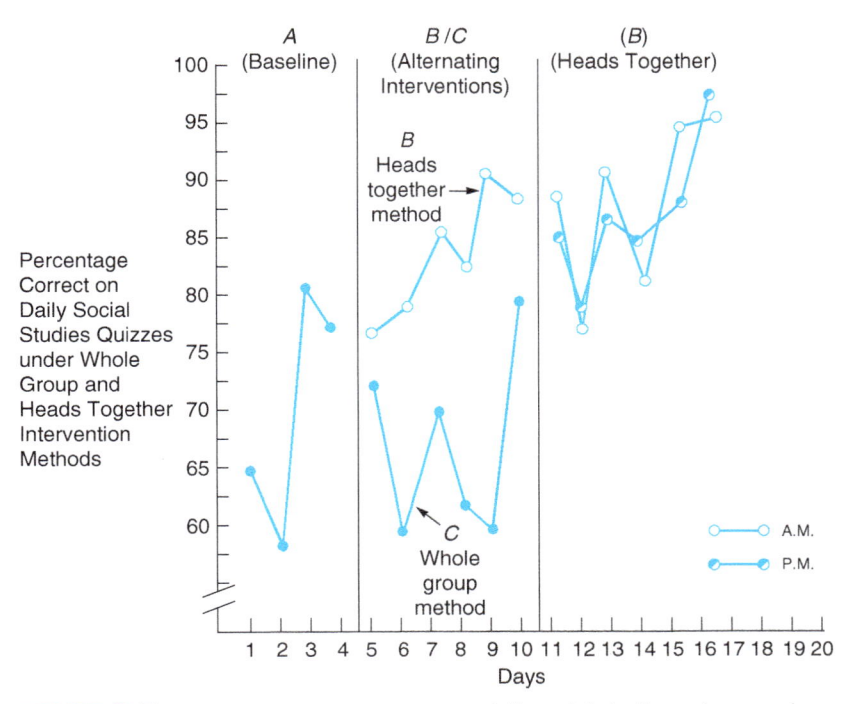

FIGURE 5 The mean percentage correct on daily social studies quizzes under alternating intervention design.

(Adapted from Maheady, Mallette, Harper, & Sacca, 1991.)

Introducing the Client to the Alternating Intervention Design

The basic similarity of the alternating intervention design to other designs means that you can use the material in previous introductions to help you begin your discussion of this design. However, for the unique element of this design, the fact that more than one intervention will be used in the same phase, we suggest the following: "*I am going to suggest that we try two approaches to help resolve your problem. We know that each will be of some help, but I can't tell without trying each which is the more effective one. Once we get some ideas about how well each method works, we'll use the better one. This will require that we continue to keep accurate records of how you are doing.*"

Let's say, however, that the techniques you use in one intervention contradict the techniques in another intervention. More explicitly, if what you tell the client in the instructions in one intervention seems nonreversible, you might try the following, once you actually get into the alternation of the interventions: "*I know that with our other approach, I suggested you do (X). Now what I'd like you to do is specifically not do (X). We will then see which way is better. When we start this next approach, be sure to specifically not do (X).*"

INTERACTION DESIGN: A-B-A-B-BC-B-BC

| A_1 | B_1 | A_2 | B_2 | BC_1 | B_3 | BC_2 |

The interaction design is rarely used in actual practice because of its complexity. However, we present it here as a model to help you understand many of the complex factors involved in deriving conclusions about causality regarding two or more interventions. The major concern of the interaction design is to sort out the differential effects of multiple interventions by comparing adjacent interventions in a logically controlled manner. We have discussed how the separate effects of two discrete interventions can be determined for one target, and we noted at that time that further design phases would be necessary in order to determine the differential or relative effect of these two interventions. For example, we considered the *A-B-A-C-A* design as representative of successive intervention designs. Although the second and third returns to baseline enabled the practitioner to determine the *separate* effects of *B* and *C*, it was not possible to make a logical comparison of the *relative* effectiveness of *B* and *C*. Without overcomplicating this point, we would like to present a strategy for studying such interactions.

The interaction design, designated as *A-B-A-B-BC-B-BC*, may be the minimal arrangement of elements from which you can determine the interactive effects of two interventions. This means they would be studied separately and in combination by comparing differences in the adjacent *B* and *BC* phases (Barlow, Nock, & Hersen, 2009). After first conducting a standard *A-B-A-B* sequence, you then add in the next phase a new intervention, *C*, to the earlier intervention, *B*. Then, the subsequent return to *B* and reintroduction of the combined *BC* would allow for analysis of the additive and controlling effects of the first intervention, *B*, and the combined intervention, *BC*.

This is the most complex of the designs we present in this book, and so we will explain why it technically appears to be the minimal arrangement for making interaction comparisons among interventions with the same client or target. The components are familiar. First of all, there are the repeated baseline and intervention phases as in an *A-B-A-B* design. This provides the kinds of causal information on the *B* intervention that we recognize from the experimental replication design. In addition, there is a set of four phases, *B-BC-B-BC* (overlapping the first *A-B-A-B* set), in which two types of interventions are alternated. These two types bear a special relationship to each other, with the *B* phase being a component of the *BC* phase package. Because the causal influence of the *B* phase has been assessed in the first *A-B-A-B* segment of the interaction design, the adjacent comparisons of the *B* with *BC* permit analysis of the additional effects of the *C* component of *BC*. The second *B* intervention, B_2, functions as if it were the baseline for the *BC* intervention, and it too requires a removal (the third *B* intervention or B_3) for a definitive analysis of the effects of the second *BC* intervention, BC_2. This design allows determination of the contributions *C* makes toward the effects obtained by *BC*, after separately analyzing the effects of *B* in the first four phases. Thus, this design allows the analysis of separate and additive effects of the interventions.

There are several possible variations of the interaction design. Two important variations involve combining the principles of the interaction design with those of the differentiating (strip) and additive (construction) designs. These combinations would provide a more convincing demonstration of which of the components is most effective than use of the more approximate strip/construction methods.

The first variation would be the *interaction/strip* design: *A-BC-A-BC-B-BC-( )*. With this design, you would begin with a baseline and then introduce a package of interventions, *BC*. The practitioner would determine the causal impact of *BC* by using an experimental design (similar to the *A-B-A-B*) in the first four phases. Then, taking this intervention of known effects, *BC*, you could differentiate between its components by stripping down the package to one intervention, *B*. By again experimentally manipulating this intervention, *BC-B-BC*, you not only can compare the effects of *BC* and *B* (because they are adjacent), but will understand the extent to which the intervention *C* contributed to the overall effects of *BC*. Then, the last step is to use what appears to be the most effective component, indicated by the parentheses. If you wanted, in addition, to do a separate comparison of the *B* and *C* interventions, the entire process would be viewed as follows: *A-BC-A-BC-B-BC-B-C-B-( )*.

The second variation is the *interaction/additive* design: *A-B-A-B-BC-B-BC-B-( )* (technically, the last *B* phase may not be necessary, since the *B* was manipulated earlier in *A-B-A-B* fashion). We have provided the basic logical analysis of the additive (or construction) design in the earlier discussion of the general interaction design. It does bear repeating, however, that at the conclusion of the use of this design you have the basis for analyzing not only the causal effects of *B* and *BC*, but the comparative effects as well, thereby ending up with the most effective component.

These variations of interaction designs provide the soundest logical basis for making complex comparisons. You might want to compare the differences between these designs and the strip/construction, successive intervention designs. The interaction design variations are rather long and fierce looking until they are broken down into their component elements and the reasons are understood regarding why they are put together as they are. We also want to emphasize that this is the way interventions often are combined in actual practice: Some techniques may be combined into a package or program, and then some are partialed out as experience reveals them to be less effective. Or, from a simple beginning that doesn't seem to be making the desired impact on the client's problems, you add other intervention components to make a new package. The interaction design in its additive or differentiating forms is simply a flow from the kind of thinking that went into the less complex designs as we move toward asking more demanding questions: What is the comparative effect of each of the interventions (or intervention packages) I have used?

Strengths of the Interaction Design

This powerful design (and its variations) is able to show change in target problems, to provide the basis for logically inferring whether the intervention had any causal relationship with that outcome, and to locate the differential effects of each element in the intervention process (the components or the combinations). This type of design also encourages practitioners to try out multiple interventions with some hope of sorting out what effects each may have. It also may be useful in testing conceptual ideas derived from practice theory. In short, the strengths of this interaction design are like those of the previously described *A-B-A-B* designs, plus the interaction design has the capacity to make a powerful differentiating or component analysis.

Limitations of the Interaction Design

It is obvious that the *A-B-A-B-BC-B-BC* design (and its variations) is complex and would require a good deal of time and control to perform adequately. That is why it is rarely used in actual practice. It requires considerable dedication to pursue this design, as more immediate practical interests might be served by a more simple design. In addition, these designs also involve the same problems as any standard removal design, compounded by the successive alternations.

Recommendations Regarding the Interaction Design

Interaction designs tend to require considerable control over variables, time, and energy. It would seem on the face of it that they only would be used in limited situations, such as studies of the effects of drugs or other practice efforts within institutions in which a high degree of control is possible. However, given the power of these designs, keep them in mind as possible designs to use when you need knowledge of the differential effects of interventions. (We will provide one illustration outside of a highly controlled environment to illustrate its possibilities.)

For our purposes, though, introducing the interaction design has another value, that of illustrating the logical extensions of the many design principles illustrated throughout this part of the book. If you understand the logic behind this design, then you should be able to use and analyze any single-system design, because all of these designs are made up of one or another of the logical principles illustrated in this interaction design.

Another value of interaction designs is that they can aid in the never-ending process of technique building. Interaction designs show great potential for helping to isolate the effective components of our practice. It is the rare practitioner who does not continually add or subtract different intervention components from his or her overall intervention plan, based on some standard as to what works and what doesn't. Interaction designs give us the potential for being *systematic* in that effort, for clearly and carefully identifying those components of practice that work or don't work with a variety of clients and problems/situations. This is the heart of professional practice, and the process of technique building—systematically identifying effective components of our practice—is one of the ways we can all add to the cumulative growth of professional knowledge.

Case Illustrations

We first will present a disguised version of one actual case in which a graduate social work student used a variation of the interaction design. A family agency ran a summer camp for emotionally frail youngsters. In one section of the camp, a group of eight boys ranging from 8 to 10 years old was under the guidance of a team of social workers who took turns with different aspects of their care and tending. The boys soon called themselves the "Ferrets," a very apt name, as these youngsters spent the better part of most days fighting with one another, crying, or clinging to the counselors.

One counselor, Greg, decided to attempt some group activities that would reduce the fighting and bickering that were threatening to the youngsters and frustrating to the staff. The camp defined fighting as hitting or throwing things at another camper, and the staff was required to record incidents of such behavior as a matter of routine work. All staff members used the same criteria regarding fighting, which made record keeping easy.

Greg used a psychodynamic model to conceptualize the events in this group. The model involved a consideration of latency-age boys having weak, incomplete egos with narcissistic, libidinal functioning and impulsivity. These factors, combined with thin emotional insulation and an inadequate protection against overstimulation, resulted in a propensity to fight. The boys chose to play team baseball, but they possessed neither the skill nor the cooperative ability to handle this sport, and it probably would have led to more frustration and fighting. In the context of ordinary summer activities at the camp, Greg made some plans involving what he termed, "mock athletic experiences", that is, those that would resemble athletics and thus appeal to these young boys, but would be harmless and would teach them some of the rules of sharing and cooperation (see Figure 6.).

Baseline (A) data collection involved measures of fighting during ordinary camp activities such as eating, swimming, arts and crafts, game time, quiet time, and so on. Greg was with the boys almost daily (with relief time supplied by his team colleagues). Greg introduced a "powder-puff volleyball game" in which a large, soft ball was to be kept in the air by the group as a whole for 1 minute at a time for the "team" to get a point. They would record their scores each day, playing against their former high score. This is termed B, the intervention. Greg and the staff continued to collect data on fighting behavior among group members. He noticed some reduction of fighting and a little more friendly interaction, but it did not appear clinically or socially meaningful.

Greg was due for a relief period in which he went home for a week. His colleague took over all of the activities, except that the colleague did not know about the powder-puff volleyball, so this activity was removed. Because fighting was recorded as usual by the staff, this period constitutes a return to baseline, A_2 (although it makes a possibly unwarranted assumption that the counselors are interchangeable).

Greg returned, noted that the fighting had returned to its former high levels, and so he reinstituted the powder-puff volleyball game, B_2. Again the rates of fighting inched downward, but not very fast nor enough to be of practical importance. Greg decided to add a campfire discussion each evening, at which time he led the boys in thinking about the day's activities, especially about how they were getting along with one another. This constitutes a C intervention, and since it took place each day along with powder-puff volleyball, the set of interventions may be described as BC. Greg noticed a much sharper reduction in fighting, and was quite pleased with himself as he went to the counselors' Fourth of July picnic. There he promptly got a bad case of poison ivy, which put him in the camp infirmary for nearly a week.

During his absence, his team colleagues took over the group, and Greg urged them to continue the powder-puff volleyball; the boys had learned the rules by now and were pretty much doing it on their own. The campfire discussions were, however, postponed until Greg returned. This period of time might be considered as a B_3 phase; fighting activity was recorded as usual.

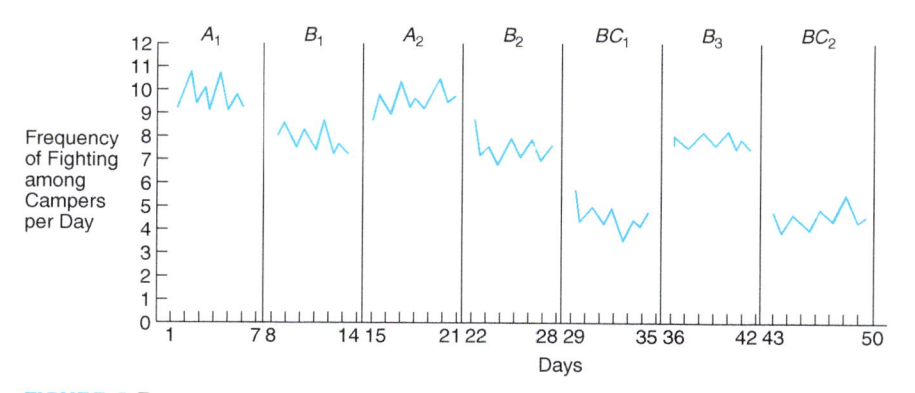

FIGURE 6 Reconstruction of camp data on the "Ferrets," illustrating an interaction design (from a disguised student case).

When Greg returned, he saw that the fighting had once again increased, and so he reinstituted the campfire discussion as well as the powder-puff volleyball, BC_2. He was pleased with the results, although he noted that as the boys prepared to leave for home, they once again broke into fights and crying bouts, just as they had on arrival. He attributed this to the stress of leaving, but recognized that the therapeutic gains were probably only temporary. Unfortunately, he did not attempt any follow-up, although he did report to the family agency his results that appeared to control the problem behaviors in the camp setting. His main consolation was that the agency was going to consider using his new game and the discussion method in their ongoing after-school programs. (See Figure 6 for a reconstruction of these camp data; Greene, personal communication, 1986.)

A variation of an interaction design was used to explore multiple interventions. Stock and Milan (1993) used this design to understand the effects of various interventions on improving dietary practices of three elderly persons at an independent living facility. Each of these individuals had a strong medical need to eat healthful foods; none was in fact following these directives. The dining room was decorated like a fine restaurant, with linen table cloths, fresh flowers, and a menu with four choices in each of the four courses—appetizers, entrees, vegetables, and desserts.

We have changed the notation of this design to conform to the practices suggested in this book (see Figure 7). Note that Stock and Milan have a *B-A-B* design in the first three phases, but it fails to produce any changes in the behavior of the three clients, probably because the initial *B* phase had been long in existence at the living facility, and it wasn't recognized by the clients as anything new; that is, "an intervention."

The first condition (*B*) involved menus already in place at the facility in which there were prompts for the healthful foods—a heart was placed by those items that were low-cholesterol and calorie-modified; and the names of these dishes were intended to sound appealing. The data show fairly low percentages of healthy choices by the three clients.

The second condition (*A*) was the removal of these prompts, which constitutes a baseline situation for this study. Note there is no deterioration in healthy choices at this time, and indeed, one client (client #2) seems to improve in her healthy choices.

The third condition was a brief reinstatement of the first condition (B_2). The data show little change from the baseline levels.

A fourth condition—various kinds of enhanced prompts, feedback, and social reinforcement—is termed *C* because it was quite different from *B*, even though it was based on *B*. The fifth condition was the introduction of a lottery, in which residents (including the three individuals) would win prizes through healthy food choices. Let us term this condition *D*, and since it is taking place concurrently with *C*, is indicated as *CD*.

A sixth condition, *E*, is added, and it, too, takes place concurrently with *C* and *D*. This involves having residents (including the three clients) serve as confederates in helping others to make healthy food choices. This addition combined with the prior intervention to form a *CDE* intervention.

Next, the authors systematically removed components to study their effects. In the seventh condition, component *E* is removed, leaving the *CD* unit. Then, in the eighth condition, the *D* is removed, leaving the *C* unit. Finally, in the ninth condition, *C* is removed and *B* is reinstated.

The results presented in Figure 7 are simpler to describe than was the design. Prompts and no prompts produced equally low percentages of healthy food choices; the three residents simply were ignoring hearts on menus or their absence. However, the enhanced prompts, feedback, and social reinforcement had a strong positive effect on the residents, but the lottery and acting as a confederate generally had little additional effect. Finally, the removal of all of these enhanced prompts and a return to only hearts on menus led to a return to low choices of healthy foods, suggesting that the experience did not leave any lasting impressions on the three clients.

From these results, the authors can sort out apparently effective from less effective interventions, and recognize the likelihood that enhanced prompts will be necessary on a continuing basis to stabilize healthy food choices in these three residents who responded in a relatively similar manner across all conditions.

Does this design provide any basis for causal inference? In addition to the inferences that indeed can be made from the designs tracking each individual's progress (based on the removals and additions and subtractions of interventions), when we find three separate individuals responding in relatively similar ways, we can begin to formulate an even stronger causal hypothesis that would need further empirical

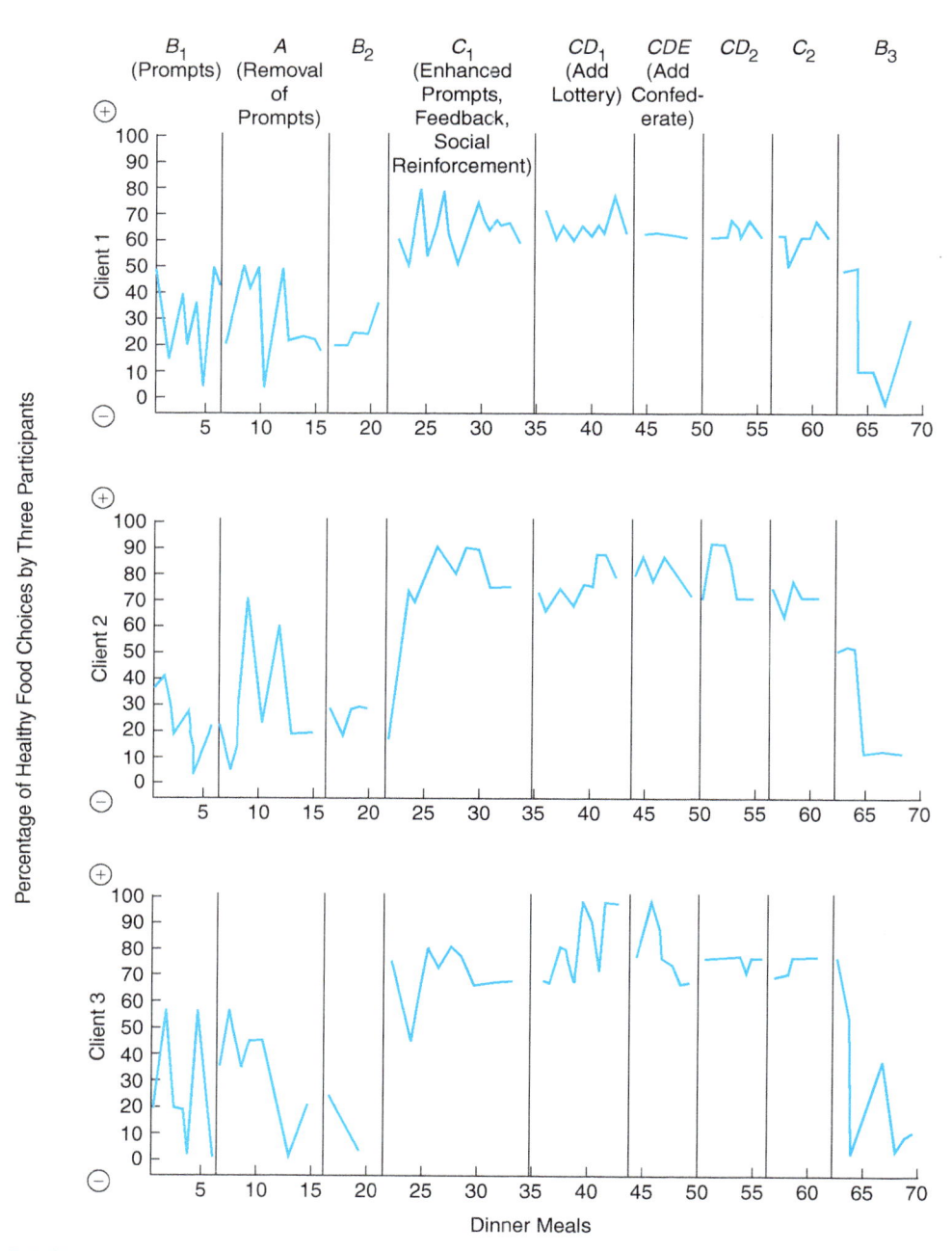

FIGURE 7 Percentage of healthy food choices made during each dinner by three participants (Amy, Beth, Carl) at an independent living facility during nine experimental conditions of the study.

(Adapted from Stock & Milan, 1993.)

Designs for Comparing Interventions

testing. This is like having three simultaneous replications in one study. It is also like a multiple-target design with removal and successive interventions.

Obesity and lack of control over weight are increasing problems in our contemporary world. VanWormer (2004) presents some ideas and single-system analyses for ways to increase physical activities for overweight adults. We will illustrate his work with one case, Jennifer, using multiple targets with an interaction design, a very complex design that should provide good evidence of practitioner-designed target changes. Briefly, VanWormer used a self-monitoring approach in which the clients employed a pedometer as one intervention (B) and some brief electronic counseling in addition to the pedometer as another intervention (B).

The resulting chart for this one client is complex, both because of the *A-B-A-B-BC-B-BC-F* design, and because he uses the left vertical axis to indicate steps taken as measured by the pedometer, while on the right vertical axis, he indicates weight, here represented approximately by stars (*). We have simplified the actual chart shown in Figure 8. to indicate basic trends of the data.

The baselines (A_1 and A_2) represent no intervention, which in this case means no self-monitoring of number of steps taken each day. The baseline lines therefore indicate estimates of steps taken. With the first intervention (B_1), there is some increase in steps walked. The second baseline (A_2) shows a slight decrease in estimated steps. And then in the second intervention (B_2), there is a repeat of the first intervention, so that this *A-B-A-B* component of VanWormer's design could have been used to indicate a basis for a causal inference about the effect of self-monitoring.

But VanWormer went further. He modified the intervention, and we identify this as a new intervention, *BC*, with the addition of electronic counseling. There appears (in the original data) to be more fluctuation in this section of the chart than before, but at a slightly higher level than with interventions B_1 or B_2. With B_3, the number of steps taken returns to prior levels. In BC_2, there is again more fluctuation, but at a higher level than with the *B* interventions. Note that we have a second kind of removal design, where the known quantity (the intervention *B* has been compared to baseline twice) is now the reference point for the added intervention, *C*, a multiple-component design (*B-C-B-C*).

At follow-up, the one observation made appears to be higher than the initial baselines, and within the range of both *B* and *BC* interventions.

From these overlapping *A-B-A-B* and *B-BC-B-BC* designs, we have some strong information about what

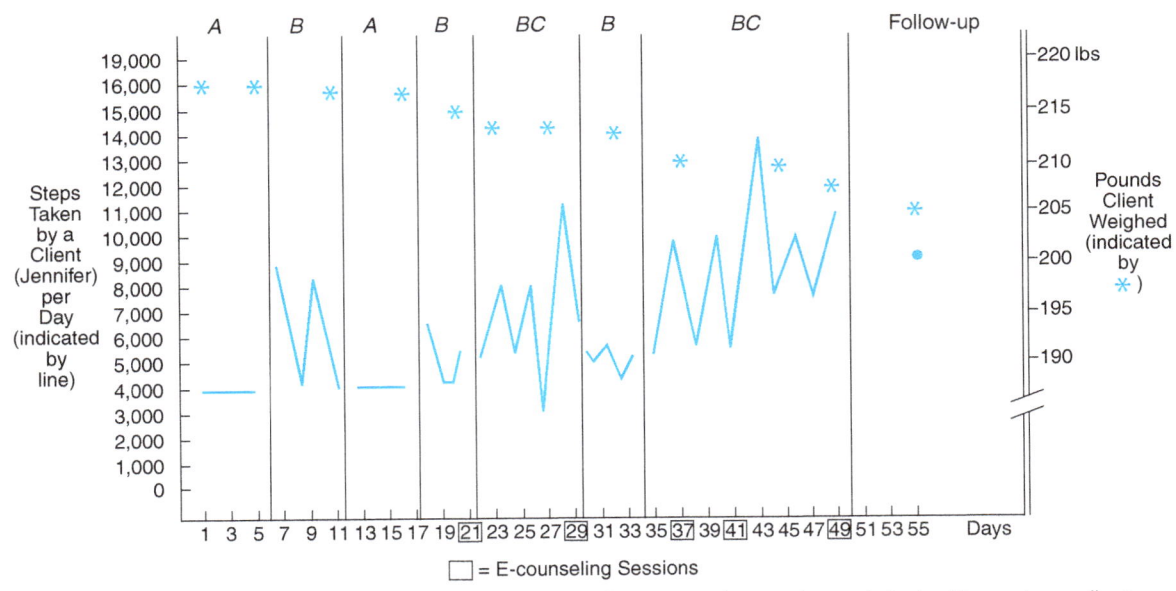

FIGURE 8 An *A-B-A-B-BC-B-BC* and follow-up design comparing steps taken and pounds lost with an obese client.

[Data and chart adapted from "Pedometers and Brief e-Couseling: Increasing Physical Activities for Overweight Adults" by J. VanWormer, 2004, *Journal of Applied Behavior Analysis, 37* (3), pp. 421–425.]

appears to be causing changes in amount of walking, even though the addition of electronic counseling does not appear to be making a large amount of difference beyond the pedometer for this client.

Now, let's look at the changes in weight. We have only 12 measures (in contrast to the 49 measures of pedometer activity), but there is a general downward trend, from about 215 pounds to about 205 pounds over 7 weeks. Looking at the two charts (lines for pedometer measures, stars for weights) we can see a trend toward more walking and a comparable trend toward lower weight, but visual analysis is not strong enough to be clear about causation. (When we discuss computer-based analyses, we may discover more that the eye can see.) However, looking at the data more closely, where the lines of steps taken and pounds lost cross, we can note that major changes appeared to occur during the *C* intervention, so that it may be argued that the electronic counseling change did produce a positive effect. It is because we have the two kinds of overlapping removal designs in one study that we can make these finer causal inferences. This design requires a cooperative client and sufficient time to observe changes that may have causal implications, especially as we plan further studies.

Introducing the Client to the Interaction Design

We recommend that you use as an introduction the approaches given previously with the *A-B-A-B*, *A-B-A-C-A*, and alternating intervention designs, especially the suggestions about trying different approaches to find better ways to solve the client's problem. We could locate little evidence that this design has been used often in actual practice. Indeed, chances are that with such a long or extended service program, you won't be in a position to give the client a full overview even in the unlikely circumstance that you had planned an interaction design. Again, we suggest that you use whatever introductions described previously fit the circumstances.

Summary

This chapter has dealt with some complex extensions of previously discussed designs that are intended to provide either quick, approximate information about the differential effects of the components of intervention or logically sound information on the same topic using an elaborate design.

The alternating intervention design, *A-B/C-(B or C)* begins from a baseline, followed by an intervention phase in which two or more interventions are randomly alternated, possibly with more than one practitioner involved. Based on your evaluation of how each intervention went, you try the "best" one and evaluate it in the regular way. This is a fast and economic approach to looking at multiple interventions to determine, approximately, the most effective one.

The interaction design is a very powerful logical design, but a cumbersome one as well. The *A-B-A-B-BC-B-BC* design is the minimum arrangement for full logical determination of the additive and separate effects of multiple interventions, and it illustrates many of the logical principles of design we have been discussing in this book.

There are other complex designs, but these essentially have been used mainly in laboratory settings and not in field settings. However, the important point is that you should feel free to be creative in constructing a design as long as your interpretation of results follows the basic principles of the design that we have described.

SELECTING A DESIGN

PURPOSE This chapter provides some specific guidelines for selecting a design most suited to your needs. It also provides a discussion of one of the most important components of effective practice and evaluation: creativity in use of single-system designs. We also discuss the use of single-system designs in minimal-contact situations and in managed care. The final section of the chapter discusses some pertinent issues related to your use of single-system designs.

Introduction
Framework for Selecting a Design
Needed: A Design for All Seasons
Creativity in Single-System Designs:
 Making Your Own Designs
    Using Single-System Designs to Analyze Unusual Problems: The Cumulative Record of Risk Model
Evaluation in Minimal-Contact Situations
    Baseline Approximations

    Intervention Data
    Involving the Client in Evaluation
    Dichotomous Data
Single-System Designs in Managed Care:
 The Stretch Design
Troubleshooting: "Okay, I Understand Everything That You Said, But My Case Is Different."
Summary

From Chapter 18 of *Evaluating Practice: Guidelines for the Accountable Professional*, Sixth Edition. Martin Bloom, Joel Fischer, John G. Orme. Copyright © 2009 by Pearson Education, Inc. All rights reserved.

INTRODUCTION

You must be wondering how you will ever sort out all of the possible designs and their infinite variations. In this chapter we present a set of general guidelines to assist you in selecting a design—or a group of designs—that most closely fits your needs. No single set of guidelines can determine exactly which design is the "best" one for a given situation. You must be willing to consider these suggestions based on your own practice wisdom. However, as points of departure, these guidelines may be useful when adjusted to the realities at hand.

FRAMEWORK FOR SELECTING A DESIGN

By asking five questions, you can be guided to one or a cluster of related designs through which you can evaluate your practice. Figure 1 represents these questions as a flow diagram; the guiding questions are framed as dichotomies that branch off and ultimately lead to one or a cluster of related designs that will fit the specifics of your case.

1. *Do you wish to conduct an evaluation of your services at all, and if yes, then with how many distinct clients or systems?* The possible answers include "Yes, with one client," "Yes, with two or more clients," and "No, I don't want to use systematic evaluation with this client." The more-than-one category refers primarily to multiple-baseline designs that will compare clients. For the most part, a single client/system will be involved, even when there are different individuals in that system. Each evaluation will relate to a given system or subsystem within the larger whole (in a family study, the child's grades could be monitored on one chart, while the parents' communication patterns could be studied on another).

2. *Are you able to collect initial baseline data?* A "yes" answer includes the determination to collect either concurrent baseline data or reconstructed baseline data if the former type are not accessible. A "no" answer leads to other designs; it may be possible to perform an evaluation even though you cannot collect baseline data at first. However, the bulk of single-system designs depend on having an initial baseline.

3. *Do you plan to intervene with one or more than one problem at the present time?* (If you change your mind, you can reconsider this question when it comes up again.) If you decide to deal with more than one problem concurrently, you have (eventually) access to a small number of possible designs. We should note that some choices will lead you to unnamed end points—that is, to points for which no identified design has been presented in this book. This merely means that no one has staked claim to such a design; it doesn't mean that no such design can exist. You simply have to construct your own design for such a set of choices.

4. *How many interventions are to be used with each problem?* If you have just one problem to deal with, then you have the bulk of the designs we have discussed at your potential disposal. However, this question potentially places further limitations on the eventual designs that might be relevant to your needs. You can choose to use either one intervention or two (or more) interventions for a given problem. (This may involve other practitioners working with you.)

5. *Do you plan to alternate new baselines and/or new interventions after completing the first intervention?* This question involves whether you intend to use any of the experimental or complex designs.

This framework is to be used by asking the questions listed in order, and then by following the branching lines connecting the answers to the end, where one or more designs are listed. In some cases you will have to choose between designs by reconsidering the distinctive characteristics of each. As noted previously, there are many unfilled slots; designs could in fact be constructed for them and may have been in experimental situations, but they are not common practice designs and so have not been described in this book. It is useful and critically important to be familiar with the literature to pick up examples of unusual or new designs (many emerge each year) and to stimulate new ways of evaluating practice as well.

The lower tier of Figure 1, involving two or more clients, has only two entries listed. In fact, you could use some of the designs listed previously with each of the multiple clients, in which case we suggest you look at a design listed in the "one client" tier and apply it for all cases. The main point to be observed about the lower tier is that these conditions could also lead to experimental/control group designs, such as those described by Kazdin (1992).

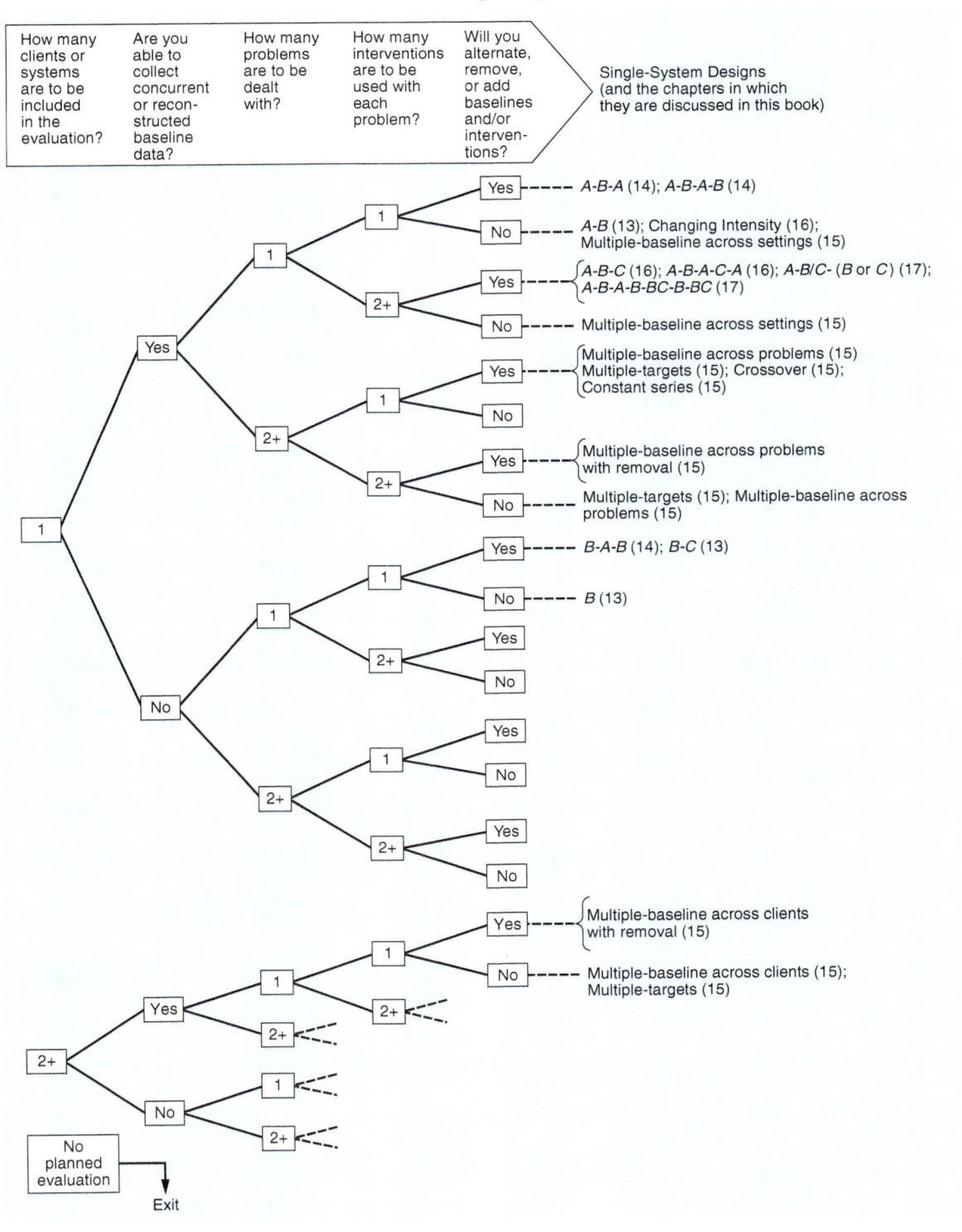

FIGURE 1 Framework for selecting a single-system design.

Some of the paths in Figure 1 lead to more than one design. We therefore suggest some further questions to help sort these out, since it would make Figure 1 unduly complicated to embed them into that framework.

Will one or more interventions be added or subtracted?

Will one or more observations be used?

Will single or combined interventions be employed?

Will the design end on an intervention or on an observation (baseline) phase?

When possible, we suggest that you attempt to select a design in advance—that is, as part of your assessment prior to the point at which intervention actually begins. This is possible in many institutional practice situations and in some less-controlled practice situations. However, again, because of the complexity of practice, it may not be possible in each and every case. In fact, in real practice you will probably modify your design as you go, changing phases and adding or subtracting interventions as the practice needs change. For example, one of our students was using an *A-B* design for a smoking-reduction program. One of the measures he was using, in addition to frequency of smoking, was an individualized rating scale dealing with the client's anxiety. The student found that as the smoking decreased the client's anxiety went up, thus leading the student to institute a technique for decreasing anxiety (relaxation). As a result the design became an *A-B-BC* design, with *B* being the smoking-reduction program and *C* being the relaxation training.

NEEDED: A DESIGN FOR ALL SEASONS

There are many variations of single-system designs as we have seen, each with its own strengths as well as limitations. Our students have told us that, as they are busy practitioners, all this information is sometimes more than they want to know or have time to digest when they are facing a client. What they want is a basic model, a point of departure that will fit most of the problems they might face every day in the field. When some complex problems emerge, they will then go "back to the books" to find an evaluation procedure commensurate with that task.

Unfortunately, there is no such thing as a perfect design for all seasons. However, we can recommend what we call an all-purpose single-system design that incorporates the basic features of this evaluation approach and yet permits the addition of other features when needed. Another way of viewing this design is as a sort of summary of much of the material.

It should come as no surprise that we recommend the basic single-system design, *A-B*, as our all-purpose design. This combination of elements—a more or less objective baseline that is compared to some clearly specified intervention addressed to an operationally defined target problem/goal—seems to us to be the rock-bottom, simplest, most easily performed, and yet reasonably helpful combination for identifying change and pointing the way to additional analysis of possible causal factors (see Figure 2).

In short, we believe that this all-purpose design can be a beginning point, not an end point, for evaluating practice. We are under few illusions about the state of perfection of single-system designs, including this basic design. However, we believe that it is a quantum leap to the *A-B* design from the subjective or intuitive approaches to evaluating practice commonly used. There are many differences between the *A-B* design and its relatives, including the experimental designs, the multiple-baselines and complex designs, and the like, but these differences are more a matter of degree than of kind. Moreover, we have emphasized throughout the book that single-system designs are highly flexible and adaptable to current circumstances in a case. This means that you can add other intervention or baseline phases to the basic *A-B* design, as portrayed in Figure 2, and thereby increase the information from the design.

In fact, we believe that once you sample the delights of using the basic design, you will be drawn to other designs as needed, because the knowledge of how well (or poorly) the intervention is progressing is a highly potent reinforcer. *The fundamental step in becoming an accountable professional is to start evaluating with the A-B design.*

CREATIVITY IN SINGLE-SYSTEM DESIGNS: MAKING YOUR OWN DESIGNS

We believe that you should feel free to construct your own practice designs. We do not make this recommendation lightly. In this book we have offered a variety of the most basic and practical designs that we think will be sufficient for most of the situations you will face. However, we recognize that client and case situations are nothing if not variable and unpredictable, so this section on creativity may be useful to all practitioners on occasion.

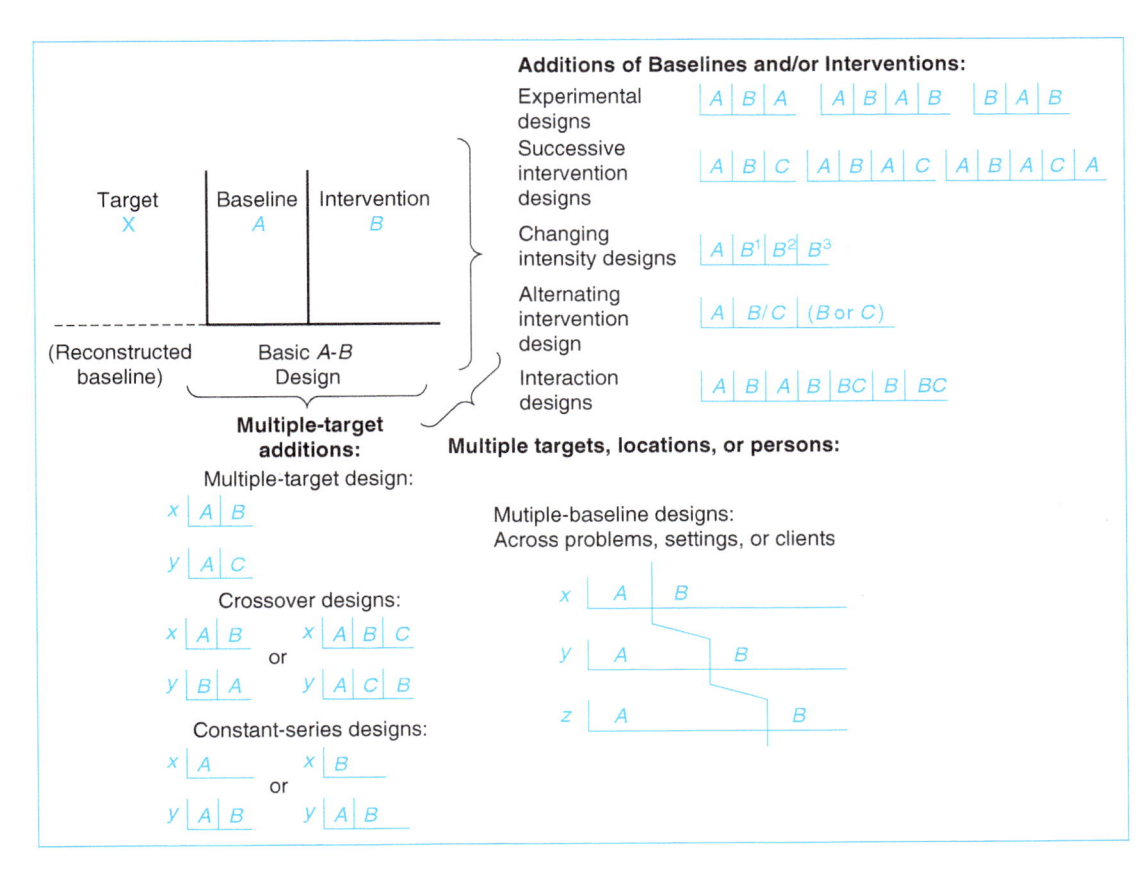

FIGURE 2 Possible additions to the all-purpose design, *A-B*.

To suggest that you can "make up" your own design is not to remove the responsibility that comes from constructing a logical structure. You must still know what you are doing and why. Indeed, the designs we presented in this book can be thought of largely as models (or "ideal" types), not the final word on designs but illustrations of some basic possibilities and principles of design construction. Examining the basic designs carefully should be sufficient background for you to understand and to apply the guidelines presented here. However, the foreground of evaluation deals with people in social and cultural settings. You must be sensitive to what is feasible, as well as to what is desirable in any evaluation context. An oppressed family may have to spend most of its available energies in holding itself together and therefore may not be able to cooperate fully in an evaluation plan; in such a case, you will have to arrange data-collection methods that are less burdensome to the family, even though such methods may be second best as empirical evaluation sources.

Thus, flexibility and sensitivity are the major dimensions of creativity in single-system designs. Consider the following guidelines for developing your own designs:

1. Obtain the original baseline conditions, if at all possible, with clear, direct measures that are culturally and socially sensitive to the people involved.

2. Plan your interventions with your clients with the same clarity and with the same sensitivity to the personal, social, and cultural structures and forces at work. Be able to define the components of your intervention plan. While it is preferable in an evaluation sense to use just one specific

intervention at a time, systems-oriented practice theory suggests the value of attending to a network of interrelated and interacting factors. The compromise between these two demands is to be clear about the interacting components, so hunches can be formed as to which seems to be the more effective (as in the alternating intervention design).

3. If progress is not occurring toward the client's goals, consider what intervention components you have, and those you have not yet employed, and speculate about other combinations. Consider interventions that are unusual by ordinary standards, to fit your unordinary client situation.

4. Let your practice observations (based on the best available information) be your guide to action, and let the evaluation design follow from those decisions. Recognize you can add *A*s, *B*s, *C*s, and *D*s . . . ad infinitum. For every combination, however, you must be responsible for the answers to questions such as:
   a. Did positive change occur in the client's target?
   b. Will changes from previous interventions be apparent or carry over? (Should you have a return to baseline to make these changes clear, or will change appear even with a new intervention?)
   c. Will your choices of designs make clear the likely causal patterns among factors?
   d. Are you sensitive enough to the client to conclude the program with a stable desired goal attained within the social and cultural definitions of what your client sees as desirable?

5. While you may distinguish minor variations in emphasis or variations in technique as distinctive interventions, it may be helpful to stand back and look at your interventions more globally in order to see whether some more basic pattern is at work, such as *A-B* or *A-B-A-C*. This will help you to interpret your design. Look for designs within designs. You may have an overall game plan, but on some specific topic you may conduct what is in effect an experiment within the larger service program. Interpret these internal or subsystem designs independently, and then apply their overall outcome as part of the larger design. At all times be imaginative, but be responsible for your designs.

Using Single-System Designs to Analyze Unusual Problems: The Cumulative Record of Risk Model

Single-system designs can be used in a wide array of situations and can be created to deal with a wide variety of cases and problems, as you have seen throughout this book. However, some situations are particularly challenging, so we would like to illustrate a model for dealing with one such class, for which problem or risk behaviors accumulate to a threshold at which special action needs to be taken. One of the authors faced such a problem with one of his students, and felt stymied for an embarrassingly long period of time, until he realized he had to turn the evaluation model upside down, so to speak, in order to fit the circumstances of the case. Here's the story: A 12-year-old boy committed suicide; the gory details were splashed all over the local newspapers. It was too late to help him, but what could be done to prevent similar situations? The instructor helped to develop this model.

The student involved in this case was seeking a method of identifying stages of risk of juvenile suicide, so as to increase the chances of preventing that fatal action. Drawing on a reported case of the suicide of this 12-year-old (Office of the Child Advocate and the Child Fatality Review Board, 2003; Santora, 2003), we proposed a single-system design model that attempts to set up alarm systems in relevant social agencies so that juveniles are less likely to slip through institutional cracks toward their self-inflicted deaths.

This design model intentionally changes the usual emphasis from accomplishment of desired objectives to one of identification of risk indicators that set off institutional alarms. In cases of juvenile suicide, often several social agencies or institutions are involved: the school system, the juvenile court, and some state department of child and family affairs or its subunits. We assume that each social system involved receives the progressive records of the other agencies' prior involvement, so that simultaneous records are available to all. (If this is not the case, then a first action step is to obtain access to confidential records of a person at risk for suicide.)

Another assumption is that there typically is no baseline in this type of case. The events have been ongoing, and the child is a member of an existing family and classroom situation, so that all of the systematic information we have is from school records, particularly grades, deportment, and tardiness/absenteeism data. We do not include any social or psychological factors, such as being bullied or having poor hygiene so that others make fun of a child, in the evaluation model because they are so individualized to the given case situation. If we were to add an intervention evaluation component to the "risk evaluation design" in Figure 3, it would be described as a *B-C-D* successive intervention design, employing three different interventions in the *B* phase to deal with the same core problems, as well as additional ones in the later phases (*C* and *D*).

Let us assume that the first level of this model involves ordinary school records of tardiness and absenteeism, as shown in Figure 3. Most school systems clearly define some number of unexcused absences as the basis for identifying "truants." When that number of absences occurs, most school systems automatically investigate the causes of this absenteeism and take some kind of action. There are, within the school system, a variety of means used to address this issue, from the homeroom teacher talking with the parents and child about the causes and possible solutions, to setting up special educational units to deal with the stresses that may have led to the absenteeism. Records ordinarily taken on tardiness and absenteeism are continued, and success would be defined as the cessation of these target behaviors.

The second level of the model would be activated when the number of unexcused absences continues to rise to a defined point where the designation such as "habitual truant" now applies, and a new social system is automatically activated: the juvenile court and its representative, the truant officer. Habitual truancy likely has a wider array of causes that the school system has not been able to handle on its own, and for which the legal system may have additional remedies, ranging from a pointed conversation among the truant officer and the parents and the legal system. Again, the regularly kept school records can indicate whether the child has ceased being truant. In addition, this level of institutional response may also target grades or deportment, as well as school attendance, so the number of targets may increase as the level of response changes.

A third level of the model may be activated when some other information emerges, possibly independent of the school records, such as a hot-line accusation of child neglect, which certain state agencies are

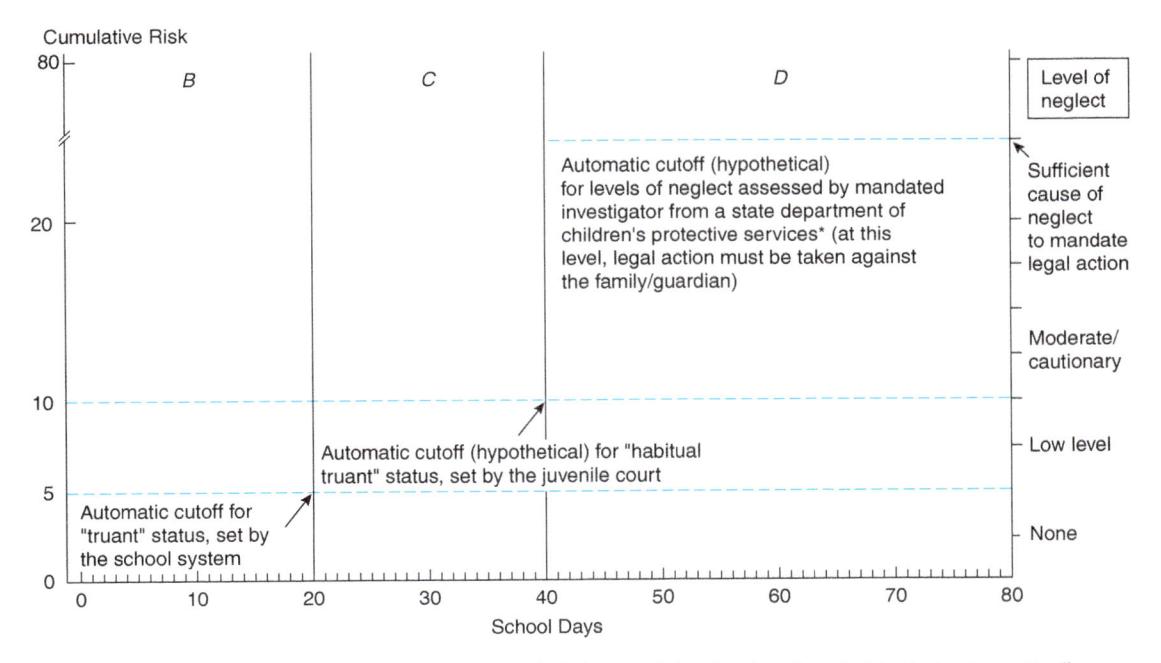

FIGURE 3 An illustration of the cumulative record of risk model indicating thresholds that automatically activate different institutions in dealing with one client-system and the several forms of target behavior.

*A hotline tip on child neglect activated a mandated investigation to assess the situation and determine the level of neglect.

mandated to investigate, along with the legal powers that this mandate holds. These legal powers may involve parents as well as children, and are as extensive as any authorization that purports to protect citizens. While tracking grades and rates of absenteeism may be part of this phase of the evaluation, there would also be studies made of levels of neglect and abuse that would activate these agencies into legal action. However, it is important to our model that the original information (on tardiness and absenteeism) be continued since successful results would include these lawful requirements of children, in addition to whatever else is being considered at this third level.

In the case under consideration, there was a breakdown at all three levels. While the school attempted to deal with many problems, from bullying attacks on this small-for-his-age child, to self-soiling, ultimately, there was no change made in the rate of absenteeism. The court and its truant officer did make contact with the child and issued strong verbal directives, but there was no change in the escalating rate of absenteeism. The state agency investigated the case, and for reasons unclear in the public record, decided that there was insufficient evidence to proceed with the case, and ultimately, there was no change made in the rate of absenteeism or any other factors contributing to the child's problems. Shortly thereafter, the child very unfortunately committed suicide by hanging himself with a tie in his closet.

Would this single-system design model have helped to prevent the suicide? This is an imponderable question, but by design, the rate of absenteeism is one important measure that required ongoing efforts by each of the levels of systems and their types of authority to demand actions on the part of the school, the family, and the child. Other targets were encountered along the way, and suitable single-system designs might have been developed to evaluate their resolution.

EVALUATION IN MINIMAL-CONTACT SITUATIONS

There are many situations in which practitioners have only brief contacts with clients such that conventional single-system evaluation methods *appear* to be unusable. For example, crises usually require rapid interventions and often referral to other agencies for additional services. Short-term services, as in acute hospitals or drug rehabilitation centers, are given to clients in a brief time period crowded with many types of activities and personnel. Hot lines have almost no sustained contact with callers—little background information, little follow-up. There are many other situations in which practitioners have minimal contact with clients, even in settings that are presumably organized for longer services—for example, where contacts require "first aid" skills or provision of concrete services. But there are a number of options for addressing these situations, which we call "minimal-contact situations" (MCS).

First, let us review the steps in the conventional practice and evaluation process in order to understand the kinds of adaptations that must be undertaken in an MCS. Ordinarily, you will make contact with a client, establish rapport, and begin to collect information about the presenting problem. When formally collected as systematic measurement, this information represents baseline data. Such information is collected until you believe that a clear and stable picture of the problems and strengths of the client or the situation has emerged. Then, continuing these same data-collection methods, you plan an intervention and monitor its progress until you see some clear and stable positive change. At this time, further analysis occurs in order to make the decision to terminate services. Then you begin a maintenance phase in order to transfer the service effects to the client's natural environment when you will no longer be in the picture. Likewise, follow-up contacts may be undertaken to ascertain whether the service effects are holding up.

Minimal contact still means that some presenting problem or challenge generally is understood by the practitioner. If a person comes in for apparent assistance with some unspecific problem that never becomes clear, the practitioner essentially is helpless to make constructive changes in that situation—unless clarifying the lack of a problem is the issue at hand. In the latter case, the presenting problem is to define the problem—or possibly the lack of a real problem. In general, minimal-contact services do address specified problems. Often, these problems are quite specific, concrete, and time-limited. Frequently, clients in MCSs do not want associations with the practitioner to be longer than necessary to deal with the specific focal problem.

Thus, all you are "given" in an MCS is the fact of an existing problem, without any dimensions of the problem; you may never know about the events leading up to the crisis, and you may never learn about what happens to the clients after they leave the office.

The core of minimal-contact services is the here-and-now problem, with the client generally seeking "while-you-wait" services. Minimal-contact services are, with good reason, difficult to evaluate objectively using conventional single-system design methods.

However, it is possible to adapt these conventional single-system evaluation methods to the MCS to obtain some minimal evaluations. We grant that minimal evaluations are not the first choice in objective assessment, but rather should be used when there are few other choices available. Not only can each evaluation provide you feedback on that particular case, but comparison of outcomes across cases—using a standardized format such as the *A-B* design—can provide information across all your cases and for the agency as a whole. And using the same format across all cases—even MCSs where you may be stretching the design a bit—keeps you in the habit of systematic evaluation.

Let us describe a variety of minimal-evaluation methods. Essential ingredients for minimal evaluations are some kind of baseline data together with some kind of equivalent intervention data, such that comparison between them can permit you to make some type of estimate of change.

Baseline Approximations

There are several ways to approximate baseline data under conditions of minimal contact. First, you can use *reconstructed* or *retrospective baseline data* derived from information the client supplies even within the MCS. For example, take the case of the distraught parent who tells the Red Cross worker that she hasn't heard from her son for over a month. A soldier stationed overseas, he had written her faithfully for the previous 6 months. Probing might reveal that the son had been in the habit of writing about once a week during that time, at least to send postcards or other souvenirs weekly. This conversation permitted the reconstruction of a baseline against which to compare the effects of the service that reestablished contact between parent and son, who in fact had been in an automobile accident. What the reconstruction of the baseline did in this case was to establish the existence of a problem, as contrasted to some minor lapse in writing home, and thus the need for immediate help rather than waiting until possibly clogged mail could be delivered.

As another example, based on an actual case of one of the author's students, a woman came to a community mental health center reporting that she was being abused by her spouse. The practitioner and the woman decided that reconciliation with the spouse would be impossible, and that the woman would have to go to the local shelter. After two contacts with the client, a place at the shelter became available. The practitioner arranged for the woman's admission, where she stayed for 2 weeks until a bond against further harassment by the spouse was obtained and a permanent placement arranged. Based on a reconstructed baseline of instances of abuse, and concurrent and follow-up recording, the chart for the case looked like the one displayed in Figure 4.

A second kind of approximate baseline can be described as *inferred baseline data* derived from parallel information known about other clients or people living in like situations. For example, a person applying for emergency food relief recently had come to town from out of state. His funds had soon been exhausted before he was able to find work. From

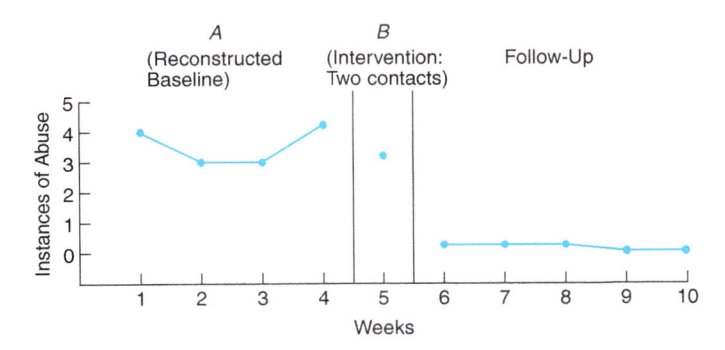

FIGURE 4 Illustration of brief contact design with instances of spousal abuse as the problem.

current censuses at the public welfare agency, it is clear that many people are in a like circumstance. You thus would be justified in presuming a baseline of fiscal need, pending additional investigation, while emergency services and aid are provided.

A third kind of comparison point is a *known end state* that can be compared with a currently unknown present state. For example, a pregnant woman comes to a homeless shelter obviously undernourished. In these circumstances, it is not possible to engage in a lengthy psychosocial and medical history, but because of the known requirements of good nutrition for pregnant women, services may be evaluated to the extent that they are able to provide her with appropriate levels and types of food.

A fourth and different kind of approximate baseline could be inferred from a minimal-contact client who clearly wants a specific goal, such as help in finding suitable housing, admission of her child to a magnet school, or other relatively precise goal. Having such a goal in mind means that the goal currently does not exist, and thus, when such a goal is reached, it is to be compared to the zero status in the baseline.

Intervention Data

Given these approximate baseline data or comparison points, you would provide services as appropriate to the situation, and repeat the information-gathering method or its equivalent. In the case of the overseas soldier who was not writing home weekly, a telephone contact was established and was equivalent to the weekly written communications. For the unemployed man, receiving financial and in-kind aid at the level presumed adequate by that state fulfilled the demand for success during the intervention period. For the pregnant woman, the provision of nutritious food also could be said to be a successful intervention as compared to norms of nutrition.

How successful are these helping actions? There are several ways to count the level or degree of success of help provided. First, one might use an agency-wide "batting average," the number of fulfilled needs (e.g., reestablished contact between mother and son, adequate food and shelter for the unemployed man and the pregnant woman, etc.) compared to all of the presenting cases for a given period of time. For example, if the Red Cross saw 10 emergency cases like that of the distraught parent each week, and was able to come to a successful resolution of 8 of these situations, then the agency batting average for that week would be .80. Such averages themselves could be averaged over a yearly fiscal period for agency accountability rates.

In the individual case, depending on the problem and how it's measured, you might be able to establish a goal and then simply note whether it was achieved. Or, if the measure involves some count, you might be able to indicate on a chart whether the problem has increased or decreased. Or, you might employ the *Goal Attainment Scale* strategy of presuming that there is in any given situation an "expected" level of success, along with several degrees above and below this expected level. So, the case of the distraught parent might have been further specified as follows (or words to this effect, according to the content of the situation):

1. Least favorable outcome thought likely
2. Less than expected success
3. Expected level of success
4. More than expected success
5. Most favorable outcome thought likely

The Red Cross worker expected that she would be able to find out through channels whether there was a problem with the soldier overseas and, thus, to reestablish communications. What she did not expect was that the soldier was in an accident and that she had to make extra arrangements through the hospital where he was staying to reestablish connections with his mother. This might constitute a rating of "more than expected success." Or, had there been no medical problem, but merely a lapse of writing, the practitioner might have set up a more reliable means of communication between parent and son, such as persuading the son to email home once a week. This solution might also have constituted a rating of "more than expected success." Had the practitioner asked the mother what an ideal communication would be in her opinion, and if the mother had reported her difficulty in getting through the international telephone system to call her son when she didn't receive weekly letters, then an intervention that taught the mother the necessary skills to master international calling might have been accorded "most favorable outcome" status. The numbers associated with given outcomes might then be combined over a practitioner's caseload to give a rating of favorable solutions overall. Individual cases that did not meet agency or practitioner averages might be reconsidered in case conferences to see how services might have been improved.

Another form of evaluation that could be used in some MCSs would be the *brief exit questionnaire* that asks clients one or two questions about the services provided, to better help clients in the future. Comparative questions could be posed, although this may require a level of sophistication that is inappropriate for some settings or types of clients. For example, one might ask:

1. How helpful or unhelpful was the service you just now received from the practitioner?
   a. Very helpful
   b. Helpful
   c. Neither helpful nor unhelpful
   d. Unhelpful
   e. Very unhelpful

2. How much of the main problem you came with has been solved (or fixed)?
   a. None of the main problem I came with has been solved (or fixed).
   b. Little of my main problem has been solved (fixed).
   c. Some of my main problem has been solved (fixed).
   d. Most of my main problem has been solved (fixed).
   e. All of my main problem has been solved (fixed).

This kind of user survey does not provide a totally objective basis for judging the effectiveness of service, but it does provide an otherwise unattainable subjective impression from the client. Of course, how much of the response will be social acquiescence and how much will reflect real change is difficult to say. Such data might best be used as a description of user responses, and correlated with other types of approximate outcome measures as described here.

A variation of this exit survey would be a *follow-up survey*, or contact by the practitioner, who would ask essentially how the situation had gone since the brief contact occurred. Ethically, the practitioner should inform the client that such follow-up contacts will be made, with the client's permission. The purpose of the follow-up is to assess the services provided, and to offer additional services as needed. This information will assist the agency to improve its services as well (by trying to expand services that have been helpful and change those that have not worked well).

Involving the Client in Evaluation

Another issue related to minimal contact is whether to involve the clients in their own evaluation. Frequently, MCSs don't easily permit the mutuality and cooperativeness of extended service work and evaluation. However, clients should be informed that some form of evaluation is being conducted as quality assurance for the agency and as a protection for the client. Also, sometimes, taking part in the approximate evaluation provides another tool that clients can take with them as they seek to solve problems on their own after the agency contact. Thus, whether or how you involve minimal-contact clients with the evaluation process depends on the context itself.

You must be prepared to take on the full evaluation role, based on whatever information can be obtained during the brief contacts. Aids like recording devices would be helpful (e.g., in a content analysis of the conversation to establish the number of times anxiety was expressed at the initial meeting, as compared with the number of times at the final meeting). But, essentially, conventional means of identifying the state of the presenting problem should be used, and then the same or equivalent method should be repeated at the end of the contacts, or, if possible, in a follow-up contact. Once this before/after approximation has been made, the choices of using a one/zero batting average approach, a modified Goal Attainment Scaling approach, or one of the other approaches can be made.

Dichotomous Data

Single-system designs also can be used when the problem is dichotomous, involving simply whether some event occurred. This is a common occurrence with minimal-contact cases with recording simply keeping track of the occurrence of some event on a "yes" or "no" basis. The case described earlier involving the soldier stationed overseas who suddenly stopped writing his mother (because he had been involved in a serious auto accident) is an instance of this dichotomous analysis, with minimal contact with the client. Figure 5 illustrates the intervention and the subsequent outcome wherein the soldier was

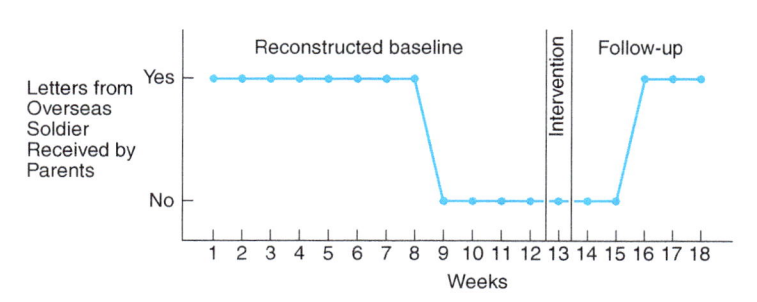

FIGURE 5 Illustration of dichotomous problem—number of letters received.

reunited with his mother by telephone and resumed his letter writing.

This example of the soldier brings up another important part of minimal-contact evaluation, the setting of practice goals or objectives whose attainment can be clearly identified. In the case of the soldier, the goal was reunion with the mother in some form, by telephone if not letter. This was attained and the case resolved for all practical purposes. In short, practical criterion goals can be used to determine when minimal-contact cases have been resolved successfully. Many examples come to mind: If clients come in for emergency fuel rations, then whether they obtain satisfaction regarding their heating problems is a practical criterion of success or nonsuccess. If a traveler gets useful aid for his or her travels, then this is a criterion for success or nonsuccess. If an information agency makes an appropriate referral to a service agency and the client follows up, then the information agency function has been accomplished successfully.

SINGLE-SYSTEM DESIGNS IN MANAGED CARE: THE STRETCH DESIGN

Managed care is imposing a wide array of demands on the helping professions (see also Bolen & Hall, 2007; Vandiver & Corcoran, 2007). Some of these new policies may reduce financial costs for various social and health services, which is generally desirable when such costs have been rising precipitously. However, these same managed care demands also will reduce services for persons in justifiable need and with preventable problems, which is very undesirable because short-term savings will lead to long-term social and financial costs in the same or related areas, as well as an unacceptable level of human misery. These are policy issues beyond the range of this book, but we have to be realistic in adapting good practice to the demands of the managed care philosophy. This includes having the evaluation tools available that can be produced in less time but with a reasonable amount of rigor, so as to provide documentable answers regarding the outcomes of services, regarding both intermediate objectives and long-term outcomes.

We believe that most of the material covered in this book can be of considerable help in documenting intervention outcomes. Yet, we also recognize that, under some circumstances, practitioners may need even briefer methods of more or less objective evaluation. For this purpose, we introduce a method we call "*stretch*" *single-system evaluations*. We will present the basic method, and then we will apply it to some of the other advanced designs we have discussed.

Imagine an ideal single-system design, with a nice, clear target and regular measures over, say, 20 sessions, once a week for 5 months. Clearly, this may soon become a distant memory for many practitioners in this era of managed care in which the pressures for accountable outcomes within 8 to 12 sessions, or even fewer, is more commonplace than a "leisurely" 5-month contact. Question: How to obtain (or approximate) the evaluation strengths of a longer period of client–practitioner contact (say, 20 sessions or more) within the managed care time-limited context (say, just 10 sessions)?

Consider the following scenarios: first, the traditional 20-session arrangement, followed by the stretch single-system evaluation within 10 sessions (see Figure 6). Both are *A-B* designs, with no training,

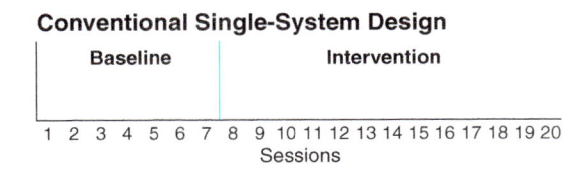

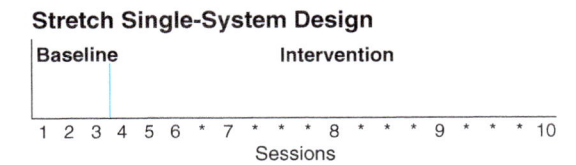

FIGURE 6 Conventional and stretch single-system designs.

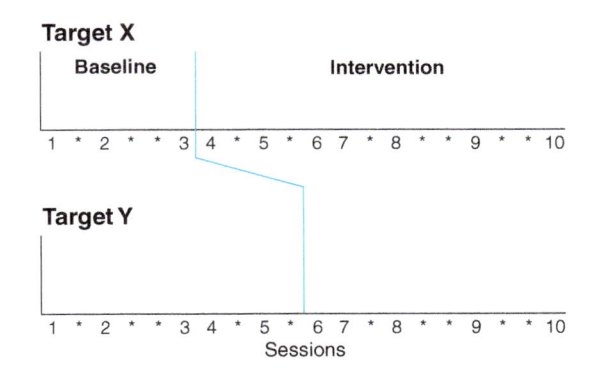

FIGURE 7 Stretch evaluation for multiple-baseline.

maintenance, booster, or follow-up phases, to keep the example simple. In place of the traditional 20 paid sessions, we now have 10 paid sessions, but stretched out over 20 time units. The asterisks represent periods of time the client does not receive professional interventive services, but which are used to continue data collection. The length of these noninterventive periods increases from 1 to 4 units over the course of intervention. There are a total of 10 such "noninterventive" units, which, along with the 10 service units, totals 20 units in which the practitioner is monitoring the ser-vice. In emergencies, sessions could be held, and in some cases, sanctioned by managed care rules.

Strictly speaking, this is a suggestion for a lean, mean design of three baseline units (#1, #2, #3) and three service units (#4, #5, #6), along with four other contact times (#7, #8, #9, #10) that can serve either as (a) more service periods, (b) maintenance training, (c) "booster shots" if needed, or (d) follow-up. The total period of time is the same 20 time units of the traditional practice evaluation; however, the actual paid contact time is just 10 time units. The ability to fine-tune practice—as service, maintenance, booster shot, or follow-up—may be an especially important advantage of the stretch method. Clients are fully informed of this arrangement and the responsibility that it implies for their own contributions to achieving their outcomes. They will be "on their own" for longer periods of time during the intervention process, even though monitoring will continue during this period. Clients could call in data during the weeks when there are no intervention services given, or they could bring in recorded data on forms on which they and the practitioner have agreed.

We recognize this stretch evaluation procedure will not be useful when continuous services and monitoring are needed for certain conditions, but because no client can be forever served and monitored, the practitioner has to begin thinking in terms of experiences in self-maintenance, and for this, the stretch evaluation may be useful.

We can expand this stretch evaluation to other single-system designs, such as the multiple-baseline across problems in one client, where the baseline period itself may need to have "noncontacts" while targeted data are still collected (see Figure 7). For example, consider the following pattern where there are stretched periods in both baseline and intervention phases, but where an intervention occurs following the change from A to B phases. In this illustration, there are 6 units of baseline data for Target X, and 10 units of baseline data for Target Y. Other patterns of noninterventive data gathering can be considered, as relevant to the content of the service.

Clearly, this "stretch" evaluation is even more approximate than the traditional single-system design, and requires case situations where valid and reliable data may be collected in the nonintervention units. However, this stretch approach does offer clients greater participation in their own service program (and especially in training for self-maintenance), so there may be some benefits from this externally imposed time-and-service constriction from managed care.

TROUBLESHOOTING: "OKAY, I UNDERSTAND EVERYTHING THAT YOU SAID, BUT MY CASE IS DIFFERENT."

Every case *is* different. The main point we have been making regarding understanding single-system designs as evaluation tools is to be able to connect them to practice. That is, we have described some of the methodological concepts and principles of evaluation and have endeavored to connect these abstractions to actual cases that appeared in the literature or that were conducted by our students. Let's look more closely at some tough cases and think through how the basic designs might be applied to complex human situations.

Case 1

"I only see my clients one or two times, and I am so busy rushing through what I have to get accomplished that I don't have any time for the luxuries of evaluation."

Response to Case 1

That *is* a tough situation. But let's think about what is possible in these kinds of cases. What basic aspects of single-system design are applicable?

Clearly this practitioner is doing something, which sounds like an intervention, *B*. So far, so good. But with one or two client contacts, it doesn't sound too promising for any kind of experimental removal, or even the addition of a new intervention.

On the other hand, the practitioner has already said she has no time for a baseline, but we can ask whether she does a rapid assessment of the presenting problems as the basis of her intervention, *B*. If so, she may have enough information to do at least a reconstructed baseline, indicated by the notation (*A*). This is not the strongest design in the world, but certainly a rough basis for identifying changes that may be occurring. What any practitioner needs in cases of brief contact is some verbal or archival description of the problem in enough detail to make a sensible and sensitive plan of intervention. In some cases, perhaps not all, this would be enough information to reconstruct a baseline.

In other cases, there may be an obvious criterion of success so that all the practitioner needs to know is that the client is not presently successful (at the first interview situation), but that by the end of this contact, the problem may be resolved according to that criterion of success. If so, this too would be the basis of evaluation.

Case 2

"I'm part of a team of workers dealing with a bunch of clients who are seen individually and in various kinds of groups. I work there part of the week, and so I don't even have continuing contact with clients. Old clients leave, and an equal number of new clients come in. How am I supposed to evaluate in this three-ring circus?"

Response to Case 2

This is another tough set of questions. Let's look at them one at a time. The team versus individual worker contribution is difficult only if you have to sort out the two for some accountability reason. If your final outcome is the resolution of client problems, then it doesn't matter who does it, so long at it is accomplished. But if you need to demonstrate your particular contribution to the team effort, that's more difficult.

You can look at the evaluation issue as being one of whether you supply information to others who do the major hands-on part, or whether others supply information to you for the same purpose. If you supply information primarily, then evaluate whether all of the needed information is made available to the direct-contact part of the team in time. You get a kind of batting average: required information presented in either a timely fashion or not. If you receive information from others primarily to make direct contact with the client regarding problem-solving issues, then evaluate in the conventional way whether these issues have been resolved, plus whether you had the relevant information in a timely fashion. (This is a polite way of saying evaluate as usual, but note whether everyone did his or her part. Your personal record should probably include only those situations where all of the essential information was available.)

Another way of looking at this problem is to think about it in terms of applying one of the designs in this book to your piece of the problem. If you are working with a client on a particular problem, and other people in your agency are working with the client as well, even on the same problem, you can still get some feedback on your contribution. All it takes is some recording of the problem, and keeping track of when you start your intervention. This will produce an *A-B* design, and if the problem starts to change only after you begin your intervention, you may begin to suspect that your intervention is crucial. If you go so far as to add a removal phase and then reinstitute the intervention (an *A-B-A-B* design), if the target problem changes in relation to these phases, you can be pretty sure your intervention is having an impact, no matter what everyone else is doing.

The next point in case 2 was evaluating part-time versus full-time work. It may be difficult to do both practice and evaluation part time, but what happens in part-time practice? Does someone else cover for you, or do you space the meetings to fit the times you can be there? Is it possible to do the same with evaluation, on the order of the stretched single-system design discussed previously? For example, what about public records (such as teachers' grade books or employers' absenteeism records)? Can the clients keep records in between times? Given your answers to these kinds of questions, can you come up with a design that accommodates these features?

The last point, about clients moving through a system, can be answered more clearly. Think about what evaluation options are available to you, and ask what designs might be used. For example, should you evaluate the progress of the entire group? If so, what baseline will you consider? Unless there are good records available, this might be problematic, as reconstructing baselines from memory is risky.

What about beginning with the new clients and running thorough evaluations on them? In time, as older clients leave, you will have full sets of data on the entire group. This also gives you a chance to do some trial evaluations to see what kinds of measurement systems work best.

Remember that there are distinctive measures of individual-level and group-level phenomena, and consider measuring both. For example, is there any measure of the morale of the clients (or staff) as a whole at different periods of time? This would be a group-level measure. Parallel measures of individual satisfaction could be obtained to compare the individual's score against the norms of the group. Changes in both group and individual scores make interesting reading because they hint at differential effectiveness with each individual and a comparison of how fast an individual is making progress relative to the group.

Case 3

"Nothing ever happens in my cases. The kind of services my agency supplies are just supportive, keeping an eye on clients just in case there is an emergency; then some other agency comes in and does the work."

Response to Case 3

If we may be so bold, we'd like to suggest you have things upside down. Your clear target is to maintain the status quo (perhaps some sort of adequate or reasonably healthy and happy living for clients). What you have to look out for are signs of change, especially deterioration. So what kinds of targets would these "no-changes" be? And by what means could you indicate states of health and healthy functioning? In short, we believe that your evaluation task is essentially the same as described previously, but you will be monitoring current levels of adequate or productive functioning. Also, consider the identifying stages of risk model, discussed previously. While we are talking about monitoring current levels of positive functioning, let us note that evaluation of primary prevention usually involves study of health and healthy functioning, and the attainment of desired new states of healthy functioning. So, remember that "targets" can refer to both problems and desired goals.

Case 4

"My client is so vague about everything that it is impossible to nail down what is troubling him. Every meeting there is a long list of new complaints, but none of them are very specific. I spend all my time getting clear about the details of one week's experiences until it is time to quit, and then I wait for a whole new set next week."

Response to Case 4

You appear to have a case of wandering targets. It is related to the doorknob syndrome, when the client, about to leave with hand on the doorknob says, "Oh, by the way, this happened to me last week," and a whole new problem suddenly appears in an untimely fashion. That is a difficult but common malady, and the only thing we can suggest (if pointing out this pattern to the client and trying to get some focus doesn't work) is to look for patterns among the diverse instances. This is where the kinds of notation from single-system designs may be helpful. Start keeping track as if each instance—trouble with the in-laws, arguments with wife, dispute with clerk in store, anger at the disobedient dog, annoyance at sullen child, etc.—were the label of a category, and then group the categories as best you can (interpersonal problems in which others are always at fault; feelings of powerlessness; etc.). Once you have a few categories, deal with them in some order of the client's priorities. This is where the client can begin to do some sorting among issues as well. Perhaps the need for training in problem-solving may itself be an underlying issue.

Case 5

"I would love to evaluate my cases, but they drop out prematurely. Is there anything I can do about this?"

Response to Case 5

This is a difficult problem, but we believe that the major issue lies in the practice area, not in the evaluation realm. If this is true of a large proportion of your caseload, and those of others in your agency, then it looks as if some institutional structures may be interfering with continuity in service. If it is mainly *your* clients that are dropping out of treatment, then use whatever data you have on whatever clients you had, and go over them in detail with a colleague or your supervisor. This is an opportunity to examine your own methods in detail. It very well may be chance, or the type of difficult problems with which you work, but it might also be that you need to brush up on certain techniques, enhance communication or interpersonal skills, and so on.

Case 6

"I was going along quite well with my client. I figured out what targets to deal with and was in the middle of the baseline period, when the client tells me that the problem has changed. Do I have to start all over again? What do I do with the old problem?"

Response to Case 6

Yes, you do have to start all over with a genuine new problem—if you are certain that it is new and not simply a variation on the original problem. Don't be surprised that problems change; that is just part of life when one is under varied stresses. But we do have to be sensitive to genuine changes in problems.

What do you do with the old target and all that work you went through to gather baseline data? First, don't throw away any data. The original problem may return, and you have some solid baseline data ready to go. Second, if the original problem is important enough in its own right, then continue monitoring it as if you were closing out a target upon completion of your work with that part of the client's problems. You also have the choice of monitoring and intervening with both problems at the same time. Also, sometimes baselining reveals that no real problem exists on one of the targets—and that in itself is vital information. The same is true with problems that change in the middle of the baseline. It is important to document that some important developments took place. You might check to see how and why the problem happened to disappear before your contributions were needed. Does the client have some resources and skills that can be put to work with other problems?

Case 7

"I am a little embarrassed to admit this, but the great problem I thought I had identified in the first session turned out by session 3 not to be the problem at all. In the meantime, I had the client involved in baselining for 3 weeks. What do I do about this first problem?"

Response to Case 7

Maybe nothing. If you did the best you could to identify a problem at the first session, and started baselining, then that may be exactly what was appropriate at the time given the information you had. If, by the third session, you learn new information, and the target now shifts to another problem entirely, then start baselining that new problem and drop the first—if it really is not a problem.

Don't be embarrassed about making a judgment with the best available information at the time and then finding new information that produces a change in judgment. Be embarrassed only if you don't change when you have new information indicating change is necessary.

Case 8

"I am taking a class at school where I am learning about these single-system designs, but when I go to my practicum, my field instructor doesn't believe in evaluation and won't support me in this. I am caught between a rock and a hard place. What am I supposed to do?"

Response to Case 8

Sadly, there are still some good practitioners out in the field who are not convinced that evaluation is a vital and necessary part of good practice. While we personally hope that these people see the light—or at least bow to the collective wisdom of accrediting bodies that mandate that students know how to evaluate their own practice in field settings—we appreciate your situation.

There are several things you might do. First, inform your advisor about these limitations on your education, and perhaps your school can apply some needed pressure. Second, failing this, try to link up with some colleagues whose agencies do permit them to evaluate their practice. You could share a case, or even better, consider attempting to be a teacher yourself to convey these skills to a cooperative practitioner at that other agency who might be willing to evaluate his or her own case. Both methods will give you the hands-on experience you need. A third method is to conduct a single-system evaluation on yourself—identify something you would like to do more or less of, read the literature on how to do this while you are keeping a baseline, then intervene and maintain the measurement of the targeted behavior and analyze the results. This way, you get to be both client and practitioner, and you might gain a useful perspective on evaluation that you might not see in any other way.

Case 9

"My client won't permit me to do any evaluation. Period. What am I supposed to do now?"

Response to Case 9

We wonder why the client has refused so strongly. He or she may have been "burned" by other evaluation or research experiences, but if you have tried your best to show how monitoring and evaluation will help you to provide better services, and the client still refuses, then by all means agree that you will not do any formal evaluation. However, consider how would you do practice without identifying a target and monitoring the progress of the target over time until resolution?

This doesn't mean that you won't do whatever good practice calls for, and part of good practice requires that you know what the problems are that require service, and how your interventions are affecting them. Consider the full range of unobtrusive and nonreactive measures—those that truly do not involve the client in participating in any evaluation process. Your evaluations are then part of case records only, as tools to guide practice interventions.

We believe that this suggestion for unobtrusive evaluation, without the client's participation or knowledge, fulfills the ethical obligations of good practice since evaluation is vital for the conduct of effective practice. However, if you feel that this indirect evaluation violates your agreement with the client, then you have several final options: (a) do not do any evaluation whatsoever (although we hope that having gotten this far in this text, it may be hard for you ever to go back again to practice without thinking about clear identification of targets and monitoring their changes); (b) terminate the case because you cannot practice without knowing exactly what the problem is or how well your intervention is working; or (c) transfer the case to a practitioner who is willing to work under these limiting restrictions.

Case 10

"My client just loves this evaluation business. She is the kind of person who makes lists and is well-organized, and when I asked her to keep track of several targets, she constructed checklists and completed them exactly as we discussed. Now I have tons of data and I don't know what to do with them all. And the client wants to do more tracking of targets!"

Response to Case 10

Sometimes clients are very helpful in evaluation because they find the activity itself useful to them. However, we find ourselves without a great deal of sympathy—and maybe even some envy—for your plight of having "tons of data." Assuming that you have three, four, five, or more targets, this still amounts mainly to putting five dots in appropriate places on graph paper for each time unit, and then keeping up-to-date about the analysis. If this gives you an accurate picture of changes in the client's condition, then that is a very small price to pay in terms of time and effort. So enjoy!

Summary

This chapter provided specific guidelines by which you can select a design or a group of designs most suited to your client's needs. Recognizing that each situation is unique, we also note that there are common issues in most situations that can be described by a set of questions:

How many clients are to be included in the evaluation?
Are you able to collect baseline data?
How many problems are to be dealt with?
How many interventions are to be used with each problem?
Will you alternate or add baselines and/or interventions?

By using this set of questions as described in this chapter, we believe you will be able to make a wise selection of a design or from a group of related designs.

As soon as you begin to use single-system designs with real clients, you will discover the necessity of being creative and adaptive; we provided some basic suggestions on the use of creativity with single-system designs. We encourage you to use the basic principles as best you can—only be responsible for dealing with the common problems people face in using single-system designs. We hope our answers provide helpful points of departure for your own creative solutions.

Single-system designs have great potential for use across the full range of contacts—from minimal to long term—with clients. They can be adapted to the types of problems just about any agency typically sees. They also have the flexibility to be adapted by practitioners to meet the needs of just about any case or situation.

BASIC PRINCIPLES OF ANALYSIS

PURPOSE This chapter introduces the general concepts and guidelines for analyzing a set of data to determine whether a significant change has taken place. The chapter discusses a number of issues that you must understand in order to analyze your results appropriately, and provides a number of tools—including the introduction to SINGWIN, the computer program that will help you analyze your results.

Introduction
Distinguishing Effort, Effectiveness, and Efficiency
    Effort, Effectiveness, and Efficiency in Single-System Designs
Significance—Practical, Statistical, and Theoretical
    Practical Significance
    Statistical Significance
        Statistical Power
    Theoretical Significance
    Comparing and Aligning the Three Types of Significance
Evaluating Goal Achievement
    Goal Determination
    Goal-Attainment Scaling
    Target Complaints
    Visual Analysis
    Statistics
Issues in Analysis of Data
    How Long Should Information Be Collected?
    When Should You Change Interventions?
    Training Phases, Maintenance Phases, and Follow-Ups
Computer Analysis of Data for Single-System Designs
    SINGWIN: A Personal Computer Program for the Analysis of Single-System Design Data
The Issue of Autocorrelation
    The Debate over Autocorrelation
    Computational Steps in Testing for Autocorrelation
    Computer Procedures in Testing for Autocorrelation
Tools in Analysis of Data
    The Transformation of Autocorrelated Data
        Moving Average Transformation
        First Differences Transformation
    Computing and Graphing Transformed Data with SINGWIN
    Probability Tables for Use in Single-System Designs
    Computing Probabilities with SINGWIN
Summary

From Chapter 19 of *Evaluating Practice: Guidelines for the Accountable Professional*, Sixth Edition. Martin Bloom, Joel Fischer, John G. Orme. Copyright © 2009 by Pearson Education, Inc. All rights reserved.

INTRODUCTION

By this point in the helping process, you've obtained some more or less objective data, as well as many subjective impressions, about the client. The task now is to analyze these data—that is, to look at them, perhaps to rearrange them in particular ways, and to perform additional operations on them as needed—to arrive at a conclusion about the data and the events in real life to which these data refer. In this chapter, we discuss the basic concepts and procedures in this analytic process.

As in the problem-solving process itself, analysis begins with a question or challenge: What do these data tell us about X? This question directs you to look at the data in certain ways that will subsequently answer that question. What form will the answers take? If you're trying to reduce a client's depression, then you should look for evidence that depression has been lowered, as well as seek evidence that no new problems have emerged. The more clearly you can formulate your first questions regarding the data, the more readily will the answers be forthcoming. However, you also may find new questions emerging as you interpret portions of the data. Question formulation is a dynamic process that continues as long as new questions are raised by your analyses of data.

Once a question is raised, the next step is to arrange the data to provide answers. From simple visual inspection of changes in the data, to simple procedures for testing logical and statistical conclusions concerning the data. The rationale and utility of each of these methods is presented.

Underlying these procedures are some basic ideas that are useful for each of them. These are the ideas that form the basis of principles of analysis for single-system designs: How can practitioners distinguish the effort they put into helping a client from the effect of that effort and the efficiency by which it's delivered? What is pragmatically significant change? What is statistically significant change? What is theoretically significant change? What if these three don't coincide? How can you be as alert to significant deterioration as you are to improvement?

We also discuss some topics both as issues and as tools to be used in the analysis of data. These topics include consideration of autocorrelation, the transformation of autocorrelated data, and the use of probability tables; procedures for calculating these analytic tools are described in the SINGWIN program.

DISTINGUISHING EFFORT, EFFECTIVENESS, AND EFFICIENCY

In analyzing what the service program has meant for a client, some practitioners point to the fact that they have worked hard on behalf of their clients, made many visits, written many reports, and so forth. This is very meaningful to those who are on the front lines delivering services, but it may carry less weight with those who either receive the services or who underwrite the programs. These latter two groups of people are more concerned with the effectiveness of these interventions and how efficiently they were delivered. We can clarify these terms—effort, effectiveness, and efficiency—by reference to the single-system design model in Figure 1. As

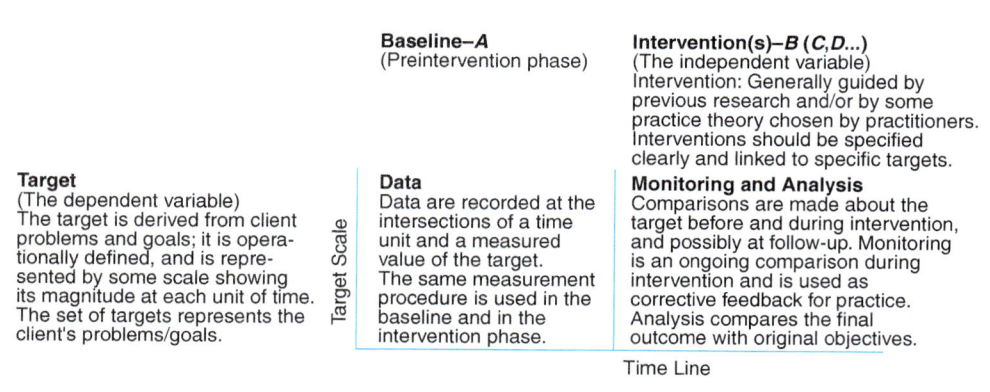

	Baseline–A (Preintervention phase)	**Intervention(s)–B (C,D...)** (The independent variable) Intervention: Generally guided by previous research and/or by some practice theory chosen by practitioners. Interventions should be specified clearly and linked to specific targets.
Target (The dependent variable) The target is derived from client problems and goals; it is operationally defined, and is represented by some scale showing its magnitude at each unit of time. The set of targets represents the client's problems/goals.	**Data** Data are recorded at the intersections of a time unit and a measured value of the target. The same measurement procedure is used in the baseline and in the intervention phase.	**Monitoring and Analysis** Comparisons are made about the target before and during intervention, and possibly at follow-up. Monitoring is an ongoing comparison during intervention and is used as corrective feedback for practice. Analysis compares the final outcome with original objectives.

Time Line

FIGURE 1 Schematic presentation of the evaluation process in single-system designs.

we'll see, effectiveness and efficiency require some form of evaluated outcome, and efficiency also requires a comparison between outcome and effort expended.

Effort refers to the work that goes into a service program. It's summarized in Figure 1 as the intervention—the range of activities that makes up the helping program. Measures of effort may include the amount of time spent with a client or with others. Effort may involve the amount of money provided during a given period of time. Sometimes agencies count the mileage practitioners travel or how far clients are transported for services. The intervention period on the chart indicates only a telescoped version of the efforts expended. For example, training each partner in a marriage to do more of what the other spouse thinks is good and to do less of what that spouse thinks is not good requires considerable teaching and role-playing time and effort. The phrase *reciprocal reinforcement* summarizes these efforts. It requires additional analysis to attach cost figures to the various efforts that go into any given intervention.

Effectiveness refers to changes that come about in a target event. Effectiveness also refers to the outcome—seen either in a positive or negative sense—that the service program has on achieving the goals of intervention. Part IV is directed primarily at describing how to determine effectiveness. In Figure 1, effectiveness is based on a comparison of a target comparing periods before, during, and after some intervention(s) relative to the intervention goals. Obviously, effectiveness requires effort to be expended. However, the focus of effectiveness is on the *outcome* of service, particularly the careful measurement and analysis of client changes, in relation to specific practitioner actions and other extraneous influences. Thus, effectiveness is a complicated affair requiring careful attention. We return to this point shortly.

Efficiency refers to how much effectiveness was attained given how much effort and how much time. Time and effort are costs to society to provide help; effectiveness is a benefit, both to the individuals involved and to society indirectly. Thus, efficiency is a ratio that compares costs and benefits. In Figure 1 efficiency would be indicated by looking at the number of time units and the measures of effort related to the determination of effectiveness. How much does it cost (in personal or material resources) to obtain so much outcome? Efficiency in organizational terms refers to optimizing this combination, achieving the best outcomes for the least costs.

Effort, Effectiveness, and Efficiency in Single-System Designs

Figure 1 casts the chart in the form of a practice hypothesis, and the various analytic procedures are ways of interpreting these results against defined criteria. We will discuss several categories of criteria against which observed results can be compared; they form a continuum from the relatively simple visual approaches to the relatively complex statistical ones, but they are all quite manageable by practitioners without mathematical backgrounds or inclinations. The basic questions the chart poses are: Did the targets change significantly from what they had been at the baseline period? Did they change for the better or for the worse? And is there a logical basis for inferring that the intervention was causally involved in these outcomes?

The causality question—was your intervention responsible for the observed changes?—is primarily a design issue. The other question, however—was there a significant change in the target problem?—is a question that can be resolved through a variety of analytic methods, including visual inspection of patterns of change in the data and the use of statistics. We use the word *analysis* as the generic term to cover the ways in which the issue of the significance of change gets addressed. Although there is overlap between the two questions—is the change significant and did my interventions cause it?—there are some clear differences as well. For example, a statistically significant change means the change probably is "real"; it did not occur by chance. But statistical significance says nothing about what *caused* the change. This is a question for the design to answer; it may or may not have been your interventions.

In this chapter, then, to prepare you for use of the analytic procedures, we discuss some basic principles of analysis, those concepts and guidelines that will help you determine whether or not change occurred in the targets of your intervention.

SIGNIFICANCE—PRACTICAL, STATISTICAL, AND THEORETICAL

A key concept in the analysis of data concerns the significance of observed changes in the data from baseline to intervention periods and to other variations. Given that life itself is a continuous series of changes, are the changes observed in the practice situation meaningful or not? The answer to this question implies another question: Meaningful to whom? There are three broad categories of answers, each with several subtypes. The broad classes will be called practical, statistical, and theoretical significance.

Practical Significance

Huff, in his wonderful book entitled *How to Lie with Statistics* (1954, p. 58), observed that "... a difference is a difference only if it makes a difference." Even if there's improvement in a target from one phase (e.g., baseline) to another (e.g., intervention), you can't conclude necessarily that the change was *sufficient* or *meaningful*. Such a conclusion requires evidence of what is known variously as *clinical significance, social validity or social significance, or practical significance* (e.g., Blanton & Jaccard, 2006; Cooper, Heron, & Heward, 2007; Dworkin et al., 2008; Friman, 2009; Ogles, Lambert, & Fields, 2002; Wise, 2004); all of these concepts include the idea that somebody—especially the client—believes that there has been sufficient or meaningful change in the target. Clinical significance is one aspect of this broader concept that we will refer to as *practical significance* because it seems to us the most comprehensive of the available terms for this concept. The basic idea here is that there is a change in a client's real-world functioning or quality of life that is sufficient or meaningful to the client, significant others, and/or society at large.

There are different methods for determining practical significance, but most involve the comparison of a client's functioning against some standard, and a determination of whether a discrepancy exists between the level of functioning and the standard. For example, the problems of a psychiatric patient may be sufficiently resolved to warrant deinstitutionalization, with appropriate medication and outpatient services, but the patient's behavior may still be inappropriate by community standards. A student's classroom behavior may show improvement over the course of intervention, but the student's teacher may still view the behavior as problematic. Even after losing a certain amount of weight, a client may decide that he or she is overweight based on his or her personal standards. Physical abuse of a partner or child may be reduced, but some abuse may still occur. Chronic pain may decrease, but still be sufficiently intense to be debilitating.

There are different types of personal and social standards that can be used to determine practical significance, depending on the target of intervention, including a comparison of a client's functioning with: (a) the average functioning of a nonproblematic peer group; (b) the average functioning of a peer group that exhibits exemplary behavior; (c) the subjective impression of the client or relevant others; (d) the expectations from theories of development or psychopathology; (e) the cultural norms or values of relevant groups; or (f) the intervention goals set by the practitioner and/or the client. Therefore, it may be appropriate to think of practical significance with a variety of terms—practical, social, clinical, personal—depending on the targeted intervention; we use the term *practical significance* to encompass all of these.

For example, Engel, Jensen, and Schwartz (2004) conducted a study on reducing chronic back pain in several clients with cerebral palsy. They used an 11-point Likert scale in a "pain diary" in which the client recorded how she felt after the biofeedback-type intervention to indicate the *clinical* changes in pain. The study by Saville, Neef, Van Norman, and Fereri (2006) compared teaching methods. Students filled out questionnaires at the end of each class where the teaching methods were alternated in which they raised questions that they were *personally* concerned with, which became the topics of the lecture in the next class period. McSweeny (1978) conducted a single-system design with over 1 million people, in order to discover the *social* impact of a local telephone assistance charge on usage, in comparison with continuing free service for long distance telephone assistance.

Criteria and procedures for determining practical significance are not well-developed. Moreover, the selection and application of criteria for determining practical significance often involve personal values, and sometimes personal values that are in conflict (e.g., husband and wife, parent and child). Therefore, the criteria for determining practical significance may require a process of discussion and negotiation among different involved parties in much the same way that targets and goals for intervention are selected. Nevertheless, such standards are necessary as a basis for making decisions concerning the course of intervention.

Statistical Significance

Any analysis involves comparisons between two or more events in connection with some valued state of affairs, such as a client's goal. For example, sets of data collected before an intervention are compared with sets of data collected during and after intervention; thus, analysis involves two sets of facts and one set of values. If we don't have any independent value or criterion to analyze these differences (such as a criterion score necessary to gain admission to school, maintaining weight within a desired range, scoring in the normal range of a standardized scale measuring depression), then we have to find our valued reference point within our sets of data. For example, with an *A-B* design where we have intervened in phase *B* to improve a client's condition as compared to the baseline *A*, in part the valued objective is built into the design. The analysis directs us to compare the intervention data with the baseline data according to some procedure, to determine whether the client's condition has improved.

Unfortunately, various haphazard or chance factors can cause a target to appear to change over time (e.g., imperfect reliability in the measurement of a target, inconsistency in the implementation of baseline or intervention activities, events in a client's life). Therefore, it's necessary to decide whether there's a systematic difference in a target under different conditions or whether the observed difference is just due to haphazard or chance factors. Many researchers have asserted that systematic differences between conditions should be so obvious that visual inspection is sufficient to analyze the data (e.g., Colon, 2006; Cooper, Heron, & Heward, 2007; Kennedy, 2005; Parsonson & Baer, 1986; Thyer & Myers, 2007). Others have argued that tests of statistical significance should be used to analyze single-system data (e.g., Onghena & Edgington, 2005; Todman & Dugard, 2001). There is considerable debate about the relative merits of visual and statistical analysis.

We believe that visual analysis is very important. We also believe that tests of statistical significance have merit. Tests of statistical significance can be used to provide the weight of standardized rules to determine whether or not there are systematic differences between phases and the size of existing differences. They also can be used to tease out subtle effects, given enough observations. Statistics also can be used, as we describe, to take account of problems such as autocorrelated data. In short, the use of statistics can help to increase the precision of our conclusions.

It is important to note that, although tests of statistical significance can provide a basis for deciding whether there's a systematic difference in a target under different conditions, they don't indicate what *caused* the difference. It might be that the intervention caused the difference, but there are other possible explanations for such a difference. The plausibility of these alternative explanations depends on the type of design used and the pattern of the results obtained.

When tests of statistical significance are used to decide whether there's a systematic difference in a target between conditions, the following steps are used, and these steps are illustrated in Figure 2:

1. State what you hope to find (e.g., the mean number of parent–child conflicts will be less during

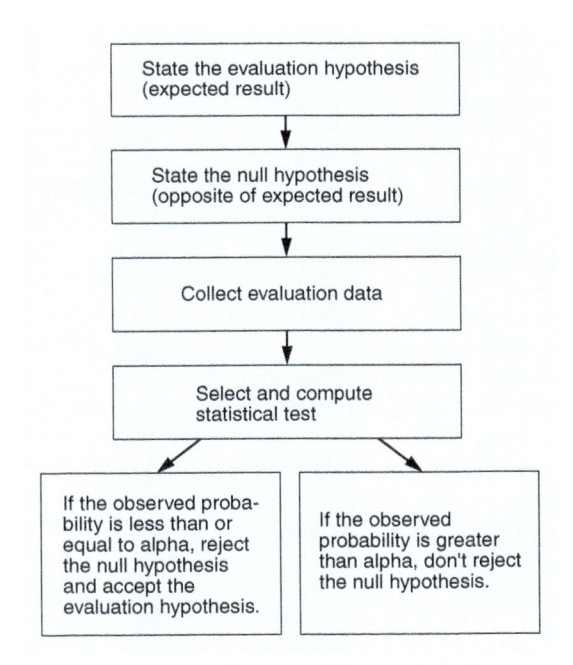

FIGURE 2 Process in determining statistical significance.

intervention than during baseline). Statisticians call this the *research* hypothesis, but because of our focus on evaluation we'll call it the *evaluation* hypothesis.

2. State the opposite of what you hope to find (e.g., the mean number of parent–child conflicts during intervention is the same or greater than the mean number of conflicts during baseline). Statisticians refer to this as the *null hypothesis*. It traditionally is stated this way to put the burden of "proof" on the intervention/evaluation. Paradoxically, this is the hypothesis that is tested. If the null hypothesis is rejected, your evaluation hypothesis is supported because it's the opposite of the null hypothesis.

3. Collect your evaluation data.

4. Select and compute the appropriate statistical test. This test will tell you how likely it is to get a difference between conditions as large as or larger than the one you actually got if the null hypothesis is true. Statisticians call this the *observed probability* (p).

5. If the observed probability is equal to or less than some small value selected before you conduct your test, typically .05 (and referred to as *alpha*), reject the null hypothesis and accept your evaluation hypothesis. Alpha also is known as the *level of significance*, and tells us how probable it is that we are incorrectly rejecting the null hypothesis (if alpha is .05, then larger values would include .06, .10, .25, etc., and smaller values would include .04, .01, or .001). If the null hypothesis is rejected, this means the outcome was statistically significant.

6. If the observed probability is greater than alpha (i.e., greater than .01, .05, .10, or whatever value you select), do not reject the null hypothesis.

Tests of statistical significance are used to make decisions, and with these or any other procedures, including visual analysis, there's always some chance that the decision will be wrong. The different types of incorrect and correct decisions are illustrated in Figure 3, and as shown in this figure there are two types of possible decision errors. First, you might conclude that a difference exists when it really doesn't; that is, you reject the null hypothesis when it shouldn't be rejected. This is called a *Type I error* by statisticians. The probability of making a Type I error is determined by your alpha level. Second, you might conclude that a difference doesn't exist when it really does; that is, you don't reject the null hypothesis

Alpha is the probability of rejecting the null when it shouldn't be rejected.
Beta is the probability of not rejecting the null when it should be rejected.
Power is the probability of correctly rejecting the null, and it is equal to 1-beta.

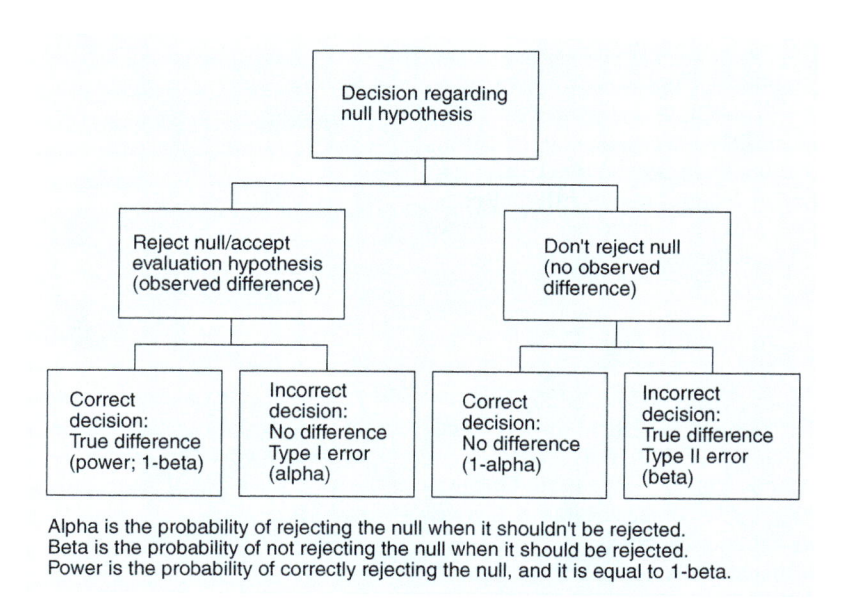

FIGURE 3 Outcomes of decisions concerning the null hypothesis.

when it should be rejected. This is called a *Type II error* by statisticians, sometimes signified as *beta*. As practitioners and evaluators, we are concerned about avoiding Type II errors because we want to correctly reject the null hypothesis when we should (when it is false), that is, find an effect of our intervention when there really is one. The probability of doing so is called *statistical power*.

Statistical Power. Statistical power is the probability of finding an effect of our intervention when there really is an effect. In single-system design terms, this is the probability that you'll correctly detect a difference between phases if there is a difference. Obviously, you want this probability to be large, and there are numerous strategies you can use to increase power (Cohen, 1988; Orme, 1991); some of these strategies are somewhat technical and beyond the scope of this book (see Allison, Silverstein, & Gorman, 1997, for a review of these strategies).

Other strategies for increasing power are somewhat impractical. For example, one of the main reasons we are concerned about power in single-system designs is that power is, in large part, a function of sample size, or, in single-system design terms, it is a function of the number of data points over time. Thus, one of the most important ways of increasing power is to try to collect as many observations as is possible, practical, and consistent with good practice. (There actually are numerous tables available to help you determine the number of data points you need to achieve a given level of power—say, .80—which allows only a 20% probability of making a Type II error. See Allison, Silverstein, & Gorman, 1997, for a review of those tables. Also, see Dattalo, 2008.)

We will indicate the number of observations that appears to be optimal. However, given the costs involved in collecting more observations, especially in this era of managed care, we think you may be better off to consider one of the following strategies. Remember that the idea here is to increase your chances of detecting a real difference between phases.

1. Implement your intervention as consistently and accurately as is possible, practical, and consistent with good practice.

2. Increase the strength of your intervention as much as possible, practical, and consistent with good practice.

3. Use the most reliable and valid outcome measures that are possible, practical, and consistent with good practice, and collect outcome measures in a consistent and careful fashion.

4. Use the most powerful test of statistical significance permitted by the assumptions of your data. Some statistical tests are better than others at detecting differences between phases. We'll have more to say about this when we discuss specific tests.

5. Increase alpha (e.g., use .10 instead of .05). Increasing alpha in order to increase the chance of detecting an existing difference is controversial and requires some brief comments here. There is a long history and very strong scientific convention about using the .05 level. Also, very importantly, increasing alpha increases the chance that you'll conclude there is a difference when there isn't (Type I error). This is an important mistake. It might result in current and future clients receiving an ineffective service, although on subsequent use the mistake might be discovered.

Why not use a value for alpha even lower than .05, if that would reduce the chance of mistakenly concluding that there is a difference between phases? Well, unfortunately, the lower the value of alpha, the less chance of detecting a difference when one actually exists (Type II error). This also is an important mistake. It might result in the intervention being abandoned and, consequently, the mistake left undiscovered, the current client receiving unneeded additional services, and subsequent clients not receiving an effective service.

Ideally, single-system designs should be undertaken that minimize the chance of either of these mistakes, and we've discussed strategies for doing this that don't involve increasing alpha. Unfortunately, sometimes these other strategies, even in combination, are impractical, insufficient, or at odds with good practice. In any case, in these situations we don't believe that you should blindly adhere to the .05 convention at the cost of having very little chance of detecting an effective intervention. In these situations you might consider setting alpha greater than .05, say perhaps .10, although this is something that you should do as a last resort, and something that you should decide before analyzing your data. We can make this recommendation most comfortably when you are trying a brand new intervention, which typically is accompanied by some degree of uncertainty on the part of the practitioner; if the intervention seems to work at the .10 level, then it can be analyzed with future clients at the .05 level.

Theoretical Significance

A third kind of significance related to changes in client behavior or changes in the environment is called theoretical significance (Bloom, 1987). The practitioner conceptualizes and plans his or her intervention with certain expectations in mind based on the theory employed. That is, the theory describes a future pattern of events, given certain initial causes. The practitioner seeks to use this theory as a guide to what is to be expected in the given case, and translates the general causal suggestions of the theory into specific events with a client. Briefly, the practitioner seeks to make the theoretical prediction come to pass in the life of the client.

For example, a cognitive-behavioral practitioner might view depression as a kind of mind-set about oneself and the world, along with associated behaviors fulfilling these mental images (McCullough, 1984). According to this cognitive-behavioral theory, if the practitioner can teach the client to think in a certain way and to do certain kinds of activities that change this negative self-view, then the depression should disappear. In McCullough's (1984) therapy system derived from this theory, there are two training stages: one involving cognitive changes, and the other, behavioral changes. According to the theory, the client should begin at one level of depressive functioning (i.e., during baseline), and eventually the depression should be reduced when the client comes to understand certain aspects of his or her depression (during the cognitively-focused intervention). However, after a subsequent intervention involving the learning of behavioral skills, the client should be doing demonstrably better than under either of the other two situations separately. Predicted changes in depression based on McCullough's therapy system are visually represented in Figure 4. Follow-ups (McCullough suggests 2-year follow-ups) should show that clients have maintained their successful resolution of the depression.

Given this theory with its clear expectations of the patterns that are likely to occur, there are several possible outcomes. First, it might be that the client performs just as the theory predicts, in which case we can say that the results exhibit theoretical significance. (Note that nothing is said about the specific degrees of change; theoretical significance generally deals in ordinal statements, as contrasted with interval or ratio statements.)

On the other hand, it may be that the client's depression lifts, but not in the way predicted by the theory. For example, suppose clients receiving McCullough's therapy got completely better (statistically and practically) during the first (cognitive) intervention. That would be fine (statistically and practically) for this one client, but it would not help you, the practitioner, to have a working theory that could be applied to other clients. The success would be a mystery

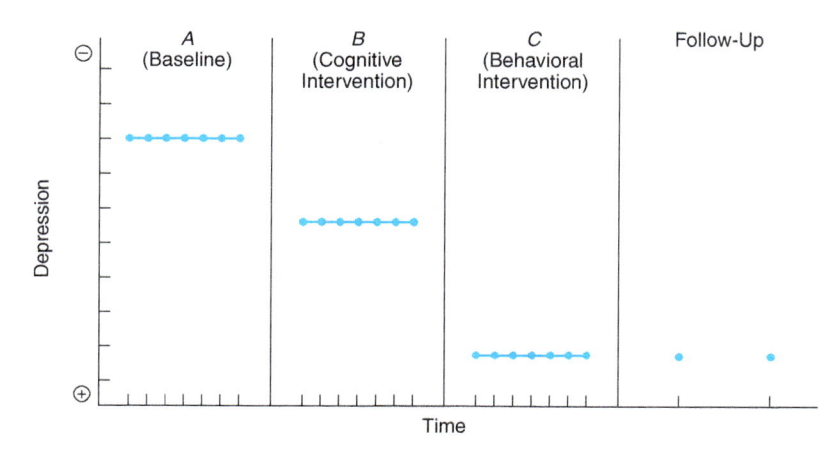

FIGURE 4 Change in depression predicted by McCullough's (1984) therapy system.

in that your theory did not lead you to expect these results in the way they came about. Theoretical significance would not be achieved.

There's a third logical possibility. If the client did not improve during the first intervention, then you have several options as dictated by the theory: You might continue with the behavioral phase to see if it eventually gains some positive change, but might intensify the intervention to see if this could bring about the expected changes. Or you might reasonably combine the cognitive and behavioral phase into a *BC* phase to see if their joint use leads to greater improvement. Or you might consider other theories that might be better suited to this particular client's situation. Perhaps a straightforward behavioral model might be needed on grounds that the client may not have the cognitive sophistication or perseverance to understand or use the cognitive tools alone. In this case, you begin again with a new set of theoretical expectations derived from the behavioral model.

Unfortunately, theories are often vague about predicted patterns of change, and especially about specific stages of such changes. It's often possible to draw on the "practice wisdom" of experienced practitioners who have some sense of the likely course of events from the perspective of a given theory (Klein & Bloom, 1995). (Indeed, we should press our theorists and our teachers of practice theories to provide the specific expectations so that we might benefit more fully from their guidance.) However, when it's not possible to obtain an expected pattern from a given theory, that is, when we have no way of testing theoretical significance, we should turn to the other two forms of significance in a given case.

Comparing and Aligning the Three Types of Significance

Practical, statistical, and theoretical significance are important for evaluation-informed practice regardless of whether the intervention is with individuals, groups, organizations, or communities. However, they are independent ideas. One may have attained practical significance, but neither statistical nor theoretical significance, nor any other combination of the three types. For example, it may be that a former psychiatric patient underwent a statistically significant change in the level of his bizarre behavior, as he was expected to do according to the theory used by his clinicians. But he may not yet be acting within an acceptable range of behaviors in his local public library.

Likewise, he may be exhibiting some very significant behavior as far as practical matters are concerned; for example, he has not made a second attempt on his own life since having therapy, but statistically and theoretically speaking, we might want to monitor him for a longer period of time, since the nonsuicidal behavior so far exhibited could have occurred by chance alone, and our theory directs us to be aware of novel stresses for which he may not be prepared.

Although independent, these three forms of significance have important implications for one another. We view theoretical and statistical significance as tools for better understanding both our interventions and what is occurring in the client's life, compared to the literature and collective wisdom about what might be expected regarding the client's type of problem. Practical significance, which is probably the most commonly used form of significance among the three, should be viewed as the "bottom line" we must achieve to validate our helping roles in society.

As an evaluation-informed practitioner, you want to try to align all three forms of significance. You must achieve practical results, resolve the problems clients come in with, and not create new social disturbances in so doing. But in order to build a repertoire of effective intervention methods for evidence-based practice, rather than reinvent the wheel with each new client, you must seek to demonstrate improvements that are unlikely to have happened by chance alone. You also must seek to understand why these results happened as they did; that is, you must seek theoretical significance. With the three combined, you approximate the ideals of the scientific practitioner—sensitive (practical significance) and effective (statistical and theoretical significance) helping. To paraphrase Kant, having statistical and theoretical significance without the practical is hollow, but having practical significance without the other two is blind. All are needed for scientific practice, since they address different but important and complementary issues.

EVALUATING GOAL ACHIEVEMENT

Assuming that your intervention has been proceeding more or less smoothly and your monitoring of data shows that your intervention is achieving positive results, at some point you will want to evaluate whether your objectives and goals have been met. There are several ways of doing this, and, in fact, most of these

Basic Principles of Analysis

Your Name	Date	Name of Person You're Evaluating

Level of Improvement

Compared to the first time I evaluated this person, the problem is now:

Problem	Much Worse	Worse	Same	Improved	Very Much Improved
1. _____	_____	_____	_____	_____	_____
2. _____	_____	_____	_____	_____	_____
3. _____	_____	_____	_____	_____	_____
4. _____	_____	_____	_____	_____	_____

FIGURE 5 Checklist for evaluating outcome.

ways can be integrated into a comprehensive evaluation package (Gingerich, 1983).

Goal Determination

If your objectives and goals have been stated in clear, operational terms regarding the client's performance, you simply may be able to check whether the client's performance or activities actually meet the stated goals using whatever measurement system you have selected. If they do, you know you have arrived. For example, if the client's goal was to maintain his weight at 145 pounds for at least 3 weeks, once he has accomplished that, you will know your goals were achieved.

Goal-Attainment Scaling

The methods of GAS are another way of evaluating overall goal achievement, since they are designed to do just that.

Target Complaints

An individualized rating scale, based on target complaints can be used to aid in evaluating overall goal achievement. If you have not used an IRS as one of your basic tools for a given client, you may establish one to be used only at the end of the intervention to supplement your other data (e.g., *very much improved, much improved, minimally improved, no change, minimally worse, much worse,* and *very much worse* compared to baseline). This allows clients or relevant others to evaluate success based on their own impressions. You can use one of the formats or a simple checklist, such as the one illustrated in Figure 5. With slight modification, this form also can be used to obtain the client's impressions of success.

Research investigating the efficacy of chronic pain treatments provides another example of how you can set goals with target complaint ratings (Dworkin et al., 2008; Ogles, Lunnen, & Bonesteel, 2001). For example, pain intensity is often measured on a scale from 0 to 10, with higher scores indicating greater pain intensity (Dworkin et al., 2008; Herr, Spratt, Garand, & Li, 2007; Moon, McMurtry, & McGrath, 2008; Morley, Williams, & Hussain, 2008; Turk, Okifuji, & Skinner, 2008). Provisional benchmarks have been developed for evaluating the magnitude of changes in pain intensity (Dworkin et al., 2008). Reductions of 30% to 49% represent *moderate* improvement, and reductions of 50% or more represent *substantial* improvement. Suppose, for example, that a client had a pretreatment rating of 8. What rating would indicate the goal of 50% reduction? The pretreatment rating, minus the pretreatment rating multiplied by .50, gives you the answer to this question (8 − [8 × .50] = 4). So, if the patient started with a rating of 8, and ended up with a rating of 4, pain intensity decreased by 50%. You also can calculate the exact percentage reduction at posttreatment with the following simple formula:

$$100\left[\frac{\text{Pretreatment} - \text{Posttreatment}}{\text{Posttreatment}}\right] = \%\text{Reduction}$$

$$100\left[\frac{8-4}{8}\right] = 50\%$$

Basic Principles of Analysis

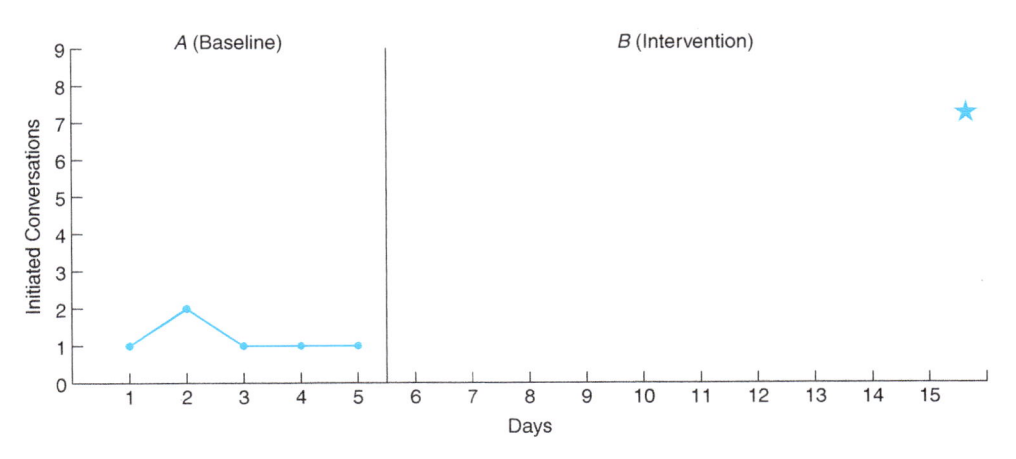

FIGURE 6 Illustration of "aim-star" technique.

This basic idea also can be used in other ways. For example, if you were interested in a 30% reduction, you would substitute .30 for .50 in the prior calculations (e.g., 8 − [8 × .3] = 5.6). Or, if you were interested in a percentage increase, you would *add*—instead of subtract—the pretreatment rating multiplied by .50 (or .30; pretreatment + posttreatment). Finally, you could use these basic ideas with other types of outcomes (e.g., percentage reduction in number of problematic behaviors), but remember that the benchmarks that apply to changes in pain intensity won't necessarily apply to reductions in other outcomes. Finally, remember that even though a 50% reduction in pain intensity might indeed represent *substantial* improvement, it might not represent *sufficient* improvement (i.e., practical significance).

Visual Analysis

Probably the most basic analytic method of single-system designs is to do a visual analysis—a comparison of the data you are collecting on your charts during the intervention phase with the data you collected during the baseline period. This provides you with ongoing feedback in evaluating goal achievement.

One variation of visual analysis is the *aim-star technique* (White, 1977). This procedure essentially synthesizes the practice of goal determination as discussed previously with the process of visual analysis. If the goal has been clearly identified in advance, you simply draw a star on your standard chart at the level of performance that you have targeted for the client at about the time that you expect the client to reach that level (as illustrated in Figure 6). You could even use a series of stars on the chart to correspond to your objectives, with each corresponding to successively greater achievements. While it may be difficult to be precise about exactly when the client will reach that point, having it plotted on the chart in advance establishes a clear goal toward which you and the client can work, and also can add to the client's motivation as he or she begins to approach that goal.

Statistics

As we said, you can use statistics to help you evaluate your goals. We said that in the absence of other clear guidelines, you can establish goals that indicate success when statistical significance is reached.

Much of the rest of the book discusses how to use some of these procedures for evaluating goal attainment, but first we provide an overview of issues in the analysis of data and the use of personal computers for conducting some of these analytic tasks.

ISSUES IN ANALYSIS OF DATA

How Long Should Information Be Collected?

How long should baselining continue? In that chapter we offered a number of suggestions, some of which, unfortunately, could not provide exact answers about the exact number of observations you need to make. We have some additional guidelines to provide at this point, and we will provide more specific answers when we discuss particular statistical tests because the exact number of observations is related to the statistical test used.

In general, as we indicated earlier in our discussion of *power*, the more information you have (i.e., the more observations you make), and the more accurate the information (e.g., reliable and valid), the better your chances of accurately detecting a real difference between phases. However, if there is a large difference in the level of the target between phases it will be easier for you to detect accurately, and you won't need to collect as many observations. Therefore, the more powerful the intervention effect, the easier it will be to detect accurately, and the fewer observations you will need. On the other hand, smaller differences between phases require more information to accurately determine whether any observed differences are real, or simply due to chance fluctuations over time. To detect subtle intervention effects you will need more information. In short, if you don't collect enough information you might miss a difference between phases, and hence, an intervention effect (Cohen, 1988; Orme, 1991).

One way to decide whether you have enough information is to wait until practical, statistical, and theoretical significance converge. Obviously, you should collect data throughout the intervention period in order to know how well the client is progressing toward his or her goals. However, practitioners collect enormous amounts of subjective impressions along with a handful of empirically defined and collected information. There may be an overpowering temptation to stop the rigorous data collection when you feel that the goals have been obtained based on subjective impressions. We don't oppose this application of practice wisdom, but we would like to offer a suggestion to make it less idiosyncratic. Based on the discussion of statistical, practical, and theoretical significance, we suggest that formal measurement of outcomes could end when these tests of significance are aligned, that is, when statistical, practical, and theoretical significance have been attained. In this way we can provide a pretty objective foundation for what essentially are subjective judgments about whether target events lie within an acceptable range, to the client, practitioner, and/or others.

When statistical, practical, and theoretical significance are not in alignment, it's likely that further monitoring of the intervention, and perhaps a change in the intervention, is needed. The lack of practical significance means that further steps are necessary in the successive approximation toward a goal of satisfying psychological and/or social functioning. The lack of statistical significance means that any observed change might be due to chance factors. The lack of theoretical significance means we have no clear conceptual framework from which to interpret the data.

If there's some doubt about the lasting quality of the outcome, it's wise to continue monitoring. This judgment may be made based on expectations derived from reviewing the literature, from other experiences with similar targets, or from knowledge of the client's background. It's also possible to make this judgment by examining the whole set of target events for a given client; if one target has improved sufficiently, it may be necessary to continue observing it until the others among the cluster of targets also improve sufficiently. It also may be reassuring to clients to note that they can maintain successful accomplishments while they're working to resolve other concerns. This use of stable data should be shared with clients.

Using the procedure of estimating efficiency by means of projecting the trends of current interventive efforts, you can make a rough prediction of how long it will take to arrive at statistical significance, at least given current trends. Then, based on client needs and agency resources, you can decide whether to continue the intervention. How that decision is made depends on the practitioner and the agency involved.

All things considered, collecting information, although it does carry a price tag, may be one of your cheapest, yet most important, investments in practice. If intervention is to continue, then we would suggest that evaluation—at least, of the major aspects of the client's situation—be continued as well.

When Should You Change Interventions?

This is a basic question for practice. It presumes that the problems and strengths of the client are being monitored, and that you are asking not only to evaluate the data collected, but also to translate these evaluations into decisions for possible changes in the intervention; this is the heart of evaluation-informed practice. There are eight logical combinations of the

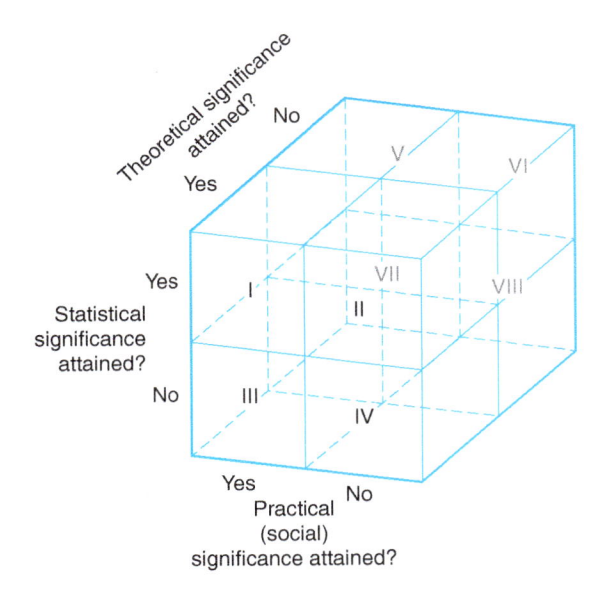

FIGURE 7 Three types of significance with eight combinations.

presence or absence of practical, statistical, and theoretical significance that can help you come to some decision, as depicted in Figure 7.

The first case is when all three forms of significance are present. This happy state of affairs should give clear direction for practice decisions, as the theory tells us what to expect to happen, the statistical analysis informs us that this has happened, and the practical meaning is clear that these are changes appropriate to function adequately in society. In the best of all possible worlds, you probably would be well-advised to continue with the intervention until this alignment of information informs you that the client's objectives have been attained.

The next three cases are when only two of the three forms of significance are present. For example, suppose practical and statistical significance have been attained, but not theoretical; then you have to decide on whether to use these other two criteria as the basis of your decision making. You should recognize that what has happened here may not support your guiding theory of practice, which means that you should consider what unique factors might explain these results, or think about how the theory might be strengthened to incorporate the events of this case. Or, you might wish to consider new theories that better explain the outcomes. A single case is not enough to discard a well-developed theory, but as information accumulates over many cases, we probably should be prepared to seek stronger theories as needed.

In the situation in which there's practical and theoretical significance, but not statistical, you should look to see if there is a trend in the data. It's possible in some cases to project how long it will take, given the present state of affairs in a case, for that case to show statistically significant results. If there's a clear positive trend, and success is predicted without considerable expenditure of time and effort, then consider completing the case by attaining statistical significance along with the other two. If there's no clear trend, then you might want to check the evidence for the other forms of significance again, as this would be an inconsistent pattern.

The last of this set of three situations would be when there's statistical and theoretical significance, but no practical outcomes. This pattern strongly suggests that the intervention be continued longer, as matters are moving in the right direction according to both theory and analysis of current data. It may be that this pattern suggests strengthening the intervention to attain the desired practical effect along with the other two forms of significance.

The next three cases occur when there's only one form of significance. For example, when practical significance alone is present, we're under great temptation to make decisions on this sole piece of information. This practical significance is very important, but it may be superficial so that once you terminate, the problems may reappear. Stronger certainty would come either when you had expected this improvement to occur early (a part of the expectations from your theory), or when the magnitude of change could not have happened by chance alone (statistical significance). However, if you had to choose one form of significance that you could not do without, then practical significance probably would be it.

If you've obtained statistically significant improvement alone, this is an indication that you're probably on the right path, although without theoretical significance you may not know what particular path it is. If you're moving in the right direction, though, you should probably continue the intervention until practical significance is achieved.

If you obtain theoretical significance only, then your theory probably will already tell you to keep on with the intervention, because this is not the end of the expectation. Such information may tide you over during rough parts of cases. For example, behavioral theory suggests that clients may react at first with a sharp rise in problematic behaviors when reinforcement for those behaviors is purposely removed and the problematic behaviors ignored (this is called an *extinction burst*). Obviously there would be no practical or statistical significance in that situation, but it could be anticipated because of the theory, along with the prediction of improvement that is to come.

The final case is where there are no forms of significance present, even after some considerable interventive efforts. Then the message is very clear that you should consider rapidly changing the intervention. Included in this situation would be sudden negative changes. You should be annotating any extreme data points on the chart so as to account for unusual happenings, and when several come in short order, this may be enough information to make major changes in the intervention.

Thus, the various patterns among the three forms of significance can be used to suggest approaches to the intervention. The general point is that this is what we mean by feedback from your evaluation to your practice, or *evaluation-informed practice*. You can use practical, statistical, and theoretical guidelines as part of the basis for making decisions about practice.

Training Phases, Maintenance Phases, and Follow-Ups

Throughout this book, we've made the point that single-system designs use some special phases in the problem-solving process. Here, we link our discussions of training, maintenance, and follow-up phases with analysis—how these distinctive parts of evaluation fit into our analysis and decision making on a case. These elements, particularly maintenance and follow-up, also are essential from the point of view of evidence-based practice.

During the *training phase* the client will often not perform immediately at the highest levels because he or she has to learn how and what to do, and learning takes time and practice. So, analysis of the training phase requires that we look for trends in the right direction, given enough time for the client to learn whatever is needed to achieve the desired outcome. If the client's target behavior shows no sign of improvement, or is getting worse, then double-check to make sure that the intervention is in fact being used as intended. If it is, then consider changing the intervention in some way—making it stronger if you're convinced by available evidence that this is the appropriate intervention for this case, or changing to something new if you're not so convinced. If the client's target behavior is moving in the right direction with reasonable speed, then be reassured and continue the intervention as planned.

Events in the *maintenance phase* tell you something quite different. In this case, you've attained a stable pattern of success in achieving the client's objectives, but you wish to ensure that this learning will be maintained over time. So, the maintenance phase contains those new learning experiences to ensure the transfer of effects. Maintenance is part of the intervention in general, even though it's not the intervention, per se. Thus, you should continue regular observations of the target behavior. However, because you're introducing something new, you should expect some variation in the pattern achieved in the regular intervention phase. If this occurs, you can look for a new steady state indicating that the client can handle the problem on his or her own, and then terminate. If, however, there's a sharp deterioration in the target event, then you may have caused a problem rather than solved one. First, double-check with the client about extraneous events that may be influencing this deterioration. If such events don't appear to be present, then monitor the maintenance intervention to see if it appears to be having an iatrogenic effect (harm caused by the practitioner). If the problems are severe, you probably should drop the maintenance activities and go back to the intervention to regain the stable, desired level of behaviors. Once that has been reachieved, you can try a new maintenance activity, or terminate while the target problem is in a desired state.

Follow-ups are probably the cheapest form of insurance the practitioner has that his or her interventions are effective. They can help answer several important questions:

1. Does the impact of the service maintain itself after the end of the intervention program? Is the client independently controlling his or her own fate?

2. Have there been any negative changes in the target, suggesting a need for a "booster shot" (i.e., the delivery of more of the intervention)?

3. Has the client incorporated the intervention experience as a way of dealing with new problems?

On a carefully planned basis you should make contact and reassess the client's functioning on the target problems, using the same form of measurement of the target events that you used throughout the baseline and intervention periods, if possible. One important method of conducting follow-ups is to select the times with progressively increasing intervals, for example, 1 month, 3 months, 6 months, and then a year following termination. Or, you can select the times randomly using a computer program such as Microsoft Excel. Random selection of the exact time for follow-ups increases the chance that the selected times will provide a representative picture of the client's functioning. No matter how you select follow-up times, though, you don't necessarily have to tell the client exactly when you plan to reassess his or her functioning, but only that you would like to check back several times for some months to see how things are going.

Be prepared for a possibly ambivalent response sometimes, because you represent a time in the former client's life that may be difficult and embarrassing for that client—and your presence may perhaps be an unhappy reminder. However, you're also showing continuing interest and availability, which should be reassuring to the former client. We suggest you accept whatever follow-up is acceptable to the client, even if it's a brief telephone call on how the client is doing on the former target behaviors. These follow-ups become "reconstructed" follow-up data, similar to reconstructed baseline data. Use them cautiously to provide a broad perspective on the persistence of results without clear detail, but do try to use them.

We would recommend a minimum of three follow-up contacts, if possible. Two follow-ups might give you a rough estimate of whether there was a trend during follow-up, but three observations would be even better because they would give you a better estimate of whether there was a stable trend or a changing trend (e.g., increasing functioning followed by decreasing functioning). Also, if you do only one or two follow-ups it might be that you just catch the client at a particularly good or bad time, whereas three (or more) follow-ups increase the chances that the follow-up data provide a clearer picture of the client's functioning.

Another consideration in determining the number and schedule of follow-ups is the nature of the target. For example, problems might be associated with a particular day of the week (e.g., "blue Mondays," caused by starting the work week), time of the month (e.g., shortage of money and resulting tensions prior to receiving monthly checks), or time of the year (e.g., holidays or personal anniversaries). Such patterns should be considered in determining the scheduling of follow-ups.

COMPUTER ANALYSIS OF DATA FOR SINGLE-SYSTEM DESIGNS

Personal computers can increase the speed, efficiency, and accuracy with which single-system data are analyzed. Personal computers also increase the range of statistical procedures that can be used because they can do certain mathematical procedures that would be too cumbersome to do by hand or with a calculator (autocorrelation and some tests of statistical significance come to mind). However, the use of personal computers to analyze single-system data requires an investment of time and money, especially initially. On the other hand, computer programs are becoming more and more user-friendly, and computers are increasingly available to practitioners in the workplace (Schoech, 2008). Therefore, personal computers can be important tools for the analysis of single-system data.

You could use a wide variety of personal computer programs to compute particular statistics for the analysis of single-system design data. There are several broad categories of such programs. First, there are commercial programs designed primarily for the analysis of group designs. These programs compute some of the statistics we discuss in this book. They include SPSS and SAS, two programs widely used by social science researchers.

Second, any search of the Internet for shareware programs will turn up a number of diverse personal computer programs that will compute some relevant statistics and charts. These programs are distributed free or for a small fee.

Third, spreadsheet programs such as Microsoft Excel can compute some relevant statistics and are especially useful for constructing line charts. For example, Microsoft Excel can be customized to compute statistics for the analysis of single-system designs (e.g., Fisher, Kelley, & Lomas, 2003; Orme & Cox, 2001; Patterson & Basham, 2006; Todman & Dugard, 2001). It also can be used easily to graph the results of single-system designs (Carr & Burkholder, 1998; Grehan & Moran, 2005; Hillman & Miller, 2004; Lo & Konrad, 2007; Moran & Hirschbine, 2002; Patterson & Basham, 2006). (Programs by Grehan & Moran, 2005, Hillman & Miller, 2004, and Moran & Hirschbine, 2002, can be downloaded for free from

"The Behavior Analyst Today" web site located at: www.behavior-analyst-today.com. (Click on "Index," search for the correct volume and issue, click on it, and scroll to the particular article.)

Finally, there are programs designed for specific limited types of analysis of single-system design data. For example, Crosbie (1993, 1995; Crosbie & Sharpley, 1991) developed a personal computer program named ITSACORR designed specifically to conduct time-series analyses of single-system data, although questions have been raised about the accuracy of this and other time-series analyses proposed for the analysis of single-system design data (Huitema, 2004). McKnight, McKean, and Huitema (2000) developed an alternative to ITSACORR for the analysis of time-series data (www.stat.wmich.edu/slab/Software/Timeseries.html). Van Damme and Onghena (Onghena & Edgington, 1994; Onghena & Van Damme, 1994) developed SCRT, a personal computer program designed specifically to conduct randomization tests for single-system designs, and other programs for randomization tests are summarized in Todman and Dugard (2001). Other specific programs have been discussed in Franklin, Allison, and Gorman (1997).

Many of the programs mentioned here are very useful and sophisticated computer programs, but most of the things they do are not relevant to the analysis of single-system designs, or they don't do some of the things needed in the analysis of single-system design data. Also, some, but not all, of these programs are quite expensive. In any case, personal computer-based data analysis is a rapidly growing area, so you should look for current developments in such journals as *Journal of Technology in Human Services*, *Social Science Computer Review*, and *Computers in Psychiatry/Psychology*; in reference books such as *Data Analysis with Spreadsheets* (Patterson & Basham, 2006); on the Internet at www.uta.edu/sswtech/husita/; and in software review sections of professional journals.

SINGWIN: A Personal Computer Program for the Analysis of Single-System Design Data

We are pleased to include with this book what we think is the most comprehensive program for the analysis of single-system design data. This program is named SINGWIN, and it is a Windows-based program designed by Charles Auerbach, David Schnall, and Heidi Heft Laporte specifically for this book.

SINGWIN computes most of the statistics we discuss, and generates most of the graphs and charts. Furthermore, SINGWIN is a program that we think you'll find very user-friendly and it only will take a small investment of your time to learn. It's menu-driven, and we believe that after a small amount of practice you won't even need the instructions.

All computer programs—no matter how carefully constructed, tested, and explained—pose problems and questions for users. Also, most computer programs grow over time to encompass new features. To address these issues, you can go to the web page for this book: www.pearsonhighered.com/bloom/. There is a button marked "Technical Support." You also can request technical support for SINGWIN by sending email to *singwin@ymail.yu.edu*. Also, the web site contains the most recent updates for SINGWIN available to users who purchased this book.

THE ISSUE OF AUTOCORRELATION

All statistical tests require certain assumptions. The violation of assumptions can result in the detection of a difference between phases when a difference doesn't really exist (Type I error), or the failure to detect a difference when it really does exist (Type II error). Furthermore, when the number of observations is small, as it often is in practice, the consequences of violating many of these assumptions are exacerbated.

One of the most troublesome assumptions underlying many statistical tests as applied to the analysis of single-system designs is the assumption that the observations are independent. *Independence* essentially means that one observation can't be predicted from other observations. For example, if a client's behavior at one time predicts behavior at a later time, the observations would not be independent. Or, if two or more clients shared a common environment or history, for example, a husband and wife or clients hospitalized on the same ward, the observations of the different clients might not be independent.

When observations are not independent they're said to be *dependent*, or correlated. Of particular importance to the analysis of single-system design data is the correlation of temporally adjacent observations within a series of observations made over time. This type of dependency is known as *serial dependency*, and is quantified by a type of correlation known as an *autocorrelation*.

When there are three or more observations in a phase, more than one autocorrelation can be computed. It might be that values for a variable are dependent on the immediately preceding values, the values before that, or the values before that, and so on. The temporal distance between two observations is known as a *lag*, so a lag 1 autocorrelation indicates the extent to which the values of a variable are dependent upon immediately preceding values; a lag 2 autocorrelation indicates the extent to which they're dependent upon values before that (i.e., that are two points away), and so on. Data can be autocorrelated at a particular lag (e.g., lag 2) but not at another lag (e.g., lag 1) and *an autocorrelation of any lag can invalidate tests of statistical significance that assume that the observations are independent*. The total number of possible autocorrelations for a series of observations is the total number of observations minus 1. However, typically the lag 1 autocorrelation is considered the most important, especially when small numbers of observations are involved.

The Debate over Autocorrelation

There's ample reason to believe that autocorrelation can increase Type I or Type II errors (depending on whether observations are positively or negatively correlated and whether they're correlated within or between phases) (Huitema & McKean, 2007). Positive autocorrelation makes it more likely that you'll find a statistically significant difference between phases when there is not a difference (Type I error), and negative autocorrelation makes it less likely that you will find a statistically significant difference between phases when there is a difference (Type II error) (Huitema & McKean, 2007).

There's some debate about the extent to which single-system design data are autocorrelated and how important autocorrelation actually is (Arnau & Bono, 2003; Busk & Marascuilo, 1988; Huitema, 1985, 1988; Matyas & Greenwood, 1991, 1997; Sharpley & Alavosius, 1988; Wampold, 1988). However, a recent study of 166 published *A-B* contrasts found that two-thirds of data sets had an undesirable level of autocorrelation (autocorrelation greater than .20); 24% of those had an undesirable level of negative autocorrelation and 43% had an undesirable level of positive autocorrelation (Parker, 2006). Indeed, one argument is that the issue is not at all whether the autocorrelation is significant, but the effect any autocorrelation has on the use of statistics. Sharpley and Alavosius (1988) have shown that even low levels of autocorrelation—statistically significant or not—can distort the data in traditional statistics, leading to Type I or Type II errors (e.g., an autocorrelation of .5 can inflate traditional statistics like the *t*-test by 173%). Thus, it appears that the presence of autocorrelation in your data really can produce distortion in your ability to understand the statistical significance of your data, and we urge you to consider this point whether or not the autocorrelation you compute is statistically significant.

We believe that the issue is broader and more complex than what the general question—are single-system design data autocorrelated?—implies. Each data set—like each client—is different. We also believe it is safest to err on the side of caution, especially given recent results reported by Parker (2006). Therefore, we present methods for detecting autocorrelation and for transforming autocorrelated data into a form suitable for statistical analyses. In fact, we will make this an issue you can explore for yourself with each set of observations in your cases.

Unfortunately, you can't necessarily see autocorrelation in a set of data (Kratochwill, 1978). Other aspects of time-series data, such as stability, variability, and overlap, are easier to discern through visual inspection. Thus, autocorrelation can complicate visual as well as statistical analysis. Fortunately, there are statistical procedures to detect autocorrelation, and we describe these procedures in the following section.

If there's reason to believe that data are autocorrelated, or that other assumptions are violated, you have a couple of different options. First, sometimes it's possible to use another statistical procedure that relies on less stringent assumptions. We describe different statistical tests. A second option is to transform the data so the required assumptions are met. For example, transformations can be used to remove autocorrelation from a set of observations. We describe several such transformations in the section on "Transforming Data," later in this chapter.

Computational Steps in Testing for Autocorrelation

There has been considerable research conducted by Huitema and his colleagues concerning how best to compute autocorrelation and test it for statistical significance with the relatively small number of observations typically available in single-system designs (Huitema & McKean, 1994a, b, c, 1996, 2007; Huitema, McKean, & Zhao, 1996). Our reading of the recent autocorrelation literature, and consultation with Huitema, leads us to recommend a version of the autocorrelation that Huitema and McKean label r_{F2} (1994a, b), and a test of statistical significance that Huitema and McKean label t_{F2} (1994b).

Let's take a hypothetical example and illustrate how to compute the r_{F2} autocorrelation and test it for statistical significance using t_{F2}. Suppose that you're working with a parent and child to increase the number of daily positive contacts. Eight days of baseline data are collected (see Figure 8). There are two ways to test for autocorrelation. The first is using the SINGWIN computer program. The second is to work out the calculations by hand, as illustrated in Exhibit 1. In this exhibit, the computational steps are identified on the left side of the page and are illustrated with data from our example on the right side of the page. (Note that if all scores within a phase are the same, the data within that phase won't be autocorrelated, and you can move on to the procedures.)

Our example only includes baseline data. Other phases also should be tested for autocorrelation because autocorrelation in any phase can lead to incorrect conclusions. However, autocorrelations should be computed separately for separate phases, because differences between phases can produce misleading estimates of the degree of autocorrelation (Gorsuch, 1983; Huitema, 1985, 1988; Huitema & McKean, 1996). (Also, you should note that when there's a trend in a set of scores—that is, they are systematically increasing or decreasing—the method outlined previously for computing an autocorrelation can produce an inaccurate autocorrelation; Huitema, 1988; Huitema & McKean, 1996.)

If you find that r_{F2} is not significantly different from zero, that is, the data don't appear to be autocorrelated, you could proceed to use the statistics with increased confidence. However, only relatively large autocorrelations are likely to be detected with the relatively small number of observations in most single-system designs (i.e., eight or nine data points per phase, even in published research; Parker & Hagan-Burke, 2007b; Parker & Vannest, in press; Parker, Vannest, &

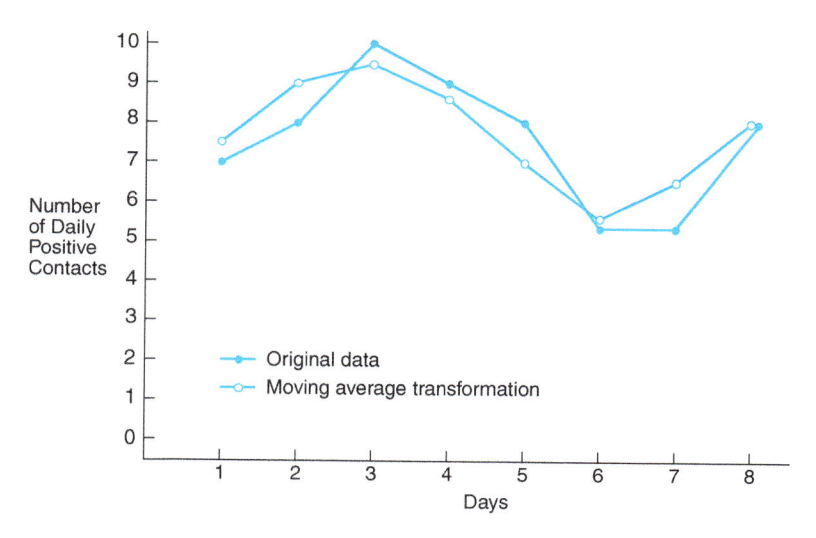

FIGURE 8 Data set for analyzing autocorrelation (Exhibit 19.1) and moving average transformations (Exhibit 3).

Brown, in press), so the failure to detect an autocorrelation may not fully justify the conclusion that the data are not autocorrelated (cf. DeCarlo & Tryon, 1993; Huitema & McKean, 1991; Matyas & Greenwood, 1991; Suen & Ary, 1987). The reason for this is that most statistical tests are not very sensitive with small numbers of observations. Our suggestion is to interpret the autocorrelation test results with caution when the number of observations is very small. In fact, with six or fewer observations, you could treat the data as though they were autocorrelated just to be on the safe side.

What do you do if the data are autocorrelated? First, you could refrain from using tests of statistical significance at all. Thus, you would simply be satisfied with visual inspection of the data and perhaps supplement this visual inspection with some of the descriptive statistics. However, you should be aware of the fact that precisely because of autocorrelation, even your visual analysis will be somewhat suspect, and again, you should interpret these data cautiously (Matyas & Greenwood, 1990). In other words, what looks like a "significant" change may really be just a function of the autocorrelation in the data.

Second, you could use tests of statistical significance that are less problematic when there is autocorrelation. We discuss one such method, the conservative dual-criteria (CDC) approach. Initial research indicates that the CDC approach works relatively well even when there is autocorrelation in the range typically found in single-system design data (i.e., between 0 and .50).

Third, you could go ahead and compute tests of statistical significance that assume the absence of autocorrelation, but use them as rougher guides than you would ordinarily because autocorrelation may have introduced errors in the eventual statistical result.

Fourth, you could try to transform the data to remove the autocorrelation. In a subsequent section we suggest methods of transforming autocorrelated data, although there are more precise, yet complicated, methods for doing this (e.g., Parker, 2006). However, we want to add a word of caution: If you do transform the data, you will be losing many of the original characteristics of those data. This may be necessary in using some analytic procedures, but you have to be careful in interpreting results because your transformation may have affected the basic character of the data.

Finally, there are a couple of things that you can do to minimize or prevent autocorrelation (Todman & Dugard, 2001). First, maximize the interval between measurements. Measurements that are closer together generally are more autocorrelated. Second, make sure that the measures you use are as reliable and valid as possible. Autocorrelation is less likely to occur with reliable and valid measures.

You can compute the autocorrelation and its associated test of statistical significance easily with SINGWIN, and in the next section we describe how to do this. However, if you have an *A-B* design, and fewer than 15 data points total for baseline and intervention, you also can compute autocorrelation with an Excel program.

We also created a set of easy-to-use interactive exercises to help you get a better understanding of autocorrelation.

Computer Procedures in Testing for Autocorrelation

Here's how to use SINGWIN to compute and test an autocorrelation for statistical significance. As you will see, this is a much easier method than hand calculation.

1. Start SINGWIN.

2. Open the "ex19-1.dbf" file (containing the Exhibit 1 data) that comes with SINGWIN (see "Opening the Existing File").

3. Follow the steps outlined in the section entitled "Computing and Testing Autocorrelation."

TOOLS IN ANALYSIS OF DATA

The Transformation of Autocorrelated Data

Transformations of autocorrelated data can reduce or remove this autocorrelation by mathematical means, making it possible to use certain statistical tests and even facilitating visual analysis. There are two general types of transformation that can rather easily be used—the *first differences transformation* and the *moving average transformation* (Gottman & Leiblum, 1974). In deciding what procedure to use, we suggest the following guidelines: (a) if the data appear to have a linear trend, then use the first differences transformation and (b) if the data appear to be fluctuating wildly, then use a moving average transformation—this is also called *smoothing* the data. (Smoothing also can be used if the first differences transformation doesn't succeed in removing the autocorrelation from the data.)

Moving Average Transformation. When the data are widely fluctuating within a phase, you can smooth the data by using the moving average transformation (smoothing). All you're doing here is plotting the means for adjacent pairs of data points. Note that in this example the moving average transformation not only did not remove the autocorrelation, but it actually increased it (the data were not wildly fluctuating in the first place). In such a case, procedures that do not assume that observations are independent, or more sophisticated transformations, may be needed.

First Differences Transformation. The data from an example of a target problem of "satisfying time spent together" are shown in Figure 9 as original data (top line). These data clearly show a linear trend (moving upward). As we noted earlier, special procedures beyond the scope of this book are needed to accurately compute an autocorrelation for data showing a trend, and so it is not even appropriate to compute r_{F2} for these data (r_{F2} = 1.34 in this case, clearly beyond the theoretical upper bound, that is, 1, of the autocorrelation). The steps for transforming these data using a first differences transformation are shown in Exhibit 4. As shown in Figure 9, though, while the first difference transformation appears graphically to be successful in removing this trend (bottom line), the autocorrelation for these transformed data is statistically significant, meaning the data still are autocorrelated ($r_{F2} = -.49$, $t_{F2} = 3.5$, $df[N + 5] = 16$; $p < .05$). Therefore, as suggested in Exhibit 4 on the CD-ROM, another transformation can be attempted (of course, the transformed data in

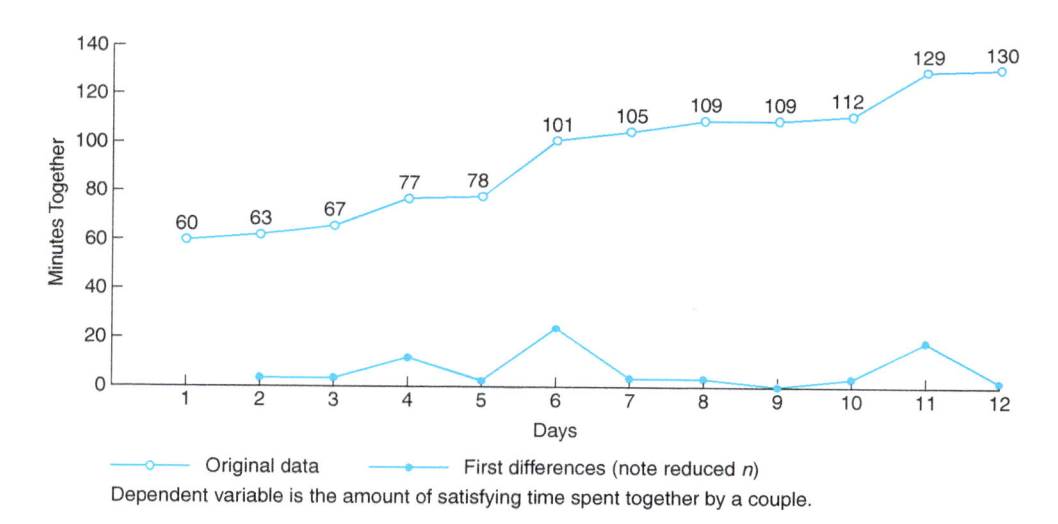

FIGURE 9 Example of first difference transformation with negative numbers.

Basic Principles of Analysis

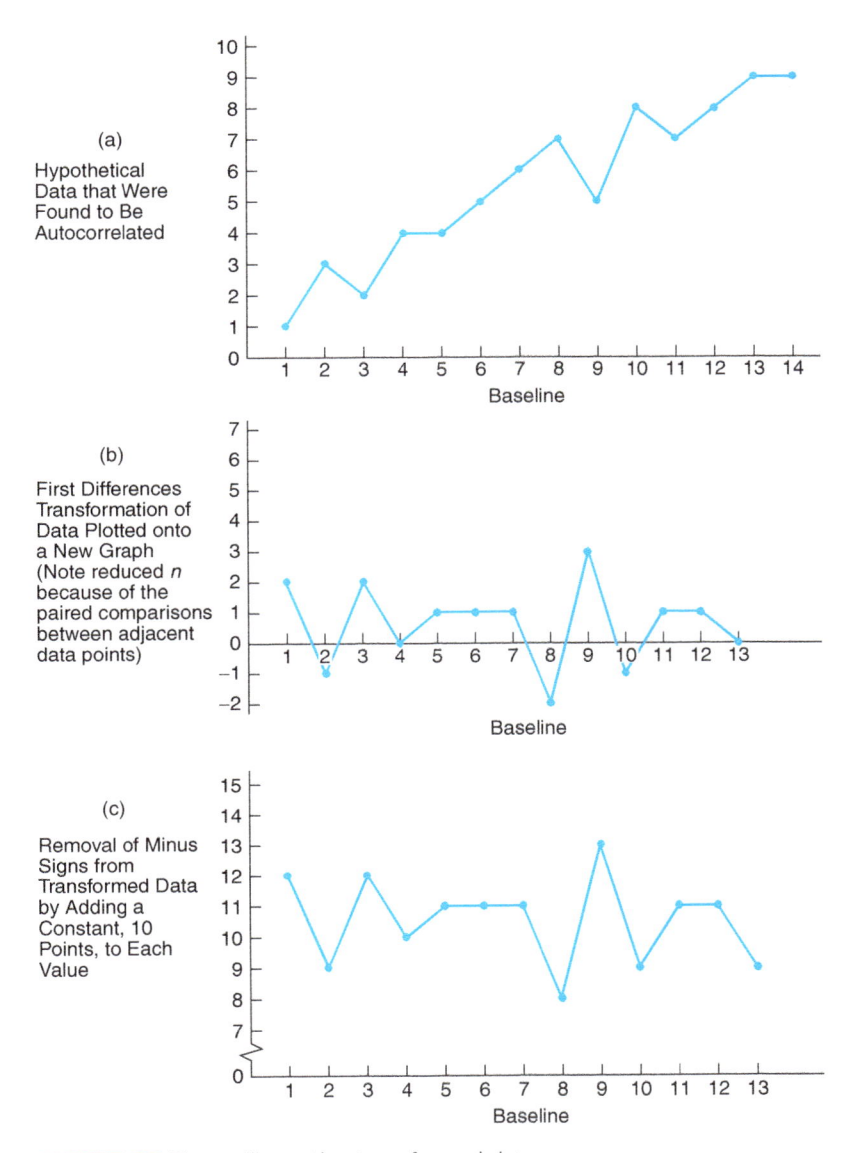

(a) Hypothetical Data that Were Found to Be Autocorrelated

(b) First Differences Transformation of Data Plotted onto a New Graph (Note reduced *n* because of the paired comparisons between adjacent data points)

(c) Removal of Minus Signs from Transformed Data by Adding a Constant, 10 Points, to Each Value

FIGURE 10 Charts illustrating transformed data.

Figure 9 could be used, but with great caution in interpreting them). Figure 10 illustrates the process of transforming data into a usable form.

Computing and Graphing Transformed Data with SINGWIN

Here's how to use SINGWIN to transform data using the moving average or first difference transformation and how to graph and compute statistics based on the transformed data.

1. Start SINGWIN.

2. Open the "ex-19-1.dbf" (containing the Exhibit 1 data) or "fig19-9.dbf" (containing the Figure 9 data) file that comes with SINGWIN (see "Opening an Existing File").

3. Read the section entitled "Creating a Line Chart" to make sure that you know how to create a basic line chart of untransformed data.

4. Follow the steps outlined in the section entitled "Creating Charts of Transformed Data" to get line charts of moving average or first difference transformed data.

5. Follow the steps outlined in the section entitled "Computing Transformations" to transform and save data using either the "*moving average*" or "*first difference transformation,*" and to then manipulate these transformed data in various ways (e.g., compute and test autocorrelation or other statistics, create graphs).

Probability Tables for Use in Single-System Designs

Probability tables summarize a large number of mathematical operations, each of which tells us how likely it is that some set of events occurred given certain conditions. These conditions are built into the structure of the tables and involve the proportion of specified events during the baseline and the number (or frequency) of observations made during intervention.

When we use probability tables (Bloom, 1975) to aid our analysis of single-system design data, we use some simple but powerful tools to determine whether a set of outcome events could have happened by chance alone, given the nature of the baseline events. As far as you are concerned, most of the statistical work has been done. They will be used in conjunction with the proportion/frequency approach. They also can be used as part of the Probability Method for determining generalizability of single-system designs.

Computing Probabilities with SINGWIN

You can compute binomial probabilities easily with SINGWIN, and following we describe how to do this.

We also created a set of easy-to-use interactive exercises to help you get a better understanding of these probabilities.

Here's how to use SINGWIN to compute probabilities with ease.

1. Start SINGWIN.

2. Follow the steps outlined in the section entitled "Computing a Proportion/Frequency Approach," and enter the following: # Baseline Points = 12; # Baseline Successes = 2; # of Intervention Points = 12; # of Intervention Successes = 5.

Summary

In this chapter we've presented some distinctions that are important in the analysis of data. We've explained effort (the amount of work performed), effectiveness (the results of the work), and efficiency (the comparison of results and efforts expended). These terms can help you understand that accountability is not simply a matter of raising effectiveness levels; accountability must also exhibit an optimal ratio of effort expended for the effectiveness obtained.

We also discussed practical, statistical, and theoretical significance. The first refers to social and personal criteria of acceptable behaviors in various social settings, the second relates to mathematical rules, and the third involves theoretical expectations. Sometimes they coincide, but not necessarily; they are independent concepts of equal importance for evaluation-informed practice. However, we want you to understand the implications of the several combinations of significance that we discussed early in this chapter.

We presented guidelines for determining the number of observations in a phase and for determining when to change an intervention. We also discussed the use of follow-ups in single-system designs, suggesting that follow-ups be used to obtain vital information on the lasting quality of your services.

We introduced the issue of autocorrelation, noting that it can be a very serious problem for rigorous evaluation. We showed how to test for the presence of autocorrelated data, and we discussed what to do about it. The latter included a presentation on how to transform autocorrelated data into data that are usable by the several analytic techniques. We also showed how to test for autocorrelation and how to transform autocorrelated data using an easy-to-use personal computer program, SINGWIN, which comes with this book. Finally, we presented a discussion of probability tables that can be used with some analytic procedures and we showed how SINGWIN could be used in place of these tables if you prefer.

VISUAL ANALYSIS OF SINGLE-SYSTEM DESIGN DATA

PURPOSE This chapter describes the most basic method of analyzing data from single-system designs: visual inspection of patterns in the data. After presenting some definitions of visual patterns, we'll describe the major patterns and their implications for evaluation, as well as the limitations of visual inspection.

Introduction
Definition of Terms
Basic Patterns and Implications
    Interpreting Several Patterns Simultaneously
Visual Inspection of Raw Data
Interpreting Ambiguous Patterns
    Guidelines for Interpretation of Ambiguous Patterns

Problems of Visual Inspection
Creating a Chart with SINGWIN
Summary

From Chapter 20 of *Evaluating Practice: Guidelines for the Accountable Professional*, Sixth Edition. Martin Bloom, Joel Fischer, John G. Orme. Copyright © 2009 by Pearson Education, Inc. All rights reserved.

INTRODUCTION

This chapter discusses the visual analysis of single-system design data—simply looking at the data and finding discontinuities and other patterns that aid in the interpretation of the results. This method is notably flexible and easy to use, and it draws its major strength from the pictorial nature of the data and the practical considerations related to them. For example, suppose that an AIDS patient took less than 10% of his daily requirement of the drug AZT before intervention during a baseline period, and then 100% during implementation of an intervention designed to increase compliance. The graphed results would provide strong visual evidence for improvement in compliance with the AZT regimen. Such "commonsense" analysis also could be treated mathematically, and very likely these results would indicate a statistically significant difference between baseline and intervention phases. But if the results are so obvious from visual inspection, why go further? As we'll see, there are circumstances that lead to problems with visual analysis, and under these circumstances, the statistical approaches can prove useful. However, a careful visual inspection of the data should be a starting point for all of the other methods of analysis discussed in Part IV because visual analysis is holistic and the breadth of patterns it can detect is not equaled by any statistical methods (Parker & Hagan-Burke, 2007a).

DEFINITION OF TERMS

There are several properties of data appearing in charts (or graphs; we use these terms interchangeably) that require careful definition. Although the ideas are simple, many terms have been used (sometimes in conflicting ways) to describe them. Let's begin by looking at a graph that presents data as simply as possible. Figure 1 shows a set of data as if they fell along straight lines. Of course, sometimes data do, in fact, appear along a straight line, but most of the time in real practice, the data will vary. To view the data in a simple form, we draw a horizontal line through a set of data that best represents their average magnitude; we call this the mean line. The mean is computed by adding all of the values, and dividing this total by the number of data points.

A first property of data can be seen in the mean line in the baseline period of Figure 1a. The first property of graphed data to be considered is *level*, which refers to the magnitude of the variable as indicated by the data at any point. When the data are increasing or decreasing, as in Figure 1b during the intervention period, the final magnitude or level is determined at the point at which the intervention ends. (However, one could examine the magnitude of the data at any point in the baseline or intervention phase to determine the level of the data at that point.) A *change in level* between the baseline and the intervention phase is called a *discontinuity*. A major discontinuity (major change in level between baseline and intervention phases) is an important indicator of change in the target, and is consistent with the hypothesis that the intervention may have produced that change, although other alternative explanations are possible. These differences in levels are indicated in Figure 11a and b by arrows.

A second property of graphed data concerns *stability*, defined as clear predictability from a prior period to a later one (note, however, that the literature

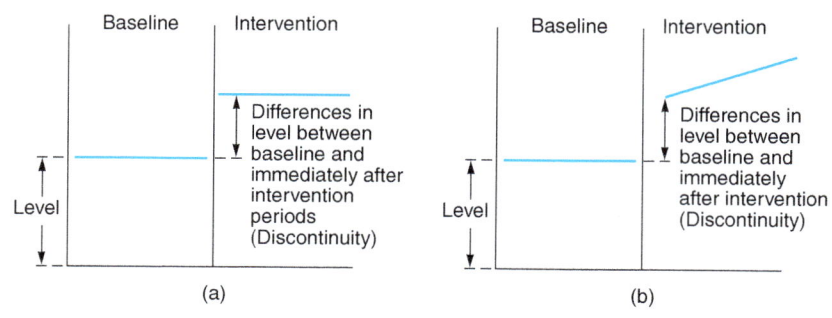

FIGURE 1 Illustration of levels of data and differences between levels in baseline and intervention periods.

Visual Analysis of Single-System Design Data

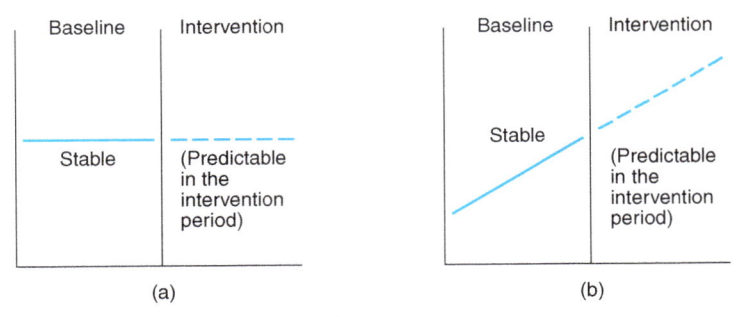

FIGURE 2 Illustrations of stability of data between baseline and intervention periods.

often refers to stable data only as flat data). Figure 2 provides some illustrations of this view of stability in data. Figure 2a shows a mean line that is projected (by a dashed line) into the intervention period. Figure 2b shows a trend line; even though it's increasing in magnitude, it's still predictable. If the baseline data cannot be represented adequately by a line, for example, if baseline data are highly irregular, then the baseline is not stable, because no clear prediction can be made as to the direction that intervention data will take.

A third property of graphed data concerns *trends* in the data, that is, *directionality* of the data. Data may show an increasing trend, a decreasing trend, no trend (flat data), or a pattern that varies irregularly. Furthermore, trends can occur both *within* a phase (sometimes called *slope*) or *across* phases (sometimes called *drift*). Figure 3 illustrates different patterns of trends. Note that for a trend across phases to exist, the slope within each phase must be in the same direction, as in Figure 3d, whether or not the angle of the slope is the same.

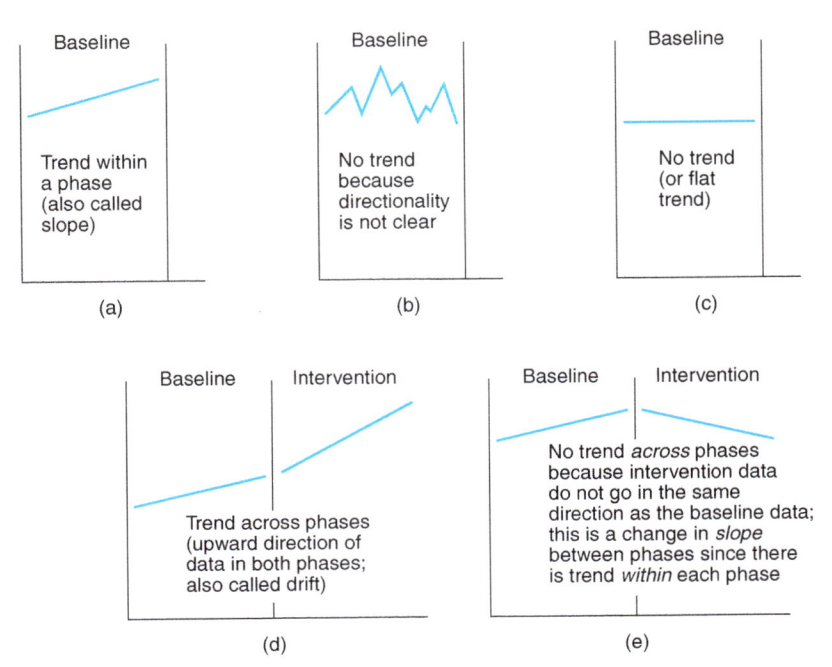

FIGURE 3 Illustrations of trends within a phase (slope) and across phases (drift).

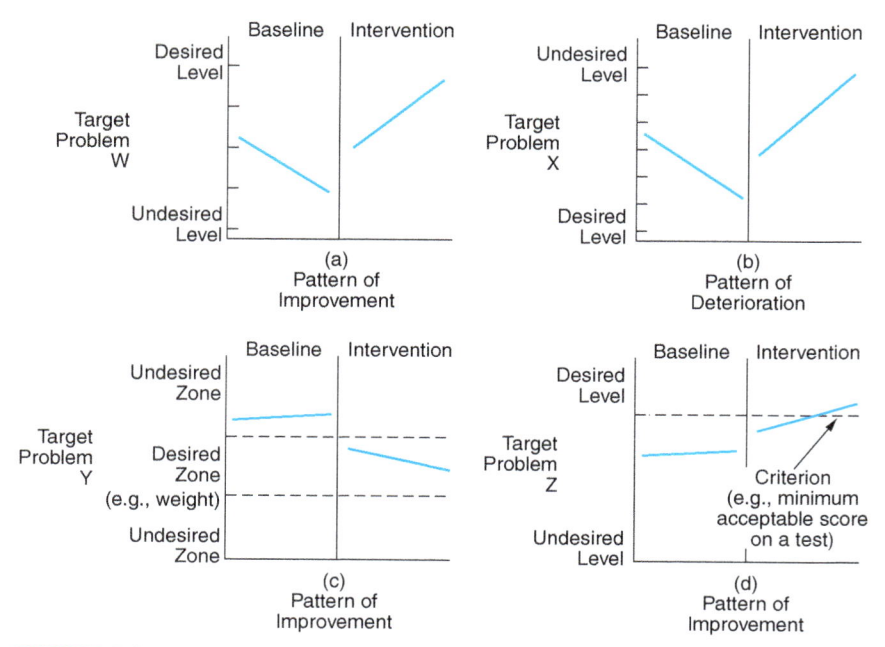

FIGURE 4 Illustrations of patterns of improvements and of deterioration, depending on defined levels or zones of desired events.

A fourth property of graphed data concerns whether there's *improvement, deterioration,* or *no change* from one phase to the next. Depending on how the target problem is defined, for example, if more of the target is desirable or if less of the target is desirable, trend and level combine to indicate improvement or deterioration. Figure 4 illustrates this property.

Figures 4a and b show exactly the same pattern of data, but the definition of desired and undesired levels of behavior are reversed, producing the overall pattern of improvement and deterioration, respectively. Figure 4c shows a situation in which some middle zone is desired, such as a client trying to maintain a desired weight level; again, the definition of improvement depends on the definition of target events. Figure 4d illustrates yet another variation in which some minimum level of acceptable performance is defined, such as in weight requirements for making a wrestling team. The direction of data in itself doesn't define improvement or deterioration; it's the nature of the target that generates these labels. This is where client and societal values are directly related to the evaluation of practice outcomes.

BASIC PATTERNS AND IMPLICATIONS

Now we can construct a figure that shows basic, but simplified, patterns in single-system design data from which change—improvement or deterioration—can be inferred. Figure 5 presents nine basic patterns, each with three subtypes (X, Y, and Z)—27 patterns in all—that will illustrate the large bulk of data patterns that you are likely to encounter. All of the data are simplified as straight-line data in order to clarify the patterns and their implications. The top three patterns assume that the baseline data are flat and at a midlevel of magnitude. (Obviously, other levels could be used, but the same patterns would be present.) The middle three patterns involve an increasing baseline, while the bottom three patterns show a decreasing baseline.

In a like manner, we've assumed that intervention periods show data that are either increasing (X), staying the same (Y), or decreasing (Z). In this way we can economically present 27 combinations of baseline and intervention patterns. More important, we can suggest the predominant interpretation of each of the various patterns of data. Figure 5 has been constructed by

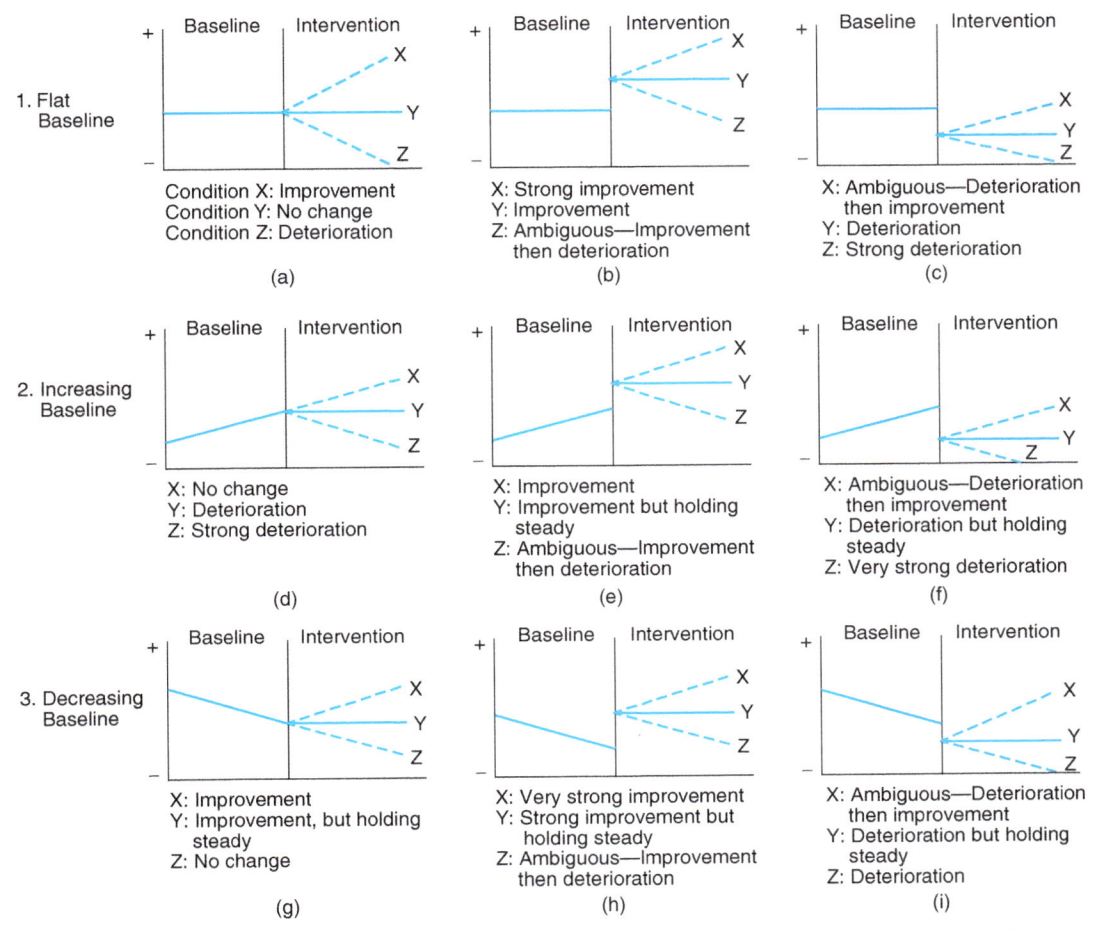

FIGURE 5 Basic patterns in data from simplified single-system designs. (This figure assumes the desired level or zone is up as indicated by +.)

varying level, discontinuities (changes in level between phases), trends within a phase (slope), and trends across phases (drift). In order to emphasize whether one, two, or three changes are occurring, we indicate the interpretation by corresponding degrees—for example, "improvement," "strong improvement," or "very strong improvement." Note also that we've arbitrarily designated (by pluses and minuses on the vertical axis) "up" as improvement and "down" as deterioration.

Figures 5a, b, and c begin with a flat baseline, and then, depending on whether there's a change in level and a change in the trend between phases, they indicate degrees of improvement or deterioration. Also noted are some ambiguous situations in which, after an initial improvement (based on a change in level), the data begin to show deterioration (see Figure 5b, condition Z); in the same manner, after an initial deterioration in the target the data begin to change in the direction of improvement (as in Figure 5c, condition X), which is another ambiguous situation. In ambiguous situations we suggest you continue the intervention phase (when conditions are improving), if possible, to see whether a clear trend develops. However, when an initial improvement shows signs of deteriorating, you should act before the deterioration gets out of hand. This could involve changing the intervention or increasing the intensity of the current intervention.

Figures 5d, e, and f begin with an increasing slope during baseline. Assuming that the high end of the vertical axis represents a desired level of events,

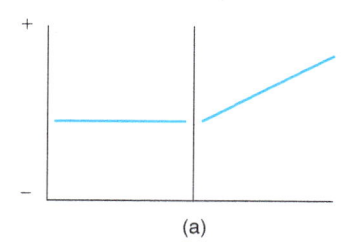

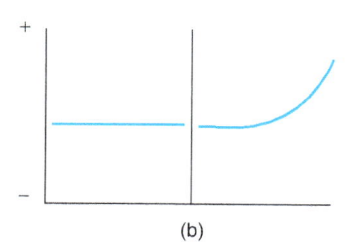

FIGURE 6 Illustrations of immediate (a) and delayed (b) effects of intervention.

then changes that take place between baseline and intervention must include consideration of the trend as well as the level. The condition Y in these three patterns is a flat line and represents an improvement or deterioration (depending on baseline conditions) that is holding steady. That is, after the initial change from baseline to intervention, there's no slope. For some conditions, such as in work with a terminally ill person, "holding one's own" (a flat line) may be a major accomplishment. However, in other cases there's an element of ambiguity in this steady state that may require you to reconsider whether the intervention is powerful enough at this time.

In Figure 5d, condition X, there's an interesting point to be made: Even though there's a trend that continues in a desired direction from the baseline and through the intervention period (drift), the general pattern is one of no change, since that same increasing pattern was present during the baseline period. It's only when, in addition to the drift, there's a change in level or in the *angle* of the slope (clearly increasing or decreasing in the intervention period), that such a pattern becomes an improvement or deterioration, depending on baseline circumstances.

In the last set of three patterns, Figures 5g, h, and i, the baseline exhibits a decreasing or worsening trend. Thus, any change toward improvement or holding steady may qualify as a desired change if the level also holds steady or improves. Very strong improvement is possible under the terms described in Figure 5h, condition X, just as very strong deterioration is possible in Figure 5f, condition Z. Both of these patterns involve changes in level and slope.

There are many other aspects of graphs that could be used as aids in interpretation, but if we were to illustrate every one, we would need to present hundreds of patterns, and that would defeat the purpose of this chapter. However, we'll mention some other variations in data that may have an impact on interpretation.

First, consider the starting level of the baseline data. Under certain conditions, such as when using a depression scale, a very high starting score limits the amount of upward change. In this case an upward change would be a negative change or signify deterioration because the higher the score, the more depressed the person could be said to be.

On the other hand, consider the timing of the changes in intervention. Either the target events change immediately after the intervention, or they change gradually after some delay, as illustrated in Figure 6. There may be a period of time during which the client is trained to perform the intervention, such as training in free association or in thought stopping. Little change would be expected during the training part of intervention; however, you may be counting this time in evaluating the intervention. Our advice is to continue monitoring the intervention after the training, or to make the training phase separate.

Another pattern of data that sometimes may be important concerns the stability of the observed change. For example, there may be an initial impact, perhaps due to the novelty of the intervention (the "honeymoon" period), but once the intervention becomes routine, the impact returns to the original level, as illustrated in Figure 7. Stopping the intervention too soon would have missed this important

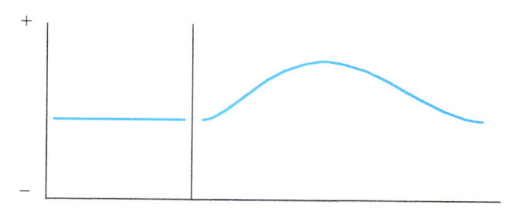

FIGURE 7 Illustration of an unstable data change.

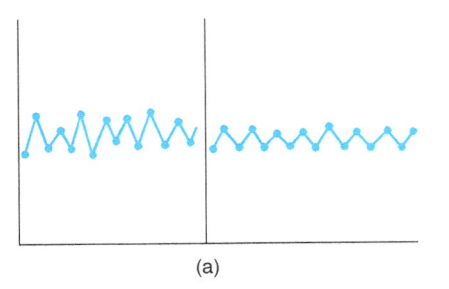

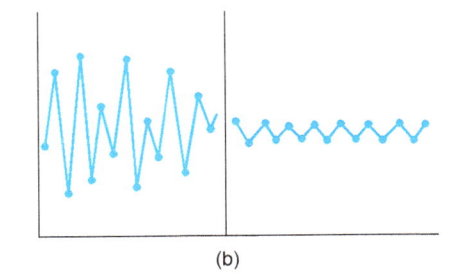

FIGURE 8 Illustrations of variability in data.

point. You would be wise to take action soon after an initially successful intervention begins to deteriorate. This situation might call for another intervention or a stronger intensity of the first intervention.

By using averages portrayed as mean or trend lines in baseline and intervention, we hide another obvious characteristic of graphs that should be considered—*variability* in data. In baselines, stability usually refers to data falling within a relatively narrow, predictable range. The more variability in baseline data, as illustrated in Figure 8b, the more caution you must use in interpreting changes during intervention. More control was exhibited over the target problem in Figure 8b than in Figure 8a relative to the starting conditions at their baselines, but it's clear that the baseline in Figure 8b was less stable.

The degree of overlap between phases is another important consideration in comparing the pattern of data in one phase to the pattern in adjacent phases (Cooper, Heron, & Heward, 2007; Kennedy, 2005; Thyer & Myers, 2007). Overlap is the degree to which data in adjacent phases share similar quantitative values (Kennedy, 2005). For example, consider Figures 9a, b, and c. There is no overlap between phases in Figure 9a, very little overlap in Figure 9b, and almost total overlap in Figure 9c. So, Figure 9a illustrates a slightly larger difference between phases than Figure 9b, and Figures 9a and b indicate a much larger difference between phases as compared to data illustrated in Figure 9c. The less overlap, the greater the difference between phases and the degree of overlap can be quantified to measure the magnitude of the difference more precisely (Parker & Hagan-Burke, 2007a, b; Parker & Vannest, in press; Parker, Vannest, & Brown, in press).

A final pattern of data that might emerge is a *cycle*. Identification of such cycles can provide clues concerning the origins of problems, which might in turn suggest interventions. For example, there might be changes in a target associated with a particular day of the week (e.g., "blue Mondays," caused by starting the work week), time of the month (e.g., shortage of money and resulting tensions prior to receiving monthly checks), or time of the year (e.g., seasonal affective disorders). Similarly, there might be changes in a target associated with holidays or personal anniversaries. Therefore, in addition to labeling time periods with sequential numbers, it also can be useful to label them with days of the week and dates.

To help you practice and learn how to visually analyze single-system design data we created an exercise with Microsoft Excel. Visual analysis takes practice, and we strongly encourage you to work through this exercise (we know it is a little challenging but we hope it also will be fun).

Interpreting Several Patterns Simultaneously

There are many times when you may be called upon to interpret the patterns of more than one graph at the same time. Just think about any multiple-target design as only one example. We would like to offer some introductory ideas on this topic.

There are three general patterns of simultaneous graphing that can be used to make overall sense of changes in the several targets you are addressing:

1. *Alignments* exist when all of the graphs that are being considered together have essentially the same pattern of improvement, no change, or deterioration. Obviously, we are interested in improvement, but simultaneous patterns of no change or deterioration also inform you as to

Visual Analysis of Single-System Design Data

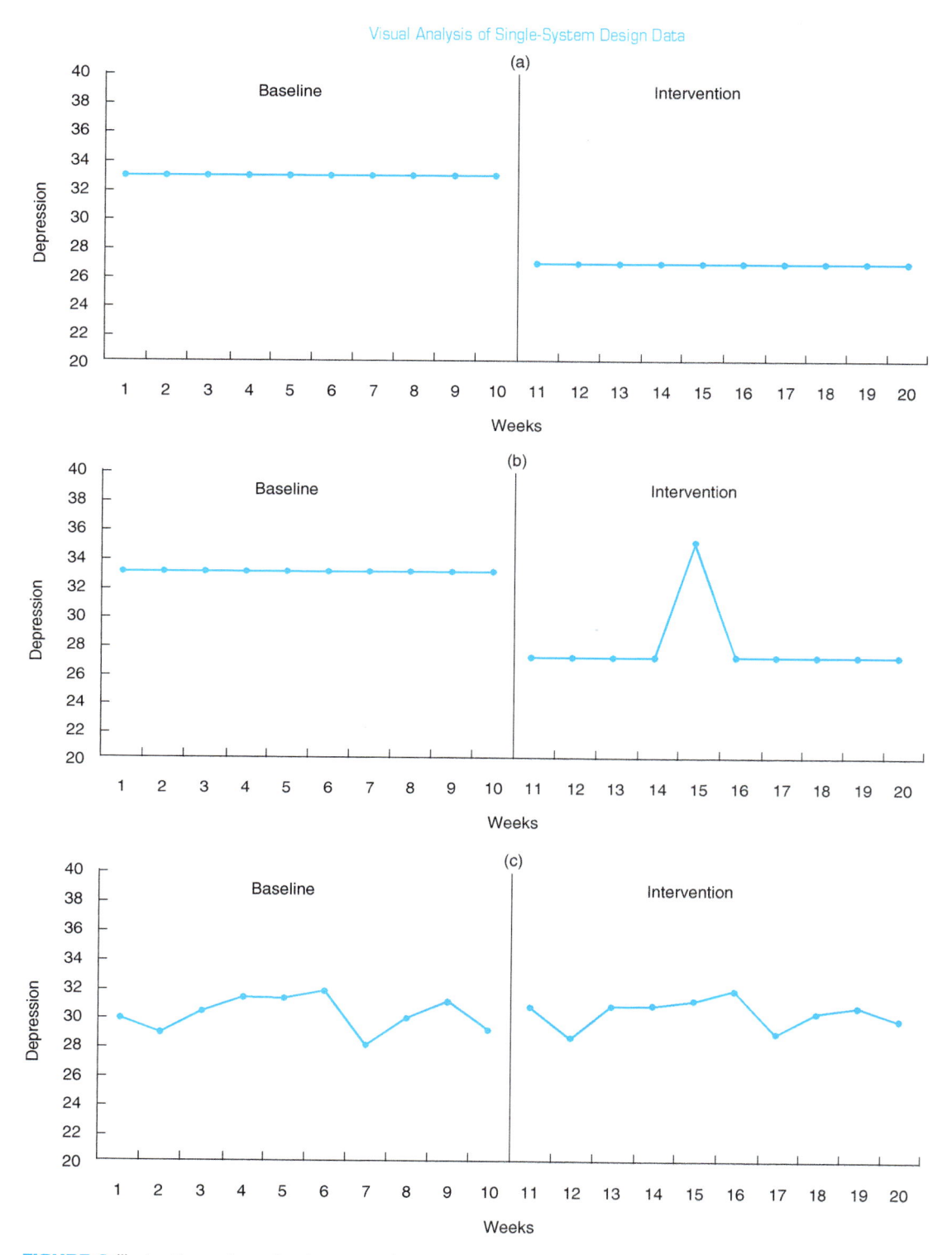

FIGURE 9 Illustrations of overlap between phases.

needed changes in intervention, as we shall see. We suggest this notation: + + +, 0 0 0, and − − − to indicate such alignment among three graphs for a single client/system, where the pluses indicate improvement, the zeroes no change, and the minuses deterioration.

2. *Dominance* exists when a majority of the graphs being considered together show a common pattern, either of improvement, no change, or deterioration. These would be represented as + + 0, + + −, 0 0 +, 0 0 −, − − +, − − 0. (When four or even numbers of graphs are used, this principle can be adapted in terms of the importance of the respective targets, as discussed later.)

3. *Disagreement* would exist when no pattern among graphs appears. These would be represented as + 0 −. (Again, adaptation to this principle has to be made for even numbers of graphs.)

Ordinarily, we seek alignment in improvements among however many graphs are being monitored simultaneously. However, there are exceptions, such as being content with the most optimal expected pattern of no change in a terminally ill patient, or a steady state of positive functioning on targets we are tracking but don't want to change. (The latter would constitute a check for "symptom substitution" phenomena; improvement in the target followed by new problems "popping up".)

When we get a pattern of dominance, we have to introduce another element into this discussion, the relative *importance* of each target. If one target is of overwhelming importance, then this weighting may be more crucial than alignment or dominance on other targets. This is a more or less subjective weighting and should be made before considering the patterns of relationship among graphs. When two out of three are important, and the third less so, then there is still a dominant trend. When the three are such that two targets are still of less importance than the strong third target, then we have in effect a pattern of disagreement.

Another consideration is the internal pattern. The +, 0, and − patterns permit us to distinguish findings that are "one step" or "two steps" discrepant. The pattern + + 0 shows two positives and one neutral result, one step apart, while the pattern + + − shows two positives and one negative result, two steps apart in the sense of the meaning of the results. (To clarify "two steps apart," visualize + as 3, 0 as 2, and − as 1. Therefore, + + − can be seen as two steps apart.) The two-step pattern + + − suggests that the negative graph may not be conceptually or practically related to events in the two positive graphs, and the entire service plan should be reconsidered. In general, any two-step discrepancy suggests reconsideration of the overall plan.

When these one- or two-step arrangements are combined with weightings, we suggest that the important successful graphs become the central focus of revised practice plans, and new targets or interventions be considered. The successful graphs become a known entity, and new service ideas can be introduced (new targets and methods) with reference to building on this success, expanding it into new aspects of the client situation.

To illustrate these simultaneous patterns, let's reconsider Figure 5. Look at the middle column of graphs, b, e, and h. The three Xs on these graphs each show improvement over baseline, and would be indicated as + + + for this discussion of simultaneous analysis of data. Likewise, the three Ys show improvement, while the Zs end in a deteriorating pattern as compared with baseline. Thus, the Zs would be indicated as − − −.

Next, consider the left column graphs, a, d, and g, with reference to the X, Y, and Z patterns. (a) X, (d) Y, and (g) Z show positive change, deterioration, and no change. If these three graphs represented one client's situation, it would indicate disagreement, and would suggest the need for reconsideration of the service plan (possibly using the one successful graph as the anchoring point for building a new approach to intervention).

In general, to identify and comprehend the configuration of outcomes on multiple targets, you must reduce each graph to its simplest pattern (such as those indicated by straight lines on Figure 5). If there are major differences in the importance or weighting of each target, include this in how you think about patterns of results. Assuming relatively equally important targets, then use the notation for alignment, dominance, or disagreement, and make the next service plans accordingly.

Another way of thinking about analyzing the results of several graphs simultaneously is to simplify several patterns by combining them. In some areas of evaluation, this, in a sense, is already done for you. For example, a standardized scale usually combines items that tap into a common domain. These items are analyzed as being statistically related to each other to justify being put into a single scale. In a similar way, we have suggested choosing targets from one client/system representing important domains of that system. Each target that is graphed may be interpreted in its own right. But we have stressed that it is the *combination* of targets that represents the whole client/system. There are no standard ways to form these combinations of targets. Some designs, such as the multiple-baseline design, make the decision for you in showing interrelationships. But when multiple targets are used, we are left with the dilemma of how to put all of the information we gather together: Overall, how well is this client/system progressing?

One way to combine targeted materials is simply to add them together, as in the following student case situation. A 7-year-old child was having serious problems at home with his mother and stepfather. He refused to do chores or be cooperative in any way. At school, he also was not completing assigned tasks, and he was throwing tantrums at the slightest provocation. The practitioner developed interventions with these various targeted behaviors, and chose to use a 5-point IRS with each. In order to provide feedback for the child (and parents), the student used individual charts but presented the family with a composite chart—the simple sum of the individual charts. There was some progress on two of the three graphs, but less on the third. But the simple additive graph showed overall success, and served to encourage the child to gain control over his behavior. The practitioner thought that this simplified chart succeeded in conveying important information to the clients that discussions of specific, individual charts could not do.

VISUAL INSPECTION OF RAW DATA

The eye tends to complete visual gestalts. That is, there's a tendency to find patterns among objects appearing in the same visual space. For example, the headlights, grill, and bumper on some cars appear to be smiling faces, and moving clouds appear to take the shape of animals.

Batches of data points on evaluation charts also often appear to be taking a particular direction, such as upward or steady. In the preceding discussion we simplified the set of data points into straight lines, some horizontal, and others with upward or downward trends. When we introduced data in Figure 8, their variability made them somewhat harder to interpret, especially if we hadn't drawn lines between adjacent points. Even so, it's sometimes difficult to find the dominant direction of a set of data points.

For example, in Figure 10, both graphs have the same mean line (indicated by the horizontal dashed lines) but differences in variability. In order to convey this difference in variability, often it's better to draw and connect the actual data points instead of drawing straight lines to indicate means or trends.

When there is an increasing or decreasing trend in the data, a mean (horizontal) line will be misleading, as illustrated in Figure 11a. Rather, what is needed is a line that follows the general trend of the data themselves, as illustrated in Figure 11b.

Another way in which sets of data are viewed is by looking for typical patterns. For example, in Figure 12 a set of data has been collected during one period of time, and although these data are quite variable, they still represent the levels of behavior that the client can exhibit. Therefore, we can ask: What is typical about this set of events? "Typical" events can be defined in different ways. For example, one way would be as data varying within some set distance around the mean. Because one standard

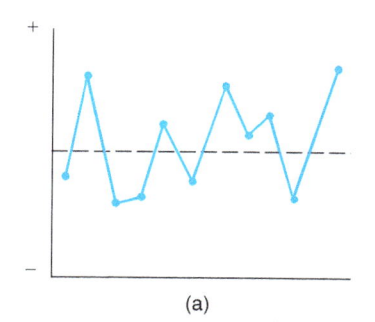

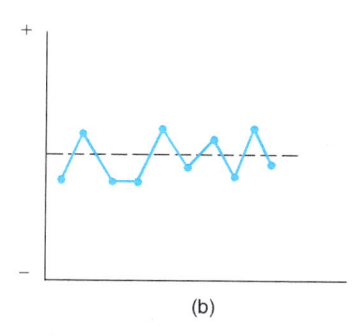

FIGURE 10 Illustrations of mean lines drawn on baseline data that differ in variability.

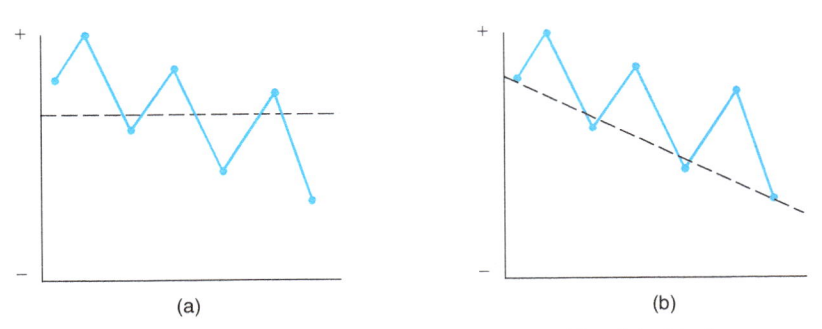

FIGURE 11 Illustrations of a mean line (a) and a trend line (b) with the same target event data.

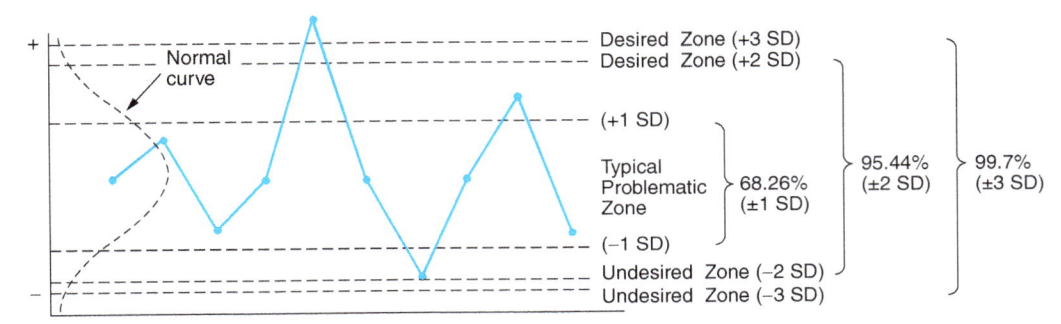

FIGURE 12 Illustration of data points in which the "typical" pattern has been indicated by the pair of dashed lines representing an approximation of a zone one standard deviation above and below the mean of these data. A normal curve is indicated by a dotted curve to show the "typical" or middle zone where about two-thirds of the data are likely to fall (i.e., ± 1 SD). The external dashed lines equal a rarer situation, ± 3 SD (99.7% of the data), representing the rarest desired and undesired zones.

deviation above and below the mean in a normal curve contains about two-thirds of all the data falling under that curve, we could define as typical an area in which two-thirds of the data points fall, and then areas above and below that line as either desired or undesired, depending on the nature of the target. This approach is used with the proportion/frequency statistic. Or, to be even more rigorous, we could establish a broader zone, say plus or minus three standard deviations, which would encompass some 99.7% of all scores. Scores outside of that zone, then, could be seen as (extremely) desired or extremely undesired (as with the 3-standard-deviation-band approach). The important point about typical events is that you would expect them to continue in their typical pattern over time unless something intervenes to change them, such as an intervention program.

INTERPRETING AMBIGUOUS PATTERNS

If only the world of visual analysis of patterns presented in Figure 5 were as clear as we have depicted it. In that figure, we illustrated 27 different patterns of data, most of which can result in relatively clear conclusions about changes between baseline and intervention periods.

But, as with our presentation of basic designs in Part III, these patterns essentially are ideal types, presented to show you optimally clear and basic patterns to help you understand key characteristics of single-system design data.

But what is intended as optimally clear and basic for a textbook does not necessarily always reflect real-life practice. In fact, if you look closely at Figure 5, you will see several patterns that we have called *ambiguous*. It is an unfortunate, but frequently true, aspect of practice that the data patterns produced in real-life single-system evaluations often are ambiguous, and the resulting implications from such a visual analysis are often unclear (Brossart, Parker, Olson, & Mahadevan, 2006; Colon, 2006; Fisher, Kelley, & Lomas, 2003; Rubin & Knox, 1996; Stewart, Carr, Brandt & McHenry, 2007).

This all-too-common result of ambiguous patterns is one of the reasons we recommend supplementing your visual analysis with statistical analysis. Ambiguous and/or wildly fluctuating patterns of data can be transformed, if need be, so that underlying patterns can be more clearly revealed. Moreover, even when the patterns are not wildly fluctuating so that transformations are not necessary, the use of the statistics we recommend can provide clear guidelines for making decisions in a number of ways, from when to change interventions to evaluations of overall effectiveness. But the use of statistics to some extent still does not directly address the issue of finding the best use and interpretation of an ambiguous data pattern.

Figure 13 presents several ambiguous patterns, building on those presented in Figure 5. In Figure 13a, we see a wildly fluctuating baseline leading to a problem in understanding the meaning and consistency of the targeted event, as well as in knowing when to stop the baseline and move to the intervention period.

Figure 13b illustrates the ambiguous pattern of apparent initial improvement followed by deterioration, leading to the problem of trying to recapture that initial improvement while not wanting to terminate while the target event is deteriorating. The opposite problem is illustrated in Figure 13c, deterioration then improvement, leaving the practitioner to wonder whether the improvement is temporary or a possible result of concomitant variation with factors other than the intervention.

Figure 13d and e show multiple variations in the intervention phase leading to ambiguous patterns. In Figure 13d, there is a pattern of improvement then deterioration then improvement, while Figure 13e shows the reverse pattern, deterioration then improvement then deterioration. Both sets of patterns leave the practitioner wondering whether a termination date is possible, whether changes are only temporary, and how to assess the real meaning of the changes.

Finally, an all-too-common pattern in real practice is the one portrayed in Figure 13f, wildly fluctuating data in the intervention period, to the point that the practitioner cannot make an informed judgment one way or another.

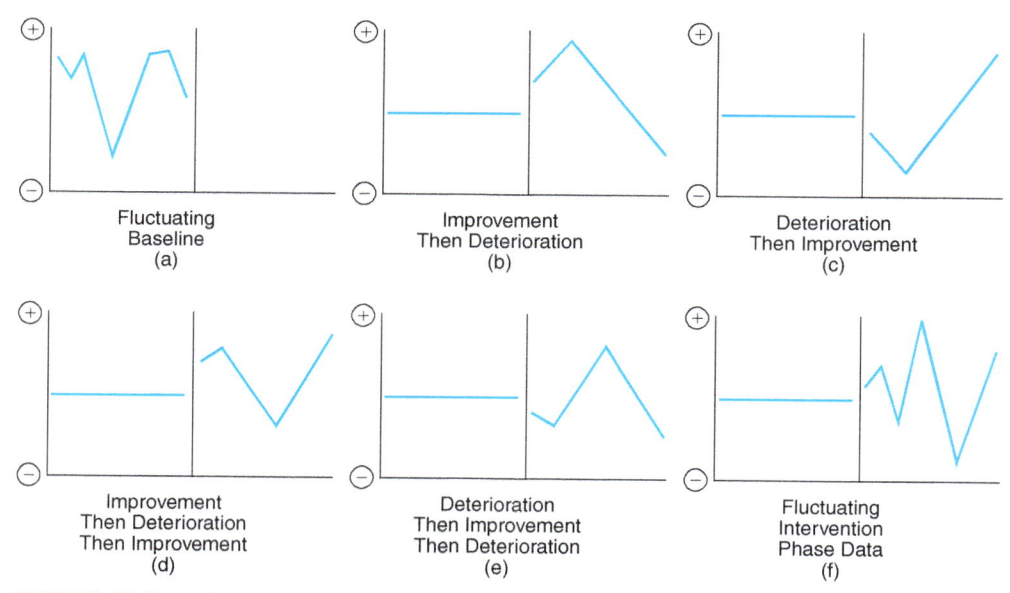

FIGURE 13 Examples of ambiguous data patterns.

Guidelines for Interpretation of Ambiguous Patterns

In many places, we've mentioned the fact that some of the procedures associated with single-system design evaluations are approximate, that is, the best we can do under the complicated circumstances of practice, but often less than perfection. There are few situations of single-system design evaluation, though, where the term "approximate" rings more true than when the data pattern and, hence, the visual analysis, is ambiguous. So, our first, admittedly less than satisfactory, guideline for dealing with an ambiguous pattern is this: Do the best you can. We've discussed this principle of utility elsewhere in the book; in this context, we mean that you can try to understand even small patterns—or trends—in the data; consider concomitant variation or events in the life of the client or client/system outside of the intervention as possible explanations for ambiguous patterns; and attempt to piece together all the evidence as systematically as possible.

Utility also implies added discussions with the client(s) about what the data mean and working together on what seems to be working and what doesn't. The client may have ideas about what is going on that may clarify ambiguous results. Indeed, variability might be due to inconsistencies in service or inconsistencies in how a client completes homework assignments. This effort to enhance communication will give the client a closer connection to, and sense of control over, the entire intervention process; this also is good practice for self-maintenance later.

Second, when the pattern is ambiguous and the potential decision you have to make on the basis of those data is particularly crucial, you might want to consider extending the phase with the ambiguous pattern to achieve more stable results with regard to unstable baselines. Of course, we recognize that some practice situations don't allow an extension of time, but other situations may permit a trade-off between the time available and the need to have a clearer pattern of results.

Third, with a consistently ambiguous data pattern, you might want to consider changing your intervention to see whether that change will produce a clearer, and, one hopes, positive, pattern.

Fourth, when ambiguous patterns are present, we suggest you pay even more attention than you might otherwise to issues of practical significance. In this context, consultations with the client and relevant others can help you make a decision that may cut through the ambiguous pattern to get at the heart of the matter: Are the changes meaningful to the people affected?

Fifth, as we discussed, we urge you to use more than one measure. Ambiguous patterns on the charted measure suggests a perfect reason for use of more than one measure: The additional measure(s) may reveal a pattern of changes that is clearer than the one you charted. Thus, a synthesis of results from several measures may produce a clearer pattern and allow greater confidence in your decision to continue with the same intervention, to change intervention, or to begin termination procedures.

Sixth, we discussed some of the consequences of the ways measures are used. Well, these consequences could include ambiguous data patterns. For example, inconsistencies in how measurements are taken (when, how, and where measurements are collected, as well as who collected the measurements) could produce considerable variability in the data resulting in ambiguous patterns. Further, variability that leads to ambiguous patterns could result from using an unreliable measure, even if it is used consistently.

Seventh, you would also want to consider what we described as theoretical significance. There may be sufficient information in the body of knowledge you used to inform your practice selections to provide some hypotheses as to what the ambiguous patterns might mean, or even as to whether you might expect such an ambiguous result to be a predictable phase of the intervention. For example, a key part of treatment of problems associated with borderline personality from a psychodynamic perspective is setting limits (Corcoran & Keeper, 1992). It follows then that a persistent problem in therapy would be some gains followed by a testing of those limits and temporary regression. Thus, the data would show an ambiguous pattern that actually involves the predictable ups and downs of the therapeutic process.

Eighth, you can try to transform ambiguous patterns. Transforming data is not a perfect solution because some of the patterns in the data may be lost. But, again, you will be able to simplify ambiguous patterns as an aid to interpretation.

Finally, probably the best way to handle ambiguous data is to use the statistics described; these statistics are made accessible, we hope, by the SINGWIN program. There is one thing you can count on when you use statistics: Subjectivity can be ruled out because the rules apply to all cases. In other words, using statistics can help you tease out actual developments in your case that ambiguous patterns hide, and statistics also can provide information about the *lack* of developments.

In all, ambiguous patterns can be frustrating, but they are just one of many challenges you face when engaging in evaluation-informed and evidence-based practice. Individually, and as a package, these several suggestions can help you overcome a great deal of the interpretation difficulties that could result from ambiguous data patterns. But ambiguity isn't the only problem that could occur in visual analysis. In the following section, we describe several additional problems in visual analysis, whether or not the pattern is ambiguous.

PROBLEMS OF VISUAL INSPECTION

Any graphic method depends on the care with which data points are graphed. Therefore, if you don't have access to a computer, we recommend that you use graph paper to construct graphs, although even with graph paper there are problems in interpreting visual representations of data (e.g., Brossart, Parker, Olson, & Mahadevan, 2006; Colon, 2006; Fisher, Kelley, & Lomas, 2003; Rubin & Knox, 1996; Stewart, Carr, Brandt, & McHenry, 2007). If you use the CASS/CAAP programs, graphs will be generated virtually automatically. Even better, you can use SINGWIN, described in this part of the book, to graph and automatically update single-system design data and at the same time compute most of the statistics described in this part of the book. Also, it is easy to graph single-system design data using Microsoft Excel (Carr & Burkholder, 1998; Grehan & Moran, 2005; Hillman & Miller, 2004; Lo & Konrad, 2007; Moran & Hirschbine, 2002; Patterson & Basham, 2006; Grehan & Moran, 2005; Hillman & Miller, 2004; and Moran & Hirschbine, 2002, can be downloaded for free from "The Behavior Analyst Today" web site located at: www.behavior-analyst-today.com; click on "Index," search for the correct volume and issue, click on it, and scroll to the particullar article).

One problem relates to how data are represented on graphs. Consider Figures 14a and b in which the same data are presented with different intervals on the vertical and horizontal axes. In Figure 14a the sharp valleys and peaks don't suggest that stable behaviors have been achieved during baseline; they also make interpretation of intervention data difficult. However, in Figure 14b the softened curves produced by using larger intervals with exactly the same data disguise these differences. Which graph is accurate? Actually, they are both accurate but for different purposes. If you wish to show the minute variations in behavior, then small intervals are preferable both on the vertical axis and on the horizontal axis (the time line). When large variations in behavior are expected, larger intervals may be useful to present the data in perspective. You should try to keep the intervals on both axes approximately the same so that no distortions are artificially produced. Imagine the distortions in presentation if the intervals on the horizontal axis in Figure 14a were used with the intervals on the vertical axis in Figure 14b.

Autocorrelation is another potential problem in the visual analysis of graphed data. Autocorrelation can bias visual judgments in the same way it can bias judgments based on conventional statistical tests (Gorsuch, 1983; Jones et al., 1978; Matyas & Greenwood, 1990). Autocorrelation can make differences between phases appear larger or smaller than they really are, depending on the nature of the autocorrelation (e.g., larger if it's positive and smaller if it's negative). In fact, positive autocorrelation tends to decrease variability, and negative autocorrelation increases variability. In general, the former probably makes it more likely that people will conclude that a difference between phases exists when it does not, and the latter makes it more likely that people will conclude that there is not a difference between phases when there is a difference. And it is also very likely that visual inspection of a set of data cannot reveal the underlying autocorrelation. Thus, observed changes may actually have been quite predictable because of the autocorrelation. Therefore, you cannot assume that even some clear visual patterns will lead to error-free interpretations. Visual analysis is a tentative evaluation approach. It is useful for making quick and approximate judgments, but when the data relate to important content or when there is any doubt about the clarity of the data, nonvisual (i.e., statistical) methods can aid in the analysis (e.g., Colon, 2006; Fisher, Kelley, & Lomas 2003; Stewart, Carr, Brandt, & McHenry, 2007).

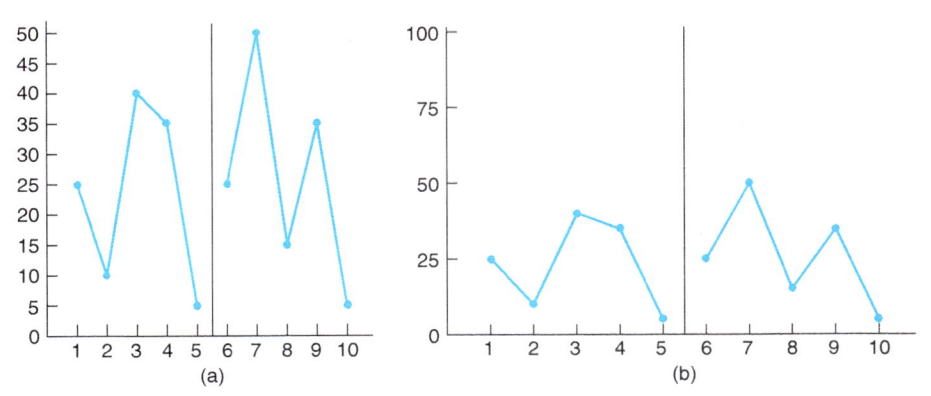

FIGURE 14 Illustrations of the same data points presented on charts with different intervals showing the exaggerated or softened effect that charting alone can produce.

There are other problems associated with visual inspection. When there are complex patterns, such as a bimodal pattern (two separate peaks) within a set of data, it is often difficult to interpret such information by simple inspection. The patterns themselves are important. Do high periods (of desired performance) come early or late in the set of data? Even more complicated is the interpretation of extremely variable data. It is difficult to make a judgment as to whether any change at all took place across phases with variable data since the variability can make it difficult to judge the level of the data. In general, when such problems arise, we recommend that you use one of the statistical procedures presented to aid in your analysis of the data.

Another problem emerges when two or more persons (including the client, as well as other helping professionals) are involved in the interpretation of visual patterns of data. A person's expectations, to say nothing about the person's values and biases, about the client's behavior may influence his or her interpretation. That is, what may appear to be major change to one observer may be considered as insignificant by another. Without clear-cut rules for analysis—which is what statistical procedures provide—there's considerable leeway in interpreting data as supporting one's practice hypotheses. In fact, our experience in working with students indicates that the visual analysis of single-system design data is more difficult and takes more practice than we might have imagined. In addition, research suggests that even experts have trouble agreeing on the visual interpretation of graphed data (see Fisher, Kelley, & Lomas, 2003, and Colon, 2006, for recent summaries of this research).

In all, then, visual inspection of data should be considered a very useful beginning, especially for *monitoring* ongoing events, because rapid feedback permits you to correct obvious problems. But unless the patterns are very clear, with sufficient numbers of observations and with stable baseline data, other methods of analysis also should be employed. Also, the possibility of autocorrelation is always present with data; it requires special techniques, such as the transformations, so that distortions can be minimized.

CREATING A CHART WITH SINGWIN

Some of the charts we discuss and charts you will want to create for your own cases can be created easily by SINGWIN. Here's how to use SINGWIN to create a chart.

1. Start SINGWIN
2. Create and open a new file, or open an existing file (see "Creating a New File" and "Opening an Existing File").
3. Follow the steps outlined in the section entitled "Creating a Line Chart."

Summary

Visual inspection of data for obvious changes in pattern is easy and should be done in all cases, especially when you seek quick, approximate information that will be used rapidly in formulating ongoing practice hypotheses. We've presented some basic patterns of data simplified as mean and trend lines to draw out these implications more clearly. We've distinguished three attributes of graphed data in particular—the level of the data, the trend or directionality of data within one phase (slope), and the trend or directionality of data across phases (drift). When baseline phases are compared to intervention phases using these three attributes, we can indicate general patterns of improvement, strong improvement, or very strong improvement (depending on the number of attributes affected), or we can indicate the same three patterns of deterioration, depending on the definition of desired or undesired events.

It's difficult to interpret data when they're variable or autocorrelated. Therefore, visual analysis contains inherent risks. We believe it is advisable to supplement visual analyses with some of the simple statistical analyses.

NOT FOR PRACTITIONERS ALONE

Evaluation for Clients, Administrators, Educators, and Students

PURPOSE This chapter reviews a number of issues about single-system evaluation. We first discuss the use of single-system designs in managed care and primary prevention. We then discuss evaluation from the perspective of clients, administrators, educators, and students, not so much referring to how it is done—but rather referring to why and under what conditions. We also present a working draft of a code of ethics for evaluating practice.

Introduction
Special Application of Single-System Designs
    Managed Care and Single-System Designs
    Using Single-System Designs in Primary Prevention
        School Dropout
        Pregnancy
        Long-Term Career
Recent Criticisms of Single-System Evaluation
    The First Set of Criticisms: Single-System Evaluation and Practice
    The Second Set of Criticisms: Research and Evaluation Issues
    The Third Set of Criticisms: Ethical Issues in Single-System Designs
    The Fourth Set of Criticisms: Meta-Issues in Philosophy, Politics, and Socioeconomics
    The Fifth Set of Criticisms: Technological Issues
For the Client
    Questions about Evaluation
    How Can Recording Help the Client (and the Practitioner)?
    Ethical Considerations in Using Single-System Designs
    A Model Consent Form
For the Administrator
    Evaluation: Do I Have a Choice?
    Staff Development
    Staff Cooperation and Deployment
    Examples of Evaluation in Agency Settings
For Educators and Students
Summary

From Chapter 25 of *Evaluating Practice: Guidelines for the Accountable Professional*, Sixth Edition. Martin Bloom, Joel Fischer, John G. Orme. Copyright © 2009 by Pearson Education, Inc. All rights reserved.

INTRODUCTION

This is the age of accountability, especially for human service professions. Scarce resources and numerous options for spending those that are available mean that the human service professions have to have a strong basis for their requests from the public treasury. The pressures to engage in evaluation-informed and evidence-based practice are growing, both from within and without our professions. This book has been directed primarily at professional *practitioners*, the people who will actually *use* these evaluation procedures in working with clients. The goal is to enable those practitioners to know how well the intervention is going both during and after the service period so that the intervention may be made more effective, more efficient, and less costly in psychological, social, and financial terms.

However, there are other audiences to whom this book is directed and other issues that have to be considered. It is directed to those who must understand the purpose of evaluating practice and the ethical issues that surround these practices. In this chapter, we address a variety of special issues as they affect clients, administrators, teachers, and students.

First, we will discuss some special applications of single-system designs. Then, we will discuss some of the recent criticisms of single-system designs and, in some cases, of evaluation itself, and provide our perspective on these criticisms. We then will address the remainder of this chapter to our several constituent groups.

SPECIAL APPLICATIONS OF SINGLE-SYSTEM DESIGNS

Although most of this book has discussed use of single-system designs in "typical" intervention situations with individuals, couples, families, groups, organizations, and communities, there are two important applications that are not quite so typical: the use of single-system designs in managed care and primary prevention, the topics of this section.

Managed Care and Single-System Designs

Managed care refers to a system of policies and procedures for connecting the quality and quantity of client care to public fiscal accountability, in what amounts to a kind of grand cost-benefit analysis and external control system. (That is, the direct service practitioner does not have much control over the nature and extent of services that will be paid for under the existing financial plan.) With the rapid increase in costs of health, education, and welfare, social critics are exploring ways to contain and reduce costs, while attaining equivalent or improved outcomes, by having a presumably disinterested party examine the proposed intervention goals and methods in light of the best available practice information so as to determine what is allowable under these general guidelines. In principle, this is a laudable social goal; the devil is in the details (Bolen & Hall, 2007; Finkelman, 2001; Rossiter, 2000; Strom-Gottfried, 1997; Vandiver & Corcoran, 2007).

While managed care is being discussed widely in the applied social sciences, there are relatively few discussions of the role of practice evaluation, the topic of this book, and its potential role under an external accountability system (for an important exception, see Hayes, Barlow, & Nelson-Gray, 1999). Nevertheless, evaluation procedures are integral to managed care (e.g., Minami et al., 2008). All managed care systems include quality assurance reviews to assess the extent to which the service provided approximates some desired form of practice. Similarly, managed care relies on utilization reviews (retrospective, concurrent, and prospective), comparing services against a set of criteria to determine the necessity and appropriateness of those services. (We, of course, recognize that there are numerous other forces that influence decisions in managed care systems, including political and economic forces that are beyond the scope of this book.) Therefore, we offer the following *tentative* assessment and suggestions, in light of the rapidly changing array of methods and populations being covered by managed care.

First, the emergence of managed care reflects events in the larger society, and is a reality that helping professionals have to address. It is written into law (P.L. 97-248); it is included in private third-party payers and corporate benefit programs; and it is becoming part of the normative thinking in society and many of its professional associations (Corcoran & Gingerich, 1994, p. 328; Finkelman, 2001; Strom-Gottfried, 1997).

Second, a distinction must be made between review processes that take place before services are rendered, called *managed care reviews*, and those that occur during or after services, called *quality assurance reviews (QARs)* (Corcoran & Gingerich, 1994; Tischler, 1990). Both involve a review process that examines the proposed and delivered services with regard to their necessity, duration, quality, and outcome, while also considering best-practice knowledge, quality of care, and reduction of unnecessary costs. Corcoran and Gingerich (1994, p. 329) note that concrete and specific short- and long-term intervention objectives and goals are required, as well as evidence of observable changes (Osman & Shueman, 1988).

Third, the philosophy and procedures for single-system designs, in general, offer individual practitioners and entire agencies a specific and useful means of attaining the highest professional standards of evaluated practice, while at the same time enabling them to provide almost all of the required information for peer reviews and managed care. All of the steps we propose in this book would be useful in achieving this dual goal of quality interventions and cost-effectiveness. While the managed care and quality assurance reviews do introduce a fiscal dimension to professional services, the procedures suggested for single-system designs also introduce client preferences and professional decisions, which both embody values underlying the helping process. These values are part of the choices made in identifying clients' short-term objectives and long-term goals, in the choice of methods used to attain them, in clients' comfort and satisfaction given in feedback on the helping process itself, and in societal satisfaction on effective problem resolution (e.g., Morgan & Morgan, 2001).

Fourth, some single-system methods provide a way to project efficiency estimates: how long it would take, under existing patterns of success, for the client to attain stable and satisfactory outcomes, and at what costs in terms of professional time and energy. It may be that this systematic thinking will need to be incorporated into the basic evaluation plans for social services.

In the following section, we will elaborate on the parallels between the demands likely to emerge from the managed care/quality assurance review perspectives and the enhanced perspective on evaluation that results from evaluation-informed practice, particularly using single-system designs, that fulfills these demands while maintaining professional standards.

Typical Demands of a Managed Care or Quality Assurance Review
(based on a review of these systems-in-change)

1. Definition of the presenting problems and the context of these problems that may require changes and amelioration.

2. Normative information will be needed on the types of interventions that have been used, their ranges of success with these kinds of problems, and the realistic goals that can be set in this regard.

Expanded Single-System Evaluation
(enhanced to clarify procedures that are likely to match external systems review)

1. Operational definitions of target behaviors, which may need to be expanded to include the context in which each target exists. This is similar to a social-ecological perspective of looking at the person in the environment, and measuring both person and environmental factors because either or both may be used as targets of intervention.

Consideration may also be given to preventive interventions, as part of a long-term cost–benefit analysis.

2. Evidence-based practice routinely is based on the best available information, and future practice may need to document this best usage. Access to information data bases and retrieval and printing of abstracts is one form of such documentation of best available information for both intervention and primary prevention services.

The setting of goals and objectives continues to be part of the client–practitioner process, so that appropriate values are incorporated into the service program.

3. Based on preliminary assessments of the client's full situation, a categorical match will be conducted by an external reviewer, who will then indicate the average time that is needed with the standard or validated methods in regard to a given condition. The practitioner has to decide whether to accept this interpretation or to provide further information on extenuating circumstances that require the provision of more or less time and/or covered services.

In addition to outcome measures, managed care thinking also will require something new in single-system designs: a continuing concern for the quality of care, including client satisfaction, and how well the intervention conforms to standard expectations for best treatment.

4. The external reviewer may be involved to some degree in observing the monitoring of changes in the targeted behaviors. This may be done by reviewing charts as described in this book, or practice evaluation forms, or computer-assisted case-recording methods (Corcoran & Gingerich, 1994).

3. The baseline for the target and for relevant factors in the context may be used as the basis for considering extenuating circumstances. While each case is different, there are still basic similarities to cases in the literature from which we can expect likely outcomes. It may be possible to take baseline data, make a projection of the likely course of events if some intervention is not undertaken, and then connect some financial estimates of the cost of the continuing or escalating problem. This will require agencies to begin analyzing their records based on their own experiences in serving a given range of cases.

Then, if there is any service being conducted, a worker could make an efficiency estimate. This would say how long (and, thus, at what cost) a given program of intervention has to be continued before statistically significant results are projected, given current rates of change. It may be necessary to expand this efficiency estimate by adding the clinical or practical significance of such changes, because this represents another way to view social costs.

The considerations of client satisfaction and service expectations for best treatment require additional data (on client satisfaction) and more explicit operationalization of actual interventions used for evidence-based practice. With regard to client satisfaction, it is simply a matter of selecting some mutually agreeable satisfaction measure, and gathering data periodically, rather than gathering data continuously (which may be reactive and counterproductive).

4. The monitoring of the progress of practice is a step ahead of the managed care/quality assurance review process. Single-system designs may have to be clearer in specifying the immediate and intermediate objectives on the path toward some long-term goal. Then, part of the charting and monitoring can be a cooperative process with the reviewer, probably on a random review basis, showing where the client is vis-à-vis a particular objective in a series of objectives toward the goal. With appropriate charting, the practitioner would be ready at any time to convey progress toward objectives, and to record mitigating circumstances if any (as in annotations on the chart). This approach requires that evaluators work with reviewers to reach agreement as to what constitutes the evidence they need.

5. Extensions, when needed, are based on further evidence that the problem has changed or the circumstances in which it exists have changed, so that more time and services are needed to achieve a predictable objective. It is also possible that changing events may mean that less time and services are needed.

6. There will likely be some record-keeping system of both process measures and outcome measures, as part of the payment for covered services.

5. The notion of a predictable objective allows for more accurate efficiency estimates. Agencies can keep track of the accuracy of their efficiency estimates and how closely practitioners succeed in achieving predicted goals in projected times. These rates of accurate efficiency estimates can be added to other information when practitioners request extensions, and so forth.

6. The nature of this final accounting system is still to be determined, but evaluators should be prepared to influence the final form by making it compatible with the range and depth of their single-system designs. That is, everything that we propose be done using evidence-based and evaluation-informed practice should be usable in any final accounting form. Moreover, as Strom-Gottried (1997, p. 14) points out with regard to social work cases, many clients have complex and long-standing difficulties that are intricately related to environmental conditions, oppression, and poverty. Regardless of the worker's skills, resources, and motivation, some problems will prove difficult and time-consuming to remediate. Strom-Gottried goes on to note that helping practitioners need to account for the efficiency and effectiveness of their services, but they must be careful that unrealistic performance standards do not set them up for failure because if they don't reach these standards, then there may be reductions in funding and services.

Using Single-System Designs in Primary Prevention

Primary prevention is the third helping modality (along with *treatment* of, or *intervention* with, existing problems or conditions, and *rehabilitation* of persons or groups involved in those treatments or interventions); it presents some special considerations for using single-system evaluations that we discuss and illustrate in this section (see Dulmus & Rapp-Paglicci, 2005, and Gullotta & Bloom, 2003, for an encyclopedia of developments in primary prevention). Primary prevention may be defined as the *coordinated actions* seeking to *prevent* predictable problems, *protect* existing states of health and healthy functioning, and *promote* desired objectives (Bloom, 1996). It is because the specific, predicted, preventable problem has not yet occurred, and the at-risk individual or group is functioning relatively well with regard to that predicted untoward condition, that we can speak of taking preventive actions. It is this "no-problem-yet" status that sometimes makes it difficult for evaluators to figure out how to measure process and outcome in prevention, especially over a long period of time. The same issues emerge when evaluating the promotion of desired objectives and the protection of existing states of health and healthy functioning.

However, in principle, primary prevention may be evaluated in exactly the same way as any other treatment or rehabilitation concern, as long as specific targets are identified, and repeated measures are employed with relevant designs. Instead of measuring problem behaviors or events, primary preventers often measure strengths in persons or environments that keep the problem from happening, or that discourage the emergence of dysfunctional or undesirable behaviors or events. For example, Van Wormer (2004) addressed the problem of obesity and lack of control over weight by focusing on walking as a target antagonistic to weight gain. He measured weight, but focused on encouraging the self-monitoring of walking (through the use of a pedometer). Austin, Weatherly, and Gravina (2005) directly encouraged safety in a restaurant through individual and group feedback regarding a checklist of activities to be performed for satisfactory closing tasks. The emphasis was on positive reinforcement for what had been done correctly, although individuals were privately informed about areas where they needed improvement.

On the other hand, some primary prevention projects have to address undesired behaviors, such as the study by Miltenberger et al. (2004) in which behavioral skills training was delivered to young children to prevent their playing with guns. Lane et al. (2006) presented a study of a boy who picked his skin. In each case, specific targets of undesired behaviors to be reduced were identified, and various methods introduced to achieve these goals.

Let's illustrate a single-system design with a primary prevention situation. Suppose a school nurse and a school counselor team formed a group with 10th-, 11th-, and 12th-grade female students who were being treated for sexually transmitted diseases (STDs) at the school-based health clinic (compare Dryfoos, 1994). The common problem involved the immediate treatment condition (STDs), but the service team was aware of some related long-term concerns as well. These young women were at high risk for school dropout, unwanted pregnancies, and limited future career options. The service team addressed the immediate STD problems first, and then arranged to deal with these longer-term risky behaviors. First, the service team redefined them as positive targets antithetical to the negative terms:

1. A *preventable* problem: The negative term, dropout, was redefined; the target would be to help the young women to stay in school, which is the antithetical and positive goal regarding dropout.

2. A *protectable* situation: The negative risk of their becoming unintentionally pregnant was redefined in its antithetical form; the protective goal consists of maintaining their existing states of health and their self-desired nonpregnancy.

3. A *promotable* concern: The negative risk of limited future career options was redefined; the promotive concern would be to enhance the potential of these young women so as to have some high-quality career options instead of dead-end, low-paying jobs.

Taking these changes of negative-to-positive goals, let us suggest some operational measures for each and see how these would be charted in a primary prevention project (also, see Lopez & Snyder's, 2003, book, *Positive Psychological Assessment: A Handbook of Models and Measures*). We will employ the distinctions between ultimate goals and intermediate objectives (or subgoals) because some primary prevention work involves long periods of time. It may be difficult to stay connected in a longitudinal project, but intermediate objectives that are on the path toward the long-term goal are valuable and worth attaining in their own right, as well as being a logical step toward the desired long-term goal.

School Dropout. Attendance is the logical antithetical measure with regard to the prevention of dropout. If there is need for rapid feedback to the counselor on nonattendance, then daily data may be necessary; once a stable pattern of attendance is obtained, then weekly or longer attendance records may be used. Daily attendance is an obvious intermediate objective to the long-term goal of a satisfactory attendance rate. However, mere attendance does not tell us how much the student has learned, and, conceptually, we would like to see students not only attend school, but also learn something. Grades in the basic subjects constitute a rough but available indicator of learning. So, by combining attendance with grades, we have an operational definition of a positive concept (perhaps "educational engagement") that is antithetical to school dropout. Note that, in effect, we measure the nonoccurrence of the risky condition (dropout) by measuring in detail the opposite positive conditions (attendance and passing grades). Dropout could occur for other than academic reasons, such as traumatic social events or pressures, but these would appear as annotations on our charts. Such dropouts would not "count" in a kind of batting-average approach with the group of high school women in our STD treatment example. We would count only the academic successes, that is, the number of students with both good attendance rates and passing grades, divided by the total number of students in the STD group, to give the rate of success in this part of the project.

Pregnancy. Protecting the existing state of health and nonpregnant status at this time are other clear objectives antithetical to unwanted teen pregnancy. We'll focus on the pregnancy issue for this discussion. "Nonpregnancy" can be attained in two ways, abstinence, and the proper use of birth control methods, but we are emphasizing the goal of not being pregnant during the person's time as a high school student. So, a monthly self-report of one's pregnancy status would be adequate. This self-report on such a personal topic is a delicate issue, but we see this as representing a kind of self-monitoring intervention that enables the young woman to demonstrate control over her own life in this area, and for which she would receive whatever program reinforcements are present, such as scholarship funds for college or technical school.

Long-Term Career. Any long-term goal, such as obtaining a job that pays a livable wage and that the worker enjoys, is difficult to evaluate because it is an ultimate, long-term goal that may occur only years after high school. However, there are clearly some intermediate steps that are necessary toward attaining the ultimate goal, and primary prevention/single-system designs can provide evaluation of the attained merit of these intermediate objectives. For young women to begin to enter high-quality life career options of their own choice, it would be necessary to obtain: (1) the requisite education (measured by mastery of relevant courses at school, as identified by the academic counselors), (2) the requisite skills (measured by achievement of relevant work or volunteer experiences, such as working for a nonprofit organization, or volunteering to help older clients at a nursing home, etc.), and (3) the requisite level of self-efficacy, or the belief that one can succeed in accomplishing the specific course of actions involved (Bandura, 1986), as measured by standardized scales tests or reports by teachers.

Figure 1 shows the charts used in this example. As with charting methods discussed earlier in this book, there are some criteria for each set, such as acceptable attendance rates, and grades adequate to pass and graduate. Sometimes multiple charts are used for one target condition; at other times, one chart will do. Thus, the same basic procedures for single-system designs in treatment/intervention and rehabilitation may be applied in primary prevention work, given a clear conceptual analysis and construction of targets.

RECENT CRITICISMS OF SINGLE-SYSTEM EVALUATION

A number of thoughtful scholars, researchers, teachers, and practitioners have offered criticisms of single-system designs and the evaluation-informed practice approach they embody (Davis, 2007; Heineman-Pieper, 1994; Laird, 1994; Nelsen, 1994; Sherman & Reid, 1994; Tyson, 1994; Wakefield & Kirk, 1996, 1997; Witkin, 1997; Witkin & Saleebey, 2007; and others). We have tried to deal with these issues in writing the current edition of this text, but we thought it might be helpful to draw together many of these criticisms so that we could address them directly, and let the readers be the judge. We count ourselves among the critics of single-system designs in the sense that we have added and subtracted to this edition, according to our sense of the best available thinking on these evaluation methods. But we appreciate these outside critics, however painful their criticisms may be, calling attention to our possible mistakes and misinterpretations, because we have been, are, and probably will be wrong in the future on some of these points, although, we would argue, not on all of them. So, critics keep us honest, and we want to share these criticisms and responses with readers of this book (see also Cone, 2001; Jordan & Franklin, 2003; Ogles, Lambert, & Fields, 2002; and Roberts & Yeager, 2003, for good discussions of the issues involved in evaluating outcomes, and recent work on evidence-based assessment, such as Kazdin, 2005, and Hunsley & Mash, 2008).

We propose to sort out the array of critical comments into five sections relating single-system designs and evaluation-informed practice to: (1) practice; (2) research; (3) ethical issues; (4) philosophical, political, and socioeconomic issues (we'll term these the meta-issues for short); and (5) technological issues. Of course, we recognize that there may be overlap among categories. We believe that readers who might use single-system designs in their own practice should read the practice (#1) and ethical issues (#3) at least, while research students who are studying or using single-system designs would also profit from

Not for Practitioners Alone

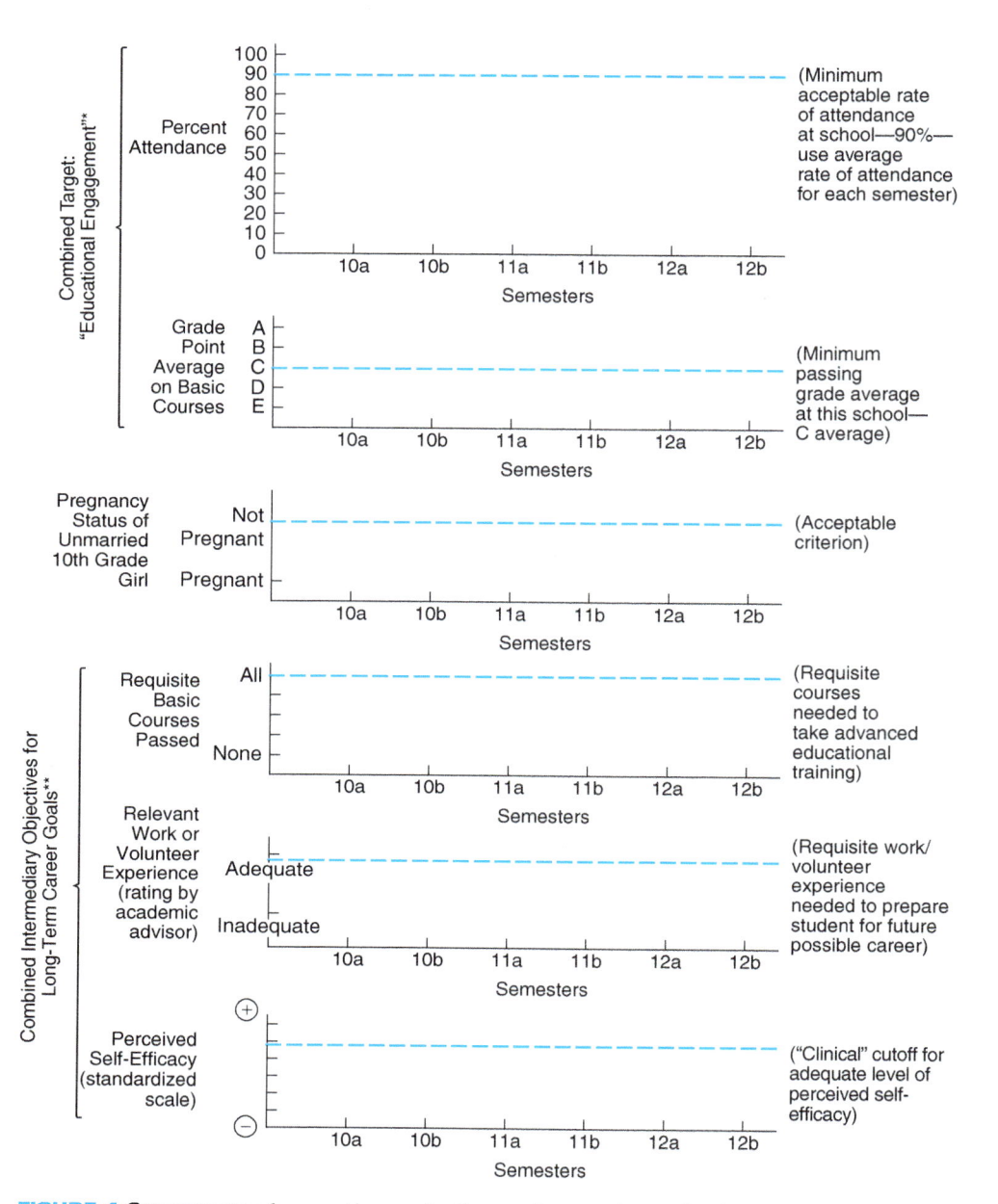

FIGURE 1 Components of preventive, protective, and promotive evaluation objective for one 10th-grade girl in an STD intervention group, viewed over a 3-year period.

*"Success" = joint occurrence of at-or-above minimal attendance and C or better grade average for each semester period.

**"Success" = joint occurrence of: (1) passing all requisite basic courses, (2) obtaining relevant work or volunteer experiences, and (3) having a perceived self-efficacy at or above the "clinical" cutoff mark.

looking at the research (#2) and the technological (#5) issues. We would suggest that the meta-issues (#4) might be most interesting to persons concerned with the larger philosophical-political-social contexts in which evaluation is practiced, because we will discuss topics on ideology, paradigms, managed care, and sociocultural and feminist issues.

We will discuss specific issues within these five sets by stating the criticisms in italics, followed by our response.

The First Set of Criticisms: Single-System Evaluation and Practice

1. *Evaluation interferes with practice because the efforts required by evaluation take too much time and effort away from practice itself.* This criticism has a grain of truth: It does take time to learn how to do single-system evaluations, but like any aspect of professional education, once learned and practiced, they become second nature. As with the learning of new intervention techniques, one cannot attain complete comfort without considerable practice. Similarly, during the process of conducting practice with a client, a group of clients, or a system, the practitioner indeed may have to take time away from the specific actions that constitute methods that change persons and environments to do other things that support these specific practice actions. Included among these supportive measures would be thinking about the meaning of events to the client and relevant others, about specific targets, about interventions that are likely to have a direct impact on those targets, about monitoring how these interventions are going, and about deciding whether and when to terminate services, and so forth. These are some of the component steps of evaluation, and thus are simply a part of good practice. Not doing evaluation, that is, not performing the actions described previously, would constitute a very strange kind of practice. Engaging in good, active listening skills, sociocultural sensitivity, good ethical behavior, and so forth, all take time away from specific practice actions in a narrow sense of the term, and yet no one complains about these components of good practice as taking time away from practice. We submit that evaluation components are exactly like these other components of good practice. Evaluation, good communication skills, cultural sensitivities, and ethical considerations are different ways to describe aspects of good practice.

2. *Evaluation imposes too rigid requirements that force practitioners to do things (such as having long baselines when the client needs immediate service) that they would not do if they weren't doing evaluation.* This criticism is misdirected. The practitioner and client have to agree that the idea of evaluation feedback will be useful in the context of service, and then they have to consider the best way to achieve this useful component of practice. (We discuss this later as part of our suggested Client Consent Form.) There are ways of evaluating practice by beginning with service, if this is needed, such as when using the B-A-B design; it is possible to begin an intervention using reconstructed baseline data if necessary; and it is always possible to drop evaluation, before or during baseline, if it proves to be harmful in any significant way to the client. One always has to balance the benefits from evaluation against the costs of doing the evaluation. We have tried to point out the flexibility in designs and methods so as to offer practitioners lots of choices in proposing and using single-system designs. We have challenged practitioners to be creative as well as sensitive in doing evaluation. But we recognize that there could be occasions when evaluation may not be helpful or may be actually harmful, and, thus, in these situations, evaluation should not be used.

3. *Evaluation doesn't add anything to practice that good practitioners don't already do.* The sense of this criticism is that evaluation is unnecessary because good practitioners already have a sense of how matters are proceeding, and merely applying numbers to this sensitivity is unnecessary. This is partly true; good practitioners *do* think about clear problem definitions and clear modes of intervention directly related to resolving client problems, and they do have some understanding of how the client is changing over time. We think using some evaluation tools may help make these good practitioners even better informed and supply them with more crisp and objective information on which to make better decisions. However, students have to learn how to be good practitioners, and perhaps these evaluation methods might be jump-starts to progress to the stage of high-level practice where clear problem definitions, clear modes of intervention, and the like become second nature. And, as we discussed earlier, managed care may demand objective methods of accountability, even from experienced practitioners. We have made the point that single-system design methods are also highly

sensitive to the practice context, and able to provide more objective accountability as well.

4. *The goals of evaluation often interfere with the goals of practice.* This is a persistent misperception that is related to another point we will discuss shortly: that evaluation, a knowledge-using enterprise, is different from research, a knowledge-building activity. The goal of evaluation is to facilitate the goals and objectives of practice. The components of, and steps in, evaluation are also the components and steps in good practice.

The Second Set of Criticisms: Research and Evaluation Issues

1. *Evaluation in practice is just another way to conduct research on practice.* This criticism is intended to show that the actual nitty-gritty practices of doing evaluation impose research-like restrictions that interfere with good practice. It is true that evaluation uses many of the same tools and methods as research (such as interobserver reliability, objective counting of target behaviors, statistical formulas in arriving at probability statements, etc.), but this criticism neglects the strong differences that distinguish evaluation from research.

Research is logically separate from practice, frequently with different goals from practice (e.g., building knowledge for the sake of knowledge), and is bound by the strict requirements of its constituent logical models, including such factors as random assignments; experimental and control groups; preidentified goals; unchanging interventions; subjects who typically are not consulted about goals, methods, or roles; and so forth.

Evaluation, on the other hand, especially single-system evaluation, has goals compatible with practice; it is intended to facilitate practice, and its underlying model demands the incorporation of client and community values, client participation in the formation of practice goals and objectives to the extent possible, a flexible logical structure that permits additions and subtractions of interventions during the service period, multidimensional contextual analyses, and so forth. All of these features that characterize the basic ingredients of research and evaluation are essentially different from each other. Evaluation is not research; research is not evaluation.

However, there are many occasions when researchers use single-system designs to conduct research (see Parker, 2006, and Parker, Hagan-Burke, & Vannest, 2007 for bibliographies of single-system designs, many of which are examples of the use of these designs for research). To take only one example, consider the research of Holden and his colleagues concerning the effectiveness of STARBRIGHT World (SBW) (www.starbright.org) in reducing the pain intensity, aversiveness, and anxiety in hospitalized children (e.g., Holden et al., 2003). Self-report, visual analog scales were used to measure children's perceptions of pain intensity, aversiveness, and anxiety. An alternating treatment design was used, randomization tests were used to analyze the data, and ultimately, a meta-analysis aggregating the results of three different studies was conducted. Results indicated that children in the SWB condition (compared to the "General Pediatric Milieu" condition) reported significantly less pain intensity, aversiveness, and anxiety and the effect was slightly stronger for females, and strongest for 11- to 13-year-olds. We accept (gladly) these kinds of knowledge-building projects, but we expect that few practitioners will organize their evaluations of practice primarily to build generalized knowledge as did Holden and his colleagues. Our book, and single-system designs in general, focuses on evaluation and the benefits of rapid feedback for stimulating good practice.

2. *Conducting an evaluation takes practitioner time and energy away from the client, who then does not get the full benefit of the services.* Apart from the fact that the entire focus of the evaluation is on and for the client, this criticism in part turns on the meaning of the word "client": whether that is only the one person sitting before you now, or whether it is the collective sense of "client." We believe that "client" means both the individual(s) before the practitioner now and also all of the individuals and groups the practitioner ever will see. Feedback from single-system designs is intended primarily to enhance practice with the immediate client/system. Practitioners should fully and directly serve the specific client before them, but they also should learn from this experience in order to serve other clients better. We believe that it is fully ethical and essentially incumbent on practitioners to learn as much as possible about their intervention methods with different categories of client problems, so as to be able to progress in their effectiveness with similar cases.

When the opportunity presents itself, it may be useful for practitioners to understand what is causing what, rather than simply determining that some desirable change has occurred. This is a kind of repertoire-of-practice-building aspect of evaluation, and it is different from the classical research approach, even though it may lead to shared knowledge of effective methods under certain circumstances. We wish more practitioners would share their practice wisdom in this way. The current client has likely benefited from prior evaluated practices, and future clients we hope also will benefit. Clients would not wish to consult with practitioners who did not learn from their practice experiences. Single-system designs provide one set of methods of developing a repertoire of effective interventions under certain conditions, supplementing the methods of evidence-based practice.

The Third Set of Criticisms: Ethical Issues in Single-System Designs

1. *Single-system designs violate the basic code of ethics of helping professionals by diverting their attention to evaluation rather than their attending exclusively to practice.* This chapter will include an extensive discussion of ethical issues, but we want to explore here some of the implications of the message of the Hippocratic Oath: Help if you can, but if not, do no harm. All of practice is predicated on the belief that performing certain methods in sensitive but systematic ways likely will help. We believe that the evaluation components added to whatever practice model the practitioner is employing will contribute to performing those methods in a sensitive and systematic way. This is the essence of the ethical code: help if you can. We also have argued that *not* using evaluation components may lead to ethical concerns (Bloom & Klein, 1994).

The second part of the ethical code, do no harm, is also part of the safety features in the single-system methodology: Clients are involved in the formulation of problems and goals, values to be considered, methods to be employed, interpretation of the data, and application of data to the next stages in client service whenever this is feasible. At each of these points, clients might break off engaging in the evaluation components because of perceived or anticipated harms. We believe that doing so will lead to a less sensitive and effective service, but clients can exert this control over evaluation so as to limit harm.

Even more to the point, it may be a violation of professional ethics *not* to evaluate. As just one example, the Code of Ethics of the National Association of Social Workers adopted by the NASW Delegate Assembly on August 15, 1996, specifically states that social workers should monitor and evaluate the implementation of programs and practice interventions. Ethical codes for other professions have similar provisions (Fisher, 2004; O'Donohue & Ferguson, 2003).

2. *Single-system designs do not help practitioners to prevent extreme cases of mortality (such as fatal child abuse).* This criticism is valid. Yet, we would argue that both research and practice share the inability of single-system evaluation to address adequately this kind of issue. However, it may be that if single-system evaluation were being conducted on, say, an abusive parent, it might seem to that parent that a more or less public spotlight is trained on his or her behaviors with regard to fundamental targets (the health and well-being of the child) on an ongoing basis; then the behaviors may not progress to the point of abuse or neglect. Does this make evaluation a kind of intervention? In the case of the abusive parent, it may be so; we are saying: "Here is what we are officially observing in your behavior toward your child." To any client, we are saying: "Here is what we agreed to observe in your behavior and the environment with your problem or goal." In general, this further suggests that evaluation components are one part of good practice.

3. *Single-system designs cannot be used to study interventions in major social problems, such as poverty, unemployment, or discrimination.* This, to some extent, is true, strictly speaking. We can't hide behind the small numbers that are commonly found in most single-system designs. However, remember that the "client" can be a system of any number, such as the millions of callers in a Cincinnati telephone system project (McSweeny, 1978), or the hundreds in an open-pit mining project (Fox, Hopkins, & Anger, 1987). Yet, this criticism is right on the mark. There are very few single-system design studies, or any kind of studies for that matter, on demonstration projects to prevent poverty, to protect existing states of healthy employment, or to promote tolerance among masses of citizens.

However, we can point to single-system evaluations of small pieces of the larger issues, such as the King, Winett, and Lovett (1986) study to enhance coping behaviors in women who were in dual-earner families; Levy and Bavandan's (1995) study promoting health care in women; the Jason, Billows, Schnopp-Wyatt, and King (1996) study on reducing illegal sales of cigarettes to minors; the Altus, Welsh, Miller, and Merrill (1993) study on evaluating an ongoing consumer cooperative over a 9-year period; the Brigham, Meier, and Goodner (1995) project to increase "designated drivers" so as to reduce alcohol-related accidents; and the Brothers, Krantz, and McClannahan (1994) effort to evaluate a recycling project. These are all instances where major social concerns were addressed using single-system design methods, focusing on specific representatives of the larger group that is involved. These successful instances should be considered as the foundation for ideas for addressing larger numbers of persons with similar problems. Indeed, Miringoff and Opdycke (1996) created a time-series model for an index on social health (measuring 16 leading indicators including infant mortality, child abuse, teenage suicide, high school dropout, adult unemployment, poverty in the over-65 age group, etc.). While this is not a single-system design as such, it does illustrate the use of this kind of methodology with regard to understanding more clearly the nature of these social problems.

The Fourth Set of Criticisms: Meta-Issues in Philosophy, Politics, and Socioeconomics

1. *Single-system designs and evaluation are part of the larger philosophy of science enterprise termed postpositivism (Reid, 1997b) and are heir to its flawed assumptions and methods.* The naturalistic, heuristic, constructivist critics of single-system designs have long lists of arguments against neopositivist approaches, including single-system designs. Readers will find the hard-hitting discussions by Heineman-Pieper (1994), Tyson (1994), and others (see various authors in Sherman & Reid, 1994; Witkin & Saleebey, 2007) to be most interesting. Rather than address every criticism, we will select representative ones.

The experimental method, including ". . . the modified form in which it is applied to single-subject studies" (Heineman-Pieper, 1994, p. 72) is said to involve prospective rather than retrospective studies, operational definitions, data gathering by structured instruments, and the like, which are best applied to closed systems or "nonhuman subjects." These methods are said to be imposed on the clients and thereby change them in unacceptable ways that damage the helping process. We would agree that there are costs for any intervention into another person's (client's) life situation that change that situation to some degree; the question is whether the intervention (and the evaluation) are worth the price. We believe that more or less objective feedback of monitored interventions, as well as the interventions themselves, are well worth that cost. Further, the hundreds of examples in the literature of single-system designs being used under the completely opposite conditions as concocted by these critics suggest that this criticism simply does not reflect the realities of practice.

Critics suggest that single-system designs are "interventionist" because ". . . they involve manipulation of the treatment process" that introduces "nontherapeutic motives and experiences into the treatment relationship, and therefore, always reduce the quality of the service being offered" (Heineman-Pieper, 1994, p. 73). We simply disagree. We suggest that good evaluation *adds* to the quality of the service being offered by documenting significant changes or lack of changes and thus supporting client change efforts far beyond just talking about change, even within a trusting relationship. No practice ideology has a monopoly on what is "good service" and who best offers it. The proof is in the reality.

Critics argue that positivist researchers (presumably including those who use single-system designs) believe their work is confirmed by Hanson's (1969, p. 74) wonderful phrase, "immaculate perceptions," using immutable formulas and numbers, while striving for absolute confirmation and total objectivity. As readers of this book will recognize, the discussion of single-system designs in the previous pages is anything but absolute, immutable, unchanging, and immaculate. Single-system designs are approximate, highly flexible, and constantly changing to fit the needs of client and practitioner.

Critics argue that the findings from single-system designs are paper-thin (rather than the "thick" knowledge of qualitative naturalistic studies), stripped of the context of real life, which leads to avoiding the role of advocate for some valued position (while remaining loyal to the "value-free" position of the positivist), and thus are a "handmaiden to the status quo" (Heineman-Pieper, 1994, p.82). In contrast to these critical remarks, the single-system designs we have been discussing involve value decisions of client and practitioner throughout, where targets are representatives of the global but unmeasurable whole, and where the set of targets may represent a "thick" understanding of the client's situation. (We call attention to the work of Secret & Bloom, 1994, for a truly multifaceted view of a typical clinical problem.) As Tyson (1994, p. 102) notes, "all data collection strategies are heuristics that give priority to one form of accuracy but sacrifice another. . . ." We have argued that single-system designs seek to balance the priorities of successful client outcome and objectivity. Losing either one while gaining the other is a mistake no ethical practitioner should ever make.

2a. *Single-system designs reflect the dominance of a positivist research establishment with its emphasis on unattainable objectivity and its selection of simplistic targets of study rather than the meaningful understanding of the whole situation; in short, the futile aping of the quantitative model and the neglect of qualitative methods.*

2b. *Single-system designs reflect the soft fuzzy thinking of qualitative methods, with its kindly efforts of deep understanding of the entire world of the objects of study at the price of losing objectivity and perspective, and its neglect of quantitative research, which is the basis of modern science.* Rather than get involved in the seemingly endless debates on the nature of contemporary applied social science (see, e.g., *Letters* in the September 1997 issue of *Social Work Research*, and Epstein's (2008) recent smashing review of Witkins & Saleebey's 2007 anthology), we would only reply that single-system designs reflect a joint origin in both qualitative and quantitative perspectives, and that we believe single-system designs contain the best of both perspectives. Along with qualitative methods, single-system designs are vitally concerned with the unique characteristics of the client's situation. Discussions with the client with regard to problems and/or goals, alternative methods and likely costs and benefits, and involvement in the process and outcome of the study as these affect practitioners' interventions and client outcomes are all the hallmarks of single-system designs in common with some forms of qualitative research. Along with quantitative methods, single-system designs share the concern for objectivity, for replicability, and for using a scientific language that communicates with all qualified persons so that our knowledge of effective ways of helping can expand and be used by other helping professionals.

We find it significant that single-system designs often are the subject of criticism by scientific positions that are, theoretically, diametrically opposed to each other. This suggests to us the folly of being too much convinced by one's own rhetoric about the truth and rightness of one's own ways, and the inconceivable stupidity of others (who disagree).

3. *Managed care will be making significant demands on practitioner accountability that will be detrimental to professional practice. Single-system evaluation is a too-willing accomplice of managed care, and is tarred by the same brush.* Managed care is a reality that we have to address, whether we want to or not, as it will likely grow to dominate many of the service areas where helping professionals are at work. Although, at this time, "managed care" is a broad label without a fixed and consistently applied meaning, it appears likely that in all forms of managed care, some form of accountability will be involved. We certainly have no complaint about accountability, and we are happy, in this specific sense, to be accomplices to the accountability movement because we believe that this will lead to greater openness and rigor in the evaluation of professional practice, to the benefit of clients, practitioners, and the payers of these services. This does not mean that we are silent about the abuses of managed care that are surfacing all about us. Rather, we hope that the incorporation of accountable methods by all practitioners might forestall an imposed set of standard methods and demanded outcomes that are difficult to achieve in any human service situation. We believe it is possible to demonstrate more or less objective outcomes and effective methods without having third-party nonprofessionals determining what practitioners can and cannot do in the actual context of service.

4. *There has never been any scientific evidence that the use of single-system designs helps in enhancing practice outcome (as distinct from the issue in which single-system designs document change and inferred causes of the change in a given case situation). Moreover, most graduates still are not using single-system design methods, after three decades of inclusion in educational curricula.* Our goal in explicating single-system designs and methods is to explicate single-system designs and methods. We assert (and cite ample literature and our own experiences) that these methods *can* help us document significant positive client changes, and in the case of using

advanced designs, also can help us infer causality regarding these changes. We also have illustrated a number of other ways that practice can be enhanced from the use of single-system evaluations, from the way we identify problems and goals to our recording of outcomes. These are tasks that are different from scientifically demonstrating that using single-system design methods versus not using them will lead practitioners to better outcomes in practice. However, studies by Faul, McMurty, and Hudson, (2001), Lambert (2007), and Slonim-Nevo and Anson, (1998), *do* suggest that adding evaluation procedures to an intervention can positively affect client outcomes beyond the effects of the intervention alone. This issue actually provides a research question, and a good one, but it is not the one we address in this book, so long as we can demonstrate hundreds of times with many different targets in many different fields that the outcome of practice efforts is significantly positive, and (when suitable designs are used) that what we did is likely to be one cause of that improvement. This, in itself, is a critically important task. However, there is an emerging, methodologically strong body of evidence which shows that such routine monitoring and receipt of feedback, as in evaluation-informed practice, can reduce deterioration, improve overall outcome, and lead to fewer treatment sessions with no worsening of outcome for clients making progress (i.e., increased cost-effectiveness) (e.g., Lambert, 2007; Lambert et al., 2002, 2003; Harmon et al., 2007). Thus, the rationale for use of single-system designs is increased dramatically to the extent that this finding is corroborated in subsequent research.

5. *Single-system evaluators largely have been silent with regard to racial and ethnic identity, national origin, cultural background, language preference, gender, age, sexual orientation, disability status, religion, extent of spirituality, and socioeconomic status, and other issues regarding oppressed persons.* In one sense, this is a justified criticism in that few studies have been conducted specifically on such topics, primarily because single-system designs are an evaluation method, not a research tool per se. However, those using and writing about single-system designs have begun to address these issues (e.g., Cheung & Canda, 1992; Nelsen, 1994; Rogers & Potocky, 1997; Rubin, 1991; Soliman, 1999; Staudt, 1997). However, classical research methods have been used extensively in the study of multicultural assessment. (See Suzuki and Ponterotto, 2008, for a recent extensive review of this topic.) However, people of different ethnic backgrounds, genders, and other social characteristics have been clients and their problems or challenges have been evaluated, as this book amply demonstrates.

It is important to continue to work to ensure that there is no systematic bias in the use of single-system designs or any evaluation or research designs against people with any particular social characteristics (Gilbert, 2003; Suzuki & Ponterotto, 2008). The goal of social and cultural competence, sensitivity to and knowledge of our clients' (and colleagues') characteristics and differences, are the same for use of single-system designs as they are for all of practice. However, there can be many places where such biases may emerge, such as in formulation of target problems or challenges. For example, if a woman is being seen by a practitioner with regard to her depressed feelings and actions, it is possible that a biased practitioner may direct attention to the woman alone as the source of her own problems, rather than exploring what part her social and cultural training and roles may play in her depression. Once a target is identified, intervention plans to address it may further continue the bias. If the woman is seen as the predominant source of her depression, then treatments will likely be addressed to the woman alone, as contrasted with making adaptive changes in her social and cultural settings. The choice of who is to collect data, and how these data are interpreted, may yet continue the bias. If the client's husband is involved in data collection, and if, in fact, he is part of the social environment creating the depressive context, then there may be bias in the data collection and, ultimately, its interpretation. All of these systematic errors in evaluation may be totally unintended and invisible to the practitioner who would claim to be free of such biases (Broverman, Broverman, Clarkson, Rosenkrantz, & Vogel, 1970). Yet, it is one of the ironies of the helping professions that we, as self-consciously open-minded persons, may be displaying unknown biases, until critics help us to see ourselves and our discriminatory actions in a clearer light. Thus, the admonition to be sensitive to one's own biases is as central to the use of single-system designs as it is in every other realm of professional service. We believe that sharing the problem identification and other aspects of intervention with the client is one of the best ways to avoid the worst of these biases. Listening carefully to critics of single-system evaluation is another way of checking ourselves against unintended biases.

The Fifth Set of Criticisms: Technological Issues

1. *There are some technological problems that strike at the very heart of single-system designs and their evaluation process. They either make these designs impossibly difficult to do on a routine basis (e.g., autocorrelation), or they challenge the logical meaning of data analysis and interpretation (for instance, definitions of significance, and methods of analyzing data).* These technological issues, such as autocorrelation, the meaning of significance, and the methods of analyses, are real and do represent important concerns regarding single-system design because they call attention to possible methodological issues that may limit the usefulness of these designs, or else they offer new ideas that force us to change how we have considered some basic topics. Whenever possible, we take a conservative position, call attention to the issues, and caution users that future study may lead to different suggestions for evaluating practice. With regard to new ideas, we approach them cautiously and offer them on an experimental basis. The main point we want to make with regard to such new ideas is that they may prove fruitful or not, and we hope to respond accordingly. Readers of more than one of these several editions of *Evaluating Practice* will notice some absences and changes in our discussion of these topics, as technical knowledge has grown, shifted, or retreated. We cannot promise the reader "truth" in these matters, only the best of present-day thinking as it applies to single-system designs. While negotiating the challenges of autocorrelation and methods of analysis may be time-consuming, we have offered advances in time-saving methods through the use of computer programs. In the end, it is a choice of balancing the costs of obtaining and analyzing valuable data against the benefits of knowing what we are doing and how well the interventions are succeeding.

We now turn to discussion of a number of other issues, in particular, ethical issues. We address these by posing a series of questions, addressed to the various groups for whom this book was written.

FOR THE CLIENT

Questions about Evaluation

What shall I expect from evaluation? What are my rights? My responsibilities? What problems and possible advantages may I expect if I cooperate with the evaluation of my own situation?

Evaluation is not new to practitioners; it has always been a part of professional helping, but often was largely a subjective judgment rather than a more or less objective procedure. Evaluation has moved from a global, poorly defined process to a more specific and empirically oriented set of procedures. It has become incorporated into the helping process as a vital adjunct to the intervention itself. However, this addition is not without costs. It often is time-consuming to collect information about one's feelings, thoughts, and behaviors, as well as those of others. Is this effort worth the costs?

We believe that it is worth the price, and that clients get more than their fair share for energies expended on behalf of evaluation. First, accountability is a pressure obliging practitioners to demonstrate their competent performance of the role that society has assigned them. After all, the helping professional often is given enormous prerogatives and independence of function, so accountability is one way of making a quality control check. Most practitioners are convinced that they have knowledge and skills that can be helpful in resolving psychosocial problems. That they are asked to demonstrate this is sometimes embarrassing for them, but it is neither more nor less than the ethics of their professions demand. It also may be embarrassing when the client participates in an evaluation because it opens up the practitioner's work to scrutiny. But this is misplaced embarrassment, since *the fundamental objective of helping is to help, and the fundamental objective of evaluation is to improve that helping.* The professional presumably is trained to try a variety of methods to attain the client's objectives if the first method does not work. Thus, accountability is a pressure to ensure competency in helping; it is a fair demand, and no party to it should feel embarrassed by results, since this is the information needed to achieve the mutual goal of client and practitioner—helping to solve the client's problems.

A second reason that evaluation is worth its weight in effort to the client is that the client is directly a party to the evaluation whenever possible. The client is as biased in favor of desired outcomes as the practitioner.

Therefore, more or less objective evaluation may be seen as a sort of way of protecting one from one's self. The attempt to achieve objectivity may prevent premature stopping of intervention, or may help terminate a fruitless process. The point is that we have more or less independent confirmation of hopes (or doubts), and this is the information that we can use to make decisions with regard to intervention. For a little bit of time and effort in collecting or participating in data collection, clients can have a more or less objective basis for making vital decisions in regard to their own lives.

How Can Recording Help the Client (and the Practitioner)?

There is a myth (not supported by actual research; see Campbell, 1988, 1990) that clients will resist recording their own problems or strengths. What the myth may really point to is the fact that practitioners may be uncomfortable about asking clients to do recording. In this section we emphasize how recording can help the client and the practitioner in addition to those benefits.

First, recording can describe the actual scope of the problem. This is protection against natural tendencies to exaggerate or to minimize. If clients are prepared to share information with practitioners at all, then sharing accurate information should be acceptable, especially if the practitioner can convince the client (and himself or herself) of the utility of collecting data. Demonstrate how these data will be used. Let the client have a real part in the intervention, and the data will become real to the client.

Second, recording helps clients be aware of their behavior. Benjamin Franklin wrote in his *Autobiography and Other Writings* that for many years he kept track of his tendencies toward being disorderly, intemperate, not silent, and so on. He kept track of these tendencies by putting down a dot for each time he exhibited one of these behaviors. He expressed surprise at how many little dots there were. However, he also wrote that it gave him much pleasure to reduce the number of those dots. Awareness can be a motivating factor.

Third, this awareness leads to another important phenomenon for clients. By getting used to thinking about a behavior, one becomes used to thinking about its impact before it happens. This is something similar to anticipatory feedback. The charting of a set of behaviors often indicates the ripple effects of one event. The awareness of this (as pointed out by the practitioner) may be helpful to the client's understanding and self-control.

Fourth, recording can be a significant step in a client's independence from professional intervention. Keeping track of events can make the intervention briefer by helping the practitioner aid the client more clearly and directly. After the program of service is over, the client might profit by keeping track of events as a way of maintaining self-awareness of problems and strengths. It is important that clients be encouraged to chart strengths so as to accentuate the positive. Recording encourages honesty with one's self and with others. As long as the operations for measurement are precise and reasonably objective, recording presents life as it actually appears, without a sugar coating; thus, the problems will not be exaggerated either.

Ethical Considerations in Using Single-System Designs

Ethical questions naturally arise as increasing numbers of people learn about single-system designs and use them in many different contexts. Each choice you make regarding what kinds of practice and what forms of evaluation to use involve ethical decisions that may not always be obvious to the people involved. In this section, we continue our exploration of ethical principles that may be helpful in a variety of service contexts. We recognize that our statements may be controversial, but they represent only our opinions; we offer them as a beginning point for the discussions that may ultimately provide clear ethical guidelines for the helping professions.

First, though, we must emphasize that we view evaluation as an intrinsic part of practice so that the ethical guidelines of practice apply also to evaluation. However, many professional codes of conduct largely involve the conduct of the professional with regard to the practitioner role: responsibilities to clients, to colleagues, and to the employing agency, as well as to the profession and society. Frequently, little is said about research and evaluation. (We noted earlier in this chapter the recent NASW Code of Ethics revision that mandates evaluation of practice interventions.) Thus, to supplement professional, practice-oriented codes of ethics, we offer 11 ethical statements focusing on evaluation in the context of practice on the grounds that, for practice to be ethically conducted, evaluation must be integral to it. As ethical principles, these statements are guidelines for identifying the social and personal benefits and risks associated with the application of single-system designs for practice purposes. They generally are constructed like a formula for estimating how to maximize the benefits and minimize the risks in making a decision about whether to evaluate and how to evaluate.

1. *Provide demonstrable help.* As we noted earlier, the Hippocratic oath begins with the basic idea of providing help to clients. The original statement that has been the basis of so much of our ethical thinking in the helping professions is translated in this form:

> As to diseases, make a habit of two things—to help, or at least to do no harm. (From *The Epidemics,* as quoted by Veatch, 1981, p. 22)

Our suggestion for a first ethical principle for evaluating practice likewise begins with the statement to offer help, but to do so in the context of *demonstrable* help. The demonstration must be as objective as possible, for, as Demosthenes noted: "Nothing is so easy as to deceive one's self; for what we wish, that we readily believe." Demonstrated help involves several components: (a) the accurate identification of the presenting problems and potentials in the client situation, (b) corroboration of the extent to which help is in fact offered as intended for these identified concerns, and (c) documentation of ongoing changes and final outcomes relative to the client's goals and the social context. This first principle restates our basic belief that practice and evaluation are intricately related; caring practice and scientific practice necessarily mean *evaluated* practice.

2. *Demonstrate that no harm is done.* The Hippocratic oath continues that if one cannot help, then at least one should do no harm. Our suggestion for evaluating practice extends this principle to situations in which you are providing service on the assumption that you are helping. Because of the complexity of human behavior and circumstances, it is often difficult to tell whether a change in the client situation has occurred, and especially whether what you did affected that change. In some client situations, holding one's own is about the best outcome attainable, and slower-than-expected deterioration may be a positive result as well.

Systematic evaluation can provide information on whether there is deterioration from the initial state before intervention began. Thus, the meaning of doing no harm has to be clarified for a given client and situation. Because of practitioner bias or blindness, intended or not, there is always a danger that problems in the case may not be observed. Systematic evaluation is a key way that the trend toward harm becomes visible and subject to change.

There is an extended sense of doing no harm when scientific practice is viewed from a systems perspective. Clearly, you would not want to do anything that leaves the client damaged. Neither would you want to perform an action that helps the client at a comparable or greater expense to others, either those directly related to the case, or to the public at large. Thus, "do no harm" must be extended to include the client and affected others.

When there is a conflict between doing good for the client and doing significant harm to some other, the general principle of doing no significant harm to anyone takes precedence over doing good for someone. Other means of serving the client must be found that will approximate the joint goals of helping and doing no harm. Evaluation follows general practice ethics in such situations, but offers a way to specify the extent of the changes that might be involved in order to think more clearly about ethical decisions that would thereby be involved.

The concept of equivalent or comparable harm can be considered in the sense of a zero-sum versus a non-zero-sum situation. In the former or closed system, what one party gains, the other party loses. For example, a child cannot be both left at home with an abusive family and removed from that home. It is an ethical decision to weigh the potential good to the child (to be removed from an abusive situation) versus the potential harm to the family (for being denied ordinary parental rights).

In the non-zero-sum situation, what one party gains is not gained at the expense of the other party. For example, it would be conceivable that the harm of removing a child may be very destructive to the parents over the long run, so this dilemma becomes a stimulus to innovative thinking, such as having a third party live with the family for a period of time, or having the whole family move into a protective/training setting where staff could model appropriate parenting while safeguarding the child.

In general, the serious consideration of not doing significant harm may stimulate innovative practice, and careful documentation. Society demands strong evidence in such situations, and the helping professions can use evaluation to test their innovative practices.

3. Because evaluation is intrinsic to good practice, the practitioner should *involve clients in the consideration of evaluation of their situation while coming to agreement on the overall practice relationship.* This principle states that clients should be guaranteed informed consent regarding the objectives and methods of practice, which includes the evaluation of that practice. Focusing on the evaluation aspect, there are some pros and cons of introducing systematic evaluation in any particular situation. The pros (such as having more or less objective information as feedback to guide the practitioner toward helping the client achieve his or her goal) and cons (such as the time and energy needed to obtain the information and interpret it) should be considered with the client, as far as practical, before entering into the task.

The practitioner's obligation is to discuss what service will entail with (and perhaps even without) evaluation, and what information will or will not be available, accordingly. If the clients, or their guardians, are not able to participate in such a consideration, then some objective review panel or ombudsman should be consulted, in the same way that a supervisor or a medical review committee double-checks a medical practitioner's specific practices.

4. *Involve the client in the identification of the specific problem or objective and in the data collection process as much as possible.* This principle emerges from the value stance of the helping professions, that client participation in the definition of the situation for which professional help is being received is part of the client's right to self-determination. Participating in the helping process is critical to most practice methods; it also is important in most single-system evaluations. Practitioners must respect the client's values as expressed in the definition of the problems to be resolved and the goals or objectives to be attained. This does not mean that you cannot add objectives that reflect the values of significant others.

Baseline and intervention data may be directly or indirectly intrusive in the lives of clients and others, and should be collected only as long as needed to gain a clear perspective on the client situation. This perspective is to be used as a basis for planning the intervention and as a basis for determining when to change interventions and to terminate practice.

For some clients, involvement in their own data collection may be a burden; for others, it will constitute another aid to problem resolution itself. Some clients cannot or will not provide accurate information. Thus, this principle emphasizes that there is no one right way for involving clients in data collection, no automatic inclusion or exclusion of the client in the evaluation process. The prior guidelines of doing demonstrable helping and doing no harm may be applied in this situation of involving clients in the evaluation to the extent possible.

5. *Evaluation should intrude as little as possible on the intervention process, while still being capable of collecting useful and usable information.* Scientific practice includes both intervention services and the monitoring of the progress and the outcome of these services. However, monitoring activities may sometimes interfere with the delivery of services. In such cases, there is no question but that the service side of practice takes precedence over the evaluation side of practice.

However, such interference must be nontrivial before evaluation is to be removed from practice because, on balance, information that evaluation provides can be vital to practice. For example, a client was asked to keep track of her developmentally challenged child's behaviors in putting on his clothes in the correct order. This took some time and energy for an already frustrated mother, but, based on her collection of data, she soon realized that the child was dressing correctly the great majority of the time, and hence realized that the source of her frustrations was in some other area. She might never have realized this without going through the effort of measuring the child's behavior. The removal of evaluation from practice means a reduction in useful and usable information for practice, and not simply the elimination of a luxury accessory.

6. *Stop evaluation whenever it is painful or harmful to the client, physically, psychologically, or socially, without prejudice to the services offered.* Clients have the right to understand that they are being evaluated as part of being served, and that the evaluation may help you to offer more effective services. However, if at any time in the practice process, including before evaluation is to begin, the client finds the

prospect or the reality of evaluation to be severely problematic, then it is incumbent upon you to find other ways of evaluating that do not so burden the client.

This principle does not mean that all evaluation will be removed, since evaluation is essential to the conduct of practice. Rather, this principle emphasizes that evaluation shall not injure the client because of the evaluation process itself. (Obviously, a corresponding practice principle emphasizes that practice shall not injure the client because of the practice process itself.) Unobtrusive and nonreactive forms of evaluation may be feasible and unoffensive to the client.

7. *Confidentiality with regard to the data resulting from evaluation of the client/situation must be maintained as stringently as possible given organizational guidelines.* Clear limits should be preset with the client's knowledge regarding who has access to information emerging from evaluation. The data should be shared with the client to the extent possible. There may be contraindications to such sharing that emerge during the time of service. For instance, one contraindication would be where shared data may exaggerate the process of deterioration.

Data may be shared with other helping professionals involved with the case, but only in the context of professional helping. For example, case conferences frequently involve a group of professionals discussing the current events of agency cases on an ongoing basis, so as to benefit from the collective thinking on client problems and available evaluation data.

Confidentiality is not an absolute; clients have to be apprised of this fact. Case records may be subpoenaed by courts when there may be life-threatening circumstances involving persons affected by the client's behaviors (see *Tarasoff v. Regents of University of California* [17 Cal. 3rd 425, 1976]; Kopels & Kagle, 1993; Wilson, 1983).

Data may be used for research reports, provided no identifying information on individual clients is present. However, this raises a special risk in which practitioners make evaluation choices for the sake of the research data rather than what is appropriate for practice. A student of one of the authors reported that she changed a successful intervention because she wanted to use an experimental design; her teacher may have contributed to this misguided enthusiasm for evaluation by urging students to come up with a strong design. Because the facts of the case did not call for such a change, the student and the teacher may have been acting beyond ethical bounds.

8. *Balance the costs and benefits of evaluating practice.* Practice itself involves a complicated assessment of the costs and benefits of various actions in the client's situation. There may be occasions when you would not perform some rational action because the costs are too high or the benefits too low. But, most of the time, a projected favorable cost–benefit ratio helps to shape interventive actions.

Likewise, with the evaluation of practice, every action has a cost and some have personal and social benefits. Evaluation requires the likelihood that there will be a favorable balance, with the benefits from monitoring change and assessing outcome outweighing the costs in client energy, tolerance, money, and agency resources. This principle requires that you be able to assign weights, at least figuratively, to these categories, reflecting the individual client situation.

It sometimes is useful to predict the length of services necessary to achieve a statistically significant outcome, which could be useful in practitioner and agency planning. Achieving the projected statistical significance would still have to be aligned with achieving practical and theoretical significance.

9. *Evaluation should proceed only in the context of sensitivity to and respect for the client's individuality, particularly ethnicity, income level, sexual orientation, and gender.* Most helping professionals are aware of the need to be respectful of the client's individuality. But evaluation adds a completely new component to how one interacts with one's client(s). Use of questionnaires or other data-gathering devices may be viewed with suspicion by members of some groups. Some people may be reluctant to provide this information, particularly if they are of a different gender or ethnic group than the practitioner, or members of oppressed minority groups. Of course, there is no substitute for empathy and sensitivity on the part of the practitioner. It is your job to be concerned about how clients perceive these evaluation efforts, to include them as much as possible in planning them, and to do whatever you can to ensure that your efforts at evaluation will not be used in oppressive ways or even be perceived in

those ways. Involving clients in the selection of measurement tools is one way of openly addressing this concern.

10. *Evaluation is practice theory-neutral and value-tinged. Any conceptual guideline may have its implications evaluated, but every strategic choice stemming from that guideline has value implications.* This statement sums up our position that single-system designs can be used with any theory of or approach to practice, as long as the targets and interventions can be clearly and accurately identified. Theories project some vision of the future, and under some conditions, predictions of that future can be tested with single-system designs, and also with classical group designs. However, every practice decision is, in effect, subjected to evaluation on a formal or informal basis. Because value questions can be raised about every professional helping action, it becomes useful to have clear evidence about the trend of events and the outcome of actions, using more or less objective measures. Thus, evaluation provides the evidence for values. You evaluate your practice not only for factual information, but to supply evidence about the values involved in your helping actions.

11. *A Client Bill of Rights is an intrinsic part of a code of ethics for evaluating practice.* The following rights are the minimum:

1. Clients have the right to know what the *problem* is (from the perspective of the practitioner) in clear language that they can understand.
2. Clients have the right to participate in selecting *goals* and *objectives* of their intervention.
3. Clients have the right to know specifically what is going to happen during the *intervention process*—who is supposed to do what to whom and under what conditions?
4. Clients have the right to know how long the intervention is likely to last (*time* dimensions).
5. Clients have the right to know *alternative methods* of dealing with their problems, and what the probability is that the one(s) selected will lead to successful resolution of the difficulties.
6. Clients have the right to know how much the intervention will *cost* them. If they do not directly pay fees, it is equally a right to know the value of the services being provided.
7. Clients have the right to know what *records* will be kept and who will have access to them.
8. Clients have the right to know in advance about conditions regarding the *termination* of services.
9. Clients have the right to take increasing *control* over their own lives, so far as they are able, or to know (or have a guardian know) why this is not so.
10. Clients have the right to have all professional interventions systematically *evaluated* and to be a part of and informed about the *evaluation* of their own situations, so that they may profit from and make decisions based on these data.
11. Clients have the right to the most *effective interventions* available, based on the practitioner's review of the most current and relevant research and other literature; this is the heart of evidence-based practice.

A Model Consent Form

Exhibit 1 provides a model consent form for use in evaluation with single-system designs. It may require variations added to reflect special service situations. But, at least, these are the categories that you should closely consider. We again want to emphasize that *separate* consent for evaluation is not necessary since we view evaluation as just one component of overall practice. Thus, consent in this context is for practice to proceed and *includes* consent for evaluation.

FOR THE ADMINISTRATOR

Do I have a choice whether to evaluate? How can I get my staff to cooperate? How can I convincingly present information to funding agencies? What about the image of our agency?

Not for Practitioners Alone

EXHIBIT 1 Model consent form.

Client Consent Form

Preamble: This is a statement of intent for services to be rendered to _____
(client) by _____ (practitioner) beginning on _____ (date).

1. The following are targets to which we will devote our cooperative efforts: (state problem or objectives as relevant)
   A. Problem: _____ Objective: _____
   B. Problem: _____ Objective: _____ etc.
2. The overall goals of service are:
   A. _____ B. _____ etc.
3. While it is difficult to know exactly how long it will take to deal effectively with these targets of service, problems like these generally take about _____ weeks.
   (Or we can agree in advance to work together for a set period of time, and in this time accomplish all we can do. Let us agree that we will work together exactly _____ weeks, and re-evaluate our timing then.)
4a. The task of the practitioner is to provide guidance in thinking about alternative approaches to solutions of these problems. Several possible alternatives have been suggested, including:
    A. _____ B. _____ etc.
4b. We (client and practitioner) have decided that _____ approach is most likely to be helpful with the least negative side effects.
4c. The practitioner will be implementing the following interventive activities:
    A. _____ B. _____ C. _____
4d. The client will be doing the following tasks/activities as part of the intervention:
    A. _____ B. _____ C. _____
5a. In considering how to monitor ongoing events in this situation, and to evaluate the outcome, the practitioner is to suggest some methods of evaluation. Several possible alternatives have been suggested, including:
    A. _____ B. _____ etc.
5b. We (client and practitioner) have considered the options and have decided that _____ is most likely to be helpful in understanding the changes in events.
6. In these evaluation methods, it is understood that
   A. _____ (name party) will give
   B. _____ (specified types of information such as measures used) to
   C. _____ (name of receiver of information) on
   D. _____ (date information is due), which will then be analyzed and interpreted by the practitioner (and shared, as appropriate, with the client and relevant others).
7. The costs or fees involved in this service are set by the agency. The total fees are as follows: _____ (break down fees, as relevant). (The client is expected to pay the fee after each visit; if the client is unable to do so, please discuss this matter with the practitioner. If the client is not directly paying for the fees, then the above information may be useful to know regarding the financial aspects of this service.)
8. Several kinds of records will be kept:
   First, a service record in which the practitioner indicates summaries of client contacts.
   Second, agency records are kept related to fiscal matters for this case and the entire caseload of the agency.
   Third, information is kept monitoring the progress of the case, and whether or not case objectives are attained. Clients may be requested to participate in providing some of these data, which will be used to monitor progress and assess the outcome of practice.
9. Access to the records on this case will be restricted to
   a. agency personnel (for case management/collective thinking, and for fiscal matters)
   b. research personnel (for collective analysis—no individual names will be identified)
   c. outside legal authorities (only when the case records are subpoenaed)
10. Special requests regarding the practice and evaluation of this situation as made by the client, and agreed to by the practitioner:
    A. _____ B. _____ etc.

Client's Signature _____ Practitioner's Signature _____ Date _____

We have presented an optimistic picture of single-system evaluation, not omitting the difficulties, but accentuating the potentials. However, there is another side of evaluation, one that the administrator has to face. It is to this special set of issues that we now turn, for evaluation is difficult for many reasons totally separate from the evaluation task itself.

Evaluation: Do I Have a Choice?

No. The question really is what kind of evaluation you will choose for your agency, not *whether* you can choose to evaluate at all. Even privately funded institutions are subjected to various kinds of overt and covert pressure in this age of accountability, and public or quasi-public agencies have numerous pressures that are, at the core, evaluative in nature.

There are many forms of evaluation. The general label "program evaluation" is given to those attempts to view the complex workings of an organization or some component (program) of an organization relative to some set of stated objectives. The evaluation of social, educational, and welfare agencies is a special subcategory in program evaluation because of the factors studied, human satisfactions, feelings, understandings, and actions. No matter how difficult the task of evaluating these variables is, there is considerable pressure to present *some* evaluation. Formal program evaluation, as represented by the classical experimental, control-group designs, is a difficult, expensive enterprise, but it can present very powerful data. We offer single-systems designs as an alternative, or more accurately, as a *complement*, to the classical program evaluations (see also Royse, Thyer, Padgett, & Logan, 2006, and Unrau, Gabor, & Grinnell, 2007).

Most program evaluation is conducted in ways that produce grouped data. This is a very efficient way of summarizing the typical pattern among a number of clients, but the problem is that this also hides individual differences. The failures tend to offset the successes, suggesting that nothing significant happened. However, in fact, many significant events may have occurred. If a means were available for identifying individual outcomes, then it may be shown that some cases were "successful." It would also have to be admitted that there were some cases of failure, and a number of individuals who did not make any changes at all. This is important information because it directs us to take differential action, learn what went wrong (as far as possible), and try to correct for this in new cases, or in present cases before the deterioration becomes serious and irreversible. For the middle group of persons who do not change appreciably, the attempt can be made to change events to turn this situation around.

Single-system designs can supply administrators with this type of information about individual clients. Indeed, several types of information, as listed here, would be available to administrators through the use of single-system designs:

1. Data on clients, including specific types of client problems and strengths, seen at their agency
2. Data on how specific practitioners succeed with selected types of problems
3. Data on how individual practitioners are succeeding in general (overall caseload performance)
4. Data on how the set of practitioners is performing (agency "batting average")

These types of data have an internal and an external face. Internally, they supply information for the relevant parties. For example, as explained previously, information on client performance can be a big boost to client morale and motivation to continue treatment. But for the practitioner, information on his or her performance is a double-edged sword. If it tells the practitioner of successes, all well and good; if it reveals less than satisfactory performance, then this becomes pressure to change. One type of change is attacking the evaluation system (as we discuss shortly), but the other type of change is accepting the information as reasonably valid and looking for ways of benefiting from its suggestions. Perhaps a given practitioner does not work well with specific types of problems; he or she can transfer a case with such problems before becoming too deeply involved. On the other hand, this same practitioner also could get some special supervision in working with these types of problems. The point is that information can produce a crisis that can serve as an opportunity for positive change or as simply a burden or negative part of one's workload. More on this shortly.

The external face of these types of data refers to how evaluators of that information react to it. Practitioners react to clients' data in ways that keep the movement of the cases flowing toward desired goals. Supervisors in agencies keep supplies and supports flowing toward practitioners based on their individualized performance record. This could include merit bonuses for those doing particularly well and extra supervision or additional training for those not doing well. The point is not to make evaluation a punitive device for the staff, but rather to have it be an opportunity for advancement along a variety of fronts. Over time, probably all practitioners need some additional support for difficult types of case problems. Most practitioners probably would benefit from demonstrated successes with certain types of cases.

Obviously, external evaluators of agency functioning are an important audience to consider when choosing how the performance of an agency is going to be evaluated. We submit that the face validity of single-system designs may be very persuasive to board members who may not be versed in the use of more complicated research and statistical procedures. Explanations of how specific client problems and strengths were targeted for measurement before, during, and after intervention with given results would go far in making the evaluation process intelligible to decision makers. With this method, summary scores such as agency batting averages would become more meaningful. There would be positive pictures to present through individual analysis, even though there would also be negative ones. Moving agency practice in the direction of successful methods suggests both goals and promise for succeeding years.

Even for sophisticated reviewers of agency programs, single-system designs offer important advantages. Through the use of more powerful designs within this group, practitioners can offer strong evidence for showing that their interventions really did bring about changes in their clients' problems. In addition, the range of cases to be evaluated likely will be much more extensive with single-system designs, as most, if not all, practitioners can take part in doing evaluations of their own cases. Certainly the costs are lower when practitioners incorporate and use evaluation information within their own practices rather than waiting for control-group designs (and these are only group averages, not individual changes) to report back to the agency. Indeed, the involvement of practitioners in evaluation is a strong point in an agency's favor showing its willingness to respond to the immediate feedback such data provide.

Staff Development

Evaluation of a practitioner's own practice is an important addition to staff development, because it has not been until relatively recently that practitioners have had courses and workshops that conveyed information on single-system designs. As students in practica and internships come to agencies ready and able to evaluate their own practice, it may be somewhat embarrassing if no one is able to provide this type of guidance. (Indeed, the students may do the teaching in these cases.) However, workshops in single-system designs for supervisors and practitioners are immediately rewarding, as practitioners may quickly and relatively easily apply the basic principles to their own practices, although they too must work at learning these principles.

It would be helpful to have a staff member who is well-trained in these methods to act as consultant to the rest of the staff in these training phases. Questions always arise as to how to specify targets, how to chart particular events, and the like, and it is useful to have some resident expert—someone well-trained in the procedures who can act as a catalyst to the other members of the staff, a consultant on particular problems, and an interpreter for boards and the public. Support like this makes evaluation easier.

An important contribution to the integration of evaluation and practice in agencies is a book by Reid (1987) that is addressed to both practitioners and administrators; it spells out how a research and/or evaluation program can be integrated into human service agencies. While the practical suggestions presented by Reid are too numerous to detail here (they did, after all, require an entire book), briefly noting some of the topics might illustrate how they can be used to integrate ideas presented here into workable strategies for conducting successful evaluation programs in agencies while simultaneously providing services to clients.

Reid (1987) illustrates how to synthesize evaluation activities into daily job responsibilities. He has suggestions about actually making evaluation enjoyable(!), avoiding some of the common organizational and practice pitfalls in conducting evaluations, and strategies for involving staff in evaluation programs. He also offers a checklist of the key points that need to be addressed to complete evaluations successfully. While not all of the suggestions in Reid's book are focused on single-system designs, the basic principles can be applied to virtually any type of research or evaluation activity in an agency to facilitate accountable, scientific practice.

Staff Cooperation and Deployment

If an administrator is convinced of the value of single-system designs in the workings of his or her agency, then the next major step is to gain the cooperation of the staff in making evaluation an integral part of agency practice. This requires careful explanation not only about how to evaluate, but about what evaluation will mean for the practitioners themselves (their salary, promotion, or even tenure at the agency). Concerning the question of how to evaluate, it is relatively easy to bring in consultants and workshops to the agency or to have some or all practitioners attend classes at nearby colleges and universities.

The other side of the coin, how will evaluation affect a practitioner's job, is a question that has to be answered carefully (Kazi, 1998; Percevic, Lambert, & Kordy, 2004). We suggest that requiring that case evaluations be positive is not appropriate and should be separated from merit rewards up to a point, because of the enormous range of forces that may be acting on clients and that are out of the control of practitioners. Every practitioner will run into difficult cases sooner or later, cases where external events are way out of the control of the practitioner. However, there is a point in attempting to increase the effectiveness of practitioners, for the good of clients and society at large. And that point starts with evaluation of all cases, no matter what the outcomes may be. Systematic evaluation of all cases should be rewarded with incentives and bonuses.

For practitioners who *can* show success, even if the success is only with particular cases or with particular problems, there may be an additional system of rewards and benefits. It is important to a professional, as with all people, that he or she be given due recognition.

Single-system designs provide the basis for clear and specific recognition on several counts: first, just for their use; second, for the success itself; and third, for the sake of learning what went right or wrong and what can be conveyed to colleagues in and beyond the agency so that they can benefit from the experience. The ethical guidelines of all the helping professions direct their practitioners to contribute to the development of their discipline through communication about their work.

One major advantage for both administrators and the whole organization is that single-system designs can be used to monitor not only an individual practitioner's practice, but also to monitor practice throughout the whole agency. This can be done most readily when similar instruments are used throughout the agency, thus allowing the accumulation of information across all practitioners (Lambert, 2007; Ogles, Lambert, & Fields, 2002; Percevic, Lambert, & Kordy, 2004). Cumulating results across practitioners provide excellent models of accountable, organizational practice. They not only can highlight an agency's strengths, but they can point to areas of practice that might need bolstering in subsequent years.

Examples of Evaluation in Agency Settings

A number of agencies across the United States and elsewhere are using a variety of different methods to monitor and evaluate client outcomes (e.g., Harmon et al., 2007; Kazi, 1998; Kazi & Wilson, 1996; Lambert, 2007; Minami et al., 2008; Neuman, 2002; Percevic, Lambert, & Kordy, 2004; Wade & Neuman, 2007). Examples are summarized here to illustrate the range of evaluation procedures and the ways they can be applied.

An early study of social workers' use of single-system evaluation in a traditional, psychodynamically oriented family agency setting was conducted by Mutschler (1979, 1984). She trained a small group of six experienced social workers to identify treatment goals using a variety of standardized measures, and to monitor their specific interventions to gain feedback on the progress toward goal attainment. A 6-month training period consisted of biweekly meetings in which 15 single-system evaluation procedures were discussed. The social workers eventually selected a portion of these for their continuing use, including the Target Problem Measure, which we call an individualized rating scale (Battle et al., 1966), Goal Attainment Scaling (Kiresuk & Sherman, 1968), and Global Ratings of Improvement or Deterioration, in which both clients and practitioners rated overall perceived changes during and at the end of treatment.

The six social workers were to use these procedures throughout the 1-year evaluation phase, with each practitioner working with four randomly assigned clients. Four months after the project ended, follow-up questionnaires were employed to see, in part, whether the social workers had continued to use any of these evaluation tools.

Mutschler found that the social workers did indeed continue use of evaluation procedures for the full 2-year project but tended to use the briefest, and those perceived as most relevant, forms of evaluation. The initially negative or neutral attitudes of experienced practitioners were changed through involvement in the development and application of the measures they were to use. This was particularly true of the single-system designs (which emphasized achievement of service outcomes) rather than control-group designs (which emphasized studies of differential effectiveness of treatments). Mutschler also emphasized the need for changes in the organizational context that encourage evaluation as a part of practice.

Kazi and Wilson (1996) built on and extended Mutschler's work to an entire British social work agency (see Kazi, 1998, for additional examples from different agencies.). Kazi and Wilson trained and encouraged 21 social workers to use single-system evaluation with their clients. The project emphasized the gradual introduction of these designs into practice and extensive collaboration among practitioners and those supporting their efforts. Practitioners were trained to break down global targets into measurable parts, select appropriate and practical measures, and use these measures to evaluate their practice. A wide range of measures was used, many of the measurement strategies described throughout this book, and practitioners were actively engaged in the selection and development of the measurement strategies. The construction of single-system graphs and the visual analysis of graphed data were taught and used, but for the most part statistical tests were not. A wide range of interventions were evaluated. Kazi and Wilson (1996) provide a number of interesting and useful case examples drawn from this project, and these examples illustrate the wide diversity of the targets addressed and the single-system designs used. Finally, Kazi and Wilson, like Mutschler, emphasized the importance of changing the agency's policies, procedures, and practices—in other words, the agency milieu and values—in order to facilitate routine use of single-system designs. Those interested in implementing single-system evaluation in an agency would be well-advised to read Kazi and Wilson's work.

Finally, in a recent program of research which provides a wonderful example of evaluation-informed practice, Lambert and his colleagues provided regular feedback to practitioners about the progress of clients (e.g., Harmon et al., 2007; Lambert, 2007; Lambert et al., 2003). All clients regularly completely the Outcome Questionnaire, a 45-item measure designed to assess symptoms of psychological disturbance, interpersonal problems, social role functioning, and quality of life. So, unlike Mutschler and Kazi, Lambert and his colleagues did not tailor the measurement strategy to the individual client, but rather used the same multidimensional measure with all clients. Results of this program of research showed, among other things, that routine client monitoring and feedback to practitioners reduced deterioration, improved overall outcome, and led to fewer treatment sessions with no worsening of outcome for clients who were making progress (i.e., increased cost-effectiveness)

These examples illustrate ways in which agencies have been getting involved in evaluation of their practices on routine bases. This kind of information can be used to evaluate how well the agency as a whole is doing, and where it needs to make further efforts toward improvement of services. The key term in all this is *routine* evaluation, undertaking systematic measurement of what is done and how well it is working as an ordinary part of agency life. Aided by computers for the management of large bodies of such information, it is now possible to know up to the minute how well the agency is doing and what more needs to be done. This is clearly a beginning picture of the future of scientific practice.

FOR EDUCATORS AND STUDENTS

Educators: Do I know enough about this type of evaluation method to teach it? What about classical research? Does teaching single-system designs mean ignoring other types of designs? Is this just a fad?

Students: Can I really learn enough of this type of evaluation to use it on my own? I have "math anxiety"; can I get through a course on single-system designs?

We and several of our colleagues have taught single-system designs in various undergraduate and graduate programs across the country for a number of years, and we feel very close to the questions raised here on behalf of educators and students. In this section we try to respond to these questions based on our own experiences.

Does anyone know enough about anything to justify teaching it? The answer is relative. We may never know "enough," but as long as we have substantial knowledge of the particular topic and a well-rounded background of which the topic is a part, we may know enough to teach a course. To put it more positively, there is no better way to learn than by teaching. We hope this book can serve as one of the inputs for courses on single-system designs.

We often hear a concern that single-system designs may replace classical research. This is unlikely, however, because both serve different functions and address different questions. There will always be a need for classical research designs and the supporting statistical procedures. Single-system designs are special forms of evaluation designs particularly appropriate for applied uses by nonresearchers who have been trained in their implementation. These single-system designs are practice-oriented; they supply rapid feedback on the course of clinical and social system events, and they evaluate differences in outcomes between nonintervention periods and intervention periods. This is applied information, and it is acknowledged as an approximation of the experimental/control group design. The latter (classical) research is to some extent a more specialized discipline, and few professional educational programs give equal educational experience in classical research and in practice. Therefore, it is unrealistic to expect less than fully prepared practitioners to engage in classical research, except for the rare individual who seeks out special training and support, or when the practitioner takes part in a supporting role. What we are suggesting, in addition to all of the other benefits, is a way to encourage you to directly experience the pleasures of evaluation in the hopes of enticing you to take more advanced courses in classical designs and statistics.

Is the single-system design merely a fad? We prefer to consider it more a part of a paradigm shift (Fischer, 1981, 1993). Practitioners have long experienced the frustration of trying to apply classical research models to their own situations in the field and coming away empty-handed. Even when research teams are brought in, their services are often too remote from everyday problems in the agency to be perceived as of much use. Their often ponderous reports are long in coming, heavy in language, and low in applicability to this or that client here and now. Therefore, there is a search for new ways of solving the problem. Certain ideas are suggested and tentatively found to be useful. Others expand on the ideas and procedures, and soon textbooks that communicate the knowledge on a broad scale are written. This is pretty much a description of the field of single-system designs, with one exception: Single-system (or time-series) designs have been around in a variety of forms for over 100 years, and they have been heavily used by some social sciences such as economics and by the physical sciences and in agriculture, from whence many evaluation procedures were derived. We therefore conclude that single-system designs are no fad, but, rather, they represent a fundamental ground swell rebelling against the misapplication of complex research models to direct practices. However, we may be biased. Our final comment on this point is: Watch the professional literature; the literature on this topic has expanded enormously in recent years, and this is one way of distinguishing between a fad and a legitimate new development.

Students have a special right to be heard. They are the ones who ultimately are asked to experiment with new evaluation and practice procedures. Is it possible to learn enough about single-system designs in one or two classes to be competent in their use? We firmly believe that it is. This is not to say that all of the nuances of this approach, especially at first, will be digested completely—is anything ever so fully and finally learned? But the basic procedures, as described in this book, are relatively clear and are, we believe, relatively simple. We know from our own experiences that we can teach these procedures to typical classes of students in a regular semester. However, we recommend an additional semester for actual practice of these evaluation skills. Most importantly, we recommend that the skills not lie dormant, remaining in a practice and/or evaluation class; they should be integrated with and tried in field experiences and with the expectations and criteria for competent performance in general.

Single-system designs make heavy use of elementary logic (such as concomitant variation as the basis for inferences of causality) and thus far have placed comparatively little emphasis on advanced statistics. Although it may not even be necessary to apply the statistics in this book, one basic course in elementary statistics usually will supply all the information needed, at least for the time being. However, the logic of practice designs is a form of mathematical reasoning, you have reason to doubt the self-stereotyping many students perpetuate, that is, that they have trouble with math or logic ("math anxiety").

Mathematics is often a rather abstract subject, exquisite in its formal characteristics and logical power, quite unlike many other aspects of the knowledge of the helping professions. However, when students are directly working with clients and observe the usefulness of applying numbers to target events, we cannot help but believe that we will make many converts to this practical application of "numbers." To master a task (especially when putting in considerable effort) is the surest way of developing a committed user. This is one of the basic assumptions of this book: That using single-system designs will lead to more effective practice, and that many of the tasks associated with it, including a small amount of numerical calculations, will add to the delight of accomplishment.

In fact, single-system designs pose a powerful challenge to students (and faculty and practitioners): the challenge of keeping up-to-date and attempting to master new knowledge and new technology to the point where you can make a reasoned decision about how helpful it is to your work. Much of the material in this book is part of the challenge: learning about the ways computers can help us in managing our practice, learning the skills of analysis of data, integrating new knowledge with old, and evaluating it all as to its utility and importance. These are all hallmarks of the new breed of scientific practitioners. We, in fact, believe that these multiple challenges are ethical prerequisites for effective practice. Indeed, the evidence for the notion that mastery of the knowledge in this book will enhance your practice is in your hands.

Summary

The utility of single-system designs in the end result really depends on what you want to make of them. There are times when their application is difficult or time-consuming or their appropriateness is even somewhat unclear. Yet, we believe the advantages of single-system designs far outweigh the potential disadvantages.

In this chapter, we reviewed a number of ethical and other issues pertinent to clients, administrators, students, and educators. Out of all this, we hope we have convinced you if not to adopt single-system evaluations lock, stock, and barrel, then to give them a try and to decide after your own experience with evaluating your practice whether the endeavor is indeed worthwhile. We hope—no, we predict—that it will be.

REFERENCES

Abramovitz, J. S. (2006). *Obsessive-compulsive disorder: Advances in psychotherapy-An evidence-based practice.* New York: Hogrefe & Huber.

Ahluwalia, M. K. (2008). Multicultural issues in computer-based assessment. In Suzuki, L. A., & Ponterotto, J. G. (Eds.), *Handbook of multicultural assessment: Clinical, psychological, and educational applications* (3rd ed.) (pp. 92–106). San Francisco: Jossey-Bass.

Aiken, L. R., & Groth-Marnat, G. (2005). *Psychological testing and assessment* (12th ed.). Boston: Allyn & Bacon.

Alessi, G. (1988). Direct observation methods for emotional/behavioral problems. In E. S. Shapiro & T. R. Kratochwill (Eds.), *Behavioral assessment in schools: Conceptual foundations and practical applications* (chap. 2). New York: Guilford Press.

Allison, D. B., Silverstein, J. M., & Gorman, B. S. (1997). Power, sample size estimation, and early stopping rules. In R. D. Franklin, D. B. Allison, & B. S. Gorman (Eds.), *Design and analysis of single-case research* (pp. 245–277). Mahwah, NJ: Lawrence Erlbaum.

Allison, H., Gripton, J., & Rodway, M. (1983). Social work services as a component of palliative care with terminal cancer patients. *Social Work in Health Care, 8,* 29–44.

Altus, D. E., Welsh, T. M., Miller, I. K., & Merrill, M. H. (1993). Efficacy and maintenance of an education program for a consumer cooperative. *Journal of Applied Behavior Analysis, 26,* 403–404.

Alvelo, J., Collazo, A. A., & Rosario, D. (2001). Comprehensive assessment tools for Hispanics: Validation of the Multi-Problem Screening Inventory (MPSI) for Puerto Ricans. *Research on Social Work Practice, 11,* 699–724.

American Educational Research Association, American Psychological Association, and National Council on Measurement in Education. (1999). *Standards for educational and psychological testing.* Washington, DC: American Educational Research Association.

American Psychiatric Association. (2000). *Diagnostic and statistical manual of mental disorders* (4th ed., text revision). Washington, DC: Author.

Anastasi, A. (1988). *Psychological testing* (6th ed.). New York: Macmillan.

Ancis, J. R. (Ed.). (2003). *Culturally responsive interventions: Innovative approaches to working with diverse populations.* New York: Brunner-Routledge.

Anesko, K. M., Schoiock, G., Ramirez, R., & Levine, F. M. (1987). The homework problem checklist: Assessing children's homework difficulties. *Behavioral Assessment, 9,* 179–185.

Antony, M. M., & Barlow, D. H. (Eds.) (2001). *Handbook of assessment and treatment planning for psychological disorders.* New York: Guilford Press.

Antony, M. M., Ledley, D. R., & Heimberg, R.G. (Eds.). (2005). *Improving outcomes and preventing relapse in cognitive-behavior therapy.* New York: Guilford Press.

Applegate, J. S. (1992). The impact of subjective measures on nonbehavioral practice research: Outcome vs. process. *Families in Society, 73,* 100–108.

Arnau, J., & Bono, R. (2003). Autocorrelation problems in short time series. *Psychological Reports, 92,* 355–364.

Arnold, L. E., Vitiello, B., McDougle, C., Scahill, L., Shah, B., Gonzalez, N. M., et al. (2003). Parent-defined target symptoms respond to Risperidone in RUPP autism study: Customer approach to clinical trials. *Journal of the American Academy of Child and Adolescent Psychiatry, 42,* 1443–1450.

Atienza, O. O., Tang, L. C., Ang, B. W. (1998). A SPC procedure for detecting level shifts of autocorrelated processes. *Journal of Quality Technology, 30,* 340–351

Atkins, D. C., Bedics, J. D., McGlinchey, J. B., & Beauchaine, T. P. (2005). Assessing clinical significance: Does it matter which method we use? *Journal of Consulting and Clinical Psychology, 73,* 982–989.

Austin, J., Alvero, A. M., & Olson, R. (1998). Prompting patron safety belt use at a restaurant. *Journal of Applied Behavior Analysis, 31,* 655–657.

Austin, J., Weatherly, N. L. & Gravina, N. E. (2005). Using task clarification, graphic feedback and verbal feedback to increase closing-task completion in a privately owned restaurant. *Journal of Applied Behavior Analysis, 38,* 117–120.

Avina, C. (2008). The use of self-monitoring as a treatment intervention. In O'Donohue, W. T., & Cummings, N. A. (Eds.), *Evidence-based adjunctive treatments* (pp. 207–222). Burlington, MA: Academic Press.

Ayllon, T. (1963). Intensive treatment of psychotic behavior by stimulus satiation and food reinforcement. *Behavior Research and Therapy, 1,* 53–61.

Ayllon, T., & Azrin, N. (1968). *The token economy: A motivational system for therapy and rehabilitation.* Englewood Cliffs, NJ: Prentice Hall.

Bachar, E., Canetti, L., Yonah, I., Bonne, O. (2004). Group versus individual supportive-expressive psychotherapy for chronic, symptomatically stabilized outpatients. *Psychotherapy Research, 14,* 244–251.

Baden, A. L., & Wong, G. (2008). Assessment issues for working with diverse populations of elderly: Multiculturally sensitive perspectives. In Suzuki, L. A., & Ponterotto, J. G. (Eds.), *Handbook of multicultural assessment: Clinical, psychological,*

From References of *Evaluating Practice: Guidelines for the Accountable Professional*, Sixth Edition. Martin Bloom, Joel Fischer, John G. Orme. Copyright © 2009 by Pearson Education, Inc. All rights reserved.

and educational applications (3rd ed.) (pp. 594–624). San Francisco: Jossey-Bass.

Baer, D. M., Harrison, R., Fradenburg, L., Petersen, D., & Milla, S. (2005). Some pragmatics in the valid and reliable recording of directly observed behavior. *Research on Social Work Practice, 15,* 440–451.

Bales, R., Cohen, S., & Williamson, S. (1979). *SYMLOG: A system for the multiple level observations of groups.* New York: Free Press.

Bandura, A. (1986). *Social foundations of thought and action: A social cognitive theory.* Englewood Cliffs, NJ: Prentice-Hall.

Barlow, D. H. (2001a). *Anxiety and its disorders* (2nd ed.). New York: Guilford Press.

Barlow, D. H. (Ed.). (2001b). *Clinical handbook of psychological disorders* (3rd ed.). New York: Guilford Press.

Barlow, D. H., Hayes, S. C., & Nelson, R. O. (1984). *The scientist practitioner: Research and accountability in clinical and educational settings.* New York: Pergamon Press.

Barone, V. J., Greene, B. F., & Lutzker, J. R. (1986). Home safety with families being treated for child abuse and neglect. *Behavior Modification, 10,* 93–114.

Barrett, P. M., & Ollendick, T. H. (Eds.). (2004). *Handbook of interventions that work with children and adolescents.* New York: Wiley.

Battle, C. C., Imber, S. D., Hoehn-Saric, R., Stone, A. R., Nash, E. R., & Frank, J. D. (1966). Target complaints as criteria of improvement. *American Journal of Psychotherapy, 20,* 184–192.

Bauer, S., & Lambert, M. J. (2004). Clinical significance methods: A comparison of statistical techniques. *Journal of Personality Assessment, 82,* 60–70.

Beaulaurier, R. L. (2005). Integrating computer content into social work curricula: A model for planning. *Journal of Teaching in Social Work, 25,* 153–171.

Beck, A. T., Steer, R. A., & Brown, G. K. (1996). *Beck depression inventory-II manual.* San Antonio, TX: Psychological Corporation.

Beidel, D. C. (1988). Goal attainment scaling. In M. Hersen & A. S. Bellack (Eds.), *Dictionary of behavioral assessment techniques* (pp. 238–241). New York: Pergamon Press.

Bellack, A. S. (Ed.) (2006). *Behavioral treatment for substance abuse in people with severe and persistent mental illness.* New York: Brunner-Routledge.

Benbenishty, R. (1988). Assessment of task-oriented family interventions with families in Israel. *Journal of Social Service Research, 11,* 19–43.

Benbenishty, R. (1989). Combining the single-system and group approaches to evaluate treatment effectiveness on the agency level. *Journal of Social Service Research, 12,* 31–47.

Benbenishty, R., & Ben-Zaken, A. (1988). Computer-aided process of monitoring task-centered family interventions. *Social Work Research and Abstracts, 24,* 7–9.

Benedict, W. (1978). *Evalutreat: A unified approach to program evaluation and direct service delivery.* Stoughton, WI: Lutheran Social Services of Wisconsin and Upper Michigan.

Bentley, K. J. (1990). An evaluation of family-based intervention using single-system research. *British Journal of Social Work, 20,* 101–116.

Berger, M. (2006). Computer assisted clinical assessment. *Child and Adolescent Mental Health, 11,* 64–75.

Berlin, S. B. (1985). Maintaining reduced levels of self-criticism through relapse-prevention treatment. *Social Work Research and Abstracts, 21,* 21–33.

Berlin, S. B., Mann, K. B., & Grossman, S. F. (1991). Task analysis of cognitive therapy for depression. *Social Work Research and Abstracts, 27,* 3–11.

Berntson, G. G., & Cacioppo, J. T. (2006). Multilevel analysis: Physiological and biochemical measures. In Eid, M., & Diener, D. (Eds.), *Handbook of multimethod measurement in psychology* (pp. 157–187). Washington, DC: American Psychological Association.

Beutler, L. E., & Groth-Marnat, G. (2003). *Integrative assessment of adult personality* (2nd ed.). New York: Guilford Press.

Beutler, L. E., & Mailik, M. L. (Eds.). (2002). *Rethinking the DSM: A psychological perspective.* Washington, DC: American Psychological Association.

Beutler, L. E., Malik, M., Alimohamed, S., Harwood, T. M., Talebi, H., Noble, S., & Wong, E. (2004). Therapist variables. In M. Lambert (Ed.), *Bergin and Garfield's handbook of psychotherapy and behavior change* (5th ed.) (pp. 227–306). New York: Wiley.

Bhopal, J. S. (1981). Simple SOAP system, *British Medical Journal, 283,* 889.

Bird, H. R., Canino, G., Rubio-Stipec, M., & Ribera, J. C. (1987). Further measures of the psychometric properties of the children's global assessment scale. *Archives of General Psychiatry, 44,* 821–824.

Bird, H. R., Andrews, H., Schwab-Stone, M., Goodman, S., Dulcan, M., Richters, J., Rubio-Stipec, M., Moore, R. E., Chiang, P. H., & Hoven, C. (1996). Global measures of impairment for epidemiologic and clinical use with children and adolescents. *International Journal of Methods in Psychiatric Research, 6,* 295–308.

Bisman, C. D., & Hardcastle, D. A. (1999). *Integrating research into practice.* Belmont, CA: Wadsworth.

Blanton, H., & Jaccard, J. (2006). Arbitrary metrics in psychology. *American Psychologist, 61,* 27–41.

Bloom, M. (1975). *The paradox of helping: Introduction to the philosophy of scientific practice.* New York: Wiley.

Bloom, M. (1987). Theoretical significance. In N. Gottlieb (Ed.), *Perspectives on direct practice evaluation,* (Monograph No. 5). Seattle: School of Social Work, University of Washington.

Bloom, M. (1996). *Primary prevention practices.* Thousand Oaks, CA: Sage.

Bloom, M., & Block, S. R. (1977). Evaluating one's own effectiveness and efficiency. *Social Work, 22,* 130–136.

Bloom, M., Butch, P., & Walker, D. (1979). Evaluation of single interventions. *Journal of Social Service Research, 2,* 301–310.

Bloom, M., & Fischer, J. (1982). *Evaluating practice: Guidelines for the accountable professional.* Englewood Cliffs, NJ: Prentice Hall.

Bloom, M., & Klein, W. (1994). Is there an ethical responsibility to use practice methods with the best empirical evidence of effectiveness? Yes. In H. Hudson & P. Nurius (Eds.), *Controversial issues in social work research* (pp. 100–105). Boston: Allyn & Bacon.

Bloom, M., & Orme, J. G. (1993). Ethics and single-system design. *Journal of Social Service Research, 18,* 161–180.

Bloomquist, M., & Schnell, S. V. (2002). *Helping children with aggression and conduct problems: Best practices for interventions.* New York: Guilford Press.

BLUMENTHAL, D. (1993). Total quality management and physicians' clinical decisions. *Journal of the American Medical Association, 269,* 2775–2778.

BLYTHE, B., TRIPODI, T., & BRIAR, S. (1994). *Direct practice research in human service agencies.* New York: Columbia University Press.

BOHART, A. C., & GREENBERG, L. (Eds.). (1997). *Empathy reconsidered: New directions in psychotherapy.* Washington, DC: American Psychological Association.

BOLEN, R. M., & HALL, J. C. (2007). Managed care and evidence-based practice: The untold story. *Journal of Social Work Education, 43,* 463–471.

BOSTWICK, N. K., & BOSTWICK, G. J., JR. (1987). Intersource consensus and outcome evaluation. In N. Gottlieb (Ed.), *Perspectives on direct practice evaluation* (chap. 6). Seattle: University of Washington, School of Social Work.

BRADSHAW, W. (2003). Use of single-system research to evaluate the effectiveness of cognitive-behavioural treatment of schizophrenia. *British Journal of Social Work, 33,* 885–899.

BRADSHAW, W., & ROSEBOROUGH, D. (2004). Evaluating the effectiveness of cognitive-behavioral treatment of residual symptoms and impairment in schizophrenia. *Research on Social Work Practice, 14,* 112–120.

BRAGER, G., & SPECHT, H. (1973). *Community organizing.* New York: Columbia University Press.

BRIGGS, H. E., & RZEPNICKI, T. L. (Eds.). (2004). *Using evidence in social work practice: Behavioral perspectives.* Chicago: Lyceum.

BRIGHAM, T. A., MEIER, S. M., & GOODNER, V. (1995). Increasing designated driving with a program of prompts and incentives. *Journal of Applied Behavior Analysis, 28* (1), 83–84.

BROSSART, D. F., PARKER, R. I., OLSON, E. A., & MAHADEVAN, L. (2006). The relationship between visual analysis and five statistical analyses in a simple AB single-case research design. *Behavior Modification, 5,* 531–563.

BROTHERS, K. J., KRANTZ, P. J., & MCCLANNAHAN, L. E. (1994). Office paper recycling: A function of container proximity. *Journal of Applied Behavior Analysis, 27,* 153–160.

BROVERMAN, I., BROVERMAN, D., CLARKSON, F., ROSENKRANTZ, P., & VOGEL, S. (1970). Sex-role stereotypes and clinical judgments of mental health. *Journal of Consulting and Clinical Psychology, 34,* 1–7.

BROWN, J. A., & BROWN, C. S. (1977). *Systematic counseling: A guide for the practitioner.* Champaign, IL: Research Press.

BROWNING, R. M., & STOVER, D. O. (1971). *Behavior modification in child treatment: An experimental and clinical approach.* Chicago: Aldine & Atherton.

BROWNSON, R. C., BAKER, E. A., LEET, T. L., & GILLESPIE, K. N. (2002). *Evidence-based public health.* New York: Oxford University Press.

BROXMEYER, N. (1978). Practitioner-research in treating a borderline child. *Social Work Research and Abstracts, 14,* 5–10.

BURRILL, G. C. (1976). The problem-oriented log in social casework. *Social Work, 21,* 67–68.

BUSK, P. L., & MARASCUILO, L. A. (1988). Autocorrelation in single-subject research: A counter-argument to the myth of no autocorrelation. *Behavioral Assessment, 10,* 229–242.

BUSSERI, M. A., & TYLER, J. D. (2004). Client-therapist agreement on target problems, working alliance, and counseling outcome. *Psychotherapy Research, 14,* 77–88.

BUTCHER, J. N., PERRY, J., HAHN, J. (2004). Computers in clinical assessment: Historical developments, present status, and future challenges. *Journal of Clinical Psychology, 60,* 331–345.

BUXTON, A. R. M., RODGER, S., & CUMMINGS, A. L. (2006). The change process in clients with high needs. *Canadian Journal of Counseling, 40,* 32–47.

CABOT, R. C. (1931). Treatment in social casework and the need of criteria and of tests of its success or failure. *Proceedings of the National Conference of Social Work.*

CALLAHAN, C. D., & BARISA, M. T. (2005). Statistical process control and rehabilitation outcome: The single-subject design reconsidered. *Rehabilitation Psychology, 50,* 24–33.

CAMPBELL, D. T., & FISKE, D. W. (1959). Convergent and discriminant validation by the multitrait-multimethod matrix. *Psychological Bulletin, 56,* 81–105.

CAMPBELL, D. T., & STANLEY, J. C. (1963). *Experimental and quasi-experimental designs for research.* Chicago: Rand McNally.

CAMPBELL, J. A. (1988). Client acceptance of single-system evaluation procedures. *Social Work Research and Abstracts, 24,* 21–22.

CAMPBELL, J. A. (1990). Ability of practitioners to estimate client acceptance of single-subject evaluation procedures. *Social Work, 35,* 9–14.

CAREY, R. G., & STAKE, L. V. (2003). *Improving healthcare with control charts: Basic and advanced SPC methods and case studies.* Milwaukee, WI: ASQ Quality Press.

CARR, A. (Ed.). (2000). *What works with children and adolescents?* London: Brunner-Routledge.

CARR, J. E., & BURKHOLDER, E. O. (1998). Creating single-subject design graphs with Microsoft Excel. *Journal of Applied Behavior Analysis, 31,* 245–251.

CASTONGUAY, L. G., & BEUTLER, L. E. (Eds.). (2006). *Principles of therapeutic change that work.* New York: Oxford University Press.

CHAMBLESS, D. L., SANDERSON, W. C., SHOHAM, V., BENNETT-JOHNSON, S., POPE, K. S., CRITS-CHRISTOPH, P., & BAKER, M. (1996). An update on empirically validated techniques. *The Clinical Psychologist, 49,* 5–18.

CHAMBLESS, D. L., BAKER, M. J., BAUCOM, D. H., BEUTLER, L. E., CALHOUN, K. S., & CRISTOPH, P. (1998). Update on empirically validated techniques, II. *The Clinical Psychologist, 51,* 3–16.

CHASSAN, J. B. (1979). *Research design in clinical psychology and psychiatry* (2nd ed.). New York: Irvington Press.

CHEUNG, K. F. M., & CANDA, E. R. (1992). Training Southeast Asian refugees as social workers: A single subject evaluation. *Social Development Issues, 14,* 88–99.

CLARKIN, J. F., & LEVY, K. N. (2004). The influence of client variables in psychotherapy. In M. L. Lambert (Ed.), *Bergin and Garfield's handbook of psychotherapy and behavior change* (5th ed.) (pp. 194–226). New York: Wiley.

COHEN, J. (1960). A coefficient of agreement for nominal scales. *Educational and Psychological Measurement, 20,* 37–46.

COHEN, J. (1988). *Statistical power analysis for the behavioral sciences* (2nd ed.). Hillsdale, NJ: Lawrence Erlbaum.

COLON, M. (2006). *Improving the reliability and validity of visual inspection of data by behavior analysis: An empirical comparison of two training methods to improve visual inspection and interpretation, the job aid and the conservative dual-criteria.* Unpublished doctoral dissertation, The Florida State University, Tallahassee.

COMBS-ORME, T. D., & ORME, J. G. (1986). Reliability of self-reported child abuse and neglect in a general population survey. *Social Work Research and Abstracts, 22,* 19–21.

Conboy, A., Auerbach, C., Beckerman, A., Schnall, D., & LaPorte, H. H. (2000). MSW student satisfaction with using single-system-design computer software to evaluate social work practice. *Research on Social Work Practice, 10,* 127–138.

Cone, J. D. (2001). *Evaluating outcomes: Empirical tools for effective practice.* Washington, DC: American Psychological Association.

Conrad, R. L. (2000). *Attributions of problem cause and solution in therapy.* Unpublished doctoral dissertation, University of Illinois at Urbana-Champaign.

Cook, T. D., & Campbell, D. T. (1976). The design and conduct of quasi-experiments and true experiments in field settings. In M. Dunnette (Ed.), *Handbook of industrial and organizational psychology* (pp. 223–326). Chicago: Rand McNally.

Cook, T. D., & Campbell, D. T. (1979). *Quasi-experimentation: Design and analysis issues for field settings.* Chicago: Rand McNally.

Cooper, J. O., Heron, T. E., Heward, W. L. (2007). *Applied behavior analysis* (2nd ed.). Upper Saddle River, NJ: Pearson Education.

Cooper, M. G. (1990). Treatment of a client with obsessive-compulsive disorder. *Social Work Research and Abstracts, 26,* 26–36.

Cooper, M. G. (2006). Integrating single-system design research into the clinical practice class. *Journal of Teaching in Social Work, 26,* 91–102.

Corcoran, J. (2003). *Clinical applications of evidence-based interventions.* New York: Oxford University Press.

Corcoran, K., & Gingerich, W. J. (1994). Practice evaluation in the context of managed care: Case-recording methods for quality assurance reviews. *Research on Social Work Practice, 4,* 326–327.

Corcoran, K., & Keeper, C. (1992). Psychodynamic treatment for persons with borderline personality disorders. In K. Corcoran (Ed.), *Structuring change: Effective practice for common client problems* (pp. 255–271). Chicago: Lyceum.

Cormier, S, Nurius, P., & Osborn, C. J. (2009). *Interviewing and change strategies for helpers: Fundamental skills and cognitive-behavioral interventions* (6th ed.). Pacific Grove, CA: Brooks/Cole.

Council on Social Work Education (2003). *Handbook of Accreditation Standards and Procedures* (5th ed.). Council on Social Work Education Commission on Accreditation (5th ed.). Alexandria, VA: Author.

Cournoyer, B. R. (2003). *The evidence-based social work skills book.* Boston: Allyn & Bacon.

Crisp, B. R. (2004). Evidence-based practice and the borders of data in the global information era. *Journal of Social Work Education, 40,* 73–86.

Crosbie, J. (1987). The inability of the binomial test to control Type I error with single-subject data. *Behavioral Assessment, 9,* 141–150.

Crosbie, J. (1993). Interrupted time-series analysis with brief single-subject data. *Journal of Consulting and Clinical Psychology, 61,* 966–974.

Crosbie, J. (1995). Interrupted time-series analysis with short series: Why it is problematic, how it can be improved. In J. M. Gottman (Ed.), *The analysis of change* (pp. 361–395). Mahwah, NJ: Lawrence Erlbaum.

Crosbie, J., & Sharpley, C. F. (1991). *DMITSA 2.0: A statistical program for analysing data from interrupted time-series.* Clayton, Australia: Monash University.

Crosland, K. A., Dunlap, G., Sager, W., Neff, B., Wilcox, C., Blanco, A., Giddings, T. (2008). The effects of staff training on the types of interactions observed at two group homes for foster care children. *Research on Social Work Practice, 18,* 410–420.

Cross, D. G., Sheehan, P. W., & Kahn, J. A. (1980). Alternative advice and counsel in psychotherapy. *Journal of Consulting and Clinical Psychology, 48,* 615–625.

Cross, D. G., Sheehan, P. W., & Kahn, J. A. (1982). Short- and long-term follow-up of clients receiving insight-oriented therapy and behavior therapy. *Journal of Consulting and Clinical Psychology, 50,* 103–112.

Cushing, L. S., & Kennedy, C. H. (1997). Academic effects of providing peer support in general education classrooms on students without disabilities. *Journal of Applied Behavior Analysis, 30,* 139–151.

Dana, R. H. (2005). *Multicultural assessment: Principles, applications, and examples.* Mahwah, NJ: Erlbaum.

Dattalo, P. (2008). *Determining sample size: Balancing power, precision, and practicality.* New York: Oxford University Press.

Dausch, B. M., Miklowitz, D. J., Richards, J. A. (1996). Global Assessment of Relational Functioning Scale (GARF), II: Reliability and validity in a sample of families of bipolar patients. *Family Process, 35,* 175–189.

Davis, L. E., & Proctor, E. K. (1995). *Race, gender and class: Guidelines for practice with individuals, families, and groups* (2nd ed.). Boston, MA: Allyn & Bacon.

Davis, T. D. (2007). Why do MSW students evaluate practice the way they do? An evidence-based theory for clinical supervisors. *The Clinical Supervisor, 26,* 159–175.

Dawes, M., Davies, P. T., Gray, A., Mant, J., Seers, K., & Snowball, R. (1999). *Evidence-based practice: A primer for healthcare professionals.* Edinburgh, UK: Churchill Livingstone.

Dean, R. G., & Reinherz, H. (1986). Psychodynamic practice and single system design: The odd couple. *Journal of Social Work Education, 22,* 71–81.

Deane, F. P., Spicer, J., & Todd, D. M. (1997). Validity of a simplified target complaints measure. *Assessment, 4,* 119–130.

DeCarlo, L. T., & Tryon, W. W. (1993). Estimating and testing autocorrelation with small samples: A comparison of the C-statistic to a modified estimator. *Behaviour Research & Therapy, 31,* 781–788.

De Los Reyes, A., Kazdin, A. E. (2005). Informant discrepancies in the assessment of childhood psychopathology: A critical review, theoretical framework, and recommendations for further study. *Psychological Bulletin, 131,* 483–509.

DeVellis, R. F. (2003). *Scale development: Theory and applications* (2nd ed.). Thousand Oaks, CA: Sage.

Dixon, M. R. (2003). Creating a portable data-collection system with Microsoft Embedded visual tools for the pocket PC. *Journal of Applied Behavior Analysis, 36,* 271–284.

Dobson, K. (Ed.). (2000). *Handbook of cognitive-behavioral therapies* (2nd ed.). New York: Guilford Press.

Dobson, K. S., & Craig, K. D. (Eds.). (1998a). *Best practice: Developing and promoting empirically supported interventions.* Newbury Park, CA: Sage.

Dobson, K. S., & Craig, K. D. (Eds.). (1998b). *Empirically supported therapies: Best practice in professional psychology.* Thousand Oaks, CA: Sage.

Donnelly, C., & Carswell, A. (2002). Individualized outcome measures: A review of the literature. *Canadian Journal of Occupational Therapy, 69,* 84–94.

References

DOTY, L. A. (1996). *Statistical process control* (2nd ed.). New York: Industrial Press.

DOUGHERTY, L. R., KLEIN, D. N., OLINO, T. M., & LAPTOOK, R. S. (2008). Depression in children and adolescents. In Hunsley, J., & Mash, E. J. (Eds.), *A guide to assessments that work* (pp. 69–95). New York, NY: Oxford University Press.

DRYFOOS, J. (1994). *Full-service schools: A revolution in health and social services for children, youth, and families.* San Francisco: Jossey-Bass.

DUGAS, M. J., & ROBICHAUD, M. (2006). *Cognitive-behavioral treatment for generalized anxiety: From science to practice.* New York: Brunner-Routledge.

DULMUS, C. N., & RAPP-PAGLICCI, L. A. (Eds.). (2005). *Handbook of preventive intervention for adults.* New York: Wiley.

DWORKIN, R. H., TURK, D. C., WYRWICH, K. W., BEATON, D., CLEELAND, C. S., FARRAR, J. T., ET AL. (2008). Interpreting the clinical importance of treatment outcomes in chronic pain clinical trials: IMMPACT recommendations. *Journal of Pain, 9*, 105–121.

D'ZURILLA, T. J., & NEZU, A. M. (2006). *Problem-solving therapy* (3rd ed.). New York: Springer.

EID, M., & DIENER, E. (Eds.) (2006). *Handbook of multimethod measurement in psychology.* Washington, DC: American Psychological Association.

ENGEL, J. M., JENSEN, M. P., & SCHWARTZ, L. (2004). Outcome of biofeedback-assisted relaxation for pain in adults with cerebral palsy: Preliminary findings. *Applied Psychophysiology and Biofeedback, 29*, 135–141.

EPSTEIN, W.M. (2008). [Book Review] The true Hypocrites: S. L. Witkin & D. Saleebey (Eds.). Social work dialogues. Alexandria, VA: Council on Social Work Education. In *Research on Social Work Practice, 18*, 82–84.

ERION, J. (2006). Parent tutoring: A meta-Analysis. *Education and Treatment of Children, 29*, 79–106.

ESADE, V. S., SOLANAS, A., & QUERA, V. (2005). Randomization tests for systematic single-case designs are not always appropriate. *The Journal of Experimental Education, 73*, 140–160.

FARRIMOND, S. J., & LELAND, JR., L. S. (2006). Increasing donations to supermarket foodbank bins using proximal prompts. *Journal of Applied Behavior Analysis, 39*, 249–251.

FASSLER, A. (2007). *Merging task-centered social work and motivational interviewing in outpatient medication assisted substance abuse treatment: Model development for social work practice.* Unpublished doctoral dissertation, Virginia Commonwealth University, Richmond.

FAUL, A. C., MCMURTY, S. L., & HUDSON, W. W. (2001). Can empirical clinical practice techniques improve social work outcomes? *Research on Social Work Practice, 11*, 277–299.

FEINGOLD, A., OLIVETO, A., SCHOTTENFELD, R., & KOSTEN, T. R. (2002). Utility of crossover designs in clinical trials: Efficacy of desipramine vs. placebo in opioid-dependent cocaine abusers. *American Journal on Addictions, 11*, 111–123.

FERGUSON, K. L., & RODWAY, M. R. (1994). Cognitive behavioral treatment of perfectionism: Initial evaluation studies. *Research on Social Work Practice, 4*, 283–308.

FERRON, J. (2002). Reconsidering the use of the general linear model with single-case data. *Behavior Research Methods, Instruments, and Computers, 34*, 324–331.

FERRON, J., & JONES, P. K. (2006). Tests for the visual analysis of response-guided multiple-baseline data. *The Journal of Experimental Education, 75*, 66–81.

FERRON, J., & ONGHENA, P. (1996). The power of randomization tests for single-case phased designs. *Journal of Experimental Education, 64* (3), 231–239.

FERRON, J., & WARE, W. (1994). Using randomization tests with responsive single-case designs. *Behaviour Research and Therapy, 23*, 787–791.

FERRON, J., & WARE, W. (1995). Analyzing single-case data: The power of randomization tests. *The Journal of Experimental Education, 63*, 167–178.

FICKLING, J. A. (1993). *The construction and testing of a measure of parental knowledge of home-based injury risks to preschool children.* Unpublished doctoral dissertation, University of Maryland, Baltimore.

FINKELMAN, A. W. (2001). *Managed care: A nursing perspective.* Englewood Cliffs, NJ: Prentice-Hall.

FINN, J. (2008). Online therapy. In Mizrahi, T. & Davis, L. (Eds.), Encyclopedia of Social Work (20th ed.). Washington, DC: NASW Press.

FISCHER, J. (1978). *Effective casework practice: An eclectic approach.* New York: McGraw-Hill.

FISCHER, J. (1981). The social work revolution. *Social Work, 26*, 199–207.

FISCHER, J. (1986). Eclectic Casework. In J. C. Norcross (Ed.), *Handbook of eclectic psychotherapy* (pp. 320–352). New York: Brunner/Mazel.

FISCHER, J. (1993). Empirically-based practice: The end of ideology? *Journal of Social Service Research, 18*, 19–64.

FISCHER, J. (2009). *Toward evidence-based practice: Variations on a theme.* Chicago: Lyceum Books.

FISCHER, J., & CORCORAN, K. (2007a). *Measures for clinical practice and research. Vol. 1. Couples, families, and children* (4th ed.). New York: Oxford University Press.

FISCHER, J., & CORCORAN, K. (2007b). *Measures for clinical practice and research. Vol. 2. Adults* (4th ed.). New York: Oxford University Press.

FISCHER, J., & GOCHROS, H. L. (1975). *Planned behavior change: Behavior modification in social work.* New York: Free Press.

FISHER, C. B. (2004). *Decoding the ethics code: A practical guide for psychologists.* Thousand Oaks, CA: Sage.

FISHER, J. E., & O'DONOHUE (Eds.). (2006). *Practitioner's guide to evidence-based psychotherapy.* New York: Springer.

FISHER, K., & HARDIE, R. J. (2002). Goal attainment scaling in evaluating a multidisciplinary pain management programme. *Clinical Rehabilitation, 16*, 191–198.

FISHER, L., HAYES, S., & O'DONOHUE, W. (Eds.). (2003). *Empirically supported techniques of cognitive-behavioral therapy: A step-by-step guide.* New York: Wiley.

FISHER, W. W., KELLEY, M. E., & LOMAS, J. E. (2003). Visual aids and structured criteria for improving visual inspection and interpretation of single-case designs. *Journal of Applied Behavior Analysis, 36*, 387–406.

FLEISS, J. L., LEVIN, B., PAIK, M. C., & FLEISS, J. (2003). *Statistical methods for rates and proportions* (3rd ed.). Hoboken, NJ: Wiley.

FONAGY P. (2003). Theory and some evidence. *Behavioral Inquiry, 22*, 412–459.

FONTES, L. A., O'NEILL-ARANA, M. R. (2008). Assessing for child maltreatment in culturally diverse families. In Suzuki, L. A., & Ponterotto, J. G. (Eds.), *Handbook of multicultural assessment: Clinical, psychological, and educational applications* (3rd ed.) (pp. 627–650). San Francisco: Jossey-Bass.

FORTUNE, A. E. (Ed.). (1985). *Task-centered practice with families and groups.* New York: Springer.

Foster, S. L., & Cone, J. D. (1986). Design and use of direct observation procedures. In A. R. Ciminero, K. S. Calhoun, & H. E. Adams (Eds.), *Handbook of behavioral assessment* (2nd ed.) (chap. 9). New York: Wiley.

Fox, D. K., Hopkins, B. L., & Anger, W. K. (1987). The long-term effects of a token economy on safety performance in open-pit mining. *Journal of Applied Behavior Analysis, 20*, 215–224.

Franklin, B. (1961). *Autobiography and other writings.* New York: Signet.

Franklin, R. D., Allison, D. B., & Gorman, B. S. (Eds.). (1997). *Design and analysis of single-case research.* Mahwah, NJ: Lawrence Erlbaum.

Franklin, R. D., Gorman, B. S., Beasley, T. M., & Allison, D. B. (1997). Graphical display and visual analysis. In R. D. Franklin, D. B. Allison, & B. S. Gorman (Eds.), *Design and analysis of single-case research* (pp. 119–158). Mahwah, NJ: Lawrence Erlbaum.

Fraser, M. W., Nelson, K. E., & Rivard, J. C. (1997). Effectiveness of family preservation services. *Social Work Research, 21*, 138–153.

Freeman, C., & Power, B. (Eds.) (2006). *Handbook of evidence-based psychotherapies.* New York: Wiley.

Frick, P. J., & McMahon, R. J. (2008). Child and adolescent conduct problems. In Hunsley, J., & Mash, E. J. (Eds.), *A guide to assessments that work* (pp. 41–68). New York, NY: Oxford University Press.

Friman, P. C. (2009). Behavior assessment. In Barlow, D., Nock, M., & Hersen, M. *Single case experimental designs: Strategies for studying behavior for change* (3rd ed.) (pp. 99–134). Boston, MA: Allyn & Bacon.

Fritsche, I., & Linneweber, V. (2006). Nonreactive methods in psychological research. In Eid, M., & Diener, D. (Eds.), *Handbook of multimethod measurement in psychology* (pp. 189–203). Washington, DC: American Psychological Association.

Fury, W., & Forehand, R. (1983). The daily child behavior checklist. *Journal of Behavioral Assessment, 5*, 83–95.

Gambrill, E. B. (1977). *Behavior modification: Handbook of assessment, intervention, and evaluation.* San Francisco: Jossey-Bass.

Gambrill, E. (1997). *Social work practice: A critical thinker's guide.* London: Oxford University Press.

Gambrill, E. (2001). Social work: An authority-based profession. *Research on Social Work Practice, 11*, 166–175.

Gambrill, E. (2006). *Critical thinking in clinical practice* (2nd ed.). New York: Wiley.

Geiger, G., Todd, D. D., Clark, H. B., Miller, R. P., & Kori, S. H. (1992). The effects of feedback and contingent reinforcement on the exercise behavior of chronic pain patients. *Pain, 49*, 179–185.

Gelfand, D., & Hartmann, D. P. (1975). *Child behavior analysis and therapy.* New York: Pergamon Press.

Gibbs, L. E. (1991). *Scientific reasoning for social workers: Bridging the gap between research and practice.* New York: Merrill/Macmillan.

Gibbs, L. E. (2003). *Evidence-based practice for the helping professions: A practical guide with integrated multimedia.* Pacific Grove, CA: Brooks/Cole.

Gibbs, L. E., & Gambrill, E. (2002). Evidence-based practice: Counterarguments to objections. *Research on Social Work Practice, 12*, 452–476.

Gilbert, D. (2003). Multicultural assessment. In Jordan, C., & Franklin, C. (Eds.), *Clinical assessment for social workers: Quantitative and Qualitative methods* (2nd ed.) (pp. 351–384). Chicago, IL: Lyceum.

Gilgun, J. F. (2005). The four cornerstones of evidence-based practice in social work. *Research on Social Work Practice, 15*, 52–61.

Gillespie, D. F., & Seaberg, J. R. (1977). Individual Problem Rating: A proposed scale. *Administration in Mental Health, 5*, 21–29.

Gingerich, W. J. (1983). Significance testing in single-case research. In A. Rosenblatt & D. Waldfogel (Eds.), *Handbook of clinical social work* (pp. 694–720). San Francisco: Jossey-Bass.

Gingerich, W., & Feyerherm, W. (1979). The celeration line technique for assessing client change. *Journal of Social Service Research, 3*, 99–113.

Gira, E. C., Kessler, M. L., & Poertner, J. (2004). Influencing social workers to use research in practice: Lessons from medicine and the allied health professions. *Research on Social Work Practice, 14*, 68–80.

Glass, G. V., McGaw, B., & Smith, M. L. (1981). *Meta-analysis in social research.* Beverly Hills, CA: Sage.

Gold, S., & Marx, B. P. (2006). Analogue and virtual reality assessment. In Hersen, M. (Ed.), *Clinicians handbook of child behavioral assessment* (pp. 82–102). St. Louis, MO: Academic Press.

Goldman, H. H., Skodol, A. E., Lave, T. R. (1992). Revising Axis V for DSM-IV: A review of measures of social functioning. *American Journal of Psychiatry, 149*, 1148–1156.

Goldstein, A. P., & Kanfer, F. H. (1979). *Maximizing treatment gains: Transfer enhancement in psychotherapy.* New York: Academic Press.

Gorsuch, R. L. (1983). Three methods of analyzing limited time-series (N of 1) data. *Behavioral Assessment, 5*, 141–154.

Gottman, J. M., & Leiblum, S. R. (1974). *How to do psychotherapy and how to evaluate it.* New York: Holt, Rinehart, & Winston.

Grant, R., & Maletzky, B. (1972). Application of the Weed system to psychiatric records. *Psychiatry in Medicine, 3*, 119–120.

Green, K., Worden, B., Menges, D., & McCrady, B. (2008). Alcohol use disorders. In Hunsley, J., & Mash, E. J. (Eds.), *A guide to assessments that work* (pp. 339–369). New York, NY: Oxford University Press.

Grehan, P., & Moran, D. J. (2005). Constructing single-subject reversal design graphs using Microsoft Word: A comprehensive tutorial. *The Behavior Analyst Today, 6*, 235–242.

Gresham, F. M. (1997). Treatment integrity in single-subject research. In R. D. Franklin, D. B. Allison, & B. S. Gorman (Eds.), *Design and analysis of single case research* (pp. 93–118). Mahwah, NJ: Lawrence Erlbaum.

Grinnel, Jr., R. M. (Ed.) (1993). Social work research and evaluation (4th ed.). Itasca, IL: Peacock.

Grohol, J. M. (2004). *The insider's guide to mental health resources online* (Rev. ed.). New York: Guilford Press.

Groth-Marnat, G. (2003). *Handbook of psychological assessment* (4th ed.). New York: Wiley.

Gullotta, T. P., & Blau, G. M. (2007). *Handbook of child behavioral issues: Evidence-based approaches to prevention and treatment.* New York: Routledge.

Gullotta, T. P., & Bloom, M. (Eds.). (2003). *Encyclopedia of primary prevention and health promotion.* New York: Kluwer/Plenum.

HALL, K. R. (2006). Using problem-based learning with victims of bullying behavior. *Professional School Counseling, 9,* 231–237.

HAMILTON, M. (1980). Rating depressive patients. *Journal of Clinical Psychiatry, 41,* 21–24.

HANSON, N. (1969). Logical positivism and the interpretation of scientific theories. In P. A. B. Achinstein (Ed.), *The legacy of logical positivism.* Baltimore: Johns Hopkins University Press.

HARMON, S. C., LAMBERT, M. J., SMART, D. M., HAWKINS, E., NIELSEN, S. L., SLADE, K., & LUTZ, W. (2007). Enhancing outcome for potential treatment failures: Therapist-client feedback and clinical support tools. *Psychotherapy Research, 17,* 379–392.

HAYES, S. C., BARLOW, D. H., & NELSON-GRAY, R. O. (1999). *The scientist practitioner: Research and accountability in the age of managed care* (2nd ed.). Boston: Allyn & Bacon.

HAYNES, J. (1977, March). *An evaluation of psychosocial casework using the single-subject design: First findings.* Paper presented at the meeting of the Council on Social Work Education, Phoenix, AZ.

HAYNES, S. N. (1978). *Principles of behavioral assessment.* New York: Gardner.

HAYNES, S. N., & HEIBY, E. M. (Eds.). (2003). *Comprehensive handbook of psychological assessment. Vol. 3. Behavioral assessment.* New York: Wiley.

HAYNES, S. N., & O'BRIEN, W. H. (2000). *Principles and practice of behavioral assessment.* New York: Kluwer/Plenum.

HEDGES, L. V., & OLKIN, I. (1985). *Statistical methods for meta-analysis.* New York: Academic Press.

HEINEMAN-PIEPER, M. (1994). Science, not scientism: The robustness of naturalistic clinical research. In E. Sherman & W. J. Reid (Eds.), *Research in social work* (pp. 71–88). New York: Columbia University Press.

HEKTNER, J. M., SCHMIDT, J. A., & CSIKSZENTMIHALYI, M. (2007). *Experience sampling: Measuring the quality of everyday life.* Thousand Oaks, CA: Sage.

HEMPHILL, J. (1956). *Group dimensions: A manual for their measurement.* Columbus, OH: Monographs of the Bureau of Business Research, Ohio State University.

HERR, K., SPRATT, K. F., GARAND, L., & LI, L. (2007). Evaluation of the Iowa Pain Thermometer and other selected pain intensity scales in younger and older adult cohorts using controlled clinical pain: A preliminary study. *Pain Medicine, 8,* 585–600.

HERSEN, M. (2004). *Psychological assessment in clinical practice: A pragmatic guide.* New York: Brunner Routledge.

HERSEN, M. (Ed.) (2006a). *Clinician's handbook of adult behavioral assessment.* St. Louis, MO: Academic Press.

HERSEN, M. (Ed.) (2006b). *Clinician's handbook of child behavioral assessment.* St. Louis, MO: Academic Press.

HERSEN, M., & BELLACK, A. S. (Eds.). (1999). *Comparative interventions for adult disorders.* Somerset, NJ: Wiley.

HIGGINS J. P. T., & GREEN S. (Eds.) (2008) *Cochrane Handbook for Systematic Reviews of Interventions* Version 5.0.0 [updated February 2008]. The Cochrane Collaboration.

HILL, W. (1977). Hill Interaction Matrix (HIM): The conceptual framework, derived rating scaled and updates bibliography. *Small Group Behavior, 8,* 251–268.

HILLMAN, H. L., & MILLER, L. K. (2004). Designing multiple baseline graphs using Microsoft Excel. The *Behavior Analyst Today, 5,* 372–380.

HOFFMAN, S. G., & OTTO, M. W. (2007). *Cognitive-behavior therapy of social phobia: Evidence-based and disorder-specific treatments.* New York: Routledge.

HOFMANN, S. G., & TOMPSON, M. C. (Eds.). (2002). *Treating chronic and severe mental disorders: A handbook of empirically supported interventions.* New York: Guilford Press.

HOLDEN, G., BEARISON, D. J., RODE, D. C., FISHMAN-KAPILOFF, M., ROSENBERG, G., & ONGHENA, P. (2003). Pediatric pain and anxiety: A meta-analysis of outcomes for a behavioral telehealth intervention. *Research on Social Work Practice, 13,* 693–704.

HOLDEN, G., BEARISON, D. J., RODE, D. L., ROSENBERG, G., & FISHMAN, M. (1999). Evaluating the effects of a virtual environment (STARBRIGHT World) with hospitalized children. *Research on Social Work Practice, 9,* 365–382.

HORNER, R. H., CARR, E. G., HALLE, J., MCGEE, G., ODOM, S., WOLERY, M. (2005). The use of single-subject research to identify evidence-based practice in special education. *Exceptional Children, 71,* 165–179.

HOULE, T. T. (2009). Statistical analyses for single-case experimental designs. In Barlow, D., Nock, M., & Hersen, M. (2009). *Single case experimental designs: Strategies for studying behavior for change* (3rd ed.) (pp. 271–305). Boston, MA: Allyn & Bacon.

HOWARD, M. O., MCMILLEN, C. J., & POLLIO, D. E. (2003). Teaching evidence-based practice: Toward a new paradigm for social work education. *Research on Social Work Practice, 13,* 234–259.

HUDSON, W. W. (1976). *Guidelines for social work practice with families and individuals.* Mimeograph. Honolulu, University of Hawaii, School of Social Work.

HUDSON, W. W. (1978). First axioms of treatment. *Social Work, 23,* 65–66.

HUDSON, W. W. (1982). *The clinical measurement package: A field manual.* Homewood, IL: Dorsey Press.

HUDSON, W. W. (1990). *MPSI technical manual.* Tallahassee, FL: WALMYR.

HUDSON, W. W., & FAUL, A. C. (1998). *The clinical measurement package: A field manual* (2nd ed.). Tallahassee, FL: WALMYR.

HUFF, D. (1954). *How to lie with statistics.* New York, NY: W. W. Norton.

HUITEMA, B. E. (1985). Autocorrelation in applied behavior analysis: A myth. *Behavioral Assessment, 7,* 107–118.

HUITEMA, B. E. (1986). Statistical analysis and single-subject designs: Some misunderstandings. In A. Poling & R. W. Fuqua (Eds.), *Research methods in applied behavior analysis: Issues and advances* (pp. 209–232). New York: Plenum Press.

HUITEMA, B. E. (1988). Autocorrelation: 10 years of confusion. *Behavioral Assessment, 10,* 253–294.

HUITEMA, B. E. (2004). Analysis of interrupted time-series experiments using ITSE: A critique. *Understanding Statistics, 3,* 27–46.

HUITEMA, B. E., & MCKEAN, J. W. (1991). Autocorrelation estimation and inference with small samples. *Psychological Bulletin, 110,* 291–304.

HUITEMA, B. E., & MCKEAN, J. W. (1994a). Two reduced-bias autocorrelation estimators: r_{F1} and r_{F2}. *Perceptual and Motor Skills, 78,* 323–330.

HUITEMA, B. E., & MCKEAN, J. W. (1994b). H_0: $\rho 1 = 0$ for autocorrelation estimators $rF1$, and $rF2$. *Perceptual and Motor Skills, 78,* 331–336.

HUITEMA, B. E., & MCKEAN, J. W. (1994c). Reduced bias autocorrelation estimation: Three jackknife methods. *Educational and Psychological Measurement, 54,* 654–665.

HUITEMA, B. E., & MCKEAN, J. W. (1996). Tests for the jackknife autocorrelation estimator r_{Q2}. *Educational and Psychological Measurement, 56* (2), 232–240.

HUITEMA, B. E., & MCKEAN, J. W. (1998). Irrelevant autocorrelation in least-squares intervention models. *Psychological Methods, 3*,104–116.

HUITEMA, B. E., & MCKEAN, J. W. (2000). A simple and powerful test for autocorrelated errors in OLS intervention models. *Psychological Reports, 87* (1), 3–20.

HUITEMA, B. E., MCKEAN, J. W., & MCKNIGHT, S. (1999). Autocorrelation effects on least-squares data: Intervention analysis of short time series. *Educational & Psychological Measurement, 59*, 767–786.

HUITEMA, B. E., MCKEAN, J. W., & ZHAO, J. (1996). A simple, effective alternative to the Durbin-Watson test for O.L.S. Intervention Models. *Journal of Educational and Behavioral Statistics, 21*, 390–404.

HUMPHREY, N., & BROOKS, A. G. (2006). An evaluation of a short cognitive-behavioural anger management intervention for pupils at risk of exclusion. *Emotional and Behavioural Difficulties, 11*, 5–23.

HUNSLEY, J., CRABB, R., & MASH, E. J. (2004). Evidence-based clinical assessment. *Clinical Psychologist, 57*, 25–32.

HURN, J., KNEEBONE, I., & CROPLEY, M. (2006). Goal setting as an outcome measure: A systematic review. *Clinical Rehabilitation, 20*, 756–772.

ICE, G. H. (2004). Technological advances in observational data collection: The advantages and limitations of computer-assisted data collection. *Field Methods, 16*, 325–375.

JACOB, T., & SEILHAMER, R. A. (1985). Adaptation of the Areas of Change Questionnaire for parent-child relationship assessment. *American Journal of Family Therapy, 13*, 28–38.

JACOBSON, N. S. (1979). Increasing positive behavior in severely distressed marital relationships: The effects of problem-solving training. *Behavior Therapy, 10*, 311–326.

JASON, L., BILLOWS, W., SCHNOPP-WYATT, D., & KING, C. (1996). Reducing the illegal sales of cigarettes to minors: Analysis of alternative reinforcement schedules. *Journal of Applied Behavior Analysis, 29* (3), 333–344.

JASON, L. A., & BRACKSHAW, E. (1999). Access to TV contingent on physical activity: Effects on reducing TV-viewing and body-weight. *Journal of Behavior Therapy and Experimental Psychiatry, 30*, 145–151.

JAYARATNE, S. (1977). Single-subject and group designs in treatment evaluation. *Social Work Research and Abstracts, 13*, 35–42.

JAYARATNE, S., & LEVY, R. L. (1979). *Empirical clinical practice.* New York: Columbia University Press.

JAYARATNE, S., TRIPODI, T., & TALSMA, E. (1988). The comparative analysis and aggregation of single-case data. *Journal of Applied Behavioral Science, 24*, 119–128.

JENSON, W. R., CLARK, E., KIRCHNER, J. C., & KRISTJANSSON, S. D. (2007). Statistical reform: Evidence-based practice, meta-analyses, and single subject designs. *Psychology in the Schools, 44*, 483–493.

JINDANI, S. G., & NEWMAN, C. P. (2006). Producing your own evidence for evidence-based practice. *Journal of Evidence-Based Social Work, 3*, 115–125.

JOHNSON, P., BECKERMAN, A., & AUERBACH, C. (2001). Researching our own practice: Single-system design for *Groupwork, 13*, 57–72.

JOHNSTON, C., & MAH, J. W. T. (2008). Child attention-deficit/hyperactivity disorder. In Hunsley, J., & Mash, E. J. (Eds.), *A guide to assessments that work* (pp. 17–40). New York, NY: Oxford University Press.

JONES, R. R., VAUGHT, R. S., & WEINROTT, M. (1977). Time-series analysis in operant research. *Journal of Applied Behavior Analysis, 10*, 151–166.

JORDAN, C., & FRANKLIN, C. (Eds.)(2003). *Clinical assessment for social workers: Quantitative and qualitative methods* (2nd ed.). Chicago, IL: Lyceum.

JUNG, R. S., & JASON, L. A. (1998). Job interview social skills training for Asian-American immigrants. *Journal of Human Behavior in the Social Environment, 1* (4), 11–25.

KAGLE, J. D., & KOPELS, S. (2008). *Social work records* (3rd ed.). Long Grove, IL: Waveland Press.

KAHNG, S., BOSCOE, J.H., & BYRNE, S. (2003). The use of an escape contingency and a token economy to increase food acceptance. *Journal of Applied Behavior Analysis, 36*, 349–353.

KANE, R. A. (1974). Look to the record. *Social Work, 17*, 412–419.

KANFER, F. H. (1975). Self-management methods. In F. H. Kanfer & A. P. Goldstein (Eds.), *Helping people change* (pp. 309–356). New York: Pergamon Press.

KAROLY, P., & STEFFEN, J. J. (Eds.). (1980). *Improving the long-term effects of psychotherapy.* New York: Gardner.

KARON, B. P. (2008). An 'incurable' schizophrenic: The case of Mr. X. *Pragmatic Case Studies in Psychotherapy, 4:* module 1, 1–24.

KASTNER, J. W., TINGSTROM, D. H., & EDWARDS, R. P. (2000). The utility of reading to boys with ADHD-CT administered at two different intervals post methylphenidate ingestion. *Psychology in the Schools, 37*, 367–377.

KAYE, J. L. (2001). *Target complaints as a measure of outcome in psychotherapy with the depressed elderly.* Unpublished doctoral dissertation, Pacific Graduate School of Psychology, Palo Alto, CA.

KAZANTIS, N. & L'ABATE, L. (Eds.) (2006). *Handbook of homework assignments in psychotherapy.* New York: Springer.

KAZDIN, A. E. (1975). *Behavior modification in applied settings.* Homewood, IL: Dorsey Press.

KAZDIN, A. E. (1977). Assessing the clinical or applied importance of behavior change through social validation. *Behavior Modification, 1*, 427–452.

KAZDIN, A. E. (1992). *Research design in clinical psychology* (2nd ed.) New York: Macmillan.

Kazdin, A. E. (2005). *Parent management training: Treatment for oppositional, aggressive and anti-social behavior in children and adults.* New York: Oxford.

Kazdin, A. E. (2005). Evidence-based assessment for children and adolescents: Issues in measurement development and clinical application. *Journal of Clinical Child and Adolescent Psychology, 34*, 548–558.

KAZDIN, A. E., & HARTMANN, D. P. (1978). The simultaneous treatment design. *Behavior Therapy, 9*, 912–922.

KAZDIN, A. E., & KOPEL, S. A. (1975). On resolving ambiguities of the multiple-baseline design: Problems and recommendations. *Behavior Therapy, 6*, 601–608.

KAZDIN, A. E., & WEISZ, J. R. (Eds.). (2003). *Evidence-based psychotherapies for children and adolescents.* New York: Guilford Press.

Kazi, M. A. F. (1998). *Single-case evaluation by social workers.* Aldershot, England: Ashgate.

KAZI, M. A. F., & WILSON, J. T. (1996). Applying single-case evaluation methodology in a British social work agency. *Research on Social Work Practice, 6*, 5–26.

KELLETT, S. (2007). A time series evaluation of the treatment of histrionic personality disorder with cognitive analytic therapy.

Psychology and Psychotherapy: Practice and Research, 80, 389–405.

KENDALL, P.C. (Ed.) (2005).*Child and adolescent therapy: Cognitive-behavioral procedures* (3rd ed.).New York: Guilford.

KENNEDY, C. H. (2005). *Single-case designs for educational research.* Boston, MA: Allyn & Bacon.

KENNY, D. A., & JUDD, C. M. (1986). Consequences of violating the independence assumption in analysis of variance. *Psychological Bulletin, 99,* 422–431.

KING, A. C., WINETT, R. A., & LOVETT, S. B. (1986). Enhancing coping behaviors in at-risk populations: The effects of time-management instruction and social support in women from dual-earner families. *Behavior Therapy, 17,* 57–66.

KINNAMAN, J. E. S., FARRELL, A. D., & BISCONER, S. W. (2006). Evaluation of the computerized assessment system for psychotherapy evaluation and research (CASPER) as a measure of treatment effectiveness with psychiatric inpatients. *Assessment, 13,* 154–167.

KIRCHNER, R. E., SCHNELLE, J. F., DOMASH, M., LARSON, L., CARR, A., & MCNEES, M. P. P. (1980). The applicability of a helicopter patrol procedure to diverse areas: A cost-benefit evaluation. *Journal of Applied Behavior Analysis, 13,* 143–148.

KIRESUK, T. J., & GARWICK, G. (1979). Basic goal attainment scaling procedures. In G. R. Compton & R. Gallaway (Eds.), *Social work process* (Rev. ed., pp. 412–420). Homewood, IL: Dorsey Press.

KIRESUK, T. J., & LUND, S. H. (1977). Goal attainment scaling: Research evaluation and utilization. In H. C. Schulberg & F. Baker (Eds.), *Program evaluation in the health fields* (Vol. 2). New York: Behavioral Publications.

KIRESUK, T. J., & LUND, S. H. (1978). Goal attainment scaling. In C. C. Attkisson, W. A. Hargreave, M. I. Horowitz, & S. E. Sorenson (Eds.), *Evaluation of human service programs.* New York: Academic Press.

KIRESUK, T. J., & SHERMAN, R. E. (1968). Goal attainment scaling: A general method for evaluating comprehensive community mental health programs. *Community Mental Health Journal, 4,* 443–453.

KIRESUK, T. J., & SHERMAN, R. E. (1977). A reply to the critique of goal attainment scaling. *Social Work Research and Abstracts, 13,* 9–11.

KIRESUK, T. J., SMITH, A., & CARDILLO, J. E. (Eds.). (1993). *Goal Attainment Scaling: Applications, Theory and Measurement.* New York: Erlbaum.

KIRK, S. (Ed.) (2005). *Mental disorders in the social environment: Critical perspectives.* New York: Columbia University Press.

KIVLIGHAN, D. M., MULTON, K. D., & PATTON, M. J. (2000). Insight and symptom reduction in time-limited psychoanalytic counseling. *Journal of Counseling Psychology, 47,* 50–58.

KJOSNESS, J. Y., BARR, L. R., & RETTMAN, S. (2004). *Research navigator guide: The helping professions.* Boston: Allyn & Bacon.

KLEIN, W. C., & BLOOM, M. (1995). Practice wisdom. *Social Work, 40,* 799–807.

KNAPCZYK, D. R. (1988). Reducing aggressive behaviors in special and regular class settings by training alternative social responses. *Behavior Disorders, 14,* 27–39.

KOLKO, D. J., & MILAN, M. A. (1983). Reframing and paradoxical instruction to overcome "resistance" in the treatment of delinquent youths: A multiple baseline analysis. *Journal of Consulting and Clinical Psychology, 51,* 655–660.

KOPELS, S., & KAGLE, J. D. (1993). Do social workers have a duty to warn? *Social Services Review, 67,* 101–126.

KRAEMER, H. C., MEASELLE, J. R., ABLOW, J. C., ESSEX, M. J., BOYCE, W. T., & KUPFER, D. J. (2003). A new approach to integrating data from multiple informants in psychiatric assessment and research: Mixing and matching contexts and perspectives. *American Journal of Psychiatry, 160,* 1566–1577.

KRATOCHWILL, T. R. (Ed.). (1978). *Single subject research: Strategies for evaluating change.* New York: Academic Press.

KRATOCHWILL, T. R., & LEVIN, J. R. (Eds.). (1992). *Single-case research design and analysis: New directions for psychology and education.* Hillsdale, NJ: Erlbaum.

LAIRD, J. (1994). "Thick description" revisited: Family therapist as anthropologist-constructivist. In E. Sherman & W. J. Reid (Eds.), *Qualitative research in social work* (pp. 175–189). New York: Columbia University Press.

LALL, V. F., & LEVIN, J. R. (2004). An empirical investigation of the statistical properties of generalized single-case randomization tests. *Journal of School Psychology, 42,* 61–86.

LAMBERT, M. J. (Ed.). (2004). *Bergin and Garfield's handbook of psychotherapy and behavior change* (5th ed.). New York: Wiley.

LAMBERT, M. J. (2007). Presidential address: What we have learned from a decade of research aimed at improving psychotherapy outcome in routine care. *Psychotherapy Research, 17,* 1–14.

LAMBERT, M. J., SHAPIRO, D. A., & BERGIN, A. E. (1986). The effectiveness of psychotherapy. In S. L. Garfield & A. E. Bergin (Eds.), *Handbook of psychotherapy and behavior change* (pp. 157–212). New York: Wiley.

LAMBERT, M. J., WHIPPLE, J. L., VERMEERSCH, D. A., SMART, D. W., HAWKINS, E. J., LARS NIELSEN, S., ET AL. (2002). Enhancing psychotherapy outcomes via providing feedback: A replication. *Clinical Psychology and Psychotherapy, 9,* 91–103.

LAMBERT, M. J., WHIPPLE, J. L., HAWKINS, E. J., VERMEERSCH, D. A., NIELSEN, S. L., SMART, D. W. (2003). Is it time for clinicians to routinely track patient outcome? A meta-analysis. *Clinical Psychology: Science and Practice, 10,* 288–301.

LANE, K. L., THOMPSON, A., RESKE, C. L., GABLE, L. M., & BARTON-ARWOOD, S. (2006). Reducing skin picking via competing activities. *Journal of Applied Behavior Analysis, 39:4,* 459–462.

LANG, N. C. (1994). Integrating the data processing of qualitative research and social work practice to advance the practitioner as knowledge builder: Tools for knowing and doing. In E. Sherman & W. J. Reid (Eds.), *Qualitative research in social work* (pp. 265–278). New York: Columbia University Press.

LARKIN, K. T. (2006). Psychophysiological assessment. In Hersen, M. (Ed.), *Clinicians handbook of adult behavioral assessment* (pp. 165–188). St. Louis, MO: Academic Press.

LAZARUS, A. A., & DAVISON, G. C. (1971). Clinical innovation in research and practice. In A. E. Bergin & S. L. Garfield (Eds.), *Handbook of psychotherapy and behavior change: An empirical analysis* (2nd ed.) (pp. 196–213). New York: Wiley.

LECROY, C.W. (Ed.) (2008). *Handbook of evidence-based practice treatment manuals for children and adolescents.* (2nd ed.). New York: Oxford.

LEVENSON, J. S., & MACGOWAN, M. J. (2004). Engagement, denial, and treatment progress among sex offenders in group therapy. *Sexual Abuse: A Journal of Research and Treatment, 16,* 49–63.

LEVITT, J. L., & REID, W. J. (1981). Rapid-assessment instruments for practice. *Social Work Research and Abstracts, 17,* 13–19.

LEVKOFF, S.E., CHEN, H., FISHER, J., MCINTYRE, J. (Eds.) (2006). *Evidence-based behavioral health practices for older adults.* New York: Springer.

Levy, R. L., & Bavendam, T. G. (1995). Promoting women's urologic self-care: Five single-case replications. *Research on Social Work Practice, 5*, 430–441.

Lieberman, M., Yalom, L., & Miles, M. (1973). *Encounter groups: First facts*. San Francisco: Jossey-Bass.

Liddle, H. A., Santisteban, D., Levant, R., & Bray, J. (Eds.). (2002). *Family psychology: Science-based interventions*. Washington, DC: APA.

Linton, J. M., & Singh, N. N. (1984). Acquisition of sign language using positive practice overcorrection. *Behavior Modification, 8*, 553–566.

Lipsey, M. W. (1990). *Design sensitivity: Statistical power for experimental research*. Newbury Park, CA: Sage.

Lipsey, M. W., & Wilson, D. B. (1993). The efficacy of psychological, educational, and behavioral treatment. *American Psychologist, 48*, 1181–1209.

Littel, J. Corcoran, J. & Pillai, V. (2008). *Systematic reviews and meta-analysis*. New York: Oxford.

Liu, R. Y., & Tang, J. (1996). Control charts for dependent and independent measurements based on bootstrap methods. *Journal of the American Statistical Association 91*, 1694–1700.

Lloyd, J. W., Eberhardt, M. J., & Drake, G. P., Jr. (1996). Group versus individual reinforcement contingencies within the context of group study conditions. *Journal of Applied Behavior Analysis, 29*, 189–200.

Lonetto, R., & Templer, D. I. (1983). The nature of death anxiety. In C. D. Spielberger & J. N. Butcher (Eds.), *Advances in personality assessment* (Vol. 3). Hillsdale, NJ: Erlbaum.

Lo, Y., & Konrad, M. (2007). A fieldtested task analysis for creating single-subject graphs using Microsoft Office Excel. *Journal of Behavioral Education, 16*, 155–189.

Lopez, S. J., & Snyder, C. R. (Eds.). (2003). *Positive psychological assessment. A handbook of models and measures*. Washington, DC: APA.

Lovaas, O. I., Koegel, R., Simmons, J. Q., & Long, J. D. (1973). Some generalization and follow-up measures on autistic children in behavior therapy. *Journal of Applied Behavior Analysis, 5*, 131–166.

Ludwig, T. D., & Geller, E. S. (1999). Behavior change among agents of a community safety program: Pizza deliverers advocate community safety belt use. *Journal of Organizational Behavior Management, 19*, 3–24.

Lyddon, W. J., & Jones, J. V. (Eds.). (2001). *Empirically supported cognitive therapies: Current and future applications*. New York: Springer.

Macdonald, G. (2001). *Effective interventions for child abuse and neglect: An evidence-based approach to planning and evaluating interventions*. New York: Wiley.

MacKay, G., & Sommerville, W. (1996). Reflections on goal attainment scaling: Cautionary notes and proposals for development. *Educational Research, 38*, 161–172.

McCullough, J. P. (1984). The need for new single-case design structure in applied cognitive psychology. *Psychotherapy, 31*, 389–400.

McDonald, M. R., & Budd, K. S. (1983). "Booster shots" following didactic parent training: Effects of follow-up using a graphic feedback and instructions. *Behavior Modification, 7*, 211–223.

McLaren, C., & Rodger, S. (2003). Goal attainment scaling: Clinical implications for paediatric occupational therapy practice. *Australian Occupational Therapy Journal, 50*, 2–17.

McNight, S. D., McKean, J. W., & Huitema, B. E. (2000). A double bootstrap method to analyze linear models with autoregressive error terms. *Psychological Methods, 5*, 87–101.

McNutt, J. G. (2008). Technology and macro social work practice. In Mizrahi, T. & Davis, L. (Eds.), *Encyclopedia of Social Work* (20th ed.). Washington, DC: NASW Press.

McSweeny, A. J. (1978). Effects of response cost on the behavior of a million persons: Charging for directory assistance in Cincinnati. *Journal of Applied Behavior Analysis, 11*, 47–51.

Maag, J. W., Rutherford, R. B., Jr., & DiGangi, S. A. (1992). Effects of self-monitoring and contingent reinforcements on-task behavior and academic productivity of learning-disabled students: A social validation study. *Psychology in the Schools, 29*, 157–172.

Macgowan, M. J. (1997). A measure of engagement for social group work: The groupwork engagement measure (GEM). *Journal of Social Service Research, 23*, 17–37.

Macgowan, M. J. (2000). Evaluation of a measure of engagement for group work. *Research on Social Work Practice, 10*, 348–361.

Macgowan, M. J. (2003). Increasing engagement in groups: A measurement based approach. *Social Work with Groups, 26*, 5–28.

Macgowan, M. J. (2008). *A guide to evidence-based group work*. New York: Oxford.

Macgowan, M. J., & Levenson, J. S. (2003). Psychometrics of the Group Engagement Measure with male sex offenders. *Small Group Research, 34*, 155–169.

Macgowan, M. J., & Newman, F. L. (2005). Factor structure of the group engagement measure. *Social Work Research, 29*, 107–118.

Mager, R. F. (1972). *Goal analysis*. Belmont, CA: Fearon.

Maheady, K., Mallette, B., Harper, G. F., & Sacca, K. (1991). Heads together: A peer-mediated option for improving the academic achievement of heterogeneous learning groups. *Remedial and Special Education, 12*, 25–33.

Malec, J. F. (1999). Goal attainment scaling in rehabilitation. *Neuropsychological Rehabilitation, 9*, 253–276.

Malgady, R. G., & Colon-Malgady, G. (2008). Building community test norms: Considerations for ethnic minority populations. In Suzuki, L. A., & Ponterotto, J. G. (Eds.), *Handbook of multicultural assessment: Clinical, psychological, and educational applications* (3rd ed.) (pp. 34–51). San Francisco: Jossey-Bass.

Margolis, C. Z., Mendelssohn, I., Barak, N., Beinart, T., & Goldsmith, J. R. (1984). Increase in relevant data after introduction of a problem-oriented record system in primary pediatric care. *American Journal of Public Health, 74*, 1410–1412.

Marlatt, G. A. & Donovan, D. M. (Eds.) (2005). *Relapse prevention: Maintenance strategies in the treatment of addictive disorders* (2nd ed.). New York: Guilford.

Martens, W. M., & Holmstrup, E. (1974). Problem-oriented recording. *Social Casework, 55*, 554–561.

Mash, E. & Barkley, D. M. (Eds.) (2006). *Treatment of childhood disorders* (3rd ed.).New York: Guilford.

Mash, E. J. & Barkley, R. A. (2007). (Eds.) *Assessment of childhood disorders* (3rd ed.).new York: Guilford Press.

Mash, E. J., & Terdal, L. G. (Eds.). (1997). *Assessment of childhood disorders* (2nd ed.). New York: Guilford Press.

Matyas, T. A., & Greenwood, K. M. (1990). Visual analysis of single-case time-series: Effects of variability, serial dependence and magnitude of intervention effect. *Journal of Applied Behavior Analysis, 23*, 341–351.

Matyas, T. A., & Greenwood, K. M. (1991). Problems in the estimation of autocorrelation in brief time-series and some implications for behavioral data. *Behavioral Assessment, 13*, 137–158.

Matyas, T. A., & Greenwood, K. M. (1997). Serial dependency in single-case time series. In R. D. Franklin, D. B. Allison, & B. S. Gorman (Eds.), *Design and analysis of single-case research* (pp. 215–243). Mahwah, NJ: Lawrence Erlbaum.

Mauszycki, S. C., & Wambaugh, J. L. (2008). The effects of rate control treatment on consonant production accuracy in mild apraxia of speech. *Aphasiology, 22*, 906–920.

Miller, M., Miller, S. R., Wheeler, J., & Selinger, J. (1989). Can a single-classroom treatment approach change academic performance and behavioral characteristics in severely behaviorally disordered adolescents: An experimental inquiry. *Behavioral Disorders, 14*, 215–225.

Miller, W. W., Combs, S. A., Fish, C., Bense, B., Owens, A., & Burch, A. (2008). Running training after stroke: A single-subject report. *Physical Therapy, 88*, 511–522.

Miltenberger, R.G., Flessner, C., Gatheridge, B., Johnson, B., Satterlund, M., & Egemo, K. (2004). Evaluation of behavioral skills training to prevent gun play in children. *Journal of applied behavior analysis, 37*, 249–251.

Minami, T., Wampold, B. E., Serlin, R. C., Hamilton, E. G., Brown G. S., & Kircher, J. C. (2008). Benchmarking the effectiveness of psychotherapy treatment for adult depression in a managed care environment: A preliminary study. *Journal of Consulting and Clinical Psychology, 76*, 116–124.

Mintz, J., & Kiesler, D. J. (1982). Individualized measures of psychotherapy outcome. In P. C. Kendall & J. N. Butcher (Eds.), *Handbook of research methods in clinical psychology* (pp. 491–534). New York: Wiley.

Mio, J. S., & Iwamasa, G. Y. (2003). *Culturally diverse mental health: The challenges of research and resistance.* New York: Brunner-Routledge.

Miringoff, M. L., & Opdycke, S. (1996). Monitoring the nation's social performance: The index of social health. In E. F. Zigler, S. L. Kagan, & N. W. Hall (Eds.), *Children, families, and government: Preparing for the twenty-first century.* New York: Cambridge University Press.

Mitchell, T., & Cusick, A. (1998). Evaluation of a client-centered paediatric rehabilitation programme using goal attainment scaling. *Australian Occupational Therapy Journal, 45*, 7–18.

Moon, E. C., McMurtry, C. M., & McGrath, P. J. (2008). Child and adolescent pain. In Hunsley, J., & Mash, E. J. (Eds.), *A guide to assessments that work* (pp. 551–575). New York, NY: Oxford University Press.

Moran, D. J., & Hirschbine, B. (2002). Constructing single-subject reversal design graphs using Microsoft Excel: A comprehensive tutorial. *The Behavior Analyst Today, 3*, 180–187.

Morgan, D. L., & Morgan, R. K. (2001). Single participant research design: Bringing science to managed care. *American Psychologist, 56*, 119–127.

Morley, S., & Adams, M. (1991). Graphical analysis of single-case time series data. *British Journal of Clinical Psychology, 30*, 97–115.

Morley, S., Williams, A., Hussain, S. (2008). Estimating the clinical effectiveness of cognitive behavioural therapy in the clinic: Evaluation of a CBT informed pain management programme. *Pain, 137*, 670–680.

Moss, A., Nicholas, M. (2006). Language rehabilitation in chronic Aphasia and time postonset: A review of single-subject data. *Stroke, 37*, 3043–3051.

Mottram, L. M., Bray, M. A., Kehle, T. J., Broudy, M., & Jenson, W. R. (2002). A classroom-based intervention to reduce disruptive behaviors. *Journal of Applied School Psychology, 19*, 65–74.

Mutschler, E. (1979). Using single-case evaluation procedures in a family and children's service agency: Integration of practice and research. *Journal of Social Service Research, 3*, 115–134.

Mutschler, E. (1984). Evaluating practice: A study of research utilization by practitioners. *Social Work Research and Abstracts, 29*, 332–337.

Mutschler, E., & Rosen, A. (1979). Evaluation of treatment outcome by client and social worker. In *The social welfare forum.* New York: Columbia University Press.

Myers, L. L., & Thyer, B. A. (1997). Should social work clients have the right to effective treatment? *Social Work, 42*, 288–298.

Nathan, P. N & Gorman, J. M. (Eds.) (2007). *Treatments that work* (3rd ed.).New York: Oxford.

National Association of Social Workers (NASW). (1996). *Code of ethics.* Silver Spring, MD: Author.

Nelsen, J. C. (1978). Use of communication theory in single-subject research. *Social Work Research and Abstracts, 14*, 12–19.

Nelsen, J. C. (1981). Issues in single-subject research for nonbehaviorists. *Social Work Research and Abstracts, 17*, 31–37.

Nelsen, J. C. (1994). Ethics, gender, and ethnicity in single-case research and evaluation. *Journal of Social Service Research, 18*, 139–152.

Neuman, K. (2002). From practice evaluation to agency evaluation: Demonstrating outcomes the United Way. *Social Work in Mental Health, 1*, 1–14.

Newman, M. G. (2004). Technology in psychotherapy: An introduction. *Journal of Clinical Psychology, 60*, 141–145.

Newman, M. G., Consoli, A., & Taylor, C. B. (1997). Computers in assessment and cognitive behavioral treatment of clinical disorders: Anxiety as a case in point. *Behavior Therapy, 28*, 211–235.

Newton, M. (2002). Evaluating the outcome of counseling in primary care using goal attainment scaling. *Counseling Psychology Quarterly, 15*, 85–90.

Neyer, F. J. (2006). Informant assessment. In Eid, M., & Diener, D. (Eds.), *Handbook of multimethod measurement in psychology* (pp. 43–60). Washington, DC: American Psychological Association.

Nezu, A. M., Ronan, G. F., Meadows, E. A., & McClure, K. S. (Eds.). (2000). *Practitioner's guide to empirically-based measures of depression.* New York: Kluwer Academic/Plenum.

Norcross, J. C. (Ed.). (2002). *Psychotherapy relationships that work.* New York: Oxford University Press.

Norcross, J. C., & Hill, C. E. (2004). Empirically-supported therapy relationships. *Clinical Psychologist, 57*, 19–24.

Norcross, J. C., Beutler, K. E., Levant, R. F. (Eds.) (2006). *Evidence-based practices in mental health: Debate and dialogue on the fundamental questions.* Washington, D.C.: American Psychological Association.

Normand, M. P., & Bailey, J. S. (2006). The effects of celeration lines on visual data analysis. *Behavior Modification, 30*, 295–314.

Nugent, W. R. (1987). Information gain through integrated research approaches. *Social Service Review, 61*, 337–364.

Nugent, W. R. (1988). A vector model of single case design data and its use in analyzing large single case design replication series. *Journal of Social Service Research, 12*, 49–82.

Nugent, W. R. (1991a). An experimental and qualitative analysis of a cognitive-behavioral intervention for anger. *Social Work Research and Abstracts, 27*, 3–8.

NUGENT, W. R. (1991b). A mathematical model for analyzing single subject design replication series. *Journal of Social Service Research, 15,* 93–129.

NUGENT, W. R. (1992a). The affective impact of a clinical social worker's interviewing style: A series of single-case experiments. *Research on Social Work Practice, 2,* 6–27.

NUGENT, W. R. (1992b). Psychometric characteristics of self-anchored scales in clinical application. *Journal of Social Service Research, 15,* 137–152.

NUGENT, W. R., SIEPPERT, J. D., & HUDSON, W. W. (2001). *Practice Evaluation for the 21st Century.* Belmont, CA: Brooks/Cole.

NUNNALLY, J. C., & BERNSTEIN, I. H. (1994). *Psychometric theory* (3rd ed.). New York: McGraw-Hill.

NURIUS, P. S., & HUDSON, W. W. (1993). *Human services: Practice, evaluation & computers.* Pacific Grove, CA: Brooks/Cole.

O'DONOHUE, W., & FERGUSON, K. E. (Eds.). (2003). *Handbook of professional ethics for psychologists: Issues, questions and controversies.* Thousand Oaks, CA: Sage.

O'DONOHUE, W., FISHER, J. E., HAYES, S. C. (Eds.). (2003). *Cognitive behavior therapy: Applying empirically supported techniques in your practice.* New York: Wiley.

OFFICE OF THE CHILD ADVOCATE AND THE CHILD FATALITY REVIEW BOARD (2003, January). *Investigation of the death of Joseph Daniel S.* Hartford, CT: Author.

OGLES, B. M., LAMBERT, M. J., FIELDS, S. A. (2002). *Essentials of outcome assessment.* New York: Wiley.

OGLES, B. M., LUNNEN, K. M., BONESTEEL, K. (2001). Clinical significance: History, application, and current practice. *Clinical Psychology Review, 21,* 421–446.

OGLES, B. M., & MASTERS, K. S. (1996). *Assessing Outcome in Clinical Practice.* Boston: Allyn & Bacon.

O'HARE, T. (2005). *Evidence-based practices for social workers: An interdisciplinary approach.* Chicago: lyceum Books.

OKAWA, J. B. (2008). Considerations for the cross-cultural evaluation of refugees and asylum seekers. In Suzuki, L. A., & Ponterotto, J. G. (Eds.), *Handbook of multicultural assessment: Clinical, psychological, and educational applications* (3rd ed.) (pp. 165–194). San Francisco: Jossey-Bass.

OLIVE, M. L., & SMITH, B. W. (2005). Effect size calculations and single subject design. *Educational Psychology, 25,* 313–324.

ONGHENA, P. (1992). Randomization tests for extensions and variations of *ABAB* single-case experimental designs: A rejoinder. *Behavioral Assessment, 14,* 153–172.

ONGHENA, P., & EDGINGTON, E. S. (1994). Randomization tests for restricted alternating treatments designs. *Behaviour Research and Therapy, 32,* 783–786.

ONGHENA, P., & EDGINGTON, E. S. (2005). Customization of pain treatments: Single-case design and analysis. *Clinical Journal of Pain, 21,* 56–68.

ONGHENA, P., & VAN DAMME, G. (1994). SCRT 1.1: Single-case randomization tests. *Behavior Research Methods, Instruments, & Computers, 26,* 369.

ORGNERO, M. I., & RODWAY, M. R. (1991). AIDS and social work treatment: A single-system analysis. *Health and Social Work, 16,* 123–141.

ORME, J. G. (1991). Statistical conclusion validity and single-system designs. *Social Service Review, 65,* 468–491.

ORME, J. G., & COX, M. E. (2001). Analyzing single-subject design data using statistical process control charts. *Social Work Research, 25,* 115–127.

OSMAN, S., & SHUEMAN, S. A. (1988). A guide to the peer review process for clinicians. *Social Work, 33,* 345–348.

OSTLE, B., TURNER, K. V., JR., HICKS, C. R., & MCELRATH, G. W. (1996). *Engineering statistics.* Belmont, CA: Duxbury Press.

PACK-BROWN, S. P., & WILLIAMS, C. B. (2003). *Ethics in a multicultural context.* Thousand Oaks, CA: Sage.

PADILLA, A. M., & BORSATO, G. N. (2008). Issues in culturally appropriate psychoeducational assessment. In Suzuki, L. A., & Ponterotto, J. G. (Eds.), *Handbook of multicultural assessment: Clinical, psychological, and educational applications* (3rd ed.) (pp. 5–21). San Francisco: Jossey-Bass.

PANIAGUA, F. A. (2005). *Assessing and treating culturally diverse clients: A practical guide* (3rd ed.). Thousand Oaks, CA: Sage.

PARITZKY, R. S., & MAGOON, T. M. (1982). Goal attainment models for assessing group counseling. *Personnel and Guidance Journal, 60,* 381–385.

PARKER, R. I., & BROSSART, D. F. (2003). Evaluating single-case research data. A comparison of seven statistical methods. *Behavior Therapy, 34,* 189–211.

PARKER, R. I., & BROSSART, D. F. (2006). Phase contrasts for multiphase single case intervention designs. *School Psychology Quarterly, 21,* 46–61.

PARKER, R. I., BROSSART, D. F., VANNEST, K. J., LONG, J. R., DE-ALBA, R. G., BAUGH, F. G., ET AL. (2005). Effect sizes in single case research: How large is large? *School Psychology Review, 34,* 116–132.

PARKER, R. I., CRYER, J., & BYRNS, G. (2006). Controlling baseline trend in single-case research. *School Psychology Quarterly, 21,* 418–443.

PARKER, R. I., & HAGAN-BURKE, S. (2007a). Useful effect size interpretations for single case research. *Behavior Therapy, 38,* 95–105.

PARKER, R. I., & HAGAN-BURKE, S. (2007b). Median-based overlap analysis for single case data: A second study. *Behavior Modification, 31,* 919–936.

PARKER, R. I, HAGAN-BURKE, S., & VANNEST, K. (2007). Percentage of all non-overlapping data (PAND): An alternative to PND. *The Journal of Special Education, 40,* 194–204.

PARKER, R. I., & VANNEST, K. (in press). Pairwise data overlap for single case research. *School Psychology Review.*

PARKER, R. I., VANNEST, K. J., & BROWN, L. (in press). The Improvement Rate Difference for single case research. *Exceptional Children.*

PARSONSON, B. S., & BAER, D. M. (1978). The analysis and presentation of graphic data. In T. R. Kratochwill (Ed.), *Single subject research: Strategies for evaluating change* (pp. 101–165). New York: Academic Press.

PARSONSON, B. S., & BAER, D. M. (1986). The graphic analysis of data. In A. Poling & R. W. Fuqua (Eds.), *Research methods in applied behavior analysis: Issues and advances* (pp. 157–186). New York: Plenum Press.

PATTERSON, D. A. (2008). Technology tools and applications. In Mizrahi, T. & Davis, L. (Eds.), *Encyclopedia of Social Work* (20th ed.). Washington, DC: NASW Press.

PATTERSON, D. A., & BASHAM, R. E. (2002). A data visualization procedure for the evaluation of group treatment outcomes across units of analysis. *Small Group Research, 33,* 209–230.

PATTERSON, D. A., & BASHAM, R. E. (2006). *Data analysis with spreadsheets.* Boston: Allyn & Bacon.

PAUL, R., & ELDER, L. (2004). *The miniature guide to critical thinking concepts and tools.* Dillon Beach, CA: Foundation for Critical Thinking.

PEARSON, C. L. (1990). Service inputs and outputs. In Y. T. Yuan & M. Rivest (Eds.), *Preserving families: Evaluation resources for practitioners and policymakers* (chap. 4). Newbury Park, CA: Sage.

PERCEVIC, R., LAMBERT, M. J., & KORDY, H. (2004). Computer supported monitoring of patient treatment response. *Journal of Clinical Psychology, 60,* 285–299.

PEREPLETCHIKOVA, F., TREAT, T. A., & KAZDIN, A. E. (2007). Treatment integrity in psychotherapy research: Analysis of the studies and examination of the associated factors. *Journal of Consulting and Clinical Psychology, 75,* 829–841.

PERSONS, J. B., DAVIDSON, J., TOMPKINS, M. A. (2001). *Essential components of cognitive-behavior therapy for depression.* Washington, DC: American Psychological Association.

PERSONS, J. B., & FRESCO, D. M. (2008). Adult depression. In Hunsley, J., & Mash, E. J. (Eds.), *A guide to assessments that work* (pp. 96–120). New York, NY: Oxford University Press.

PFADT, A., COHEN, I. L., SUDHALTER, V., ROMANCZYK, R. G., & WHEELER, D. J. (1992). Applying statistical process control to clinical data: An illustration. *Journal of Applied Behavior Analysis, 25,* 551–560.

PFADT, A. & WHEELER, D. J. (1995). Using statistical process control to make data-based clinical decisions. *Journal of Applied Behavior Analysis, 28,* 349–370.

PIKOFF, H. B. (1996). *Treatment effectiveness handbook: A reference guide to the key research reviews in mental health and substance abuse.* Buffalo, NY: Data for Decisions.

PITT, H. (1999). *SPC for the rest of us: A personal path to statistical process control.* King of Prussia, PA: K. W. Tunnell Company.

POLANSKY, N., CHALMERS, M. A., BUTTENWEISSER, E., & WILLIAMS, D. P. (1981). *Damaged parents—An anatomy of child neglect.* Chicago: University of Chicago Press.

POLSTER, R. A., & COLLINS, D. (1988). Measuring variables by direct observations. In R. M. Grinnell, Jr. (Ed.), *Social work research and evaluation* (3rd ed., chap. 8). Itasca, IL: Peacock.

POZNANSKI, E. O., & MOKROS, H. G. (1999). *Children's Depression Rating Scale-Revised (CDRS-R).* Los Angeles, CA: Western Psychological Services.

PROCIDANO, M. E., & HELLER, K. (1983). Measures of perceived social support from friends and from family: Three validation studies. *American Journal of Community Psychology, 11,* 1–24.

PROCTOR, E. K. (1990). Evaluating clinical practice: Issues of purpose and design. *Social Work Research and Abstracts, 26,* 32–40.

RAMSEY, P. P., & RAMSEY, P. H. (2006). Robust testing of level changes in interrupted time-series analysis. *Journal of Statistical Consulting and Simulation, 76,* 913–923.

REID, T. R. (1987, February 28). Can New Mexico's population lose 35,000 pounds by spring? *The Washington Post,* p. 43.

REID, W. J. (1977). Process and outcome in the treatment of family problems. In W. J. Reid & L. Epstein (Eds.), *Task-centered practice* (chap. 4). New York: Columbia University Press.

REID, W. J. (1978). *The task-centered system.* New York: Columbia University Press.

REID, W. J. (1997a). Evaluating the dodo's verdict: Do all interventions have equal outcomes? *Research on Social Work Practice, 21,* 5–16.

REID, W. J. (1997b). Is neo-positivism a suitable epistemological framework for HOSE courses? Yes. In M. Bloom & W. C. Klein (Eds.), *Controversial issues in human behavior in the social environment* (pp. 2–7). Boston: Allyn & Bacon.

REID, W. J., & DAVIS, I. P. (1987). Qualitative methods in single-case research. In N. Gottlieb (Ed.), *Perspectives on direct practice evaluation* (chap. 4). Seattle: University of Washington, School of Social Work.

REID, W. J., & HANRAHAN, P. (1988). Measuring implementation of social treatment. In K. J. Conrad & C. Roberts-Gray (Eds.), *Evaluating program environments* (chap. 6). San Francisco: Jossey-Bass.

REID, W. J., & SMITH, A. D. (1989). *Research in social work* (2nd ed.). New York: Columbia University Press.

REISER, R.P. & THOMPSON, (2005). *Bipolar disorder: Advances in psychotherapy – Evidence-based practice.* New York: Hofgrefe & Huber.

RHODES, K. W., COX, M. E., ORME, J. G., COAKLEY, T., BUEHLER, C., CUDDEBACK, G. S. (2006). *Casey Home Assessment Protocol (CHAP): User's manual* (2nd ed.). Knoxville, TN: University of Tennessee, Children's Mental Health Services Research Center (http://utcmhsrc.csw.utk.edu/caseyproject/).

RICHARD, D. C. S., & GLOSTER, A. (2006). Technology integration and behavioral assessment. In Hersen, M. (Ed.), *Clinicians handbook of adult behavioral assessment* (pp. 461–496). St. Louis, MO: Academic Press.

RIDLEY, C. R., TRACY, M. L., PRUITT-STEPHENS, L., WIMSATT, M. K., & BEARD, J. (2008). Multicultural assessment validity: The preeminent ethical issue in psychological assessment. In Suzuki, L. A., & Ponterotto, J. G. (Eds.), *Handbook of multicultural assessment: Clinical, psychological, and educational applications* (3rd ed.) (pp. 22–33). San Francisco: Jossey-Bass.

RIVERA, L. M. (2008). Acculturation and multicultural assessment: Issues, trends, and practice. In Suzuki, L. A., & Ponterotto, J. G. (Eds.), *Handbook of multicultural assessment: Clinical, psychological, and educational applications* (3rd ed.) (pp. 73–91). San Francisco: Jossey-Bass.

ROBERTS, A. R. & YEAGER, K. R. (Eds.) (2003). *Evidence-based practice manual: Research and outcome measures in health and human services.* Oxford: Oxford University Press.

ROBERTS, A. R., & YEAGER, K. R. (Eds.). (2004). *Evidence-based practice manual: Research and outcome measures in health and human services.* New York: Oxford.

ROBERTS, A. R & YEAGER, K. R. (Eds.) (2006). *Foundations of evidence-based practice in social work.* New York: Oxford.

ROCK, B. D., & COOPER, M. (2000). Social work in primary care: A demonstration student unit utilizing practice research. *Social Work in Health Care, 31,* 1–17.

ROGERS, A. Y., & POTOCKY, M. (1997). Evaluating culturally sensitive practice through single-system design: Methodological issues and strategies. *Research on Social Work Practice, 7,* 391–400.

ROHSENOW, D. J. (2008). Substance use disorders. In Hunsley, J., & Mash, E. J. (Eds.), *A guide to assessments that work* (pp. 319-338). New York, NY: Oxford University Press.

ROSE, S., & TOLMAN, R. (1985). Evaluation of client outcomes in groups. In M. Sundel et al. (Eds.), *Individual change through small groups.* New York: Free Press.

ROSE, S. D. (1988). Practice experiments for doctoral dissertations: Research training and knowledge building. *Journal of Social Work Education, 24,* 115–122.

ROSE, S. D. (1989). *Working with adults in groups: Integrating cognitive-behavioral and small group strategies.* San Francisco: Jossey-Bass.

ROSEN, A. (1992). Facilitating clinical decision making and evaluation. *Families in Society: The Journal of Contemporary Human Services, 73,* 522–532.

ROSEN, A. (1993). Systematic planned practice. *Social Service Review, 67,* 84–100.

ROSEN, A., & PROCTOR, E. K. (1981). Distinctions between treatment outcomes and their implications for treatment evaluation. *Journal of Consulting and Clinical Psychology, 49*, 418–425.

ROSEN, D., & ZYTOWSKI, D. G. (1977). An individualized, problem-oriented self-report of change as a follow-up of a university counseling service. *Journal of Counseling Psychology, 24*, 437–439.

ROSENTHAL, R. (1991). *Meta-analytic procedures for social research* (Rev. ed.). Newbury Park, CA: Sage.

ROSENTHAL, R., & ROSNOW, R. L. (1991). *Essentials of behavioral research: Methods and data analysis* (2nd ed.). New York: McGraw-Hill.

ROSQVIST, J. (2005). *Exposure treatment for anxiety disorders: A practitioner's guide to concepts, methods, and evidence-based practice.* New York: Routledge.

ROSQVIST, J., SUNDSMO, A., MACLANE, C., CULLEN, K., NORLING, D. C., DAVIES, M., & MAACK, D. (2006). Analogue and virtual reality assessment. In Hersen, M. (Ed.), *Clinicians handbook of adult behavioral assessment* (pp. 43–62). St. Louis, MO: Academic Press.

ROSSITER, L. F. (2001). *Understanding medicare managed care: Meeting economic, strategic, and policy challenges.* Chicago: Health Administration Press.

ROTH, A., & FONAGY, P. (Eds.). (2004). *What works for whom? A critical review of psychotherapy research.* New York: Guilford.

ROYSE, D., THYER, B. A., PADGETT, D. K., & LOGAN, T. K. (2006). *Program evaluation: An introduction* (4th ed.). Thomson Brooks/Cole: Belmont, CA.

RUBIN, A. (1991). The effectiveness of outreach counseling and support groups for battered women: a preliminary evaluation. *Research on Social Work Practice, 1*, 332–357.

RUBIN, A. (2008). *Practitioner's guide to using research for evidence-based practice.* New York: Wiley.

RUBIN, A., & BABBIE, E. (2007). *Research methods for social work* (6th ed.). Belmont, CA: Wadsworth.

RUBIN, A., & KNOX, K. S. (1996). Data analysis problems in single-case evaluation: Issues for research on social work practice. *Research on Social Work Practice, 6*, 40–65.

RUBIO-STIPEC, M., CANINO, I., HICKS, M. H., & TSUANG, M. T. (2008). Cultural factors influencing the selection, use, and interpretation of psychiatric measures. In Rush, A. J., Jr., First, M. B., & Blacker, D. (Eds.), *Handbook of psychiatric measures* (2nd ed.) (pp. 23–32). Washington, DC: American Psychiatric Association.

RUSH, A. J., JR., FIRST, M. B., & BLACKER, D. (Eds.) (2008). *Handbook of psychiatric measures* (2nd ed.). Washington, DC: American Psychiatric Association.

RYBACK, R. S. (1974). *The problem-oriented record in psychiatry and mental health care.* New York: Grune & Stratton.

RYGH, J. L., & SANDERSON, W. C. (2004). *Treating generalized anxiety disorder: Evidence-based strategies, tools, and techniques.* New York: Guilford.

RZEPNICKI, T. L. (1991). Enhancing the durability of the intervention gains: A challenge for the 1990's. *Social Service Review, 65*, 92–111.

SACKETT, D. L., STRAUS, S. E., RICHARDSON, W. S., ROSENBERG, W., & HAYNES, R. B. (2000). *Evidence-based medicine: How to practice and teach EBM* (2nd ed.). New York: Churchill Livingstone.

SANTORA, M. (2003, October 7). After son's suicide, mother is convicted over unsafe home. *New York Times*, p. A27.

SAVAGE, P. (2001). Problem-oriented medical records. *British Medical Journal, 322*, 275.

SAVILLE, B. K., ZINN, T. E., NEEF, N. A., VAN NORMAN, R., & FERRERI, S. J. (2006). A comparison of interteaching and lecture in the college curriculum. *Journal of Applied Behavior Analysis, 39*, 49–61.

SCHAEFER, B. A., KOETER, M. W. J., WOUTERS, L., EMMELKAMP, P. M. G., SCHENE, A. H. (2003). What patient characteristics make clinicians recommend brief treatment? *Acta Psychatrica Scandinavica, 107*, 188–196.

SCHILLER, P. (2005). *Information technology for social work: Practice skills for the 21st century.* Boston: Allyn & Bacon.

SCHOECH, R. (2008). Technology tools and applications. In Mizrahi, T. & Davis, L. (Eds.), *Encyclopedia of Social Work* (20th ed.). Washington, DC: NASW Press.

SCHWARTZ, A., & GOLDIAMOND, I. (1975). *Social casework: A behavioral approach.* New York: Columbia University Press.

SECRET, M., & BLOOM, M. (1994). Evaluating a self-help approach to helping a phobic child: A profile analysis. *Research on Social Work Practice, 4*, 338–348.

SELIGMAN, L. (1999). *Selecting effective treatments: A comprehensive, systematic guide for treating mental disorders* (Rev. ed.). San Francisco: Jossey-Bass.

SELIGMAN, L. (2004). *Diagnosis and treatment planning in counseling* (3rd ed.). New York: Plenum.

SEXTON, T. L., GILMAN, L., JOHNSON-ERICKSON, C. (2005). Evidence-based practices. In Gullotta, T. P. & Adams, G. R. (Eds), *Handbook of adolescent behavior problems: Evidence-based approaches to prevention and treatment* (pp. 101–128). New York: Springer.

SHABINI, D. B., KATZ, R. C., WILDER, D. A., BEAUCHAMP, K., TAYLOR, C. R., & FISCHER, K. J. (2002). Increasing social interactions in children with autism: Effects of a tactile prompt. *Journal of Applied Behavior Analysis, 35*, 79–83.

SHADISH, W. R., COOK, T. D., & CAMPBELL, D. T. (2002). *Experimental and quasi-experimental designs for generalized causal inference.* Boston: Houghton-Mifflin.

SHADISH, W. R., & RINDSKOPF, D. M. (2007). Methods for evidence-based practice: Quantitative synthesis of single-subject designs. *New Directions for Evaluation, 113*, 95–109.

SHAFFER, D., GOULD, M. S., BRASIC, J., AMBROSINI, P., FISHER, P., BIRD, H., & ALUWAHLIA, S. (1983). A Children's Global Assessment Scale (CGAS). *Archives of General Psychiatry, 40*, 1228–1231.

SHARPLEY, C. F. (1986). Fallibility in the visual assessment of behavioural interventions: Time-series statistics to analyze time-series data. *Behaviour Change, 3*, 26–33.

SHARPLEY, C. F., & ALAVOSIUS, M. P. (1988). Autocorrelation in behavioural data: An alternative perspective. *Behavioural Assessment, 10*, 243–251.

SHEAFOR, B. W., HOREJSI, G. R., & HOREJSI, G. A. (1991). *Techniques and guidelines for social work practice* (2nd ed.). Boston: Allyn & Bacon.

SHEFLER, G., CANETTI, L., & WISEMAN, H. (2001). Psychometric properties of goal attainment scaling in the assessment of Mann's time-limited therapy. *Journal of Clinical Psychology, 57*, 971–979.

SHERMAN, E., & REID, W. J. (Eds.). (1994). *Qualitative research in social work.* New York: Columbia University Press.

SHEWHART, W. A. (1931). *Economic control of quality of manufactured products.* New York: Van Nostrand Reinhold.

SIDENER, T. M., SHABANI, D. B., & CARR, J. E. (2004). A review of the behavioral evaluation strategy and taxonomy (BEST)

software application. *Behavioral Interventions, 19,* 275–285.
SIDMAN, M. (1960). *Tactics of scientific research: Evaluating experimental data in psychology.* New York: Basic Books.
SIGMON, S. T., & LAMATTINA, S. M. (2006). Self-assessment. In Hersen, M. (Ed.), *Clinicians handbook of adult behavioral assessment* (pp. 145–164). St. Louis, MO: Academic Press.
SILBERGELD, S., KOENIG, G.R., MANDERSCHEID, R.W., MEEKER, B.F., & HORNUNG, C.(1975). Assessment of environment-theory systems: The group atmosphere scale. *Journal of Consulting and Clinical Psychology, 43,* 460–469.
SILVERSTEIN, S. M., SPAULDING, W. D., MENDITO, A. A. (2006). *Schizophrenia: Advances in Psychotherapy – Evidence-based practice.* New York: Hogrefe & Huber.
SISCO, C. B., & PEARSON, C. L. (1994). Prevalence of alcoholism and drug abuse among female AFDC recipients. *Health and Social Work, 19,* 75–77.
SLADECZEK, I. E., ELLIOT, S. N., KRATOCHWILL, T. R., ROBERTSON-MJAANES, S., & CALLAN, K. (2001). Application of goal attainment scaling to a conjoint behavioral consultation case. *Journal of Educational and Psychological Consultation, 12,* 45–49.
SLONIM-NEVO, V., & ANSON, Y. (1998). Evaluating practice: Does it improve outcome? *Social Work Research, 22,* 66–74.
SLONIM-NEVO, V., & VOSLER, N. R. (1991). The use of single-system design with systemic brief problem-solving therapy. *Families in Society, 72,* 38–44.
SMITH, S. R. (2007). Making sense of multiple informants in child and adolescent psychopathology: A guide for clinicians. *Journal of Psychoeducational Assessment, 25,* 139–149.
SNYDER, D. K., HEYMAN, R. E., & HAYNES, S. N. (2008). Couple distress. In Hunsley, J., & Mash, E. J. (Eds.), *A guide to assessments that work* (pp. 439–463). New York, NY: Oxford University Press.
SOLIMAN, H. H. (1999). Post traumatic stress disorder: Treatment outcomes for a Kuwaiti child. *International Social Work, 42,* 163–175.
SORENSON, R. L., GORSUCH, R. L., & MINTZ, J. (1985). Moving targets: Patients' changing complaints during psychotherapy. *Journal of Consulting and Clinical Psychology, 53,* 49–54.
SPIES, R. A., PLAKE, B. S., GEISINGER, K. F., & CARLSON, J. F. (2007). *The seventeenth mental measurements yearbook.* Lincoln, NE: Buros Institute, University of Nebraska.
STAUDT, M. (1997). Pseudoissues in practice evaluation: Impediments to responsible practice. *Social Work, 47,* 99–106.
STEWART, K. K., CARR, J. E., BRANDT, C. W., & MCHENRY, M. M. (2007). An evaluation of the conservative dual-criterion method for teaching university students to visually inspect AB-design graphs. *Journal of Applied Behavior Analysis, 40,* 713–718.
STILES, W. B. (2006). Case studies. In Norcross, J.C., Beutler, K. E., Levant, R. F. (Eds.) (2006). *Evidence-based practices in mental health: Debate and dialogue on the fundamental questions* (pp. 57–64). Washington, D.C.: American Psychological Association.
STOBER, J., & BITTENCOURT, J. (1998). Weekly assessment of worry: An adaptation of the Penn State Worry Questionnaire for monitoring changes during treatment. *Behavior Research and Therapy, 36,* 645–656.
STOCK, L. Z., & MILAN, M. A. (1993). Improving dietary practices of elderly individuals: The power of prompting, feedback, and social reinforcement. *Journal of Behavior Analysis, 26,* 379–387.

STOCKS, J. T., & WILLIAMS, M. (1995). Evaluation of single subject data using statistical hypothesis tests versus visual inspection of charts with and without celeration lines. *Journal of Social Service Research, 20,* 105–126.
STONE, A. A., SHIFFMAN, S., ATIENZA, A. A., & NEBELING, L. (Eds.) (2007). *The science of real-time data capture: Self-reports in health research.* New York: Oxford University Press.
STONE, M., LEWIS, C., & BECK, A. (1994). The structure of Yalom's Curative Factors Scale. *International Journal of Group Psychotherapy, 44,* 239–245.
STOUT, C. E., & HAYES, R. A. (Eds.). (2004). *The evidence-based practice: Methods, models, and tools for mental health professionals.* New York: Wiley.
STREINER, D. L., & NORMAN, G. R. (1989). *Health measurement scales: A practical guide to their development and use.* New York: Oxford University Press.
STROM-GOTTFRIED, K. (1997). The implications of managed care for social work education. *Journal of Social Work Education, 33,* 7–18.
SUE, D. W., & SUE, D. (2004). *Counseling the culturally diverse: Theory and practice.* New York: Wiley.
SUEN, H. K., & ARY, D. (1987). Application of statistical power in assessing autocorrelation. *Behavioral Assessment, 9,* 125–130.
SUNDEL, M. & SUNDEL, S. S. (1975). *Behavioral modification in the human services.* New York: Wiley.
SUZUKI, L. A., & PONTEROTTO, J. G. (Eds.) (2008). Handbook of multicultural assessment: Clinical, psychological, and educational applications (3rd ed.). San Francisco: Jossey-Bass.
SWITZER, E. B., DEAL, T. E., & BAILEY, J. S. (1977). The reduction of stealing in second graders using a group contingency. *Journal of Applied Behavior Analysis, 10,* 267–272.
SYSKO, R. (2008). Eating disorders. In Hunsley, J., & Mash, E. J. (Eds.), *A guide to assessments that work* (pp. 515–534). New York, NY: Oxford University Press.
TAYLOR, C. B. (2003). Computer- and internet-based psychotherapy interventions. *Current Directions in Psychological Science, 12,* 18–22.
THOMAS, E. J. (1975). Uses of research methods in interpersonal practice. In N. A. Polansky (Ed.). *Social work research* (Rev. ed.) (pp. 254–283). Chicago: University of Chicago Press.
THOMAS, E. J. (1978). Research and service in single-case experimentation: Conflicts and choices. *Social Work Research and Abstracts, 14,* 20–31.
THOMLISON, B. & CORCORAN, K. (2008). *The evidence-based internship: A field manual.* New York: Oxford.
THYER, B. A. (1993). Single-system research designs. In R. M. Grinnel, Jr. (Ed.), *Social work research and evaluation* (4th ed.) (pp. 94–117). Itasca, IL: Peacock.
THYER, B. A. (2001). What is the role of theory in research on social work practice? *Journal of Social Work Education, 37,* 9–25.
THYER, B. A., & CURTIS, G. C. (1983). The repeated pretest-posttest single-subject experiment: A new design for empirical clinical practice. *Journal of Behavior Therapy and Experimental Psychiatry, 14,* 311–315.
Thyer, B. A., & Myers, L. L. (2007). *A social worker's guide to evaluating practice outcomes.* Alexandria, VA: Council on Social Work Education.
Thyer, B. A., & Wodarski, J. S. (Eds.) (2007). *Social work in mental health: An evidence-based approach.* Hoboken, NJ: Wiley.
THYER, B. A., & WODARSKI, J. S. (Eds.). (1998). *Handbook of empirical social work practice: Mental disorders.* New York: Wiley.

TISCHLER, G. L. (1990). Utilization management and the quality of care. *Hospital and Community Psychiatry, 41,* 1099–1102.

TODMAN, J. B. (2002). Randomisation in single-case experimental designs. *Advances in Clinical Neuroscience and Rehabilitation, 2,* 18–19.

TODMAN, J. B., & DUGARD, P. (2001). *Single-case and small-n experimental designs: A practical guide to randomization tests.* Mahwah, NJ: Lawrence Erlbaum.

TOLSON, E. R. (1977). Alleviating marital communication problems. In W. J. Reid & L. Epstein (Eds.), *Task centered practice* (pp. 100–112). New York: Columbia University Press.

TOOTHAKER, L. E., BANZ, M., NOBLE, C., CAMP, J., & DAVIS, D. (1983). N = 1 designs: The failure of ANOVA-based tests. *Journal of Educational Statistics, 8,* 289–309.

TOSELAND, R. W., & RIVAS, R. F. (2009). *An introduction to group work practice* (6th ed.). Boston: Allyn & Bacon.

TOULIATOS, J., PERLMUTTER, B. F., STRAUS, M. A., & HOLDEN, G. W. (2001). *Handbook of family measurement techniques.* Newbury Park, CA: Sage.

TRIPODI, T. (1980). Replication in clinical experimentation. *Social Work Research and Abstracts, 16,* 35.

TRUAX, C. B., & CARKHUFF, R. R. (1965). Experimental manipulation of therapeutic conditions. *Journal of Consulting Psychology, 29,* 119–124.

TURK, D. C., OKIFUJI, A., SKINNER, M. (2008). Chronic pain in adults. In Hunsley, J., & Mash, E. J. (Eds.), *A guide to assessments that work* (pp. 576–592). New York, NY: Oxford University Press.

TYSON, K. (1994). Heuristic guidelines for naturalistic qualitative evaluations of child treatment. In E. Sherman & W. J. Reid (Eds.), *Qualitative research in social work* (pp. 89–112). New York: Columbia University Press.

ULMAN, J. D., & SULZER-AZAROFF, B. (1975). Multi-element baseline design in educational research. In E. Ramp & G. Semb (Eds.), Behavior analysis: Areas of research and application. Englewood Cliffs, NJ: Prentice Hall.

UNRAU, Y. A., GABOR, P. A., & GRINNELL, R. M., JR. (2007). *Evaluation in social work: The art and science of practice.* Oxford University Press: New York.

UTSEY, S. O., & BOLDEN, M. A. (2008). Cross-cultural considerations in quality-of-life assessment. In Suzuki, L. A., & Ponterotto, J. G. (Eds.), *Handbook of multicultural assessment: Clinical, psychological, and educational applications* (3rd ed.) (pp. 299–318). San Francisco: Jossey-Bass.

VAN CAMP, C. M., VOLLMER, T. R., GOH, H. L., WHITEHOUSE, C. M., REYES, J., MONTGOMERY, J. L., ET AL. (2008). Behavioral parent training in child welfare: Evaluations of skills acquisition. *Research on Social Work Practice, 18,* 377–391.

VANCE, H. B. (1997). (Ed.) *Psychological assessment of children. Best practices for school and clinical settings* (2nd ed.). New York: Wiley.

VANCE, H. B., & PUMARIEGA, A. (Eds.). (2001). *Clinical assessment of child and adolescent behavior.* New York: Wiley.

VAN DAMME, G., & ONGHENA, P. (1992). *Single-case randomization tests.* Department of Psychology, Center for Mathematical Psychology and Psychological Methodology, Tiensestraat, 102, B-300 Leuven, Belgium.

VANDIVER, V. & CORCORAN, K. (2007). *Maneuvering the maze of managed care* (2nd ed.).New York: Free Press.

VAN HASSELT. V. & HERSEN, M. (Eds.) (1996). *Sourcebook of psychological treatment manuals for adult disorders.* New York: Plenum.

VAN WORMER, J. (2004). Pedometers and brief e-counseling: Increasing physical activities for overweight adults. *Journal of applied behavior analysis, 37,* 421–425.

VEATCH, R. M. (1981). *Theory of medical ethics.* New York: Basic Books.

VERA, M. I. (1990). Effects of divorce groups on individual adjustment: A multiple methodology approach. *Social Work Research and Abstracts, 26,* 11–20.

WADE, K., & NEUMAN, K. (2007). Practice-based research: Changing the professional culture and language of social work. *Social Work in Mental Health Care, 44,* 49–64.

WAKEFIELD, J. C., & KIRK, S. A. (1996). Unscientific thinking about scientific practice: Evaluating the scientist-practitioner model. *Social Work Research, 20,* 83–95.

WAKEFIELD, J. C., & KIRK, S. A. (1997). Science, dogma, and the scientist-practitioner model. *Social Work Research, 21,* 129–208.

WAMBAUGH, J. L., & FERGUSON, M. (2007). Application of semantic feature analysis to retrieval of action names in aphasia. *Journal of Rehabilitation Research & Development, 44,* 381–394.

WAMPOLD, B. E. (Ed.). (1988). The autocorrelation debate [Special issue]. *Behavioral Assessment, 10.*

WARD, P., JOHNSON, L. A., WARD, M. C., & JONES, D. L. (1997). Comparison of the effects of formal and informal accountability on the correct performance of a lifeguard rescue. *Journal of Behavioral Education, 7,* 359–371.

WATSON, D. L., & THARP, R. G. (2007). *Self-directed behavior* (9th ed.). Belmont, CA: Thomson Wadsworth.

WATSON-PERCZEL, M., LUTZKER, J. R., GREENE, B. F., & MCGIMPSEY, B. J. (1988). Assessment and modification of home cleanliness among families adjudicated for child neglect. *Behavior Modification, 12,* 57–81.

WEBB, E. J., CAMPBELL, D. T., SCHWARTZ, R. D., & SECHREST, L. (1966). *Unobtrusive measures: Nonreactive research in the social sciences.* Chicago: Rand McNally.

WEBB, E. J., CAMPBELL, D. T., SCHWARTZ, R. D., SECHREST, L., & GROVE, J. B. (1981). *Nonreactive measures in the social sciences* (2nd ed.). Boston: Houghton Mifflin.

WEDDING, D. BEUTLER, L. E., FREEDLAND, K. E., & SOBELL, L. C. (Eds.) (2005). *Advances in psychotherapy: Evidence-based practice (Book Series).* Ashland, OH: Hofgrefe & Huber.

WEED, L. L. (1968). Medical records that guide and teach. *New England Journal of Medicine, 278,* 593–599, 652–657.

WEED, L. L. (1969). *Medical records, medical education, and patient care: The problem-oriented record as a basic tool.* Cleveland: Case Western Reserve University Press.

WEED, L. L. (1972). Questions often asked about the problem-oriented record: Does it guarantee quality? In J. W. Hurst & H. K. Walker (Eds.), *The problem-oriented system* (pp. 51–56). New York: Medcom.

WEISS, R. L., HOPS, H., & PATTERSON, G. R. (1973). A framework for conceptualizing marital conflict, a technology for altering it, some data for evaluating it. In L. A. Hamerlynck, L. C. Handy, & E. J. Mash (Eds.), *Behavior change: Methodology, concepts, and practice.* Champaign, IL: Research Press.

WEHMEYER, M. L., PALMER, S. B., SMITH, S. J., PARENT, W., DAVIES, D. K., & STOCK, S. (2006). Technology use by people with intellecual and developmental disabilities to support employment activities: A single-subject design meta analysis. *Journal of Vocational Rehabilitation, 24,* 81–86.

WEISZ, J. R., & HAWLEY, K. M. (1998). Finding, evaluating, refining, and applying empirically supported treatments for children and adolescents. *Journal of Clinical Child Psychology, 27,* 206–216.

WHEELER, D. J., & CHAMBER, D. S. (1992). *Understanding statistical process control* (2nd ed.). Knoxville, TN: SPC Press.

WHITE, O. R. (1974). *The "split middle"—A "quickie" method of trend estimation.* University of Washington, Experimental Educational Unit, Child Development and Mental Retardation Center.

WHITE, O. R. (1977). Data-based instruction: Evaluating educational progress. In J. D. Cone & R. P. Hawkins (Eds.), *Behavioral assessment: New directions in clinical psychology.* New York: Brunner/Mazel.

WHITTAKER, J. K., OVERSTREET, E. J., GRASSO, A., TRIPODI, T., & BOYLAN, F. (1988). Multiple indicators of success in residential youth care and treatment. *American Journal of Orthopsychiatry, 58,* 143–148.

WILSON, S. J. (1983). Confidentiality. In A. Rosenblatt & D. Waldfogel (Eds.), *Handbook of clinical social work.* San Francisco: Jossey-Bass.

WISE, E. A. (2004). Methods for analyzing psychotherapy outcomes: A review of clinical significance, reliable change, and recommendations for future change. *Journal of Personality Assessment, 82,* 50–59.

WITKIN, S. L. (1997). Another visit to empirical practice land. *Social Work Research, 21,* 205–207.

WITKIN, S. L., & SALEEBEY, D. (Eds.) (2007). *Social work dialogues: Transforming the canon in inquiry, practice, and education.* Alexandria, VA: Council on Social Work Education.

WODARSKI, J. S., & THYER, B. A. (Eds.). (1998). *Handbook of empirical practice. Social problems and practice issues.* New York: Wiley.

WOODY, S. A., DETWEILER-BEDELL, J., TEACHMAN, B. A., O'HEARN, TS. (2004). *Treatment planning in psychotherapy: Taking the guesswork out of clinical care.* New York: Guilford.

WOODY, S. R., & SANDERSON, W. C. (1998). Manual for empirically supported treatments: 1998 Update. *The Clinical Psychologist, 51,* 17–21.

XIN, Y. P., GRASSO, E., DIPIPI-HOY, C. M., & JITENDRA, A. (2005). The effects of purchasing skill instruction for individuals with developmental disabilities: A meta-analysis. *Exceptional Children, 71,* 379–400.

YARBROUGH, J. L., & THOMPSON, C. L. (2002). Using single-participant research to assess counseling approaches on children's off-task behavior. *Professional School Counseling, 5,* 308–315.

ZALD, D. H., & CURTIN, C. (2006). Brain imaging and related methods. In Eid, M., & Diener, D. (Eds.), *Handbook of multimethod measurement in psychology* (pp. 173–188). Washington, DC: American Psychological Association.

ZARIT, S. H., REEVER, K. E., & BACH-PETERSON, J. (1980). Relatives of the impaired elderly: Correlates of feelings of burden. *Gerontology, 20,* 649–655.

ZIMMERMAN, S. M., & ICENOGLE, M. L. (2003). *Statistical quality control using EXCEL* (2nd ed.). Milwaukee: ASQ Quality Press.

Index

Page references followed by "f" indicate illustrated figures or photographs; followed by "t" indicates a table.

A

Abuse
  alcohol and drug, 41, 156, 171
  child, 41-42, 44, 61, 65, 88, 172-173, 186, 278, 343-344, 394, 408, 455-456, 474-475, 477, 481-482, 485, 487
  of children, 394, 477
Academic press, 189, 473, 478-479, 481, 484-487
Acceptance, 358-359, 475, 480
Accessibility, 27, 50, 155, 160, 166, 241
Accidents, 143, 320, 343, 456
Accountability, 6, 17, 19, 23, 82, 84, 112, 246, 286, 396, 400, 426, 446, 453-454, 457, 459, 466, 474, 479, 488
Accounting, 63, 449
Accreditation, 476
Acting out, 71
Action system, 18
Active listening, 247-248, 250, 453
Adaptations, 3, 16, 205, 298, 394
Addictions
  research on, 477
Administration
  basic principles, 27, 36-38, 48, 269
  types of, 36-38, 48, 160, 163, 170, 187, 269, 370, 374
Adolescents
  nature of, 216
Advice, 42, 324, 434, 476
Advocacy
  email, 100
Advocate, 392, 456, 482, 484
African Americans
  health and, 284
After-school programs, 383
Age, 2, 40, 45, 49, 158, 160, 168, 177, 223, 228, 240, 266-267, 343, 347-348, 367, 382, 394, 446, 456, 458, 466, 479
Agencies
  advantages of, 22
  responsibility to, 72
Agency
  funding sources, 82
  host, 226
  primary, 131, 278, 401, 445, 474, 483
  private, 84, 267, 293
  public, 226, 263, 267, 293, 394, 396, 401, 466-467
Agency setting, 468
Agriculture, 470
Alcohol abuse
  student, 61
alcoholism
  assessment of, 171, 487
Alignments, 435
Alzheimer's, 284
Ambiguity, 48, 434, 442
American Academy of Child and Adolescent Psychiatry, 473
American Medical Association, 475
American Psychiatric Association, 30, 183, 190, 473, 486
Anger, 55, 89, 264, 321-322, 326, 402, 455, 478, 480, 483
Anger management, 264, 480
Animal abuse, 126
Announcements, 311
Antisocial behavior, 37, 184
Anxiety disorder, 486
Anxiety disorders, 486
Anxiety scale, 172
Array, 37, 136, 218, 221, 287, 298, 307, 392-393, 398, 446, 451

Art, 13, 75, 234, 488
as professionals, 287
Assessment
  activities, 19, 63, 67, 72, 78, 83, 100, 152, 183-184, 205, 231, 238, 278-279, 332, 450, 481, 488
  and intervention, 12, 67, 82, 84, 90, 97, 133, 170, 216, 218, 249, 277, 286, 291, 296, 303
  communication in, 133
  comprehensive, 12, 56, 102, 189, 191, 276, 473, 478-479, 481, 483, 486
  culture and, 488
  data, 18-19, 62, 67, 82-85, 90-91, 98-100, 102, 105, 128, 130, 152, 156, 169-170, 181, 184-185, 191, 202, 205, 216, 218, 231, 276-280, 284-287, 290, 295, 332, 342, 360, 377, 395, 450, 458, 463, 475-478, 480-489
  ecological, 133, 202
  evidence-based, 12, 18-19, 100, 190, 249, 295, 446, 451, 473, 475-488
  group members, 152
  Identifying strengths, 55
  in counseling, 486
  in schools, 473
  intake, 156, 290
  interdisciplinary, 484
  multidisciplinary, 477
  of family functioning, 238
  of parents, 169
  of practice, 12, 19, 55, 83, 249, 277, 290-291, 295-296, 390, 446, 458, 463, 483, 488
  process of, 19, 55, 62, 83, 202, 238, 276, 295-296, 463, 474
  terms, 63, 67, 72, 91, 98, 123, 128, 156-157, 159, 203, 277, 291, 360, 400, 446, 450, 482
Assessment techniques, 474
Association, 30, 35, 183, 189-190, 350, 434, 455, 473-478, 482-483, 485-487, 489
Assumption, 8, 17, 20, 29, 31, 131, 133-134, 149, 218, 250, 257, 269, 284, 286, 292, 295, 306, 309, 382, 392, 420, 461, 481
Asylum, 484
Attention, 20, 29, 66, 145-146, 161, 176, 223, 240-241, 245, 263-264, 268-269, 284, 286, 291, 301, 318, 367, 376, 407, 441, 451, 455, 457-459, 480
Attributions, 476
Australia, 476
Authority
  for change, 478
  in practice, 478
  psychological, 478
Autism, 268, 322, 473, 486
Automatic thoughts, 321
Awareness
  self, 83, 128, 267, 374, 460

B

Baseline, 1, 3-6, 8, 10, 18-19, 37, 39, 43, 45-46, 48, 65-66, 69, 71, 81, 83-84, 86, 88-91, 94-97, 129-130, 133-134, 138, 149, 161-163, 165, 170, 177-178, 180-181, 212, 215, 217, 225-230, 243-245, 247-251, 253-262, 266-267, 270-273, 275-287, 289, 291-293, 295-303, 306-312, 315, 317, 319-324, 326-328, 329-348, 351-352, 354-370, 372-380, 382-383, 385-386, 387-392, 394-396, 398-404, 406-410, 412, 414-415, 419, 422-423, 425-426, 430-440, 442-444, 448, 453, 462, 477, 479-481, 484, 488
Baseline phase, 5, 251, 253, 271, 276, 281, 286, 310, 317, 326-327, 364
Beck Depression Inventory, 46, 171, 474
Behavior
  change and, 2, 238, 253, 355
  change in, 6, 45, 126, 136, 151, 163, 171, 235-236, 239, 253-254, 256, 260, 301-302, 310, 317, 332-333, 338-339, 343, 360, 369, 408, 412-413, 461
  control of, 338, 486
  matrix, 187, 475, 479
  target, 2-3, 6, 30, 37, 43, 45, 55-57, 61, 65, 70, 76, 82-84, 91, 93, 125-126, 128-135, 137, 140, 143, 145, 147, 149, 151, 153, 163, 167, 169, 184-185, 202, 216, 222-225, 229-230, 232, 235-236, 238-239, 241-242, 250, 253-256, 260, 264, 267, 271, 276, 284, 293, 301-302, 309-311, 316-317, 323, 326, 328, 329, 332-333, 343, 347-348, 355, 357, 367-369, 385, 393, 403, 408, 418, 432, 438, 473-476, 480
Behavioral model, 413
Best practices, 474, 488
Bias, 34, 85, 168, 174, 182, 185, 216, 254, 264, 270, 292, 442, 458, 461, 479
Birth control, 216, 451
Bono, 421, 473
Boundary, 159
Buffalo, 485
Bullying behavior, 479

C

Cabinets, 44
Campaigns, 62
Canada, 182
cancer, 473
Caring, 1, 13, 31-32, 165-166, 264, 313, 461
Case conferences, 397, 463
Case management
  goals of, 465
Case study method, 289, 291-293
Causality
  reciprocal, 407
Celeration lines, 483, 487
Cerebral palsy, 298-299, 408, 477
Challenge, 11, 14-15, 24, 33, 91, 248-249, 292, 394, 406, 459, 471, 486
Change
  ability to, 44, 66, 88-89, 158, 253, 261, 264, 274, 326, 399
  agents, 9, 311, 482
  behavior, 2-3, 6, 29-30, 37, 44-45, 57, 68, 76, 82-84, 126, 128-129, 133-134, 136-137, 139-140, 149, 151, 163, 171, 202, 216, 222, 224-225, 231, 235-236, 238-239, 241, 250, 253-256, 260, 264, 268, 271, 276, 284, 301-302, 309-311, 317, 326, 328, 332-333, 338-339, 343, 348, 355, 360, 366-367, 369, 383, 408, 412-413, 432, 443, 453, 455, 461-462, 474-486, 488-489
  commitment to, 286, 311
  cost of, 448
  domains of, 437
  identifying, 4-5, 29, 66, 78, 247, 381, 390, 392, 397, 401, 447, 463, 466
  importance of, 12, 23, 34, 50, 133, 139, 166, 218, 237, 240, 254, 260, 263, 284, 286, 437, 477, 480
  methods of, 3, 9, 12, 45, 88, 128, 139, 159, 218, 264, 309, 351, 414, 423, 430, 443, 453, 455, 459, 462, 478
  positive, 5-6, 23, 48, 54, 57, 68, 89, 126, 171, 177, 222, 224, 231, 238, 244, 246, 249-250, 252-254, 260, 276, 280, 292, 299-300, 306-310, 315, 319, 324, 327, 332-333, 336, 338-339, 350, 352, 362-364, 383, 386, 392, 394, 401, 407, 413, 417, 437, 441, 457, 461, 466, 480, 482
  resistance to, 9
  stages of, 164, 171-172, 392, 401, 413
  suggestions for, 29, 280, 287, 459

491

theory, 3-4, 6-7, 22, 29-30, 40, 44, 239, 292, 295, 302, 324, 326, 348-349, 366, 381, 392, 406, 412-413, 417, 474, 476-477, 481, 483-484, 488
   theory of, 3, 295, 349, 417, 488
   therapeutic, 186, 231, 238, 383, 441, 475, 488
Charting, 81-82, 90, 95, 98, 101, 202, 212, 260, 351, 443, 448, 451, 460
Chicago, 189, 475-478, 480, 484-488
Child abuse
   physical, 41
   reports, 344
   service delivery, 474
   sexual, 41
Child abuse and neglect
   effects of, 482
   fatalities, 343
   primary prevention, 474
Child Behavior Checklist, 163, 478
Child development
   and treatment, 489
Children
   African American, 338
   at-risk, 481
   behavior of, 44, 126, 146, 482
Clarification, 22, 54, 473
Clarifying, 22, 31, 53, 55, 394
Clarity, 53, 57, 60, 78, 160, 254, 258, 282, 286, 296, 391, 442
Clients
   collaboration with, 12
Client(s)
   reluctant, 463
Clients
   rights and, 222
Climate, 262
Clinical care, 489
Clinical significance, 179-180, 408, 473-474, 484, 489
Clinical social worker, 484
Closeness, 9, 23
Cocaine, 42, 222, 350-351, 477
Codes of ethics
   NASW, 2, 460
Cognitive analytic therapy, 480
Collaboration
   in social work, 479
Commission on Accreditation, 476
Commissions, 311
Commitment, 11, 13, 15, 286, 311
Common problems, 268, 282, 349, 404
Communication
   effective, 99, 183, 383, 483
   focus on, 18, 89, 131, 238
   improved, 264
   levels of, 298
   methods, 9, 89, 99, 131, 150, 238, 264, 295, 298, 402, 453, 468, 483
   modes of, 453
   written, 150, 396
Community
   development of, 291
   integration, 3, 485
   intentional, 247
   intervention, 1-3, 8, 18, 33, 55-57, 64, 66, 71, 247, 265-266, 291-292, 306, 311, 323, 340, 395, 408, 454, 482
   organization, 56
   problems, 2, 18, 20, 33, 55-57, 64, 66, 71, 247, 265-266, 291-292, 306, 311, 323, 408, 454, 475, 482, 485, 488
   programs, 2, 100, 311, 481
   projects, 454
   school and, 488
   sense of, 3, 454
   technology and, 482
   virtual, 100
Community Mental Health
   Journal, 481
Community values, 454
Comparison group, 358
Competence
   practice and, 7
   professional, 458
Competency, 459
Complex, 4, 6-7, 12, 16, 30, 33, 37, 54, 131, 135-138, 240, 246, 253, 260, 265, 268, 273-274, 283, 293, 297, 306, 315, 336, 349, 354, 358, 370, 371-372, 379-381, 385-386, 388, 390, 400, 407, 421, 443, 449, 466, 470

Comprehensive assessment, 56, 276, 473
Computers
   issues, 9, 49, 90, 375, 415, 420, 471, 475, 483-484
Conflict
   role, 71
Confrontation, 123
Construct validity, 9, 27, 43-47, 138-139, 151, 164-166, 174, 186, 218, 243, 261, 264
Consultant, 218, 467
Consultants, 82, 85, 185, 468
Consumers, 13, 23
Content analysis, 397
Content validity, 9, 27, 41-42, 47, 137, 164
Context
   systemic, 3
Contraception, 43
Contract, 18-19
Contributions, 11, 259, 364, 370, 380, 399, 402
Control
   possibility of, 306
Control group, 3, 7-11, 247, 250, 270, 301-302, 311-312, 316, 318, 338-340, 388, 470
Cooperatives, 312-313
Coping, 150, 300-301, 313-314, 373, 456, 481
Coping behaviors, 301, 456, 481
Correlation coefficient
   formula, 38
Cost-effectiveness, 2, 50, 311, 447, 458, 469
Counseling
   Internet, 487
Creative thinking, 349
Credentials, 265
Crises, 394
Crisis, 278, 284-285, 313, 326-327, 394, 466
Criterion-related validity, 9
Critical value, 269
Cues, 137, 283
Cultural
   context, 16, 49, 158, 391, 453, 458, 484
   diversity, 49
cultural competence
   gender, 458
   religion, 458
   sexual orientation, 458
   socioeconomic status, 458

D

Dangerous situations, 326
Data
   clinical, 6, 69, 170, 177-178, 215, 255, 268-269, 271, 292, 338, 342, 350-351, 359, 408, 448, 457, 475-478, 480-489
   collecting, 9, 18, 24, 67, 69, 81, 84, 87-90, 130, 135-137, 215, 217, 240, 250, 267, 276-277, 279, 283-284, 286, 294, 308, 315, 336, 411, 415-416, 460, 462
   presenting, 22, 67, 81, 91, 250, 253-254, 278, 280, 290, 293-294, 336, 394, 396-397, 429, 447
Data analysis, 319, 375, 420, 459, 483-484, 486
Data collection
   methods for, 67, 84
   preparation for, 315
Data set
   working with, 422
Databases, 16
Day care
   adult, 333
Defining, 20, 32, 53, 56-57, 59, 78, 126, 129, 167, 205, 267, 295
Delegate Assembly, 455
Delusions, 183
Democracy, 222
Demonstrations, 124
Denial, 481
Department of Education, 182
Dependent variable, 262, 322, 357, 406, 424
Depression
   reactive, 45, 127, 241
Describing, 11, 20-21, 30, 32, 57, 79, 91, 104, 193, 221, 234, 243, 247, 326, 347, 362, 407
Desensitization
   systematic, 373
Detoxification, 259
Diagnostic and Statistical Manual of Mental Disorders, 473
Dialogue, 483, 487
Diaries, 201-202, 219, 241
Dichotomies, 388

Differential reinforcement, 369
Dignity, 13
Direct practice
   evaluation, 474-475, 485
Disease, 2
Displaying data, 96
Distribution, 123, 269
Diversity
   multiple, 49, 342
Do no harm, 310, 324, 455, 461
Dropping out, 402
Drug abuse, 65, 156, 172, 259, 487
Drugs
   control, 350, 381
DSM, 181-182, 474, 478
DSM-IV-TR, 181

E

Eating disorders, 202, 487
Education
   trends, 366, 485
Effectiveness
   studies, 11-12, 15, 29, 266, 302, 333, 454, 458, 469, 475, 485
Efficacy, 29, 260, 298, 306, 316, 351-352, 366, 414, 451-452, 473, 477, 482
Efficiency, 32, 82, 101, 157, 188, 348, 405-407, 416, 419, 426, 447-449, 474
Ego, 59, 298
Ego psychology, 298
Email, 16, 100, 122, 170, 182, 293, 396, 420
Emotional insulation, 382
Emotions, 45
Empirical evidence, 17, 347, 474
Employees, 124, 267
Empowerment
   definitions of, 21
Enactment, 149-150
Encounter groups, 482
Encouragement, 84, 86
Encouraging, 54, 87, 137, 170, 218, 223, 307, 336, 378, 450
Energy, 9, 14, 28, 57, 89, 157, 166, 169, 186, 240, 271, 278, 319, 381, 447, 454, 462-463
Environmental
   obstacles, 18
   opportunities, 133
   stressors, 183
Ethical principles, 460
Ethics
   health care, 488
   NASW code of, 460
   of helping, 455, 459, 461, 474
Ethnic group, 266, 463
Evaluation
   case study methods, 292, 298
   developmental, 488
   formal, 2, 5, 18, 51, 160, 215, 249, 267, 276, 290, 294-295, 297, 319, 403, 416, 464, 466, 488
   informal, 293, 306, 320, 464, 488
   measures, 1, 3, 5, 8-9, 11, 18, 22-24, 27-28, 32, 34, 36, 46, 49-51, 54, 62, 68-69, 101, 151, 156, 164-166, 170, 186, 188-189, 212, 216, 221-222, 228-229, 231-232, 235, 239, 258, 262-264, 286, 293, 295-297, 299, 302, 313, 386, 390-391, 397-398, 401, 403, 441, 448-449, 453, 464-465, 468-469, 474, 476-478, 482-483, 485-486, 488
   of research, 6-8, 12-13, 15-17, 20, 23, 249, 261, 294, 454, 467, 469, 481, 483, 487-488
   of staff, 476
   practice, 1-9, 11-26, 27-29, 32, 34, 50-51, 54-55, 68, 81, 91, 98-101, 124, 151, 155, 166, 170, 186, 188-189, 201-202, 215, 219, 221-222, 232, 243-247, 249, 251, 257-259, 261, 263, 265-269, 274, 276, 278, 282, 284-286, 290, 292-293, 295-296, 298-299, 302, 305-308, 311, 319-320, 349, 356, 358, 364, 377, 386, 387-388, 390, 392, 394, 398-403, 406, 413, 416, 418, 427, 429, 432, 437, 441-442, 445-449, 451, 453-465, 467-470, 474-488
   product, 229
   program, 5, 7-8, 11-12, 22, 25, 81, 91, 99-101, 124, 135, 155, 169, 188, 202, 228-229, 231, 245, 250, 257-258, 260, 263-264, 266,

268, 276, 278, 282, 285-286, 292, 295-297, 302, 307-308, 311, 313, 319-320, 327, 356, 369, 386, 390, 392, 399, 406, 418, 427, 441, 447-448, 451, 460, 466-467, 469, 474-476, 481-482, 485-486
progress, 2, 4-8, 12, 22-23, 50, 70, 81, 98-99, 101, 135, 205, 215-216, 244-245, 249, 259, 276, 279, 292, 302, 349, 392, 394, 401, 403, 438, 448, 453-455, 458, 462, 465, 468-469, 481
reasons for, 170, 232, 246, 286
research and, 7, 9, 13, 16, 20-21, 28, 261, 369, 406, 445, 454-455, 460, 464, 467, 470, 474-481, 483-485, 487-488
Evidence-based
assessments, 448, 477-478, 480, 483, 485, 487-488
evaluations, 7, 269, 449, 488
evidence-based practice
prediction, 418
Exceptions
seeking, 86, 168, 284
Existing data
using, 156, 235
Expectations
negative, 222, 412
Experimental design, 3, 305, 307-309, 316, 326, 362, 365, 380, 463
Experimental group, 8, 10, 270, 311-312
External validity, 243, 261-262, 265-267, 308, 375
Extraneous variables, 45, 262
Eye contact, 150, 223

F

Face validity, 9, 27, 41-42, 47, 137, 153, 163-164, 467
Facilitating, 284, 424, 485
Fading, 257, 322-323
Families
extended, 85, 301
strength of, 151
work and, 477
Families in Society, 473, 485, 487
Family
interaction, 173, 264, 381, 383, 391
intervention with, 262, 295
preservation, 184, 236, 240, 478
preservation of, 184
roles, 70
rules, 295
systems, 69, 139, 342-344, 388, 392-394, 461
therapies, 476, 482
Family life education, 70
Family preservation, 236, 240, 478
Family Relations, 156, 172, 183
Family therapy
functional, 295
Fantasy, 348
Fear, 30, 62, 214
feedback
monitoring and evaluating, 276
real-time, 487
Feelings
List of, 4, 61, 156
Field practicum, 173
Flashbacks, 126
Flexibility, 3-4, 8, 19, 33, 298, 352, 356, 374-375, 391, 404, 453
Florida, 185, 475
Food
sufficient, 319
Formal evaluation, 290, 295, 403
Formulation, 18, 406, 455, 458
Foster care
long-term, 476
Foster parents, 150
Foundations, 190, 473-474, 485
Franklin, Benjamin, 460
Freedom, 9
Full-service schools, 477
Functional family therapy, 295
Funding
sources, 23, 82

G

generalization, 49, 257, 267-271, 274, 311, 360, 482
Generalized Contentment Scale (GCS), 172, 176, 196
Generate hypotheses, 204-206

Genuineness, 4
Global Assessment of Functioning (GAF), 181, 183
Global Assessment of Functioning (GAF) Scale, 181, 183
Global Assessment of Relational Functioning (GARF), 181
Goals
organizational, 57, 407, 467-468
problem solving, 4, 67
Goals and objectives
definitions, 78, 447
intermediate objectives, 72
linking, 64
Goal-setting, 9, 64, 66-67, 72
Group Atmosphere Scale, 187, 487
Group, The, 7-8, 11, 70-71, 99, 133, 146, 151-152, 158, 187, 232, 299, 301, 306, 341, 365, 382, 401, 450, 482, 487
Groups
dimensions, 186-187, 226
diversity in, 49
gender and, 476
Growth, 202, 381
Guns, 333, 450

H

Hallucinations, 183
Handbook of Psychiatric Measures, 190, 486
Harassment, 173, 395
Health
profession, 478
Health and Social Work, 314, 484, 487
Health care
behavioral, 16, 473, 485-486, 488
global, 486
settings, 488
social work in, 473, 485, 488
Helping professions
related, 67, 287, 398, 461
Hill Interaction Matrix, 187, 479
Hippocrates, 291, 324
History
mental health, 266
of social work, 484
public welfare, 396
Hits, 141
HOME, 32, 39, 41, 44, 65, 71, 85, 89-90, 99-100, 105, 127, 133, 137, 149-151, 163, 169, 181, 183-184, 217-218, 230, 232, 236-238, 263, 293, 295, 298, 320, 327, 333, 335, 340-341, 343-344, 360, 382-383, 395-396, 438, 451, 461, 474, 477, 485-486, 488
Home visits, 39, 85, 149, 181, 237
Homework, 38, 43, 58, 61, 72, 112, 116, 126, 138, 141, 163, 169, 227-228, 257, 441, 473, 480
Honesty, 23, 460
Humanism, 19
Hypotheses
generate, 201-202, 204-206, 212, 216, 219, 237, 347

I

Ideas
new, 20-22, 99, 271, 354, 362, 381, 385, 406, 413, 437, 459, 470
Identity
racial, 48, 458
Illusions, 390
Imagination, 136, 231
Immigrants
illegal, 480
Impairment, 159, 161, 172, 182-184, 474-475
Incorporation, 454, 457
Independence, 35-36, 340, 420, 459-460, 481
Independent living, 323, 325, 383-384
Independent variable, 262, 310, 406
Individuals, 2, 30, 36, 49, 62, 67, 70, 83, 98, 140, 227, 265, 284, 296, 301, 365, 383, 388, 407, 413, 446, 450, 454, 466, 476, 479, 487, 489
Infant mortality, 456
Inference, 9, 22, 232, 260, 273, 302, 307-308, 310, 315, 326, 331, 336-337, 342, 348, 363, 383, 385, 479, 486
Information technology, 100, 187, 486
Informed consent, 462
Ingredients, 7, 32, 292, 350, 369, 395, 454
Input, 102, 186
Insight, 336, 348, 476, 481

institutions, 85, 87, 226, 381, 392-393, 466
Instructions, 37, 39, 48, 82, 87, 103, 106-107, 119, 124, 130, 158, 168-169, 192, 195, 222, 224, 254, 299, 308, 317, 323, 332-333, 338, 374, 379, 420, 482
Insurance, 418
Integrity, 249, 478, 485
Interdisciplinary, 484
Intermediate objectives, 65, 72, 354-355, 398, 448, 450-451
Intermittent reinforcement, 355
Internal factors, 250
Internal validity, 243, 253, 261-263, 273, 296, 316, 351
Internships, 12, 467
Interrater reliability, 38, 61, 223, 311
Intervention
bullying, 126, 394, 479
contract, 18-19
crisis, 278, 284-285, 313, 326-327, 394
documentation of, 167, 447, 461
early, 55-56, 63, 266, 268, 294, 326-327, 361, 417, 427, 473
ineffective, 63, 207, 254, 262, 411
with families, 343, 474, 477, 479
with groups, 3, 70, 482
Intervention(s)
objectives, 406
interventions
paradoxical, 20, 299
Interviewing
recording, 218, 476
skill, 341
Introductions, 327, 346, 360-361, 379, 386
Intrusiveness, 20
Invasion of privacy, 222
Investigation, 13, 20, 260, 292, 302, 393, 396, 481, 484
Iowa, 479
Isolation, 268
Israel, 474

J

Jail, 71
Journal of Applied Behavior Analysis, 320, 335, 359, 385, 473, 477-478, 480-483, 485-488
Journal of Social Work Education, 475-476, 485, 487
Judgments, 31, 38, 40, 159, 223, 292, 416, 442, 475
Juvenile court
variations in, 392

K

Knowledge
intuitive, 390

L

Language
through, 7, 101, 223, 231, 483
Latency, 143, 150, 382
Law
degree, 86
Learning theory, 366
Letter writing, 398
Level of functioning, 408
Linear relationship, 36
Linkage, 29, 363
Logs, 24, 42, 156, 158, 201-207, 212-219, 235, 237, 241-242, 244
London, 475, 478
Loneliness, 88
Long-term care, 295

M

Mailed questionnaires, 258
Mainstreaming, 344
Maintenance, 10, 21, 99, 143, 243, 252, 257-258, 296-298, 309, 316-317, 319, 323, 327, 343-344, 350, 360-363, 372, 394, 399, 405, 418, 441, 473, 482
Manager, 116-117, 124
Mapping, 16
Marijuana, 42
Marital satisfaction, 34, 37, 41, 44, 46, 95, 156-158, 161, 172, 177-178, 218, 238
Marital therapy, 263
Markers, 66
Maryland, 477
Maturation, 263, 316
Mean

493

deviation, 179-180, 270-271, 439
Measuring, 1, 4, 8-9, 11, 23-24, 31, 33-36, 39, 41, 44-46, 49-51, 55, 62, 64-65, 82-83, 126, 139-141, 143, 156, 159, 161, 167, 182, 189-190, 194, 222, 225, 229-230, 232, 235, 237, 240-241, 259, 261, 292-293, 401, 409, 447, 449-450, 456, 462, 479, 485
Median, 484
Mediator, 294, 302, 316
Mental health
   services, 101, 182, 190, 266, 395, 474, 478, 481, 485, 487
Mental health professionals, 487
Mental health programs, 481
Mental hospitals, 177
Mental illness
   most common, 28
Mental Measurements Yearbook, 160, 187, 190, 487
Meta-analysis, 14, 16, 23, 243, 267, 269-271, 477-479, 481-482, 489
Metacommunication, 291
Methodology, 7, 15, 21, 28, 299-300, 455-456, 480, 488
Milwaukee, 475, 489
Minority group, 266
Mirroring, 22
Modem, 187
Monitoring
   technology, 3, 99, 128, 473, 482-483, 485
mores, 222
Mortality, 455-456
Multicultural, 49, 189-190, 458, 473, 476-478, 482, 484-485, 487-488
Mutuality, 397

N
National Association of Social Workers, 455, 483
National Association of Social Workers (NASW) of, 483
Naturalistic observation, 139
Negative correlation, 36
Negative reinforcement, 358-359
Neglect
   measurement of, 41
Negotiations, 237
Neighborhood
   school, 266, 350
Networks
   helping, 20
   response, 20
New Mexico, 171, 485
New Zealand, 319-320
Newspapers, 293, 392
nonverbal communication, 231
Null hypothesis, 409-411

O
Obesity, 385, 450
Objective data, 99, 406
Objective measures, 464
Objectivity, 22, 58, 456-457, 460
Observational measures, 42
Observer, 8, 20-21, 36, 44, 83, 127-133, 135-146, 149, 151-152, 163, 166, 169, 182, 222-223, 225, 229-232, 235, 238, 241, 245, 377, 443
Operationalization, 33, 43, 54, 448
Opiates, 350
Opinion, 9, 20, 41, 238-239, 396
Organization, 14, 16, 24, 56, 58, 67, 90, 98, 102, 185, 191, 222, 228, 284, 451, 466, 468
Orientation, 5, 13, 19, 33, 49, 56, 59, 98, 127, 168, 172, 181, 236-237, 241, 297, 458, 463
Output, 186

P
Palliative care, 473
Parenting skills, 161, 217, 236
Patience, 308
Perception, 4, 202
Performance standards, 449
Perseverance, 413
Personal values, 408
Personnel, 350, 394, 465, 484
Physical abuse, 88, 161, 172-173, 278, 408
Placebo, 318, 350-351, 477
Planned comparison, 249, 296
Police, 61, 222, 226
Positive change, 177, 246, 299, 308, 310, 319, 350, 352, 362-363, 392, 394, 413, 437, 466
Positive correlation, 36
Positive reinforcement, 252, 338, 358, 377-378, 450
Positivism, 479, 485
Postpositivism, 456
Poverty
   absolute, 456
   measuring, 449, 456
   rates, 449
   rates of, 449
   reducing, 456
Power
   changing, 252, 292, 365, 487
Practice
   field of, 302, 323, 470
Practice evaluation, 2, 91, 124, 151, 186, 221-222, 244, 296, 399, 446, 448, 474-476, 483-485, 487
Practice methods
   multimethod, 474
Practice theory, 3, 20-22, 381, 392, 406, 464
Practice wisdom, 29, 246, 388, 413, 416, 455, 481
Pragmatics, 474
Pregnancy
   teen, 451
Prescribing the symptom, 342
Pretest, 7, 22, 178-180, 375-376
Prevention
   focusing on, 167, 450
   relapse, 474, 482
   suicide, 486
Primary prevention, 2, 320, 401, 445-447, 449-451, 474, 478
Privilege, 86, 168
Problem solving
   training, 259, 332-333
Problems
   agency and, 55, 296, 397-398
   solving, 4, 13, 20, 23, 67, 231, 259, 297, 332-333, 366, 402, 406, 418, 470
Problem-solving, 3, 13, 23, 31, 93, 231, 332-333, 402, 406, 418, 477, 487
Professional associations, 446
Professional culture, 488
Professional ethics, 307, 455, 484
Professional psychology, 476
Program evaluation, 11, 99, 466, 474, 481, 486
Program evaluations, 7, 466
Programs, 2, 7, 11, 15, 31, 90-91, 99-101, 119, 126, 130, 133, 187-188, 226-227, 229-230, 257-258, 264, 307, 310-311, 316, 344, 353, 361, 363, 370, 373, 383, 406, 419-420, 442, 446, 455, 459, 467, 469-470, 481
Project MATCH, 171
Projection, 448
Projects, 84, 186, 450, 454-455
Prompt, 132, 296, 322-323, 486
Prompting, 324, 473, 487
Protective services, 83, 181, 344, 393
Psychiatry, 100, 172, 187, 420, 473-475, 478-481, 486-488
Psychoanalytic approach, 30
Psychoanalytic theory, 298
Psychological disorders, 189, 194, 473-474
Psychological testing, 160, 189, 473
Psychological trauma, 190
Psychology
   ego, 298
Psychometrics, 167, 482
PsycINFO, 16
Public housing, 293
Public Welfare, 396
Publications, 16, 156, 185, 481
Punishment, 139

Q
Qualities, 183, 255
Quality of life, 49, 180, 408, 469
Quantitative research, 1, 20-21, 457
Questions
   change, 23, 30, 34-35, 37, 40, 44, 47, 50, 54, 114, 161, 166, 186, 246-247, 250, 261-263, 274, 296-297, 302, 327, 362, 381, 388, 390, 392, 397, 401, 406-408, 459, 483-484, 488
   circular, 59
   difference, 15, 41, 246, 262, 375, 408, 420, 484
   effect, 14-15, 23, 37, 246, 261-262, 266, 269, 297, 302, 362, 381, 392, 406, 418, 464, 484
   esteem, 37, 44, 262, 267
   exception, 40, 50, 470
   exploratory, 14
   indirect, 50, 161
   meaning, 32, 54, 59, 72, 246, 250, 266, 459
   order of, 23, 47, 401
   possibility, 14, 59, 246, 269, 375
   responses to, 157, 161, 168-169, 327
   scaling, 397, 483, 487
   selecting, 20, 30, 34, 42, 50, 169, 388, 390, 392, 397, 400-401, 404, 464
   support, 40, 44, 71, 161, 166, 246, 327, 420, 467, 470, 488

R
Radio, 311
Random error, 34-35, 41
Random sampling, 203
Randomization, 133, 373, 375, 420, 454, 477, 481, 484, 488
Range, 2-3, 5, 7, 33, 36, 39-42, 45, 49, 65, 67-68, 76, 78, 82, 88, 95, 98-100, 114, 126-128, 133, 141, 149, 151, 156-158, 160, 163-165, 170, 174-175, 177-180, 182-184, 186, 188, 200, 204, 216, 225-227, 230, 234, 236, 270, 385, 398, 403-404, 407, 409, 413, 416, 419, 423, 435, 448-449, 456, 467-469
Rapid assessment instruments, 157
Ratio, 27, 30-31, 216, 407, 412, 426, 463
Raw data, 134, 429, 438
Reaction, 23, 43, 87, 150, 168, 203-204, 206-207, 212, 217, 294
Reactivity, 24, 45, 48, 137, 181, 221-232, 234, 287, 316, 342, 366
Reading, 2, 9, 34, 45, 90, 143, 166, 168, 245, 247, 375-377, 401, 422, 480
Reality
   flawed, 456
Reasoning, 59-60, 291, 470, 478
Reassuring, 416, 419
Recidivism, 71
Reciprocal reinforcement, 407
Recycling, 344-345, 350, 456, 475
Red Cross, 395-396
Referral, 18-19, 226, 394, 398
Reflecting, 22, 70, 274, 309, 359, 463
Refugees, 475, 484
Rehabilitation
   vocational, 263, 488
Reinforcement, 65, 71, 152, 224, 252, 257, 312, 315, 325, 338, 355, 357-359, 361, 365-369, 377-378, 383-384, 407, 418, 450, 473, 478, 480, 482, 487
Reinforcers, 334
Relationship, 5, 12, 18, 21-22, 27, 36, 47, 51, 58, 63, 82, 84-85, 139, 158, 165, 172-173, 177, 185, 205, 214, 237, 249, 251, 260, 264, 287, 291, 296-297, 307-308, 316, 319, 321, 330-331, 333, 343-344, 380-381, 437, 456, 462, 475, 480
Relationships
   parallel, 291, 316, 347
Relaxation, 298-299, 357, 373, 390, 477
Relaxation training, 298, 390
Reliability
   of information, 48-49, 156-158, 178, 218-219, 225, 238, 241, 311, 322
Research
   applied, 1, 6, 17, 20-22, 159, 170-171, 189, 249, 300, 350, 366, 369, 375, 451, 457, 467, 470, 473, 475-488
   experimental, 3, 7-9, 11-12, 15, 23, 189, 247, 265, 270, 302, 311-312, 322, 339, 358, 366, 369, 454, 463, 470, 475, 477-480, 482-484, 486-489
   experiments, 476, 479, 484-485
   in mental health, 190, 478, 483, 485, 487-488
   pure, 21
   qualitative, 1, 20-22, 26, 158, 189, 231, 300, 322, 457, 478, 480-481, 483, 485-486, 488
   understanding of, 2, 15-16, 20, 35, 45, 156, 231, 302, 423, 453, 457
Resources
   insufficient, 101
   scarce, 446
Responding, 323, 383
Rewards, 365, 468
Rights
   Children's, 473

civil, 123, 222
Ritalin, 376-377
Rogers, Carl, 249
Role playing, 82-83
Role-playing, 137, 149-150, 181, 257, 407
Roles
    conflict, 18

S
Salary, 468
Sample
    representative, 41, 72, 129, 131-133, 149, 265
Sampling, 41, 125, 129-134, 145, 202-203, 205, 265, 479
Sanctions, 83, 181
Schedules, 480
Scheduling, 224, 376, 419
Scheme, 139
School counselors, 85
School dropout, 445, 450, 456
Schools
    child maltreatment in, 477
Scientism, 479
Self
    false, 29, 187
Self-assessment, 487
self-care, 302, 482
Self-disclosure, 216
Self-efficacy, 29, 451-452
Self-esteem
    supervisors and, 82
Self-evaluation, 276
Separation, 76, 251, 254
Sex, 4, 56, 89, 160, 222, 231, 266, 475, 481-482
Sexually transmitted diseases (STDs), 450
Shaping, 354
Siblings, 16, 85, 184, 337
Significance
    statistical, 3, 24, 66, 234, 269, 271, 313-314, 375, 405, 407-411, 413, 415-419, 421-423, 426, 463, 473-474, 484, 489
    visual, 24, 375, 405, 407, 409-410, 415, 421, 423, 441, 478
Single-system designs
    A-B design, 246-247, 251-252, 254, 259, 265, 273, 290, 295, 298-299, 301, 305, 309-311, 315-324, 326-327, 349, 352, 354, 390-391, 453
    A-B-C design, 251, 258
    B design, 246-247, 251-252, 254, 259, 265, 273, 290, 295, 298-299, 301, 305, 309-311, 315-324, 326-327, 349, 352, 354, 390-391, 453
    combined, 3, 13, 20, 247-250, 254-255, 273, 290, 300-301, 306, 321, 352, 369, 390
Skills
    interviewing, 4, 249, 339, 341, 476
    observation, 82, 89, 149-150, 236
Smoking, 224, 230, 390
Social context, 3, 295, 334, 366, 461
Social group work, 482
Social research, 478, 486
Social role, 171, 469
Social Service Review, 483-486
Social status, 45
Social support, 161, 165-166, 300-301, 481, 485
Social Work
    assessment and, 100, 473, 481, 483, 488
    counseling and, 486
    psychiatry and, 486
    social welfare, 483
Social work practice
    group work, 482, 488
Social Work Research
    observational, 480
Society
    responsibilities to, 460
Solutions
    technical, 253
Speculation, 292
Standard deviation, 178-180, 270-271, 314, 439
Standard deviation (SD), 179
Standard error of measurement (SEM), 27, 36, 39
Standardized instruments, 8
Standardized tests, 227
Statistical analyses
    case, 6, 475, 479
    meta-analysis, 479
    single-system research, 475

Statistical power, 262, 405, 411, 475, 482, 487
Statistics
    analysis of, 15, 78, 91, 405, 407-408, 415, 419-421, 426, 440-442, 479-480, 484
Status quo, 29, 401, 456
Stressors, 183
Stroke, 295, 483
Structure
    interview, 17-18, 157, 169, 215
    participation, 454
Study
    descriptive, 9, 24
Subjective data, 99
Subjectivity, 218, 441
Substance abuse
    alcohol abuse, 171
Subsystem, 388, 392
Successive approximation, 370, 416
Suggesting, 31, 38, 46, 51, 54, 63-64, 139, 180, 185, 224, 230, 239, 282-283, 295, 313-314, 316, 321, 323, 360, 367, 369, 383, 418, 427, 466, 470
Suggestions, 28-29, 49, 84, 86, 98, 123, 128, 214, 223-225, 266, 280, 283, 287, 290, 293-294, 349, 386, 388, 404, 412, 415, 442, 446, 459, 466-467
Summarizing, 466
Supervision
    other forms of, 184
System
    focal, 394
Systematic desensitization, 373
Systematic error, 34-35, 41
Systems perspective, 461

T
Tactics, 222, 244, 487
Target behavior, 129, 131, 133, 137, 140, 145, 147, 224-225, 229, 250, 255-256, 260, 271, 293, 301, 309, 328, 343, 393, 418
Targets, 2, 4-6, 8-9, 22, 24, 28, 31-33, 49-50, 53-72, 76-79, 81-83, 87-90, 97, 101, 128-129, 131, 133, 139, 151, 156, 158-159, 161, 166-167, 170, 201-202, 212, 216-219, 223, 225, 235-241, 244, 246, 249, 251, 259, 271, 273, 275, 277, 283, 286, 295-296, 311-312, 329-332, 336-338, 342, 347, 349, 351-352, 355, 385, 389, 391, 393-394, 401-403, 406-407, 409, 416, 435, 437-438, 447, 449-451, 453, 455-458, 464-465, 467, 469, 487
Teachers, 42-43, 64, 85, 151, 185, 190, 238, 326-327, 343, 374, 401, 413, 446, 451
Teams, 378, 470
techniques of, 13, 30, 249, 277, 307, 342, 477
Technological problems, 459
Teen pregnancy, 451
Teenage suicide, 456
Television, 133, 232, 293
Texts, 158, 269, 351
The Depression, 37, 64, 412
Theoretical orientation, 5, 19, 33, 56, 98, 127, 236-237
Theories
    activity, 5
    critical, 2, 5, 20
    psychoanalytic, 30
Theory
    for practice, 30, 298, 406, 417, 464, 476, 481
Therapeutic change, 475
Thought, 3, 30, 37, 60-62, 68-69, 97, 157, 184, 238, 263, 276, 278, 284, 290, 293, 310, 355, 391, 396, 402, 434, 438, 451, 474
Thought stopping, 434
Time out, 356
Time-outs, 355
Token economy, 230, 338, 359, 473, 478, 480
Touch, 333, 367
Treatment
    duration of, 152, 202, 215
Treatment planning, 189, 473, 486, 489
Trend lines, 435, 444
Truancy, 55, 126, 183, 342, 393
True baseline, 273, 324
t-test, 421

U
Unconscious, 309
unemployed, 266, 373, 396

United Fund, 354-355
United Way, 483
University of Chicago, 485, 487

V
Validation, 40, 42, 160, 182, 343, 365, 473, 475, 480, 482, 485
Validity
    construct, 9, 27, 35, 42-47, 49, 138-139, 151, 160, 164-166, 174, 186, 217-218, 243, 261, 264
    content, 9, 27, 35, 41-42, 47, 49, 61, 137, 160, 164, 201, 216-217, 229, 231, 375
    criterion-related, 9, 164
    face, 9, 27, 35, 41-42, 47, 137, 153, 163-164, 168, 174, 244, 266, 367, 467
Value statements, 30, 224
Values
    clients and, 13, 462
    presenting problems and, 447
    societal values, 66, 432
Variables
    dependent, 9, 262, 266
    describing, 11
    extraneous, 45, 262, 266, 316
    independent, 9, 36, 44, 151, 262
    relationships between, 9, 316
Videotapes, 85, 185, 231
Virginia, 477
Visualization, 152, 484
Volunteers, 60, 85, 340, 378

W
Washington, 156, 189-190, 473-478, 482-487, 489
Web sites, 133, 135, 373
Welfare
    policies, 446
    spending, 446
Whole person, 4
Wisdom, 16, 29, 246, 251, 388, 403, 413, 416, 455, 481
Withdrawal, 184, 253, 307, 309, 315
Women
    battered, 486
Work
    varying, 268, 302, 372
Working Alliance Inventory (WAI), 182
World Health Organization, 185

Y
Yale University, 156